A HISTORY OF WORLD SOCIETIES

A HISTORY OF WORLD SOCIETIES

THIRD EDITION

VOLUME C
FROM
THE FRENCH
REVOLUTION TO
THE PRESENT

John P. McKay
UNIVERSITY OF ILLINOIS AT URBANA-CHAMPAIGN

Bennett D. Hill
GEORGETOWN UNIVERSITY

John Buckler
UNIVERSITY OF ILLINOIS AT URBANA-CHAMPAIGN

HOUGHTON MIFFLIN COMPANY   BOSTON   TORONTO
DALLAS   GENEVA, ILLINOIS
PALO ALTO   PRINCETON, NEW JERSEY

Sponsoring Editor: John Weingartner
Senior Development Editor: Lance Wickens
Project Editor: Christina Horn
Electronic Production Specialist: Karla K. Grinnell
Production Coordinator: Frances Sharperson
Manufacturing Coordinator: Priscilla Bailey
Marketing Manager: Diane Gifford

Printed in the U.S.A.

Library of Congress Catalog Card Number: 91 71972

ISBN: 0–395–60794–9

ABCDEFGHIJ—VH—987654321

About the Authors

John P. McKay Born in St. Louis, Missouri, John P. McKay received his B.A. from Wesleyan University (1961), his M.A. from the Fletcher School of Law and Diplomacy (1962), and his Ph.D. from the University of California, Berkeley (1968). He began teaching history at the University of Illinois in 1966 and became a professor there in 1976. John won the Herbert Baxter Adams Prize for his book *Pioneers for Profit: Foreign Entrepreneurship and Russian Industrialization, 1885–1913* (1970). He has also written *Tramways and Trolleys: The Rise of Urban Mass Transport in Europe* (1976) and has translated Jules Michelet's *The People* (1973). His research has been supported by fellowships from the Ford Foundation, the Guggenheim Foundation, the National Endowment for the Humanities, and IREX. His articles and reviews have appeared in numerous journals, including *The American Historical Review, Business History Review, The Journal of Economic History,* and *Slavic Review.* He edits *Industrial Development and the Social Fabric: An International Series of Historical Monographs.*

Bennett D. Hill A native of Philadelphia, Bennett D. Hill earned an A.B. at Princeton (1956) and advanced degrees from Harvard (A.M., 1958) and Princeton (Ph.D., 1963). He taught history at the University of Illinois at Urbana, where he was department chairman from 1978 to 1981. He has published *English Cistercian Monasteries and Their Patrons in the Twelfth Century* (1968) and *Church and State in the Middle Ages* (1970); and articles in *Analecta Cisterciensia, The New Catholic Encyclopaedia, The American Benedictine Review,* and *The Dictionary of the Middle Ages.* His reviews have appeared in *The American Historical Review, Speculum, The Historian, The Catholic Historical Review,* and *Library Journal.* He has been a fellow of the American Council of Learned Societies and has served on committees for the National Endowment for the Humanities. Now a Benedictine monk of St. Anselm's Abbey, Washington, D.C., he is also a Visiting Professor at Georgetown University.

John Buckler Born in Louisville, Kentucky, John Buckler received his B.A. from the University of Louisville in 1967. Harvard University awarded him the Ph.D. in 1973. From 1984 to 1986 he was the Alexander von Humboldt Fellow at Institut für Alte Geschichte, University of Munich. He is currently a professor at the University of Illinois. In 1980 Harvard University Press published his *The Theban Hegemony, 371–362 B.C.* He has also published *Philip II and the Sacred War* (Leiden 1989), and co-edited *BOIOTIKA: Vorträge vom 5. International Böotien-Kolloquium* (Munich 1989). His articles have appeared in journals both here and abroad, like the *American Journal of Ancient History, Classical Philology, Rheinisches Museum für Philologie, Classical Quarterly, Wiener Studien,* and *Symbolae Osloenses.*

Contents in Brief

Contents

Maps

Timelines/Genealogies

Note: *Italics* indicate comparative tables.

Preface

A HISTORY OF WORLD SOCIETIES grew out of the authors' desire to infuse new life into the study of world civilizations. We knew full well that historians were using imaginative questions and innovative research to open up vast new areas of historical interest and knowledge. We also recognized that these advances had dramatically affected the subject of economic, intellectual, and, especially, social history, while new research and fresh interpretations were also revitalizing the study of the traditional mainstream of political, diplomatic, and religious development. Despite history's vitality as a discipline, however, it seemed to us that both the broad public and the intelligentsia were generally losing interest in the past. The mathematical economist of our acquaintance who smugly quipped "What's new in history?"—confident that the answer was nothing and that historians were as dead as the events they examine—was not alone.

It was our conviction, based on considerable experience introducing large numbers of students to the broad sweep of civilization, that a book reflecting current trends could excite readers and inspire a renewed interest in history and the human experience. Our strategy was twofold. First, we made social history the core element of our work. Not only did we incorporate recent research by social historians, but also we sought to re-create the life of ordinary people in appealing human terms. A strong social element seemed to us especially appropriate in a world history, for identification with ordinary people of the past allows today's reader to reach an empathetic understanding of different cultures and civilizations. At the same time we were determined to give great economic, political, intellectual, and cultural developments the attention they unquestionably deserve. We wanted to give individual readers and instructors a balanced, integrated perspective, so that they could pursue on their own or in the classroom those themes and questions that they found particularly exciting and significant.

Second, we made a determined effort to strike an effective global balance. We were acutely aware of the great drama of our times—the passing of the European era and the simultaneous rise of Asian and African peoples in world affairs. Increasingly, the whole world interacts, and to understand that interaction and what it means for today's citizens we must study the whole world's history. Thus we adopted a comprehensive yet realistic global perspective. We studied all geographical areas and the world's main civilizations, conscious of their separate identities and unique contributions. Yet we also stressed the links between civilizations, for these links eventually transformed multicentered world history into a complex interactive process of different continents, peoples, and civilizations in recent times. Finally, it was our place neither to praise nor to vilify our own civilization's major role in the growth of global integration, accepting it rather as part of our world heritage and seeking to understand it and the consequences for all concerned. Four years ago, in an effort to realize fully the potential of our fresh yet balanced perspective, we made many changes, large and small, in the second edition.

Changes in the New Edition

In preparing the third edition we have worked hard to keep our book up-to-date and to make it still more effective. First, we have carefully examined the entire book and each of its sections for organization, clarity, and balance. Above all, the treatment of non-European societies has been expanded and enriched, while the history of European developments has been tightened and condensed. In the new edition, therefore, the history of Africa from 400 to 1500 receives a full chapter-length treatment in Chapter 15, permitting a more extensive analysis of early African kingdoms, and an expanded discussion of Mesoamerican civilizations is included in Chapter 16, the Americas before European intrusion. Similarly, in order to do justice to the complex developments occurring in Africa and western Asia in the early modern period, Africa is discussed in Chapter 22 of the new edition and the Middle East and India are the subject of Chapter 23.

As for Europe, Chapter 14 now brings together the history of the high and later Middle Ages in a single chapter. The emergence of royal absolutism and constitutionalism in western and eastern Europe in the early modern period is similarly combined in a reorganized and more sharply focused Chapter 19. For greater clarity, recent social developments in the West have been integrated into the larger, fully up-dated discussion of recovery and crisis in Europe after 1945 in Chapter 36. This chapter covers the transforming events in eastern Europe of recent years, including the revolutions of 1989.

Other major changes include a new section on the study of history and the meaning of civilization in Chapter 1. Islam and Islamic societies receive expanded and reworked coverage throughout the book. Chapter 34 contains a revised discussion of twentieth-century intellectual trends that emphasizes the connection between these movements and subsequent political developments, and Chapter 35 provides a unified account of the Second World War. With these changes and with numerous modifications highlighting crosscultural linkages, we feel we have improved the geographical and cultural balance of our text and written a more integrated and effective world history.

Second, every chapter has been carefully revised to incorporate recent scholarship. Many of our revisions relate to the ongoing explosion in social history, and once again important findings on such subjects as class relations, population, and the family have been integrated into the text. We have made a special effort to keep up with the rapidly growing and increasingly sophisticated scholarship being done in women's history, adding or revising sections on women in early Jewish society and in the Crusades, as well as in the Renaissance, the Reformation, and the Industrial Revolution. The roots of modern feminism have been explored. The revised discussion of the origins and early development of Islam reflects recent scholarship, as does the extended reconsideration of the Ottomans and their cultural and intellectual achievements. Japanese feudalism is also reconsidered in the light of current scholarly thinking.

A major effort has also been made to improve the treatment of economic development and accompanying social changes in the light of new research and fresh concepts. We are proud of the resulting changes, which include a consideration of early Islamic capitalism and agricultural innovation in Chapter 10, a new discussion of early modern crises in Chapter 19, a reexamination of the social and demographic effects of the slave trade in Africa in Chapter 22, and a fundamental rethinking of European industrialization in Chapter 26 and its global significance in Chapter 30. Other subjects not mentioned above that incorporate new scholarship in this edition include early human evolution, Germanic tribes, the Inquisition, industrial progress in early modern China, French industrialization and utopian socialism, and the development of modern Arab nationalism. New topics designed to keep the work fresh and appealing include *I-Ching* thinking in ancient China, Greek federalism, Sufism in the Islamic world, the early European reaction to knowledge of China and Japan, the settlement and the emergence of Australia, reform and revolution in the Soviet Union and eastern Europe in the 1980s, and the recent breakthrough in the struggle for racial equality in South Africa.

Third, the addition of more problems of historical interpretation in the second edition was well received, and we have continued in that direction in this edition. We believe that the problematic element helps the reader develop the critical-thinking skills that are among the most precious benefits of studying history. New examples of this more open-ended, more interpretive approach include the significance of Chinese economic development in the eighteenth century (Chapter 24), the social costs of English enclosure and the impact of industrialization on women and the standard of living (Chapter 26), and the impact of slavery on the black family in the United States (Chapter 31).

Finally, the illustrative component of our work has been completely revised. There are many new illustrations, including nearly two hundred color reproductions that let both great art and important events come alive. As in earlier editions, all illustrations have been carefully selected to complement the text, and all carry captions that enhance their value. Artwork remains an integral part of our book, for the past can speak in pictures as well as in words.

The use of full color throughout this edition also serves to clarify the maps and graphs and to enrich the textual material. Again for improved clarity, maps from the second edition have been completely redesigned to provide easily read and distinguished labels and prominent boundaries and topographical relief. We have also added new maps that illustrate social as well as political developments, including maps on Europe at 1715, the Safavid Empire, the ethnic and political boundaries of the Soviet republics, the reform movements of 1989 in eastern Europe, the world drug trade, and the Persian Gulf War.

In addition to the many maps that support text discussion, we offer a new, full-color map essay at the beginning of each volume. Our purpose is twofold. First, by reproducing and describing such cartographic landmarks as the Babylonian world map, the Islamic al-Idrisi map, the medieval Ebstorf map, the twelfth-century map of China, maps of the Americas and Africa based on Ptolemy and Mercator, the Japanese world map of 1645, and contemporary global projections and satellite images, we hope to demonstrate for students the evolution of cartography and to guide them toward an understanding of the varied functions and uses of maps. Second, the map essay is intended to show depictions of the world from different cultural perspectives and to reveal the changing concepts of our world and its interrelated parts from antiquity to the present. In a real sense, the map essay may serve as an introduction to the course as well as to cartography.

Distinctive Features

Distinctive features from earlier editions remain in the third. To help guide the reader toward historical understanding we have posed specific historical questions at the beginning of each chapter. These questions are then answered in the course of the chapter, each of which concludes with a concise summary of the chapter's findings. The timelines have proved useful, and the double-page comparative timelines, which allow students to compare simultaneous developments within different world areas, have been revised and updated.

We have also tried to suggest how historians actually work and think. We have quoted extensively from a wide variety of primary sources and have demonstrated in our use of these quotations how historians sift and weigh evidence. We want the reader to think critically and to realize that history is neither a list of cut-and-dried facts nor a sense-less jumble of conflicting opinions. It is our further hope that the primary quotations, so carefully fitted into their historical context, will give the reader a sense that even in the earliest and most remote periods of human experience, history has been shaped by individual men and women, some of them great aristocrats, others ordinary folk.

Each chapter concludes with carefully selected suggestions for further reading. These suggestions are briefly described to help readers know where to turn to continue thinking and learning about the world. The chapter bibliographies have been revised and expanded to keep them current with the vast and complex new work being done in many fields.

World civilization courses differ widely in chronological structure from one campus to another. To accommodate the various divisions of historical time into intervals that fit a two-quarter, three-quarter, or two-semester period, *A History of World Societies* is published in three versions, each set embracing the complete work:

One-volume hardcover edition, A HISTORY OF WORLD SOCIETIES; a two-volume paperback, A HISTORY OF WORLD SOCIETIES *Volume I: To 1715* (Chapters 1–19), *Volume II: Since 1500* (Chapters 18–39); and a three-volume paperback, A HISTORY OF WORLD SOCIETIES *Volume A: From Antiquity Through the Middle Ages* (Chapters 1–16), *Volume B: From 1100 Through the French Revolution* (Chapters 14–25), *Volume C: From the French Revolution to the Present* (Chapters 25–39).

Note that overlapping chapters in the two- and three-volume sets permit still wider flexibility in matching the appropriate volume with the opening and closing dates of a course term.

Ancillaries

Learning and teaching ancillaries, including a *Study Guide, MicroStudy Plus* (a computerized version of the *Study Guide*), *Instructor's Resource Manual, Test Items, MicroTest* (a computerized version of the *Test Items*), and *Map Transparencies,* also contribute to the usefulness of the text. The excellent *Study Guide* has been thoroughly revised by Professor James Schmiechen of Central Michigan University. Professor Schmiechen has been a tower of strength ever since he critiqued our initial prospectus, and he has continued to give us many valuable suggestions and his warmly appreciated support. His *Study Guide* contains chapter summaries, chapter outlines, review questions, extensive multiple-choice exercises, self-check lists of important concepts and events, and a variety of study aids and suggestions. New to the third edition are study-review exercises on the interpretation of visual sourc es and major political ideas as well as suggested issues for discussion and essay and chronology reviews. Another major addition is the section, Understanding the Past Through Primary Sources. Seven primary source documents widely used by historians are included, each preceded by a description of the author and source and followed by questions for analysis. The *Study Guide* also retains the very successful sections on studying effectively. These sections take the student by ostensive example through reading and studying activities like underlining, summarizing, identifying main points, classifying information according to sequence, and making historical comparisons. To enable both students and instructors to use the *Study Guide* with the greatest possible flexibility, the guide is available in two volumes, with considerable overlapping of chapters. Instructors and students who use only Volumes A and B of the text have all the pertinent study materials in a single volume, *Study Guide, Volume 1* (Chapters 1–25); likewise, those who use only Volumes B and C of the text also have all the necessary materials in one volume, *Study Guide, Volume 2* (Chapters 14–39).

The multiple-choice sections of the *Study Guide* are also available as *MicroStudy Plus,* a computerized, tutorial version that tells students not only which response is correct but also why each of the other choices is wrong and provides the page numbers of the text where each question is discussed. *MicroStudy Plus* is available for both IBM and Macintosh computers.

The *Instructor's Resource Manual,* prepared by Professor John Marshall Carter of Oglethorpe University, contains learning objectives, chapter synopses, suggestions for lectures and discussion, paper and class activity topics, and lists of audiovisual resources. Professor Carter also offers suggestions for the instructor who is teaching world history for the first time. The accompanying *Test Items,* by Professor Charles Crouch of St. John's University in Collegeville, Minnesota, offer identification, multiple-choice, and essay questions for a total of approximately two thousand test items. These test items are available to adopters in both IBM and Macintosh versions, both of which include editing capabilities. In addition, a set of full-color *Map Transparencies* of all the maps in the text is available on adoption.

JOHN P. MCKAY

BENNETT D. HILL

JOHN BUCKLER

Acknowledgments

It is a pleasure to thank the many instructors who have read and critiqued the manuscript through its development:

Martin Berger
Youngstown State University

Elton Daniel
University of Hawaii, Manoa

Ronald Davis
Western Michigan University

Joseph Dorinson
Long Island University

Surjit Dulai
Michigan State University

Bruce Garver
University of Nebraska, Omaha

Robert Gowen
East Carolina University

Bruce Haight
Western Michigan University

Hines Hall
Auburn University

Deanna Haney
Lansing Community College

Eugene Huck
Kennesaw State College

Margaret Hutton
Jackson State University

Jim Jackson
Point Loma Nazarene College

Gregory Kozlowski
DePaul University

Glenn Nichols
Sul Ross State University

William Ochsenwald
Virginia Polytechnic Institute and State University

Donathan Olliff
Auburn University

Oliver Pollak
University of Nebraska, Omaha

Donald Reid
Georgia State University

John Ruedy
Georgetown University

Lowell Satre
Youngstown State University

Martin Seedorf
Eastern Washington University

Anita Shelton
Eastern Illinois University

Sara Sohmer
University of Hawaii, Manoa

Alexander Sydorenko
Arkansas State University

Joanne Van Horne
Fairmont State College

James Weland
Bentley College

Many colleagues at the University of Illinois provided information and stimulation for our book, often without even knowing it. N. Frederick Nash, Rare Book Librarian, gave freely of his time and made many helpful suggestions for illustrations. The World Heritage Museum at the University continued to allow us complete access to its sizable holdings. James Dengate kindly supplied information on objects from the museum's collection. Caroline Buckler took many excellent photographs of the museum's objects and generously helped us at crucial moments in production. We greatly appreciate such wide-ranging expertise. Bennett Hill wishes to express his sincere appreciation to Ramón de la Fuente of Washington, D.C., for his support, encouragement, and research assistance in the preparation of this third edition.

Each of us has benefited from the generous criticism of his co-authors, although each of us assumes responsibility for what he has written. John Buckler has written Chapters 1–8 and 11; Bennett Hill has continued the narrative in Chapters 9–10, 12–18, part of 19, 23–24, and 31; and John McKay has written part of 19 and Chapters 20–21, 25–30, and 32–39. Finally, we continue to welcome from our readers comments and suggestions for improvements, for they have helped us greatly in this ongoing endeavor.

Expanding Horizons:
*M*apmaking in the World

Today cartography, the art of making maps, is as widespread as typography, the process of printing. Maps are so much a part of daily life that people take them for granted. But people are not born with maps in their heads, as they are with fingers on their hands. The very concept of a map is a human invention of vast intellectual and practical importance. Like writing itself, cartography depends on people's use of visual and symbolic means to portray reality. Earth is not a flat table. Instead it is marked by features such as mountains, valleys, rivers, and oceans and by the distances that separate them all. Knowledge of these physical features and the accurate mapping of them allow people to understand their relationship to the planet on which they live.

Cartographers contribute something singular to the understanding of peoples. Human beings, no matter where they live, have a natural curiosity about their world and find joy in discovering new parts of it or in learning more about regions not well known. The Roman statesman and orator Cicero once asked, "Ubinam gentium sumus?" ("Where in the world are we?") Although he used this question as a figure of speech, many people have been quite serious about finding an accurate answer to it. Such curiosity and desire have led people to examine not only the earth but its relation to the cosmos of which it is a part. Early cartographers learned to use the stars as fixed points for the measurement of place and distance. Even today American nuclear submarines depend on

MAP 1 Babylonian world map, ca 600 B.C. (*Source: Courtesy of the Trustees of the British Museum*)

celestial navigation, transmitted by satellite, to determine their course and position. Once people looked to the stars, they began to wonder about the shape, nature, and content of the universe itself. Mapping of the earth was no longer enough; people began to chart the cosmos. The Hubble space satellite, launched in May 1990, is a sign that the quest continues today.

For ordinary purposes cartography fills a host of practical needs. Maps were first used to describe people's immediate environment—to illustrate the shape of villages and the boundaries of fields. As knowledge of the earth grew, maps became indispensable for travel, both on land and at sea. It was necessary for people to know where their destination lay, how to reach it, and what to expect along the way. Mariners used the geographical knowledge provided by maps to sail from one port to another.

Other uses of early maps were economic. As people came into contact with one another, they saw new opportunities for barter and trade. It was no longer enough to know how to travel to different locations. Merchants needed to understand the geography of their markets and to know what foreign lands produced and what trading partners wanted in return for their goods. In short, economic contact itself increased knowledge of the face of the land, and that knowledge could be preserved on maps by symbols to indicate the natural resources and products of various lands.

Another important function of early maps was military. Rulers and generals needed information about distances and the terrain through which their armies would move and fight. This need spurred interest in *topography,* the detailed description and representation of the natural and artificial features of a landscape, and led to greater accuracy of maps and better definition of the physical environment.

The demands of empire were not only military but also administrative. An area cannot be governed effectively unless the ruler knows where each part of it is located and what its importance is. Rulers need precise maps to enforce their authority, dispatch commands, collect taxes, and maintain order. Thus the value to historians of some maps lies in their illustration of people's knowledge of the world in relation to the needs of government and the exercise of authority over broad distances.

Those are only a few of the uses of cartography. But what of the maps themselves? How do cartographers visually and accurately depict large sections of land or the entire face of the globe? The ways are numerous and some more exact than others.

The earliest maps are pictures of towns showing spatial relationships within a very limited area. A more accurate way of making a map was derived from land surveys. Beginning about 1500 B.C., surveyors trained in geometry and trigonometry began to study the land in question and to divide its physical features into a series of measured angles and elevations. Cartographers then placed this information on a grid so that they could represent visually, according to a consistent and logical system, relations among areas. Although the method sounds simple, it presented a daunting problem, one that still exists. Mapmakers must represent on a two-dimensional surface the face of a three-dimensional globe. To complicate matters even further, the earth is not a perfect sphere. How cartographers have grappled with these problems can be seen from the maps reproduced here.

Since maps are basically visual, it is best to trace their evolution in their own context. People of all cultures have mapped their lands, and in many cases their approaches have been strikingly similar. The earliest known representation of the world is a Babylonian world map that dates to about 600 B.C. (Map 1). It is not a map of the entire globe, for the Babylonians were ignorant of the existence of many people beyond their immediate frontiers. Instead, Babylon, with its neighbors around it, lies at the center of the world. Surrounding the land is the ocean, depicted as a circle. The triangles beyond the ocean indicate that the Babylonians knew something of the peoples beyond the ocean. Here for the first time is evidence of a people who attempted to put themselves geographically into the context of their larger world.

The greatest geographer of the Greco-Roman period was Claudius Ptolemaeus, better known as Ptolemy, who lived in Alexandria in the second century A.D. He advanced far beyond the schematic Babylonian world map to produce a scientific atlas based on data. He knew from previous scholars that the world was spherical, so he devised a way of using conic lines of *longitude,* angular distances east and west, and *latitude,* angular distances north and south, to plot the positions and distances of the earth's features. Despite its distortions, Ptolemy's *Geographia* became the standard Western work on geography until Europeans sailed out to explore the broader world around them (ca 1450–1650). The best illustration of Ptolemy's brilliant vision actually dates much later than its first representation. It dates to a manuscript produced in the German city of Ulm in 1482 (Map 2). Ptolemy put cartography on a scientific basis.

Some of the fruits of Ptolemy's labor can be seen in the series of maps known as the Peutinger Table, which probably dates to ca A.D. 500. The Table is a good example of how cartography served the Roman Empire. The section shown here is typical of the entire series: it indicates roads, rivers, mountains, cities, and towns in Greece (Map 3). In that respect it is an ancient road map, for its purpose was not to define the known world, as Ptolemy had done, but to inform the emperor and his bureaucracy how they could most easily administer and communicate with the provinces. Although alien to modern notions of the shape of Europe, the Peutinger Table is a remarkably accurate atlas of routes and distances and thus displays vividly and beautifully one of the most practical functions of cartography. The table received its name from Konrad Peutinger of Augsburg, an owner of the maps in the sixteenth century.

Islamic cartographers also drew heavily on Ptolemy's research, but they relied on exploration as well. The most famous of them as al-Idrisi, who lived in the twelfth century. His atlas depicted the entire known world and was accompanied by a

MAP 2 Map from Ptolemy's *Geographica* (Source: Michael Holford)

MAP 3 Section of the Peutinger Table illustrating Greece, ca A.D. 500 *(Source: Oster-reichische Nationalbibliothek)*

MAP 4 Portion of the map of al-Idrisi, thirteenth century *(Source: Reproduced by per-mission of Norman J. W. Thrower, Department of Geography, UCLA)*

MAP 5 Ebstorf Map, thirteenth century *(Source: Niedersächsische Landesbibliothek Hannover)*

written commentary about the places illustrated. The portion shown here represents the eastern Mediterranean and the Middle East (Map 4). As in the Peutinger Table, physical features such as rivers and mountains are stylized, but al-Idrisi made a serious effort to delineate the general features of the landmass. His map looks different from modern maps because he used south as his basic point of orientation, not north as do modern cartographers. As a result, the atlas appears upside down to our eyes, with south being at the top of the map.

Europeans in the Middle Ages, like their predecessors, drew maps of the world, but religion became an ingredient of cartography. Ptolemy's concepts of geography remained in force, but maps also served another and different purpose for society. The Ebstorf Map, drawn during the thirteenth century, shows the world surrounded by the ocean, a conception dating to antiquity (Map 5). Yet the map has several novel features. In its background is the crucified Jesus. His head, portrayed at the top, signifies the east. His outstretched arms point north and south. His feet, at the bottom, signify the west. Jerusalem occupies the center of the map to represent the place of Jesus's death as the center of the Christian world. The Ebstorf Map, unlike the practical maps of the Peutinger Table, was intended to convey a religious message, a declaration of faith.

Like the Romans, the Chinese early found it necessary to draw maps to administer efficiently the vast tracts of land under their control. The Chinese so successfully mastered the problem of reducing a huge amount of territory into a visually manageable scale that in the twelfth century they produced the Yü Chi Thu Map (Map of the Tracks of Yü the Great) (Map 6). Although the name of the geographer is unknown, his achievement is monumental. He used a system of uniform square grids to locate features of the land in exact and measured relationship to one another. The outline of the coast and the courses of the rivers are remarkably accurate. As in the case of early European maps of Africa (see Map 10), knowledge of the interior was somewhat scanty. Nonetheless, the geographer devised a reliable system in which new discoveries could be easily fitted into what was already known.

In the Americas, maps were sometimes put to a novel use. The pre-Columbian picture map (Map 7) at first sight does not look like a map at all. Dating from sometime before the sixteenth century, it portrays the history of the Mixtec people of Mexico, who can be traced from about 800. Geographical features are incidental to the historical narrative. Nevertheless, the map amply demonstrates the originality of the pre-Columbian Americans in the art of mapmaking.

Meanwhile, the people of the European Middle Ages continued to draw maps along the lines set out by Ptolemy, yet they made improvements on the work of the master. Indeed, they explored the concept of triangulation to survey the land and to navigate the seas. Cartographers chose several major points to serve as hubs of a series of lines extended to other major points. The face of the globe was thereby cut up into a pattern of triangles, rectangles, and occasionally squares. Al-

Map 6 After the Yü Chi Thu Map, twelfth century *(Source: Pei Lin Museum, Sian, China)*

MAP 7 The Dominions of Quetzalcoatl 9 Wind, *Lord of the Toltecs. From the Codex Zouche-Nuttall (Source: Courtesy of the Trustees of the British Museum (Museum of Mankind))*

though this system proved complicated and unwieldy, triangulation did improve the utility of maps for explorers. An excellent example of a triangulated map comes from the Catalan Atlas of 1375 (Map 8). The atlas is more functional than other early maps because the cartographer indicated orientation, so that users could locate their position according to the points of a compass.

Only when the Europeans began to explore the broader world around them did they make significant advances over Ptolemy's view of the world. Sailors and navigators who voyaged to find new lands or to learn more about familiar places had to be able to calculate where they were. They knew that the world was curved, and they used the stars as fixed points to guide them. It is thus ironic that one of the most important advances in geographic knowledge came by mistake. In 1492 Christopher Columbus, looking for a sea passage to India, discovered the New World by sailing westward from Europe. Although Columbus himself did not immediately recognize the full significance of his achievement, his discovery revolutionized geographical thinking: there was more to the world than Ptolemy had known; and the basic features of the earth had to be explored, relationships rethought, and a new way of looking at the globe found.

Perhaps nothing better indicates the fluid state of geography and cartography at the end of the fifteenth century than Juan de la Cosa's map of Columbus's second voyage to the Americas (Map 9). A navigator and an explorer, de la Cosa charted the newly found coast of Central America using the points of the compass to orient the fall of the land and triangulation to project his findings inland. Although he could depict the coastline accurately because of direct observation, he could reveal little about the land beyond.

The discoveries of the European explorers opened a new era in the West and throughout the rest of the world, both in how people thought of the world and in how mapmakers depicted the new findings. These pioneers were also on the threshold of uniting European, American, and Asian traditions of cartography. The real breakthrough came with Geradus Mercator (1512–1594). Mercator improved Ptolemy's system of latitude and longitude by substituting straight lines for Ptolemy's curved lines. In that respect, Mercator's cartographic organization was similar to that used by the Chinese geographer of the Yü Chi Thu Map, but Mercator's plan applied over the face of the globe. Mercator used this grid to incorporate the discoveries in a completely new atlas. Admittedly, his method distorts the actual physical relations of the landmasses over broad spaces. Areas in the polar regions appear larger than lands near the equator. For instance, Greenland on his grid is larger than South America. More important, however, Mercator showed that every portion of the world may be portrayed as possessing four right angles to orient users of any one of his maps to any portion of his other maps. Mercator's grid, in one form or another, endures as a cartographic staple to this day.

The cumulative effects of the advance of knowledge in geography and cartography can best be

MAP 8 Catalan Atlas of 1375 *(Source: Bibliothèque Nationale, Paris/Photo Hubert Josse)*

MAP 9   Juan de la Cosa's map of Columbus's discoveries, 1493 *(Source: Museo Naval de Madrid)*

MAP 10 Blaeu's map of Africa, from *Grooten Atlas*, 1648–65 *(Source: The British Library, Department of Maps)*

seen in two maps that demonstrate increasing familiarity with Africa. The map of Dutch cartographer Willem Blaeu, dating to the early seventeenth century, brings together the concepts of scale maps and picture maps (Map 10). Explorers had an accurate idea only of the shape of the continent. The inland was *terra incognita,* unknown territory where dwelt fabulous beasts and peoples. The amazing progress of human knowledge of the land and how to map it can be seen by comparing Blaeu's map of Africa with the one of French cartographer Jean-Baptiste d'Anville published in 1747 (Map 11). D'Anville made excellent use of Mercator's system to produce a profile of Africa that could find its place in any modern atlas. Yet

d'Anville was intellectually honest enough to leave the interior of Africa largely blank. D'Anville's map is not so visually delightful as Blaeu's, but in terms of cartography it is far more important. It showed its users what was yet to be discovered and how to proceed with finding it.

European penetration of Asia excited another desire for maps. In 1822 the Frenchman J. B. J. Gentil published a map of India (Map 12) that bears some slight similarity to Blaeu's earlier map of Africa. The map, which dates from 1770, is actually a drawing by an Indian of Chadjeanabad province. Like Blaeu's map, it contains drawings of animals, fruits, and costumes of the local natives. It is also similar to the pre-Columbian map of the

MAP 11 D'Anville's map of Africa, 1747 *(Source: Library of Congress, Department of Maps)*

MAP 12 Map of Chadjeanabad province, India, 1770 *(Source: The British Library, Oriental and India Office Collections)*

MAP 13 Shanawdithit's map of central Newfoundland, 1829 *(Source: Newfoundland Museum)*

MAP 14 Kiangsi province in southeast China, eighteenth century *(Source: The British Library, Department of Maps)*

dominions of Quetzalcoatl (see Map 7) in that it possesses little geographical significance. Yet it portrays many of the salient human, zoological, and botanical features of the region.

An excellent example of the combination of pictorial and geographical features of a landscape comes from a map drawn in 1829 by Shanawdithit, a woman who was the last of the Beothuk Indians of Newfoundland (Map 13). This historico-pictorial map depicts the trek of her tribe crossing an ice-covered lake along the Exploits River in central Newfoundland. It tells the story of the journey while giving an impression of the geographical features of the land through which she and her people passed.

A beautiful early-eighteenth-century Chinese map of Kiangsi province (Map 14) shows a single prefecture, at the center of which is a walled town. The mapmaker carefully depicted the features of Kiangsi, to the point of showing individual buildings in their geographical setting. Thus the nature of the landscape, both rivers and mountains, is pictorially displayed, not as on a map but rather as a view seen from above. Although this is a picture-map, unlike the more technical map by al-Idrisi (see Map 4), it gives the user a vivid sense of the landscape.

Interesting by contrast is the Bankoku Sozu (or World Map) drawn in Japan in 1645, a half-century earlier than the Chinese map of Kiangsi.

MAP 15 Bankoku Sozu, Map of the World, 1645 *(Source: Kobe City Museum)*

This map (Map 15) resembles Ptolemy's map of the world in its definition of landmasses, their configurations, and their major features. Like d'Anville (see Map 11), the Japanese cartographer indicated candidly—in the legends at the top and bottom of the map—that geographical knowledge of these regions was hazy because few people had explored them. Yet in its basics the concept behind this map is Ptolemy's. Both were more interested in portraying the nature of the landmass and the physical relation of one place to another than in drawing a picture of the landscape.

Mapmakers still grapple with the problem of accurately depicting landmasses—their shapes and their spatial relationships—on an earth that is not a perfect sphere. No matter what projection they use, some geographical areas are distorted. In struggling with this problem, cartographers have used circles, ovals, and rectangles to display regions of the earth on a flat surface. The orthographic projection (the circular maps at the four corners of Map 16) uses circles and is one of the oldest projections. Because it shows only one hemisphere at a time, distortion is minimized, especially at the center of the map, where attention is focused. It allows a realistic view of the globe, but it makes possible the display of only one hemisphere at a time. One way to minimize distortion while showing more than one hemisphere is to represent the tops of the poles as lines rather than as points, as shown in the Robinson projection (the center image of Map 16). There is still some distortion (note how large Antarctica is), but cutting off the poles diminishes it. The Robinson projection is a compromise because it sacrifices some accuracy in area to achieve less distortion in shape.

Modern attempts to depict visually the nearly spherical earth on flat maps remind people that the problems first perceived by early cartographers remain to be solved. Yet contemporary cartographers enjoy the use of a new and unusual tool for

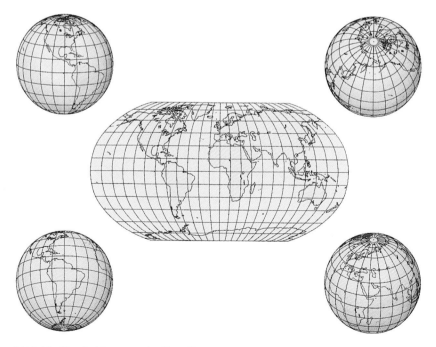

MAP 16 The Robinson projection *(Source: Reproduced with permission from WHICH MAP IS BEST? © 1988, by the American Congress on Surveying and Mapping)*

MAP 17 Landsat image of Brazil *(Source: GEOPIC™*, Earth Satellite Corporation)

mapping the globe and exploring the universe: the orbiting satellite. Technology has become so precise within the past ten years that the parts of the earth difficult to enter or too remote and forbidding to explore can be examined with minute accuracy from space. The Landsat satellite image of Brazil (Map 17) gives an excellent idea of how much more there is to learn about the earth.

JOHN BUCKLER

SUGGESTED READING

Bagrow, Leo. *History of Cartography.* 2d ed. Chicago: Precedent Publishing, 1985. Brown, Lloyd A. *The Story of Maps.* New York: Dover, 1979. Dilke, O. A. W. *Greek and Roman Maps.* Ithaca: Cornell University Press, 1985. Harley, J. B., and D. Woodward, eds. *The History of Cartography,* Vol. 1: *Cartography in Prehistoric, Ancient and Medieval Europe and the Mediterranean.* Chicago: University of Chicago Press, 1967. Harvey, Paul D. A. *The History of Topographical Maps.* London: Thames & Hudson, 1980. Hodgkiss, Alan G. *Understanding Maps: A Systematic History of Their Use and Development.* Folkestone, England: Dawson, 1981. Skelton, Raleigh A. *Decorative Printed Maps of the Fifteenth to Eighteenth Centuries.* London: Staples Press, 1952, reprinted by Spring Books, 1970. Skelton, Raleigh A. *Explorers' Maps: Chapters in the Cartographic Record of Geographical Discovery.* London: Routledge and Kegan Paul, 1958, reprinted by Spring Books, 1970. Thrower, Norman J. W. *Maps & Man: An Examination of Cartography in Relation to Culture and Civilization.* Englewood Cliffs, N.J.: Prentice-Hall, 1978, Tooley, R. V., Cand Bricker, and G. R. Crone. *A History of Cartography: 2500 Years of Maps and Mapmakers.* London: Thames & Hudson, 1969.

25

The Revolution in
Western Politics,
1775–1815

The Tennis Court Oath. Members of the Third Estate meet at an indoor tennis court, June 20, 1789

The last years of the eighteenth century were a time of great upheaval. A series of revolutions and revolutionary wars challenged the old order of kings and aristocrats. The ideas of freedom and equality, ideas that have not stopped shaping the world since that era, flourished and spread. The revolution began in North America in 1775. Then in 1789 France, the most influential country in Europe, became the leading revolutionary nation. It established first a constitutional monarchy, then a radical republic, and finally a new empire under Napoleon. The armies of France also joined forces with patriots and radicals abroad in an effort to establish new governments based on new principles throughout much of Europe. The world of modern domestic and international politics was born.

- What caused this era of revolution?
- What were the ideas and objectives of the men and women who rose up violently to undo the established system?
- What were the gains and losses for privileged groups and for ordinary people in a generation of war and upheaval?

These are the questions underlying this chapter's examination of the French and American revolutions.

LIBERTY AND EQUALITY

Two ideas fueled the revolutionary period in both America and Europe: liberty and equality. What did eighteenth-century politicians and other people mean by liberty and equality, and why were those ideas so radical and revolutionary in their day?

The call for liberty was first of all a call for individual human rights. Even the most enlightened monarchs customarily claimed that it was their duty to regulate what people wrote and believed. Liberals of the revolutionary era protested such controls from on high. They demanded freedom to worship according to the dictates of their consciences instead of according to the politics of their prince. They demanded the end of censorship and the right to express their beliefs freely in print and at public meetings. They demanded freedom from arbitrary laws and from judges who simply obeyed orders from the government.

These demands for basic personal freedoms, which were incorporated into the American Bill of Rights and other liberal constitutions, were very far-reaching. Indeed, eighteenth-century revolutionaries demanded more freedom than most governments today believe it is desirable to grant. The Declaration of the Rights of Man, issued at the beginning of the French Revolution, proclaimed, "Liberty consists in being able to do anything that does not harm another person." A citizen's rights had, therefore, "no limits except those which assure to the other members of society the enjoyment of these same rights." Liberals called for the freedom of the individual to develop and to create to the fullest possible extent. In the context of the aristocratic and monarchial forms of government that then dominated Europe, this was a truly radical idea.

The call for liberty was also a call for a new kind of government. The revolutionary liberals believed that the people were sovereign—that is, that the people alone had the authority to make laws limiting an individual's freedom of action. In practice, this system of government meant choosing legislators who represented the people and who were accountable to them. Moreover, liberals of the revolutionary era believed that every people—in other words, every ethnic group—had this right of self-determination and, thus, the right to form a free nation.

By equality, eighteenth-century liberals meant that all citizens were to have identical rights and civil liberties. Above all, the nobility had no right to special privileges based on the accident of birth.

Liberals did not define equality as meaning that everyone should be equal economically. Quite the contrary. As Thomas Jefferson wrote in an early draft of the American Declaration of Independence, before changing "property" to the more noble-sounding "happiness," everyone was equal in "the pursuit of property." Jefferson and other liberals certainly did not expect equal success in that pursuit. Great differences in wealth and income between rich and poor were perfectly acceptable to liberals. The essential point was that everyone should legally have an equal chance. French liberals and revolutionaries said that they wanted "careers opened to talent." They wanted employment in government, in business, and in the professions to be based on ability, not on family background or legal status.

Equality of opportunity was a very revolutionary idea in eighteenth-century Europe. Legal inequality between classes and groups was the rule, not the exception. Society was still legally divided into groups with special privileges, such as the nobility and the clergy, and groups with special burdens, like the peasantry. In many countries, various middle-class groups—professionals, business people, townspeople, and craftsmen—enjoyed privileges that allowed them to monopolize all sorts of economic activity. It was this kind of economic inequality, an inequality based on artificial legal distinctions, against which liberals protested.

The Roots of Liberalism

The ideas of liberty and equality—the central ideas of classical liberalism—have deep roots in Western history. The ancient Greeks and the Judeo-Christian tradition had affirmed for hundreds of years the sanctity and value of the individual human being. The Judeo-Christian tradition, reinforced by the Reformation, had long stressed the personal responsibility of both common folk and exalted rulers, thereby promoting the self-discipline without which liberty becomes anarchy. The hounded and persecuted Protestant radicals of the late sixteenth century had died for the revolutionary idea that individuals were entitled to their own religious beliefs.

Although the liberal creed had roots deep in the Western tradition, classical liberalism first crystallized at the end of the seventeenth century and during the Enlightenment of the eighteenth century. Liberal ideas reflected the Enlightenment's stress on human dignity and human happiness on earth. Liberals shared the Enlightenment's general faith in science, rationality, and progress: the adoption of liberal principles meant better government and a better society for all. Almost all the writers of the Enlightenment were passionately committed to greater personal liberty. They preached religious toleration, freedom of press and speech, and fair and equal treatment before the law.

Certain English and French thinkers were mainly responsible for joining the Enlightenment's concern for personal freedom and legal equality to a theoretical justification of liberal self-government. The two most important were John Locke and the baron de Montesquieu. Locke (see page 648) maintained that England's long political tradition rested on "the rights of Englishmen" and on representative government through Parliament. Locke admired especially the great Whig nobles who had made the bloodless revolution of 1688 to 1689, and he argued that if a government oversteps its proper function of protecting the natural rights of life, liberty, and private property, it becomes a tyranny. Montesquieu (see page 672) was also inspired by English constitutional history. He, too, believed that powerful "intermediary groups"—such as the judicial nobility of which he was a proud member—offered the best defense of liberty against despotism.

The Marquis de Lafayette was the most famous great noble to embrace the liberal revolution. Shown here directing a battle in the American Revolution, he returned to champion liberty and equality in France. For admirers he was the "hero of two worlds." (Source: Jean-Loup Charmet)

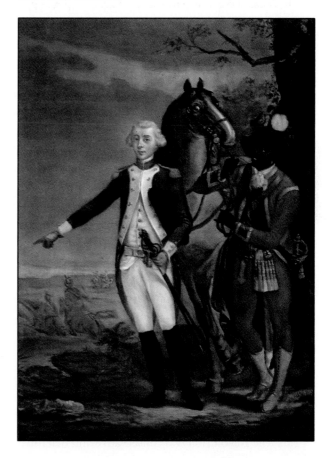

The Attraction of Liberalism

The belief that representative institutions could defend their liberty and interests appealed powerfully to ambitious and educated bourgeois. Yet it is important to realize that liberal ideas about individual rights and political freedom, as formulated by Montesquieu, also appealed to much of the aristocracy, at least in western Europe. Representative government did not mean democracy, which liberal thinkers tended to equate with mob rule. Rather, they envisioned voting for representatives as being restricted to those who owned property, those with a stake in society. England had shown the way. After 1688 it had combined a parliamentary system and considerable individual liberty with a restricted franchise and unquestionable aristocratic pre-eminence. During the eighteenth century, many French nobles, led by a judicial nobility inspired by Montesquieu, were increasingly eager to follow the English example.

Eighteenth-century liberalism, then, appealed not only to the middle class but also to some aristocrats. It found broad support among the educated elite and the substantial classes in western Europe. What it lacked from the beginning was strong mass support. For comfortable liberals, the really important questions were theoretical and political. They had no need to worry about their stomachs and the price of bread. For the much more numerous laboring poor, the great questions were immediate and economic. Getting enough to eat was the crucial challenge. These differences in outlook and well-being were to lead to many misunderstandings and disappointments for both groups in the revolutionary era.

THE AMERICAN REVOLUTION (1775–1789)

The era of liberal revolution began in the New World. The thirteen mainland colonies of British North America revolted against their home country and then succeeded in establishing a new unified government.

Americans have long debated the meaning of their revolution. Some have even questioned whether it was a real revolution, as opposed to a war for independence. According to some scholars, the Revolution was conservative and defensive in that its demands were for the traditional liberties of English citizens; Americans were united against the British, but otherwise they were a satisfied people, not torn by internal conflict. Other scholars have argued that, on the contrary, the American Revolution was quite radical. It split families between patriots and loyalists and divided the country. It achieved goals that were fully as advanced as those obtained by the French in their great revolution a few years later.

How does one reconcile these positions? Both contain large elements of truth. The American revolutionaries did believe that they were demanding only the traditional rights of English men and women. But those traditional rights were liberal rights, and in the American context they had very strong democratic and popular overtones. Thus the American Revolution was fought in the name of established ideals that were still quite radical in the context of the times. And in founding a government firmly based on liberal principles, the Americans set an example that had a forceful impact on Europe and speeded up political development there.

The Origins of the Revolution

The American Revolution had its immediate origins in a squabble over increased taxes. The British government had fought and decisively won the Seven Years' War (see page 680) on the strength of its professional army and navy. The American colonists had furnished little real aid. The high cost of the war to the British, however, had led to a doubling of the British national debt. Anticipating further expense defending its recently conquered western lands from Indian uprisings like that of Pontiac, the British government in London set about reorganizing the empire with a series of bold, largely unprecedented measures. Breaking with tradition, the British decided to maintain a large army in North America after peace was restored in 1763. Moreover, they sought to exercise strict control over their newly conquered western lands and to tax the colonies directly. In 1765 the government pushed through Parliament the Stamp Act, which levied taxes on a long list of commercial and legal documents, diplomas, pamphlets, newspapers, almanacs, dice, and playing cards. A stamp glued to each article indicated that the tax had been paid.

The Boston Tea Party This contemporary illustration shows men disguised as Indians dumping East India Company tea into Boston's harbor. The enthusiastic crowd cheering from the wharf indicates widespread popular support. *(Source: Library of Congress)*

The effort to increase taxes as part of tightening up the empire seemed perfectly reasonable to the British. Heavier stamp taxes had been collected in Great Britain for two generations, and Americans were being asked only to pay a share of their own defense costs. Moreover, Americans had been paying only very low local taxes. The Stamp Act would have doubled taxes to about 2 shillings per person per year. No other people in the European or colonial world (except the Poles) paid so little. The British, meanwhile, paid the highest taxes in the Western world in about 1765—26 shillings per person. Nevertheless, the colonists protested the Stamp Act vigorously and violently; and after riots and boycotts against British goods, Parliament reluctantly repealed the new tax.

As the fury of the Stamp Act controversy revealed, much more was involved than taxes. The key question was political. To what extent could the home government refashion the empire and reassert its power while limiting the authority of colonial legislatures and their elected representatives? Accordingly, who should represent the colonies, and who had the right to make laws for

Americans? While a troubled majority of Americans searched hard for a compromise, some radicals began to proclaim that "taxation without representation is tyranny." The British government replied that Americans were represented in Parliament, albeit indirectly (like most English people themselves), and that the absolute supremacy of Parliament throughout the empire could not be questioned. Many Americans felt otherwise. As John Adams put it, "A Parliament of Great Britain can have no more rights to tax the colonies than a Parliament of Paris." Thus imperial reorganization and parliamentary supremacy came to appear as grave threats to Americans' existing liberties and time-honored institutions.

Americans had long exercised a great deal of independence and gone their own way. In British North America, unlike England and Europe, no powerful established church existed, and personal freedom in questions of religion was taken for granted. The colonial assemblies made the important laws, which were seldom overturned by the home government. The right to vote was much more widespread than in England. In many parts of colonial Massachusetts, for example, as many as 95 percent of the adult males could vote.

Moreover, this greater political equality was matched by greater social and economic equality. Neither a hereditary nobility nor a hereditary serf population existed, although the slavery of the Americas consigned blacks to a legally oppressed caste. Independent farmers were the largest group in the country and set much of its tone. In short, the colonial experience had slowly formed a people who felt themselves separate and distinct from the home country. The controversies over taxation intensified those feelings of distinctiveness and separation and brought them to the fore.

In 1773 the dispute over taxes and representation flared up again. The British government had permitted the financially hard-pressed East India Company to ship its tea from China directly to company agents in the colonies, rather than through London middlemen who sold to independent merchants in the colonies. Thus the company secured a vital monopoly on the tea trade, and colonial merchants were suddenly excluded from a highly profitable business. The colonists were quick to protest.

In Boston, men disguised as Indians had a rowdy "tea party" and threw the company's tea into the harbor. This led to extreme measures. The so-called Coercive Acts closed the port of Boston, curtailed local elections and town meetings, and greatly expanded the royal governor's power. County conventions in Massachusetts protested vehemently and urged that the acts be "rejected as the attempts of a wicked administration to enslave America." Other colonial assemblies joined in the denunciations. In September 1774, the First Continental Congress met in Philadelphia, where the most radical members argued successfully against concessions to the Crown. Compromise was also rejected by the British Parliament; and in April 1775, fighting began at Lexington and Concord in Massachusetts.

The Signing of the Declaration, July 4, 1776 John Trumbull's famous painting shows the dignity and determination of America's revolutionary leaders. An extraordinarily talented group, they succeeded in rallying popular support without losing power to more radical forces in the process. *(Source: Yale University Art Gallery)*

Independence

The fighting spread, and the colonists moved slowly but inevitably toward open rebellion and a declaration of independence. The uncompromising attitude of the British government and its use of German mercenaries helped dissolve long-standing loyalties to the home country and rivalries among the separate colonies. *Common Sense* (1775), a brilliant attack by the recently arrived English radical Thomas Paine (1737–1809), also mobilized public opinion in favor of independence. A runaway best-seller with sales of 120,000 copies in a few months, Paine's tract ridiculed the idea of a small island ruling a great continent. In his call for freedom and republican government, Paine expressed Americans' growing sense of separateness and moral superiority.

On July 4, 1776, the Second Continental Congress adopted the Declaration of Independence. Written by Thomas Jefferson, the Declaration of Independence boldly listed the tyrannical acts committed by George III (r. 1760–1820) and confidently proclaimed the natural rights of humankind and the sovereignty of the American states. Sometimes called the world's greatest political editorial, the Declaration of Independence in effect universalized the traditional rights of English people and made them the rights of all humanity. It stated that "all men are created equal . . . they are endowed by their Creator with certain unalienable rights . . . among these are life, liberty, and the pursuit of happiness." No other American political document has ever caused such excitement, both at home and abroad.

Many American families remained loyal to Britain; many others divided bitterly. After the Declaration of Independence, the conflict often took the form of a civil war—pitting patriot against loyalist. The loyalists tended to be wealthy and politically moderate. Many patriots, too, were wealthy—individuals such as John Hancock and George Washington—but willingly allied themselves with farmers and artisans in a broad coalition. This coalition harassed the loyalists and confiscated their property to help pay for the American war effort. The broad social base of the revolutionaries tended to make the liberal revolution democratic. State governments extended the right to vote to many more people in the course of the war and re-established themselves as republics.

On the international scene, the French sympathized with the rebels from the beginning. They wanted revenge for the humiliating defeats of the Seven Years' War. Officially neutral until 1778, they supplied the great bulk of guns and gunpowder used by the American revolutionaries, very much as neutral great powers supply weapons for "wars of national liberation" in our day. By 1777 French volunteers were arriving in Virginia, and a dashing young nobleman, the marquis de Lafayette (1757–1834), quickly became one of Washington's most trusted generals. In 1778 the French government offered a formal alliance to the American ambassador in Paris, Benjamin Franklin, and in 1779 and 1780 the Spanish and Dutch declared war on Britain. Catherine the Great of Russia helped organize a League of Armed Neutrality in order to protect neutral shipping rights, which Britain refused to recognize.

Thus by 1780 Great Britain was engaged in an imperial war against most of Europe as well as against the thirteen colonies. In these circumstances, and in the face of severe reverses in India, the West Indies, and at Yorktown in Virginia, a new British government decided to cut its losses. American negotiators in Paris were receptive. They feared that France wanted a treaty that would bottle up the new United States east of the Alleghenies and give British holdings west of the Alleghenies to France's ally, Spain. The American negotiators ditched the French and accepted the extraordinarily favorable terms offered by Britain.

By the Treaty of Paris of 1783, Britain recognized the independence of the thirteen colonies and ceded all its territory between the Appalachians and the Mississippi River to the Americans. Out of the bitter rivalries of the Old World, the Americans snatched dominion over half a continent.

Framing the Constitution

The liberal program of the American Revolution was consolidated by the federal Constitution, the Bill of Rights, and the creation of a national republic. Assembling in Philadelphia in the summer of 1787, the delegates to the Constitutional Convention were determined to end the period of economic depression, social uncertainty, and very weak central government that had followed independence. The delegates decided, therefore, to grant the federal, or central, government important powers: regulation of domestic and foreign trade, the right to levy taxes, and the means to enforce its laws.

Strong rule was placed squarely in the context of representative self-government. Senators and congressmen would be the lawmaking delegates of the voters, and the president of the republic would be an elected official. The central government was to operate in Montesquieu's framework of checks and balances. The executive, legislative, and judicial branches would systematically balance each other. The power of the federal government would in turn be checked by the powers of the individual states.

When the results of the secret deliberations of the Constitutional Convention were presented to the states for ratification, a great public debate began. The opponents of the proposed constitution—the Anti-Federalists—charged that the framers of the new document had taken too much power from the individual states and made the federal government too strong. Moreover, many Anti-Federalists feared for the personal liberties and individual freedoms for which they had just fought. In order to overcome these objections, the Federalists solemnly promised to spell out these basic freedoms as soon as the new constitution was adopted. The result was the first ten amendments to the Constitution, which the first Congress passed shortly after it met in New York in March 1789. These amendments formed an effective bill of rights to safeguard the individual. Most of them—trial by jury, due process of law, right to assemble, freedom from unreasonable search—had their origins in English law and the English Bill of Rights of 1689. Others—the freedoms of speech, the press, and religion—reflected natural-law theory and the American experience.

The American Constitution and the Bill of Rights exemplified the great strengths and the limits of what came to be called "classical liberalism." Liberty meant individual freedoms and political safeguards. Liberty also meant representative government but did not necessarily mean democracy with its principle of one person, one vote.

Equality—slaves excepted—meant equality before the law, not equality of political participation or economic well-being. Indeed, economic inequality was resolutely defended by the elite who framed the Constitution. The right to own property was guaranteed by the Fifth Amendment, and if the government took private property, the owner was to receive "just compensation." The radicalism of liberal revolution in America was primarily legal and political, not economic or social.

The Revolution's Impact on Europe

Hundreds of books, pamphlets, and articles analyzed and romanticized the American upheaval. Thoughtful Europeans noted, first of all, its enormous long-term implications for international politics. A secret report by the Venetian ambassador to Paris in 1783 stated what many felt: "If only the union of the Provinces is preserved, it is reasonable to expect that, with the favorable effects of time, and of European arts and sciences, it will become the most formidable power in the world."[1] More generally, American independence fired the imaginations of the few aristocrats who were uneasy with their privileges and of commoners who yearned for greater equality. Many Europeans believed that the world was advancing and that America was leading the way. As one French writer put it in 1789: "This vast continent which the seas surround will soon change Europe and the universe."

Europeans who dreamed of a new era were fascinated by the political lessons of the American Revolution. The Americans had begun with a revolutionary defense against tyrannical oppression, and they had been victorious. They had then shown how rational beings could assemble together to exercise sovereignty and write a permanent constitution—a new social contract. All this gave greater reality to the concepts of individual liberty and representative government. It reinforced one of the primary ideas of the Enlightenment, the idea that a better world was possible.

THE FRENCH REVOLUTION (1789–1791)

No country felt the consequences of the American Revolution more directly than France. Hundreds of French officers served in America and were inspired by the experience. The most famous of these, the young and impressionable marquis de Lafayette, left home as a great aristocrat determined only to fight France's traditional foe, England. He returned with a love of liberty and firm republican convictions. French intellectuals and publicists engaged in passionate analysis of the federal Constitution and the constitutions of the various states of the new United States. The American Revolution undeniably hastened upheaval in France. Yet the French Revolution did not mirror the American example. It was more violent and more complex, more influential and more controversial, more loved and more hated. For Europeans and most of the rest of the world, it was the great revolution of the eighteenth century, the revolution that opened the modern era in politics.

The Breakdown of the Old Order

Like the American Revolution, the French Revolution had its immediate origins in the financial difficulties of the government. The efforts of Louis XV's ministers to raise taxes had been thwarted by the Parlement of Paris, strengthened in its opposition by widespread popular support (see pages 683–684). When renewed efforts to reform the tax system met a similar fate in 1776, the government was forced to finance all of its enormous expenditures during the American war with borrowed money. The national debt and the annual budget deficit soared. By the 1780s fully half of France's annual budget went for ever-increasing interest payments on the ever-increasing debt. Another quarter went to maintain the military, and 6 percent was absorbed by the costly and extravagant king and his court at Versailles. Less than one-fifth of the entire national budget was available for the productive functions of the state, such as transportation and general administration. It was an impossible financial situation.

One way out would have been for the government to declare partial bankruptcy, forcing its creditors to accept greatly reduced payments on the debt. The powerful Spanish monarchy had regularly repudiated large portions of its debt in earlier times, and France had done likewise after an attempt to establish a French national bank ended in financial disaster in 1720. Yet by the 1780s the French debt was held by an army of aristocratic and bourgeois creditors, and the French monarchy, though absolute in theory, had become far too weak for such a drastic and unpopular action.

Nor could the king and his ministers, unlike modern governments, print money and create inflation to cover their deficits. Unlike England and Holland, which had far larger national debts relative to their populations, France had no central bank, no paper currency, and no means of creating credit. French money was good gold coin. Therefore, when a depressed economy and a lack of public confidence made it increasingly difficult for the government to obtain new gold loans in 1786, it had no alternative but to try to increase taxes. And since France's tax system was unfair and out of date, increased revenues were possible only through fundamental reforms. Such reforms, which would affect all groups in France's complex and fragmented society, opened a Pandora's box of social and political demands.

Legal Orders and Social Realities

As in the Middle Ages, France's 25 million inhabitants were still legally divided into three orders, or "estates"—the clergy, the nobility, and everyone else. As the nation's first estate, the clergy numbered about 100,000 and had important privileges. It owned about 10 percent of the land and paid only a "voluntary gift" to the government every five years; moreover, the church levied on landowners a tax (the tithe) that averaged somewhat less than 10 percent. Much of the church's income was drained away from local parishes by political appointees and worldly aristocrats at the top of the church hierarchy, to the intense dissatisfaction of the poor parish priests.

The second legally defined estate consisted of some 400,000 noblemen and noblewomen—the descendants of "those who fought" in the Middle Ages. The nobles owned outright about 25 percent of the land in France, and they, too, were taxed very lightly. Moreover, nobles continued to enjoy certain manorial rights, or privileges of lordship, that dated back to medieval times and allowed them to tax the peasantry for their own profit—through exclusive rights to hunt and fish, village monopolies on baking bread and pressing grapes for wine, fees for justice, and other "useful privileges." Nobles also had "honorific privileges," such as the right to precedence on public occasions and the right to wear a sword. These rights conspicuously proclaimed the nobility's legal superiority and exalted social position.

Everyone else was a commoner, a member of the third estate. A few commoners were rich merchants or highly successful doctors and lawyers. Many more were urban artisans and unskilled day laborers. The vast majority of the third estate consisted of the peasants and agricultural workers in the countryside. Thus the third estate was a conglomeration of vastly different social groups, united only by their shared legal status as distinct from the privileged nobility and clergy.

In discussing the long-term origins of the French Revolution, historians have long focused on growing tensions between the nobility and the comfortable members of the third estate, usually known as the *bourgeoisie,* or middle class. A dominant historical interpretation has held sway for at least two generations. According to this interpretation, the bourgeoisie was basically united by economic position and class interest. Aided by the general economic expansion discussed in Chapter 21, the middle class grew rapidly in the eighteenth century, tripling to about 2.3 million persons, or about 8 percent of France's population. Increasing in size, wealth, culture, and self-confidence, this rising bourgeoisie became progressively exasperated by archaic "feudal" laws restraining the economy and by the growing pretensions of a reactionary nobility, which was closing ranks against middle-class needs and aspirations. As a result, the French bourgeoisie eventually rose up to lead the entire third estate in a great social revolution, a revolution that destroyed feudal privileges and established a capitalist order based on individualism and a market economy.

In recent years, a flood of new research has challenged these views, and once again the French Revolution is a subject of heated scholarly debate. Above all, revisionist historians have questioned the existence of a growing social conflict between a progressive capitalistic bourgeoisie and a reactionary feudal nobility in eighteenth-century France. Instead, these historians see both bourgeoisie and nobility as highly fragmented, riddled with internal rivalries. The great nobility, for example, was profoundly separated from the lesser nobility by differences in wealth, education, and world view. Moreover, the old military nobility—known as the "nobility of the sword"—eyed with suspicion the more recent bureaucratic and judicial nobility—the so-called "nobility of the robe." Differences within the bourgeoisie—between wealthy financiers and local lawyers, for example—were no less profound. Rather than standing as unified blocs against each other, nobility and bourgeoisie formed two parallel social ladders, increasingly linked together at the top by wealth, marriage, and Enlightenment culture.

Revisionist historians stress three developments in particular. First, the nobility remained a fluid and relatively open order. Throughout the eighteenth century, substantial numbers of successful commoners continued to seek and obtain noble status through government service and purchase of expensive positions conferring nobility. Thus the nobility of the robe continued to attract the wealthiest members of the middle class and to permit social mobility. Second, key sections of the nobility were no less liberal than the middle class, which, until revolution actually began, generally supported the judicial opposition led by the Parlement of Paris. Finally, the nobility and the bourgeoisie were not really at odds in the economic sphere. Both looked to investment in land and to government service as their preferred activities, and the ideal goal of the merchant-capitalist was to gain enough wealth to retire from trade, purchase estates, and live nobly as a large landowner. At the same time, wealthy nobles often acted as aggressive capitalists, investing especially in mining, metallurgy, and foreign trade.

The revisionists have clearly shaken the belief that the bourgeoisie and the nobility were inevitably locked in growing conflict before the Revolution. But in stressing the similarities between the two groups, especially at the top, revisionists have also reinforced the view, long maintained by historians, that the Old Regime had ceased to reflect social reality by the 1780s. Legally, society was still based on rigid orders inherited from the Middle Ages. In reality, France had moved far toward being a society based on wealth and economic achievement, and an emerging elite that included both aristocratic and bourgeois notables was frustrated by a bureaucratic monarchy that had long claimed the right to absolute power.

The Formation of the National Assembly

The Revolution was under way by 1787, though no one could have realized what was to follow. Spurred by a depressed economy and falling tax receipts, Louis XVI's minister of finance revived old proposals to impose a general tax on all landed property and to develop provincial assemblies to help administer the tax, and he convinced the king to call an Assembly of Notables to gain support for the idea. The assembled notables, who were mainly important noblemen and high-ranking clergy, were not in favor of it. In return for their support, they demanded that control over all government spending be given to the provincial assemblies, which they expected to control. When the government refused, the notables responded that such sweeping tax changes required the approval of the Estates General, the representative body of all three estates, which had not met since 1614.

Facing bankruptcy, the king tried to reassert his authority. He dismissed the notables and established new taxes by decree. In stirring language, the Parlement of Paris promptly declared the royal initiative null and void. The Parlement went so far as to specify some of the "fundamental laws" against which no king could transgress, such as national consent to taxation and freedom from arbitrary arrest and imprisonment. When the king tried to exile the judges, a wave of protest swept the country. Frightened investors also refused to advance more loans to the state. Finally, in July 1788, a beaten Louis XVI called for a spring session of the Estates General. Absolute monarchy was collapsing.

What would replace it? Throughout the unprecedented election campaign of 1788 and 1789, that question excited France. All across the country, clergy, nobles, and commoners came together in their respective orders to draft petitions for change and to elect their respective delegates to the Estates General. The local assemblies of the clergy showed considerable dissatisfaction with the church hierarchy, and two-thirds of the delegates were chosen from among the poorest parish priests, who were commoners by birth. The nobles, already badly split by wealth and education, remained politically divided. A conservative majority was drawn from the poorest and most numerous provincial nobility, but fully a third of the nobility's representatives were liberals committed to major changes.

As for the third estate, there was great popular participation in the elections. Almost all male commoners twenty-five years or older had the right to vote. However, voting required two stages, which meant that most of the representatives finally selected by the third estate were well-educated, prosperous members of the middle class. Most were not businessmen but lawyers and

Fan: Opening of the Legislature In 1789 the first meeting of the Estates General since 1614 was recorded not only in the annals of French history but in the most ordinary objects, including this painted fan. *(Source: Musée Carnavalet/Bulloz)*

government officials. Status and prestige were of particular concern to this elite. There were no delegates from the great mass of laboring poor, which included the peasants and the artisans.

The petitions for change from the three estates showed a surprising degree of agreement on most issues, as recent research has clearly revealed. There was general agreement that royal absolutism should give way to constitutional monarchy, in which laws and taxes would require the consent of an Estates General meeting regularly. All agreed that, in the future, individual liberties must be guaranteed by law and that the position of the parish clergy had to be improved. It was generally acknowledged that economic development required reforms, such as the abolition of internal trade barriers. The striking similarities in the grievance petitions of the clergy, nobility, and third estate reflected the broad commitment of France's elite to liberalism.

Yet an increasingly bitter quarrel undermined this consensus during the intense campaign: how would the Estates General vote, and precisely who would lead in the political reorganization that was generally desired? The Estates General of 1614 had sat as three separate houses. Any action had required the agreement of at least two branches, a requirement that had guaranteed control by the privileged orders—the nobility and the clergy. Immediately after its victory over the king, the aristocratic Parlement of Paris, mainly out of respect for tradition but partly to enhance the nobility's political position, ruled that the Estates General should once again sit separately. The ruling was quickly denounced by certain middle-class intellectuals and some liberal nobles. They demanded instead a single assembly dominated by representatives of the third estate, to ensure fundamental reforms. Reflecting a growing hostility toward aristocratic aspirations, the abbé Sieyès argued in 1789, in his famous pamphlet *What Is the Third Estate?*, that the nobility was a tiny, overprivileged minority and that the neglected third estate constituted the true strength of the French nation. When the government agreed that the third estate should have as many delegates as the clergy and the nobility combined but then rendered its act meaningless by upholding voting by separate order, middle-class leaders saw fresh evidence of an aristocratic conspiracy.

In May 1789 the twelve hundred delegates of the three estates paraded in medieval pageantry through the streets of Versailles to an opening session resplendent with feudal magnificence. The estates were almost immediately deadlocked. Delegates of the third estate refused to transact any business until the king ordered the clergy and nobility to sit with them in a single body. Finally, after a six-week war of nerves, a few parish priests began to go over to the third estate, which on June 17 voted to call itself the "National Assembly." On June 20, excluded from their hall because of "repairs," the delegates of the third estate moved to a large indoor tennis court. There they swore the famous Oath of the Tennis Court, pledging never to disband until they had written a new constitution.

The king's actions were then somewhat contradictory. On June 23 he made a conciliatory speech to a joint session, urging reforms, and then ordered the three estates to meet together. At the same time, he apparently followed the advice of relatives and court nobles who urged him to dissolve the Estates General by force. The king called an army of eighteen thousand troops toward Versailles, and on July 11 he dismissed his finance minister and his other more liberal ministers. Faced with growing opposition since 1787, Louis XVI had resigned himself to bankruptcy. Now he sought to reassert his divine and historic right to rule. The middle-class delegates had done their best, but they were resigned to being disbanded at bayonet point. One third-estate delegate reassured a worried colleague: "You won't hang—you'll only have to go back home."[2]

The Revolt of the Poor and the Oppressed

While the third estate pressed for symbolic equality with the nobility and clergy in a single legislative body at Versailles, economic hardship gripped the masses of France. Grain was the basis of the diet of ordinary people, and in 1788 the harvest had been extremely poor. The price of bread, which had been rising gradually since 1785, began to soar. By July 1789 the price of bread in the provinces climbed as high as eight sous per pound. In Paris, where bread was subsidized by the government in an attempt to prevent popular unrest, the price rose to four sous. The poor could scarcely afford to pay two sous per pound, for even at that price a laborer with a wife and three children had to spend half of his wages to buy bread.

Storming the Bastille   This representation by an untrained contemporary artist shows civilians and members of the Paris militia—the "conquerors of the Bastille"—on the attack. This successful action had enormous practical and symbolic significance, and July 14 has long been France's most important national holiday. (*Source: Musée Carnavalet/ Photo Hubert Josse*)

Harvest failure and high bread prices unleashed a classic economic depression of the preindustrial age. With food so expensive and with so much uncertainty, the demand for manufactured goods collapsed. Thousands of artisans and small traders were thrown out of work. By the end of 1789, almost half of the French people would be in need of relief. One person in eight was a pauper, living in extreme want. In Paris the situation was desperate in July 1789: perhaps 150,000 of the city's 600,000 people were without work.

Against this background of dire poverty and excited by the political crisis, the people of Paris entered decisively onto the revolutionary stage. They believed in a general, though ill-defined, way that the economic distress had human causes. They believed that they should have steady work and enough bread to survive. Specifically, they feared that the dismissal of the king's moderate finance minister would throw them at the mercy of aristocratic landowners and grain speculators. Stories like one quoting the wealthy financier Joseph François Foulon as saying that the poor "should eat grass, like my horses," and rumors that the king's troops would sack the city began to fill the air. Angry crowds formed, and passionate voices urged action. On July 13 the people began to seize arms for the defense of the city, and on July 14 several hundred of the most determined people marched to the Bastille to search for gunpowder.

A medieval fortress with walls 10 feet thick and eight great towers each 100 feet high, the Bastille had long been used as a prison. It was guarded by eighty retired soldiers and thirty Swiss guards. The governor of the fortress-prison refused to hand over the powder, panicked, and ordered his men to fire, killing ninety-eight people attempting to enter. Cannon were brought to batter the main gate, and fighting continued until the governor of the prison surrendered. While he was being taken under guard to city hall, a band of men broke through and hacked him to death. His head and that of the mayor of Paris, who had been slow to give the crowd arms, were stuck on pikes and paraded through the streets. The next day, a committee of citizens appointed the marquis de Lafayette commander of the city's armed forces. Paris was lost to the king, who was forced to recall the finance minister and to disperse his troops. The uprising had saved the National Assembly.

As the delegates resumed their long-winded and inconclusive debates at Versailles, the people in the countryside sent them a radical and unmistakable message. All across France, peasants began to rise in spontaneous, violent, and effective insurrection against their lords, ransacking manor houses and burning feudal documents that recorded the peasants' obligations. Neither middle-class landowners, who often owned manors and village monopolies, nor the larger, more prosperous farmers were spared. In some areas, the nobles and bourgeoisie combined forces and organized patrols to protect their property. Yet the peasant insurrection went on. Recent enclosures were undone; old common lands were reoccupied; and the forests were seized. Taxes were not paid. Fear of vagabonds and outlaws—the so-called Great Fear—seized the countryside and fanned the flames of rebellion. The long-suffering peasants were doing their best to free themselves from aristocratic privilege and exploitation.

Faced with chaos yet afraid to call on the king to restore order, some liberal nobles and middle-class delegates at Versailles responded to peasant demands with a surprise maneuver on the night of August 4, 1789. The duke of Aiguillon, one of France's greatest noble landowners, declared that

in several provinces the whole people forms a kind of league for the destruction of the manor houses, the ravaging of the lands, and especially for the seizure of the archives where the title deeds to feudal properties are kept. It seeks to throw off at last a yoke that has for many centuries weighted it down.[3]

He urged equality in taxation and the elimination of feudal dues. In the end, all the old exactions were abolished, generally without compensation:

serfdom where it still existed, exclusive hunting rights for nobles, fees for justice, village monopolies, the right to make peasants work on the roads, and a host of other dues. Though a clarifying law passed a week later was less generous, the peasants ignored the "fine print." They never paid feudal dues again. Thus the French peasantry, which already owned about 30 percent of all the land, quickly achieved a great and unprecedented victory. Henceforth, the French peasants would seek mainly to consolidate their triumph. As the Great Fear subsided, they became a force for order and stability.

A Limited Monarchy

The National Assembly moved forward. On August 27, 1789, it issued the Declaration of the Rights of Man. This great liberal document had a very American flavor, and Lafayette even discussed his draft in detail with the American ambassador in Paris, Thomas Jefferson, the author of the American Declaration of Independence. According to the French declaration, "men are born and remain free and equal in rights." Humankind's natural rights are "liberty, property, security, and resistance to oppression." Also, "every man is presumed innocent until he is proven guilty." As for law, "it is an expression of the general will; all citizens have the right to concur personally or through their representatives in its formation. . . . Free expression of thoughts and opinions is one of the most precious rights of mankind: every citizen may therefore speak, write, and publish freely." In short, this clarion call of the liberal revolutionary ideal guaranteed equality before the law, representative government for a sovereign people, and individual freedom. This revolutionary credo, only two pages long, was propagandized throughout France and Europe and around the world.

Moving beyond general principles to draft a constitution proved difficult. The questions of how much power the king should retain and whether he could permanently veto legislation led to another deadlock. Once again the decisive answer came from the poor, in this instance the poor women of Paris.

To understand what happened, one must remember that the work and wages of women and children were essential in the family economy of the laboring poor. In Paris great numbers of women worked, particularly within the putting-out system in the garment industry—making lace, fancy dresses, embroidery, ribbons, bonnets, corsets, and so on. Many of these goods were beautiful luxury items destined for an aristocratic and international clientele.[4] Immediately after the fall of the Bastille, many of France's great court nobles began to leave Versailles for foreign lands, so a plummeting demand for luxuries intensified the general economic crisis. International markets also declined, and the church was no longer able to give its traditional grants of food and money to the poor. Unemployment and hunger increased further, and the result was another popular explosion.

On October 5 some seven thousand desperate women marched the 12 miles from Paris to Versailles to demand action. A middle-class deputy looking out from the Assembly saw "multitudes arriving from Paris including fishwives and bullies from the market, and these people wanted nothing but bread." This great crowd invaded the Assembly, "armed with scythes, sticks and pikes." One coarse, tough old woman directing a large group of younger women defiantly shouted into the debate: "Who's that talking down there? Make the chatterbox shut up. That's not the point: the point is that we want bread."[5] Hers was the genuine voice of the people, essential to any understanding of the French Revolution.

The women invaded the royal apartments, slaughtered some of the royal bodyguards, and furiously searched for the despised queen, Marie Antoinette. "We are going to cut off her head, tear out her heart, fry her liver, and that won't be the end of it," they shouted, surging through the palace in a frenzy. It seems likely that only the intervention of Lafayette and the National Guard saved the royal family. But the only way to calm the disorder was for the king to go and live in Paris, as the crowd demanded.

The next day, the king, the queen, and their son left for Paris in the midst of a strange procession. The heads of two aristocrats, stuck on pikes, led the way. They were followed by the remaining members of the royal bodyguard, unarmed and surrounded and mocked by fierce men holding sabers and pikes. A mixed and victorious multitude surrounded the king's carriage, hurling crude insults at the queen. There was drinking and eating among the women. "We are bringing the baker, the baker's wife, and the baker's boy," they joyfully sang. The National Assembly followed the king to Paris. Reflecting the more radical environment, it adopted a constitution that gave the virtually imprisoned "baker" only a temporary veto in the lawmaking process. And, for a time, he and the government made sure that the masses of Paris did not lack bread.

The next two years, until September 1791, saw the consolidation of the liberal Revolution. Under middle-class leadership, the National Assembly abolished the French nobility as a legal order and pushed forward with the creation of a constitutional monarchy, which Louis XVI reluctantly agreed to accept in July 1790. In the final constitution, the king remained the head of state, but all lawmaking power was placed in the hands of the National Assembly, elected by the economic upper half of French males. Eighty-three departments of approximately equal size replaced the complicated old patchwork of provinces with their many historic differences. The jumble of weights and measures that varied from province to province was reformed, leading to the introduction of the simple, rational metric system in 1793. The National Assembly promoted economic freedom. Monopolies, guilds, and workers' combinations were prohibited, and barriers to trade within France were abolished in the name of economic liberty. Thus the National Assembly applied the critical spirit of the Enlightenment to reform France's laws and institutions completely.

The Assembly also threatened nobles who had emigrated from France with the loss of their lands. It nationalized the property of the church and abolished the monasteries as useless relics of a distant past. The government used all former church property as collateral to guarantee a new paper currency, the *assignats*, and then sold these properties in an attempt to put the state's finances on a solid footing. Although the church's land was sold in large blocks, a procedure that favored nimble speculators and the rich, peasants eventually purchased much of it as it was subdivided. These purchases strengthened their attachment to the revolutionary state.

The most unfortunate aspect of the reorganization of France was that it brought the new government into conflict with the Catholic church. Many middle-class delegates to the National Assembly, imbued with the rationalism and skepticism of the eighteenth-century philosophes, harbored a deep distrust of popular piety and "superstitious religion." They were interested in the church only to the extent that they could seize its land and use the church to strengthen the new state. Thus they established a national church, with priests chosen by voters. In the face of resistance, the National Assembly required the clergy to take a loyalty oath to the new government. The clergy became just so many more employees of the state. The pope formally condemned this attempt to subjugate the church. Against such a backdrop, it is not surprising that only half of the priests of France took the oath of allegiance. The result was a deep division within both the country and the clergy itself on the religious question, and confusion and hostility among French Catholics were pervasive. The attempted reorganization of the Catholic church was the revolutionary government's first important failure.

WORLD WAR AND REPUBLICAN FRANCE (1791–1799)

When Louis XVI accepted the final version of the completed constitution in September 1791, a young and still obscure provincial lawyer and member of the National Assembly named Maximilien Robespierre (1758–1794) evaluated the work of two years and concluded, "The Revolution is over." Robespierre was both right and wrong. He was right in the sense that the most constructive and lasting reforms were in place. Nothing substantial in the way of liberty and equality would be gained in the next generation, though much would be lost. He was wrong in the sense that a much more radical stage lay ahead. New heroes and new ideologies were to emerge in revolutionary wars and international conflict.

Foreign Reactions and the Beginning of War

The outbreak and progress of revolution in France produced great excitement and a sharp division of opinion in Europe and the United States. Liberals and radicals saw a mighty triumph of liberty over despotism. In Great Britain especially, they hoped that the French example would lead to a fundamental reordering of the political system. That system, which had been consolidated in the revo-

lution of 1688 to 1689 (see pages 643–649), placed Parliament in the hands of the aristocracy and a few wealthy merchants; the great majority of people had very little say in the government. After the French Revolution began, conservative leaders like Edmund Burke (1729–1797) were deeply troubled by the aroused spirit of reform. In 1790 Burke published *Reflections on the Revolution in France,* one of the great intellectual defenses of European conservatism. He defended inherited privileges in general and those of the English monarchy and aristocracy in particular. He glorified the unrepresentative Parliament and predicted that thoroughgoing reform like that occurring in France would lead only to chaos and tyranny. Burke's work sparked vigorous debate.

One passionate rebuttal came from a young writer in London, Mary Wollstonecraft (1759–1797). Born into the middle class, Wollstonecraft was schooled in adversity by a mean-spirited father who beat his wife and squandered his inherited fortune. Determined to be independent in a society that generally expected women of her class to become homebodies and obedient wives, she struggled for years to earn her living as a governess and teacher—practically the only acceptable careers for single, educated women—before attaining success as a translator and author. Interested in politics and believing that "A desperate disease requires a powerful remedy" in Great Britain as well as France, Wollstonecraft was incensed by Burke's book. She immediately wrote a blistering, widely read attack, *A Vindication of the Rights of Man* (1790).

Then, fired up on controversy and commitment, she made a daring intellectual leap. She developed for the first time the logical implications of natural-law philosophy in her masterpiece, *A Vindication of the Rights of Woman* (1792). To fulfill the liberating promise of the French Revolution and to eliminate the economic and sexual inequality she had felt so keenly, she demanded that

the Rights of Women be respected . . . [and] JUSTICE for one-half of the human race. . . . It is time to effect a revolution in female manners, time to restore to them their lost dignity, and make them, as part of the human species, labor, by reforming themselves, to reform the world.

Setting high standards for women—"I wish to persuade women to endeavor to acquire strength, both of mind and body"—Wollstonecraft broke with those who had a low opinion of women's intellectual potential. She advocated rigorous coeducation, which would make women better wives and mothers, good citizens, and even economically independent. "Women might certainly study the art of healing, and be physicians, as well as nurses." Women could manage businesses and enter politics. Men themselves would benefit from women's rights, for Wollstonecraft believed that "the two sexes mutually corrupt and improve each other."[6] Marking the birth of the modern women's movement for equal rights, Wollstonecraft's strikingly original analysis testified to the power of the Revolution to excite and inspire outside of France.

The kings and nobles of continental Europe, who had at first welcomed the revolution in France as weakening a competing power, began to feel no less threatened than Burke and his supporters. At their courts they listened to the diatribes of great court nobles who had fled France and were urging intervention in France's affairs. When Louis XVI and Marie Antoinette were arrested and returned to Paris after trying unsuccessfully to slip out of France in June 1791, the monarchs of Austria and Prussia issued the Declaration of Pillnitz. This carefully worded statement declared their willingness to intervene in France, but only with the unanimous agreement of all the Great Powers, which they did not expect to receive. Austria and Prussia expected their threat to have a sobering effect on revolutionary France without causing war.

The crowned heads of Europe misjudged the revolutionary spirit in France. When the National Assembly disbanded, it sought popular support by decreeing that none of its members would be eligible for election to the new Legislative Assembly. As a result, the new representative body that was duly elected and convened in October 1791 had a different character. The great majority of members were still prosperous, well educated, and middle class, but they were younger and less cautious than their predecessors. Loosely allied as "Jacobins," so named after their political club, the new representatives to the Assembly were passionately committed to liberal revolution.

The Jacobins increasingly lumped "useless aristocrats" and "despotic monarchs" together, and they easily whipped themselves into a patriotic fury with bombastic oratory. Were the courts of

Mary Wollstonecraft Painted by an unknown artist when Mary Wollstonecraft was thirty-two and writing her revolutionary *Vindication of the Rights of Woman*, this portrait highlights the remarkable strength of character that energized Wollstonecraft's brilliant intellect. *(Source: The Board of Trustees of the National Museums and Galleries on Merseyside, Walker Art Gallery)*

Europe attempting to incite a war of kings against France? Well then, "we will incite a war of people against kings. . . . Ten million Frenchmen, kindled by the fire of liberty, armed with the sword, with reason, with eloquence would be able to change the face of the world and make the tyrants tremble on their thrones."[7] Only Robespierre and a very few others argued that people do not welcome liberation at the point of a gun. Such warnings were brushed aside. France would "rise to the full height of her mission," as one deputy urged. In April 1792 France declared war on Francis II, archduke of Austria and king of Hungary and Bohemia.

France's crusade against tyranny went poorly at first. Prussia joined Austria in the Austrian Netherlands (present-day Belgium), and French forces broke and fled at their first encounter with armies of this First Coalition. The road to Paris lay open, and it is possible that only conflict between the eastern monarchs over the division of Poland saved France from defeat.

Military reversals and Austro-Prussian threats caused a wave of patriotic fervor to sweep France. The Legislative Assembly declared the country in danger. Volunteer armies from the provinces streamed through Paris, fraternizing with the people and singing patriotic songs like the stirring "Marseillaise," later the French national anthem.

In this supercharged wartime atmosphere, rumors of treason by the king and queen spread in Paris. Once again, as in the storming of the Bastille, the common people of Paris acted decisively. On August 10, 1792, a revolutionary crowd attacked the royal palace at the Tuileries, capturing it after heavy fighting with the Swiss guards. The king and his family fled for their lives to the nearby Legislative Assembly, which suspended the king from all his functions, imprisoned him, and called for a new National Convention to be elected by universal male suffrage. Monarchy in France was on its deathbed, mortally wounded by war and revolt.

The Second Revolution

The fall of the monarchy marked a rapid radicalization of the Revolution, a phase that historians often call the "second revolution." Louis's imprisonment was followed by the September Massacres, which sullied the Revolution in the eyes of most of its remaining foreign supporters. Wild stories spread through the city that imprisoned counterrevolutionary aristocrats and priests were plotting with the allied invaders. As a result, angry crowds invaded the prisons of Paris and summarily slaughtered half of the men and women they found. In late September 1792, the new, popularly elected National Convention proclaimed France a republic. The republic adopted a new revolutionary calendar, and citizens were expected to address each other with the friendly "thou" of the people, rather than with the formal "you" of the rich and powerful.

All of the members of the National Convention were Jacobins and republicans, and the great majority continued to come from the well-educated middle class. But the convention was increasingly divided into two well-defined, bitterly competitive

groups—the Girondists, named after a department in southwestern France, and the Mountain, led by Robespierre and another young lawyer, Georges Jacques Danton. The "Mountain" was so called because its members sat on the uppermost left-hand benches of the assembly hall. Many indecisive Convention members seated in the "Plain" below floated between the rival factions.

This division was clearly apparent after the National Convention overwhelmingly convicted Louis XVI of treason. By a single vote, 361 of the 720 members of the Convention then unconditionally sentenced him to death in January 1793. Louis died with tranquil dignity on the newly invented guillotine. One of his last statements was, "I am innocent and shall die without fear. I would that my death might bring happiness to the French, and ward off the dangers which I foresee."[8]

Both the Girondists and the Mountain were determined to continue the "war against tyranny." The Prussians had been stopped at the indecisive Battle of Valmy on September 20, 1792, one day before the First Republic was proclaimed. Republican armies then successfully invaded Savoy and captured Nice. A second army corps invaded the German Rhineland and took the city of Frankfurt. To the north, the revolutionary armies won their first major battle at Jemappes and occupied the entire Austrian Netherlands by November 1792. Everywhere they went, French armies of occupation chased the princes, "abolished feudalism," and found support among some peasants and middle-class people.

But the French armies also lived off the land, requisitioning food and supplies and plundering local treasures. The liberators looked increasingly like foreign invaders. International tensions mounted. In February 1793 the National Convention, at war with Austria and Prussia, declared war on Britain, Holland, and Spain as well. Republican France was now at war with almost all of Europe, a great war that would last almost without interruption until 1815.

As the forces of the First Coalition drove the French from the Austrian Netherlands, peasants in western France revolted against being drafted into the army. They were supported and encouraged in their resistance by devout Catholics, royalists, and foreign agents.

In Paris the quarrelsome National Convention found itself locked in a life-and-death political struggle between the Girondists and the Mountain. The two groups were in general agreement on questions of policy. Sincere republicans, they hated privilege and wanted to temper economic liberalism with social concern. Yet personal hatreds ran deep. The Girondists feared a bloody dictatorship by the Mountain, and the Mountain was no less convinced that the more moderate Girondists would turn to conservatives and even royalists in order to retain power. With the middle-class delegates so bitterly divided, the laboring poor of Paris emerged as the decisive political factor.

The great mass of the Parisian laboring poor always constituted—along with the peasantry in the summer of 1789—the elemental force that drove the Revolution forward. It was the artisans, shopkeepers, and day laborers who had stormed the Bastille, marched on Versailles, driven the king from the Tuileries, and carried out the September Massacres. The petty traders and laboring poor were often known as the *sans-culottes,* "without breeches," because they wore trousers instead of the knee breeches of the aristocracy and the solid middle class. The immediate interests of the sans-culottes were mainly economic, and in the spring of 1793 the economic situation was as bad as the military situation. Rapid inflation, unemployment, and food shortages were again weighing heavily on the poor.

In addition, by the spring of 1793, the sans-culottes were keenly interested in politics. Encouraged by the so-called angry men, such as the passionate young former priest and journalist Jacques Roux, the sans-culottes were demanding radical political action to guarantee them their daily bread. At first the Mountain joined the Girondists in violently rejecting these demands. But in the face of military defeat, peasant revolt, and hatred of the Girondists, the Mountain and especially Robespierre became more sympathetic. The Mountain joined with sans-culottes activists in the city government to engineer a popular uprising that forced the Convention to arrest thirty-one Girondist deputies for treason on June 2. All power passed to the Mountain.

Robespierre and others from the Mountain joined the recently formed Committee of Public Safety, to which the Convention had given dictatorial power to deal with the national emergency. These developments in Paris triggered revolt in leading provincial cities, such as Lyons and Marseilles, where moderates denounced Paris and demanded a decentralized government. The peasant revolt spread, and the republic's armies were driven back on all fronts. By July 1793 only the areas around Paris and on the eastern frontier were firmly controlled by the central government. Defeat appeared imminent.

Total War and the Terror

A year later, in July 1794, the Austrian Netherlands and the Rhineland were once again in the hands of conquering French armies, and the First Coalition was falling apart. This remarkable change of fortune was due to the revolutionary government's success in harnessing in a total war effort, for perhaps the first time in history, three explosive forces: a planned economy, revolutionary terror, and modern nationalism.

Robespierre and the Committee of Public Safety advanced with implacable resolution on several fronts in 1793 and 1794. In an effort to save revolutionary France, they collaborated with the fiercely patriotic and democratic sans-culottes. They established, as best they could, a planned economy with egalitarian social overtones. Rather than let supply and demand determine prices, the government decreed the maximum allowable prices, fixed in paper assignats, for a host of key products. Although the state was too weak to enforce all its price regulations, it did fix the price of bread in Paris at levels the poor could afford. Rationing and ration cards were introduced to make sure that the limited supplies of bread were shared fairly. Quality was also controlled. Bakers were permitted to make only the "bread of equality"—a rough brown bread made of a mixture of all available flours. Fine wheat bread and pastries were outlawed as frivolous luxuries. The poor of Paris may not have eaten well, but at least they ate.

They also worked, mainly to produce arms and munitions for the war effort. Craftsmen and small manufacturers were told what to produce and when to deliver. The government nationalized many small workshops and requisitioned raw materials and grain from the peasants. Sometimes planning and control did not go beyond orders to meet the latest emergency: "Ten thousand soldiers lack shoes. You will take the shoes of all the aristocrats in Strasbourg and deliver them ready for transport to headquarters at 10 A.M. tomorrow."

Failures to control and coordinate were failures of means and not of desire: seldom if ever before had a government attempted to manage an economy so thoroughly. The second revolution and the rise of the sans-culottes had produced an embryonic emergency socialism, which was to have great influence on the development of socialist ideology.

While radical economic measures supplied the poor with bread and the armies with weapons, a Reign of Terror (1793–1794) was solidifying the home front. Special revolutionary courts, responsible only to Robespierre's Committee of Public Safety, tried rebels and "enemies of the nation" for political crimes. Drawing on popular, sans-culottes support in the local Jacobin clubs, these local courts ignored normal legal procedures and judged severely. Some 40,000 French men and women were executed or died in prison. Another 300,000 suspects crowded the prisons and often brushed close to death in a revolutionary court.

Robespierre's Reign of Terror was one of the most controversial phases of the French Revolution. Most historians now believe that the Reign of Terror was not directed against any single class. Rather, it was a political weapon directed impartially against all who might oppose the revolutionary government. For many Europeans of the time, however, the Reign of Terror represented a terrifying perversion of the generous ideals that existed in 1789. It strengthened the belief that France had foolishly replaced a weak king with a bloody dictatorship.

The third and perhaps most decisive element in the French republic's victory over the First Coalition was its ability to continue drawing on the explosive power of patriotic dedication to a national state and a national mission. This dedication is the essence of modern nationalism. With a common language and a common tradition newly reinforced by the ideas of popular sovereignty and democracy, the French people were stirred by a common loyalty. The shared danger of foreign foes and internal rebels unified all classes in a heroic defense of the nation.

The Reign of Terror   A man, woman, and child accused of political crimes are brought before a special revolutionary committee for trial. The Terror's iron dictatorship crushed individual rights as well as treason and opposition. *(Source: Photo Flammarion)*

In such circumstances, war was no longer the gentlemanly game of the eighteenth century but a life-and-death struggle between good and evil. Everyone had to participate in the national effort. According to a famous decree of August 23, 1793,

The young men shall go to battle and the married men shall forge arms. The women shall make tents and clothes, and shall serve in the hospitals; children shall tear rags into lint. The old men will be guided to the public places of the cities to kindle the courage of the young warriors and to preach the unity of the Republic and the hatred of kings.

Like the wars of religion, war in 1793 was a crusade; this war, though, was fought for a secular rather than a religious ideology.

Because all unmarried young men were subject to the draft, the French armed forces swelled to one million men in fourteen armies. A force of this size was unprecedented in the history of European warfare. The soldiers were led by young, impetuous generals, many of whom had risen rapidly from the ranks and personified the opportunities that the Revolution seemed to offer gifted sons of the people. These generals used mass attacks at bayonet point by their highly motivated forces to overwhelm the enemy. By the spring of 1794, French armies were victorious on all fronts. The republic was saved.

The Thermidorian Reaction and the Directory (1794–1799)

The success of the French armies led Robespierre and the Committee of Public Safety to relax the emergency economic controls, but they extended the political Reign of Terror. Their lofty goal was increasingly an ideal democratic republic, where justice would reign and there would be neither rich nor poor. Their lowly means were unrestrained despotism and the guillotine, which struck down any who might seriously question the new order. In March 1794, to the horror of many sans-culottes, Robespierre's Terror wiped out many of the "angry men," led by the radical social democrat Jacques Hébert. Two weeks later, several of Robespierre's long-standing collaborators, led by the famous orator Danton, marched up the steps to the guillotine. Knowing that they might be next, a strange assortment of radicals and mod-

erates in the Convention organized a conspiracy. They howled down Robespierre when he tried to speak to the National Convention on 9 Thermidor (July 27, 1794). On the following day, it was Robespierre's turn to be shaved by the revolutionary razor.

As Robespierre's closest supporters followed their leader, France unexpectedly experienced a thorough reaction to the despotism of the Reign of Terror. In a general way, this "Thermidorian reaction" recalled the early days of the Revolution. The respectable middle-class lawyers and professionals who had led the liberal revolution of 1789 reasserted their authority, drawing support from their own class, the provincial cities, and the better-off peasants. The National Convention abolished many economic controls, printed more paper currency, and let prices rise sharply. It severely restricted the local political organizations where the sans-culottes had their strength. And all the while, the wealthy bankers and newly rich speculators celebrated the sudden end of the Terror with an orgy of self-indulgence and ostentatious luxury.

The collapse of economic controls, coupled with runaway inflation, hit the working poor very hard. The gaudy extravagance of the rich wounded their pride. The sans-culottes accepted private property, but they believed passionately in small business and the right of all to earn a decent living. Increasingly disorganized after Robespierre purged their radical leaders, the common people of Paris finally revolted against the emerging new order in early 1795. The Convention quickly used the army to suppress these insurrections. For the first time since the fall of the Bastille, bread riots and uprisings by Parisians living on the edge of starvation were effectively put down by a government that made no concessions to the poor.

In the face of all these catastrophes, the revolutionary fervor of the laboring poor finally subsided. As far as politics was concerned, their interest and influence would remain very limited until 1830. There arose, especially from the women, a great cry for peace and a turning toward religion. As the government looked the other way, the women brought back the Catholic church and the worship of God. In one French town, women fought with each other over which of their children should be baptized first. After six tumultuous years, the women of the poor concluded that the Revolution was a failure.

THE FRENCH REVOLUTION

May 5, 1789	Estates General convene at Versailles
June 17, 1789	Third Estate declares itself the National Assembly
June 20, 1789	Oath of the Tennis Court
July 14, 1789	Storming of the Bastille
July–August 1789	The Great Fear in the countryside
August 4, 1789	National Assembly abolishes feudal privileges
August 27, 1789	National Assembly issues Declaration of the Rights of Man
October 5, 1789	Parisian women march on Versailles and force royal family to return to Paris
November 1789	National Assembly confiscates church lands
July 1790	Civil Constitution of the Clergy establishes a national church
	Louis XVI reluctantly agrees to accept a constitutional monarchy
June 1791	Arrest of the royal family while attempting to flee France
August 1791	Declaration of Pillnitz by Austria and Prussia
April 1792	France declares war on Austria
August 1792	Parisian mob attacks palace and takes Louis XVI prisoner
September 1792	September Massacres
	National Convention declares France a republic and abolishes monarchy
January 1793	Execution of Louis XVI
February 1793	France declares war on Britain, Holland, and Spain
	Revolts in provincial cities
March 1793	Bitter struggle in the National Convention between Girondists and the Mountain
April–June 1793	Robespierre and the Mountain organize the Committee of Public Safety and arrest Girondist leaders
September 1793	Price controls to aid the sans-culottes and mobilize war effort
1793–1794	Reign of Terror in Paris and the provinces
Spring 1794	French armies victorious on all fronts
July 1794	Execution of Robespierre
	Thermidorean Reaction begins
1795–1799	The Directory
1795	End of economic controls and suppression of the sans-culottes
1797	Napoleon defeats Austrian armies in Italy and returns triumphant to Paris
1798	Austria, Great Britain, and Russia form the Second Coalition against France
1799	Napoleon overthrows the Directory and seizes power

As for the middle-class members of the National Convention, they wrote yet another constitution, which they believed would guarantee their economic position and political supremacy. The mass of the population could vote only for electors, who were men of means. Electors then elected the members of a reorganized Legislative Assembly, and key officials throughout France. The Assembly chose a five-man executive—the Directory.

The Directory continued to support French military expansion abroad. War was no longer so much a crusade as a means to meet the ever-present, ever-unsolved economic problem. Large, victorious French armies reduced unemployment at home, and they were able to live off the territories they conquered and plundered.

The unprincipled action of the Directory reinforced widespread disgust with war and starvation. This general dissatisfaction revealed itself clearly in the national elections of 1797, which returned a large number of conservative and even monarchist deputies who favored peace at almost any price. Fearing for their skins, the members of the Directory used the army to nullify the elections and began to govern dictatorially. Two years later, Napoleon Bonaparte ended the Directory in a coup d'état and substituted a strong dictatorship for a weak one. Truly, the Revolution was over.

THE NAPOLEONIC ERA (1799–1815)

For almost fifteen years, from 1799 to 1814, France was in the hands of a keen-minded military dictator of exceptional ability. One of history's most fascinating leaders, Napoleon Bonaparte realized the need to put an end to civil strife in France in order to create unity and consolidate his rule. And he did. But Napoleon saw himself as a man of destiny, and the glory of war and the dream of universal empire proved irresistible. For years he spiraled from victory to victory; but in the end he was destroyed by a mighty coalition united in fear of his restless ambition.

Napoleon's Rule of France

In 1799, when he seized power, young General Napoleon Bonaparte was a national hero. Born in Corsica into an impoverished noble family in 1769, Napoleon left home to become a lieutenant in the French artillery in 1785. After a brief and unsuccessful adventure fighting for Corsican independence in 1789, he returned to France as a French patriot and a dedicated revolutionary. Rising rapidly in the new army, Napoleon was placed in command of French forces in Italy and won brilliant victories there in 1796 and 1797. His next campaign, in Egypt, was a failure, but Napoleon made his way back to France before the fiasco was well-known. His reputation remained intact.

Napoleon soon learned that some prominent members of the Legislative Assembly were plotting against the Directory. The dissatisfaction of these plotters stemmed not so much from the fact that the Directory was a dictatorship as from the fact that it was a weak dictatorship. Ten years of upheaval and uncertainty had made firm rule much more appealing than liberty and popular politics to these disillusioned revolutionaries. The abbé Sieyès personified this evolution in thinking. In 1789 he had written in *What Is the Third Estate?* that the nobility was grossly overprivileged and that the entire people should rule the French nation. Now Sieyès's motto was "confidence from below, authority from above."

Like the other members of his group, Sieyès wanted a strong military ruler. The flamboyant thirty-year-old Napoleon was ideal. Thus the conspirators and Napoleon organized a takeover. On November 9, 1799, they ousted the Directors, and the following day soldiers disbanded the Assembly at bayonet point. Napoleon was named first consul of the republic, and a new constitution consolidating his position was overwhelmingly approved in a plebiscite in December 1799. Republican appearances were maintained, but Napoleon was already the real ruler of France.

The essence of Napoleon's domestic policy was to use his great and highly personal powers to maintain order and put an end to civil strife. He did so by working out unwritten agreements with powerful groups in France, whereby these groups received favors in return for loyal service. Napoleon's bargain with the solid middle class was codified in the famous Civil Code of 1804, which reasserted two of the fundamental principles of the liberal and essentially moderate revolution of 1789: equality of all citizens before the law and absolute security of wealth and private property. Napoleon and the leading bankers of Paris established a privately owned Bank of France, which loyally served the interests of both the state and the financial oligarchy. Napoleon's defense of the economic status quo also appealed to the peasants, who had bought some of the lands confiscated from the church and nobility. Thus Napoleon reconfirmed the gains of the peasantry and reassured the middle class, which had already lost a large number of its revolutionary illusions in the face of social upheaval.

At the same time, Napoleon accepted and strengthened the position of the French bureaucracy. Building on the solid foundations that revolutionary governments had inherited from the Old Regime, he perfected a thoroughly centralized state. A network of prefects, subprefects, and centrally appointed mayors depended on Napoleon and served him well. Nor were members of the old nobility slighted. In 1800 and again in 1802, Napoleon granted amnesty to a hundred thousand émigrés on the condition that they return to France and take a loyalty oath. Members of this returning elite soon ably occupied many high posts in the expanding centralized state. Only a thousand diehard monarchists were exempted and remained abroad. Napoleon also created a new imperial nobility in order to reward his most talented generals and officials.

Napoleon's great skill in gaining support from important and potentially hostile groups is illustrated by his treatment of the Catholic church in

THE NAPOLEONIC ERA

November 1799	Napoleon overthrows the Directory
December 1799	French voters overwhelmingly approve Napoleon's new constitution
1800	Napoleon founds the Bank of France
1801	France defeats Austria and acquires Italian and German territories in the Treaty of Lunéville
	Napoleon signs a concordat with the pope
1802	Treaty of Amiens with Britain
December 1804	Napoleon crowns himself emperor
October 1805	Battle of Trafalgar: Britain defeats the French and Spanish fleets
December 1805	Battle of Austerlitz: Napoleon defeats Austria and Prussia
1807	Treaties of Tilsit: Napoleon redraws the map of Europe
1810	Height of the Grand Empire
June 1812	Napoleon invades Russia with 600,000 men
Winter 1812	Disastrous retreat from Russia
March 1814	Russia, Prussia, Austria, and Britain form the Quadruple Alliance to defeat France
April 1814	Napoleon abdicates and is exiled to Elba
February–June 1815	Napoleon escapes from Elba and rules France until suffering defeat at the Battle of Waterloo

France. In 1800 the French clergy was still divided into two groups: those who had taken an oath of allegiance to the revolutionary government and those in exile or hiding who had refused to do so. Personally uninterested in religion, Napoleon wanted to heal the religious division so that a united Catholic church in France could serve as a bulwark of order and social peace. After long and arduous negotiations, Napoleon and Pope Pius VII (r. 1800–1823) signed the Concordat of 1801. The pope gained for French Catholics the precious right to practice their religion freely, but Napoleon gained the most politically. His government now nominated bishops, paid the clergy, and exerted great influence over the church in France.

The domestic reforms of Napoleon's early years were his greatest achievement. Much of his legal and administrative reorganization has survived in France to this day. More generally, Napoleon's domestic initiatives gave the great majority of French people a welcome sense of order and stability. And when Napoleon added the glory of military victory, he rekindled a spirit of national unity that would elude France throughout most of the rest of the nineteenth century.

Order and unity had their price: Napoleon's authoritarian rule. Women, who had participated actively in revolutionary politics, had no political rights under the Napoleonic Code. Under the law, women were dependents, of either their fathers or their husbands, and they could not make contracts or even have bank accounts in their own names. Free speech and freedom of the press—fundamental rights of the liberal revolution enshrined in the Declaration of the Rights of Man—were continually violated. Napoleon constantly reduced the number of newspapers in Paris. By 1811 only four were left—organs of government propaganda. The occasional elections were a farce. Later laws prescribed harsh penalties for political offenses.

These changes in the law were part of the creation of a police state in France. Since Napoleon was usually busy making war, this task was largely left to Joseph Fouché, an unscrupulous opportunist who had earned a reputation for brutality during the Reign of Terror. As minister of police, Fouché organized a ruthlessly efficient spy system, which kept thousands of citizens under continuous police surveillance. People suspected of subversive activities were arbitrarily detained, placed under house arrest, or even consigned to insane asylums. After 1810 political suspects were held in state prisons, as during the Terror. There were about 2,500 such political prisoners in 1814.

Napoleon's Wars and Foreign Policy

Napoleon was above all a military man, and a great one. After coming to power in 1799, he sent peace feelers to Austria and Great Britain, the two remaining members of the Second Coalition, which had been formed against France in 1798. When these overtures were rejected, French armies led by Napoleon decisively defeated the Austrians. In the Treaty of Lunéville (1801) Austria accepted the loss of its Italian possessions, and German territory on the west bank of the Rhine was incorporated into France. Once more, as in 1797, the British were alone, and war-weary, like the French.

Still seeking to consolidate his regime domestically, Napoleon concluded the Treaty of Amiens with Great Britain in 1802. Britain agreed to return Trinidad and the Caribbean islands, which it had seized from France in 1793. The treaty said very little about Europe, though. France remained in control of Holland, the Austrian Netherlands, the west bank of the Rhine, and most of the Italian peninsula. Napoleon was free to reshape the German states as he wished. To the dismay of British business people, the Treaty of Amiens did not provide for expansion of the commerce between Britain and the Continent. It was a diplomatic triumph for Napoleon, and peace with honor and profit increased his popularity at home.

In 1802 Napoleon was secure but unsatisfied. Ever a romantic gambler as well as a brilliant administrator, he could not contain his power drive. Aggressively redrawing the map of Germany so as to weaken Austria and attract the secondary states of southwestern Germany toward France, Napoleon was also mainly responsible for renewed war with Great Britain. Regarding war with Britain as inevitable, he threatened British interests in the eastern Mediterranean and tried to restrict British trade with all of Europe. Britain had technically violated the Treaty of Amiens by failing to evacuate the island of Malta, but it was Napoleon's decision to renew war in May 1803. He concentrated his armies in the French ports on the English Channel in the fall of 1803 and began making preparations to invade England. Yet Great Britain remained dominant on the seas. When Napoleon tried to bring his Mediterranean fleet around Gibraltar to northern France, a combined French and Spanish fleet was, after a series of mishaps, virtually annihilated by Lord Nelson at the Battle of Trafalgar on October 21, 1805. Invasion of England was henceforth impossible. Renewed fighting had its advantages, however, for the first consul used the wartime atmosphere to have himself proclaimed emperor in late 1804.

Austria, Russia, and Sweden joined with Britain to form the Third Coalition against France shortly before the Battle of Trafalgar. Actions like Napoleon's assumption of the Italian crown had convinced both Alexander I of Russia and Francis II of Austria that Napoleon was a threat to their interests and to the European balance of power. Yet the Austrians and the Russians were no match for Napoleon, who scored a brilliant victory over them at the Battle of Austerlitz in December 1805. Alexander I decided to pull back, and Austria accepted large territorial losses in return for peace as the Third Coalition collapsed.

Victorious at Austerlitz, Napoleon proceeded to reorganize the German states to his liking. In

David: Napoleon Crossing the Alps Bold and commanding, with flowing cape and surging stallion, the daring young Napoleon Bonaparte leads his army across the Alps from Italy to battle the Austrians in 1797. This painting by the great Jacques-Louis David (1748–1825) is a stirring glorification of Napoleon, a brilliant exercise in mythmaking. *(Source: Louvre/Cliché des Musées Nationaux, Paris)*

Moscow

×Borodino
1812

St. Petersburg

Smolensk

R U S S I A N   E M P I R E

Kiev

Dnieper

Black Sea

O T T O M A N   E M P I R E

Cyprus

Constantinople

Athens

Crete

Baltic Sea

Stockholm

KINGDOM
OF
SWEDEN

Tilsit

×Friedland 1807

Königsberg

Danzig

GRAND DUCHY
OF WARSAW

Warsaw

Vistula

Oder

PRUSSIA

Austerlitz
1805×

Pressburg

Buda

Pest

A U S T R I A N   E M P I R E

Danube

IONIAN IS.
(Gr. Br.)

Mediterranean Sea

KINGDOM OF
NORWAY

AND

DENMARK

Copenhagen

Lübeck

Hamburg

Bremen

Berlin

SAXONY

×Leipzig 1813

Wagram
1809×

Vienna

ILLYRIAN PROVINCES

KINGDOM
OF
NAPLES

Naples

Rome

KINGDOM
OF SICILY

MALTA
(Gr. Br.)

WESTPHALIA

Auerstädt 1806×

Jena 1806×

CONFEDERATION
OF THE RHINE

BAVARIA

WÜRTTEMBERG

BADEN

KINGDOM
OF
ITALY

Milan

Elba

HELGOLAND
(Gr. Br.)

Brussels

×Waterloo
1815

Antwerp

Amiens

Paris

Lunéville

Zurich

SWITZERLAND

Marengo
1800×

Genoa

Corsica

SARDINIA

North Sea

Thames

London

ENGLAND

SCOTLAND

GREAT BRITAIN

IRELAND

Seine

Loire

Rhône

FRANCE

Marseilles

ATLANTIC

OCEAN

SPAIN

Madrid

Tagus

PORTUGAL

Lisbon

Trafalgar×
1805

GIBRALTAR
(Gr. Br.)

French empire

Dependent states

Allied with Napoleon

At war with Napoleon

× Major battles

0   150   300 Km.

0   150   300 Mi.

1806 he abolished many of the tiny German states, as well as the ancient Holy Roman Empire, whose emperor had traditionally been the ruler of Austria. Napoleon established by decree a German Confederation of the Rhine, a union of fifteen German states minus Austria, Prussia, and Saxony. Naming himself "protector" of the confederation, Napoleon firmly controlled western Germany.

Napoleon's intervention in German affairs alarmed the Prussians, who had been at peace with France for more than a decade. Expecting help from his ally Russia, Frederick William III of Prussia mobilized his armies. Napoleon attacked and won two more brilliant victories in October 1806 at Jena and Auerstädt, where the Prussians were outnumbered two to one. The war with Prussia and Russia continued into the following spring, and after Napoleon's larger armies won another victory, Alexander I of Russia wanted peace.

For several days in June 1807, the young tsar and the French emperor negotiated face to face on a raft anchored in the middle of the Niemen River. All the while, the helpless Frederick William rode back and forth on the shore, anxiously awaiting the results. As the German poet Heinrich Heine said later, Napoleon had but to whistle and Prussia would have ceased to exist. In the subsequent treaties of Tilsit, Prussia lost half of its population while Russia accepted Napoleon's reorganization of western and central Europe. Alexander also promised to enforce Napoleon's recently decreed economic blockade against British goods and to declare war on Britain if Napoleon could not make peace on favorable terms with his island enemy.

After the victory of Austerlitz and even more after the treaties of Tilsit, Napoleon saw himself as the emperor of Europe, not just of France. The so-called Grand Empire he built had three parts. The core was an ever-expanding France, which by 1810 included Belgium, Holland, parts of northern Italy, and much German territory on the east bank of the Rhine (Map 25.1). Beyond French borders Napoleon established a number of dependent satellite kingdoms, on the thrones of which he placed (and replaced) the members of his large family. Last, there were the independent but allied states of Austria, Prussia, and Russia. Both satellites and allies were expected after 1806 to

support Napoleon's continental system and cease trade with Britain.

The impact of the Grand Empire on the peoples of Europe was considerable. In the areas incorporated into France and in the satellites, Napoleon introduced many French laws, abolishing feudal dues and serfdom where French revolutionary armies had not already done so. Some of the peasants and middle class benefited from these reforms. Yet while he extended progressive measures to his cosmopolitan empire, Napoleon had to put the prosperity and special interests of France first in order to safeguard his power base. Levying heavy taxes in money and men for his armies, Napoleon came to be regarded more as a conquering tyrant than as an enlightened liberator.

The first great revolt occurred in Spain. In 1808 a coalition of Catholics, monarchists, and patriots rebelled against Napoleon's attempts to make Spain a French satellite with a Bonaparte as its king. French armies occupied Madrid, but the foes of Napoleon fled to the hills and waged uncompromising guerrilla warfare. Spain was a clear warning. Resistance to French imperialism was growing.

Yet Napoleon pushed on, determined to hold his complex and far-flung empire together. In 1810, when the Grand Empire was at its height, Britain still remained at war with France, helping the guerrillas in Spain and Portugal. The continental system, organized to exclude British goods from the Continent and force that "nation of shopkeepers" to its knees, was a failure. Instead, it was France that suffered from Britain's counter-blockade, which created hard times for French artisans and the middle class. Perhaps looking for a scapegoat, Napoleon turned on Alexander I of Russia, who had been fully supporting Napoleon's war of prohibitions against British goods.

Napoleon's invasion of Russia began in June 1812 with a force that eventually numbered 600,000, probably the largest force yet assembled in a single army. Only one-third of this force was French, however; nationals of all the satellites and allies were drafted into the operation. Originally planning to winter in the Russian city of Smolensk if Alexander did not sue for peace, Napoleon reached Smolensk and recklessly pressed on. The great battle of Borodino that followed was a draw, and the Russians retreated in good order. Alexander ordered the evacuation of Moscow, which then

MAP 25.1 Napoleonic Europe in 1810

burned, and refused to negotiate. Finally, after five weeks in the burned-out city, Napoleon ordered a retreat. That retreat was one of the great military disasters in history. The Russian army and the Russian winter cut Napoleon's army to pieces. Only 30,000 men returned to their homelands.

Leaving his troops to their fate, Napoleon raced to Paris to raise yet another army. Possibly he might still have saved his throne if he had been willing to accept a France reduced to its historical size—the proposal offered by Austria's foreign minister Metternich. But Napoleon refused. Austria and Prussia deserted Napoleon and joined Russia and Great Britain in the Fourth Coalition. All across Europe, patriots called for a "war of liberation" against Napoleon's oppression, and the well-disciplined regular armies of Napoleon's enemies closed in for the kill. This time the coalition held together, cemented by the Treaty of Chaumont, which created a Quadruple Alliance to last for twenty years. Less than a month later, on April 4, 1814, a defeated, abandoned Napoleon abdi-

cated his throne. After this unconditional abdication, the victorious allies granted Napoleon the island of Elba off the coast of Italy as his own tiny state. Napoleon was even allowed to keep his imperial title, and France was required to pay him a large yearly income of 2 million francs.

The allies also agreed to the restoration of the Bourbon dynasty, in part because demonstrations led by a few dedicated French monarchists indicated some support among the French people for that course of action. The new monarch, Louis XVIII (r. 1814–1824), tried to consolidate that support by issuing the Constitutional Charter, which accepted many of France's revolutionary changes and guaranteed civil liberties. Indeed, the Charter gave France a constitutional monarchy roughly similar to that established in 1791, although far fewer people had the right to vote for representatives to the resurrected Chamber of Deputies. Moreover, after Louis XVIII stated firmly that his government would not pay any war reparations, France was treated leniently by the al-

Goya: The Third of May, 1808 This great painting screams in outrage at the horrors of war, which Goya witnessed in Spain. Spanish rebels, focused around the Christ-like figure at the center, are gunned down by anonymous French soldiers, grim forerunners of modern death squads and their atrocities. *(Source: Museo del Prado, Madrid)*

lies, who agreed to meet in Vienna to work out a general peace settlement.

Louis XVIII—old, ugly, and crippled by gout—totally lacked the glory and magic of Napoleon. Hearing of political unrest in France and diplomatic tensions in Vienna, Napoleon staged a daring escape from Elba in February 1815. Landing in France, he issued appeals for support and marched on Paris with a small band of followers. French officers and soldiers who had fought so long for their emperor responded to the call. Louis XVIII fled, and once more Napoleon took command. But Napoleon's gamble was a desperate long shot, for the allies were united against him. At the end of a frantic period known as the Hundred Days, they crushed his forces at Waterloo on June 18, 1815, and imprisoned him on the rocky island of St. Helena, far off the western coast of Africa. Old Louis XVIII returned again—this time "in the baggage of the allies," as his detractors scornfully put it—and recommenced his reign. The allies now dealt more harshly with the apparently incorrigible French (see pages 865–868). And Napoleon, doomed to suffer crude insults at the hands of sadistic English jailers on distant St. Helena, could take revenge only by writing his memoirs, nurturing the myth that he had been Europe's revolutionary liberator, a romantic hero whose lofty work had been undone by oppressive reactionaries. An era had ended.

SUMMARY

The revolution that began in America and spread to France was a liberal revolution. Inspired by English history and some of the teachings of the Enlightenment, revolutionaries on both sides of the Atlantic sought to establish civil liberties and equality before the law within the framework of representative government. Success in America was subsequently matched by success in France. There, liberal nobles and an increasingly class-conscious middle class overwhelmed declining monarchial absolutism and feudal privilege, thanks to the common people—the sans-culottes and the peasants. The government and society established by the Declaration of the Rights of Man and the French constitution of 1791 were remarkably similar to those created in America by the federal Constitution and the Bill of Rights. Thus the new political system, based on electoral competition and civil equality, came into approximate harmony with France's evolving social structure, which had become increasingly based on wealth and achievement rather than on tradition and legal privileges.

Yet the Revolution in France did not end with the liberal victory of 1789 to 1791. As Robespierre led the determined country in a total war effort against foreign foes, French revolutionaries became more democratic, radical, and violent. Their effort succeeded, but at the price of dictatorship—first by Robespierre himself and then by the Directory and Napoleon. Some historians blame the excesses of the French revolutionaries for the emergence of dictatorship; others hold the conservative monarchs of Europe responsible. In any case, historians have often concluded that the French Revolution ended in failure.

This conclusion is highly debatable, though. After the fall of Robespierre, the solid middle class, with its liberal philosophy and Enlightenment world view, reasserted itself. Under the Directory, it salvaged a good portion of the social and political gains that it and the peasantry had made between 1789 and 1791. In so doing, the middle-class leaders repudiated the radical social and economic measures associated with Robespierre, but they never re-established the old pattern of separate legal orders and absolute monarchy. Napoleon built on the policies of the Directory. With considerable success he sought to add the support of the old nobility and the church to that of the middle class and the peasantry. And though Napoleon sharply curtailed thought and speech, he effectively promoted the reconciliation of old and new, of centralized government and careers open to talent, of noble and bourgeois in a restructured property-owning elite. Louis XVIII had no choice but to accept a French society solidly based on wealth and achievement. In granting representative government and civil liberties to facilitate his restoration to the throne in 1814, Louis XVIII submitted to the rest of the liberal triumph of 1789 to 1791. The core of the French Revolution had survived a generation of war and dictatorship. Old Europe would never be the same.

NOTES

1. Quoted in R. R. Palmer, *The Age of the Democratic Revolution,* vol. 1 (Princeton, N.J.: Princeton University Press, 1959), p. 239.

2. Quoted in G. Lefebvre, *The Coming of the French Revolution* (New York: Vintage Books, 1947), p. 81.

3. Quoted in P. H. Beik, ed., *The French Revolution* (New York: Walker, 1970), p. 89.

4. O. Hufton, "Women in Revolution," *Past and Present* 53 (November 1971): 91–95.

5. Quoted in G. Pernoud and S. Flaisser, eds., *The French Revolution* (Greenwich, Conn.: Fawcett, 1960), p. 61.

6. Quotations from Wollstonecraft are drawn from E. W. Sunstein, *A Different Face: The Life of Mary Wollstonecraft* (New York: Harper & Row, 1975), pp. 208, 211; and H. R. James, *Mary Wollstonecraft: A Sketch* (London: Oxford University Press, 1932), pp. 60, 62, 69.

7. Quoted in L. Gershoy, *The Era of the French Revolution, 1789–1799* (New York: Van Nostrand, 1957), p. 150.

8. Quoted in Pernoud and Flaisser, pp. 193–194.

SUGGESTED READING

For fascinating eyewitness reports on the French Revolution, see the edited works by Beik and Pernoud and Flaisser mentioned in the Notes. In addition, A. Young *Travels in France During the Years 1787, 1788 and 1789* (1969), offers an engrossing contemporary description of France and Paris on the eve of revolution. Edmund Burke, *Reflections on the Revolution in France*, first published in 1790, is the classic conservative indictment. The intense passions generated by the French Revolution may be seen in the nineteenth-century French historians, notably the enthusiastic Jules Michelet, *History of the French Revolution;* the hostile Hippolyte Taine; and the judicious Alexis de Tocqueville, whose masterpiece, *The Old Regime and the French Revolution*, was first published in 1856. Important general studies include the work of R. R. Palmer, cited in the Notes, which paints a comparative international picture; E. J. Hobsbawm, *The Age of Revolution, 1789–1848* (1962); C. Breunig, *The Age of Revolution and Reaction, 1789–1850* (1970); O. Connelly, *French Revolution—Napoleonic Era* (1979); and L. Dehio, *The Precarious Balance: Four Centuries of the European Power Struggle* (1962).

Recent decades have seen a wealth of new scholarship and interpretation, culminating in a profusion of works published to coincide with the French Revolution's bicentenary of 1989. A. Cobban, *The Social Interpretation of the French Revolution* (1964), and F. Furet, *Interpreting the French Revolution* (1981), are major reassessments of long-dominant ideas that are admirably presented in N. Hampson, *A Social History of the French Revolution* (1963), and in the volume by Lefebvre listed in the Notes. R. Chartier, *The Cultural Origins of the French Revolution* (1989), and W. Doyle, *Origins of the French Revolution* (1981), are excellent on long-term developments. Among recent studies, which generally are often quite critical of revolutionary developments, several are noteworthy: J. Bosher, *The French Revolution* (1988); S. Schama, *Citizens: A Chronicle of the French Revolution* (1989); W. Doyle, *The Oxford History of the French Revolution* (1989); and D. Sutherland, *France, 1789–1815: Revolution and Counterrevolution* (1986).

Two valuable anthologies concisely presenting a range of interpretations are F. Kafker and J. Laux, eds., *The French Revolutions: Conflicting Interpretations*, 4th ed. (1989), and G. Best, ed., *The Permanent Revolution: The French Revolution and Its Legacy, 1789–1989* (1988). G. Rude makes the men and women of the great days of upheaval come alive in his *The Crowd in the French Revolution* (1959), and R. R. Palmer studies sympathetically the leaders of the Terror in *Twelve Who Ruled* (1941). Four other particularly interesting, detailed works are D. Jordan, *The Revolutionary Career of Maximilien Robespierre* (1985); J. P. Bertaud, *The Army of the French Revolution: From Citizen-Soldier to Instrument of Power* (1988); C. L. R. James, *The Black Jacobins* (1938, 1980), on black slave revolt in Haiti; and J. C. Herold, *Mistress to an Age* (1955), on the remarkable Madame de Staël. Other significant studies on aspects of revolutionary France include P. Jones's pathbreaking *The Peasantry in the French Revolution* (1988); D. Jordan's vivid *The King's Trial: Louis XVI vs. the French Revolution* (1979); W. Sewell Jr.'s imaginative *Work and Revolution in France: The Language of Labor from the Old Regime to 1848* (1980); and L. Hunt's innovative *Politics, Culture, and Class in the French Revolution* (1984). Mary Wollstonecraf is the subject of several biographies, including those by Sunstein and James cited in the Notes.

Two important works placing political developments in a comparative perspective are P. Higonnet, *Sister Republics: The Origins of French and American Republicanism* (1988), and E. Morgan, *Inventing the People: The Rise of Popular Sovereignty in England and America* (1988). B. Bailyn, *The Ideological Origins of the American Revolution* (1967), is also noteworthy.

The best synthesis on Napoleonic France is L. Bergeron, *France Under Napoleon* (1981). P. Geyl, *Napoleon, For and Against* (1949), is a delightful discussion of changing historical interpretations of Napoleon, which may be compared with a more recent treatment by R. Jones, *Napoleon: Man and Myth* (1977). Good biographies are J. M. Thompson, *Napoleon Bonaparte: His Rise and Fall* (1952); F. H. M. Markham, *Napoleon* (1964); and V. Cronin, *Napoleon Bonaparte* (1972). Wonderful novels inspired by this period include Raphael Sabatini's *Scaramouche*, a swashbuckler of revolutionary intrigue with accurate historical details; Charles Dickens's classic *Tale of Two Cities;* and Leo Tolstoy's saga of Napoleon's invasion of Russia, *War and Peace.*

26

The Industrial Revolution in Europe

Paddington Station, London. William-Powell Frith, *The Railway Station* (detail)

While the Revolution in France was opening a new political era, another revolution was transforming economic and social life. This was the Industrial Revolution, which began in England around the 1780s and started to influence continental Europe and the rest of the world after 1815. Because the Industrial Revolution was less dramatic than the French Revolution, some historians see industrial development as basically moderate and evolutionary. From a long perspective, however, it was rapid and brought about radical changes. Perhaps only the development of agriculture during Neolithic times had a similar impact and significance.

The Industrial Revolution profoundly modified much of human experience. It changed patterns of work, transformed the social class structure, and even altered the international balance of political and military power, giving added impetus to ongoing Western expansion into non-Western lands. The Industrial Revolution also helped ordinary people gain a higher standard of living as the widespread poverty of the preindustrial world was gradually reduced.

Unfortunately, improvement in the European standard of living was quite limited until about 1850, for at least two reasons. First, even in England only a few key industries experienced a technological revolution. Many more industries continued to use old methods, especially on the Continent, and this held down the increase in total production. Second, the increase in total population, which began in the eighteenth century (see pages 695–697), continued all across Europe as the era of the Industrial Revolution unfolded. As a result, the rapid growth in population threatened—quite literally—to eat up the growth in production and to leave individuals poorer than ever. Thus rapid population growth formed a somber background for European industrialization and made the wrenching transformation even more difficult.

- What was the Industrial Revolution?
- What were the origins of the Industrial Revolution, and how did it develop?
- How did the changes brought by the Industrial Revolution affect people and society in an era of continued rapid population growth?

These are the questions that this chapter seeks to answer. Chapter 28 examines in detail the emergence of accompanying changes in urban civilization, and Chapter 30 probes the consequences of industrialization in Europe for non-Western peoples.

THE INITIAL BREAKTHROUGH IN ENGLAND

The Industrial Revolution began in England. It was something new in history, and it was quite unplanned. With no models to copy and no idea of what to expect, England had to pioneer not only in industrial technology but also in social relations and urban living. Between 1793 and 1815, these formidable tasks were complicated by almost constant war with France. The trailblazer in economic development, as France was in political change, England must command special attention.

Eighteenth-Century Origins

Although many aspects of the Industrial Revolution are still matters for scholarly debate, it is generally agreed that the industrial changes that did occur grew out of a complex combination of factors. These factors came together in eighteenth-century England and initiated a decisive breakthrough, a breakthrough that many place in the 1780s—after the American war for independence and just before the French Revolution.

In analyzing the causes of the late-eighteenth-century acceleration in the English economy, historians have paid particular attention to dramatic changes in agriculture, foreign trade, technology, energy supplies, and transportation. Although this chapter focuses on those issues, one must first understand that England had other, less conspicuous, assets that favored the long process of development that culminated in industrial breakthrough.

Relatively good government was one such asset. The monarchy and the aristocratic oligarchy, which jointly ruled the country after the constitutional settlement of 1688 (see pages 648–649), provided stable and predictable government. Neither civil strife nor invading armies threatened the peace of the realm. Thus the government let the domestic economy operate fairly freely and with few controls, encouraging personal initiative, technological change, and a free market.

A related asset was an experienced business class with very modern characteristics. This business class, which traced its origins to the High Middle Ages, eagerly sought to make profits and to accumulate capital.

England also had a large class of hired agricultural laborers, whose numbers were further increased by agricultural changes in the eighteenth century. These rural wage earners were relatively mobile—compared with village-bound peasants in France and western Germany, for example—and along with cottage workers they formed a potential labor force for capitalist entrepreneurs.

Several other assets supporting English economic growth stand out. First, unlike France and most other countries, England had an effective central bank and well-developed credit institutions. Second, although England may seem a rather small country today, it undoubtedly enjoyed the largest effective domestic market in eighteenth-century Europe. In an age when shipping goods by water was much cheaper than shipping goods by land, no part of England was more than twenty miles from navigable water. Beginning in the 1770s, a canal-building boom greatly enhanced this natural advantage (Map 26.1). Nor were there any tariffs within the country to hinder trade, as there were in France before 1789 and in politically fragmented Germany and Italy. Finally, only in Holland did the lower classes appear to live as well as in England. The ordinary English family did not have to spend almost everything it earned just to buy bread. It could spend more on other items, thereby adding significantly to the total demand for manufactured goods. And growing demand for manufactured goods was probably the critical factor in initiating England's industrial breakthrough.

All these factors combined to initiate the Industrial Revolution, a term first coined by awed contemporaries in the 1830s to describe the burst of major inventions and technical changes that they had witnessed in certain industries. This technical revolution went hand in hand with an impressive quickening in the annual rate of industrial growth in England. Thus industry grew at only 0.7 per-

MAP 26.1 Cottage Industry and Transportation in Eighteenth-Century England England had an unusually good system of navigable waterways even before river-linking canals made it better.

cent per year between 1700 and 1760—before the Industrial Revolution—but it grew at the much higher rate of 3 percent between 1801 and 1831, when industrial transformation was in full swing.[1] The decisive quickening of growth probably came in the 1780s, after the American war of independence and just before the French Revolution.

The great economic and political revolutions that shaped the modern world occurred almost simultaneously, though they began in different countries. The Industrial Revolution, however, was a longer process. It was not complete in England until 1830 at the earliest, and it had no real impact on continental countries until after the Congress of Vienna ended the era of revolutionary wars in 1815.

The Agricultural Revolution

According to an older generation of historians, England's industrial transformation depended on an earlier revolution in agriculture and rural life. Although scholars no longer believe that radical agricultural change was a necessary precondition for the industrial breakthrough, the general stress on the importance of agricultural improvement remains valid. A gradual but profound revolution in agricultural methods did promote accelerated economic growth, and that revolution mirrored the general economic leadership underpinning England's epoch-making industrial surge.

In essence, the Agricultural Revolution eliminated the traditional pattern of village agriculture found in northern and central Europe. It replaced the medieval open-field system (see page 377) with a new system of continuous rotation that resulted in more food for humans and their animals. The new agricultural system had profound implications, for it eliminated long-standing common rights as well as the fallow. But whereas peasants and rural laborers checked the spread of the new system on the Continent in the eighteenth century, large landowners and powerful market forces overcame such opposition in England.

The new methods of agriculture originated in the Low Countries. The vibrant, dynamic middle-class society of seventeenth-century republican Holland was the most advanced in Europe in many areas of human endeavor, including agriculture. By 1650 intensive farming was well established throughout much of the Low Countries. Enclosed fields, continuous rotation, heavy manuring, and a wide variety of crops—all these innovations were present. Agriculture was highly specialized and commercialized. The same skills that grew turnips produced flax to be spun into linen for clothes and tulip bulbs to lighten the heart with beautiful flowers. The fat cattle of Holland, so beloved by Dutch painters, gave the most milk in Europe.

The reasons for early Dutch leadership in farming were basically threefold. First, the Low Countries were densely populated, and the Dutch were forced at an early date to seek maximum yields from their land and to increase land area through the steady draining of marshes and swamps. Second, the growth of towns and cities—Amsterdam grew from 30,000 to 200,000 in its golden seventeenth century—provided Dutch peasants with good markets and encouraged each region to specialize in what it did best. Finally, there was the quality of the people. Oppressed by neither grasping nobles nor war-minded monarchs, the Dutch could develop their potential in a free and capitalistic society. The Low Countries became "the Mecca of foreign agricultural experts who came . . . to see Flemish agriculture with their own eyes, to write about it and to propagate its methods in their home lands."[2]

The English were the best students. They learned about water control from the Dutch, the world's leaders after centuries of effort in the skills of drainage. In the seventeenth century, Dutch experts made a great contribution to draining the extensive marshes, or fens, of wet and rainy England. On such new land, where traditions and common rights were not established, farmers introduced new crops and new rotations fairly easily.

Dutch experience was also important to Viscount Charles Townsend (1674–1738), one of the pioneers of English agriculture improvement. This lord from the upper reaches of the English aristocracy learned about turnips and clover while serving as English ambassador to Holland. In the 1710s, he was growing these crops in the sandy soil of his large estates in Norfolk in eastern England, already one of the most innovative agricultural areas in the country. When Lord Charles retired from politics in 1730 and returned to Norfolk, it was said that he spoke of turnips, turnips, and nothing but turnips. This led some wit to nickname his lordship "Turnip" Townsend. But Townsend had the last laugh. Draining extensively, manuring heavily, and sowing crops in regular rotation without fallowing, the farmers who leased Townsend's lands produced larger crops. They and he earned higher incomes. Those who had scoffed reconsidered. By 1740 agricultural improvement had become a craze among the English aristocracy.

Jethro Tull (1674–1741), part crank and part genius, was another important English innovator. A true son of the early Enlightenment, Tull constantly tested accepted ideas about farming in an effort to develop better methods through empirical research. He was especially enthusiastic about using horses for plowing, in preference to slower-moving oxen. He also advocated sowing seed with drilling equipment rather than scattering it by hand. Drilling distributed seed evenly and at the proper depth. There were also improvements in livestock, inspired in part by the earlier successes of English country gentlemen in breeding ever-faster horses for the races and fox hunts that were their passions. Selective breeding of ordinary livestock was a marked improvement over the old pattern, which has been graphically described as little more than "the haphazard union of nobody's son with everybody's daughter."

By the mid-eighteenth century, English agriculture was in the process of a radical and technologically desirable transformation. The eventual result was that by 1870 English farmers produced 300 percent more food than they had produced in 1700, although the number of people working the land had increased by only 14 percent. This great surge of agricultural production provided food for England's rapidly growing urban population. It was a tremendous achievement.

The Cost of Enclosure

What was the cost of technical progress in England, and to what extent did its payment result in social injustice? Scholars agree that the impetus for enclosing the fields came mainly from the powerful ruling class, the English landowning aristocracy. Owning large estates, the aristocracy benefited directly from higher yields that could support higher rents, and it was able and ready to make expensive investments in the new technology. Beyond these certainties, there are important differences of interpretation among historians.

Many historians contrast the initiative and enterprise of the big English landowners with the inertia and conservatism of continental landowners, big and small. They also assert that the open fields were enclosed fairly and that both large and small owners received their fair share after the strips were surveyed and consolidated.

Other historians argue that fairness was more apparent than real. The large landowners controlled Parliament, which made the laws. They had Parliament pass hundreds of "enclosure acts," each of which authorized the fencing of open fields in a given village and the division of the common in proportion to one's property in the open fields. The heavy legal and surveying costs of enclosure were also divided among the landowners. This meant that many peasants who had small holdings had to sell out to pay their share of the expenses. Similarly, the landless cottagers lost their age-old access to the common pasture but received no compensation whatsoever. Landless families were dealt a serious blow, for women were deprived of the means to raise animals for market and to earn vital income. In the spirited words of one critical historian, "Enclosure (when all the sophistications are allowed for) was a plain enough case of class robbery, played according to the fair rules of property and law laid down by a Parliament of property-owners and lawyers."[3]

In assessing these conflicting interpretations, one needs to put eighteenth-century developments in a longer historical perspective. In the first place, as much as half of English farmland was already enclosed by 1750. A great wave of enclosure of English open fields into sheep pastures had occurred in the sixteenth and early seventeenth centuries, a wave that had dispossessed many English peasants in order to produce wool for the thriving textile industry. In the later seventeenth and early eighteenth centuries, many open fields were enclosed fairly harmoniously by mutual agreement among all classes of landowners in English villages. Thus parliamentary enclosure, the great bulk of which occurred after 1760 and particularly during the Napoleonic wars, only completed a process that was in full swing. Nor did an army of

Surveyors Measuring Enclosing open farmland met with much resistance, especially from poorer peasants and some nobility. It was more successful in England as illustrated in this scene from a nineteenth-century map of Bedfordshire. (Source: Courtesy, Bedfordshire County Council)

landless cottagers and farm laborers appear only in the last years of the eighteenth century. Much earlier, and certainly by 1700, there were perhaps two landless agricultural workers in England for every independent farmer.

Indeed, by 1700 a highly distinctive pattern of landownership and production existed in England. At one extreme were a few large landowners, at the other a large mass of landless cottagers who labored mainly for wages and who could graze only a pig or a cow on the village common. In between stood two other groups: small, independent peasant farmers who owned their own land, and substantial tenant farmers who rented land from the big landowners, hired wage laborers, and sold their output on a cash market. Yet the small, independent English farmers had been declining in numbers since the sixteenth-century enclosures (and even before), and they continued to do so in the eighteenth century. They could not compete with the profit-minded, market-oriented tenant farmers.

These tenant farmers, many of whom had formerly been independent owners, were the key to mastering the new methods of farming. Well financed by the large landowners, the tenant farmers fenced fields, built drains, and improved the soil with fertilizers. Such improvements and new methods of farming actually increased employment opportunities for wage workers. Thus enclosure did not force people off the land by eliminating jobs.

At the same time, by eliminating common rights and greatly reducing the access of poor men and women to the land, the eighteenth-century enclosure movement marked the completion of two major historical developments in England: the rise of market-orientated estate agriculture and the emergence of a landless proletariat. By 1815 a tiny minority of wealthy English (and Scottish) landowners held most of the land and pursued profits aggressively, leasing their holdings through agents at competitive prices to middle-sized farmers. These farmers produced mainly for cash markets and relied on landless laborers for their workforce. In strictly economic terms, these landless laborers may have lived as well in 1800 as in 1700, but they had lost that bit of independence and self-respect that common rights had provided. They had become completely dependent on cash wages. In no other European country had this "proletarianization"—this transformation of large numbers of

small peasant farmers into landless rural wage earners—gone so far as it had in England by the late eighteenth century. And, as in the earlier English enclosure movement, the village poor found the cost of economic change and technical progress heavy and unjust.

The Growth of Foreign Trade

In addition to leading Europe in agricultural improvement, Great Britain (formed in 1707 by the union of England and Scotland into a single kingdom) gradually became the leading maritime power. In the eighteenth century, British ships and merchants succeeded in dominating long-distance trade, particularly intercontinental trade across the Atlantic. This foreign trade stimulated the economy.

Britain's commercial leadership in the eighteenth century had its origins in the mercantilism of the seventeenth century (see page 614). European mercantilism was a system of economic regulations aimed at increasing the power of the state. What distinguished English mercantilism was the unusual idea that government economic regulations could and should serve the private interest of individuals and groups as well as the public needs of the state. As Josiah Child, a very wealthy brewer and director of the East India Company, put it, in the ideal economy "Profit and Power ought jointly to be considered."[4]

The seventeenth-century Navigation Acts reflected the desire of Great Britain to increase both its military power and its private wealth. The initial target of these instruments of economic warfare was the Dutch, who were far ahead of the English in shipping and foreign trade in the mid-seventeenth century. The Navigation Acts, in conjunction with three Anglo-Dutch wars between 1652 and 1674, did seriously damage the Dutch. By the later seventeenth century, the Netherlands was falling behind England in shipping, trade, and colonies. France then stood clearly as England's most serious rival in the competition for overseas empire. Rich in natural resources and endowed with a population three or four times that of England, continental Europe's leading military power was already building a powerful fleet and a worldwide system of rigidly monopolized colonial trade. And France, aware that Great Britain coveted large parts of Spain's American em-

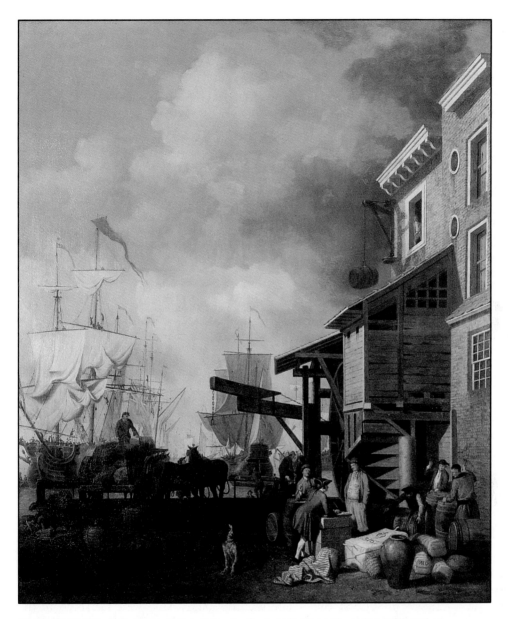

The East India Dock, London This painting by Samuel Scott captures the spirit and excitement of British maritime expansion. Great sailing ships line the quay, bringing profit and romance from far-off India. London grew in population from 350,000 in 1650 to 900,000 in 1800, when it was twice as big as Paris, its nearest rival. *(Source: Courtesy of Board of Trustees of the Victoria & Albert Museum)*

pire, was determined to revitalize its Spanish ally. Thus from 1701 to 1763, Britain and France were locked in a series of wars to decide, in part, which nation would become the leading maritime power and claim the lion's share of the profits of Europe's overseas expansion (Map 26.2).

The first round was the War of the Spanish Succession (see page 617), which resulted in major gains for Great Britain in the Peace of Utrecht (1713). France ceded Newfoundland, Nova Scotia, and the Hudson Bay territory to Britain. Spain was compelled to give Britain control of the lucrative West African slave trade—the so-called *asiento*—and to let Britain send one ship of merchandise into the Spanish colonies annually. In the course of the War of the Austrian Succession

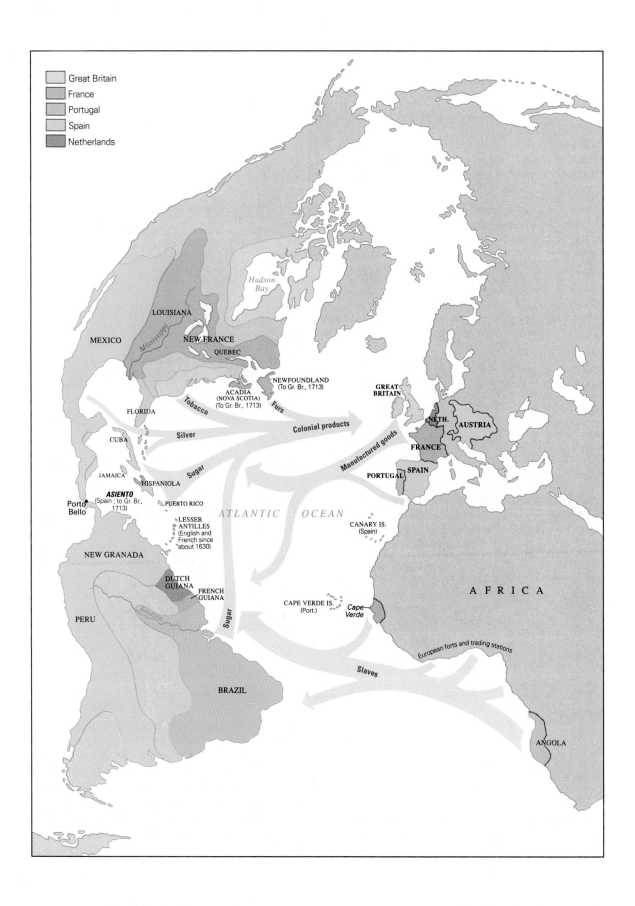

Great Britain
France
Portugal
Spain
Netherlands

Hudson
Bay

LOUISIANA

MEXICO   NEW FRANCE

QUEBEC

NEWFOUNDLAND
(To Gr. Br., 1713)
ACADIA
(NOVA SCOTIA)
(To Gr. Br., 1713)

GREAT
BRITAIN

Tobacco   Furs

FLORIDA   Colonial products

CUBA   Silver   Manufactured goods   NETH.   AUSTRIA

JAMAICA   Sugar   FRANCE

HISPANIOLA   PORTUGAL   SPAIN

Porto   ASIENTO
Bello   (Spain ; to Gr. Br.,   PUERTO RICO
           1713)

LESSER   ATLANTIC   OCEAN   CANARY IS.
ANTILLES   (Spain)
(English and
French since
NEW GRANADA   about 1630)

DUTCH
GUIANA   CAPE VERDE IS.   Cape
FRENCH   (Port.)   Verde
GUIANA   A F R I C A
PERU
Amazon   Sugar

                                                     European forts and trading stations

                          Slaves

BRAZIL

                                                                          ANGOLA

(1740–1748), New England colonists momentarily seized French territory in Canada.

This stand-off helped set the stage for the Seven Years' War (1756–1763), which was the decisive round in the Franco-British competition for colonial empire. Led by William Pitt, whose grandfather had made a fortune as a trader in India, the British concentrated on using superior sea power to destroy the French fleet and choke off French commerce around the world. With the Treaty of Paris (1763), France lost all its possessions on the mainland of North America and gave up most of its holdings in India as well. By 1763, Britain had realized its goal of monopolizing a vast trade and colonial empire for its benefit.

This interconnected expansion of trade and empire marked a major step toward the Industrial Revolution, although people could not know it at the time. Since the late Middle Ages, England had successfully manufactured woolen cloth, which had provided an outstanding opportunity for profit and economic growth. By 1700 much of this cloth was exported abroad, and fully 90 percent of it was sold to Europeans. In the course of the eighteenth century, however, the states of continental Europe were trying to develop their own cottage textile industries in an effort to deal with the growth of rural poverty and population. Like England earlier, these states adopted protectionist, mercantilist policies. They tried, with some success, by means of tariffs and other measures to exclude competing goods from abroad, and by 1773 England was selling only about two-thirds as much woolen cloth to northern and western Europe as it had sold in 1700. The English economy badly needed new markets and new products in order to develop and prosper.

Protected colonial markets came to the rescue and provided a great stimulus for many branches of English manufacturing. The value of sales of manufactured products to the Atlantic economy—primarily the mainland colonies of North America and the West Indian sugar islands, with an important assist from West Africa and Latin America—soared from £475,000 in 1700 to £3.9 million in 1773 (Figure 26.1). English exports of manufac-

MAP 26.2 The Economy of the Atlantic Basin in 1701 The growth of trade encouraged both economic development and military conflict in the Atlantic Basin.

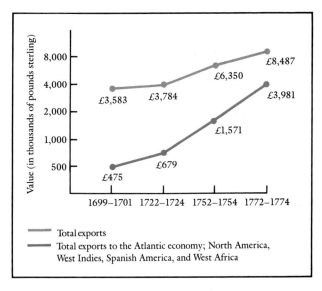

FIGURE 26.1 Exports of English Manufactured Goods, 1700–1774 While trade between England and Europe stagnated after 1700, English exports to Africa and the Americas boomed and greatly stimulated English economic development. *(Source: Based on information from R. Davis, "English Foreign Trade, 1700–1774," Economic History Review, 2d series, 15 (1962): 302–303. Used with permission of Basil Blackwell Ltd.)*

tured goods to continental Europe grew hardly at all in these years.

English exports became much more balanced and diversified. To America and Africa went large quantities of metal items—axes to frontiersmen, firearms, chains for slaveowners. Also exported were clocks and coaches, buttons and saddles, china and furniture, musical instruments and scientific equipment, and a host of other things. By 1750 half of the nails made in England were going to the colonies. Foreign trade became the bread and butter of some industries. Thus the mercantile system established in the seventeenth century to attack the Dutch and to win power and profit for England continued to shape trade in the eighteenth century. The English concentrated in their hands much of the demand for manufactured goods from the growing Atlantic economy. Sales to other "colonies"—Ireland and India—also rose substantially in the eighteenth century. Nor was this all. Demand from the well-integrated home market was also rising. The English were relatively well-off, and their population was growing. Moreover, new methods of farming and good weather brought a period of bountiful crops and low food prices, especially before 1760. Ordinary people could buy more manufactured goods. Rising demand from home and abroad put intense pressure on the whole system of production.

Land and Wealth in North America

Britain's colonies on the North American mainland proved particularly valuable in the long run (Map 26.3). Because the settlements along the Atlantic coast provided an important outlet for surplus population, migration abroad limited poverty in England, Scotland, and Northern Ireland. The settlers benefited because for most of the eighteenth century they had privileged access to virtually free and unlimited land. The abundance of almost-free land resulted in a rapid increase in the white population, which multiplied a staggering ten times between 1700 and 1774 as immigrants arrived and colonial couples raised large families. In 1774, 2.2 million whites and 330,000 blacks inhabited what would soon become the independent United States.

Rapid population growth did not reduce the settlers to poverty. On the contrary, agricultural development resulted in fairly high standards of living. It has been estimated that between 1715 and 1775 the real income of the average American was increasing about 1 percent per year per person, almost two-thirds as fast as it increased with massive industrialization between 1840 and 1959.[5] There was also an unusual degree of economic equality, by European standards. Few people were extremely rich and few were extremely poor. On the eve of the American Revolution, the average white man or woman in the mainland British colonies probably had the highest income and standard of living in the world.

The availability of land made labor expensive. This encouraged the growth of black slavery in the southern colonies and created a wealthy planter class with a taste for home-country luxuries.

The First Factories

The pressure to produce more goods for a growing market was directly related to the first decisive breakthrough of the Industrial Revolution—the creation of the world's first large factories in the English cotton textile industry. Technological innovations in the manufacture of cloth led to a whole new pattern of production and social relationships. Since no other industry experienced such a rapid or complete transformation before 1830, these trailblazing developments deserve special consideration.

Although the putting-out system of merchant capitalism (see page 699) was expanding all across Europe in the eighteenth century, this pattern of rural industry was most fully developed in England. Thus it was in England, under the pressure of growing demand, that the system's shortcomings first began to outweigh its advantages—especially in the cottage textile industry after about 1760.

There was always a serious imbalance in this family enterprise: the work of four or five spinners was needed to keep one weaver steadily employed. The wife and the husband had constantly to try to find more thread and more spinners. Widows and unmarried women—"spinsters" who spun for their living—were recruited by the wife. Or perhaps the weaver's son went off on horseback to seek thread. The need for thread might even lead the weaver and his wife to become small capitalist employers, putting out raw wool or cotton to other cottagers.

Deep-seated conflict between workers and employers complicated increased production. In "The Clothier's Delight, or the Rich Men's Joy and the Poor Men's Sorrow," an English popular song written about 1700, a merchant boasts of his countless tricks used to "beat down wages":

We heapeth up riches and treasure great store
Which we get by griping and grinding the poor.
And this is a way for to fill up our purse
Although we do get it with many a curse.[6]

There were constant disputes over the weights of materials and the quality of the cloth. Merchants accused workers of stealing raw materials, and weavers complained that merchants delivered underweight bales. Both were right; each tried to cheat the other, even if only in self-defense.

There was another problem, at least from the merchant-capitalist's point of view. Rural labor was cheap, scattered, and poorly organized; thus it was hard to control. Cottage workers tended to work in spurts. After they got paid on Saturday af-

MAP 26.3 European Claims in North America Before and After the Seven Years' War, 1756–1763   France lost its vast claims in North America, though the British government then prohibited colonists from settling west of a line drawn in 1763. The British wanted to avoid costly wars with Indians living in the newly conquered territory.

ternoon, the men in particular tended to drink and carouse for two or three days. Indeed, Monday was called "holy Monday" because inactivity was so religiously observed. By the end of the week the weaver was probably working feverishly to make his quota. But if he did not succeed, there was little the merchant could do. When times were good and the merchant could easily sell everything produced, the weaver and his family did fairly well and were particularly inclined to loaf, to the dismay of the capitalist. Thus, in spite of its early virtues, the putting-out system in the textile industry revealed growing limitations, and the merchant-capitalist's search for more efficient methods of production intensified.

Attention focused on ways to improve spinning. Many a merchant and tinkering worker knew that

a better spinning wheel promised rich rewards. Spinning of the traditional raw materials—wool and flax—proved hard to change, but cotton was different. Cotton textiles had first been imported into England from India by the East India Company, and by 1760 there was a tiny domestic industry in northern England. After many experiments over a generation, a gifted carpenter and jack-of-all-trades, James Hargreaves, invented his cotton-spinning jenny about 1765. At almost the same moment a barber-turned-manufacturer, Richard Arkwright, invented (or possibly pirated) another kind of spinning machine, the water frame. These breakthroughs produced an explosion in the infant industry. By 1790 the new machines produced ten times as much cotton yarn as had been made in 1770. By 1800 the production of cotton thread had become England's most important industry.

Hargreaves's jenny was simple and inexpensive. It was also operated by hand. In early models, from six to twenty-four spindles were mounted on a sliding carriage, and each spindle spun a fine, slender thread. A woman moved the carriage back and forth with one hand and turned a wheel to supply power with the other. Now it was the weaver who could not keep up with his vastly more efficient wife.

Arkwright's water frame employed a different principle. It quickly acquired a capacity of several hundred spindles and demanded much more power—water power. The water frame thus required large specialized mills, factories that employed hundreds of workers from the very beginning. The water frame could spin only coarse, strong thread, which was then put out for respinning on hand-powered cottage jennies. Around 1790 another innovation, Samuel Crompton's "mule"— which combined the best aspects of the jenny and the water frame—began to require more power than the human arm could supply. Thus all cotton spinning gradually became concentrated in factories.

The first consequences of these revolutionary developments were more beneficial than is generally believed. Cotton goods became much cheaper, and they were bought and treasured by all classes. In the past, only the wealthy could afford the comfort and cleanliness of underwear, which was called "body linen" because it was made from expensive linen cloth. Now millions of poor people, who had earlier worn nothing underneath their coarse, filthy outer garments, could afford to wear cotton slips and underpants.

Families using cotton in cottage industry were freed from their constant search for adequate yarn from scattered, part-time spinners, since all the

Hargreave's Spinning Jenny The loose cotton strands on the slanted bobbins passed up to the sliding carriage and then on to the spindles in back for fine spinning. By 1783 one woman could spin by hand a hundred threads at a time on an improved model. *(Source: University of Illinois, Champaign)*

thread needed could be spun in the cottage on the jenny or obtained from a nearby factory. The wages of weavers, now hard pressed to keep up with the spinners, rose markedly until about 1792. Weavers were among the best-paid workers in England. They were known to walk proudly through the streets with £5 notes stuck in their hatbands, and they dressed like the middle class.

One result of this unprecedented prosperity was that large numbers of agricultural laborers became weavers. Meanwhile, however, mechanics and capitalists were seeking to invent a power loom to save on labor costs. This Edmund Cartwright achieved in 1785. But the power looms of the factories worked poorly at first, and handloom weavers continued to receive good wages until at least 1800.

Working conditions in the early factories were less satisfactory than those of cottage weavers and spinners. But until the late 1780s, most English factories were in rural areas, where they had access to water power. These factories employed a relatively small percentage of all cotton textile workers. Since people were reluctant to work in them, factory owners often turned to children who had been abandoned by their parents and put in the care of local parishes. The parish officers often "apprenticed" such unfortunate orphans to factory owners. The parish thus saved money, and the factory owners gained workers over whom they exercised almost the authority of slaveowners.

Apprenticed as young as five or six years of age, the boy and girl workers were forced by law to labor for their "master" for as many as fourteen years. Clothed, fed, and locked up nightly in factory dormitories, the young workers received little or no pay for their toil. Hours were appalling— commonly thirteen or fourteen hours a day, six days a week. Harsh physical punishment maintained brutal discipline. To be sure, poor children had typically worked long hours from an early age in the eighteenth century—and frequently outside the home for a brutal master. But the wholesale coercion of orphans as factory apprentices constituted exploitation on a truly unprecedented scale. This exploitation ultimately piqued the conscience of reformers and reinforced humanitarian attitudes toward children and their labor in the early nineteenth century.

The creation of the world's first modern factories in the English cotton textile industry in the 1770s and 1780s, which grew out of the putting-out system of cottage production, was a momentous development. Both symbolically and in substance, the big new cotton mills marked the beginning of the Industrial Revolution in England. By 1831 the largely mechanized cotton textile industry towered above all others, accounting for fully 22 percent of the country's entire industrial production.

ENERGY AND TRANSPORTATION

If water from rivers and streams had remained the primary source of power for the new factories, the growth of the cotton textile industry might have been stunted or cut short. This did not occur because an epoch-making solution was found to the age-old problem of energy and power. This solution to the energy problem—a problem that has reappeared in recent times—permitted continued rapid development in cotton textiles, the gradual generalization of the factory system, the revolution in transportation, and the triumph of the Industrial Revolution.

The Problem of Energy

Human beings, like all living organisms, require energy. Adult men and women need 2,000 to 4,000 calories (units of energy) daily simply to fuel their bodies, work, and survive. Energy comes from a variety of sources; it also takes different forms, and one form may be converted into another. Plants have been converting solar energy into caloric matter for eons. Human beings have used their toolmaking abilities to construct machines that convert one form of energy into another for their own benefit.

Prehistoric people relied on plants and plant-eating animals as their sources of energy. With the development of agriculture, early civilizations were able to increase the number of useful plants and thus the supply of energy. Some plants could be fed to domesticated animals, like the horse. Stronger than human beings, these animals converted the energy in the plants into work. In the medieval period, people began to develop water mills to grind their grain and windmills to pump water and drain swamps. In the sixteenth and seventeenth centuries, more efficient use of water and wind enabled human beings, especially Europeans, to accomplish somewhat more; intercontinental sailing ships are a prime example. Nevertheless, even into the eighteenth century, European society continued to rely for energy mainly on plants, and human beings and animals continued to perform most work. This dependence meant that Western civilization remained poor in energy and power.

Lack of power lay at the heart of the poverty that afflicted the large majority of people worldwide. The man behind the plow and the woman at the spinning wheel could employ only horsepower and human muscle in their labor. No matter how hard they worked, they could not produce very much. What people needed were new sources of energy and more power at their disposal; then they would be able to work more efficiently, produce more, and live better.

Where was more energy to be found? Almost all energy came directly or indirectly from plants and therefore from the land: grain for people, hay for animals, and wood for heat. The land was also the principal source of raw materials needed for industrial production: wool and flax for clothing; leather for shoes; wood for housing, tools, and ironmaking. Although the land's yield could be increased—through the elimination of fallow, for example—there were definite limits to such improvements.

The shortage of energy was becoming particularly severe in England by the eighteenth century. Because of the growth of population, most of the great forests of medieval England had long ago been replaced by fields of grain and hay. Wood was in ever shorter supply; yet it remained tremendously important. In addition to serving as the primary source of heat and as a basic raw material, processed wood (charcoal) was mixed with iron ore in a blast furnace to produce pig iron. The iron industry's appetite for wood was enormous, and by 1740 the English iron industry was stagnating. Vast forests enabled Russia in the eighteenth century to become the world's leading producer of iron, much of which was exported to England. But Russia's potential for growth was limited, too, and in a few decades Russia would reach the barrier of inadequate energy that was already holding back England.

The Steam Engine Breakthrough

As this early energy crisis grew worse, England looked toward its abundant and widely scattered reserves of coal as an alternative to wood. Coal was first used in England in the late Middle Ages as a source of heat. By 1640 most homes in London were heated with it, and it also provided heat for making beer, glass, soap, and other products. Coal was not used, however, to produce mechanical energy or to power machinery. It was there that coal's potential was enormous, as a simple example shows.

One pound of good bituminous coal contains about 3,500 calories of heat energy. A miner who eats 3,500 calories of food can produce about 1 horsepower-hour as he digs out 500 pounds of coal in the course of a day using hand tools. Even an extremely inefficient converter, which transforms only 1 percent of the heat energy in coal into mechanical energy, will produce 27 horsepower-hours of work from the 500 pounds of coal that the miner cut out of the earth. Much more energy is consumed by the converter, but much more work can be done. Early steam engines were just such inefficient converters.

As more coal was produced, mines were dug deeper and deeper and were constantly filling with water. Mechanical pumps, usually powered by animals walking in circles at the surface, had to be installed. At one mine, fully five hundred horses were used for pumping. Such power was expensive and bothersome. In an attempt to overcome these disadvantages, Thomas Savery in 1698 and Thomas Newcomen in 1705 invented the first primitive steam engines.

These engines were extremely inefficient. Both burned coal to produce steam, which was then injected into a cylinder or reservoir. In Newcomen's engine, the steam in the cylinder was cooled, creating a partial vacuum in the cylinder. This vacuum allowed the pressure of the earth's atmosphere to push the piston in the cylinder down and operate a pump. By the early 1770s, many of the Savery engines and hundreds of the Newcomen engines were operating successfully, though inefficiently, in English and Scottish mines.

In the early 1760s, a gifted young Scot named James Watt (1736–1819) was drawn to a critical study of the steam engine. Watt was employed at

Making Charcoal   After wood was carefully cut and stacked, iron masters slowly burned it to produce charcoal. Before the Industrial Revolution, a country's iron industry depended greatly on the size of its forests. *(Source: University of Illinois, Champaign)*

the time by the University of Glasgow as a skilled craftsman making scientific instruments. The Scottish universities were pioneers in practical technical education, and in 1763 Watt was called on to repair a Newcomen engine being used in a physics course. After a series of observations, Watt saw why the Newcomen engine wasted so much energy: the cylinder was being heated and cooled for every single stroke of the piston. To remedy this problem, Watt added a separate condenser, where the steam could be condensed without cooling the cylinder. This splendid invention greatly increased the efficiency of the steam engine.

To invent something in a laboratory is one thing; to make it a practical success is quite another. Watt needed skilled workers, precision parts, and capital. The relatively advanced nature of the English economy proved essential. A partnership with a wealthy, progressive toymaker provided risk capital and a manufacturing plant. In the craft tradition of locksmiths, tinsmiths, and millwrights, Watt found skilled mechanics who could install, regulate, and repair his sophisticated engines. From ingenious manufacturers like the cannonmaker John Wilkinson, who learned to bore cylinders with a fair degree of accuracy, Watt was gradually able to purchase precision parts. This support allowed him to create an effective vacuum and regulate a complex engine. In more than twenty years of constant effort, Watt made many further improvements. By the late 1780s, the steam engine was a practical and commercial success in England.

The steam engine of Watt and his followers was the Industrial Revolution's most fundamental advance in technology. For the first time in history, humanity had—at least for a few generations—almost unlimited power at its disposal. For the first time, inventors and engineers could devise and implement all kinds of power equipment to aid people in their work. For the first time, abundance was at least possible for ordinary men and women.

The steam engine was quickly put to use in many industries in England. It made possible the production of even more coal to feed steam engines elsewhere. The steam-power plant began to replace the use of waterpower in the cotton-spinning mills during the 1780s, as well as in the flour, malt, and sugar mills.

Steam power promoted important breakthroughs in other industries. The English iron industry was radically transformed. The use of powerful, steam-driven bellows in blast furnaces helped ironmakers switch over rapidly from limited charcoal to unlimited coke (which is made from coal) in the smelting of pig iron after 1770. In the 1780s Henry Cort developed the puddling furnace, which allowed pig iron to be refined in turn with coke. Strong, skilled ironworkers—the puddlers—"cooked" molten pig iron in a great vat, raking off globs of refined iron for further processing. Cort also developed heavy-duty steam-powered rolling mills capable of spewing out finished iron in every shape and form.

The economic consequence of these technical innovations was a great boom in the English iron industry. In 1740 annual British iron production was only 17,000 tons. With the spread of coke smelting and the first impact of Cort's inventions, production reached 68,000 tons in 1788, 125,000 tons in 1796, and 260,000 tons in 1806. In 1844 Britain produced 3 million tons of iron. This was truly phenomenal expansion. Once scarce and expensive, iron became the cheap, basic building block of the economy.

The Coming of the Railroads

Sailing ships had improved noticeably since the Age of Discovery, and the second half of the eighteenth century saw extensive construction of hard and relatively smooth roads in Europe. Yet passenger traffic benefited most from this construction. Overland shipment of freight, relying solely on horsepower, was still quite limited and frightfully expensive; shippers used rivers and canals for heavy freight whenever possible. It was logical therefore that inventors would try to use steam power.

As early as 1800, an American ran a "steamer on wheels" through city streets. Other experiments followed. In the 1820s, English engineers perfected steam cars capable of carrying fourteen passengers at ten miles an hour—as fast as the mail coach. But the noisy, heavy steam automobiles frightened passing horses and damaged themselves as well as the roads with their vibrations. For the rest of the century, horses continued to reign on highways and city streets.

The coal industry had long been using plank roads and rails to move coal wagons within mines and at the surface. Rails reduced friction and allowed a horse or a human being to pull a heavier load. Thus, once a rail capable of supporting a heavy locomotive was developed in 1816, all sorts of experiments with steam engines on rails went forward. In 1825, after ten years of work, George Stephenson built an effective locomotive. In 1830 his Rocket sped down the track of the just-completed Liverpool and Manchester Railway at sixteen miles per hour. This was the world's first important railroad, fittingly steaming in the heart of industrial England.

The line from Liverpool to Manchester was a financial as well as a technical success, and many private companies were quickly organized to build more rail lines. These companies had to get permission for their projects from Parliament and pay for the rights of way they needed; otherwise, their freedom was great. Within twenty years, they had completed the main trunk lines of Great Britain. Other countries were quick to follow.

The significance of the railroad was tremendous. The railroad dramatically reduced the cost and uncertainty of shipping freight overland. This advance had many economic consequences. Previously, markets had tended to be small and local. As the barrier of high transportation costs was lowered, they became larger and even nationwide. Larger markets encouraged larger factories with more sophisticated machinery. Such factories could make goods cheaper, enabling people to pay less for them. They also tended to drive most cottage workers, many urban artisans, and other manufacturers out of business.

In all countries, the construction of railroads contributed to the growth of a class of urban workers. Cottage workers, farm laborers, and small peasants did not generally leave their jobs and homes to go directly to work in factories. However, the building of railroads created a strong demand for labor, especially unskilled labor, throughout a country. Like farm work, hard work on construction gangs was done in the open air with animals and hand tools. Many farm laborers and poor peasants, long accustomed to leaving their villages for temporary employment, went to build railroads. By the time the work was finished, life back home in the village often seemed dull and

unappealing, and many men drifted to towns in search of work with the railroad companies, in construction, in factories. By the time they sent for their wives and sweethearts to join them, they had become urban workers.

The railroad changed the outlook and values of the entire society. The last and culminating invention of the Industrial Revolution, the railroad dramatically revealed the power and increased the speed of the new age. Racing down a track at sixteen miles per hour or, by 1850, at a phenomenal fifty miles per hour was a new and awesome experience. As a noted French economist put it after a ride on the Liverpool and Manchester in 1833, "There are certain impressions that one cannot put into words!"

The Liverpool and Manchester Railway This hand-colored engraving celebrates the opening of the world's first major railroad on September 15, 1830. Railroad construction reshaped the built environment and proclaimed the coming of a new age. *(Source: Mr. and Mrs. M. G. Powell)*

The Third-Class Carriage The French artist Honoré Daumier was fascinated by the railroad and its human significance. This great painting focuses on the peasant grandmother, absorbed in memories. The nursing mother represents love and creativity; the sleeping boy, innocence. *(Source: The Metropolitan Museum of Art. Bequest of Mrs. H. O. Havemeyer, 1929. The H. O. Havemeyer Collection (29.100.129))*

Some great painters, notably J. M. W. Turner (1775–1851) and Claude Monet (1840–1926), succeeded in expressing this sense of power and awe. So did the massive new train stations, the cathedrals of the industrial age. Leading railway engineers like Isambard Kingdom Brunel and Thomas Brassey, whose tunnels pierced mountains and whose bridges spanned valleys, became public idols—the astronauts of their day. Everyday speech absorbed the images of railroading. After you got up a "full head of steam," you "highballed" along. And if you did not "go off the track," you might "toot your own whistle." The railroad fired the imagination.

Industry and Population

In 1851 London was the site of a famous industrial fair. This Great Exposition was held in the newly built Crystal Palace, an architectural masterpiece made entirely of glass and iron, both of which were now cheap and abundant. For the millions who visited, one fact stood out. The little island of Britain—England, Wales, and Scotland—was the "workshop of the world." It alone produced two-thirds of the world's coal and more than half of its iron and cotton cloth. More generally, it has been carefully estimated that, in 1860, Britain produced a truly remarkable 20 percent of the entire world's output of industrial goods, whereas it had produced only about 2 percent of the world's total in 1750.[7] Experiencing revolutionary industrial change, Britain became the first industrial nation (Map 26.4).

As the British economy significantly increased its production of manufactured goods, the gross national product (GNP) rose roughly fourfold at constant prices between 1780 and 1851. In other words, the British people increased their wealth and their national income dramatically. At the same time, the population of Great Britain boomed, growing from about 9 million in 1780 to almost 21 million in 1851. Thus growing numbers consumed much of the increase in total production. According to one recent study, average consumption per person increased by only 75 percent between 1780 and 1851, as the growth in the total population ate up a large part of the fourfold increase in gross national product in those years.[8]

Although the question is still debated, many economic historians now believe that rapid population growth in Great Britain was not harmful because it facilitated industrial expansion. More people meant a more mobile labor force, with a wealth of young workers in need of employment and ready to go where the jobs were. Contemporaries were much less optimistic. In his influential *Essay on the Principle of Population* (1798), Thomas Malthus (1766–1834) argued that population would always tend to grow faster than the food supply. In Malthus's opinion, the only hope of warding off such "positive checks" to population growth as war, famine, and disease was "prudential restraint"—that is, young men and women had to limit the growth of population by the old tried-and-true means of marrying late in life. But Malthus was not optimistic about this possibility. The powerful attraction of the sexes would cause most people to marry early and have many children.

The wealthy English stockbroker and leading economist David Ricardo (1772–1823) coldly spelled out the pessimistic implications of Malthus's thought. Ricardo's depressing "iron law of wages" posited that, because of the pressure of population growth, wages would always sink to the subsistence level—that is, wages would be just high enough to keep the workers from starving. With Malthus and Ricardo setting the tone, there

is little wonder that economics was soon dubbed "the dismal science."

Malthus, Ricardo, and their many followers were proved wrong—in the long run. However, as the great economist John Maynard Keynes quipped in the Great Depression of the 1930s, "we are all dead in the long run." Those who lived through the Industrial Revolution could not see the long run in advance. As modern quantitative studies show, until the 1820s, or even the 1840s, contemporary observers might reasonably conclude that the economy and the total population were racing neck and neck, with the outcome very much in doubt. The closeness of the race added to

MAP 26.4 The Industrial Revolution in England, ca 1850 Industry concentrated in the rapidly growing cities of the north and the Midlands, where rich coal and iron deposits were in close proximity.

the difficulties inherent in the unprecedented journey toward industrial civilization.

There was another problem as well. Perhaps workers, farmers, and ordinary people did not get their rightful share of the new wealth. Perhaps only the rich got richer while the poor got poorer or made no progress at all. We will turn to this great issue after looking at the process of industrialization in continental countries in the nineteenth century.

INDUSTRIALIZATION IN CONTINENTAL EUROPE

The new technologies developed in the British Industrial Revolution were adopted rather slowly by businesses in continental Europe. Yet by the end of the nineteenth century several European countries, as well as the United States, had industrialized their economies to a considerable but variable degree. This meant that the process of Western industrialization proceeded gradually, with uneven jerks and national (and regional) variations.

Scholars are still struggling to explain these variations, especially since good answers may offer valuable lessons in our own time for poor countries seeking to improve their material condition through industrialization and economic development. The latest findings on the Western experience are encouraging. They suggest that there were alternative paths to the industrial world in the nineteenth century and that, today as then, there is no need to follow a rigid, predetermined British model.

National Variations

European industrialization, like most economic developments, requires some statistical analysis as part of the effort to understand it. Comparative data on industrial production in different countries over time help to give an overview of what happened. One set of data, the work of a Swiss scholar, compares the level of industrialization on a per capita basis in several countries from 1750 to 1913. These data are far from perfect because there are gaps in the underlying records. But they reflect basic trends and are presented in Table 26.1 for closer study.

As the heading of Table 26.1 makes clear, this is a per capita comparison of levels of industrialization—a comparison of how much industrial product was available, on average, to each person in a given country in a given year. Thus, all the numbers in the table are expressed in terms of a single index number of 100, which equals the per capita level of industrial goods in Great Britain (and Ireland) in 1900. Every number is a percentage of the 1900 level in Great Britain and is directly comparable with every other number in the table. The countries are listed in roughly the order in which they began to use large-scale, power-driven technology.

What does this overview of European industrialization tell us? First, and very significantly, in 1750 all countries were fairly close together and Britain was only slightly ahead of its archenemy, France. Second, by 1800 Britain had opened up a noticeable lead over all continental countries, and that gap progressively widened as the British Industrial Revolution accelerated to 1830 and reached full maturity by 1860. In 1830, the British level of per capita industrialization was twice the French level, for example; in 1860, it was more than three times the French level. At both dates, all other large countries, except the United States, had fallen even further behind Britain than France had. Sophisticated quantitative history confirms the primacy and relative rapidity of Britain's Industrial Revolution.

Third, variations in the timing and in the extent of industrialization among the continental powers and the United States are also apparent. Belgium, independent in 1831 and rich in iron and coal, led in adopting Britain's new technology. France developed factory production more gradually, and most historians now detect no burst in French mechanization and no acceleration in the growth of overall industrial output that may accurately be called revolutionary. They stress instead France's relatively good pattern of early industrial growth, which has been unjustly tarnished by the spectacular rise of Germany and the United States after 1860. By 1913 Germany was rapidly closing in on Britain and the United States had already passed Britain in per capita production.

	1750	1800	1830	1860	1880	1900	1913
Great Britain	10	16	25	64	87	100	115
Belgium	9	10	14	28	43	46	88
United States	4	9	14	21	38	69	126
France	9	9	12	20	28	39	59
Germany	8	8	9	15	25	52	85
Austria-Hungary	7	7	8	11	15	23	32
Italy	8	8	8	10	12	17	26
Russia	6	6	7	8	10	15	20

Note: All entires are based on an index value of 100, equal to the per capita level of industrialization in Great Britain in 1900.

Source: P. Bairoch, "International industrialization Levels from 1750 to 1980," *Journal of European Economic History* 11 (Spring 1982): 294. Used with permission. Data for Great Britain are actually for the United Kingdom, thereby including Ireland with England, Wales, and Scotland.

TABLE 26.1 Per Capita Levels of Industrialization, 1750–1913

All European states (as well as the United States, Canada, and Japan) managed to raise per capita industrial levels in the nineteenth century. These continent-wide increases stood in stark contrast to the large and tragic decreases that occurred at the same time in most non-Western countries, and most notably in China and India. European countries industrialized to a greater or lesser extent even as most of the non-Western world deindustrialized. Thus differential rates of wealth- and power-creating industrial development, which heightened disparities within Europe, also greatly magnified existing inequalities between Europe and the rest of the world. We return to this momentous change in Chapter 30.

The Challenge of Industrialization

The different patterns of industrial development suggest that the process of industrialization was far from automatic. Indeed, building modern industry was an awesome challenge. To be sure, the eighteenth century was throughout Europe an era of agricultural improvement, population increase, expanding foreign trade, and growing cottage industry. England led in these developments, but other countries participated in the general trend. Thus, when the pace of English industry began to accelerate in the 1780s, continental businesses began to adopt the new methods as they proved their profitability. English industry enjoyed clear superiority, but at first the Continent was not very far behind.

By 1815, however, the situation was quite different. In spite of wartime difficulties, English industry maintained the momentum of the 1780s and continued to grow and improve between 1789 and 1815. On the Continent, the unending political and economic upheavals that began with the French Revolution had another effect. They disrupted trade, created runaway inflation, and fostered social anxiety. War severed normal communications between England and the Continent, severely handicapping continental efforts to use new British machinery and technology. Moreover, the years from 1789 to 1815 were, even for the privileged French economy, a time of "national catastrophe"—in the graphic words of a leading French scholar.[9] Thus, whatever the French Revolution and the Napoleonic era meant politically, economically and industrially they meant that France and the rest of Europe were further behind Britain in 1815 than in 1789.

The Crystal Palace   The Great Exhibition of 1851 attracted more than six million visitors, many of whom journeyed to London on the newly built railroads. Companies and countries displayed their products and juries awarded prizes in the strikingly modern Crystal Palace. *(Source: The Bridgeman Art Library)*

This widening gap made it more difficult if not impossible for other countries to follow the British pattern in energy and industry after 1815. Above all, in the newly mechanized industries British goods were being produced very economically, and these goods had come to dominate world markets completely while the continental states were absorbed in war between 1792 and 1815. Continental firms had little hope of competing with mass-produced British goods in foreign markets for a long time. In addition, British technology had become so advanced and complicated that very few engineers or skilled technicians outside England understood it. Moreover, the technology of steam power had grown much more expensive. It involved large investments in the iron

and coal industries and, after 1830, required the existence of railroads, which were very costly. Continental business people had great difficulty finding the large sums of money demanded by the new methods, and there was a shortage of laborers accustomed to working in factories. Landowners and government officials were often so suspicious of the new form of industry and the changes it brought that they did little at first to encourage it. All these disadvantages slowed the spread of modern industry (Map 26.5).

After 1815, however, when continental countries began to face up to the British challenge, they had at least three important advantages. First, most continental countries had a rich tradition of putting-out enterprise, merchant-capitalists, and skilled urban artisans. Such a tradition gave continental firms the ability to adapt and survive in the face of new market conditions. Second, continental capitalists did not need to develop, ever so slowly and expensively, their own advanced technology. Instead, they could simply "borrow" the new methods developed in Great Britain, as well as engineers and some of the financial resources they lacked. European countries like France and Russia also had a third asset that many non-Western areas lacked in the nineteenth century. They had strong independent governments, which did not fall under foreign political control. These governments could fashion economic policies to serve their own interests, and they proceeded to do so. They would eventually use the power of the state to promote the growth of industry and catch up with Britain.

Agents of Industrialization

The British realized the great value of their technical discoveries and tried to keep their secrets to themselves. Until 1825 it was illegal for artisans and skilled mechanics to leave Britain; until 1843 the export of textile machinery and other equipment was forbidden. Many talented, ambitious workers, however, slipped out of the country illegally and introduced the new methods abroad.

MAP 26.5 Continental Industrialization, ca 1850 Although continental countries were beginning to make progress by 1850, they still lagged far behind England. For example, continental railroad building was still in an early stage, whereas the English rail system was essentially complete.

One such man was William Cockerill, a Lancashire carpenter. He and his sons began building cotton-spinning equipment in French-occupied Belgium in 1799. In 1817 the most famous son, John Cockerill, purchased the old summer palace of the deposed bishops of Liège in southern Belgium. Cockerill converted the palace into a large industrial enterprise that produced machinery, steam engines, and then railway locomotives. He also established modern ironworks and coal mines.

Cockerill's plants in the Liège area became an industrial nerve center, continually gathering new information and transmitting it across Europe. Many skilled British workers came, illegally, to work for Cockerill, and some went on to found their own companies throughout Europe. Newcomers brought the latest plans and secrets and Cockerill could boast that ten days after an industrial advance occurred in Britain, he knew all about it in Belgium. Thus British technicians and

skilled workers were a powerful force in the spread of early industrialization.

Another agent of industrialization was Fritz Harkort, a pioneer in the German machinery industry. Serving in England as a Prussian army officer during the Napoleonic wars, Harkort was impressed and enchanted with what he saw. He concluded that Germany had to match all these English achievements as quickly as possible. Setting up shop in an abandoned castle in the still-tranquil Ruhr Valley, Harkort felt an almost religious calling to build steam engines and become the "Watt of Germany."

Harkort's basic idea was simple, but it was enormously difficult to carry out. Lacking skilled laborers to do the job, Harkort turned to England for experienced, though expensive, mechanics. He could not be choosy, and he longed for the day when he could afford to replace the haughty foreigners with his fellow Germans. Getting materials

A Silesian Ironworks, 1841   This plant is using the new British method of smelting iron with coke. Silesia and the Ruhr region emerged as the main centers of German heavy industry in the nineteenth century, but that development was only beginning when this picture was painted. *(Source: Deutsches Museum, Munich)*

also posed a great problem. At great cost, he had to import from England the thick iron boilers that he needed. Moreover, German roads were so bad that steam engines had to be built at the works, dismantled and shipped piece by piece to the buyer, and then reassembled by Harkort's technicians. In spite of all these problems, Harkort built and sold engines, winning fame and praise. His ambitious efforts over sixteen years also resulted in large financial losses for himself and his partners, and in 1832 he was forced out of his company by his financial backers, who cut back operations to reduce losses. His career illustrates both the great efforts of a few important business leaders to duplicate the British achievement and the difficulty of the task.

Entrepreneurs like Harkort were obviously exceptional. Most continental businesses adopted factory technology slowly, and handicraft methods lived on. Recent research on France has shown that continental industrialization usually brought substantial but uneven expansion of handicraft industry in both rural and urban areas for a time. Artisan production of luxury items grew in France, as the rising income of the international middle class created foreign demand for silk scarfs, embroidered needlework, perfumes, and fine wines.

Support from the government often helped business people in continental countries to overcome some of their difficulties. Tariff protection was one such support. For example, after Napoleon's wars ended in 1815, France was suddenly flooded with cheaper and better English goods. In order to protect the French economy, the French government responded by laying high tariffs on many English imports. After 1815 continental governments bore the cost of building roads and canals to improve transportation, and they also bore to a significant extent the cost of building railroads.

The career of the German journalist and thinker Friedrich List (1789–1846) reflects government's greater role in industrialization on the Continent than in England. List considered the growth of modern industry of the utmost importance because manufacturing was a primary means of increasing people's well-being and relieving their poverty. Moreover, List was a dedicated nationalist. He wrote that the "wider the gap between the backward and advanced nations becomes, the more dangerous it is to remain behind," for an ag-

ricultural nation was not only poor but weak, increasingly unable to defend itself and maintain its political independence. To promote industry was to defend the nation.

The practical policy that List focused on in articles and in his *National System of Political Economy* (1841) was the tariff. He supported the formation of a customs union, or *Zollverein,* among the separate German states. Such a tariff union came into being in 1834. It allowed goods to move between the German member states without tariffs, and a single uniform tariff was erected against all other nations. List wanted a high protective tariff, which would encourage infant industries, allowing them to develop and eventually to hold their own against their more advanced British counterparts. List denounced the English doctrine of free trade as little more than England's attempt "to make the rest of the world, like the Hindus, its serfs in all industrial and commercial relations." By the 1840s List's ideas were increasingly popular in Germany and elsewhere.

Banks, like governments, also played a larger and more creative role on the Continent than in England. Previously, almost all banks in Europe had been private, organized as secretive partnerships. Such banks were content to deal with a few rich clients and a few big merchants. They avoided industry. In the 1830s two important Belgian banks pioneered in a new direction. They operated as big corporations with many stockholders, large and small. Thus their financial resources were large. The banks were able to use that money to develop industrial companies. They became, in short, industrial banks.

Similar banks became important in France and Germany in the 1850s. They established and developed many railroads and many companies working in heavy industry. The most famous such bank was the Crédit Mobilier of Paris, founded by Isaac and Émile Pereire, two young Jewish journalists from Bordeaux. The Crédit Mobilier advertised extensively. It used the savings of thousands of small investors, as well as the resources of big ones. The activities of the bank were far-reaching; it built railroads all over France and Europe. As Émile Pereire had said in 1835, "It is not enough to outline gigantic programs on paper. I must write my ideas on the earth."

Industrial banks like the Crédit Mobilier mobilized the savings of thousands of small investors and invested those savings in industry and transportation, particularly in the 1850s. In doing so, the directors of these banks helped their countries find the capital needed for industrialization. They also often made themselves very wealthy.

CAPITAL AND LABOR

Industrial development brought new social relations and intensified problems between capital and labor. A new group of factory owners and industrial capitalists arose. These men strengthened the wealth and size of the middle class, which had previously been made up mainly of merchants and professional people. The nineteenth century became the golden age of the middle class. Modern industry also created a much larger group, the factory workers. For the first time, large numbers of men and women came together under one roof to work with complicated machinery for major capitalists and large companies. What was the nature of relations between these two new groups—capital and labor? Did the new industrial middle class ruthlessly exploit the workers, as Karl Marx and others have charged?

The New Class of Factory Owners

Early industrialists operated in a highly competitive economic system. As the careers of Watt and Harkort illustrate, there were countless production problems, and success and large profits were by no means certain. Manufacturers, therefore, waged a constant battle to cut their production costs and stay afloat. Much of the profit had to go back into the business for new and better machinery. "Dragged on by the frenzy of this terrible life," according to one of the dismayed critics, the struggling manufacturer had "no time for niceties. He must conquer or die, make a fortune or drown himself."[10]

The early industrialists came from a variety of backgrounds. Many, like Harkort, were from well-established merchant families who provided capital and contacts. Others, like Watt and Cockerill, were of modest means, especially in the early days. Artisans and skilled workers of exceptional ability had unparalleled opportunities. The ethnic

and religious groups that had been discriminated against in the traditional occupations controlled by the landed aristocracy jumped at the new chances. Quakers and Scots were tremendously important in England; Protestants and Jews dominated banking in Catholic France. Many of the industrialists were newly rich, and, not surprisingly, they were very proud and self-satisfied.

As factories grew larger, opportunities declined, at least in well-developed industries. It became considerably harder for a gifted but poor young mechanic to end up as a wealthy manufacturer. Formal education became more important as a means of advancement, and formal education at the advanced level was expensive. In England by 1830 and in France and Germany by 1860, leading industrialists were more likely to have inherited their well-established enterprises, and they were financially much more secure than their fathers and grandfathers. They were also aware of a greater gap between themselves and their workers.

The New Factory Workers

The social consequences of the Industrial Revolution have long been hotly debated. The condition of English workers during the transformation has always generated the most controversy among historians because England was the first country to industrialize and because the social consequences seem harshest there. Before 1850, other countries had not proceeded very far with industrialization, and almost everyone agrees that the economic conditions of European workers improved after 1850. The countries that followed England were able to benefit from English experience in social as well as technical matters. Thus the experience of English workers to about 1850 deserves special attention. (Industrial growth also promoted rapid European urbanization with its own awesome problems, as is shown in Chapter 28.)

From the beginning, the Industrial Revolution in England had its critics. Among the first were the romantic poets. William Blake (1757–1827) called the early factories "satanic mills" and protested against the hard life of the London poor. William Wordsworth (1770–1850) lamented the destruction of the rural way of life and the pollution of the land and water. Some handicraft workers—notably the Luddites, who attacked whole factories in northern England in 1812 and after—smashed the new machines, which they believed were putting them out of work. Doctors and reformers wrote eloquently of problems in the factories and new towns, and Malthus and Ricardo (see page 845) concluded that workers would earn only enough to stay alive.

This pessimistic view was accepted and reinforced by Friedrich Engels (1820–1895), the future revolutionary and colleague of Karl Marx. After studying conditions in northern England, this young middle-class German published in 1844 *The Condition of the Working Class in England,* a blistering indictment of the middle classes. "At the bar of world opinion," he wrote, "I charge the English middle classes with mass murder, wholesale robbery, and all the other crimes in the calendar."[11] The new poverty of industrial workers was worse than the old poverty of cottage workers and agricultural laborers, according to Engels. The culprit was industrial capitalism, with its relentless competition and constant technical change. Engels's charge of middle-class exploitation and increasing worker poverty was embellished by Marx and later socialists. It was extremely influential.

Meanwhile, other observers believed that conditions were improving for the working class. Andrew Ure wrote in 1835 in his study of the cotton industry that conditions in most factories were not harsh and were even quite good. Edwin Chadwick, a great and conscientious government official well acquainted with the problems of the working class, concluded that the "whole mass of the laboring community" was increasingly able "to buy more of the necessities and minor luxuries of life."[12] Nevertheless, if all the contemporary assessments were counted up, those who thought conditions were getting worse for working people would probably be the majority.

In an attempt to go beyond the contradictory judgments of contemporaries, some historians have looked at different kinds of sources. Statistical evidence is one such source. If working people suffered a great economic decline, as Engels and later socialists asserted, then they must have bought less and less food, clothing, and other necessities as time went on. The purchasing power of the working person's wages must have declined drastically.

Scholarly statistical studies, which continue to multiply rapidly in an age of easy calculations with computer technology, have weakened the idea that the condition of the working class got much worse with industrialization. On the other hand, the most recent studies also confirm the view that the early years of the Industrial Revolution were hard ones for English and Scottish workers. There was little or no increase in the purchasing power of the average British worker from about 1780 to about 1820. The years from 1792 to 1815, a period of almost constant warfare with France, were particularly difficult. Food prices rose faster than wages, and the living conditions of the laboring poor declined. Only after 1820, and especially after 1840, did real wages rise substantially, so that the average worker earned and consumed roughly 50 percent more in real terms in 1850 than in 1770.[13] In short, there was considerable economic improvement for workers throughout Great Britain by 1850, but that improvement was hard-won and slow in coming.

This important conclusion must be qualified, though. Increased purchasing power meant more goods, but it did not necessarily mean greater happiness. More goods may have provided meager compensation for work that was more dangerous and monotonous. Also, statistical studies do not say anything about how the level of unemployment may have risen, for the simple reason that there are no good unemployment statistics from this period. Furthermore, the hours in the average workweek increased; to an unknown extent, workers earned more simply because they worked more. Finally, the wartime decline was of great importance. The war years were formative years for the new factory labor force. They were also some of the hardest yet experienced. They colored the early experience of modern industrial life in somber tones.

Another way to consider workers' standard of living is to look at the goods that they purchased. Again the evidence is somewhat contradictory. Speaking generally, workers ate somewhat more food of higher nutritional quality as the Industrial Revolution progressed, except during wartime. Diets became more varied; people ate more potatoes, dairy products, fruits, and vegetables. Clothing improved, but housing for working people probably deteriorated somewhat. Per capita use of specific goods supports the position that the standard of living of the working classes rose, at least moderately, after the long wars with France.

Cotton Mill Workers Family members often worked side by side in industry. Here women and children are combing raw cotton and drawing it into loose strands called rovings, which will then be spun into fine thread. *(Source: The Mansell Collection)*

Conditions of Work

What about working conditions? Did workers eventually earn more only at the cost of working longer and harder? Were workers exploited harshly by the new factory owners?

The first factories were cotton mills, which began functioning along rivers and streams in the 1770s. Cottage workers, accustomed to the putting-out system, were reluctant to work in factories even when they received relatively good wages, because factory work was different from what they were used to and unappealing. In the factory, workers had to keep up with the machine and follow its tempo. They had to show up every day and work long, monotonous hours. Factory workers had to adjust their daily lives to the shrill call of the factory whistle.

Cottage workers were not used to that kind of life and discipline. All members of the family worked hard and long, but in spurts, setting their own pace. They could interrupt their work when they wanted to. Women and children could break up their long hours of spinning with other tasks. On Saturday afternoon the head of the family delivered the week's work to the merchant-manufacturer and got paid. Saturday night was a time of relaxation and drinking, especially for the men. Recovering from his hangover on Tuesday, the weaver bent to his task on Wednesday and then worked frantically to meet his deadline on Saturday. Like some students today, he might "pull an all-nighter" on Thursday or Friday in order to get his work in.

Also, early factories resembled English poorhouses, where totally destitute people went to live on welfare. Some poorhouses were industrial prisons, where the inmates had to work in order to receive their food and lodging. The similarity between large brick factories and large stone poorhouses increased the cottage workers' fear of factories and their hatred of factory discipline.

It was cottage workers' reluctance to work in factories that prompted the early cotton mill owners to turn to abandoned and pauper children for their labor (see page 707). They contracted with local officials to employ large numbers of these children, who had no say in the matter. Pauper children were often badly treated and terribly overworked in the mills, as they were when they were apprenticed as chimney sweeps, market girls, shoemakers, and so forth. In the eighteenth century, semiforced child labor seemed necessary and was socially accepted. From our modern point of view, it was cruel exploitation and a blot on the record of the new industrial system.

By 1790 the early pattern was rapidly changing. The use of pauper apprentices was in decline, and in 1802 it was forbidden by Parliament. Many more factories were being built, mainly in urban areas, where they could use steam rather than waterpower and attract a workforce more easily than in the countryside. The need for workers was great. Indeed, people came from near and far to work in the cities, both as factory workers and as laborers, builders, and domestic servants. Yet, as they took these new jobs, working people did not simply give in to a system of labor that had formerly repelled them. Rather, they helped modify the system by carrying over old, familiar working traditions.

For one thing, they often came to the mills and the mines as family units. This was how they had worked on farms and in the putting-out system. The mill or mine owner bargained with the head of the family and paid him or her for the work of the whole family. In the cotton mills, children worked for their mothers or fathers, collecting wastes and "piecing" broken threads together. In the mines, children sorted coal and worked the ventilation equipment. Their mothers hauled coal in the narrow tunnels below the surface while their fathers hewed with pick and shovel at the face of the seam.

The preservation of the family as an economic unit in the factories from the 1790s on made the new surroundings more tolerable, both in Great Britain and in other countries during the early stages of industrialization. Parents disciplined their children, making firm measures socially acceptable, and directed their upbringing. The presence of the whole family meant that children and adults worked the same long hours (twelve-hour shifts were normal in cotton mills in 1800). In the early years, some very young children were employed solely to keep the family together. Jedediah Strutt, for example, believed children should be at least ten years old to work in his mills, but he reluctantly employed seven-year-olds to satisfy their parents. Adult workers were not particularly interested in limiting the minimum working age or hours of their children as long as they worked side by side. Only when technical changes threatened to place control and discipline in the hands of impersonal managers and foremen did they protest against inhuman conditions in the name of their children.

Some enlightened employers and social reformers in Parliament argued that more humane standards were necessary, and they used widely circulated parliamentary reports to influence public opinion. For example, Robert Owen (1771–1858), a very successful manufacturer in Scotland, testified in 1816 before an investigating committee on the basis of his experience. He stated that "very strong facts" demonstrated that employing children under ten years of age as factory workers was "injurious to the children, and not beneficial to the proprietors." The parliamentary committee asked him to explain, and the testimony proceeded as follows:

"Seventeen years ago, a number of individuals, with myself, purchased the New Lanark establishment from the late Mr. Dale, of Glasgow. At that period I find that there were 500 children, who had been taken from poor-houses, chiefly in Edinburgh. . . . The hours of work at that time were thirteen, inclusive of meal times, and an hour and a half was allowed for meals. I very soon discovered that although those children were very well fed, well clothed, well lodged, and very great care taken of them when out of the mills, their growth and their minds were materially injured by being employed at those ages within the cotton mills for eleven and a half hours per day. . . . Their limbs were generally deformed, their growth was stunted, and although one of the best school-masters upon the old plan was engaged to instruct those children every night, in general they made but a very slow progress, even in learning the common alphabet. . . ."

"Do you think the age of ten the best period for the admission of children into full and constant employment for ten or eleven hours per day, within woollen, cotton, and other mills or manufactories?"

"I do not."

"What other period would you recommend for their full admission to full work?"

"Twelve years." [14]

Owen's testimony rang true because he had already raised the age of employment in his mills and was promoting education for young children. Workers also provided graphic testimony at such hearings as the reformers pressed Parliament to pass corrective laws. The reformers scored some important successes.

Their first major accomplishment was the Factory Act of 1833. It limited the factory workday for children between nine and thirteen to eight hours and that of adolescents between fourteen and eighteen to twelve hours, although the act made no effort to regulate hours of work for children at home or in small businesses. The law also prohibited the factory employment of children under nine; they were to be enrolled in the elementary schools that factory owners were required to establish. The employment of children declined rapidly. The Factory Act broke the pattern of whole families working together in the factory because efficiency required standardized shifts for all workers.

Ties of blood and kinship were important in other ways in Great Britain in the formative years between about 1790 and 1840. Many manufacturers and builders hired workers not directly but through subcontractors. They paid the subcontractors on the basis of what the subcontractors and their crews produced—for smelting so many tons of pig iron or moving so much dirt or gravel for a canal or roadbed. Subcontractors in turn hired and fired their own workers, many of whom were friends and relations. The subcontractor might be as harsh as the greediest capitalist, but the relationship between subcontractor and work crew was close and personal. This kind of personal relationship had traditionally existed in cottage industry and in urban crafts, and it was more acceptable to many workers than impersonal factory discipline. This system also provided people an easy way to find a job. Even today, a friend or relative who is a supervisor is frequently worth a hundred formal application forms.

Ties of kinship were particularly important for newcomers, who often traveled considerable distances to find work. Many urban workers in Great Britain were from Ireland. Forced out of rural Ireland by population growth and deteriorating economic conditions from 1817 on, Irish in search of jobs could not be choosy; they took what they could get. As early as 1824, most of the workers in the Glasgow cotton mills were Irish; in 1851 one-sixth of the population of Liverpool was Irish. Even when Irish workers were not related directly by blood, they were held together by ethnic and religious ties. Like other immigrant groups elsewhere, they worked together, formed their own neighborhoods, and not only survived but thrived.

It is important to remember that many kinds of employment changed slowly during and after the Industrial Revolution in Great Britain. Within industry itself, the pattern of small-scale production with artisan skills lived on in many trades even as some other trades were revolutionized. For example, as in the case of cotton and coal, the British iron industry was completely dominated by large-scale capitalist firms by 1850. One iron magnate in Wales employed six thousand workers in his plant, and many large ironworks had over a thousand people on their payroll. Yet the firms that fashioned iron into small metal goods, such as tools, tableware, and toys, employed on average fewer than ten workers, who used time-honored handicraft skills. Only gradually after 1850 did some owners find ways to reorganize such handicraft industries with new machines and new patterns of work. The survival of small workshops and artisan crafts gave many workers an alternative to factory employment.

Old, familiar jobs outside industry provided other alternatives for individual workers. In 1850 more British people still worked on farms than in any other occupation. The second largest occupation was domestic service, which counted more than a million household servants, 90 percent of whom were women. Thus many traditional jobs lived on, and this also helped ease the transition to industrial civilization.

In Great Britain and in other countries later on, workers gradually built a labor movement to improve working conditions and to serve their needs. In 1799, partly in panicked reaction to the French Revolution, Parliament had passed the Combination Acts outlawing unions and strikes. These acts were widely disregarded by workers. Societies of skilled factory workers organized unions, as printers, papermakers, carpenters, and other such craftsmen had long since done. The unions sought to control the number of skilled workers, limit apprenticeship to members' own children, and bargain with owners over wages. They were not afraid to strike; there was, for example, a general strike of adult cotton spinners in Manchester in 1810. In the face of widespread union activity, Parliament repealed the Combination Acts in 1824, and unions were tolerated though not fully accepted after 1825.

The next stage in the development of the British trade-union movement was the attempt to create a single large national union. This effort was led not so much by working people as by social reformers like Robert Owen. Owen, the self-made cotton manufacturer quoted earlier, had pioneered in industrial relations by combining firm discipline with concern for the health, safety, and hours of his workers. After 1815 he experimented with cooperative and socialist communities, including one at New Harmony, Indiana. Then, in 1834, Owen organized one of the largest and most visionary of the early national unions, the Grand National Consolidated Trades Union. When this and other grandiose schemes collapsed, the British labor movement moved once again after 1851 in the direction of craft unions. The most famous of these "new model unions" was the Amalgamated Society of Engineers. These unions won real bene-

fits for members by fairly conservative means and thus became an accepted part of the industrial scene.

British workers also engaged in direct political activity in defense of their own interests. After the collapse of Owen's national trade union, a great deal of the energy of working people went into the Chartist movement, whose goal was political democracy. The key Chartist demand—that all men be given the right to vote—became the great hope of millions of aroused people. Workers were also active in campaigns to limit the workday in the factories to ten hours and to permit duty-free importation of wheat into Great Britain to secure cheap bread. Thus working people played an active role in shaping the new industrial system. Clearly, they were neither helpless victims nor passive beneficiaries.

The Sexual Division of Labor

The era of the Industrial Revolution witnessed major changes in the sexual division of labor. In preindustrial Europe most people generally worked in family units. By tradition, certain jobs were defined by sex—women and girls for milking and spinning, men and boys for plowing and weaving. But many tasks might go to either sex

Girl Dragging Coal Tubs   Published by reformers in Parliament in 1842, this picture shocked public opinion and contributed to the Mines Act of 1842. *(Source: The British Library)*

because particular circumstances dictated a family's response in its battle for economic survival. This pattern of family employment carried over into early factories and subcontracting, but it collapsed as child labor was restricted and new attitudes emerged. A different sexual division of labor gradually arose to take its place. The man emerged as the family's primary wage earner, and the woman found only limited job opportunities. Generally denied good jobs at good wages in the growing urban economy, women were expected to concentrate on unpaid housework, child care, and craft work at home.

"Be United and Industrious"   This handsome membership certificate of the "new model" Amalgamated Society of Engineers exalts the nobility of skilled labor and the labor movement. Union members are shown rejecting the call of Mars, the God of War, and accepting well-deserved honors from the Goddess of Peace. Other figures represent the strength of union solidarity, famous English inventors, and the trades of the members. *(Source: E. T. Archive)*

This new pattern of "separate spheres" had several aspects. First, all studies agree that married women were much less likely to work full-time for wages outside the house after the first child arrived, although they often earned small amounts doing putting-out handicrafts at home and taking in boarders. Second, when married women did work for wages outside the house, they usually came from the poorest, most desperate families, where the husbands were poorly paid, sick, unemployed, or missing. Third, these poor married (or widowed) women were joined by legions of young unmarried women, who worked full-time but only in certain jobs. Fourth, all women were generally confined to low-paying, dead-end jobs. Virtually no occupation open to women paid a living wage—a wage sufficient for a person to live independently. Men predominated in the better-paying, more promising employments. Evolving gradually as family labor declined, but largely in place in the urban sector of the British economy by 1850, the new sexual division of labor constituted a major development in the history of women and of the family.

If the reorganization of paid work along gender lines is widely recognized, there is as yet no agreement on its causes. One school of scholars sees little connection with industrialization and finds the answer in the deeply ingrained sexist attitudes of a "patriarchal tradition" that predated the economic transformation. These scholars stress the role of male-dominated craft unions in denying women access to good jobs and in reducing them to unpaid maids dependent on their husbands. Other scholars, believing that the gender roles of women and men can vary enormously with time and culture, look more to a combination of economic and biological factors in order to explain why the mass of women were either unwilling or unable to halt the emergence of a sex-segregated division of labor.

Three ideas stand out in this more recent interpretation. First, the new and unfamiliar discipline of the clock and the machine was especially hard on married women. Above all, relentless factory discipline conflicted with child care in a way that labor on the farm or in the cottage had not. A woman operating ear-splitting spinning machinery could mind a child of seven or eight working beside her (until such work was outlawed), but she could no longer pace herself through pregnancy, even though overwork during pregnancy heightened the already high risks of childbirth. Nor could a woman breast-feed her baby on the job, although breast-feeding saved lives. Thus a working-class woman had strong incentives to concentrate on child care within her home, if her family could afford for her to do so.

Second, running a household in conditions of primitive urban poverty was an extremely demanding job in its own right. There were no supermarkets or discount department stores; there was no running water or public transportation. Everything had to be done on foot. As in the poor sections of many inner cities today, shopping and feeding the family constituted a never-ending challenge. The woman marched from one tiny shop to another, dragging her tired children (for who was to watch them?) and struggling valiantly with heavy sacks, tricky shopkeepers, and walk-up apartments. Yet another brutal job outside the house—a "second shift"—had limited appeal for the average married woman. Thus women might well accept the emerging division of labor as the best available strategy for family survival in the industrializing society.[15]

Third, why were the women who did work for wages outside the home segregated and confined to certain "women's jobs"? No doubt the desire of males to monopolize the best opportunities and hold women down provides part of the answer. Yet, as the English women's historian Jane Humphries has argued, sex-segregated employment also formed a collective response to the new industrial system. Previously, at least in theory, young people worked under a watchful parental eye. The growth of factories and mines brought unheard-of opportunities for girls and boys to mix on the job, free of familial supervision. Continuing to mix after work, they were "more likely to form liaisons, initiate courtships, and respond to advances."[16] Such intimacy also led to more unplanned pregnancies and fueled the illegitimacy explosion that had begun in the late eighteenth century and that gathered force until at least 1850 (see pages 702–704). Thus segregation of jobs by gender was partly an effort by older people to help control the sexuality of working-class youth.

Parliamentary investigations into the British coal industry before 1842 provide a graphic example of this concern. The middle-class men leading the inquiry often failed to appreciate the physical effort of the girls and women who dragged with belt and chain the unwheeled carts of coal along narrow underground passages. But they professed horror at the sight of girls and women working without shirts, which was a common practice because of the heat, and they quickly assumed the prevalence of licentious sex with the male miners, who also wore very little clothing. In fact, most girls and married women worked for related males in a family unit that provided considerable protection and restraint. Yet many witnesses from the working class believed that "blackguardism and debauchery" were common and that "They are best out of the pits, the lasses." Some miners stressed particularly the sexual danger of letting girls work past puberty. As one explained when corrective legislation was being considered,

"I consider it a scandal for girls to work in the pits. Till they are 12 or 14 they may work very well but after that it's an abomination. . . . The work of the pit does not hurt them, it is the effect on their morals that I complain of, and after 14 they should not be allowed to go. . . . [A]fter that age it is dreadful for them."[17]

The Mines Act of 1842 prohibited underground work for all women, as well as for boys under ten.

Some women who had to support themselves protested against being excluded from coal mining, which paid higher wages than most other jobs open to women. But if they were part of families that could manage economically, the girls and the women who had worked underground were generally pleased with the law. In explaining her satisfaction in 1844 to a follow-up investigator, one mother of four provided a real insight into why many women accepted the emerging sexual division of labor:

While working in the pit I was worth to my [miner] husband seven shillings a week, out of which we had to pay 2 $^{1}/_{2}$ shillings to a woman for looking after the younger children. I used to take them to her house at 4 o'clock in the morning, out of their own beds, to put them into hers. Then there was one shilling a week for washing; besides, there was mending to pay for, and other things. The house was not guided. The other children broke things; they did not go to school when they were sent; they would be playing about, and get ill-used by other children, and their clothes torn. Then when I came home in the evening, everything was to do after the day's labor, and I was so tired I had no heart for it; no fire lit, nothing cooked, no water fetched, the house dirty, and nothing comfortable for *my husband. It is all far better now, and I wouldn't go down again.*[18]

SUMMARY

Western society's industrial breakthrough grew out of a long process of economic and social change in which the rise of capitalism, overseas expansion, and the growth of rural industry stand out as critical preparatory developments. Eventually taking the lead in all of these developments, and also profiting from stable government, abundant natural resources, and a flexible labor force, England experienced between roughly the 1780s and the 1850s an epoch-making transformation that is still aptly termed the "Industrial Revolution."

Building on technical breakthroughs, power-driven equipment, and large-scale enterprise, the Industrial Revolution in England greatly increased output in certain radically altered industries, stimulated the large handicraft and commercial sectors, and speeded up overall economic growth. Rugged Scotland industrialized at least as fast as England, and Great Britain became the first industrial nation. By 1850 the level of British per capita industrial production surpassed continental levels by a growing margin, and Britain savored a near monopoly in world markets for mass-produced goods. Thus continental countries inevitably took rather different paths to the urban industrial society. They relied more on handicraft production in both towns and villages, and only in the 1840s did railroad construction begin to create a strong demand for iron, coal, and railway equipment that speeded up the process of industrialization.

The rise of modern industry had a profound impact on people and their lives. In the early stages Britain again led the way, experiencing in a striking manner the long-term social changes accompanying the economic transformation. Factory discipline and Britain's stern capitalist economy weighed heavily on working people, who, however, actively fashioned their destinies, refusing to be passive victims. Improvements in the standard of living came slowly, although they were substantial by 1850. The era of industrialization fostered new attitudes toward child labor, encouraged protective factory legislation, and called forth an as-

sertive labor movement. Within the family it also promoted a more rigid division of roles and responsibilities that was detrimental to women, another gradual but profound change of revolutionary proportions.

NOTES

1. N. F. R. Crafts, *British Economic Growth During the Industrial Revolution* (Oxford: Oxford University Press, 1985), p. 32. These estimates are for Great Britain as a whole.
2. B. H. Slicher van Bath, *The Agrarian History of Western Europe, A.D. 500–1850* (New York: St. Martin's Press, 1963), p. 240.
3. E. P. Thompson, *The Making of the English Working Class* (New York: Vintage Books, 1966), p. 218.
4. Quoted in C. Wilson, *England's Apprenticeship, 1603–1763* (London: Longmans, Green, 1965), p. 169.
5. G. Taylor, "America's Growth Before 1840," *Journal of Economic History* 24 (December 1970): 427–444.
6. Quoted in P. Mantoux, *The Industrial Revolution in the Eighteenth Century* (New York: Harper & Row, 1961), p. 75.
7. P. Bairoch, "International Industrialization Levels from 1750 to 1980," *Journal of European Economic History* 11 (Spring 1982): 269–333.
8. Crafts, pp. 45, 95–102.
9. M. Lévy-Leboyer, *Les banques européennes et l'industrialisation dans la première moitié du XIXe siècle* (Paris: Presses Universitaires de France, 1964), p. 29.
10. J. Michelet, *The People,* trans. with an introduction by J. P. McKay (Urbana: University of Illinois Press, 1973; original publication, 1846), p. 64.
11. F. Engels, *The Condition of the Working Class in England,* trans. and ed. W. O. Henderson and W. H. Chaloner (Stanford, Calif.: Stanford University Press, 1968), p. xxiii.
12. Quoted in W. A. Hayek, ed., *Capitalism and the Historians* (Chicago: University of Chicago Press, 1954), p. 126.
13. Crafts, p. 95.
14. Quoted in E. R. Pike, *"Hard Times": Human Documents of the Industrial Revolution* (New York: Praeger, 1966), p. 109.
15. See especially J. Brenner and M. Rama, "Rethinking Women's Oppression," *New Left Review* 144 (March–April 1984): 33–71, and sources cited there.
16. J. Humphries, " '. . . The Most Free from Objection . . .' The Sexual Division of Labor and Wom-

en's Work in Nineteenth-Century England," *Journal of Economic History* 47 (December 1987): 948.

17. Quoted in Ibid., p. 941; quoted in Pike, p. 266.
18. Quoted in Pike, p. 208.

SUGGESTED READING

There is a vast and exciting literature on the Industrial Revolution. R. Cameron, *A Concise Economic History of the World* (1989), provides an introduction to the issues and has a carefully annotated bibliography. J. Goodman and K. Honeyman, *Gainful Pursuits: The Making of Industrial Europe, 1600–1914* (1988); D. S. Landes, *The Unbound Prometheus: Technological Change and Industrial Development in Western Europe from 1750 to the Present* (1969); and S. Pollard, *Peaceful Conquest: The Industrialization of Europe* (1981), are excellent general treatments of European industrial growth. These studies also suggest the range of issues and interpretations. M. Berg, *The Age of Manufactures: Industry, Innovation and Work in Britain, 1700–1820* (1985); P. Mathias, *The First Industrial Nation: An Economic History of Britain, 1700–1914* (1969); and P. Mantoux, *The Industrial Revolution in the Eighteenth Century* (1961), admirably discuss the various aspects of the English breakthrough and offer good bibliographies, as does the work by Crafts mentioned in the Notes. J. de Vries, *The Dutch Rural Economy in the Golden Age, 1500–1700* (1974), examines the causes of early Dutch Leadership in farming, and E. L. Jones, *Agriculture and Economic Growth in England* (1967), shows the importance of the Agricultural Revolution for England. W. Rostow, *The Stages of Economic Growth: A Non-Communist Manifesto* (1960), is a well-known, provocative study.

H. Kirsch, *From Domestic Manufacturing to Industrial Revolution: The Case of the Rhineland Textile Districts* (1989), and M. Neufield, *The Skilled Metalworkers of Nuremberg: Craft and Class in the Industrial Revolution* (1985), examine the persistence and gradual transformation of handicraft techniques. R. Cameron brilliantly traces the spread of railroads and industry across Europe in *France and the Economic Development of Europe, 1800–1914* (1961). The works of A. S. Milward and S. B. Saul, *The Economic Development of Continental Europe, 1780–1870* (1973) and *The Development of the Economies of Continental Europe, 1850–1914* (1977), may be compared with J. Clapham's old-fashioned classic, *Economic Development of France and Germany* (1963). C. Kindleberger, *Economic Growth in France*

and Britain, 1851–1950 (1964), is a stimulating study, especially for those with some background in economics. Other important works on industrial developments are C. Tilly and E. Shorter, *Strikes in France, 1830–1848* (1974); D. Ringrose, *Transportation and Economic Stagnation in Spain, 1750–1850* (1970); L. Schofer, *The Formation of a Modern Labor Force* (1975), which focuses on the Silesian part of Germany; and W. Blackwell, *The Industrialization of Russia,* 2d ed. (1982). L. Moch, *Paths to the City: Regional Migration in Nineteenth-Century France* (1983), and W. Schivelbusch, *Disenchanted Night: The Industrialization of Light in the Nineteenth Century* (1983), imaginatively analyze different aspects of industrialization's many consequences.

The debate between "optimists" and "pessimists" about the consequences of industrialization in England goes on. P. Taylor, ed., *The Industrial Revolution: Triumph or Disaster?* (1970), is a useful introduction to different viewpoints. Hayek's collection of essays, cited in the Notes, stresses positive aspects. It is also fascinating to compare Friedrich Engels's classic condemnation, *The Condition of the Working Class in England,* with Andrew Ure's optimistic defense, *The Philosophy of Manufactures,* first published in 1835 and reprinted recently. E. P. Thompson continues and enriches the Engels tradition in *The Making of the English Working Class* (1963), an exciting book rich in detail and early working-class lore. E. R. Pike's documentary collection, *"Hard Times,"* cited in the Notes, provides fascinating insights into the lives of working people. An unorthodox but moving account of a doomed group is D. Bythell, *The Handloom Weavers* (1969). F. Klingender, *Art and the Industrial Revolution,* rev. ed. (1968), is justly famous, and M. Ignatieff, *A Just Measure of Pain* (1980), is an engrossing study of prisons during English industrialization. D. S. Landes, *Revolution in Time: Clocks and the Making of the Modern World* (1983), is a brilliant integration of industrial and cultural history.

Among general studies, G. S. R. Kitson Clark, *The Making of Victorian England* (1967), is particularly imaginative. A. Briggs, *Victorian People* (1955), provides an engrossing series of brief biographies. H. Ausubel discusses a major reformer in *John Bright* (1966), and B. Harrison skillfully illuminates the problem of heavy drinking in *Drink and the Victorians* (1971). The most famous contemporary novel dealing with the new industrial society is Charles Dickens's *Hard Times,* an entertaining but exaggerated story. *Mary Barton* and *North and South* by Elizabeth Gaskell are more realistic portrayals, and both are highly recommended, as is Émile Zola's *Germinal,* a grim, powerful story of love and hate during a violent strike by French coal miners.

27

Ideologies and Upheavals in Europe, 1815–1850

Citizens of Vienna astride the barricades during the revolution of 1848

The momentous economic and political transformation of modern times began in the late eighteenth century with the Industrial Revolution in England and then the French Revolution. Until about 1815, these economic and political revolutions were separate, involving different countries and activities and proceeding at very different paces. The Industrial Revolution created the factory system and new groups of capitalists and industrial workers in northern England, but almost continuous warfare with France checked its spread to continental Europe. Meanwhile, England's ruling aristocracy suppressed all forms of political radicalism at home and joined with crowned heads abroad to oppose and eventually defeat revolutionary and Napoleonic France. The economic and political revolutions worked at cross-purposes and even neutralized each other.

After peace returned in 1815, the situation changed. Economic and political changes tended to fuse, reinforcing each other and bringing about what the historian Eric Hobsbawm has incisively called the "dual revolution." For instance, the growth of the industrial middle class encouraged the drive for representative government, while the demands of the French sans-culottes in 1793 and 1794 inspired many socialist thinkers. Gathering strength and threatening almost every aspect of the existing political and social framework, the dual revolution rushed on to alter completely first Europe and then the entire world. Much of world history in the last two centuries can be seen as the progressive unfolding of the dual revolution.

Yet three qualifications must be kept firmly in mind. In Europe in the nineteenth century, as in Asia and Africa in more recent times, the dual revolution was not some inexorable mechanical monster grinding peoples and cultures into a homogenized mass. The economic and political transformation it wrought was built on complicated histories, strong traditions, and highly diverse cultures. Radical change was eventually a constant, but the particular results varied enormously.

Nor should the strength of the old forces be underestimated. In central and eastern Europe especially, the traditional elites—the monarchs, noble landowners, and bureaucrats—long proved capable of defending their privileges and even of redirecting the dual revolution to serve their interests.

Finally, the dual revolution posed a tremendous intellectual challenge. The meanings of the economic, political, and social changes that were occurring, as well as the ways they could be shaped by human action, were anything but clear. These questions fascinated observers and stimulated new ideas and ideologies.

- What ideas did thinkers develop to describe and shape the transformation going on?
- How did the artists and writers of the romantic movement reflect and influence changes in this era?
- How did the political revolution, derailed in France and resisted by European monarchs, eventually break out again after 1815?
- Why did the revolutionary surge triumph briefly in 1848, then fail almost completely?

These are the questions explored in this chapter.

PEACE SETTLEMENT

The eventual triumph of revolutionary economic and political forces was by no means certain in 1814. Quite the contrary. The conservative, aristocratic monarchies with their preindustrial armies and economies (Great Britain excepted) appeared firmly in control once again. France had been decisively defeated by the off-again, on-again alliance of Russia, Prussia, Austria, and Great Britain. That alliance had been strengthened and reaffirmed in March 1814, when the allies pledged not only to defeat France but to hold it in line for twenty years thereafter. The Quadruple Alliance had then forced Napoleon to abdicate in April 1814 and restored the Bourbon dynasty to the French throne (see page 822). But there were many other international questions outstanding, and the allies agreed to meet in Vienna to fashion a general peace settlement. Interrupted by Napoleon's desperate gamble during the Hundred Days, the allies concluded their negotiations at the Congress of Vienna after Napoleon's defeat at Waterloo.

Most people felt a profound longing for peace. The great challenge for political leaders in 1814

The Great Powers negotiated the main questions of the peace settlement in intimate sessions at the Congress of Vienna. This painting shows the Duke of Wellington, standing at the far left; seated at far left is the Prussian Prince of Hardinberg. Wellington had just led the allied forces to victory against Napoleon at Waterloo. *(Source: Windsor Castle, Royal Library © 1990. Her Majesty Queen Elizabeth II)*

was to construct a peace settlement that would last and not sow the seeds of another war. Their efforts were largely successful and contributed to a century unmarred by destructive, generalized war (Map 27.1).

The Congress of Vienna

The allied powers were concerned first and foremost with the defeated enemy, France. Agreeing to the restoration of the Bourbon dynasty, the allies signed the first Peace of Paris with Louis XVIII on May 30, 1814.

The allies were quite lenient toward France. France was given the boundaries it possessed in 1792, which were larger than those of 1789.

France lost only the territories it had conquered in Italy, Germany, and the Low Countries, in addition to a few colonial possessions. Although there was some sentiment for levying a fine on France to pay for the war, the allies did not press the matter when Louis XVIII stated firmly that his government would not pay any reparations. France was even allowed to keep the art treasures that Napoleon's agents had looted from the museums of Europe. Thus the victorious powers did not punish harshly, and they did not foment a spirit of injustice and revenge in the defeated country.

When the four allies met together at the Congress of Vienna, assisted in a minor way by a host of delegates from the smaller European states, they also agreed to raise a number of formidable barriers against renewed French aggression. The Low

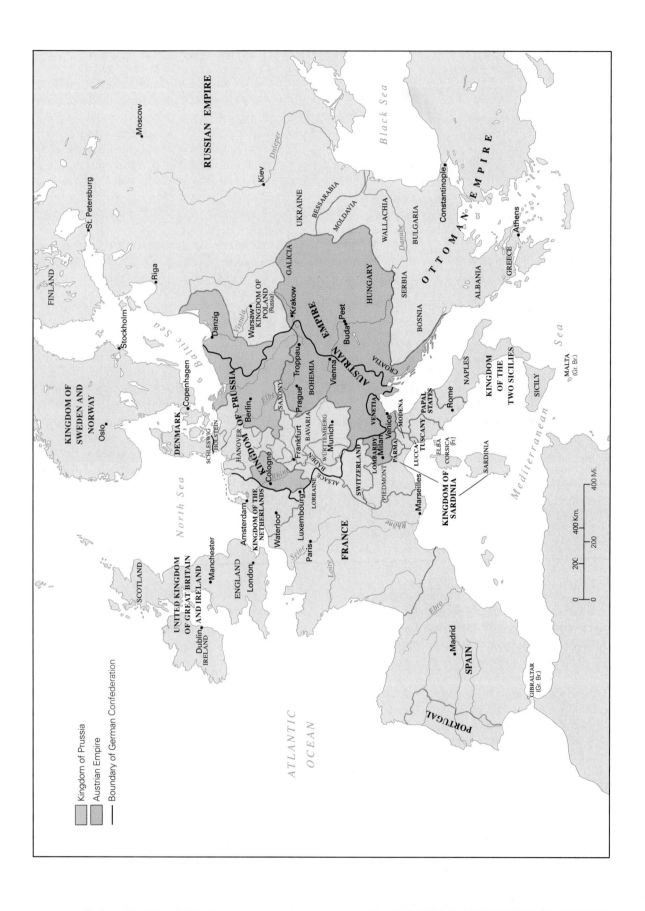

RUSSIAN EMPIRE

Moscow

Kiev

St. Petersburg

Riga

FINLAND

Stockholm

OTTOMAN EMPIRE

Black Sea

Dnieper

UKRAINE

BESSARABIA

MOLDAVIA

WALLACHIA

Danube

BULGARIA

Constantinople

GALICIA

SERBIA

HUNGARY

BOSNIA

CROATIA

ALBANIA

GREECE

Athens

Danzig

Warsaw

KINGDOM OF POLAND (Russia)

Krakow

AUSTRIAN EMPIRE

Vistula

KINGDOM OF SWEDEN AND NORWAY

Oslo

Baltic Sea

Copenhagen

DENMARK

SCHLESWIG

HOLSTEIN

KINGDOM OF PRUSSIA

Berlin

Troppau

BOHEMIA

Prague

Buda Pest

Vienna

Elbe

SAXONY

Frankfurt

HANOVER

North Sea

Amsterdam

KINGDOM OF THE NETHERLANDS

Cologne

Rhine

BAVARIA

WÜRTTEMBERG

Munich

BADEN

SWITZERLAND

LOMBARDY

Milan

PIEDMONT

VENETIA

Venice

PARMA

MODENA

KINGDOM OF THE TWO SICILIES

NAPLES

Rome

PAPAL STATES

TUSCANY

LUCCA

ELBA

CORSICA (Fr.)

SARDINIA

SICILY

MALTA (Gr. Br.)

Mediterranean Sea

KINGDOM OF SARDINIA

Marseilles

ALSACE

LORRAINE

Luxembourg

Waterloo

Seine

Paris

FRANCE

Loire

Rhône

Ebro

Madrid

SPAIN

GIBRALTAR (Gr. Br.)

PORTUGAL

UNITED KINGDOM OF GREAT BRITAIN AND IRELAND

Manchester

ENGLAND

London

Dublin

IRELAND

SCOTLAND

ATLANTIC OCEAN

Kingdom of Prussia

Austrian Empire

Boundary of German Confederation

400 Mi.

400 Km.

200

200

0

0

Countries—Belgium and Holland—were united under an enlarged Dutch monarchy capable of opposing France more effectively. Moreover, Prussia received considerably more territory on France's eastern border so as to stand as "sentinel on the Rhine" against France. In these ways the Quadruple Alliance combined leniency toward France with strong defensive measures. They held out a carrot with one hand and picked up a bigger stick with the other.

In their moderation toward France the allies were motivated by self-interest and traditional ideas about the balance of power. To Metternich and Castlereagh, the foreign ministers of Austria and Great Britain, as well as their French counterpart Talleyrand, the balance of power meant an international equilibrium of political and military forces that would preserve the freedom and independence of each of the Great Powers. Such a balance would discourage aggression by any combination of states or, worse, the domination of Europe by any single state. As they saw it, the task of the powers was thus twofold. They had to make sure that France would not dominate Europe again, and they also had to arrange international relations so that none of the victors would be tempted to strive for domination in its turn. Such a balance involved many considerations and all of Europe.

The balance of power was the mechanism used by the Great Powers—Austria, Britain, Prussia, Russia, and France—to settle their own dangerous disputes at the Congress of Vienna. There was general agreement among the victors that each of them should receive compensation in the form of territory for their successful struggle against the French. Great Britain had already won colonies and strategic outposts during the long wars, and these it retained. Metternich's Austria gave up territories in Belgium and southern Germany but expanded greatly elsewhere, taking the rich provinces of Venetia and Lombardy in northern Italy as well as its former Polish possessions and new lands on the eastern coast of the Adriatic (see Map 27.1). There was also agreement that Prussia and Russia should be compensated. But where, and to

what extent? That was the ticklish question that almost led to renewed war in January 1815.

The vaguely progressive, impetuous Alexander I of Russia had already taken Finland and Bessarabia on his northern and southern borders. Yet he burned with ambition to restore the ancient kingdom of Poland, on which he expected to bestow the benefits of his rule. The Prussians were willing to go along and give up their Polish territories, provided they could swallow up the large and wealthy kingdom of Saxony, their German neighbor to the south.

These demands were too much for Castlereagh and Metternich, who feared an unbalancing of forces in central Europe. In an astonishing about-face, they turned for diplomatic support to the wily Talleyrand and the defeated France he represented. On January 3, 1815, Great Britain, Austria, and France signed a secret alliance directed against Russia and Prussia. As Castlereagh concluded somberly, it appeared that the "peace we have so dearly purchased will be of short duration."[1]

The outcome, however, was compromise rather than war. When rumors of the alliance were intentionally leaked, the threat of war caused the rulers of Russia and Prussia to moderate their demands. They accepted Metternich's proposal: Russia established a small Polish kingdom, and Prussia received two-fifths rather than all of Saxony (see Map 27.1). This compromise was very much within the framework of balance-of-power ideology and eighteenth-century diplomacy: Great Powers became greater, but not too much greater. In addition, France had been able to intervene and tip the scales in favor of the side seeking to prevent undue expansion of Russia and Prussia. In so doing, France regained its Great Power status and was no longer isolated, as Talleyrand gleefully reported to Louis XVIII.

Unfortunately for France, as the final touches were being put on the peace settlement at Vienna, Napoleon suddenly reappeared on the scene. Escaping from his "comic kingdom" on the island of Elba in February 1815 and rallying his supporters for one last campaign during the Hundred Days, Napoleon was defeated at Waterloo and exiled to St. Helena. Yet the resulting peace—the second Peace of Paris—was still relatively moderate toward France. Fat old Louis XVIII was restored to his throne for a second time. France lost some

MAP 27.1 Europe in 1815 Europe's leaders re-established a balance of political power after the defeat of Napoleon.

territory, had to pay an indemnity of 700 million francs, and had to support a large army of occupation for five years.

The rest of the settlement already concluded at the Congress of Vienna was left intact. The members of the Quadruple Alliance, however, did agree to meet periodically to discuss their common interests and to consider appropriate measures for the maintenance of peace in Europe. This agreement marked the beginning of the European "congress system," which lasted long into the nineteenth century and settled international crises through diplomatic conferences.

Intervention and Repression

There was also a domestic political side to the re-establishment of peace. Within their own countries, the leaders of the victorious states were much less flexible. In 1815, under Metternich's leadership, Austria, Prussia, and Russia embarked on a crusade against the ideas and politics of the dual revolution. The crusade lasted until 1848.

The first step was the Holy Alliance, formed by Austria, Prussia, and Russia in September 1815. First proposed by Russia's Alexander I, the alliance proclaimed the intention of the three eastern monarchs to rule exclusively on the basis of Christian principles and to work together to maintain peace and justice on all occasions. Castlereagh refused to sign, characterizing the vague statement of principle as "a piece of sublime mysticism and nonsense." Yet it soon became a symbol of the repression of liberal and revolutionary movements all over Europe.

In 1820 revolutionaries succeeded in forcing the monarchs of Spain and the southern Italian kingdom of the Two Sicilies to grant liberal constitutions against their wills. Metternich was horrified: revolution was rising once again. Calling a conference at Troppau in Austria, under the provisions of the Quadruple Alliance he and Alexander I proclaimed the principle of active intervention to maintain all autocratic regimes whenever they were threatened. Austrian forces then marched into Naples and restored Ferdinand I to the throne of the Two Sicilies. The French armies of Louis XVIII likewise restored the Spanish regime—after the Congress of Troppau had rejected Alexander's offer to send his Cossacks across Europe to teach the Spanish an unforgettable lesson.

Great Britain remained aloof, arguing that intervention in the domestic politics of foreign states was not an object of British diplomacy. In particular, Great Britain opposed any attempts by the restored Spanish monarchy to reconquer its former Latin American possessions, which had gained their independence during and after the Napoleonic wars. Encouraged by the British position, the young United States proclaimed its celebrated Monroe Doctrine in 1823. This bold document declared that European powers were to keep their hands off the New World and in no way attempt to re-establish their political system there. In the United States, constitutional liberalism, which was an ongoing challenge to the conservatism of continental Europe, retained its cutting edge.

In the years following the crushing of liberal revolution in southern Italy in 1821 and in Spain in 1823, Metternich continued to battle against liberal political change. Sometimes he could do little, as in the case of the new Latin American republics. Nor could he undo the dynastic changes of 1830 and 1831 in France and Belgium. Nonetheless, until 1848 Metternich's system proved quite effective in central Europe, where his power was the greatest.

Metternich's policies dominated not only Austria and the Italian peninsula but the entire German Confederation, which the peace settlement of Vienna had called into being. The confederation was composed of thirty-eight independent German states, including Prussia and Austria. (Neither Prussia's eastern territories nor the Hungarian half of the Austrian Empire was included in the confederation.) These states met in complicated assemblies dominated by Austria, with Prussia a willing junior partner in the planning and execution of repressive measures.

It was through the German Confederation that Metternich had the infamous Carlsbad Decrees issued in 1819. The decrees required the thirty-eight German member states to root out subversive ideas in their universities and newspapers. The decrees also established a permanent committee with spies and informers to investigate and punish any liberal or radical organizations. Metternich's ruthless imposition of repressive internal policies on the governments of central Europe contrasted with the intelligent moderation he had displayed in the general peace settlement of 1815.

Metternich and Conservatism

Metternich's determined defense of the status quo made him a villain in the eyes of most progressive, optimistic historians of the nineteenth century. Yet rather than denounce the man, it is more useful to try to understand him and the general conservatism he represented.

Born into the middle ranks of the landed nobility of the Rhineland, Prince Klemens von Metternich (1773–1859) was an internationally oriented aristocrat. In 1795 his splendid marriage to Eleonora von Kaunitz, granddaughter of a famous Austrian statesman and heiress to vast estates, opened the door to the highest court circles and a brilliant diplomatic career. Austrian ambassador to Napoleon's court in 1806 and Austrian foreign minister from 1809 to 1848, the cosmopolitan Metternich always remained loyal to his class and jealously defended its rights and privileges to the day he died. Like most other conservatives of his time, he did so with a clear conscience. The nobility was one of Europe's most ancient institutions, and conservatives regarded tradition as the basic source of human institutions. In their view, the proper state and society remained that of pre-1789 Europe, which rested on a judicious blend of monarchy, bureaucracy, and aristocracy.

Metternich's commitment to conservatism was coupled with a passionate hatred of liberalism. He firmly believed that liberalism, as embodied in revolutionary America and France, had been responsible for a generation of war with untold bloodshed and suffering. Liberal demands for representative government and civil liberties had unfortunately captured the imaginations of some middle-class lawyers, business people, and intellectuals. Metternich thought that these groups had been and still were engaged in a vast conspiracy to impose their beliefs on society and destroy the existing order. Like many other conservatives then and since, Metternich blamed liberal revolutionaries for stirring up the lower classes, whom he believed to be indifferent or hostile to liberal ideas, desiring nothing more than peace and quiet.

The threat of liberalism appeared doubly dangerous to Metternich because it generally went with national aspirations. Liberals, especially liberals in central Europe, believed that each people, each national group, had a right to establish its own independent government and seek to fulfill its own destiny. The idea of national self-determination was repellent to Metternich. It not only threatened the existence of the aristocracy, but it also threatened to destroy the Austrian Empire and revolutionize central Europe.

The vast Austrian Empire of the Habsburgs was a great dynastic state. Formed over centuries by war, marriage, and luck, it was made up of many peoples speaking many languages (Map 27.2). The Germans, long the dominant element, had supported and profited by the long-term territorial expansion of Austria, yet they accounted for only a quarter of the population. The Magyars (Hungarians), a substantially smaller group, dominated the kingdom of Hungary—which was part of the Austrian Empire—though they did not account for a majority of the population even there.

The Czechs, the third major group, were concentrated in Bohemia and Moravia. There were

Metternich This portrait by Sir Thomas Lawrence reveals much of Metternich the man. Handsome, refined, and intelligent, Metternich was a great aristocrat passionately devoted to the defense of his class and its interests. *(Source: Copyright reserved to Her Majesty Queen Elizabeth II)*

RUSSIA

POLAND

SILESIA

GERMAN
STATES

GALICIA

MORAVIA

Prague
BOHEMIA

Vienna

SILESIA

BAVARIA

TYROL

SALZBURG

SWITZERLAND

CORINTHIA

AUSTRIA

STYRIA

Danube

Tisza

Budapest

HUNGARY

TRANSYLVANIA

ROMANIA

Danube

OTTOMAN   EMPIRE

SERBIA

CROATIA-SLAVONIA

BOSNIA

ILLYRIA

VENETIA

Venice

LOMBARDY

Milan

Po

Adriatic Sea

ITALIAN
STATES

Germans
Hungarians
Italians
Romanians
Poles
Czechs

Carpatho-Ukrainians
(Ruthenians)
Serbs and Croats
Slovaks
Slovenes
Habsburg Monarchy
boundaries

0   50   100 Km.

0   50   100 Mi.

also large numbers of Italians, Poles, and Ukrainians, as well as smaller groups of Slovenes, Croats, Serbs, Ruthenians, and Romanians. The various Slavic peoples, together with the Italians and the Romanians, represented a widely scattered and completely divided majority in an empire dominated by Germans and Hungarians. Different ethnic groups often lived in the same provinces and even the same villages. Thus the different parts and provinces of the empire differed in languages, customs, and institutions. They were held together primarily by their ties to the Habsburg emperor.

The multinational state that Metternich served was both strong and weak. It was strong because of its large population and vast territories; it was weak because of its many and potentially dissatisfied nationalities. In these circumstances, Metternich virtually had to oppose liberalism and nationalism, for Austria was simply unable to accommodate those ideologies of the dual revolution. Other conservatives supported Austria because they could imagine no better fate for the jumble of small nationalities wedged precariously between masses of Germans and hordes of Russians in east central Europe. Castlereagh even went so far as to say that Austria was the "great hinge upon which the fate of Europe must ultimately depend." Metternich's repressive conservatism may not hold appeal for many people today, but it had understandable roots in the dilemma of a multinational state in an age of rising nationalism.

RADICAL IDEAS AND EARLY SOCIALISM

The years following the peace settlement of 1815 were years of profound intellectual activity. Intellectuals and social observers were seeking to understand the revolutionary changes that had occurred and were still taking place. These efforts led to ideas that still motivate the world.

Almost all of these basic ideas were radical. In one way or another they opposed the old, deeply

MAP 27.2 Peoples of the Habsburg Monarchy, 1815 The old dynastic state was a patchwork of nationalities. Notice the widely scattered pockets of Germans and Hungarians.

felt conservatism that Metternich exemplified so well. The revived conservatism, with its stress on tradition, a hereditary monarchy, a strong and privileged landowning aristocracy, and an official church, was rejected by radicals. Instead, radicals developed and refined alternative visions—alternative ideologies—and tried to convince society to act on them. With time, they were very successful.

Liberalism

The principal ideas of liberalism—liberty and equality—were by no means defeated in 1815. First realized successfully in the American Revolution and then achieved in part in the French Revolution, this political and social philosophy continued to pose a radical challenge to revived conservatism. Liberalism demanded representative government as opposed to autocratic monarchy, equality before the law as opposed to legally separate classes. The idea of liberty also continued to mean specific individual freedoms: freedom of the press, freedom of speech, freedom of assembly, and freedom from arbitrary arrest. In Europe, only France with Louis XVIII's Constitutional Charter and Great Britain with its Parliament and historic rights of English men and women had realized much of the liberal program in 1815. Even in those countries, liberalism had not fully succeeded; and elsewhere, liberal demands were still a call for revolutionary change.

Although liberalism still had its cutting edge, it was not as sharp a tool as it had been. This was true because liberalism in the early nineteenth century resolutely opposed government intervention in social and economic affairs, even if the need for action seemed great to social critics and reformers. This form of liberalism is often called "classical" liberalism in the United States, in order to distinguish it sharply from modern American liberalism, which usually favors more government programs to meet social needs and to regulate the economy. Classical liberalism's decline in radicalism was especially evident in its economic principles, which called for unrestricted private enterprise and no government interference in the economy. This philosophy was popularly known as the doctrine of *laissez faire*.

The idea of a free economy had first been persuasively formulated by a Scottish professor of philosophy, Adam Smith (1723–1790). Smith, whose *Inquiry into the Nature and Causes of the Wealth of Nations* (1776) founded modern economics, was highly critical of eighteenth-century mercantilism. Mercantilism, he said, meant stifling government regulations as well as unjust privileges for private monopolies and government favorites. Far preferable was free competition, which would give all citizens an equal opportunity to do what they did best. Smith argued effectively that freely competitive private enterprise would bring greater income for everyone, not just the rich.

Unlike some of his contemporaries, Smith applauded the modest rise in real wages of British workers in the eighteenth century and went so far as to say, "No society can surely be flourishing and happy, of which the far greater part of the members are poor and miserable." Smith also believed that greater competition meant higher wages for workers, since manufacturers and "masters are always and everywhere in a sort of tacit, but constant and uniform, combination, not to raise the wages of laborers above their actual rate." In short, Adam Smith was a spokesman for general economic development, not narrow business interests.

In the early nineteenth century, the British economy was progressively liberalized as old restrictions on trade and industry were relaxed or eliminated. This liberalization promoted continued economic growth in the Industrial Revolution. At the same time, however, economic liberalism and laissez-faire economic thought were tending to become a doctrine serving business interests. Businessmen used the doctrine to defend their right to do exactly as they wished in their factories. Labor unions were outlawed because they supposedly restricted free competition and the individual's "right to work."

The teachings of Thomas Malthus (1766–1834) and David Ricardo (1772–1823) helped especially to make economic liberalism an ideology of business interests in many people's minds (see page 845). Malthus argued that population would always tend to grow faster than the supply of food. This led Ricardo to formulate his "iron law of wages," which said that, because of the pressure of population growth, wages would be just high enough to keep the workers from starving. Malthus and Ricardo thought of themselves as objective social scientists. Yet their teachings were often used by industrial and middle-class in-

terests in England, the Continent, and the United States to justify opposing any kind of government action to protect or improve the lot of workers: if workers were poor, it was their own fault, the result of their breeding like rabbits.

In the early nineteenth century, liberal political ideals also became more closely associated with narrow class interests. Early-nineteenth-century liberals favored representative government, but they generally wanted property qualifications attached to the right to vote. In practice, this meant limiting the vote to well-to-do aristocratic landowners, substantial businessmen, and successful members of the professions. Workers and peasants as well as the lower middle class of shopkeepers, clerks, and artisans did not own the necessary property and thus could not vote.

As liberalism became increasingly middle class after 1815, some intellectuals and foes of conservatism felt that it did not go nearly far enough. Inspired by memories of the French Revolution and the contemporary example of exuberant Jacksonian democracy in the young American republic, they called for universal voting rights, at least for males. Giving all men the vote, they felt, would allow the masses to join in government and would lead to democracy.

Many people who believed in democracy also believed in the republican form of government. They detested the power of the monarchy, the privileges of the aristocracy, and the great wealth of the upper middle class. These democrats and republicans were more radical than the liberals. Taking for granted much of the liberal program, they sought to go beyond it. Democrats and republicans were also more willing than most liberals to endorse violent upheaval to achieve goals. All of this meant that liberals and radical, democratic republicans could join forces against conservatives only up to a point.

Nationalism

Nationalism was a second radical idea in the years after 1815, an idea destined to have an enormous influence in the modern world. In a summation of this complex ideology, three points stand out. First, nationalism has normally evolved from a real or imagined cultural unity, manifesting itself especially in a common language, history, and territory. Second, nationalists have usually sought to turn this cultural unity into political reality so that the territory of each people coincides with its state boundaries. It was this goal that made nationalism so potentially explosive in central and eastern Europe after 1815, when there were either too few states (Austria, Russia, and the Ottoman Empire) or too many (the Italian peninsula and the German Confederation) and when different peoples overlapped and intermingled. Third, modern nationalism had its immediate origins in the French Revolution and the Napoleonic wars. Nationalism was effectively harnessed by the French republic during the Reign of Terror to help repel foreign foes, and all across Europe patriots tried to kindle nationalist flames in the war against Napoleon. Thus by 1815 there were already hints of nationalism's remarkable ability to spread and develop.

Between 1815 and 1850, most people who believed in nationalism also believed in either liberalism or radical, democratic republicanism. In more recent times, however, many governments have been very nationalistic without favoring liberty and democracy. Why, then, was love of liberty almost synonymous with love of nation in the early nineteenth century?

A common faith in the creativity and nobility of the people was perhaps the single most important reason for linking these two concepts. Liberals and especially democrats saw the people as the ultimate source of all government. The people (or some of them) elected their officials and governed themselves within a framework of personal liberty. Yet such self-government would be possible only if the people were united by common traditions and common loyalties. In practice, common loyalties rested above all on a common language. Thus liberals and nationalists agreed that a shared language forged the basic unity of a people, a unity that transcended local or provincial interests and even class differences.

Early nationalists usually believed that every nation, like every citizen, had the right to exist in freedom and to develop its character and spirit. They were confident that the independence and freedom of other nations, as in the case of other citizens within a nation, would not lessen the freedom of their own country. Rather, the symphony of nations would promote the harmony and ultimate unity of all peoples. As the French historian Jules Michelet put it in *The People* in 1846, each

citizen "learns to recognize his country . . . as a note in the grand concert; through it he himself participates and loves the world." Similarly, the Italian patriot Giuseppe Mazzini believed that "in laboring according to the true principles of our country we are laboring for Humanity." Thus individual liberty and love of a free nation overlapped greatly in the early nineteenth century.

Nationalism also had a negative side to it. Even as they talked of serving the cause of humanity, early nationalists stressed the differences among peoples. The German pastor and philosopher Johann Herder (1744–1803) had argued that every people has its own particular spirit and genius, which it expresses through its culture and language. Yet Herder (and others after him) could not define the uniqueness of the French, German, and Slavic peoples without comparing and contrasting one people with another. Thus, even early nationalism developed a strong sense of "we" and "they."

"They" were often the enemy. The leader of the Czech cultural revival, the passionate democrat and nationalist historian Francis Palacký, is a good example of this tendency. In his histories he lauded the achievements of the Czech people, which he characterized as a long struggle against brutal German domination. To this "we-they" outlook, it was all too easy for nationalists to add two other highly volatile ingredients: a sense of national mission and a sense of national superiority. As Mazzini characteristically wrote, "Peoples never stop before they have achieved the ultimate aim of their existence, before having fulfilled their mission." Even Michelet, so alive to the aspirations of other peoples, could not help speaking in 1846 of the "superiority of France"; the principles espoused in the French Revolution had made France the "salvation of mankind."

German and Spanish nationalists had a very different opinion of France. To them the French often seemed as oppressive as the Germans seemed to the Czechs, as hateful as the Russians seemed to the Poles. The despised enemy's mission might seem as oppressive as the American national mission seemed to the Mexicans after the U.S. annexation of Texas. In 1845 the American journalist and strident nationalist John Louis O'Sullivan wrote that taking land from an "imbecile and distracted Mexico" was a laudable step in the "fulfillment of our manifest destiny to overspread the continent allotted by Providence for the free development of our yearly multiplying millions."[2]

Early nationalism was thus ambiguous. Its main thrust was liberal and democratic. But below the surface lurked ideas of national superiority and national mission that could lead to aggressive crusades and counter-crusades, as had happened in the French Revolution and in the "wars of liberation" against Napoleon.

French Utopian Socialism

Despite the fact that France lagged far behind Great Britain in developing modern industry, almost all the early socialists were French. Although they differed on many specific points, these French thinkers were acutely aware that the political revolution in France and the rise of modern industry in England had begun a transformation of society. Yet they were disturbed by what they saw. Liberal practices in politics and economics appeared to be fomenting selfish individualism and splitting the community into isolated fragments. There was, they believed, an urgent need for a further reorganization of society to establish cooperation and a new sense of community. Starting from this shared outlook, individual French thinkers went in many different directions. They searched the past, analyzed existing conditions, and fashioned luxurious utopias. Yet certain ideas tied their critiques and visions together.

Early French socialists believed in economic planning. Inspired by the emergency measures of 1793 and 1794 in France, they argued that the government should rationally organize the economy and not depend on destructive competition to do the job. Early socialists also shared an intense desire to help the poor and to protect them from the rich. With passionate moral fervor, they preached that the rich and the poor should be more nearly equal economically. Finally, socialists believed that most private property should be abolished and replaced by state or community ownership. Planning, greater economic equality, and state ownership of property: these were the key ideas of early French socialism and of all socialism since.

One of the most influential early socialist thinkers was a nobleman, Count Henri de Saint-Simon (1760–1825). A curious combination of radical thinker and successful land speculator, Saint-

Simon optimistically proclaimed the tremendous possibilities of industrial development: "The age of gold is before us!" The key to progress was proper social organization. Such an arrangement of society required the "parasites"—the court, the aristocracy, lawyers, churchmen—to give way, once and for all, to the "doers"—the leading scientists, engineers, and industrialists. The doers would carefully plan the economy and guide it forward by undertaking vast public works projects and establishing investment banks. Saint-Simon also stressed in highly moralistic terms that every social institution ought to have as its main goal improved conditions for the poor. Saint-Simon's stress on industry and science inspired middle-class industrialists and bankers, like the Pereire brothers, founders of the Crédit Mobilier (see page 851).

After 1830 the socialist critique of capitalism became sharper. Charles Fourier (1772–1837), a lonely, saintly man with a tenuous hold on reality, described a socialist utopia in lavish mathematical detail. Hating the urban wage system, Fourier envisaged self-sufficient communities of 1,620 people living communally on 5,000 acres devoted to a combination of agriculture and industry. Although Fourier waited in vain each day at noon in his apartment for a wealthy philanthropist to endow his visionary schemes, he was very influential. Several utopian communities were founded along the lines he prescribed, mainly in the United States.

Fourier was also an early proponent of the total emancipation of women. Extremely critical of middle-class family life, Fourier believed that most marriages were only another kind of prostitution. According to Fourier, young single women were shamelessly "sold" to their future husbands for dowries and other financial considerations. Thus Fourier called for the abolition of marriage, free unions based only on love, and complete sexual freedom. Many middle-class men and women found these ideas, which were shared and even practiced by some followers of Saint-Simon, shocking and immoral. The socialist program for the liberation of women as well as workers appeared to them as doubly dangerous and revolutionary.

Louis Blanc (1811–1882), a sharp-eyed, intelligent journalist, was much more practical. In his *Organization of Work* (1839), he urged workers to agitate for universal voting rights and to take control of the state peacefully. Blanc believed that the full power of the state should be directed at setting up government-backed workshops and factories to guarantee full employment. The right to work had to become as sacred as any other right. Finally, there was Pierre Joseph Proudhon (1809–1865), a self-educated printer, who wrote a pamphlet in 1840 entitled *What Is Property?* His answer was that it was nothing but theft. Property was profit that was stolen from the worker, who was the source of all wealth. Unlike most socialists, Proudhon feared the power of the state and was often considered an anarchist.

Thus a variety of French thinkers blazed the way with utopian socialism in the 1830s and 1840s. Their ideas were very influential, particularly in Paris, where poverty-stricken workers with a revolutionary tradition were attentive students. Yet the economic arguments of the French utopians were weak, and their specific programs usually seemed too fanciful to be taken seriously. To Karl Marx was left the task of establishing firm foundations for modern socialism.

The Birth of Marxian Socialism

In 1848 the thirty-year-old Karl Marx (1818–1883) and the twenty-eight-year-old Friedrich Engels (1820–1895) published the *Communist Manifesto,* the bible of socialism. The son of a Jewish lawyer who had converted to Christianity, the atheistic young Marx had studied philosophy at the University of Berlin before turning to journalism and economics. He read widely in French socialist thought and was influenced by it. He shared Fourier's view of middle-class marriage as legalized prostitution, and he too looked forward to the emancipation of women and the abolition of the family. But by the time he was twenty-five, he was developing his own socialist ideas.

Early French socialists often appealed to the middle class and the state to help the poor. Marx ridiculed such appeals as naive. He argued that the interests of the middle class and those of the industrial working class are inevitably opposed to each other. Indeed, according to the *Manifesto,* the "history of all previously existing society is the history of class struggles." In Marx's view, one class had always exploited the other, and with the advent of modern industry, society was split more clearly than ever before: between the middle class—the *bourgeoisie*—and the modern working

The Marx Family   In 1849 the exiled Marx settled in London. There he wrote *Capital,* the weighty exposition of his socialist theories, and worked to organize the working class. With his coauthor and financial supporter Friedrich Engels (right), Marx is shown here with his daughters, ironically a picture of middle-class respectability. *(Source: Culver Pictures)*

class—the *proletariat.* Moreover, the bourgeoisie had reduced everything to a matter of money and "naked self-interest." "In a word, for exploitation, veiled by religious and political illusions, the bourgeoisie had substituted naked, shameless, direct brutal exploitation."

Just as the bourgeoisie had triumphed over the feudal aristocracy, Marx predicted, the proletariat was destined to conquer the bourgeoisie in a violent revolution. While a tiny minority owned the means of production and grew richer, the ever-poorer proletariat was constantly growing in size and in class consciousness. In this process, the proletariat was aided, according to Marx, by a portion of the bourgeoisie who had gone over to the proletariat and who (like Marx and Engels) "had raised themselves to the level of comprehending theoretically the historical moment." And the critical moment was very near. "Let the ruling classes tremble at a Communist revolution. The proletarians have nothing to lose but their chains. They have a world to win. WORKING MEN OF ALL COUNTRIES, UNITE!" So ends the *Communist Manifesto*.

In brief outline, Marx's ideas may seem to differ only slightly from the wild and improbable ideas of the utopians of his day. Yet whatever one may think of the validity of Marx's analysis, he must be taken seriously. He united sociology, economics, and all human history in a vast and imposing edifice. He synthesized in his socialism not only French utopian schemes but English classical economics and German philosophy—the major intellectual currents of his day. Moreover, after the young Marx fled to England as a penniless political refugee after the revolutions of 1848, he continued to show a rare flair for combining complex theorization with both lively popular writing and practical organizational ability. This combination of theoretical and practical skills contributed greatly to the subsequent diffusion of Marx's socialist synthesis after 1860 (see pages 953–956).

Marx's debt to England was great. He was the last of the classical economists. Following David Ricardo, who had taught that labor was the source of all value, Marx went on to argue that profits were really wages stolen from the workers. Moreover, Marx incorporated Engels's charges of terrible oppression of the new class of factory workers in England; thus his doctrines seemed to be based on hard facts.

Marx's theory of historical evolution was built on the philosophy of the German Georg Hegel (1770–1831). Hegel believed that history is "ideas in motion": each age is characterized by a dominant set of ideas, which produces opposing ideas and eventually a new synthesis. The idea of *being* had been dominant initially, for example, and it had produced its antithesis, the idea of *nonbeing*. This idea in turn had resulted in the synthesis of *becoming*. Thus history has pattern and purpose.

Marx retained Hegel's view of history as a dialectic process of change but made economic relationships between classes the driving force. This dialectic explained the decline of agrarian feudal-ism and the rise of industrial capitalism. And Marx stressed again and again that the "bourgeoisie, historically, has played a most revolutionary part. . . . During its rule of scarcely one hundred years the bourgeoisie has created more massive and more colossal productive forces than have all preceding generations together." Here was a convincing explanation for people trying to make sense of the dual revolution. Marx's next idea, that it was now the bourgeoisie's turn to give way to the socialism of revolutionary workers, appeared to many the irrefutable capstone of a brilliant interpretation of humanity's long development. Thus Marx pulled together powerful ideas and insights to create one of the great secular religions out of the intellectual ferment of the early nineteenth century.

THE ROMANTIC MOVEMENT

Radical concepts of politics and society were accompanied by comparable changes in literature and other arts during the dual revolution. The early nineteenth century marked the acme of the romantic movement, which profoundly influenced the arts and enriched European culture immeasurably.

The romantic movement was in part a revolt against classicism and the Enlightenment. Classicism was essentially a set of artistic rules and standards that went hand in glove with the Enlightenment's belief in rationality, order, and restraint. The classicists believed that the ancient Greeks and Romans had discovered eternally valid esthetic rules and that playwrights and painters should continue to follow them. Classicists could enforce these rules in the eighteenth century because they dominated the courts and academies for which artists worked.

Forerunners of the romantic movement appeared from about 1750 on. Of these, Rousseau (see page 676)—the passionate advocate of feeling, freedom, and natural goodness—was the most influential. Romanticism then crystallized fully in the 1790s, primarily in England and Germany. The French Revolution kindled the belief that radical reconstruction was also possible in cultural and artistic life (even though many early English and German romantics became disillusioned with events in France and turned from liberalism to conservatism in politics). Romanticism gained strength until the 1840s.

Romanticism

Romanticism was characterized by a belief in emotional exuberance, unrestrained imagination, and spontaneity in both art and personal life. In Germany early romantics of the 1770s and 1780s called themselves the "Storm and Stress" *(Sturm und Drang)* group, and many romantic artists of the early nineteenth century lived lives of tremendous emotional intensity. Suicide, duels to the death, madness, and strange illnesses were not uncommon among leading romantics. Romantic artists typically led bohemian lives, wearing their hair long and uncombed in preference to powdered wigs and living in cold garrets rather than frequenting stiff drawing rooms. They rejected materialism and sought to escape to lofty spiritual heights through their art. Great individualists, the romantics believed the full development of one's unique human potential to be the supreme purpose in life. The romantics were driven by a sense of an unlimited universe and by a yearning for the unattained, the unknown, the unknowable.

Nowhere was the break with classicism more apparent than in romanticism's general conception of nature. Classicism was not particularly interested in nature. In the words of the eighteenth-century English author Samuel Johnson, "A blade of grass is always a blade of grass; men and women are my subjects of inquiry." Nature was

Constable: The Hay Wain Constable's love of a spiritualized and poetic nature radiates from this masterpiece of romantic art. Exhibited in Paris in 1824, *The Hay Wain* created a sensation and made a profound impression on the young Delacroix. *(Source: Courtesy of the Trustees, The National Gallery, London)*

portrayed by classicists as beautiful and chaste, like an eighteenth-century formal garden. The romantics, on the other hand, were enchanted by nature. Sometimes they found it awesome and tempestuous, as in Théodore Géricault's painting *The Raft of the Medusa,* which shows the survivors of a shipwreck adrift in a turbulent sea. Others saw nature as a source of spiritual inspiration. As the great English landscape artist John Constable declared, "Nature is Spirit visible."

Most romantics saw the growth of modern industry as an ugly, brutal attack on their beloved nature and on the human personality. They sought escape—in the unspoiled Lake District of northern England, in exotic North Africa, in an idealized Middle Ages. Yet some romantics found a vast, awesome, terribly moving power in the new industrial landscape. In ironworks and cotton mills they saw the flames of hell and the evil genius of Satan himself. One of John Martin's last and greatest paintings, *The Great Day of His Wrath* (1850), vividly depicts the Last Judgment foretold in Revelation 6, when the "sun became black as sackcloth of hair, and the moon became as blood; and the stars of heaven fell unto the earth." Martin's romantic masterpiece was inspired directly by a journey through the "Black country" of the industrial Midlands in the dead of night. According to Martin's son:

The glow of the furnaces, the red blaze of light, together with the liquid fire, seemed to him truly sublime and awful. He could not imagine anything more terrible even in the regions of everlasting punishment. All he had done or attempted in ideal painting fell far short, very far short, of the fearful sublimity.[3]

Fascinated by color and diversity, the romantic imagination turned toward the study and writing of history with a passion. For romantics, history was not a minor branch of philosophy from which philosophers picked suitable examples to illustrate their teachings. History was beautiful, exciting, and important in its own right. It was the art of change over time—the key to a universe that was now perceived to be organic and dynamic. It was no longer perceived to be mechanical and static as it had seemed to the philosophes of the eighteenth-century Enlightenment.

Historical studies supported the development of national aspirations and encouraged entire peoples to seek in the past their special destinies. This trend was especially strong in Germany and eastern Europe. As the famous English historian Lord Acton put it, the growth of historical thinking associated with the romantic movement was a most fateful step in the story of European thought.

Literature

Britain was the first country where romanticism flowered fully in poetry and prose, and the British romantic writers were among the most prominent in Europe. William Wordsworth, Samuel Taylor Coleridge, and Sir Walter Scott were all active by 1800, to be followed shortly by Percy Bysshe Shelley, John Keats, and George Gordon, Lord Byron. All were poets: romanticism found its distinctive voice in poetry, as the Enlightenment had in prose.

A towering leader of English romanticism, William Wordsworth (1770–1850) traveled in France after his graduation from Cambridge. There he fell passionately in love with a French woman, who bore him a daughter. He was deeply influenced by the philosophy of Rousseau and the spirit of the early French Revolution. Back in England, prevented by war and the Terror from returning to France, Wordsworth settled in the countryside with his sister Dorothy and Samuel Taylor Coleridge (1772–1834).

In 1798 the two poets published their *Lyrical Ballads,* one of the most influential literary works in the history of the English language. In defiance of classical rules, Wordsworth and Coleridge abandoned flowery poetic conventions for the language of ordinary speech, simultaneously endowing simple subjects with the loftiest majesty. This twofold rejection of classical practice was at first ignored and then harshly criticized, but by 1830 Wordsworth had triumphed.

One of the best examples of Wordsworth's romantic credo and genius is "Daffodils":

I wandered lonely as a cloud
That floats on high o'er vales and hills,
When all at once I saw a crowd,
A host, of golden daffodils;
Beside the lake, beneath the trees,
Fluttering and dancing in the breeze.

.   .   .

The waves beside them danced, but they
Out-did the sparkling waves in glee:

Heroes of Romanticism   Observed by a portrait of Byron and a bust of Beethoven, Liszt plays for friends. From left to right sit Alexander Dumas, George Sand (characteristically wearing men's garb), and Marie d'Agoult, Liszt's mistress. Standing are Victor Hugo, Paganini, and Rossini. *(Source: Bildarchiv Preussischer Kulturbesitz)*

A poet could not but be gay,
In such a jocund company:
I gazed—and gazed—but little thought
What wealth the show to me had brought:

For oft, when on my couch I lie
In vacant or in pensive mood,
They flash upon that inward eye
Which is the bliss of solitude;
And then my heart with pleasure fills,
And dances with the daffodils.

Here are simplicity and love of nature in commonplace forms. Here, too, is Wordsworth's romantic conviction that nature has the power to elevate and instruct, especially when interpreted by a high-minded poetic genius. Wordsworth's conception of poetry as the "spontaneous overflow of powerful feeling recollected in tranquility" is well illustrated by the last stanza.

At first, the strength of classicism in France inhibited the growth of romanticism there. Then, between 1820 and 1850, the romantic impulse broke through in the poetry and prose of Alphonse de Lamartine, Alfred de Vigny, Victor Hugo, Alexander Dumas, and George Sand. Of these, Victor Hugo (1802–1885) was the greatest in both poetry and prose.

Son of a Napoleonic general, Hugo achieved an amazing range of rhythm, language, and image in his lyric poetry. His powerful novels exemplified the romantic fascination with fantastic characters, strange settings, and human emotions. The hero of Hugo's famous *Hunchback of Notre Dame* (1831) is the great cathedral's deformed bell-ringer, a "human gargoyle" overlooking the teeming life of fifteenth-century Paris. A great admirer of Shakespeare, whom classical critics had derided as undisciplined and excessive, Hugo also championed romanticism in drama. His play *Hernani* (1830) consciously broke all the old rules as Hugo renounced his early conservatism and equated freedom in literature with liberty in politics and society. Hugo's political evolution was thus exactly the opposite of Wordsworth's, in whom youthful radicalism gave way to middle-aged caution. As the contrast between the two artists suggests, romanticism was a cultural movement compatible with many political beliefs.

Amandine Aurore Lucie Dupin (1804–1876), a strong-willed and gifted woman generally known by her pen name, George Sand, defied the narrow conventions of her time in an unending search for self-fulfillment. After eight years of unhappy marriage in the provinces, she abandoned her dullard of a husband and took her two children to Paris to pursue a career as a writer. There Sand soon achieved fame and wealth, eventually writing over eighty novels on a variety of romantic and social themes. All were shot through with a typically romantic love of nature and moral idealism. George Sand's striking individualism went far beyond her flamboyant preference for men's clothing and cigars and her notorious affairs with the poet Alfred de Musset and the composer Frédéric Chopin, among others. Her semi-autobiographical novel *Lélia* was shockingly modern, delving deeply into her tortuous quest for sexual and personal freedom.

In central and eastern Europe, literary romanticism and early nationalism often reinforced each other. Seeking a unique greatness in every people, well-educated romantics plumbed their own histories and cultures. Like modern anthropologists, they turned their attention to peasant life and transcribed the folk songs, tales, and proverbs that the cosmopolitan Enlightenment had disdained. The brothers Jacob and Wilhelm Grimm were particularly successful at rescuing German fairy tales from oblivion. In the Slavic lands, romantics played a decisive role in converting spoken peasant languages into modern written languages. The greatest of all Russian poets, Alexander Pushkin (1799–1837), rejecting eighteenth-century attempts to force Russian poetry into a classical straitjacket, used his lyric genius to mold the modern literary language.

Art and Music

The greatest and most moving romantic painter in France was Eugène Delacroix (1798–1863), probably the illegitimate son of the French foreign minister Talleyrand. Delacroix was a master of dramatic, colorful scenes that stir the emotions. He was fascinated with remote and exotic subjects, whether lion hunts in Morocco or the languishing, sensuous women of a sultan's harem. Yet he was also a passionate spokesman for freedom. His masterpiece, *Liberty Leading the People,* celebrated the nobility of popular revolution in general and revolution in France in particular.

In England the most notable romantic painters were J. M. W. Turner (1775–1851) and John Constable (1776–1837). Both were fascinated by nature, but their interpretations of it contrasted sharply, aptly symbolizing the tremendous emotional range of the romantic movement. Turner depicted nature's power and terror; wild storms and sinking ships were favorite subjects. Constable painted gentle Wordsworthian landscapes in which human beings were at one with their environment, the comforting countryside of unspoiled rural England.

It was in music that romanticism realized most fully and permanently its goals of free expression and emotional intensity. Whereas the composers of the eighteenth century had remained true to well-defined structures like the classical symphony, the great romantics used a great range of forms to create a thousand musical landscapes and evoke a host of powerful emotions. Romantic composers also transformed the small classical orchestra, tripling its size by adding wind instruments, percussion, and more brass and strings. The crashing chords evoking the surge of the masses in Chopin's "Revolutionary" etude, the bottomless despair of the funeral march in Beethoven's Third Symphony, the solemn majesty of a great religious event in Schumann's *Rhenish* Symphony—such were the modern orchestra's musical paintings that plumbed the depths of human feeling.

This range and intensity gave music and musicians much greater prestige than in the past. Music no longer simply complemented a church service or helped a nobleman digest his dinner. Music became a sublime end in itself. It became for many the greatest of the arts, precisely because it achieved the most ecstatic effect and most perfectly realized the endless yearning of the soul. It was worthy of great concert halls and the most dedicated sacrifice. The unbelievable one-in-a-million performer—the great virtuoso who could transport the listener to ecstasy and hysteria—became a cultural hero. The composer Franz Liszt (1811–1886) vowed to do for the piano what Nicolo Paganini (1782–1840) had done for the violin, and he was lionized as the greatest pianist of his age. People swooned for Liszt as they scream for rock stars today.

Though romanticism dominated music until late in the nineteenth century, no composer ever surpassed its first great master, Ludwig van Beethoven (1770–1827). Extending and breaking open classical forms, Beethoven used contrasting themes and tones to produce dramatic conflict and inspiring resolutions. As the contemporary German novelist Ernst Hoffmann (1776–1822) wrote, "Beethoven's music sets in motion the lever of fear, of awe, of horror, of suffering, and awakens just that infinite longing which is the essence of Romanticism." Beethoven's range was tremendous; his output included symphonies, chamber music, sonatas for violin and piano, masses, an opera, and a great many songs.

At the peak of his fame, in constant demand as a composer and recognized as the leading concert pianist of his day, Beethoven began to lose his hearing. He considered suicide but eventually overcame despair: "I will take fate by the throat; it will not bend me completely to its will."[4] Beethoven continued to pour out immortal music. Among other achievements, he fully exploited for the first time the richness and beauty of the piano. Beethoven never heard much of his later work, including the unforgettable choral finale to the Ninth Symphony, for his last years were silent, spent in total deafness.

REFORMS AND REVOLUTIONS

While the romantic movement was developing, liberal, national, and socialist forces battered against the conservatism of 1815. In some countries, change occurred gradually and peacefully. Elsewhere, pressure built up like steam in a pressure cooker without a safety valve and eventually caused an explosion—in 1848. Three important countries—Greece, Great Britain, and France—experienced variations on this basic theme.

National Liberation in Greece

National, liberal revolution, frustrated in Italy and Spain by conservative statesmen, succeeded first after 1815 in Greece. Since the fifteenth century, the Greeks had been living under the domination of the Ottoman Turks. In spite of centuries of foreign rule, the Greeks had survived as a people, united by their language and the Greek Orthodox religion. It was perfectly natural that the general growth of national aspirations and a desire for independence would inspire some Greeks in the early nineteenth century. This rising national movement led to the formation of secret societies and then to revolt in 1821, led by Alexander Ypsilanti, a Greek patriot and a general in the Russian army.

The Great Powers, particularly Metternich, were opposed to all revolution, even revolution against the Islamic Turks. They refused to back Ypsilanti and supported the Ottoman Empire. Yet for many Europeans the Greek cause became a holy one. Educated Americans and Europeans were in love with the culture of classical Greece; Russians were stirred by the piety of their Orthodox brethren. Writers and artists, moved by the romantic impulse, responded enthusiastically to the Greek struggle. The flamboyant, radical poet Lord Byron went to Greece and died there in the struggle "that Greece might still be free." Turkish atrocities toward the rebels fanned the fires of European outrage and Greek determination. One of Delacroix's romantic masterpieces memorialized the massacre at Chios, where the Turks slaughtered nearly 100,000 Greeks.

The Greeks, though often quarreling among themselves, battled on against the Turks and hoped for the eventual support of European governments. In 1827 Great Britain, France, and Russia responded to popular demands at home and directed Turkey to accept an armistice. When the Turks refused, the navies of these three powers trapped the Turkish fleet at Navarino and destroyed it. Russia then declared another of its

Delacroix: Massacre at Chios   The Greek struggle for freedom and independence won the enthusiastic support of liberals, nationalists, and romantics. The Ottoman Turks were seen as cruel oppressors holding back the course of history, as in this powerful masterpiece by Delacroix. *(Source: Louvre/Cliché des Musées Nationaux, Paris)*

periodic wars of expansion against the Turks. This led to the establishment of a Russian protectorate over much of present-day Romania, which had also been under Turkish rule. Great Britain, France, and Russia finally declared Greece independent in 1830 and installed a German prince as king of the new country in 1832. In the end the Greeks won: a small nation gained its independence in a heroic war against a foreign empire.

Liberal Reform in Great Britain

Eighteenth-century British society had been both flexible and remarkably stable. It was dominated by the landowning aristocracy, but that class was neither closed nor rigidly defined. Successful business and professional people could buy land and become gentlefolk, and the common people had more than the usual opportunities of the preindustrial world. Basic civil rights for all were balanced by a tradition of deference to one's social superiors. Parliament was manipulated by the king and was thoroughly undemocratic. Only about 6 percent of the population could vote for representatives to Parliament, and by the 1780s there was growing interest in some kind of political reform.

But the French Revolution threw the aristocracy into a panic for a generation, making it extremely hostile to any attempts to change the status quo. The Tory party, completely controlled by the landed aristocracy, was particularly fearful of radical movements at home and abroad. Castlereagh initially worked closely with Metternich to restrain France and restore a conservative balance in central Europe. This same intense conservatism motivated the Tory government at home. After 1815 the aristocracy defended its ruling position by repressing every kind of popular protest.

The first step in this direction began with revision of the Corn Laws in 1815. Corn Laws to regulate the foreign grain trade had long existed, but they were not needed during a generation of war with France because the British had been unable to import cheap grain from eastern Europe. As shortages occurred and agricultural prices skyrocketed, a great deal of marginal land had been brought under cultivation. This development had been a bonanza for the landed aristocracy, whose fat rent rolls became even fatter. Peace meant that grain could be imported again and that the price of wheat and bread would go down. To almost everyone except the aristocracy, lower prices seemed highly desirable. The aristocracy, however, rammed far-reaching changes in the Corn Laws through Parliament. The new law prohibited the importation of foreign grain unless the price at home rose above 80 shillings per quarter-ton—a level reached only in time of harvest disaster before 1790. Seldom has a class legislated more selfishly for its own narrow economic advantage.

The change in the Corn Laws, coming at a time of widespread unemployment and postwar adjustment, led to protests and demonstrations by urban laborers. They were supported by radical intellectuals, who campaigned for a reformed House of Commons that would serve the nation and not just the aristocracy. In 1817 the Tory government responded by temporarily suspending the traditional rights of peaceable assembly and habeas corpus. Two years later, Parliament passed the infamous Six Acts, which among other things controlled a heavily taxed press and practically eliminated all mass meetings. These acts followed an enormous but orderly protest, at Saint Peter's Fields in Manchester, that had been savagely broken up by armed cavalry. Nicknamed the "Battle of Peterloo," in scornful reference to the British victory at Waterloo, this incident expressed the government's determination to repress and stand fast.

Ongoing industrial development was not only creating urban and social problems but also strengthening the upper middle classes. The new manufacturing and commercial groups insisted on a place for their new wealth alongside the landed wealth of the aristocracy in the framework of political power and social prestige. They called for certain kinds of liberal reform: reform of town government, organization of a new police force, and more rights for Catholics and dissenters. In the 1820s a less frightened Tory government moved in the direction of better urban administration, greater economic liberalism, and civil equality for Catholics. The prohibition on imports of foreign grain was replaced by a heavy tariff. These actions encouraged the middle classes to press on for reform of Parliament so that they could have a larger say in government and perhaps repeal the revised Corn Laws, that symbol of aristocratic domination.

The Whig party, though led like the Tories by great aristocrats, had by tradition been more responsive to commercial and manufacturing interests. In 1830 a Whig ministry introduced "an act to amend the representation of the people of England and Wales." Defeated, then passed by the House of Commons, this reform bill was rejected by the House of Lords. But when in 1832 the Whigs got the king to promise to create enough new peers to pass the law, the House of Lords reluctantly gave in rather than see its snug little club ruined by upstart manufacturers and plutocrats. A mighty surge of popular protest had helped the king and lords make up their minds.

The Reform Bill of 1832 had profound significance. The House of Commons emerged as the all-important legislative body. In the future, an obstructionist House of Lords could always be brought into line by the threat of creating new peers. The new industrial areas of the country gained representation in the Commons, and many

THE PRELUDE TO 1848

March 1814	Russia, Prussia, Austria, and Britain form the Quadruple Alliance to defeat France
April 1814	Napoleon abdicates
May–June 1814	Restoration of the Bourbon monarchy; Louis XVIII issues Constitutional Charter providing for civil liberties and representative government
	First Peace of Paris: allies combine leniency with defensive posture toward France
October 1814–June 1815	Congress of Vienna peace settlement: establishes balance-of-power principle and creates the German Confederation
February 1815	Napoleon escapes from Elba and marches on Paris
June 1815	Battle of Waterloo
September 1815	Austria, Prussia, and Russia form the Holy Alliance to repress liberal and revolutionary movements
November 1815	Second Peace of Paris and renewal of Quadruple Alliance: punishes France and establishes the European "congress system"
1819	Carlsbad Decrees: Metternich imposes harsh measures throughout the German Confederation
1820	Revolution in Spain and the Kingdom of the Two Sicilies
	Congress of Troppau: Metternich and Alexander I of Russia proclaim principle of intervention to maintain autocratic regimes
1821	Austria crushes liberal revolution in Naples and restores the Sicilian autocracy
	Greek revolt against the Ottoman Turks
1823	French armies restore the Spanish regime
	United States proclaims the Monroe Doctrine
1824	Reactionary Charles X succeeds Louis XVIII in France
1830	Charles X repudiates the Constitutional Charter; insurrection and collapse of government; Louis Philippe succeeds to the throne and maintains a narrowly liberal regime until 1848
	Greece wins independence from the Ottoman Empire
1832	Reform Bill expands British electorate and encourages the middle class
1839	Louis Blanc, *Organization of Work*
1840	Pierre Joseph Proudhon, *What Is Property?*
1846	Jules Michelet, *The People*
1848	Karl Marx and Friedrich Engels, *The Communist Manifesto*

old "rotten boroughs"—electoral districts with very few voters that the landed aristocracy had bought and sold—were eliminated.

The redistribution of seats reflected the shift in population to the northern manufacturing counties and the gradual emergence of an urban society. As a result of the Reform Bill of 1832, the number of voters increased about 50 percent. Comfortable middle-class groups in the urban population, as well as some substantial farmers who leased their land, received the vote. Thus the pressures building in Great Britain were successfully—though only temporarily—released. A major reform had been achieved peacefully,

without revolution or civil war. More radical reforms within the system appeared difficult but not impossible.

The principal radical program was embodied in the "People's Charter" of 1838 and the Chartist movement (see page 857). Partly inspired by the economic distress of the working class, the Chartists' core demand was universal male (not female) suffrage. They saw complete political democracy and rule by the common people as the means to a good and just society. Hundreds of thousands of people signed gigantic petitions calling on Parliament to grant all men the right to vote, first and most seriously in 1839, again in 1842, and yet again in 1848. Parliament rejected all three petitions. In the short run, the working poor failed with their Chartist demands, but they learned a valuable lesson in mass politics.

While calling for universal male suffrage, many working-class people joined with middle-class manufacturers in the Anti–Corn Law League, founded in Manchester in 1839. Mass participation made possible a popular crusade against the tariff on imported grain and against the landed aristocracy. People were fired up by dramatic popular orators such as John Bright and Richard Cobden. These fighting liberals argued that lower food prices and more jobs in industry depended on repeal of the Corn Laws. Much of the working class agreed. The climax of the movement came in 1845. In that year Ireland's potato crop failed, and rapidly rising food prices marked the beginning of the Irish famine. Famine prices for food and even

famine itself also seemed likely in England. To avert the impending catastrophe, the Tory prime minister Robert Peel joined with the Whigs and a minority of his own party to repeal the Corn Laws in 1846. England escaped famine. Thereafter, free trade became almost sacred doctrine in Great Britain.

The following year, the Tories passed a bill designed to help the working classes, but in a different way. This was the Ten Hours Act of 1847, which limited the workday for women and young people in factories to ten hours. Tory aristocrats continued to champion legislation regulating factory conditions. They were competing vigorously with the middle class for the support of the working class. This healthy competition between a still-vigorous aristocracy and a strong middle class was a crucial factor in Great Britain's peaceful evolution. The working classes could make temporary

Evictions of Irish Peasants who could not pay their rent continued for decades after the famine. Surrounded by a few meager possessions, this family has been turned out of its cottage in the 1880s. The door is nailed shut to prevent their return. *(Source: Lawrence Collection, National Library of Ireland, Dublin)*

alliances with either competitor to better their own conditions.

The people of Ireland did not benefit from this political competition. Long ruled as a conquered people, the great mass of the population (outside the northern counties of Ulster, which were partly Presbyterian) were Irish Catholic peasants who rented their land from a tiny minority of Church of England Protestants, many of whom lived in England (see page 642). Ruthlessly exploited and growing rapidly in numbers, Irish peasants depended on the potato crop, the size of which varied substantially from year to year. Potato failures cannot be detected in time to plant other crops, nor can potatoes be stored for more than a year. Moreover, Ireland's precarious potato economy was a subsistence economy, which therefore lacked a well-developed network of roads and trade capable of distributing other foods in time of disaster. When the crop failed in 1845, the Irish were very vulnerable.

In 1846, 1848, and 1851, the potato crop failed again in Ireland and throughout much of Europe. The general result was high food prices, widespread suffering, and, frequently, social upheaval. In Ireland, the result was unmitigated disaster— the Great Famine. Blight attacked the young plants, and the tubers rotted. Widespread starvation and mass fever epidemics followed. Total losses of population were staggering. Fully 1 million emigrants fled the famine between 1845 and 1851, going primarily to the United States and Great Britain, and at least 1.5 million people died or went unborn because of the disaster. The British government's efforts at famine relief were too little and too late. At the same time, the government energetically supported the heartless demands of landowners with armed force. Tenants who could not pay their rents were evicted and their homes broken up or burned. Famine or no, Ireland remained a conquered province, a poor agricultural land that had gained little from the liberal reforms and the industrial developments that were transforming Great Britain.

The Revolution of 1830 in France

Louis XVIII's Constitutional Charter of 1814—theoretically a gift from the king but actually a response to political pressures—was basically a liberal constitution (see page 822). The economic gains of the middle class and the prosperous peasantry were fully protected; great intellectual and artistic freedom was permitted; and a real parliament with upper and lower houses was created. Immediately after Napoleon's abortive Hundred Days, the moderate, worldly wise king refused to bow to the wishes of diehard aristocrats like his brother Charles, who wished to sweep away all the revolutionary changes and return to a bygone age of royal absolutism and aristocratic pretension. Instead, Louis appointed as his ministers moderate royalists who sought and obtained the support of a majority of the representatives elected to the lower Chamber of Deputies between 1816 and Louis's death in 1824.

Louis XVIII's charter was anything but democratic. Only about 100,000 of the wealthiest people out of a total population of 30 million had the right to vote for the deputies who, with the king and his ministers, made the laws of the nation. Nonetheless, the "notable people" who did vote came from very different backgrounds. There were wealthy businessmen, war profiteers, successful professionals, former revolutionaries, large landowners from the middle class, Bourbons, and Bonapartists.

The old aristocracy with its pre-1789 mentality was a minority within the voting population. It was this situation that Louis's successor, Charles X (r. 1824–1830), could not abide. Crowned in a lavish, utterly medieval, five-hour ceremony in the cathedral of Reims in 1824, Charles was a true reactionary. He wanted to re-establish the old order in France. Increasingly blocked by the opposition of the deputies, Charles finally repudiated the Constitutional Charter in an attempted coup in July 1830. He issued decrees stripping much of the wealthy middle class of its voting rights, and he censored the press. The reaction was an immediate insurrection. In "three glorious days" the government collapsed. Paris boiled with revolutionary excitement, and Charles fled. Then the upper middle class, which had fomented the revolt, skillfully seated Charles's cousin, Louis Philippe, duke of Orléans, on the vacant throne.

Louis Philippe (r. 1830–1848) accepted the Constitutional Charter of 1814, adopted the red, white, and blue flag of the French Revolution, and admitted that he was merely the "king of the French people." In spite of such symbolic actions, the situation in France remained fundamentally unchanged. Casimir Périer, a wealthy banker and

Delacroix: Liberty Leading the People This great romantic painting glorifies the July Revolution in Paris in 1830. Raising high the revolutionary tricolor, Liberty unites the worker, bourgeois, and street child in a righteous crusade against privilege and oppression. *(Source: Louvre/Cliché des Musées Nationaux, Paris)*

Louis Philippe's new chief minister, bluntly told a deputy who complained when the vote was extended only from 100,000 to 170,000 citizens, "The trouble with this country is that there are too many people like you who imagine that there has been a revolution in France."[5] The wealthy "notable" elite actually tightened its control as the old aristocracy retreated to the provinces to sulk harmlessly. For the upper middle class there had been a change in dynasty in order to protect the status quo and the narrowly liberal institutions of 1815. Republicans, democrats, social reformers, and the poor of Paris were bitterly disappointed.

They had constructed a revolution, but it seemed for naught.

THE REVOLUTIONS OF 1848

In 1848 revolutionary political and social ideologies combined with economic crisis and the romantic impulse to produce a vast upheaval. Only the most advanced and the most backward major countries—reforming Great Britain and immobile Russia—escaped untouched. Governments toppled; monarchs and ministers bowed or fled. National independence, liberal-democratic constitutions, and social reform: the lofty aspirations of a generation seemed at hand. Yet, in the end, the revolutions failed. Why was this so?

A Democratic Republic in France

The late 1840s in Europe were hard economically and tense politically. The potato famine in Ireland in 1845 and in 1846 had echoes on the Continent. Bad harvests jacked up food prices and caused misery and unemployment in the cities. "Prerevolutionary" outbreaks occurred all across Europe: an abortive Polish revolution in the northern part of Austria in 1846, a civil war between radicals and conservatives in Switzerland in 1847, and an armed uprising in Naples, Italy, in January 1848. Revolution was almost universally expected, but it took revolution in Paris—once again—to turn expectations into realities.

From its beginning in 1830, Louis Philippe's "bourgeois monarchy" was characterized by stubborn inaction. There was a glaring lack of social legislation, and politics was dominated by corruption and selfish special interests. The king's chief minister in the 1840s, François Guizot, was complacency personified. Guizot was especially satisfied with the electoral system. Only the rich could vote for deputies, and many of the deputies were docile government bureaucrats. It was the government's stubborn refusal to consider electoral reform that touched off popular revolt in Paris. Barricades went up on the night of February 22, 1848, and by February 24 Louis Philippe had abdicated in favor of his grandson. But the common people in arms would tolerate no more monarchy. This refusal led to the proclamation of a provisional republic headed by a ten-man executive committee and certified by cries of approval from the revolutionary crowd.

In the flush of victory, there was much about which Parisian revolutionaries could agree. A generation of historians and journalists had praised the First French Republic, and their work had borne fruit: the revolutionaries were firmly committed to a republic as opposed to any form of constitutional monarchy, and they immediately set about drafting a constitution for France's Second Republic. Moreover, they wanted a truly popular

and democratic republic so that the healthy, life-giving forces of the common people—the peasants and the workers—could reform society with wise legislation. In practice, building such a republic meant giving the right to vote to every adult male, and this was quickly done. Revolutionary compassion and sympathy for freedom were expressed in the freeing of all slaves in French colonies, abolition of the death penalty, and the establishment of a ten-hour workday for Paris.

Yet there were profound differences within the revolutionary coalition in Paris. On the one hand, there were the moderate, liberal republicans of the middle class. They viewed universal manhood suffrage as the ultimate concession to be made to popular forces, and they strongly opposed any further radical social measures. On the other hand were the radical republicans. Influenced by the critique of capitalism and unbridled individualism elaborated by a generation of utopian socialists, and appalled by the poverty and misery of the urban poor, the radical republicans were committed to socialism. To be sure, socialism came in many utopian shapes and sizes for the Parisian working poor and their leaders, but that did not make their commitment to it any less real. Finally, wedged in between these groups were individuals like the poet Lamartine and the democrat Alexandre Auguste Ledru-Rollin, who were neither doctrinaire socialists nor stand-pat liberals and who sought to escape an impending tragedy.

Worsening depression and rising unemployment brought these conflicting goals to the fore. Louis Blanc (see page 874), who along with a worker named Albert represented the republican socialists in the provisional government, pressed for recognition of a socialist right to work. Blanc asserted that permanent government-sponsored cooperative workshops should be established for workers. Such workshops would be an alternative to capitalist employment and a decisive step toward a new social order.

The moderate republicans wanted no such thing. They were willing to provide only temporary relief. The resulting compromise set up national workshops—soon to become a vast program of pick-and-shovel public works—and established a special commission under Louis Blanc to "study the question." This satisfied no one. As bad as the national workshops were, though, they were better than nothing. An army of desperate poor from the French provinces and even from foreign countries streamed into Paris to sign up. The number enrolled in the workshops soared from 10,000 in March to 120,000 by June, and another 80,000 were trying unsuccessfully to join.

While the workshops in Paris grew, the French masses went to the polls in late April. Voting in most cases for the first time, the people elected to the new Constituent Assembly about five hundred moderate republicans, three hundred monarchists, and one hundred radicals who professed various brands of socialism. One of the moderate republicans was the author of *Democracy in America,* Alexis de Tocqueville (1805–1859), who had predicted the overthrow of Louis Philippe's government. To this brilliant observer, socialism was the most characteristic aspect of the revolution in Paris.

This socialist revolution was evoking a violent reaction not only among the frightened middle and upper classes but also among the bulk of the population—the peasants. The French peasants owned land, and according to Tocqueville, "private property had become with all those who owned it a sort of bond of fraternity."[6] The countryside, Tocqueville wrote, had been seized with a universal hatred of radical Paris. Returning from Normandy to take his seat in the new Constituent Assembly, Tocqueville saw that a majority of the members were firmly committed to the republic and strongly opposed to the socialists, and he shared their sentiments.

The clash of ideologies—of liberal capitalism and socialism—became a clash of classes and arms after the elections. The new government's executive committee dropped Louis Blanc and thereafter included no representative of the Parisian working class. Fearing that their socialist hopes were about to be dashed, the workers invaded the Constituent Assembly on May 15 and tried to proclaim a new revolutionary state. But the government was ready and used the middle-class National Guard to squelch this uprising. As the workshops continued to fill and grow more radical, the fearful but powerful propertied classes in the Assembly took the offensive. On June 22 the government dissolved the national workshops in Paris, giving the workers the choice of joining the army or going to workshops in the provinces.

The result was a spontaneous and violent uprising. Frustrated in their attempts to create a socialist society, masses of desperate people were now

Daumier: The Legislative Belly   Protected by freedom of the press after 1830, French radicals bitterly attacked the do-nothing government of Louis Philippe. Here Daumier savagely ridicules the corruption of the Chamber of Deputies. *(Source: ©1990 The Art Institute of Chicago. All Rights Reserved)*

losing even their life-sustaining relief. As a voice from the crowd cried out when the famous astronomer François Arago counseled patience, "Ah, Monsieur Arago, you have never been hungry!"[7] Barricades sprang up in the narrow streets of Paris, and a terrible class war began. Working people fought with the courage of utter desperation, but the government had the army and the support of peasant France. After three terrible "June Days" and the death or injury of greater than ten thousand people, the republican army under General Louis Cavaignac stood triumphant in a sea of working-class blood and hatred.

The revolution in France thus ended in spectacular failure. The February coalition of the middle and working classes had in four short months become locked in mortal combat. In place of a generous democratic republic, the Constituent Assembly completed a constitution featuring a strong executive. This allowed Louis Napoleon, nephew of Napoleon Bonaparte, to win a landslide victory in the election of December 1848. The appeal of his great name, as well as the desire of the propertied classes for order at any cost, had produced a semi-authoritarian regime.

The Austrian Empire in 1848

Throughout central Europe, news of the upheaval in France evoked feverish excitement and eventually revolution. Liberals demanded written constitutions, representative government, and greater civil liberties. When governments hesitated, popular revolts followed. Urban workers and students served as the shock troops, but they were allied with middle-class liberals and peasants. In the face of this united front, monarchs collapsed and granted almost everything. The popular revolutionary coalition, having secured great and easy victories, then broke down as it had in France. The traditional forces—the monarchy, the aristocracy, and the regular army—recovered their nerve, reasserted their authority, and took back many though not all of the concessions. Reaction was everywhere victorious.

The revolution in the Austrian Empire began in Hungary. Nationalism had been growing among Hungarians since about 1790. In 1848, under the leadership of Louis Kossuth, the Hungarians demanded national autonomy, full civil liberties, and universal suffrage. When the monarchy in Vienna

hesitated, Viennese students and workers took to the streets on March 13 and added their own demands. Peasant disorders broke out in parts of the empire. The Habsburg emperor Ferdinand I (r. 1835–1848) capitulated and promised reforms and a liberal constitution. Metternich fled in disguise toward London. The old order seemed to be collapsing with unbelievable rapidity.

The coalition of revolutionaries was not completely stable, though. The Austrian Empire was overwhelmingly agricultural, and serfdom still existed. On March 20, as part of its capitulation before upheaval, the monarchy abolished serfdom with its degrading forced labor and feudal services. Peasants throughout the empire felt that they had won a victory reminiscent of that in France in 1789. Newly free, men and women of the land lost interest in the political and social questions agitating the cities. The government had in the peasants a potential ally of great importance, especially since, in central Europe as in France, the army was largely composed of peasants.

The coalition of March was also weakened—and ultimately destroyed—by conflicting national aspirations. In March the Hungarian revolutionary leaders pushed through an extremely liberal, almost democratic, constitution granting widespread voting rights and civil liberties and ending feudal obligations. So far, well and good. Yet the Hungarian revolutionaries were also nationalists with a mission. They wanted the ancient Crown of Saint Stephen, with its mosaic of provinces and nationalities, transformed into a unified, centralized Hungarian nation. To the minority groups that formed half of the population of the kingdom of Hungary—the Croats, the Serbs, and the Romanians—such unification was completely unacceptable. Each felt entitled to political autonomy and cultural independence. The Habsburg monarchy in Vienna exploited the fears of the minority groups, and they were soon locked in armed combat with the new Hungarian government.

In a somewhat different way, Czech nationalists based in Bohemia and the city of Prague, led by the Czech historian Palacký, came into conflict with German nationalists. Like the minorities in Hungary, the Czechs saw their struggle for autonomy as a struggle against a dominant group, the Germans. Thus the national aspirations of different peoples in the Austrian Empire came into sharp conflict, and the monarchy was able to play off one group against the other.

THE REVOLUTIONS OF 1848

February	Revolt in Paris against Louis Philippe's "bourgeois monarchy"; Louis Philippe abdicates; proclamation of a provisional republic
February–June	Establishment and rapid growth of government-sponsored workshops in France
March 3	Hungarians under Kossuth demand autonomy from Austrian Empire
March 13	Uprising of students and workers in Vienna; Metternich flees to London
March 19–21	Frederick William IV of Prussia is forced to salute the bodies of slain revolutionaries in Berlin and agrees to a liberal constitution and merger into a new German state
March 20	Ferdinand I of Austria abolishes serfdom and promises reforms
March 26	Workers in Berlin issue a series of socialist demands
April 22	French voters favor moderate republicans over radicals 5:1
May 15	Parisian socialist workers invade the Constitutional Assembly and unsuccessfully proclaim a new revolutionary state
May 18	Frankfurt National Assembly begins writing a new German constitution
June 17	Austrian army crushes working-class revolt in Prague
June 22–26	French government abolishes the national workshops, provoking an uprising
	June Days: republican army defeats rebellious Parisian working class
October	Austrian army besieges and retakes Vienna from students and working-class radicals
December	Conservatives force Ferdinand I of Austria to abdicate in favor of young Francis Joseph
	Frederick William IV disbands Prussian Constituent Assembly and grants Prussia a conservative constitution
	Louis Napoleon wins a landslide victory in French presidential elections
March 1849	Frankfurt Assembly elects Frederick William IV of Prussia emperor of the new German state; Frederick William refuses and reasserts royal authority in Prussia
June–August 1849	Habsburg and Russian forces defeat the Hungarian independence movement

Nor was this all. The urban working classes of poor artisans and day laborers were not as radical in the Austrian Empire as they were in France, but then neither were the middle class and lower middle class. Throughout Austria and the German states, where Metternich's brand of absolutism had so recently ruled supreme, the middle class wanted liberal reform, complete with constitutional monarchy, limited voting rights, and modest social measures. They wanted a central European equivalent of the English Reform Bill of 1832 and the Corn Laws repeal of 1846. When the urban poor rose in arms—as they did in the Austrian cities of Vienna, Prague, and Milan and throughout the German Confederation as well, presenting their own demands for socialist workshops and universal voting rights for men—the prosperous middle classes recoiled in alarm. As in Paris, the union of

the urban poor and the middle class was soon a mere memory, and a bad memory at that.

Finally, the conservative aristocratic forces gathered around Emperor Ferdinand I regained their nerve and reasserted their great strength. The archduchess Sophia, a conservative but intelligent and courageous Bavarian princess married to the emperor's brother, provided a rallying point. Deeply ashamed of the emperor's collapse before a "mess of students,"[8] she insisted that Ferdinand, who had no heir, abdicate in favor of her eighteen-year-old son, Francis Joseph. Powerful nobles who held high positions in the government, the army, and the church agreed completely. They organized around Sophia in a secret conspiracy to reverse and crush the revolution.

Their first breakthrough came when one of the most dedicated members of the group, Prince

Alfred Windischgrätz, bombarded Prague and savagely crushed a working-class revolt there on June 17. Other Austrian officials and nobles began to lead the minority nationalities of Hungary against the revolutionary government proclaimed by the Hungarian patriots. In late July 1848 another Austrian army reconquered Austria's possessions in northern Italy, where Italian patriots had seized power in March. Thus revolution failed as miserably in Italy as everywhere else. At the end of October, the well-equipped, predominantly peasant troops of the regular Austrian army attacked the student and working-class radicals in Vienna and retook the city at the cost of more than four thousand casualties. Thus the determination of the Austrian aristocracy and the loyalty of its army were the final ingredients in the triumph of reaction and the defeat of revolution.

Sophia's son Francis Joseph (r. 1848–1916) was crowned emperor of Austria immediately after his eighteenth birthday in December 1848. Only in Hungary were the Austrian forces at first unsuccessful in establishing control on the new emperor's behalf. Yet another determined conservative, Nicholas I of Russia (r. 1825–1855), obligingly lent his iron hand. On June 6, 1849, 130,000 Russian troops poured into Hungary. After bitter fighting—in which the Hungarian army supported the revolutionary Hungarian government—they subdued the country. For a number of years the Habsburgs ruled Hungary as a conquered territory.

Prussia and the Frankfurt Assembly

The rest of the states in the German Confederation generally recapitulated the ebb and flow of developments in France and Austria. The key difference was the additional goal of unifying the thirty-eight states of the German Confederation, with the possible exception of Austria, into a single sovereign nation. Thus events in Germany were extraordinarily complex, for they were occurring not only in the individual principalities but at the all-German level as well.

After Austria, Prussia was the largest and most influential German kingdom. Prior to 1848, the goal of middle-class Prussian liberals had been to transform absolutist Prussia into a liberal constitutional monarchy. Such a monarchy would then take the lead in merging itself and all the other

German states into a liberal, unified nation. The agitation following the fall of Louis Philippe encouraged Prussian liberals to press their demands. When these were not granted, the artisans and factory workers in Berlin exploded, joining temporarily with the middle-class liberals in the struggle against the monarchy. The autocratic yet paternalistic Frederick William IV (r. 1840–1861), already displaying the instability that later became insanity, vacillated. Humiliated by the revolutionary crowd, which forced him to salute from his balcony the blood-spattered corpses of workers who had fallen in an uprising on March 18, the nearly hysterical king finally caved in. On March 21 he promised to grant Prussia a liberal constitution and to merge it into a new national German state. He appointed two wealthy businessmen from the Rhineland—perfect representatives of moderate liberalism—to form a new government.

The situation might have stabilized at this point if the workers had not wanted much more and the Prussian aristocracy much less. On March 26 the workers issued a series of radical and vaguely socialist demands that troubled their middle-class allies: universal voting rights, a ministry of labor, a minimum wage, and a ten-hour day. At the same time, a wild-tempered Prussian landowner and aristocrat, Otto von Bismarck, joined the conservative clique gathered around the king to urge counter-revolution. While these tensions in Prussia were growing, an elected assembly met in Berlin to write a constitution for the Prussian state.

To add to the complexity of the situation, a self-appointed committee of liberals from various German states successfully called for the formation of a national constituent assembly to begin writing a federal constitution for a unified German state. That body met for the first time on May 18 in Saint Paul's Church in Frankfurt. The Frankfurt National Assembly was a most curious revolutionary body. It was really a serious middle-class body whose 820 members included some 200 lawyers; 100 professors; many doctors, judges, and officials; and 140 businessmen for good measure.

Convened to write a constitution, the learned body was soon absorbed in a battle with Denmark over the provinces of Schleswig and Holstein. Jurisdiction over them was a hopelessly complicated issue from a legal point of view. Britain's foreign minister Lord Palmerston once said that only three people had ever understood the Schleswig-Holstein question, and of those one had died, another had gone mad, and he himself had forgotten the answer. The provinces were inhabited primarily by Germans but were ruled by the king of Denmark, although Holstein was a member of the German Confederation. When Frederick VII, the new nationalistic king of Denmark, tried to integrate both provinces into the rest of his state, the Germans there revolted.

Hypnotized by this conflict, the National Assembly at Frankfurt debated ponderously and fi-

nally called on the Prussian army to oppose Denmark in the name of the German nation. Prussia responded and began war with Denmark. As the Schleswig-Holstein issue demonstrated, the national ideal was a crucial factor motivating the German middle classes in 1848.

Almost obsessed with the fate of Germans under Danish rule, many members of the National Assembly also wanted to bring the German-speaking provinces of Austria into the new German state.

Revolutionary Justice in Vienna   As part of the conservative resurgence, in October 1848 the Austrian minister of war ordered up reinforcements for an army marching on Hungary. In a last defiant gesture the outraged revolutionaries in Vienna seized the minister and lynched him from a lamppost for treason. The army then reconquered the city in a week of bitter fighting. *(Source: Mary Evans Picture Library/Photo Researchers)*

Yet resurgent Austria resolutely opposed any division of its territory. Once this Austrian action made a "big German state" impossible, the National Assembly completed its drafting of a liberal constitution. Finally, in March 1849, the Assembly elected King Frederick William of Prussia emperor of the new German national state (minus Austria and Schleswig-Holstein).

By early 1849, however, reaction had been successful almost everywhere. Frederick William reasserted his royal authority, disbanded the Prussian Constituent Assembly, and granted his subjects a limited, essentially conservative, constitution. Reasserting that he ruled by divine right, Frederick William contemptuously refused to accept the "crown from the gutter." The reluctant revolutionaries in Frankfurt had waited too long and acted too timidly.

When Frederick William, who really wanted to be emperor but only on his own authoritarian terms, tried to get the small monarchs of Germany to elect him emperor, Austria balked. Supported by Russia, Austria forced Prussia to renounce all its schemes of unification in late 1850. The German Confederation was re-established. After two turbulent years, the political map of the German states remained unchanged. Attempts to unite the Germans—first in a liberal national state and then in a conservative Prussian empire—had failed completely.

SUMMARY

In 1814 the victorious allied powers sought to restore peace and stability in Europe. Dealing moderately with France and wisely settling their own differences, the allies laid the foundations for beneficial international cooperation throughout much of the nineteenth century. Led by Metternich, the conservative powers also sought to prevent the spread of subversive ideas and radical changes in domestic politics. Yet European thought has seldom been more powerfully creative than after 1815, and ideologies of liberalism, nationalism, and socialism all developed to challenge the existing order. The romantic movement, breaking decisively with the dictates of classicism, reinforced the spirit of change and revolutionary anticipation.

All of these forces culminated in the liberal and nationalistic revolutions of 1848. Political, economic, and social pressures that had been building since 1815 exploded dramatically, but the upheavals of 1848 were abortive and very few revolutionary goals were realized. The moderate, nationalistic middle classes were unable to consolidate their initial victories in France or elsewhere in Europe. Instead, they drew back when artisans, factory workers, and radical socialists rose up to present their own much more revolutionary demands. This retreat facilitated the efforts of dedicated aristocrats in central Europe and made possible the crushing of Parisian workers by a coalition of solid bourgeoisie and landowning peasantry in France. A host of fears, a sea of blood, and a torrent of disillusion had drowned the lofty ideals and utopian visions of a generation. The age of romantic revolution was over.

NOTES

1. Quoted in A. J. May, *The Age of Metternich, 1814–1848,* rev. ed. (New York: Holt, Rinehart & Winston, 1963), p. 11.
2. Quoted in H. Kohn, *Nationalism* (New York: Van Nostrand, 1955), pp. 141–142.
3. Quoted in F. D. Klingender, *Art and the Industrial Revolution* (St. Albans, England: Paladin, 1972), p. 117.
4. Quoted in F. B. Artz, *From the Renaissance to Romanticism: Trends in Style in Art, Literature, and Music, 1300–1830* (Chicago: University of Chicago Press, 1962), pp. 276, 278.
5. Quoted in G. Wright, *France in Modern Times* (Chicago: Rand McNally, 1960), p. 145.
6. A. de Tocqueville, *Recollections* (New York: Columbia University Press, 1949), p. 94.
7. M. Agulhon, *1848* (Paris: Éditions du Seuil, 1973), pp. 68–69.
8. Quoted in W. L. Langer, *Political and Social Upheaval, 1832–1852* (New York: Harper & Row, 1969), p. 361.

SUGGESTED READING

All of the works cited in the Notes are highly recommended. May's book is a good brief survey, and Kohn has written perceptively on nationalism in many books. Wright's *France in Modern Times* is a lively introduction to French history with stimulating biographical discussions; Langer's work is a balanced synthesis with an excellent bibliography. Among general studies, C. Moraze, *The Triumph of the Middle Classes* (1968), a wide-ranging procapitalist interpretation, may be compared with E. J. Hobsbawm's flexible *Marxism in the Age of Revolution, 1789–1848* (1962). For English history, A. Briggs, socially oriented *The Making of Modern England, 1784–1867* (1967), and D. Thomson, *England in the Nineteenth Century, 1815–1914* (1951), are excellent. Restoration France is sympathetically portrayed by G. de Bertier de Sauvigny in *The Bourbon Restoration* (1967), and R. Price, *A Social History of Nineteenth-Century France* (1987), is a fine synthesis incorporating recent research. T. Hamerow studies the social implications of the dual revolution in *Germany in Restoration, Revolution, Reaction 1815–1871* (1966), which may be compared with H. Treitschke's bombastic, pro-Prussian *History of Germany in the Nineteenth Century* (1915–1919), a classic of nationalistic history, and L. Snyder, *Roots of German Nationalism* (1978). H. James, *A German Identity, 1770–1990* (1989), and J. Sheehan, *Germany, 1770–1866* (1989), are stimulating general histories that skillfully incorporate recent research. E. Kedourie, *Nationalism* (1960), is a stimulating critique of the new faith. H. Kissinger, *A World Restored* (1957), offers not only a provocative interpretation of the Congress of Vienna but also insights into the mind of Richard Nixon's famous secretary of state. Compare that volume with H. Nicolson's entertaining *The Congress of Vienna* (1946). On 1848, L. B. Namier's highly critical *1848: The Revolution of the Intellectuals* (1964) and P. Robertson's *Revolutions of 1848: A Social History* (1960) are outstanding. I. Deak, *The Lawful Revolution: Louis Kossuth and the Hungarians, 1848–49* (1979), is a noteworthy study of an interesting figure.

On early socialism and Marxism, there are A. Lindemann's stimulating survey, *A History of European Socialism* (1983), and W. Sewell Jr.'s *Work and Revolution in France: The Language of Labor from the Old Regime to 1848* (1980), as well as G. Lichtheim's high-powered *Marxism* (1961) and his *Short History of Socialism* (1970). Fourier is treated sympathetically in J. Beecher, *Charles Fourier* (1986). J. Schumpeter, *Capitalism, Socialism and Democracy* (1947), is magnificent but difficult, a real mind-stretcher. Also highly recommended is B. Taylor, *Eve and the New Jerusalem: Socialism and Feminism in the Nineteenth Century* (1983), which explores fascinating English attempts to emancipate workers and women at the same time. On liberalism, there are R. Heilbroner's entertaining *The Worldly Philosophers* (1967) and G. de Ruggiero's classic *History of European Liberalism* (1959). J. Barzun, *Classic, Romantic and Modern* (1961), skillfully discusses the emergence of romanticism. R. Stromberg, *An Intellectual History of Modern Europe,* 3d ed. (1981), and F. Baumer, *Modern European Thought: Continuity and Change in Ideas, 1600–1950* (1970), are valuable surveys. The important place of religion in nineteenth-century thought is considered from different perspectives in H. McLeod, *Religion and the People of Western Europe* (1981), and O. Chadwick, *The Secularization of the European Mind in the Nineteenth Century* (1976). Two good church histories with useful bibliographies are J. Altholz, *The Churches in the Nineteenth Century* (1967), and A. Vidler, *The Church in an Age of Revolution: 1789 to the Present Day* (1961).

The thoughtful reader is strongly advised to delve into the incredibly rich writing of contemporaries. J. Bowditch and C. Ramsland, eds., *Voices of the Industrial Revolution* (1961), is an excellent starting point, with well-chosen selections from leading economic thinkers and early socialists. H. Hugo, ed., *The Romantic Reader,* is another fine anthology. Mary Shelley's *Frankenstein,* a great romantic novel, draws an almost lovable picture of the famous monster and is highly recommended. Jules Michelet's compassionate masterpiece *The People,* a famous historian's anguished examination of French social divisions on the eve of 1848, draws one into the heart of the period and is highly recommended. Alexis de Tocqueville covers some of the same ground less romantically in his *Recollections,* which may be compared with Karl Marx's white-hot "instant history," *Class Struggles in France, 1848–1850* (1850). Great novels that accurately portray aspects of the times are Victor Hugo, *Les Misérables,* an exciting story of crime and passion among France's poor; Honoré de Balzac, *La Cousine Bette* and *Le Père Goriot;* and Thomas Mann, *Buddenbrooks,* a wonderful historical novel that traces the rise and fall of a prosperous German family over three generations during the nineteenth century.

28

Life in European Urban Society

Nineteenth-century London. John O'Connor, *St. Pancras Hotel and Station from Pentonville Road*

The era of intellectual and political upheaval that culminated in the revolutions of 1848 was also an era of rapid urbanization. After 1848, Western political development veered off in a novel and uncharted direction, but the growth of towns and cities rushed forward with undiminished force. Thus Western society was urban and industrial in 1900, as surely as it had been rural and agrarian in 1800. The urbanization of society was both a result of the Industrial Revolution and a reflection of its enormous long-term impact.

- What was life like in the cities, and how did it change?
- What did the emergence of urban industrial society mean for rich and poor and those in between?
- How did families cope with the challenges and respond to the opportunities of the developing urban civilization?
- What changes in science and thought inspired and gave expression to this new urban society?

These questions are investigated in this chapter.

TAMING THE CITY

The growth of industry posed enormous challenges for all elements of Western society, from young factory workers confronting relentless discipline to aristocratic elites maneuvering to retain political power. As we saw in Chapter 26, the early consequences of economic transformation were mixed and far-reaching and by no means wholly negative. By 1850 at the latest, working conditions were improving and real wages were definitely rising for the mass of the population, and they continued to do so until 1914. Thus, given the poverty and uncertainty of preindustrial life, some historians maintain that the history of industrialization in the nineteenth century is probably better written in terms of increasing opportunities than of greater hardships.

Critics of this relatively optimistic view of industrialization claim that it neglects the quality of life in urban areas. They stress that the new industrial towns and cities were awful places, where people,

especially poor people, suffered from bad housing, lack of sanitation, and a sense of hopelessness. They ask if these drawbacks did not more than cancel out higher wages and greater opportunity. An examination of urban development provides some answers to this complex question.

Industry and the Growth of Cities

Since the Middle Ages, European cities had been centers of government, culture, and large-scale commerce. They had also been congested, dirty, and unhealthy. People were packed together almost as tightly as possible within the city limits. The typical city was a "walking city": for all but the wealthiest classes, walking was the only available form of transportation.

Infectious disease spread with deadly speed in cities, and people were always more likely to die in the city than in the countryside. In the larger towns, more people died each year than were born, on the average, and urban populations were able to maintain their numbers only because newcomers were continuously arriving from rural areas. Little could be done to improve these conditions. Given the pervasive poverty, absence of urban transportation, and lack of medical knowledge, the deadly and overcrowded conditions could only be accepted fatalistically. They were the urban equivalents of bad weather and poor crops, the price of urban excitement and opportunity.

Clearly, deplorable urban conditions did not originate with the Industrial Revolution. What the Industrial Revolution did was to reveal those conditions more nakedly than ever before. The steam engine freed industrialists from dependence on the energy of fast-flowing streams and rivers, so that by 1800 there was every incentive to build new factories in urban areas. Cities had better shipping facilities than the countryside and thus better supplies of coal and raw materials. There were also many hands wanting work in the cities, for cities drew people like a magnet. And it was a great advantage for a manufacturer to have other factories nearby to supply the business's needs and buy its products. Therefore, as industry grew, there was also a rapid expansion of already overcrowded and unhealthy cities.

The challenge of the urban environment was felt first and most acutely in Great Britain. The number of people living in cities of 20,000 or more in

MAP 28.1 European Cities of 100,000 or More, 1800 and 1900 There were more large cities in Great Britain in 1900 than in all of Europe in 1800.

England and Wales jumped from 1.5 million in 1801 to 6.3 million in 1851 and reached 15.6 million by 1891. Such cities accounted for 17 percent of the total English population in 1801, for 35 percent as early as 1851, and for fully 54 percent in 1891. Other countries duplicated the English pattern as they industrialized. An American observer was hardly exaggerating when he wrote in 1899 that "the most remarkable social phenomenon of the present century is the concentration of population in cities" (Map 28.1).[1]

In the 1820s and 1830s, people in Britain and France began to worry about the condition of their cities. In those years, the populations of a number of British cities were increasing by 40 to 70 percent each decade. With urban areas expanding at such previously undreamed-of rates, people's fatalistic acceptance of overcrowded, unsanitary urban living conditions began to give way to active concern. Something had to be done.

On one point everyone could agree: except on the outskirts, each town and city was using every scrap of land to the fullest extent. Parks and open areas were almost nonexistent. A British parliamentary committee reported in 1833 that "with a rapidly increasing population, lodged for the most part in narrow courts and confined streets, the means of occasional exercise and recreation in fresh air are every day lessened, as inclosures [of vacant areas] take place and buildings spread themselves on every side."[2] Buildings were erected on the smallest possible lots in order to pack the maximum number of people into a given space. Narrow houses were built wall to wall, in long rows. These row houses had neither front nor back yards, and only a narrow alley in back separated one row from the next. Or buildings were built around tiny courtyards completely enclosed on all four sides. Many people lived in cellars and attics. These tiny rooms were often overcrowded. "Six, eight, and even ten occupying one room is anything but uncommon," wrote a doctor from Aberdeen in Scotland for a government investigation in 1842.

These highly concentrated urban populations lived in extremely unsanitary and unhealthy conditions. Open drains and sewers flowed alongside or down the middle of unpaved streets. Because of poor construction and an absence of running water, the sewers often filled with garbage and excrement. Toilet facilities were primitive in the extreme. In parts of Manchester, as many as two hundred people shared a single outhouse. Such privies filled up rapidly, and since they were infrequently emptied, sewage often overflowed and seeped into cellar dwellings.

The extent to which filth lay underfoot and the smell of excrement filled the air is hard to believe,

A COURT FOR KING CHOLERA.

Filth and Disease This 1852 drawing from *Punch* tells volumes about the unhealthy living conditions of the urban poor. In the foreground children play with a dead rat and a woman scavenges a dungheap. Cheap rooming houses provide shelter for the frightfully overcrowded population. *(Source: The British Library)*

yet it was abundantly documented between 1830 and 1850. One London construction engineer found, for example, that the cellars of two large houses on a major road were "full of night-soil [human excrement], to the depth of three feet, which had been permitted for years to accumulate from the overflow of the cesspools." Moreover, some courtyards in poorer neighborhoods became dunghills, collecting excrement that was sometimes sold as fertilizer. In the provocative words of a leading historian, by the 1840s there was among the better-off classes a growing, shocking "realization that, to put it as mildly as possible, millions of English men, women, and children were living in shit."[3]

Who or what was responsible for these awful conditions? The crucial factors were the tremendous pressure of more people and the total ab-

sence of public transportation. People simply had to jam themselves together if they were to be able to walk to shops and factories. Another factor was that government in Great Britain, both local and national, was slow to provide sanitary facilities and establish adequate building codes. This slow pace was probably attributable more to a need to explore and identify what precisely should be done than to rigid middle-class opposition to government action. Certainly Great Britain had no monopoly on overcrowded and unhealthy urban conditions; many continental cities were as bad.

Most responsible of all was the sad legacy of rural housing conditions in preindustrial society, combined with appalling ignorance. As the author of a major study concludes, there "were rural slums of a horror not surpassed by the rookeries of London. . . . The evidence shows that the decent cottage was the exception, the hovel the rule."[4] Thus housing was far down on the newcomer's list of priorities, and it is not surprising that many people carried the filth of the mud floor and the dung of the barnyard with them to the city.

Indeed, ordinary people generally took dirt and filth for granted, and some even prized it. One English miner told an investigator, "I do not think it usual for the lasses [in the coal mines] to wash their bodies; my sisters never wash themselves." As for the men, "their legs and bodies are as black as your hat." When poor people were admitted to English workhouses, they often resisted the required bath. One man protested that it was "equal to robbing him of a great coat which he had had for some years."[5]

The Public Health Movement

Although cleanliness was not next to godliness in most people's eyes, it was becoming so for some reformers. The most famous of these was Edwin Chadwick, one of the commissioners charged with the administration of relief to paupers under the revised Poor Law of 1834. Chadwick was a follower of the radical philosopher Jeremy Bentham (1748–1832). Bentham had taught that public problems ought to be dealt with on a rational, scientific basis and according to the "greatest good for the greatest number." Applying these principles, Chadwick soon saw that much more than economics was involved in the problems of poverty and the welfare budget. Indeed, he soon became convinced that disease and death actually caused poverty, simply because a sick worker was an unemployed worker and orphaned children were poor children. Most important, Chadwick believed that disease could be prevented by quite literally cleaning up the urban environment. That was his "sanitary idea."

Building on a growing number of medical and sociological studies, Chadwick collected detailed reports from local Poor Law officials on the "sanitary conditions of the laboring population." After three years of investigation, these reports and Chadwick's hard-hitting commentary were published in 1842 to wide publicity. This mass of evidence proved that disease was related to filthy environmental conditions, which were in turn caused largely by lack of drainage, sewers, and garbage collection. Putrefying, smelly excrement was no longer simply disgusting. For reformers like Chadwick, it was a threat to the entire community. It polluted the atmosphere and caused disease.

The key to the energetic action that Chadwick proposed was an adequate supply of clean piped water. Such water was essential for personal hygiene, public bathhouses, street cleaning, firefighting, and industry. Chadwick correctly believed that the stinking excrement of communal outhouses could be carried off by water through sewers at less than one-twentieth the cost of removing it by hand. The cheap iron pipes and tile drains of the industrial age would provide running water and sewerage for all sections of town, not just the wealthy ones. In 1848, with the cause strengthened by the cholera epidemic of 1846, Chadwick's report became the basis of Great Britain's first public health law, which created a national health board and gave cities broad authority to build modern sanitary systems.

The public health movement won dedicated supporters in the United States, France, and Germany from the 1840s on. As in Great Britain, governments accepted at least limited responsibility for the health of all citizens. Moreover, they adopted increasingly concrete programs of action, programs that broke decisively with the age-old fatalism of urban populations in the face of shockingly high mortality. Thus, despite many people's skepticism about sanitation, European cities were making real progress toward adequate water supplies and sewage systems by the 1860s and 1870s. And city dwellers were beginning to reap the reward of better health.

The Bacterial Revolution

Effective control of communicable disease required a great leap forward in medical knowledge and biological theory as well as a clean water supply and good sewers. Reformers like Chadwick were seriously handicapped by the prevailing *miasmatic theory* of disease—the belief that people contract disease when they breathe the bad odors of decay and putrefying excrement; in short, the theory that smells cause disease. The miasmatic theory was a reasonable deduction from empirical observations: cleaning up filth did produce laudable results. Yet the theory was very incomplete.

Keen observation by doctors and public health officials in the 1840s and 1850s pinpointed the role of bad drinking water in the transmission of disease and suggested that contagion was spread through filth and not caused by it. Moreover, some particularly horrid stenches, such as that of the sewage-glutted Thames River at London in 1858, did not lead to widely feared epidemics, and this fact also weakened the miasmatic idea.

The breakthrough was the development of the *germ theory* of disease by Louis Pasteur (1822–1895), a French chemist who began studying fermentation in 1854. For ages people had used fermentation to make bread and wine, beer and cheese, but without really understanding what was going on. And from time to time, beer and wine would mysteriously spoil for no apparent reason. Responding to the calls of big brewers for help, Pasteur used his microscope to develop a simple test that brewers could use to monitor the fermentation process and avoid spoilage. Continuing his investigations, Pasteur found that fermentation depended on the growth of living organisms and that the activity of these organisms could be sup-

FIGURE 28.1 The Decline of Death Rates in England and Wales, Germany, France, and Sweden, 1840–1913 A rising standard of living, improvements in public health, and better medical knowledge all contributed to the dramatic decline of death rates in the nineteenth century.

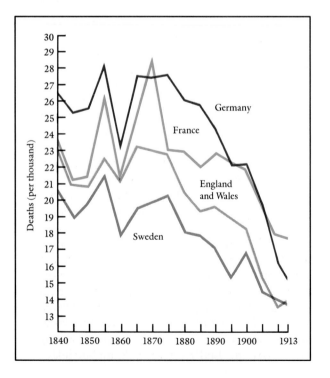

pressed by heating the beverage—by pasteurizing it. The breathtaking implication was that specific diseases were caused by specific living organisms—germs—and that those organisms could be controlled in people as well as in beer, wine, and milk.

By 1870 the work of Pasteur and others had demonstrated the general connection between germs and disease. When, in the middle of the 1870s, the German country doctor Robert Koch and his coworkers developed pure cultures of harmful bacteria and described their life cycles, the dam broke. Over the next twenty years, researchers—mainly Germans—identified the organisms responsible for disease after disease, often identifying several in a single year. These discoveries led to the development of a number of effective vaccines and the emergence of modern immunology.

Acceptance of the germ theory brought about dramatic improvements in the deadly environment of hospitals and surgery. The English surgeon Joseph Lister (1827–1912) had noticed that patients with simple fractures were much less likely to die than those with compound fractures, in which the skin was broken and internal tissues were exposed to the air. In 1865, when Pasteur showed that the air was full of bacteria, Lister immediately grasped the connection between aerial bacteria and the problem of wound infection. He reasoned that a chemical disinfectant applied to a wound dressing would "destroy the life of the floating particles." Lister's "antiseptic principle" worked wonders. In the 1880s, German surgeons developed the more sophisticated practice of sterilizing not only the wound but everything—hands, instruments, clothing—that entered the operating room.

The achievements of the bacterial revolution coupled with the ever-more-sophisticated public health movement saved millions of lives, particularly after about 1890. As the awful death sentences of the past—diphtheria, typhoid and typhus, cholera, yellow fever—became vanishing diseases, mortality rates began to decline dramatically in European countries (Figure 28.1). City dwellers benefited especially from these developments. By 1910 the death rates for people of all ages in urban areas were generally no greater than in rural areas, and sometimes they were less. Particularly striking was the decline in infant mortality in the cities after 1890. By 1910, in many countries, an urban mother was less likely than a rural mother to see her child die before its first birthday. A great silent revolution had occurred: the terrible ferocity of death from disease-carrying bacteria in the cities had almost been tamed.

Urban Planning and Public Transportation

Public health was only part of the urban challenge. Overcrowding, bad housing, and lack of transportation could not be solved by sewers and better medicine; yet in these areas, too, important transformations significantly improved the quality of urban life after midcentury.

More effective urban planning was one of the keys to improvement. Urban planning was in decline by the early nineteenth century, but after 1850 its practice was revived and extended. France took the lead during the rule of Napoleon III (r. 1848–1870), who sought to stand above class conflict and promote the welfare of all his subjects through government action (see pages 930–933). He believed that rebuilding much of Paris would provide employment, improve living conditions, and testify to the power and glory of his empire. In the baron Georges Haussmann, an aggressive, impatient Alsatian whom he placed in charge of Paris, Napoleon III found an authoritarian planner capable of bulldozing both buildings and opposition. In twenty years Paris was quite literally transformed (Map 28.2).

The Paris of 1850 was a labyrinth of narrow, dark streets, the results of desperate overcrowding. In a central city not twice the size of New York's Central Park lived more than one-third of the city's one million inhabitants. Terrible slum conditions and extremely high death rates were facts of life. There were few open spaces and only two public parks for the entire metropolis. Public transportation played a very small role in this enormous walking city.

Haussmann and his fellow planners proceeded on many interrelated fronts. With a bold energy that often shocked their contemporaries, they razed old buildings in order to cut broad, straight, tree-lined boulevards through the center of the city as well as in new quarters on the outskirts. These boulevards, designed in part to prevent the easy construction and defense of barricades by revolutionary crowds, permitted traffic to flow freely. Their creation also demolished some of the worst slums. New streets stimulated the construction of better housing, especially for the middle classes. Small neighborhood parks and open spaces were created throughout the city, and two very large parks suitable for all kinds of holiday activities were developed on either side of the city. The city also improved its sewers, and a system of aqueducts more than doubled the city's supply of good fresh water.

Haussmann and Napoleon III tried to make Paris a more beautiful city, and to a large extent they succeeded. The broad, straight boulevards, such as those radiating out like the spokes of a wheel from the Arch of Triumph and those centering on the new Opera House, afforded impressive vistas. If for most people Paris remains one of the world's most beautiful and enchanting cities, it is in part because of the transformations of Napoleon III's Second Empire.

Rebuilding Paris provided a new model for urban planning and stimulated modern urbanism throughout Europe, particularly after 1870. In city after city, public authorities mounted a coordinated attack on many of the interrelated problems of the urban environment. As in Paris, improvements in public health through better water supplies and waste disposal often went hand in hand with new boulevard construction. Cities like Vienna and Cologne followed the Parisian example of tearing down old walled fortifications and replacing them with broad, circular boulevards on which office buildings, town halls, theaters, opera houses, and museums were erected. These ring roads and the new boulevards that radiated out from them toward the outskirts eased movement and encouraged urban expansion (see Map 28.2).

The development of mass public transportation was also of great importance in the improvement of urban living conditions. Such transportation came late but in a powerful rush. In the 1870s, many European cities authorized private companies to operate horse-drawn streetcars, which had been developed in the United States, to carry riders along the growing number of major thoroughfares. Then, in the 1890s, occurred the real revolution: European countries adopted another American transit innovation, the electric streetcar.

Electric streetcars were cheaper, faster, more dependable, and more comfortable than their horse-drawn counterparts. Service improved dramatically. Millions of Europeans—workers, shoppers, schoolchildren—hopped on board during the workweek. And on weekends and holidays,

Apartment Living in Paris This drawing shows how different social classes lived close together in European cities about 1850. Passing the middle-class family on the first (American second) floor, the economic condition of the tenants declined until one reached abject poverty in the garret. *(Source: Bibliothèque Nationale, Paris)*

MAP 28.2 The Modernization of Paris, ca 1850–1870 Broad boulevards, large parks, and grandiose train stations transformed Paris. The cutting of the new north-south axis—known as the Boulevard Saint-Michel—was one of Haussmann's most controversial projects. It razed much of Paris's medieval core and filled the Île de la Cité with massive government buildings.

streetcars carried millions on happy outings to parks and countryside, racetracks and music halls. In 1886 the horse-drawn streetcars of Austria-Hungary, France, Germany, and Great Britain were carrying about 900 million riders. By 1910 electric streetcar systems in those four countries were carrying 6.7 billion riders. Each man, woman, and child was using public transportation four times as often in 1910 as in 1886.[6]

Good mass transit helped greatly in the struggle for decent housing. The new boulevards and horse-drawn streetcars had facilitated a middle-class move to better housing in the 1860s and 1870s; similarly, after 1890, electric streetcars gave people of modest means access to new, improved housing. The still-crowded city was able to expand and become less congested. In England in 1901, only 9 percent of the urban population was "overcrowded" in terms of the official definition of more than two persons per room. On the Continent, many city governments in the early twentieth century were building electric streetcar systems that provided transportation for the working classes to new public and private housing developments in outlying areas of the city. Poor, overcrowded housing, long one of the blackest blots on the urban landscape, was in retreat—another example of the gradual taming of the urban environment.

RICH AND POOR AND IN BETWEEN

General improvements in health and in the urban environment had beneficial consequences for all kinds of people. Yet differences in living conditions between social classes remained gigantic.

Social Structure

How much had the almost-completed journey to an urban, industrialized world changed the social framework of rich and poor? The first great change was a substantial and undeniable increase in the standard of living for the average person. The real wages of British workers, for example, which had already risen by 1850, almost doubled between 1850 and 1906. Similar unmistakable increases occurred in continental countries as industrial development quickened after 1850. Ordinary people took a major step forward in the centuries-old battle against poverty, reinforcing efforts to improve many aspects of human existence.

There is another side to the income coin, however, and it must be stressed as well. Greater economic rewards for the average person did not eliminate poverty, nor did they make the wealth and income of the rich and the poor significantly more nearly equal. In almost every advanced country around 1900, the richest 5 percent of all households in the population received one-third of all national income. The richest one-fifth of households received anywhere from 50 to 60 percent of all national income, and the entire bottom four-fifths received only 40 to 50 percent. Moreover, the bottom 30 percent of households received 10 percent or less of all income. These

enormous differences are illustrated in Figure 28.2.

The middle classes, smaller than they are today, accounted for less than 20 percent of the population; thus the statistics show that the upper and middle classes alone received more than one-half of all income. The poorest four-fifths—the working classes, including peasants and agricultural laborers—received less altogether than the two richest classes. And since many wives and teenagers in poor families worked for wages, these figures actually understate the enduring gap between rich and poor. Moreover, income taxes on the wealthy were light or nonexistent. Thus the gap between rich and poor remained enormous at the beginning of the twentieth century. It was probably almost as great as it had been in the age of agriculture and aristocracy, before the Industrial Revolution.

The great gap between rich and poor endured, in part, because industrial and urban development made society more diverse and less unified. By no means did society split into two sharply defined opposing classes, as Marx had predicted. Instead, economic specialization enabled society to produce more effectively and in the process created more new social groups than it destroyed. There developed an almost unlimited range of jobs, skills, and earnings; one group or subclass shaded off into another in a complex, confusing hierarchy. Thus the tiny elite of the very rich and the sizable mass of the dreadfully poor were separated from each other by many subclasses, each filled with individuals struggling to rise or at least to hold their own in the social order. In this atmosphere of competition and hierarchy, neither the middle classes nor the working classes acted as a unified force. The age-old pattern of great economic inequality remained firmly intact.

The Middle Classes

By the beginning of the twentieth century, the diversity and range within the urban middle class were striking. Indeed, it is more meaningful to think of a confederation of middle classes, loosely united by occupations requiring mental rather than physical skill. At the top stood the *upper middle class,* composed mainly of the most successful business families from banking, industry, and large-scale commerce. These families were the prime beneficiaries of modern industry and scientific progress. As people in the upper middle class gained in income and progressively lost all traces of radicalism after the trauma of 1848, they were strongly drawn toward the aristocratic lifestyle.

As the aristocracy had long divided the year between palatial country estates and lavish townhouses during "the season," so the upper middle class purchased country places or built beach houses for weekend and summer use. (Little wonder that a favorite scenario in late-nineteenth-century middle-class novels was a mother and children summering gloriously in the country home, with only sporadic weekend intrusions by a distant, shadowy father.) The number of servants was an important indicator of wealth and standing for the middle class, as it had always been for the aristocracy. Private coaches and carriages, ever an expensive item in the city, were also signs of rising social status. More generally, the rich businessman and certainly his son devoted less time to business and more to "culture" and easy living than was the case in less wealthy or well-established commercial families.

The topmost reaches of the upper middle class tended to shade off into the old aristocracy to form a new upper class. This was the 5 percent of the population that received roughly one-third of the national income in European countries before 1914. Much of the aristocracy welcomed this development. Having experienced a sharp decline in its relative income in the course of industrialization, the landed aristocracy had met big business coming up the staircase and was often delighted to trade titles, country homes, and snobbish elegance for good hard cash. Some of the best bargains were made through marriages to American heiresses. Correspondingly, wealthy aristocrats tended increasingly to exploit their agricultural and mineral resources as if they were business people. Bismarck was not the only proud nobleman to make a fortune distilling brandy on his estates.

Below the wealthy upper middle class were much larger, much less wealthy, and increasingly diversified middle-class groups. Here one found the moderately successful industrialists and merchants, as well as professionals in law and medicine. This was the *middle middle class,* solid and quite comfortable but lacking great wealth. Below them were independent shopkeepers, small traders, and tiny manufacturers—the *lower middle class.* Both of these traditional segments of the

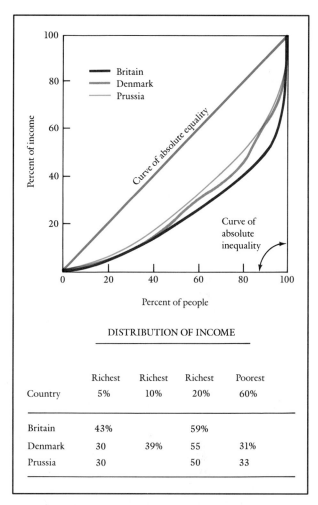

DISTRIBUTION OF INCOME

Country	Richest 5%	Richest 10%	Richest 20%	Poorest 60%
Britain	43%		59%	
Denmark	30	39%	55	31%
Prussia	30		50	33

FIGURE 28.2 The Distribution of Income in Britain, Denmark, and Prussia in 1913 The so-called Lorenz curve is useful for showing the degree of economic inequality in a given society. The closer the actual distribution of income lies to the (theoretical) curve of absolute equality, where each 20 percent of the population receives 20 percent of all income, the more nearly equal are incomes. European society was very far from any such equality before the First World War. Notice that incomes in Prussia were somewhat more equal than those in Britain. *(Source: Based on information from S. Kuznets,* Modern Economic Growth, *Yale University Press, New Haven, 1966, pp. 208–209. Copyright © 1966 by Yale University Press. Used with permission.)*

middle class expanded modestly in size with economic development.

Meanwhile, the traditional middle class was gaining two particularly important additions. The expansion of industry and technology created a growing demand for experts with specialized knowledge. The most valuable of the specialties became solid middle-class professions. Engineering, for example, emerged from the world of skilled labor as a full-fledged profession of great importance, considerable prestige, and many branches. Architects, chemists, accountants, and surveyors—to name only a few—first achieved professional standing in this period. They established criteria for advanced training and certification and banded together in organizations to promote and defend their interests.

Management of large public and private institutions also emerged as a kind of profession, as governments provided more services and as very large corporations like railroads came into being. Government officials and many private executives were not capitalists in the sense that they owned business enterprises. But public and private managers did have specialized knowledge and the capacity to earn a good living. And they shared most of the values of the business-owning entrepreneurs and the older professionals.

Industrialization also expanded and diversified the lower middle class. The number of independent, property-owning shopkeepers and small business people grew and so did the number of white-collar employees—a mixed group of traveling salesmen, bookkeepers, store managers, and clerks who staffed the offices and branch stores of large corporations. White-collar employees were propertyless and often earned no more than the better-paid skilled or semiskilled workers did. Yet white-collar workers were fiercely committed to the middle class and to the ideal of moving up in society. In the Balkans, for example, clerks let their fingernails grow very long to distinguish themselves from people who worked with their hands. The tie, the suit, and soft clean hands were no-less-subtle marks of class distinction than wages.

Relatively well educated but without complex technical skills, many white-collar groups aimed at achieving professional standing and the accompanying middle-class status. Elementary school teachers largely succeeded in this effort. From being miserably paid part-time workers in the early nineteenth century, teachers rode the wave of mass education to respectable middle-class status and income. Nurses also rose from the lower ranks of unskilled labor to precarious middle-class standing. Dentistry was taken out of the hands of the working-class barbers and placed in the hands of highly trained (and middle-class) professionals.

In spite of their growing occupational diversity and conflicting interests, the middle classes were loosely united by a certain style of life. Food was the largest item in the household budget, for middle-class people liked to eat very well. In France and Italy, the middle classes' love of good eating meant that, even in large cities, activity ground almost to a halt between half past twelve and half past two on weekdays, as husbands and schoolchildren returned home for the midday meal. Around eight in the evening, the serious business of eating was taken up once again.

The English were equally attached to substantial meals, which they ate three times a day if income allowed. The typical English breakfast of bacon and eggs, toast and marmalade, and stewed fruits—not to mention sardines, kidneys, or fresh fish—always astonished French and German travelers, though large-breakfast enthusiasts like the Dutch and Scandinavians were less awed. The European middle classes consumed meat in abundance, and a well-off family might spend 10 percent of its substantial earnings on meat alone. In the 1890s, even a very prosperous English family—with an income of, say, $10,000 a year (the average working-class family earned perhaps $400 a year)—spent fully a quarter of its income on food and drink.

Spending on food was also great because the dinner party was the favored social occasion of the middle classes. A wealthy family might give a lavish party for eight to twelve almost every week; more modest households would settle for once a month. Throughout middle-class Europe, such dinners were served in the "French manner" (which the French had borrowed from the Russian aristocracy): eight or nine separate courses, from appetizers at the beginning to coffee and liqueurs at the end. In summer, a picnic was in order. But what a picnic! For a party of ten, one English cookbook suggested 5 pounds of cold salmon, a quarter of lamb, 8 pounds of pickled brisket, a beef tongue, a chicken pie, salads, cakes, and 6 pounds of strawberries. An ordinary family meal normally consisted of only four courses—soup, fish, meat, and dessert.

A middle-class wife could cope with this endless procession of meals, courses, and dishes because she had both servants and money at her disposal. The middle classes were solid members of what some contemporary observers called the "servant-keeping classes." Indeed, the employment of

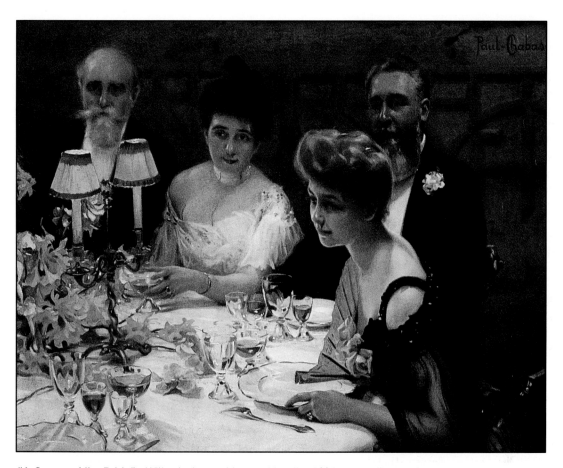

"A Corner of the Table"   With photographic precision this 1904 oil painting by French academic artist Paul-Émile Chabas (1867–1937) skillfully idealizes the elegance and intimacy of a sumptuous dinner party. *(Source: Bibliothèque des Arts Decoratifs/Jean-Loup Charmet)*

at least one enormously helpful full-time maid to cook and clean was the best single sign that a family had crossed the vague line separating the working classes from the middle classes. The greater its income, the greater was the number of servants a family employed. The all-purpose servant gave way to a cook and a maid, then to a cook, a maid, and a boy, and so on. A prosperous English family, far up the line with $10,000 a year, in 1900 spent fully one-fourth of its income on a hierarchy of ten servants: a manservant, a cook, a kitchen maid, two housemaids, a serving maid, a governess, a gardener, a coachman, and a stable boy. Domestic servants were the second largest item in the budget of the middle classes. Food and servants together absorbed about one-half of income at all levels of the middle classes.

Well fed and well served, the middle classes were also well housed by 1900. Many quite prosperous families rented rather than owned their homes. Apartment living, complete with tiny rooms for servants under the eaves of the top floor, was commonplace (outside Great Britain), and wealthy investors and speculative builders found good profits in middle-class housing. By 1900 the middle classes were also quite clothes-conscious. The factory, the sewing machine, and the department store had all helped to reduce the cost and expand the variety of clothing. Middle-class women were particularly attentive to the fickle dictates of fashion.

Education was another growing expense, as middle-class parents tried to provide their children with ever-more-crucial advanced education. The keystones of culture and leisure were books, music, and travel. The long realistic novel, the heroics of Wagner and Verdi, the diligent striving of the dutiful daughter on a piano, and the packaged tour to a foreign country were all sources of middle-class pleasure.

Finally, the middle classes were loosely united by a shared code of expected behavior and morality. This code was strict and demanding. It laid great stress on hard work, self-discipline, and personal achievement. Men and women who fell into crime or poverty were generally assumed to be responsible for their own circumstances. Traditional Christian morality was reaffirmed by this code and preached tirelessly by middle-class people who took pride in their own good conduct and regular church attendance. Drinking and gambling were denounced as vices; sexual purity and fidelity were celebrated as virtues. In short, the middle-class person was supposed to know right from wrong and was expected to act accordingly.

The Working Classes

About four out of five people belonged to the working classes at the turn of the century. Many members of the *working classes*—that is, people whose livelihoods depended on physical labor and who did not employ domestic servants—were still small landowning peasants and hired farm hands. This was especially true in eastern Europe. In western and central Europe, however, the typical worker had left the land. In Great Britain, less than 8 percent of the people worked in agricul-

FIGURE 28.3 The Urban Social Hierarchy

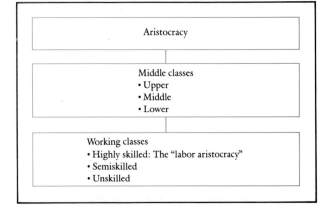

ture, and in rapidly industrializing Germany only one person in four was employed in agriculture and forestry. Even in less industrialized France, less than half of the people depended on the land in 1900.

The urban working classes were even less unified and homogeneous than the middle classes. In the first place, economic development and increased specialization expanded the traditional range of working-class skills, earnings, and experiences. Meanwhile, the old sharp distinction between highly skilled artisans and unskilled manual workers was gradually breaking down. To be sure, highly skilled printers and masons, as well as unskilled dock workers and common laborers, continued to exist. But between these extremes there were ever-more semiskilled groups, many of which were composed of factory workers and machine tenders (Figure 28.3).

In the second place, skilled, semiskilled, and unskilled workers had widely divergent lifestyles and cultural values, and their differences contributed to a keen sense of social status and hierarchy within the working classes. The result was great variety and limited class unity.

Highly skilled workers, who constituted about 15 percent of the working classes, were a real "labor aristocracy." By 1900 they were earning about £2 a week in Great Britain, or roughly $10 a week and $500 per year. This was only about two-thirds the income of the bottom ranks of the servant-keeping classes. But it was fully twice as much as the earnings of unskilled workers, who averaged about $5 per week, and substantially more than the earnings of semiskilled workers, who averaged perhaps $7 per week. Other European countries had a similar range of earnings.

The most "aristocratic" of the highly skilled workers were construction bosses and factory foremen, men who had risen from the ranks and were fiercely proud of their achievement. The labor aristocracy also included members of the traditional highly skilled handicraft trades that had not been mechanized or placed in factories. These included makers of scientific and musical instruments, cabinetmakers, potters, jewelers, bookbinders, engravers, and printers. This group as a whole was under constant long-term pressure. Irregularly but inexorably, factory methods were being extended to more crafts, and many skilled artisans were being replaced by lower-paid semiskilled factory workers. Traditional woodcarvers and watchmakers virtu-

Sweated Industry About 1900 This moving photograph shows an English family making cheap toys at home for low wages. Women and children were the backbone of sweated industry, and this husband may be filling in while unemployed. *(Source: University of Reading, Institute of Agricultural History and Museum of English Rural Life)*

ally disappeared, for example, as the making of furniture and timepieces was put into the factory.

At the same time, a contrary movement was occurring. The labor aristocracy was consistently being enlarged by the growing need for highly skilled workers, such as shipbuilders, machine-tool makers, railway locomotive engineers, fine cotton textile spinners, and some metalworkers. Thus the labor elite was in a state of flux as individuals and whole crafts moved in and out of it.

To maintain its precarious standing, the upper working class adopted distinctive values and strait-laced, almost puritanical, behavior. Like the middle classes, the labor aristocracy was strongly committed to the family and to economic improvement. Families in the upper working class saved money regularly, worried about their children's education, and valued good housing. Despite these similarities, which superficial observers were quick to exaggerate, skilled workers viewed themselves not as aspirants to the middle class but as the pacesetters and natural leaders of all the working classes. Well aware of the degradation not

so far below them, they practiced self-discipline and stern morality.

The upper working class in general frowned on heavy drinking and sexual permissiveness. The organized temperance movement was strong in the countries of northern Europe, such as Great Britain, where a generation advocated tea as the "cup that cheers but does not inebriate." As one German labor aristocrat somberly warned, "the path to the brothel leads through the tavern" and from there quite possibly to drastic decline or total ruin for person and family.[7]

Below the labor aristocracy stood *semiskilled* and *unskilled urban workers* (see Figure 28.3). The enormous complexity of this sector of the world of labor is not easily summarized. Workers in the established crafts—carpenters, bricklayers, pipefitters—stood near the top of the semiskilled hierarchy, often flirting with (or having backslid from) the labor elite. A large number of the semiskilled were factory workers, who earned highly variable but relatively good wages and whose relative importance in the labor force was increasing.

Below the semiskilled workers was the larger group of unskilled, who included day laborers such as longshoremen, wagon-driving teamsters, teenagers, and every kind of "helper." Many of these people had real skills and performed valuable services, but they were unorganized and divided, united only by the common fate of meager earnings. The same lack of unity characterized street vendors and market people—self-employed workers who competed savagely with each other and with the established shopkeepers of the lower middle class.

One of the largest components of the unskilled group was domestic servants, whose numbers grew steadily in the nineteenth century. In Great Britain, for example, in 1911 one out of every seven employed persons was a domestic servant. The great majority were women; indeed, one out of every three girls in Britain between the ages of fifteen and twenty was a domestic servant. Throughout Europe and America, a great many female domestics in the cities were recent migrants from rural areas. As in earlier times, domestic service was still hard work at low pay with limited personal independence.

Nonetheless, domestic service had real attractions for "rough country girls" with strong hands and few specialized skills. Marriage prospects were better, or at least more varied, in the city. And though wages were low, they were higher and more regular than in hard agricultural work. Finally, as one London observer noted, young girls and other migrants were drawn to the city by "the contagion of numbers, the sense of something going on, the theaters and the music halls, the brightly lighted streets and busy crowds—all, in short, that makes the difference between the Mile End fair on a Saturday night, and a dark and muddy country lane, with no glimmer of gas and with nothing to do."[8]

Many young domestics from the countryside made a successful transition to working-class wife and mother. Yet, with an unskilled or unemployed husband and a growing family, such a woman often had to join the broad ranks of working women in the "sweated industries." These industries resembled the old putting-out and cottage industries of the eighteenth and early nineteenth centuries. The women normally worked at home, though sometimes together in some loft or garret, for tiny merchant-manufacturers. Paid by the piece and not by the hour, these women (and their young daughters), for whom organization was impossible, earned pitiful wages and lacked any job security.

Some women did hand-decorating of every conceivable kind of object; the majority, however, made clothing, especially after the advent of the sewing machine. Foot-powered sewing machines allowed the poorest wife or widow in the foulest dwelling to rival and eventually supplant the most highly skilled male tailor. By 1900 only a few such tailors lingered on in high-priced "tailor-made" shops. An army of poor women accounted for the bulk of the inexpensive "ready-made" clothes displayed on department store racks and in tiny shops. All of these considerations graphically illustrate the rise and fall of groups and individuals within the working classes.

The urban working classes sought fun and recreation, and they found it. Across the face of Europe, drinking was unquestionably the favorite leisure-time activity of working people. For many middle-class moralists, as well as moralizing historians since, love of drink has been a curse of the modern age—a sign of social dislocation and popular suffering. Certainly, drinking was deadly serious business. One English slum dweller recalled that "drunkenness was by far the commonest cause of dispute and misery in working class homes. On account of it one saw many a decent family drift down through poverty into total want."[9]

Generally, however, heavy "problem" drinking declined by the late nineteenth century, as it became less and less socially acceptable. This decline reflected in part the moral leadership of the upper working class. At the same time, drinking became more public and social, especially as on-the-job drinking, an ancient custom of field laborers and urban artisans, declined. Cafés and pubs became increasingly bright, friendly places. Working-class political activities, both moderate and radical, were also concentrated in taverns and pubs. Moreover, social drinking by married couples and sweethearts became an accepted and widespread practice for the first time. This greater participation by women undoubtedly helped to civilize the world of drink and hard liquor.

The two other leisure-time passions of the working classes were sports and music halls. By the late nineteenth century there had been a great decline in "cruel sports," such as bullbaiting and cockfighting, throughout Europe. Their place was filled by modern spectator sports, of which racing and soccer were the most popular. There was a great deal of gambling on sports events, and for many a working person the desire to decipher the racing forms was a powerful incentive toward literacy. Music halls and vaudeville theaters, the working-class counterparts of middle-class opera and classical theater, were enormously popular throughout Europe. In the words of one English printer, "It is to the music halls that the vast body of working people look for recreation and entertainment."[10] In 1900 there were more than fifty in London alone. Music hall audiences were thoroughly mixed, which may account for the fact that drunkenness, sexual intercourse and pregnancy before marriage, marital difficulties, and problems with mothers-in-law were favorite themes of broad jokes and bittersweet songs.

In more serious moments, religion and the Christian churches continued to provide working people with solace and meaning. The eighteenth-century vitality of popular religion in Catholic countries and the Protestant rejuvenation exemplified by German Pietism and English Methodism (see pages 720–721) carried over into the nineteenth century. Indeed, many historians see the early nineteenth century as an age of religious revival. Yet historians also recognize that, by the last two or three decades of the nineteenth century, a considerable decline in both church attendance and church donations was occurring in

Renoir: Le Moulin de la Galette à Montmartre In this 1876 masterpiece the impressionist painter Auguste Renoir (1841–1919) has transformed a popular outdoor dance hall of the Parisian masses into an enchanted fairyland. Renoir was a joyous artist, and his work optimistically affirmed the beauty and value of modern life. *(Source: Musée d'Orsay/ Cliché des Musées Nationaux, Paris)*

most European countries. And it seems clear that this decline was greater for the urban working classes than for their rural counterparts or for the middle classes.

What did the decline in working-class church attendance really mean? Some have argued that it accurately reflected a general decline in faith and religious belief. Others disagree, noting correctly that most working-class families still baptized their children and considered themselves Christians. Although more research is necessary, it appears that the urban working classes in Europe did become more secular and less religious in the late nineteenth and early twentieth centuries. They rarely repudiated the Christian religion, but it tended to play a diminishing role in their day-to-day lives.

Part of the reason was that the construction of churches failed to keep up with the rapid growth of urban population, especially in new working-class neighborhoods. Thus the vibrant, materialistic urban environment undermined popular religious impulses, which were poorly served in the cities. Equally important, however, was the fact that throughout the nineteenth century both Catholic and Protestant churches were normally seen as they saw themselves—as conservative institutions defending social order and custom. Therefore, as the European working classes became more politically conscious, they tended to see the established (or quasi-established) "territorial church" as defending what they wished to change and allied with their political opponents. Especially the men of the urban working classes developed vaguely antichurch attitudes, even though they remained neutral or positive toward religion. They tended to regard regular church attendance as "not our kind of thing"—not part of urban working-class culture.

The pattern was different in the United States. There, most churches also preached social conservatism in the nineteenth century. But because church and state had always been separate and because there was always a host of competing denominations and even different religions, working people identified churches much less with the political and social status quo. Instead, individual churches in the United States were often closely identified with an ethnic group rather than with a social class; and churches thrived, in part, as a means of asserting ethnic identity.

THE FAMILY

Urban life wrought many fundamental changes in the family. Although much is still unknown, it seems clear that by the late nineteenth century the family had stabilized considerably after the disruption of the late eighteenth and early nineteenth centuries. The home became more important for both men and women. The role of women and attitudes toward children underwent substantial change, and adolescence emerged as a distinct stage of life. These are but a few of the transformations that affected all social classes in varying degrees.

Premarital Sex and Marriage

By 1850 the preindustrial pattern of lengthy courtship and mercenary marriage was pretty well dead among the working classes. In its place, the ideal of romantic love had triumphed. Couples were ever more likely to come from different, even distant, towns and to be more nearly the same age, further indicating that romantic sentiment was replacing tradition and financial considerations.

Economic considerations in marriage long remained much more important to the middle classes than to the working classes. In France, dowries and elaborate legal marriage contracts were standard practice among the middle classes, and marriage was for many families life's most crucial financial transaction. A popular author advised young Frenchmen that "marriage is in general a means of increasing one's credit and one's fortune and of insuring one's success in the world."[11] This preoccupation with money led many middle-class men, in France and elsewhere, to marry late, after they were established economically, and to choose women considerably younger and less sexually experienced than themselves. These differences between husband and wife became a source of tension in many middle-class marriages.

A young woman of the middle class found her romantic life carefully supervised by her well-meaning mother, who schemed for a proper marriage and guarded her daughter's virginity like the family's credit. After marriage, middle-class morality sternly demanded fidelity.

Middle-class boys were watched, too, but not as vigilantly. By the time they reached late adolescence, they had usually attained considerable sexual experience with maids or prostitutes. With marriage a distant, uncertain possibility, it was all too easy for a young man of the middle classes to turn to the urban underworld of whoredom and sexual exploitation to satisfy his desires.

Sexual experimentation before marriage had also triumphed, as had illegitimacy. There was an "illegitimacy explosion" between 1750 and 1850 (see page 703). By the 1840s, as many as one birth in three was occurring outside of wedlock in many large cities. Although poverty and economic uncertainty undoubtedly prevented many lovers from marrying, there were also many among the poor and propertyless who saw little wrong with having illegitimate offspring. One young Bavarian woman answered happily when asked why she kept having illegitimate children: "It's O.K. to make babies. . . . The king has o.k.'d it!"[12] Thus the pattern of romantic ideals, premarital sexual activity, and widespread illegitimacy was firmly established by midcentury among the urban working classes.

It is hard to know how European couples managed sex, pregnancy, and marriage after 1850, because such questions were considered improper both in polite conversation and in public opinion polls. Yet there are many telltale clues. In the second half of the century the rising rate of illegitimacy was reversed: more babies were born to married mothers. Some observers have argued that this shift reflected the growth of puritanism and a lessening of sexual permissiveness among the unmarried. This explanation, however, is unconvincing.

The percentage of brides who were pregnant continued to be high and showed little or no tendency to decline. In many parts of urban Europe around 1900, as many as one woman in three was going to the altar an expectant mother. Moreover, unmarried people almost certainly used the cheap condoms and diaphragms that the industrial age had made available to prevent pregnancy, at least in predominantly Protestant countries.

Unmarried young people were probably engaging in just as much sexual activity as their parents and grandparents who had created the illegitimacy explosion of 1750 to 1850. But toward the end of the nineteenth century, pregnancy usually meant marriage and the establishment of a two-parent household. This important development reflected the growing respectability of the working classes, as well as their gradual economic improvement. Skipping out was less acceptable, and marriage was less of an economic disaster. Thus the urban working-class couple became more stable, and this stability strengthened the family as an institution.

Prostitution

In Paris alone, 155,000 women were registered as prostitutes between 1871 and 1903, and 750,000 others were suspected of prostitution in the same years. Men of all classes visited prostitutes, but the middle and upper classes supplied much of the motivating cash. Thus, though many middle-class men abided by the publicly professed code of stern puritanical morality, others indulged their appetites for prostitutes and sexual promiscuity.

My Secret Life, the anonymous eleven-volume autobiography of an English sexual adventurer from the servant-keeping classes, provides a remarkable picture of such a man. Beginning at an early age with a maid, the author becomes progressively obsessed with sex and devotes his life to living his sexual fantasies. In almost every one of his innumerable encounters all across Europe, this man of wealth simply buys his pleasure. Usually meetings are arranged in a businesslike manner: regular and part-time prostitutes quote their prices; working-class girls are corrupted by hot meals and baths.

At one point, he offers a young girl six pence for a kiss and gets it. Learning that the pretty, unskilled working girl earns nine pence a day, he offers her the equivalent of a week's salary for a few moments of fondling. When she finally agrees, he savagely exults that "her want was my opportunity."[13] Later he offers more money for more gratification, and when she refuses, he tries unsuccessfully to rape her in a hackney cab.

Obviously atypical in its excesses, the encyclopedic thoroughness of *My Secret Life* does reveal the dark side of sex and class in urban society. Thinking of their wives largely in terms of money and social position, the men of the comfortable classes often purchased sex and even affection from poor girls both before and after marriage. Moreover, the great continuing differences between rich and poor made for every kind of debauchery and sexual exploitation, including the brisk trade in poor virgins that the author of *My Secret Life* particularly relished. Brutal sexist behavior was part of life—a part the sternly moral women (and men) of the upper working class detested and tried to shield their daughters from. For many poor young women, prostitution, like domestic service, was a stage of life. Having passed through it for two or three years in their early twenties, they went on in their mid-twenties to marry (or live with) men of their own class and establish homes and families.

Kinship Ties

Within working-class homes, ties to relatives after marriage—kinship ties—were in general much stronger than superficial social observers have recognized. Most newly-weds tried to live near their parents, though not in the same house. Indeed, for many married couples in the cities, ties to mothers and fathers, uncles and aunts, became more important, and ties to nonrelated acquaintances became weaker.

People turned to their families for help in coping with sickness, unemployment, death, and old age. Although governments were generally providing more welfare services by 1900, the average couple and their children inevitably faced crises. Funerals, for example, were an economic catastrophe requiring a sudden large outlay for special clothes, carriages, and burial services. Unexpected death or desertion could leave the bereaved or abandoned, especially widows and orphans, in need of financial aid or perhaps a foster home. Relatives responded to such crises, knowing full well that their own time of need would come.

Relatives were also valuable at less tragic moments. If a couple was very poor, an aged relation often moved in to cook and mind the children so the wife could earn badly needed income outside the home. Sunday dinners were often shared, as were outgrown clothing and useful information. Often the members of a large family group all lived in the same neighborhood.

Women and Family Life

Industrialization and the growth of modern cities brought great changes to the lives of European women. These changes were particularly consequential for married women, and in the nineteenth century most women did marry.

The work of most wives became quite distinct and separate from the work of their husbands. Husbands became wage earners in factories and offices; wives tended to stay home and manage the household and care for the children. The preindustrial pattern among both peasants and cottage workers, in which husbands and wives worked together and divided up household duties and child rearing, declined. Only in a few occupations, such as retail trade, did married couples live where they worked and struggle together to make their mom-and-pop operations a success. Factory employment for married women also declined as the early practice of hiring entire families in the factory disappeared.

As economic conditions improved late in the nineteenth century, only married women in poor families tended to work outside the home. One old English worker recalled that "the boy wanted to get into a position that would enable him to keep a wife and family, as it was considered a thoroughly unsatisfactory state of affairs if the wife had to work to help maintain the home."[14] The ideal was a strict division of labor by sex: the wife as mother and homemaker, the husband as wage earner.

This rigid division of labor meant that married women faced great injustice if they tried to move into the man's world, the world of employment outside the home. Husbands were unsympathetic or hostile. Well-paying jobs were off-limits to women, and a woman's wage was almost always less than a man's, even for the same work.

Moreover, married women were subordinated to their husbands by law and lacked many basic legal rights. In England, the situation was summed up in a famous line from the jurist William Blackstone: "In law husband and wife are one person, and the husband is that person." Thus a wife in England had no legal identity and hence no right to own property in her own name. Even the wages she might earn belonged to her husband. In France, the Napoleonic Code also enshrined the principle of female subordination and gave the wife few legal rights regarding property, divorce, and custody of the children. Legal inferiority for women permeated Western society.

With middle-class women suffering, sometimes severely, from a lack of legal rights and with all

Women Workers   Founded in 1869, the German Social Democratic party became the strongest socialist party in Europe. Women were active in the socialist movement, as this engraving from 1890 of a meeting of workers in Berlin illustrates. *(Source: Bildarchiv Preussischer Kulturbesitz)*

women facing discrimination in education and employment, there is little wonder that some women rebelled and began the long-continuing fight for equality of the sexes and the rights of women. Their struggle proceeded on two main fronts. First, following in the steps of women like Mary Wollstonecraft (see page 810), organizations founded by middle-class feminists campaigned for equal legal rights for women as well as access to higher education and professional employment. These organizations scored some significant victories, like the law giving English married women full property rights in 1882. In the years before 1914, middle-class feminists increasingly shifted their attention to securing the right to vote for women.

Women inspired by utopian and particularly Marxian socialism blazed a second path. Often scorning the programs of middle-class feminists, socialist women leaders argued that the liberation of (working-class) women would come only with the liberation of the entire working class through revolution. In the meantime, they championed the cause of working women and won some practi-

cal improvements, especially in Germany, where the socialist movement was most effectively organized. In a general way, these different approaches to women's issues reflected the diversity of classes in the urban society.

If the ideology and practice of rigidly separate roles undoubtedly narrowed women's horizons and caused some women to rebel, there was a brighter side to the same coin. As home and children became the typical wife's main concerns, her control and influence there apparently became increasingly strong throughout Europe. Among the English working classes, it was the wife who generally determined how the family's money was spent. In many families the husband gave all his earnings to his wife to manage, whatever the law might read. She returned to him only a small allowance for carfare, beer, tobacco, and union dues. All the major domestic decisions, from the children's schooling and religious instruction to the selection of new furniture or a new apartment, were hers. In France women had even greater power in their assigned domain. One English feminist noted in 1908 that "though legally women occupy

A Working-Class Home, 1875   Emotional ties within ordinary families grew stronger in the nineteenth century. (Source: Illustrated London News, LXVI, 1875. Photo courtesy of Boston Public Library)

a much inferior status than men [in France], in practice they constitute the superior sex. They are the power behind the throne."[15]

Women ruled at home partly because running the urban household was a complicated, demanding, and valuable task. Twice-a-day food shopping, penny-pinching, economizing, and the growing crusade against dirt—not to mention child rearing—constituted a full-time occupation. Nor were there any labor-saving appliances to help. Working yet another job for wages outside the home had limited appeal for most married women, unless such earnings were essential for family survival.

The wife also guided the home because a good deal of her effort was directed toward pampering her husband as he expected. In humble households she saw that he had meat while she ate bread, that he relaxed by the fire while she did the dishes.

The woman's guidance of the household went hand in hand with the increased emotional importance of home and family. The home she ran was idealized as a warm shelter in a hard and impersonal urban world. By the 1820s one observer of the comfortable middle classes in Marseilles had noted, for example, that "the family father, obliged to occupy himself with difficult business

problems during the day, can relax only when he goes home. . . . Family evenings together are for him a time of the purest and most complete happiness."[16]

In time the central place of the family spread down the social scale. For a child of the English slums in the early 1900s,

home, however poor, was the focus of all love and interests, a sure fortress against a hostile world. Songs about its beauties were ever on people's lips. "Home, sweet home," first heard in the 1870s, had become "almost a second national anthem." Few walls in lower-working-class houses lacked "mottoes"—colored strips of paper, about nine inches wide and eighteen inches in length, attesting to domestic joys: EAST, WEST, HOME'S BEST; BLESS OUR HOME; GOD IS MASTER OF THIS HOUSE; HOME IS THE NEST WHERE ALL IS BEST.[17]

By 1900 home and family were what life was all about for millions of people of all classes.

Women also developed stronger emotional ties to their husbands. Even in the comfortable classes, marriages were increasingly founded on sentiment and sexual attraction rather than on money and calculation. Affection and eroticism became more central to the couple after marriage. Gustave Droz, whose best seller *Mr., Mrs., and Baby* went through 121 editions between 1866 and 1884, saw love within marriage as the key to human happiness. He condemned men who made marriage sound dull and practical, men who were exhausted by prostitutes and rheumatism and who wanted their young wives to be little angels. He urged women to follow their hearts and marry a man more nearly their own age:

A husband who is stately and a little bald is all right, but a young husband who loves you and who drinks out of your glass without ceremony, is better. Let him, if he ruffles your dress a little and places a kiss on your neck as he passes. Let him, if he undresses you after the ball, laughing like a fool. You have fine spiritual qualities, it is true, but your little body is not bad either and when one loves, one loves completely. Behind these follies lies happiness.[18]

Many French marriage manuals of the late 1800s stressed that women had legitimate sexual needs, such as the "right to orgasm." Perhaps the French were a bit more enlightened in these matters than other nationalities. But the rise of public socializing by couples in cafés and music halls, as well as franker affection within the family, suggest a more erotic, pleasurable intimate life for women throughout Western society. This, too, helped make the woman's role as mother and homemaker acceptable and even satisfying.

Child Rearing

One of the most striking signs of deepening emotional ties within the family was the mother's love and concern for her tiny infants. This was a sharp break with the past. It may seem scarcely believable today that the typical mother in preindustrial Western society was very often indifferent toward her baby. This indifference—unwillingness to make real sacrifices for the welfare of the infant—was giving way among the comfortable classes by the later part of the eighteenth century, but the ordinary mother adopted new attitudes only as the nineteenth century progressed. The baby became more important, and women became better mothers.

Mothers increasingly breast-fed their infants, for example, rather than paying wet nurses to do

so. Breast-feeding involved sacrifice—a temporary loss of freedom, if nothing else. Yet in an age when there was no good alternative to mother's milk, it saved lives. The surge of maternal feeling also gave rise to a wave of specialized books on child rearing and infant hygiene, such as Droz's phenomenally successful book. Droz urged fathers to get into the act and pitied those "who do not know how to roll around on the carpet, play at being a horse and a great wolf, and undress their baby."[19] Another sign, from France, of increased affection is that fewer illegitimate babies were abandoned as foundlings, especially after about 1850. Moreover, the practice of swaddling disappeared completely. Instead, ordinary mothers allowed their babies freedom of movement and delighted in their spontaneity.

The Drawing Room The middle-class ideal of raising cultured, educated, and properly protected young women is captured in this illustration. A serious mother lovingly teaches her youngest child while the older daughters practice their genteel skills. A drawing room was a kind of nineteenth-century family room, mercifully spared the tyranny of television. *(Source: Bettmann/Hulton)*

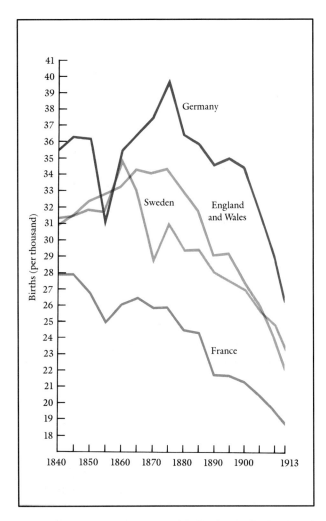

FIGURE 28.4 The Decline of Birthrates in England and Wales, France, Germany, Sweden, 1840–1913 Women had fewer babies for a variety of reasons, including the fact that their children were increasingly less likely to die before reaching adulthood. Compare with Figure 28.1.

The loving care lavished on infants was matched by greater concern for older children and adolescents. They, too, were wrapped in the strong emotional ties of a more intimate and protective family. For one thing, European women began to limit the number of children they bore, in order to care adequately for those they had. It was evident by the end of the century that the birthrate was declining across Europe, as Figure 28.4 shows, and it continued to do so until after the Second World War. An Englishwoman who married in the 1860s, for example, had an average of about six children; her daughter marrying in the 1890s had

only four; and her granddaughter marrying in the 1920s had only two or possibly three.

The most important reason for this revolutionary reduction in family size, in which the comfortable and well-educated classes took the lead, was parents' desire to improve their economic and social position and that of their children. Children were no longer an economic asset. By having fewer youngsters, parents could give those they had valuable advantages, from music lessons and summer vacations to long, expensive university educations and suitable dowries. A young German skilled worker with only one child spoke for many in his class when he said, "We want to get ahead, and our daughter should have things better than my wife and sisters did."[20] Thus the growing tendency of couples in the late nineteenth century to use a variety of contraceptive methods—rhythm, withdrawal, and mechanical devices—certainly reflected increased concern for children.

Indeed, many parents were probably too concerned about their children, unwittingly subjecting them to an emotional pressure cooker of almost unbearable intensity. The result was that many children and especially adolescents came to feel trapped, longing for greater independence.

Biological and medical theories led parents to believe in the possibility that their own emotional characteristics were passed on to their offspring and that they were thus directly responsible for any abnormality in a child. The moment a child was conceived was thought to be of enormous importance. "Never run the risk of conception when you are sick or over-tired or unhappy," wrote one influential American woman. "For the bodily condition of the child, its vigor and magnetic qualities, are much affected by conditions ruling this great moment."[21] So might the youthful "sexual excess" of the father curse future generations. Although this was true in the case of syphilis, which could be transmitted to unborn children, the rigid determinism of such views left little scope for the child's individual development.

Another area of excessive parental concern was the sexual behavior of the child. Masturbation was viewed with horror, for it represented an act of independence and even defiance. Diet, clothing, games, and sleeping were carefully regulated. Girls were discouraged from riding horses and bicycling because rhythmic friction simulated masturbation. Boys were dressed in trousers with shallow and widely separated pockets.

These and less blatant attempts to repress the child's sexuality were a source of unhealthy tension, often made worse by the rigid division of sexual roles within the family. It was widely believed that mother and child love each other easily but relations between father and child are necessarily difficult and often tragic. The father was a stranger; his world of business was far removed from the maternal world of spontaneous affection. Moreover, the father was demanding, often expecting the child to succeed where he himself had failed and making his love conditional on achievement. Little wonder that the imaginative literature of the late nineteenth century came to deal with the emotional and destructive elements of father-son relationships. In the Russian Feodor Dostoevsky's great novel *The Brothers Karamazov* (1880–1881), for example, four sons work knowingly or unknowingly to destroy their father. Later, at the murder trial, one of the brothers claims to speak for all mankind and screams out: "Who doesn't wish his father dead?"

Sigmund Freud (1856–1939), the Viennese founder of psychoanalysis, formulated the most striking analysis of the explosive dynamics of the family, particularly the middle-class family in the late nineteenth century. A physician by training, Freud began his career treating mentally ill patients. He noted that the hysteria of his patients appeared to originate in bitter early childhood experiences, wherein the child had been obliged to repress strong feelings. When these painful experiences were recalled and reproduced under hypnosis or through free association of ideas, the patient could be brought to understand his or her unhappiness and eventually to deal with it.

One of Freud's most influential ideas concerned the Oedipal tensions resulting from the son's instinctive competition with the father for the mother's love and affection. More generally, Freud postulated that much of human behavior is motivated by unconscious emotional needs, whose nature and origins are kept from conscious awareness by various mental devices that he called "defense mechanisms." Freud concluded that much unconscious psychological energy is sexual energy, which is repressed and precariously controlled by rational thinking and moral rules. If Freud exaggerated the sexual and familial roots of adult behavior, that exaggeration was itself a reflection of the tremendous emotional intensity of family life in the late nineteenth century.

The working classes probably had more avenues of escape from such tensions than did the middle classes. Unlike their middle-class counterparts, who remained economically dependent on their families until a long education was finished or a proper marriage secured, working-class boys and girls went to work when they reached adolescence. Earning wages on their own, by the time they were sixteen or seventeen they could bargain with their parents for greater independence within the household. If they were unsuccessful, they could and did leave home, to live cheaply as paying lodgers in other working-class homes. Thus a young person from the working classes broke away from the family more easily when emotional ties became oppressive. In the twentieth century, middle-class youth would follow this lead.

SCIENCE AND THOUGHT

Major changes in Western thought accompanied the emergence of urban society. Two aspects of these complex intellectual developments stand out as especially significant. Scientific knowledge expanded rapidly and came to influence the Western world view even more profoundly than it had since the scientific revolution and the early Enlightenment. And, between about the 1840s and the 1890s, European literature underwent a shift from soaring romanticism to tough-minded realism.

The Triumph of Science

As the pace of scientific advance quickened and as theoretical advances resulted in great practical benefits, science exercised growing influence on human thought. The intellectual achievements of the scientific revolution had resulted in few such benefits, and theoretical knowledge had also played a relatively small role in the Industrial Revolution in England. But breakthroughs in industrial technology enormously stimulated basic scientific inquiry, as researchers sought to explain theoretically how such things as steam engines and blast furnaces actually worked. The result was an explosive growth of fundamental scientific discoveries from the 1830s onward. And in contrast to earlier periods, these theoretical discoveries were increasingly transformed into material improvements for the general population.

A perfect example of the translation of better scientific knowledge into practical human benefits was the work of Pasteur and his followers in biology and the medical sciences. Another was the development of the branch of physics known as "thermodynamics." Building on Newton's laws of mechanics and on studies of steam engines, thermodynamics investigated the relationship between heat and mechanical energy. By midcentury, physicists had formulated the fundamental laws of thermodynamics, which were then applied to mechanical engineering, chemical processes, and many other fields. The *law of conservation of energy* held that different forms of energy—such as heat, electricity, and magnetism—could be converted but neither created nor destroyed. Nineteenth-century thermodynamics demonstrated that the physical world is governed by firm, unchanging laws.

Chemistry and electricity were two other fields characterized by extremely rapid progress. Chemists devised ways of measuring the atomic weight of different elements, and in 1869 the Russian chemist Dmitri Mendeleev (1834–1907) codified the rules of chemistry in the periodic law and the periodic table. Chemistry was subdivided into many specialized branches, such as organic chemistry—the study of the compounds of carbon. Applying theoretical insights gleaned from this new field, researchers in large German chemical companies discovered ways of transforming the dirty, useless coal tar that accumulated in coke ovens into beautiful, expensive synthetic dyes for the world of fashion. The basic discoveries of Michael Faraday (1791–1867) in electromagnetism in the 1830s and 1840s resulted in the first dynamo (generator) and opened the way for the subsequent development of electric motors, electric lights, and electric streetcars.

The triumph of science and technology had at least three significant consequences. First, though ordinary citizens continued to lack detailed scientific knowledge, everyday experience and innumerable popularizers impressed the importance of science on the popular mind.

As science became more prominent in popular thinking, the philosophical implications of science formulated in the Enlightenment spread to broad sections of the population. Natural processes appeared to be determined by rigid laws, leaving little room for either divine intervention or human will. Yet scientific and technical advances had also fed the Enlightenment's optimistic faith in human progress, which now appeared endless and automatic to many middle-class minds.

Finally, the methods of science acquired unrivaled prestige after 1850. For many, the union of careful experiment and abstract theory was the only reliable route to truth and objective reality. The "unscientific" intuitions of poets and the revelations of saints seemed hopelessly inferior.

Social Science and Evolution

From the 1830s onward, many thinkers tried to apply the objective methods of science to the study of society. In some ways these efforts simply perpetuated the critical thinking of the philosophes. Yet there were important differences. The new "social scientists" had access to the massive sets of numerical data that governments had begun to collect on everything from children to crime, from population to prostitution. In response, they developed new statistical methods to analyze these facts "scientifically" and supposedly to test their theories. And the systems of the leading nineteenth-century social scientists were more unified, all-encompassing, and dogmatic than those of the philosophes. Marx was a prime example (see pages 875–876).

Another extremely influential system builder was the French philosopher Auguste Comte (1798–1857). Initially a disciple of the utopian socialist Saint-Simon (see page 874), Comte wrote the six-volume *System of Positive Philosophy* (1830–1842), largely overlooked during the romantic era. But when the political failures of 1848 completed the swing to realism, Comte's philosophy came into its own. Its influence has remained great to this day.

Comte postulated that all intellectual activity progresses through predictable stages:

The great fundamental law . . . is this:—that each of our leading conceptions—each branch of our knowledge—passes successively through three different theoretical conditions: the Theological, or fictitious; the Metaphysical, or abstract; and the Scientific, or positive. . . . The first is the necessary point of departure of human understanding, and the third is the fixed and definitive state. The second is merely a transition.[22]

By way of example, Comte noted that, as knowledge of astronomy developed, the prevailing explanation of cosmic patterns had shifted from the will of God (the theological) to the will of an orderly Nature (the metaphysical) to the rule of unchanging laws (the scientific). Later, this same intellectual progression took place in increasingly complex fields—physics, chemistry, and finally the study of society. By applying the scientific or positivist method, Comte believed, his new discipline of sociology would soon discover the eternal laws of human relations. This colossal achievement would in turn enable expert social scientists to impose a disciplined harmony and well-being on less enlightened citizens. Dismissing the "fictions" of traditional religions, Comte became the chief priest of the religion of science and rule by experts.

Comte's stages of knowledge exemplify the nineteenth-century fascination with the idea of evolution and dynamic development. Thinkers in many fields, like the romantic historians and "scientific" Marxists, shared and applied this basic concept. In geology, Charles Lyell (1797–1875) effectively discredited the long-standing view that the earth's surface had been formed by short-lived cataclysms, such as biblical floods and earthquakes. Instead, according to Lyell's principle of uniformitarianism, the same geological processes that are at work today slowly formed the earth's surface over an immensely long time. The evolutionary view of biological development, first proposed by the Greek Anaximander in the sixth century B.C., re-emerged in a more modern form in the work of Jean Baptiste Lamarck (1744–1829). Lamarck asserted that all forms of life had arisen through a long process of continuous adjustment to the environment.

Lamarck's work was flawed—he believed that characteristics that parents acquired in the course of their lives could be inherited by their children—and was not accepted, but it helped prepare the way for Charles Darwin (1809–1882), the most influential of all nineteenth-century evolutionary thinkers. As the official naturalist on a five-year scientific cruise to Latin America and the South Pacific beginning in 1831, Darwin carefully collected specimens of the different animal species that he encountered on the voyage. Back in England, convinced by fossil evidence and by his friend Lyell that the earth and life on it were immensely ancient, Darwin came to doubt the general belief in a special divine creation of each species of animals. Instead, he concluded, all life had gradually evolved from a common ancestral origin in an unending "struggle for survival." After long hesitation, Darwin published his research, which immediately attracted wide attention.

Darwin's great originality lay in suggesting precisely how biological evolution might have occurred. His theory is summarized in his title, *On the Origin of Species by the Means of Natural Selection* (1859). Decisively influenced by Malthus's gloomy theory that populations naturally grow faster than their food supplies, Darwin argued that chance differences among the members of a given species help some to survive while others die. Thus the variations that prove useful in the struggle for survival are selected naturally and gradually spread

Attracting Females was an integral part of the struggle for survival, according to Charles Darwin. He theorized that those males who were most attractive to females would have the most offspring, like this type of monkey that had developed ornamental hair with devastating sex appeal. Darwin used this illustration in *The Descent of Man* (1871). *(Source: Library of Congress)*

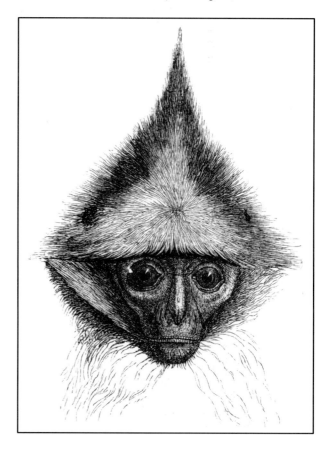

to the entire species through reproduction. Darwin did not explain why such variations occurred in the first place, and not until the early twentieth century did the study of genetics and the concept of mutation provide some answers.

As the capstone of already-widespread evolutionary thinking, Darwin's theory had a powerful and many-sided influence on European thought and the European middle classes. Darwin was hailed as the great scientist par excellence, the "Newton of biology," who had revealed once again the powers of objective science. Darwin's findings also reinforced the teachings of secularists like Comte and Marx, who scornfully dismissed religious belief in favor of agnostic or atheistic materialism. In the great cities especially, religion was on the defensive. Finally, many writers applied the theory of biological evolution to human affairs. Herbert Spencer (1820–1903), an English disciple of Auguste Comte, saw the human race as driven forward to ever-greater specialization and progress by the brutal economic struggle that efficiently determined the "survival of the fittest." The poor were the ill-fated weak, the prosperous the chosen strong. Understandably, Spencer and other Social Darwinists were especially popular with the upper middle class.

Realism in Literature

In 1868 Émile Zola (1840–1902), the giant of the realist movement in literature, defended his violently criticized first novel against charges of pornography and corruption of morals. Such accusations were meaningless, Zola claimed: he was only a purely objective scientist using "the modern method, the universal instrument of inquiry of which this age makes such ardent use to open up the future":

I chose characters completely dominated by their nerves and their blood, deprived of free-will, pushed to each action of their lives by the fatality of their flesh. . . . I have simply done on living bodies the work of analysis which surgeons perform on corpses.[23]

Zola's literary manifesto articulated the key themes of realism, which had emerged in the 1840s and dominated Western culture and style until the 1890s. Realist writers believed that literature should depict life exactly as it was. Forsaking poetry for prose and the personal, emotional viewpoint of the romantics for strict, scientific objectivity, the realists simply observed and recorded—content to let the facts speak for themselves.

The major realist writers focused their extraordinary powers of observation on contemporary everyday life. Emphatically rejecting the romantic search for the exotic and the sublime, they energetically pursued the typical and the commonplace. Beginning with a dissection of the middle classes, from which most of them sprang, many realists eventually focused on the working classes, especially the urban working classes, which had been neglected in imaginative literature before this time. They put a microscope to many unexplored and taboo subjects—sex, strikes, violence, alcoholism—and hastened to report that slums and factories teemed with savage behavior. Many shocked middle-class critics denounced realism as ugly sensationalism wrapped provocatively in pseudoscientific declarations and crude language.

The realists' claims of objectivity did not prevent the elaboration of a definite world view. Unlike the romantics, who had gloried in individual freedom and an unlimited universe, realists such as Zola were strict determinists. Human beings, like atoms, were components of the physical world, and all human actions were caused by unalterable natural laws. Heredity and environment determined human behavior; good and evil were merely social conventions.

The realist movement began in France, where romanticism had never been completely dominant, and three of its greatest practitioners—Balzac, Flaubert, and Zola—were French. Honoré de Balzac (1799–1850) spent thirty years writing a vastly ambitious panorama of postrevolutionary French life. Known collectively as *The Human Comedy,* this series of nearly one hundred books vividly portrays more than two thousand characters from virtually all sectors of French society. Balzac pictures urban society as grasping, amoral, and brutal, characterized by a Darwinian struggle for wealth and power. In *Le Père Goriot* (1835), the hero, a poor student from the provinces, eventually surrenders his idealistic integrity to feverish ambition and society's all-pervasive greed.

Madame Bovary (1857), the masterpiece of Gustave Flaubert (1821–1880), is far narrower in scope than Balzac's work but unparalleled in its depth and accuracy of psychological insight. Unsuccessfully prosecuted as an outrage against public morality and religion, Flaubert's carefully crafted novel tells the ordinary, even banal, story of a frustrated middle-class housewife who has an adulterous love affair and is betrayed by her lover. Without moralizing, Flaubert portrays the provincial middle class as petty, smug, and hypocritical.

Zola was most famous for his seamy, animalistic view of working-class life. But he also wrote gripping, carefully researched stories featuring the stock exchange, the big department store, and the army, as well as urban slums and bloody coal strikes. Like many later realists, Zola sympathized with socialism, a sympathy evident in his overpowering *Germinal* (1885).

Realism quickly spread beyond France. In England, Mary Ann Evans (1819–1880), who wrote under the pen name George Eliot, brilliantly achieved a more deeply felt, less sensational kind of realism. "It is the habit of my imagination," George Eliot wrote, "to strive after as full a vision of the medium in which a character moves as one of the character itself." Her great novel *Middlemarch: A Study of Provincial Life* examines masterfully the ways in which people are shaped by their social medium as well as by their own inner strivings, conflicts, and moral choices. Thomas Hardy (1840–1928) was more in the Zola tradition. His novels, such as *Tess of the D'Urbervilles* and *Return of the Native*, depicted men and women frustrated and crushed by fate and bad luck.

The greatest Russian realist, Count Leo Tolstoy (1828–1910), combined realism in description and character development with an atypical moralizing, which came to dominate his later work. Tolstoy's greatest work was *War and Peace*, a monumental novel set against the historical background of Napoleon's invasion of Russia in 1812. Tolstoy probes deeply into the lives of a multitude of unforgettable characters: the ill-fated Prince Andrei; the shy, fumbling Pierre; and the enchanting, level-headed Natasha. Tolstoy goes to great pains to develop his fatalistic theory of history, which regards free will as an illusion and the achievements of even the greatest leaders as only the channeling of historical necessity. Yet Tolstoy's central message is one that most of the people discussed in this chapter would readily accept: human love, trust, and everyday family ties are life's enduring values.

Degas: Women Ironing   Realism replaced romanticism as the dominant trend in the visual arts for a long generation after 1850. This French work by Edgar Degas (1834–1917) accurately captures the hard work and fatigue of unskilled labor. *(Source: Musée d'Orsay/Cliché des Musées Nationaux, Paris)*

SUMMARY

The Industrial Revolution had a decisive influence on the urban environment. The populations of towns and cities grew rapidly because it was economically advantageous to locate factories and offices in urban areas. This rapid growth worsened long-standing overcrowding and unhealthy living conditions and posed a frightening challenge for society. Eventually government leaders, city planners, reformers, scientists, and ordinary citizens responded. They took effective action in public health and provided themselves with other badly needed urban services. Gradually they tamed the ferocious savagery of the traditional city.

As urban civilization came to prevail, there were major changes in family life. Especially among the lower classes, family life became more stable, more loving, and less mercenary. These improvements had a price, though. Sex roles for men and women became sharply defined and rigidly separate.

Women especially tended to be locked into a subordinate and stereotypical role. Nonetheless, on balance, the quality of family life improved for all family members. Better, more stable family relations reinforced the benefits for the masses of higher real wages, increased social security, political participation, and education.

While the quality of urban and family life improved, the class structure became more complex and diversified than before. Urban society featured many distinct social groups, which existed in a state of constant flux and competition. In mature urban society, the gap between rich and poor remained enormous and really quite traditional, although there were countless gradations between the extremes. Large numbers of poor women in particular continued to labor as workers in sweated industries, as domestic servants, and as prostitutes in order to satisfy the demands of their masters in the servant-keeping classes. Urban society in the late nineteenth century represented a great step forward for humanity, but it remained very unequal.

Inequality was a favorite theme of realist novelists like Balzac and Zola. More generally, literary realism reflected Western society's growing faith in science, progress, and evolutionary thinking. The emergence of urban, industrial civilization accelerated the secularization of the Western world view.

NOTES

1. A. Weber, *The Growth of Cities in the Nineteenth Century* (New York: Columbia University Press, 1899), p. 1.
2. Quoted in W. Ashworth, *The Genesis of Modern British Town Planning* (London: Routledge & Kegan Paul, 1954), p. 17.
3. S. Marcus, "Reading the Illegible," in *The Victorian City: Images and Realities,* vol. 1, ed. H. J. Dyos and Michael Wolff, (London: Routledge & Kegan Paul, 1973), p. 266.
4. E. Gauldie, *Cruel Habitations: A History of Working-Class Housing, 1780–1918* (London: Allen & Unwin, 1974), p. 21.
5. Quoted in E. Chadwick, *Report on the Sanitary Condition of the Labouring Population of Great Britain,* ed. M. Flinn (Edinburgh: University of Edinburgh Press, 1965; original publication, 1842), pp. 315–316.
6. J. P. McKay, *Tramways and Trolleys: The Rise of Urban Mass Transport in Europe* (Princeton, N.J.: Princeton University Press, 1976), p. 81.
7. Quoted in R. P. Neuman, "The Sexual Question and Social Democracy in Imperial Germany," *Journal of Social History* 7 (Winter 1974): 276.
8. Quoted in J. A. Banks, "The Contagion of Numbers," in Dyos and Wolff, vol. 1, p. 112.
9. Quoted in R. Roberts, *The Classic Slum: Salford Life in the First Quarter of the Century* (Manchester, England.: University of Manchester Press, 1971), p. 95.
10. Quoted in B. Harrison, "Pubs," in Dyos and Wolff, vol. 1, p. 175.
11. Quoted in T. Zeldin, *France, 1848–1945,* vol. 1 (Oxford, England.: Clarendon Press, 1973), p. 288.
12. Quoted in J. M. Phayer, "Lower-Class Morality: The Case of Bavaria," *Journal of Social History* 8 (Fall 1974): 89.
13. Quoted in S. Marcus, *The Other Victorians: A Study of Sexuality and Pornography in Mid-Nineteenth-Century England* (New York: Basic Books, 1966), p. 142.
14. Quoted in G. S. Jones, "Working-Class Culture and Working-Class Politics in London, 1870–1900: Notes on the Remaking of a Working Class," *Journal of Social History* 7 (Summer 1974): 486.
15. Quoted in Zeldin, vol. 1, p. 346.
16. Quoted in E. Shorter, *The Making of the Modern Family* (New York: Basic Books, 1975), pp. 230–231.
17. Roberts, p. 35.
18. Quoted in Zeldin, vol. 1, p. 295.
19. Ibid., p. 328.
20. Quoted in Neuman, p. 281.
21. Quoted by S. Kern, "Explosive Intimacy: Psychodynamics of the Victorian Family," *History of Childhood Quarterly* 1 (Winter 1974): 439.
22. A. Comte, *The Positive Philosophy of Auguste Comte,* vol. 1, trans. H. Martineau (London: J. Chapman, 1853), pp. 1–2.
23. Quoted in G. J. Becker, ed., *Documents of Modern Literary Realism* (Princeton, N.J.: Princeton University Press, 1963), p. 159.

SUGGESTED READING

All of the books and articles cited in the Notes are highly recommended; each in its own way is an important contribution to social history and the study of life in the urban society. Note that the *Journal of Social History,* which has a strong European orientation, is excellent both for its articles and for its reviews of new books.

The book by T. Zeldin, *France, 1848–1945,* 2 vols. (1973, 1977), is a pioneering social history that opens many doors, as is the ambitious synthesis by T. Hamerow, *The Birth of a New Europe: State and Society in the Nineteenth Century* (1983).

On the European city, D. Harvey, *Consciousness and the Urban Experience* (1985), is provocative, and D. Pickney, *Napoleon III and the Rebuilding of Paris* (1972), is fascinating, as are G. Masur, *Imperial Berlin* (1970), and M. Hamm, ed., *The City in Russian History* (1976). So also are N. Evenson's beautifully illustrated *Paris: A Century of Change, 1878–1978* (1979) and D. Grew's authoritative *Town in the Ruhr: A Social History of Bochum, 1860–1914* (1979). J. Siegel, *Bohemian Paris: Culture, Politics, and the Boundaries of Bourgeois Life, 1830–1930* (1986), and J. Merriman, ed., *French Cities in the Nineteenth Century: Class, Power, and Urbanization* (1982), are important works on France. D. Olsen's scholarly *Growth of Victorian London* (1978) complements H. Mayhew's wonderful contemporary study, *London Labour and the Labouring Poor* (1861), reprinted recently. M. Crichton's realistic historical novel on organized crime, *The Great Train Robbery* (1976), is excellent. J. J. Tobias, *Urban Crime in Victorian England* (1972), is a lively, scholarly approach to declining criminal activity in the nineteenth century, with a wealth of detail. J. P. Goubert, *The Conquest of Water: The Advent of Health in the Industrial Age* (1989), and G. Rosen, *History of Public Health* (1958), are excellent introductions to sanitary and medical developments. For society as a whole, J. Burnett, *History of the Cost of Living* (1969), cleverly shows how different classes spent their money, and B. Tuchman, *The Proud Tower* (1966), draws an unforgettable portrait of people and classes before 1914. J. Laver's handsomely illustrated *Manners and Morals in the Age of Optimism, 1848–1914* (1966) investigates the urban underworld and relations between the sexes. Sexual attitudes are also examined by E. Trudgill, *Madonnas and Magdalenas: The Origin and Development of Victorian Sexual Attitudes* (1976), and J. Phayer, *Sexual Liberation and Religion in Nineteenth Century Europe* (1977). G. Alter, *Family and Female Life Course: The Women of Verviers, Belgium, 1849–1880* (1988), and A. McLaren, *Sexuality and Social Order: Birth Control in Nineteenth-Century France* (1982), explore attitudes toward family planning.

Women are coming into their own in historical studies. In addition to the general works by Shorter, Wrigley, Stone, and Tilly and Scott cited in Chapter 21, there are a growing number of eye-opening specialized investigations. These include L. Davidoff, *The Best Circles* (1973), and P. Jalland, *Women, Marriage and Politics, 1860–1914* (1986), on upper-class society types; O.

Banks, *Feminism and Family Planning in Victorian England* (1964); and P. Branca, *Women in Europe Since 1750* (1978). M. J. Peterson, *Love and Work in the Lives of Victorian Gentlewomen* (1989), and L. Holcombe, *Victorian Ladies at Work* (1973), examine middle-class women at work. M. Vicinus, ed., *Suffer and Be Still* (1972), and *A Widening Sphere* (1981), are far-ranging collections of essays on women's history, as is R. Bridenthal, C. Koonz, and S. Stuard, eds., *Becoming Visible: Women in European History,* 2d ed. (1987). Feminism is treated perceptively in R. Evans, *The Feminists: Women's Emancipation in Europe, America, and Australia* (1979); K. Blair, *The Clubwoman as Feminist: True Womanhood Redefined, 1868–1914* (1980); and C. Moses, *French Feminism in the Nineteenth Century* (1984). J. Gillis, *Youth and History* (1974), is a good introduction. D. Ransel, ed., *The Family in Imperial Russia* (1978), is an important work on the subject, as is J. Donzelot, *The Policing of Families* (1979), which stresses the loss of family control of all aspects of life to government agencies.

Among studies of special groups, J. Scott, *The Glass-Workers of Carmaux* (1974), is outstanding on skilled French craftsmen, and D. Lockwood, *The Black-coated Worker* (1958), carefully examines class consciousness in the English lower middle class. J. R. Wegs, *Growing Up Working Class: Continuity and Change Among Viennese Youth, 1890–1938* (1989), is recommended. Two fine studies on universities and their professors are S. Rothblatt, *Revolution of the Dons: Cambridge and Society in Victorian England* (1968), and F. Ringer, *The Decline of the German Mandarins* (1969). Servants and their employers receive excellent treatment in T. McBride, *The Domestic Revolution: The Modernization of Household Service in England and France, 1820–1920* (1976), and B. Smith, *Ladies of the Leisure Class: The Bourgeoises of Northern France in the Nineteenth Century* (1981), which may be compared with the innovative study by M. Miller, *The Bon Marché: Bourgeois Culture and the Department Store, 1869–1920* (1981).

On Darwin, M. Ruse, *The Darwinian Revolution* (1979), is a good starting point, as are P. Bowler, *Evolution: The History of an Idea,* rev. ed. (1989), and G. Himmelfarb, *Darwin and the Darwinian Revolution* (1968). O. Chadwick, *The Secularization of the European Mind in the Nineteenth Century* (1976), analyzes the impact of science (and other factors) on religious belief. The masterpieces of the great realist social novelists remain one of the best and most memorable introductions to nineteenth-century culture and thought. In addition to the novels discussed in this chapter and those cited in the Suggested Reading for Chapters 26 and 27, I. Turgenev's *Fathers and Sons* and Zola's *The Dram-Shop (L'Assommoir)* are especially recommended.

29

The Age of Nationalism
in Europe, 1850–1914

The meeting of Garibaldi and Victor Emmanuel

The revolutions of 1848 closed one era and opened another. Urban industrial society began to take strong hold on the Continent, as it already had in Great Britain. Internationally, the repressive peace and diplomatic stability of Metternich's time was replaced by a period of war and rapid change. In thought and culture, soaring romanticism gave way to tough-minded realism. In the European economy, the hard years of the 1840s were followed by good times and prosperity throughout most of the 1850s and 1860s. Perhaps most important of all, European society progressively found, for better or worse, a new and effective organizing principle, capable of coping with the many-sided challenge of the dual revolution and the emerging urban civilization. That principle was *nationalism:* dedication to and identification with the nation-state.

The triumph of nationalism in Europe after 1850 is a development of enormous historical significance. It was by no means completely predictable. After all, nationalism had been a powerful force since at least 1789. Yet it had repeatedly failed to realize its goals, most spectacularly so in 1848.

- Why did nationalism become in one way or another an almost universal faith in Europe between 1850 and 1914?
- How did nationalism evolve so that it appealed not only to predominantly middle-class liberals but to the broad masses of society as well?

These are the weighty questions that this chapter seeks to answer.

NAPOLEON III IN FRANCE

Early nationalism was at least liberal and idealistic and was often democratic and radical as well. The ideas of nationhood and popular sovereignty posed an awesome revolutionary threat to conservatives like Metternich. Yet from the vantage point of the twentieth century, it is clear that nationalism wears many masks. It may be democratic and radical, as it was for Mazzini and Michelet; but it can also flourish in dictatorial states, which may be

conservative, fascist, or communist. Napoleon I's France had already combined national devotion with authoritarian rule. Significantly, it was Napoleon's nephew, Louis Napoleon, who revived and extended this merger. It was he who showed how governments could reconcile popular and conservative forces in an authoritarian nationalism. In doing so, he provided a model for political leaders elsewhere.

The Second Republic and Louis Napoleon

The overwhelming victory of Louis Napoleon Bonaparte in the French presidential elections of December 1848 has long puzzled historians. The nephew of Napoleon I, Louis Napoleon had lived most of his life outside of France and played no part in French politics before 1848. Why did universal manhood suffrage give such an unproven nobody 5.5 million votes while the runner-up, General Cavaignac of June Days fame, polled only 1.5 million and the other three candidates (including the poet Lamartine) received insignificant support?

The usual explanation is that, though Louis Napoleon had only his great name in common with his uncle, that was enough. According to some historians, the Napoleonic legend—a monument to the power of romanticism between 1820 and 1848—had transformed a dictator into a demigod in the minds of the unsophisticated French masses. Another explanation, popularized by Karl Marx, has stressed the fears of middle-class and peasant property owners in the face of the socialist challenge of urban workers. These classes wanted protection. They wanted a tough cop with a big stick on the beat. They found him in Louis Napoleon, who had indeed served briefly as a special constable in London during the Chartist agitation.

These explanations are not wrong, but there was more to Louis Napoleon's popularity than stupidity and fear. In late 1848, Louis Napoleon had a positive "program" for France—a plan that was to guide him throughout most of his long reign. He had elaborated his program in two pamphlets, *Napoleonic Ideas* and *The Elimination of Poverty,* which he had written while imprisoned for a farcical attempt to overthrow Louis Philippe's government. The pamphlets had been widely circulated prior to the presidential election.

Louis Napoleon believed that the government should represent the people and that it should also try hard to help them economically. How was this to be done? Parliaments and political parties were not the answer, according to Louis Napoleon. Politicians represented special-interest groups, particularly middle-class ones. When they ran a parliamentary government, they stirred up class hatred because they were not interested in helping the poor. This had occurred under Louis Philippe, and it was occurring again under the Second Republic. The answer was a strong, even authoritarian, national leader, like the first Napoleon, who would serve all the people, rich and poor. This leader would be linked to the people by direct democracy and universal male suffrage. Sovereignty would flow from the entire population to the leader and would not be diluted or corrupted by politicians and legislative bodies.

These political ideas went hand in hand with Louis Napoleon's vision of national unity and social progress. Unlike his uncle, who had reduced unemployment and social tensions by means of foreign wars, Louis Napoleon favored peaceful measures to relieve the awful poverty of the poor. Rather than doing nothing or providing only temporary relief, the state and its leader had a sacred duty to provide jobs and stimulate the economy. All classes would benefit by such action.

Louis Napoleon's political and social ideas were at least vaguely understood by large numbers of French peasants and workers in December 1848. To many common people he appeared to be both a strong man and a forward-looking champion of their interests, and that is why they voted for him.

Elected to a four-year term, President Louis Napoleon had to share power with a conservative National Assembly. With some misgivings he signed a bill to increase greatly the role of the Catholic church in primary and secondary education. In France as elsewhere in Europe after 1848, the anxious well-to-do saw religion as a bulwark against radicalism. As one leader of the church in France put it, "There is only one recipe for making those who own nothing believe in property-rights: that is to make them believe in God, who dictated the Ten Commandments and who promises eternal punishment to those who steal."[1] Very reluctantly, Louis Napoleon also signed another conservative law, depriving many poor men of the right to vote. He took these conservative measures for two main

reasons: he wanted the Assembly to vote funds to pay his personal debts, and he wanted it to change the constitution so he could run for a second term.

The Assembly did neither. Thus in 1851, Louis Napoleon began to organize a conspiracy with key army officers. On December 2, 1851, he illegally dismissed the Assembly and seized power in a coup d'état. There was some armed resistance in Paris and other cities, but the conservative actions of the Assembly had left the Second Republic with few defenders. Restoring universal male suffrage, Louis Napoleon called on the French people to legalize his actions as his uncle had done. They did: 92 percent voted to make him a strong president for ten years. A year later, 97 percent agreed in a national plebiscite to make him hereditary emperor. For the third time, and by the greatest margin yet, the authoritarian Louis Napoleon was overwhelmingly elected to lead the French nation.

Napoleon III's Second Empire

Louis Napoleon—now Emperor Napoleon III—experienced both success and failure between 1852 and 1870. His greatest success was with the economy, particularly in the 1850s. His government encouraged the new investment banks and massive railroad construction that were at the heart of the Industrial Revolution on the Continent. General economic expansion was also fostered by the government's ambitious program of public works, which included the rebuilding of Paris to improve the urban environment (see pages 903–906). The profits of businessmen soared with prosperity, and the working classes did not fare poorly either. Their wages more than kept up with inflation, and jobs were much easier to find. France's economy benefited from a worldwide economic boom and from other external events, such as gold discoveries in California and Australia. Yet the contribution of Napoleon III's economic policies was real all the same.

Louis Napoleon always hoped that economic progress would reduce social and political tensions. This hope was at least partially realized. Until the mid-1860s, there was little active opposition and even considerable support for his government from France's most dissatisfied group, the urban workers. Napoleon III's regulation of pawnshops and his support of credit unions and

Rebuilding Paris Expensive and time consuming, boulevard construction in Paris brought massive demolition, considerable slum clearance, and protests of ruin to the old city. In addition to expecting economic benefits, Napoleon III rightly believed that broad boulevards would be harder for revolutionaries to barricade than narrow twisting streets. *(Source: The Monsell Collection)*

better housing for the working class were evidence of positive concern in the 1850s. In the 1860s, he granted workers the right to form unions and the right to strike—important economic rights denied by earlier governments.

At first, political power remained in the hands of the emperor. He alone chose his ministers, and they had great freedom of action. At the same time, Napoleon III restricted but did not abolish the Assembly. To be sure, the French parliament in the 1850s had little power. It could not initiate legislation, and it did not control the budget. Yet the members of the Assembly were elected by universal male suffrage every six years, and Louis Napoleon and his government took the parliamentary elections very seriously. They tried to entice notable people, even those who had opposed the

regime, to stand as government candidates in order to expand its base of support. Moreover, the government used its officials and appointed mayors to spread the word that the election of the government's candidates—and the defeat of the opposition—was the key to roads, schools, tax rebates, and a thousand other local concerns.

In 1857 and again in 1863, Louis Napoleon's system worked well and produced overwhelming electoral victories. The poet-politician Alphonse de Lamartine was convinced that Louis Napoleon was France's greatest politician since Talleyrand, and possibly even greater than he. Yet in the course of the 1860s Napoleon III's electoral system gradually disintegrated, for several reasons. France's problems in Italy and the rising power of Prussia led to increasing criticism at home from his

Catholic and nationalist supporters. With increasing effectiveness, the middle-class liberals who had always detested his dictatorship denounced his rule as a disgrace to France's republican tradition.

Napoleon III was always sensitive to the public mood. Public opinion, he once said, always wins the last victory. Thus in the 1860s, he progressively "liberalized" his empire. He gave the Assembly greater powers and the opposition candidates greater freedom, which they used to good advantage. In 1869 the opposition, consisting of republicans, monarchists, and liberals, polled almost 45 percent of the vote.

The following year, a sick and weary Louis Napoleon once again granted France a new constitution, which combined a basically parliamentary regime with a hereditary emperor as chief of state. In a final great plebiscite on the eve of a disastrous war with Prussia, 7.5 million Frenchmen voted in favor of the new constitution, and only 1.5 million opposed it. Napoleon III's attempt to reconcile a strong national state with universal manhood suffrage was still evolving, in a democratic direction.

NATION BUILDING IN ITALY AND GERMANY

Louis Napoleon's triumph in 1848 and his authoritarian rule in the 1850s provided the old ruling classes of Europe with a new model in politics. To what extent was it possible that the expanding urban middle classes and even the growing working classes might, like people in rural areas, rally to a strong and essentially conservative national state? This was one of the great political questions in the 1850s and 1860s. In central Europe, a resounding and definitive answer came with the national unification of Italy and Germany.

Italy to 1850

Italy had never been a united nation prior to 1860. Part of Rome's great empire in ancient times, the Italian peninsula was divided in the Middle Ages into competing city-states, which led the commercial and cultural revival of the West with amazing creativity. A battleground for great powers after 1494, Italy had been reorganized in 1815 at the Congress of Vienna. The rich northern provinces of Lombardy and Venetia were taken by Metternich's Austria. Sardinia and Piedmont were under the rule of an Italian monarch, and Tuscany with its famous capital of Florence shared north central Italy with several smaller states. Central Italy and Rome were ruled by the papacy, which had always considered an independent political existence necessary to fulfill its spiritual mission. Naples and Sicily were ruled, as they had been for almost a hundred years, by a branch of the Bourbons. Metternich was not wrong in dismissing Italy as "a geographical expression" (Map 29.1).

Between 1815 and 1848, the goal of a unified Italian nation captured the imaginations of increasing numbers of Italians. There were three basic approaches. The first was the radical program of the idealistic patriot Giuseppi Mazzini (1805–1872), who preached a centralized democratic republic based on universal suffrage and the will of the people. The second was that of Vincenzo Gioberti (1801–1852), a Catholic priest, who called for a federation of existing states under the presidency of a progressive pope. Finally, there were those who looked for leadership toward the autocratic kingdom of Sardinia-Piedmont, much as many Germans looked toward Prussia.

The third alternative was strengthened by the failures of 1848, when Austria smashed and discredited Mazzini's republicanism. Almost by accident, Sardinia's monarch Victor Emmanuel II (1849–1878) retained the liberal constitution granted under duress in March 1848. This constitution provided for a fair degree of civil liberties and real parliamentary government, complete with elections and parliamentary control of taxes. To the Italian middle classes, Sardinia appeared to be a liberal, progressive state, ideally suited to achieve the goal of national unification. By contrast, Mazzini's brand of democratic republicanism seemed quixotic and too radical. As for the papacy, the initial cautious support by Pius IX (r. 1846–1878) for unification had given way to fear and hostility after he was temporarily driven from Rome during the upheavals of 1848. For a long generation, the papacy would stand resolutely opposed not only to national unification but to most modern trends. In 1864, in the *Syllabus of Errors,* Pius IX strongly denounced rationalism, socialism, separation of church and state, and religious liberty, denying that "the Roman pontiff can and ought to reconcile and align himself with progress, liberalism, and modern civilization."

MAP 29.1 The Unification of Italy, 1859–1870 The leadership of Sardinia-Piedmont and nationalist fervor were decisive factors in the unification of Italy.

Cavour and Garibaldi

The kingdom of Sardinia (see Map 29.1) had the good fortune of being led by a brilliant statesman, Count Camillo Benso di Cavour (1810–1861), the dominant figure in the Sardinian government from 1850 until his death. Cavour's rise to promi-

nence presaged the coming tacit alliance between the aristocracy and the solid middle class throughout much of Europe. Beginning as a successful manager of his father's landed estates in Piedmont, Cavour was also an economic liberal. He turned toward industry and made a fortune in sugar mills, steamships, banks, and railroads. Economically secure, he then entered the world of politics and became chief minister in the liberalized Sardinian monarchy. Cavour's national goals were limited and realistic. Until 1859 he sought unity only for the states of northern and perhaps central Italy in a greatly expanded kingdom of Sardinia. It was *not* one of his goals to incorporate the papal states or the kingdom of the Two Sicilies, with their very different cultures and governments, into an Italy of all the Italians. Cavour was a moderate nationalist.

In the 1850s Cavour worked to consolidate the kingdom of Sardinia as a liberal state capable of leading northern Italy. His program of highways and railroads, of civil liberties and opposition to clerical privilege, increased support for Sardinia throughout northern Italy. Yet Cavour realized that Sardinia could not drive Austria out of Lombardy and Venetia and unify northern Italy under Victor Emmanuel without the help of a powerful ally. He sought that ally in the person of Napoleon III, who sincerely believed in the general principle of nationality as well as in modest expansion for France.

In a complicated series of diplomatic maneuvers, Cavour worked for a diplomatic alliance with Napoleon III against Austria. Finally, in July 1858, he succeeded and goaded Austria into attacking Sardinia. Napoleon III came to Sardinia's defense. Then, after the victory of the combined Franco-Sardinian forces, Napoleon III did a complete about-face. Nauseated by the gore of war and criticized by French Catholics for supporting the pope's declared enemy, Napoleon III abandoned Cavour. He made a compromise peace with the Austrians at Villafranca in July 1859. The kingdom of Sardinia received only Lombardy, the area around Milan. The rest of the map of Italy remained essentially unchanged. Cavour resigned in a rage.

Garibaldi and His Red Shirts Four days after landing in western Sicily, Garibaldi's forces won the Battle of Calatafimi, pictured here with the flamboyant patriot exhorting his troops at the center. Within two weeks Garibaldi took Palermo and established a provisional government in Sicily. *(Source: Museo del Risorgimento, Milan. Photo: Giancarlo Costa)*

Yet Cavour's plans were salvaged by popular revolts and Italian nationalism. While the war against Austria had raged in the north, dedicated nationalists in central Italy had risen and driven out their rulers. Nationalist fervor seized the urban masses. Large crowds demonstrated, chanting, "Italy and Victor Emmanuel!" and singing passionately, "Foreigners, get out of Italy!" Buoyed by this enthusiasm, leaders of the nationalist movement in central Italy ignored the compromise peace of Villafranca and called for fusion with Sardinia. This was not at all what France and the other Great Powers wanted, but the nationalists held firm and eventually had their way. Cavour returned to power in early 1860 and worked out a diplomatic deal with Napoleon III. The people of central Italy voted overwhelmingly to join a greatly enlarged kingdom of Sardinia. Cavour had achieved his original goal of a north Italian state (see Map 29.1).

Superpatriots like Giuseppe Garibaldi (1801–1882) believed that the job of unification was still only half done. The son of a poor sailor, Garibaldi personified the romantic, revolutionary nationalism of Mazzini and 1848. As a lad of seventeen, he had traveled to Rome and been converted to the "New Italy, the Italy of all the Italians." As he later wrote in his *Autobiography,* "The Rome that I beheld with the eyes of youthful imagination was the Rome of the future—the dominant thought of my whole life." Sentenced to death in 1834 for his part in an uprising in Genoa, Garibaldi escaped to South America. For twelve years he led a guerrilla band in Uruguay's struggle for independence. "Shipwrecked, ambushed, shot through the neck," he found in a tough young woman, Anna da Silva, a mate and companion in arms. Their first children nearly starved in the jungle while Garibaldi, clad in a long red shirt, fashioned a legend not unlike that of the Cuban Che Guevara in recent times. He returned to Italy to fight in 1848 and led a corps of volunteers against Austria in 1859. By the spring of 1860, Garibaldi had emerged as a powerful independent force in Italian politics.

Partly to use Garibaldi and partly to get rid of him, Cavour secretly supported Garibaldi's bold plan to "liberate" Sicily. Landing in Sicily in May 1860, Garibaldi's guerrilla band of a thousand "Red Shirts" captivated the Sicilian peasantry. Outwitting the 20,000-man royal army, the guerrilla leader took Palermo. Then he and his men crossed to the mainland, marched triumphantly toward Naples, and prepared to attack Rome and the pope. But the wily Cavour quickly sent Sardinian forces to occupy most of the Papal States (but not Rome) and to intercept Garibaldi.

Cavour realized that an attack on Rome would bring about war with France, and he also feared Garibaldi's popular appeal. Thus he immediately organized a plebiscite in the conquered territories. The patriotic Garibaldi did not oppose Cavour, despite the urging of some of his more radical supporters, and the people of the south voted to join the kingdom of Sardinia. When Garibaldi and Victor Emmanuel rode through Naples to cheering crowds, they symbolically sealed the union of north and south, of monarch and people.

Cavour had succeeded. He had controlled Garibaldi and had turned popular nationalism in a conservative direction. The new kingdom of Italy, which did not include Venice until 1866 or Rome until 1870, was neither radical nor democratic. Italy was a parliamentary monarchy under Victor Emmanuel, but in accordance with the Sardinian constitution only a small minority of Italians had the right to vote. There was a definite division between the propertied classes and the common people. There was also a great social and cultural gap between the progressive, industrializing north and the stagnant, agrarian south. This gap would increase, since peasant industries in the south would not be able to survive. Italy was united politically. Other divisions remained.

Germany Before Bismarck

In the aftermath of 1848, while Louis Napoleon consolidated his rule and Cavour schemed, the German states were locked in a political stalemate. With Russian diplomatic support, Austria had blocked the halfhearted attempt of Frederick William IV of Prussia (r. 1840–1861) to unify Germany "from above" This action contributed to growing tension between Austria and Prussia, as each power sought to block the other within the reorganized German Confederation (pages 868 and 894). Stalemate also prevailed in the domestic politics of the individual states, as Austria, Prussia, and the smaller German kingdoms entered a period of reaction and immobility.

At the same time, powerful economic forces were undermining the political status quo. Modern industry grew rapidly in Europe throughout the 1850s (see pages 846–852). Nowhere was this growth more rapid than within the German customs union *(Zollverein)*. Developing gradually under Prussian leadership after 1818 and founded officially in 1834 to stimulate trade and increase the revenues of member states, the Zollverein did not include Austria. After 1848 it became a crucial factor in the Austro-Prussian rivalry.

Prussia convinced the Zollverein to reduce substantially its tariff duties, so that Austria's highly protected industry could not afford to join the customs union. In retaliation, Austria tried to destroy the Zollverein by inducing the south German states to leave it, but without success. Indeed, by the end of 1853 all the German states except Austria had joined the customs union. A new Germany excluding Austria was becoming an economic reality, and the middle class and business groups were finding solid economic reasons to bolster their idealistic support of national unification. Thus economic developments helped Prussia greatly in its struggle against Austria's traditional supremacy in German affairs.

The national uprising in Italy in 1859 made a profound impression in the German states. In Prussia, great political change and war—perhaps with Austria, perhaps with France—seemed quite possible. The tough-minded William I of Prussia (r. 1861–1888), had replaced the unstable Frederick William IV as regent in 1858 and become king in 1861. He and his top military advisers were convinced of the need for major army reforms. William I wanted to double the size of the highly disciplined regular army. He also wanted to reduce the importance of the reserve militia, a semipopular force created during the Napoleonic wars. Of course, reform of the army meant a bigger defense budget and higher taxes.

Prussia had emerged from 1848 with a parliament of sorts, and by 1859 the Prussian parliament was in the hands of the liberal middle class. The middle class, like the landed aristocracy, was overrepresented by the Prussian electoral system, and it wanted society to be less, not more, militaristic. Above all, middle-class representatives wanted to establish once and for all that parliament, not the king, had the ultimate political power. They also wanted to ensure that the army was responsible to the people and not a "state within a state." These demands were popular. The parliament rejected the military budget in 1862,

Otto von Bismarck A fierce political fighter with a commanding personality and a brilliant mind, Bismarck was devoted to Prussia and its king and aristocracy. Uniforms were worn by civilian officials as well as by soldiers in Prussia. *(Source: Brown Brothers)*

and the liberals triumphed so completely in new elections that the conservatives "could ride to the parliament building in a single coach." King William considered abdicating in favor of his more liberal son. In the end, he called on Count Otto von Bismarck to head a ministry and defy the parliament. It was a momentous choice.

Bismarck Takes Command

The most important figure in German history between Luther and Hitler, Otto von Bismarck (1815–1898) has been the object of enormous interest and debate. Like his contemporary Abraham Lincoln, who successfully led the North against the South in the American Civil War between

1861 and 1865, Bismarck used military victory to forge a strong, unified national state.

A great hero to some, a great villain to others, Bismarck was above all a master of politics. Born into the Prussian landowning aristocracy, the young Bismarck was a wild and tempestuous student, given to duels and drinking. Proud of his Junker heritage—"my fathers have been born and have lived and died in the same rooms for centuries"—and always devoted to his Prussian sovereign, Bismarck had a strong personality and an unbounded desire for power.

Bismarck entered the civil service—the only socially acceptable career, except the army, for a Prussian aristocrat. But he soon found bureaucratic life unbearable and fled to his ancestral estate. The civil servant was like a musician in an orchestra, he said, and, "I want to play the tune the way it sounds to me or not at all. . . . My pride bids me command rather than obey."[2] Yet in his drive for power, power for himself and for Prussia, Bismarck was extraordinarily flexible and pragmatic. "One must always have two irons in the fire," he once said. He kept his options open, pursuing one policy and then another as he moved with skill and cunning toward his goal.

Bismarck first honed his political skills as a diplomat. Acquiring a reputation as an ultraconservative in the Prussian assembly in 1848, he fought against Austria as the Prussian ambassador to the German Confederation from 1851 to 1859. Transferred next to St. Petersburg and then to Paris, Bismarck had an excellent opportunity to evaluate Tsar Alexander II and Emperor Napoleon III at close range. A blunt, expansive talker, especially after a few drinks, Bismarck's basic goal was well known in 1862: to build up Prussia's strength and consolidate Prussia's precarious Great Power status.

To achieve this goal, Bismarck was convinced that Prussia had to control completely the northern, predominantly Protestant part of the German Confederation. He saw three paths open before him. He might work with Austria to divide the smaller German states lying between them (see Map 29.2). Or he might combine with foreign powers—France and Italy, or even Russia—against Austria. Or he might ally with the forces of German nationalism to defeat and expel Austria from German affairs. Each possibility was explored in many complicated diplomatic maneuvers, but in the end the last path was the one Bismarck took.

That Bismarck would join with the forces of German nationalism to increase Prussia's power seemed unlikely when he took office in 1862. Bismarck's appointment made a strong but unfavorable impression. One of the liberal middle-class members of the Prussian parliament expressed enlightened public opinion throughout Prussia and the other German states: "Bismarck, that is to say: government without budget, rule by the sword in home affairs, and war in foreign affairs. I consider him the most dangerous Minister for Prussia's liberty and happiness."[3]

Bismarck's speeches were a sensation and a scandal. Declaring that the government would rule without parliamentary consent, Bismarck lashed out at the middle-class opposition: "The great questions of the day will not be decided by speeches and resolutions—that was the blunder of 1848 and 1849—but by blood and iron." In 1863 he told the Prussian parliament, "If a compromise cannot be arrived at and a conflict arises, then the conflict becomes a question of power. Whoever has the power then acts according to his opinion." Denounced for his view that "might makes right," Bismarck and the bureaucracy went right on collecting taxes, even though the parliament refused to approve the budget, and reorganized the army. And for four years, from 1862 to 1866, the voters of Prussia continued to express their opposition by sending large liberal majorities to the parliament.

The Austro-Prussian War of 1866

Opposition at home spurred the search for success abroad. The ever-knotty question of Schleswig-Holstein (see page 892) provided a welcome opportunity. When the Danish king tried again, as in 1848, to bring the provinces into a centralized Danish state against the will of the German Confederation, Prussia joined Austria in a short and successful war against Denmark in 1864. Then, rather than following nationalist sentiment and allowing the conquered provinces to become another medium-size independent state within the German Confederation, Bismarck maneuvered Austria into a tricky position. Prussia and Austria agreed to joint administration of the conquered provinces, thereby giving Bismarck a weapon he could use either to force Austria into peacefully accepting Prussian domination in northern Germany or to start a war against Austria.

MAP 29.2 The Unification of Germany, 1866–1871 Prussian expansion, Austrian expulsion from the old German Confederation, and the creation of a new German Empire all went together. Austria lost no territory, but Prussia's neighbors in the north suffered grievously or simply disappeared.

Bismarck knew that a war with Austria would have to be localized war. He had to be certain that Prussian expansion did not provoke a mighty armed coalition, such as the coalition that had almost crushed Frederick the Great in the eighteenth century. Russia, the great bear to the east, was no problem. Bismarck had already gained Alexander II's gratitude by supporting Russia's repression of a Polish uprising in 1863. Napoleon III—the "sphinx without a riddle," according to Bismarck—was another matter. But Bismarck charmed him into neutrality with vague promises of more territory along the Rhine. Thus, when Austria proved unwilling to give up its historic role in German affairs, Bismarck was in a position to engage in a war of his own making.

The Austro-Prussian War of 1866 lasted only seven weeks. Utilizing railroads to mass troops and the new breechloading needle gun for maximum firepower, the reorganized Prussian army overran northern Germany and defeated Austria decisively at the battle of Sadowa in Bohemia. Anticipating Prussia's future needs, Bismarck offered Austria realistic, even generous, peace terms. Austria paid no reparations and lost no territory to Prussia, although Venice was ceded to Italy. But Hanover was seized by Prussia, the German Confederation was dissolved, and Austria agreed to withdraw from German affairs. The states north of the Main River were grouped in a new North German Confederation led by an expanded Prussia. The mainly Catholic states of the south were permitted to remain independent while forming military alliances with Prussia. Bismarck's fundamental goal of Prussian expansion was being realized (Map 29.2).

The Taming of Parliament

Bismarck had long been convinced that the old order he so ardently defended should make peace— on its own terms—with the liberal middle class and the nationalist movement. Inspired somewhat by Louis Napoleon, he realized that nationalism was not necessarily hostile to conservative, authoritarian government. Moreover, Bismarck believed that, because of the events of 1848, the German middle class could be led to prefer the reality of national unity to a long, uncertain battle for truly liberal institutions. During the constitutional struggle over army reform and parliamentary authority, he had delayed but not abandoned this goal. Thus, during the attack on Austria in 1866, he increasingly identified Prussia's fate with the "national development of Germany."

In the aftermath of victory, Bismarck fashioned a federal constitution for the new North German Confederation. Each state retained its own local government, but the king of Prussia was to be president of the confederation and the chancellor—Bismarck—was to be responsible only to the president. The federal government—William I and

Bismarck—controlled the army and foreign affairs. There was also a legislature, consisting of an upper house, whose delegates were appointed by the different states, and a lower house. Both houses shared equally in the making of laws. Members of the lower house were elected by universal, equal manhood suffrage. With this radical innovation, Bismarck opened the door to popular participation and went over the head of the middle class directly to the people. All the while, however, ultimate power rested as securely as ever in the hands of Prussia and its king and army.

Events within Prussia itself were even more significant than those at the federal level. In the flush of victory, the ultraconservatives expected Bismarck to suspend the Prussian constitution or perhaps abolish the Prussian parliament altogether. Yet he did nothing of the sort. Instead, he held out an olive branch to the parliamentary opposition. Marshaling all his diplomatic skill, Bismarck asked the parliament to pass a special indemnity bill to approve after the fact all of the government's spending between 1862 and 1866. Most of the liberals snatched at the chance to cooperate. For four long years, they had opposed and criticized Bismarck's "illegal" measures. And what had happened? Bismarck, the king, and the army had persevered, and in the end these conservative forces had succeeded beyond the wildest dreams of the liberal middle class. In 1866 German unity was in sight, and the people were going to be allowed to participate actively in the new state. Many liberals repented their "sins" and were overjoyed that Bismarck would forgive them.

None repented more ardently or more typically than Hermann Baumgarten, a mild-mannered, thoroughly decent history professor and member of the liberal opposition. In an essay entitled "A Self Criticism of German Liberalism," he confessed in 1866:

We thought by agitation we could transform Germany. But . . . almost all the elements of our political system have been shown erroneous by the facts themselves. . . . Yet we have experienced a miracle almost without parallel. The victory of our principles would have brought us misery, whereas the defeat of our principles has brought boundless salvation.[4]

The constitutional struggle was over. The German middle class was bowing respectfully before

Bismarck and the monarchial authority and aristocratic superiority that he represented. They did not stand upright again in the years before 1914.

The Franco-Prussian War of 1870 to 1871

The rest of the story of German unification is anticlimactic. In 1867 Bismarck brought the four south German states into the customs union and established a customs parliament. The south Germans, led by the anti-Prussian Bavarians, were reluctant to go further because of their different religious and political traditions. Bismarck realized that a patriotic war with France would drive the south German states into Prussia's arms. The French obligingly played their part. The apparent issue—whether a distant relative of Prussia's William I (and France's Napoleon III) might become king of Spain—was only a diplomatic pretext. By 1870 the French leaders of the Second Empire, alarmed by their powerful new neighbor on the Rhine, had decided on a war to teach Prussia a lesson.

As soon as war against France began in 1870, Bismarck had the wholehearted support of the south German states. With other governments standing still—Bismarck's generosity to Austria in 1866 was paying big dividends—German forces under Prussian leadership decisively defeated Louis Napoleon's armies at Sedan on September 1, 1870. Three days later, French patriots in Paris proclaimed yet another French republic (the third) and vowed to continue fighting. But after five months, in January 1871, a starving Paris surrendered and France went on to accept Bismarck's harsh peace terms. By this time, the south German states had agreed to join a new German Empire. The victorious William I was proclaimed emperor of Germany in the Hall of Mirrors in the palace of Versailles. Europe had a nineteenth-century German "sun king." As in the 1866 constitution, the king of Prussia and his ministers had ultimate power in the new empire, and the lower house of the legislature was elected popularly by universal male suffrage.

The Franco-Prussian War of 1870 to 1871, which Europeans generally saw as a test of nations in a pitiless Darwinian struggle for existence, released an enormous surge of patriotic feeling in Germany. Bismarck's genius, the invincible Prussian army, the solidarity of king and people in a unified nation—these and similar themes were trumpeted endlessly during and after the war. The weakest of the Great Powers in 1862—after Austria, Britain, France, and Russia—Prussia (fortified by the other German states) had become the most powerful state in Europe in less than a decade. Most Germans were enormously proud, enormously relieved. And they were somewhat drunk with success, blissfully imagining themselves the fittest and best of the European species.

"His First Thought"   This 1896 cartoon provides a brilliant commentary on German middle-class attitudes. Suddenly crippled, the man's first thought is "Disaster! Now I can no longer be an army reserve officer." Being a part-time junior officer, below the dominant aristocratic career officers, became a great middle-class status symbol. *(Source: Caroline Buckler)*

Semi-authoritarian nationalism had triumphed. Only a few critics remained dedicated to the liberal ideal of truly responsible parliamentary government.

THE MODERNIZATION OF RUSSIA

In Russia, unlike in Italy and Germany, there was no need to build a single state out of a jumble of principalities. The Russian Empire was already an enormous multinational state, a state that contained all the ethnic Russians and many other nationalities as well. The long-term challenge facing the government was to hold the existing state together, either by means of political compromise or by military force. Thus Russia's rulers saw nationalism as a subversive ideology in the early nineteenth century, and they tried with some success to limit its development among their non-Russian subjects.

Yet old, autocratic Russia found itself in serious trouble after 1853. It became clear to Russia's leaders that the country had to embrace the process of modernization. A vague and often overworked term, "modernization" is a great umbrella under which some writers place most of the major developments of the last two hundred or even five hundred years. Yet defined narrowly—as changes that enable a country to compete effectively with the leading countries at a given time—modernization can be a useful concept. It fits Russia after the Crimean War particularly well.

The "Great Reforms"

In the 1850s Russia was a poor agrarian society. Industry was little developed, and almost 90 percent of the population lived on the land. Agricultural techniques were backward: the ancient open-field system reigned supreme. Serfdom was still the basic social institution. Bound to the lord on a hereditary basis, the peasant serf was little more than a slave. In the early nineteenth century, individual serfs and serf families were regularly sold, with and without land. Serfs were obliged to furnish labor services or money payments as the lord saw fit. Moreover, the lord could choose freely among them for army recruits, who had to serve for twenty-five years, and he could punish a serf with deportation to Siberia whenever he wished. Sexual exploitation of female serfs by their lords was common.

Serfdom had become the great moral and political issue for the government by the 1840s, but it might still have lasted many more years had it not been for the Crimean War of 1853 to 1856. The war began as a dispute with France over who should protect certain Christian shrines in the Ottoman Empire. Because the fighting was concentrated on the Crimean peninsula in the Black Sea, Russia's transportation network of rivers and wagons failed to supply the distant Russian armies adequately. France and Great Britain, aided by Sardinia, inflicted a humiliating defeat on Russia.

The military defeat marked a turning point in Russian history. The Russian state had been built on the military, and Russia had not lost a major war for a century and a half. This defeat demonstrated that Russia had fallen behind the rapidly industrializing nations of western Europe in many areas. At the very least, Russia needed railroads, better armaments, and reorganization of the army if it was to maintain its international position as a Great Power. Moreover, the disastrous war had caused hardship and raised the specter of massive peasant rebellion. Reform of serfdom was imperative. And, as the new tsar, Alexander II (r. 1855–1881), told the serf owners, it would be better if reform came from above rather than from below. Military disaster thus forced Alexander II and his ministers along the path of rapid social change and general modernization.

The first and greatest of the reforms was the freeing of the serfs in 1861. Human bondage was abolished forever, and the emancipated peasants received, on the average, about half of the land. Yet they had to pay fairly high prices for their land, and because the land was owned collectively, each peasant village was jointly responsible for the payments of all the families in the village. The government hoped that collective responsibility would strengthen the peasant village as a social unit and prevent the development of a class of landless peasants. In practice, collective ownership and responsibility made it very difficult for individual peasants to improve agricultural methods or leave their villages. Thus the effects of the reform were limited, for it did not encourage peasants to change their old habits and attitudes.

Most of the later reforms were also halfway measures. In 1864 the government established a new institution of local government, the *zemstvo*. Members of this local assembly were elected by a three-class system of towns, peasant villages, and noble landowners. A zemstvo executive council dealt with local problems. The establishment of the zemstvos marked a significant step toward popular participation, and Russian liberals hoped that it would lead to a national parliament. They were soon disappointed. The local zemstvo remained subordinate to the traditional bureaucracy and the local nobility, which were heavily favored by the property-based voting system. More successful was reform of the legal system, which established independent courts and equality before the law. Education was also liberalized somewhat, and censorship was relaxed but not removed.

The Industrialization of Russia

Until the twentieth century, Russia's greatest strides toward modernization were economic rather than political. Industry and transport, both so vital to the military, were transformed in two industrial surges. The first came after 1860. The government encouraged and subsidized private railway companies, and construction boomed. In 1860 the empire had only about 1,250 miles of railroads; by 1880 it had about 15,500 miles. The railroads enabled agricultural Russia to export grain and thus earn money for further industrialization. Domestic manufacturing was stimulated, and by the end of the 1870s Russia had a sophisticated and well-developed railway-equipment industry. Industrial suburbs grew up around Moscow and St. Petersburg, and a class of modern factory workers began to take shape.

Industrial development strengthened Russia's military forces and gave rise to territorial expansion to the south and east. Imperial expansion greatly excited many ardent Russian nationalists and superpatriots, who became some of the government's most enthusiastic supporters. Industrial development also contributed mightily to the spread of Marxian thought and the transformation of the Russian revolutionary movement after 1890.

In 1881 Alexander II was assassinated by a small group of terrorists. The era of reform came to an abrupt end, for the new tsar, Alexander III (r. 1881–1894), was a determined reactionary. Russia, and indeed all of Europe, experienced hard times economically in the 1880s. Political modernization remained frozen until 1905, but economic modernization sped forward in the 1890s, in the massive second industrial surge. As it had after the Crimean War, nationalism played a decisive role. The key leader was Sergei Witte (1849–1915), the tough, competent minister of finance from 1892 to 1903. Early in his career, Witte had found in the writings of Friedrich List (page 851) an analysis and a program for action. List had stressed the peril for Germany of remaining behind England in the 1830s and 1840s. Witte saw the same threat of industrial backwardness hindering Russia's power and greatness.

Witte moved forward on several fronts. A railroad manager by training, he believed that railroads were "a very powerful weapon . . . for the direction of the economic development of the country."[5] Thus the Russian government built railroads rapidly, doubling the network to 35,000 miles by the end of the century. The gigantic trans-Siberian line connecting Moscow with Vladivostok on the Pacific Ocean 5,000 miles away was Witte's pride, and it was largely completed during his term of office. Following List's advice, Witte raised high protective tariffs to build Russian industry, and he put the country on the gold standard of the "civilized world" in order to strengthen Russian finances.

Witte's greatest innovation, however, was to use the West to catch up with the West. He aggressively encouraged foreigners to use their abundant capital and advanced technology to build great factories in backward Russia. As he told the tsar, "The inflow of foreign capital is . . . the only way by which our industry will be able to supply our country quickly with abundant and cheap products."[6] This policy was brilliantly successful, especially in southern Russia. There, in the eastern Ukraine, foreign capitalists and their engineers built an enormous and very modern steel and coal industry almost from scratch in little more than a decade. By 1900 only the United States, Germany, and Great Britain were producing more steel than Russia. The Russian petroleum industry had even pulled up alongside that of the United States and was producing and refining half of the world's output of oil.

Novgorod Merchants Drinking Tea This late nineteenth-century photograph suggests how Russian businessmen were slow to abandon traditional dress and attitudes. Stern authoritarians and staunchly devoted to church and tsar, they were often suspicious of foreigners as well as the lawyers and journalists who claimed to speak for the nation's middle class. *(Source: Bettmann/Hulton)*

Witte knew how to keep foreigners in line. Once a leading foreign businessman came to him and angrily demanded that the Russian government fulfill a contract that it had signed and pay certain debts immediately. Witte asked to see the contract. He read it and then carefully tore it to pieces and threw it in the wastepaper basket without a word of explanation. It was just such a fiercely independent Russia that was catching up with the advanced nations of the West.

The Revolution of 1905

In part, catching up meant vigorous territorial expansion, for this was the age of Western imperialism (see Chapter 30). By 1903 Russia had established a sphere of influence in Chinese Man-churia and was casting greedy eyes on northern Korea. When the protests of equally imperialistic Japan were ignored, the Japanese launched a surprise attack in February 1904. To the world's amazement, Russia suffered repeated losses and was forced in August 1905 to accept a humiliating defeat.

As is often the case, military disaster abroad brought political upheaval at home. The business and professional classes had long wanted to match economic with political modernization. Their minimal goal was to turn the last of Europe's absolutist monarchies into a liberal, representative regime. Factory workers, strategically concentrated in the large cities, had all the grievances of early industrialization and were organized in a radical labor movement. Peasants had gained little from the era of reforms and were suffering from poverty and overpopulation. Nationalist sentiment was emerging among the empire's minorities. The politically and culturally dominant ethnic Russians were only about 45 percent of the population, and by 1900 some intellectuals among the subject nationalities were calling for self-rule and autonomy. Separatist nationalism was strongest among the Polish and Ukrainians. With the army pinned down in Manchuria, all these currents of discontent converged in the revolution of 1905.

The beginning of the revolution pointed up the incompetence of the government. On a Sunday in January 1905, a massive demonstration of workers and their families converged peacefully on the Winter Palace in St. Petersburg to present a petition to the tsar. The workers were led by a trade-unionist priest named Father Gapon, who had been secretly supported by the police as a preferable alternative to more radical unions. Carrying icons and respectfully singing "God Save the Tsar," the workers did not know that Nicholas II had fled the city. Suddenly troops opened fire, killing and wounding hundreds. The "Bloody Sunday" massacre turned ordinary workers against the tsar and produced a wave of general indignation.

Outlawed political parties came out into the open, and by the summer of 1905 strikes, peasant uprisings, revolts among minority nationalities, and troop mutinies were sweeping the country. The revolutionary surge culminated in October 1905 in a great paralyzing general strike, which forced the government to capitulate. The tsar issued the October Manifesto, which granted full civil rights and promised a popularly elected *Duma* (parliament) with real legislative power. The manifesto split the opposition. It satisfied most moderate and liberal demands, but the Social Democrats rejected it and led a bloody workers' uprising in Moscow in December 1905. Frightened middle-class moderates helped the government repress the uprising and survive as a constitutional monarchy.

On the eve of the opening of the first Duma in May 1906, the government issued the new constitution, the Fundamental Laws. The tsar retained great powers. The Duma, elected indirectly by universal male suffrage, and a largely appointive upper house could debate and pass laws, but the tsar had an absolute veto. As in Bismarck's Germany, the emperor appointed his ministers, who did not need to command a majority in the Duma.

The disappointed, predominantly middle-class liberals, the largest group in the newly elected Duma, saw the Fundamental Laws as a great step backward. Efforts to cooperate with the tsar's ministers soon broke down. The government then dismissed the Duma, only to see a more hostile and radical opposition elected in 1907. After three months of deadlock, the second Duma was also dismissed. Thereupon the tsar and his reactionary advisers unilaterally rewrote the electoral law so as to increase greatly the weight of the propertied classes at the expense of workers, peasants, and national minorities.

The new law had the intended effect. With landowners assured half of the seats in the Duma, the government secured a loyal majority in 1907 and again in 1912. Thus armed, the tough, energetic chief minister, Peter Stolypin, pushed through important agrarian reforms designed to break down collective village ownership of land and to encourage the most enterprising peasants—the so-called wager on the strong. On the eve of the First World War, Russia was partially modernized, a conservative constitutional monarchy with a peasant-based but industrializing economy.

THE RESPONSIVE NATIONAL STATE (1871–1914)

For central and western Europe, the unification of Italy and Germany by "blood and iron" marked the end of a dramatic period of nation building. After 1871 the heartland of Europe was organized in strong national states. Only on the borders of Europe—in Ireland and Russia, in Austria-Hungary and the Balkans—did subject peoples still strive for political unity and independence. Despite national differences, European domestic politics after 1871 had a common framework: the firmly established national state. The common themes within that framework were the emergence of mass politics and growing mass loyalty toward the national state.

For good reason, ordinary people—the masses of an industrializing, urbanizing society—felt increasing loyalty to their governments. More and more people could vote. By 1914 universal manhood suffrage was the rule rather than the exception. This development had as much psychological as political significance. Ordinary men were no longer denied the right to vote because they lacked wealth or education. They counted; they could influence the government to some extent. They could feel that they were becoming "part of the system."

Women began to demand the right to vote. The women's suffrage movement achieved its first success in the western United States, and by 1913 women could vote in twelve states. Europe, too, moved slowly in this direction. In 1914 Norway gave the vote to most women. Elsewhere, women like the English Emmeline Pankhurst were very militant in their demands. They heckled politicians and held public demonstrations. These efforts generally failed before 1914, but they prepared the way for the triumph of the women's suffrage movement immediately after the First World War.

As the right to vote spread, politicians and parties in national parliaments represented the people more responsively. Most countries soon had many political parties. The multiparty system meant that parliamentary majorities were built on shifting coalitions, which were unstable but did give parties leverage. They could obtain benefits for their supporters. Governments increasingly passed laws to alleviate general problems and to help specific groups. Governments seemed to care, and they seemed more worthy of support.

The German Empire

Politics in Germany after 1871 reflected many of these developments. The new German Empire was a federal union of Prussia and twenty-four smaller states. Much of the everyday business of government was conducted by the separate states, but there was a strong national government with a chancellor—until 1890, Bismarck—and a popularly elected parliament, called the *Reichstag*. Although Bismarck refused to be bound by a parliamentary majority, he tried nonetheless to maintain such a majority. This situation gave the political parties opportunities. Until 1878 Bismarck relied mainly on the National Liberals, who had rallied to him after 1866. They supported legislation useful for further economic and legal unification of the country.

Less wisely, they backed Bismarck's attack on the Catholic church, the so-called *Kulturkampf,* or "struggle for civilization." Like Bismarck, the middle-class National Liberals were particularly alarmed by Pius IX's declaration of papal infallibility in 1870. That dogma seemed to ask German Catholics to put loyalty to their church above loyalty to their nation. Only in Protestant Prussia did the Kulturkampf have even limited success. Catholics throughout the country generally voted for the Catholic Center party, which blocked passage of national laws hostile to the church. Finally in 1878, Bismarck abandoned his attack. Indeed, he and the Catholic Center party entered into an uneasy but mutually advantageous alliance. The reasons were largely economic.

After a worldwide financial bust in 1873, European agriculture was in an increasingly difficult position. Wheat prices plummeted as cheap grain poured in from the United States, Canada, and Russia. New lands were opening up in North America and Russia, and the combination of railroads and technical improvements in shipping cut freight rates for grain drastically. European peasants with their smaller, less efficient farms could not compete in cereal production, especially in western and southern Germany. The peasantry there was largely Catholic, and the Catholic Center party was thus converted to the cause of higher tariffs to protect the economic interests of its supporters.

The same competitive pressures caused the Protestant Junkers, who owned large estates in eastern Germany, to embrace the cause of higher tariffs. They were joined by some of the iron and steel magnates of the Prussian Rhineland and Westphalia, who had previously been for free trade. With three such influential groups lobbying energetically, Bismarck was happy to go along with a new protective tariff in 1879. In doing so, he won new supporters in the Reichstag—the Center party of the Catholics and the Conservative party of the Prussian landowners—and he held on to most of the National Liberals.

Bismarck had been looking for a way to increase taxes and raise more money for the government. The solution was higher tariffs. Many other governments acted similarly. The 1880s and 1890s saw a widespread return to protectionism. France in particular established very high tariffs to protect agriculture and industry, peasants and manufacturers. Thus the German government and other

Bismarck and William II   Shown here visiting Bismarck's country estate in 1888, shortly after he became emperor of Germany (and king of Prussia), the young and impetuous William II soon quarrelled with his chief minister. Determined to rule, not merely to reign, his dismissal of Bismarck in 1890 was a fatal decision. *(Source: Bildarchiv Preussicher Kulturbesitz)*

governments responded to a major economic problem and simultaneously won greater loyalty.

At the same time, Bismarck tried to stop the growth of German socialism because he genuinely feared its revolutionary language and allegiance to a movement transcending the nation-state. In 1878, after two attempts on the life of William I by radicals (though not socialists), Bismarck succeeded in ramming through the Reichstag a law repressing socialists. Socialist meetings and publications were strictly controlled. The Social Democratic party was outlawed and driven underground. However, German socialists displayed a discipline and organization worthy of the Prussian army itself. Bismarck had to try another tack.

Thus Bismarck's state pioneered with social measures that were designed to win the support of working-class people. In 1883 he pushed through parliament the first of several modern social security laws to help wage earners. The laws of 1883 and 1884 established national sickness and acci-

dent insurance; the law of 1889 established old-age pensions and retirement benefits. Henceforth sick, injured, and retired workers could look forward to regular weekly benefits from the state. This national social security system, paid for through compulsory contributions by wage earners and employers as well as grants from the state, was the first of its kind anywhere. It was to be fifty years before similar measures would be taken in the United States. Bismarck's social security system did not wean workers from socialism, but it did protect them from some of the uncertainties of the complex urban industrial world. This enormously significant development was a product of political competition and government efforts to win popular support.

Increasingly, the great issues in German domestic politics were socialism and the Marxian Social Democratic party. In 1890 the new emperor, the young, idealistic, and unstable William II (r. 1888–1918), opposed Bismarck's attempt to renew the law outlawing the Social Democratic party. Eager to rule in his own right, as well as to earn the support of the workers, William II forced Bismarck to resign. After the "dropping of the pilot," German foreign policy changed profoundly and mostly for the worse, but the government did pass new laws to aid workers and to legalize socialist political activity.

Yet William II was no more successful than Bismarck in getting workers to renounce socialism. Indeed, socialist ideas spread rapidly, and more and more Social Democrats were elected to the parliament in the 1890s. After opposing a colonial war in German Southwest Africa in 1906 and thus suffering important losses in the general elections of 1907, the German Social Democratic party broadened its base in the years before the First World War. In the elections of 1912, the party scored a great victory, becoming the largest single party in the Reichstag. The "revolutionary" socialists, however, were becoming less and less revolutionary in Germany. In the years before the First World War, the strength of socialist opposition to greater military spending and imperialist expansion declined greatly. German socialists marched under the national banner.

Republican France

In 1871 France seemed hopelessly divided once again. The patriotic republicans who proclaimed the Third Republic in Paris after the military disaster at Sedan refused to admit defeat. They defended Paris with great heroism for weeks, living off rats and zoo animals, until they were quite literally starved into submission by German armies in January 1871. When national elections then sent a large majority of conservatives and monarchists to the National Assembly, the traumatized Parisians exploded and proclaimed the Paris Commune in March 1871. Vaguely radical, the leaders of the Commune wanted to govern Paris without interference by the conservative French countryside. The National Assembly, led by the aging politician Adolphe Thiers, would hear none of it. The Assembly ordered the French army into Paris and brutally crushed the Commune. Twenty thousand people died in the fighting. As in June 1848, it was Paris against the provinces, French against French.

Out of this tragedy France slowly formed a new national unity, achieving considerable stability before 1914. How is one to account for this? Luck played a part. Until 1875 the monarchists in the "republican" National Assembly had a majority but could not agree about who should be king. The compromise Bourbon candidate refused to rule except under the white flag of his ancestors—a completely unacceptable condition. In the meantime, Thiers's slaying of the radical Commune and his other firm measures showed the fearful provinces and the middle class that the Third Republic might be moderate and socially conservative. France therefore retained the republic, though reluctantly. As President Thiers cautiously said, it was "the government which divides us least."

Another stabilizing factor was the skill and determination of the moderate republican leaders in the early years. The most famous of these was Léon Gambetta, the son of an Italian grocer, a warm, easygoing, unsuccessful lawyer turned professional politician. A master of emerging mass politics, Gambetta combined eloquence with the personal touch as he preached a republic of truly equal opportunity. Gambetta was also instrumental in establishing absolute parliamentary supremacy between 1877 and 1879, when the somewhat autocratic president Marie Edmé MacMahon was forced to resign. By 1879 the great majority of members of both the upper and the lower houses of parliament were republicans. Although these republicans were split among many parliamentary groups and later among several parties—a situation that led to constant coalition politics and the rapid turnover of ministers—the Third Republic had firm foundations after almost a decade.

The moderate republicans sought to preserve their creation by winning the hearts and minds of the next generation. Trade unions were fully legalized, and France acquired a colonial empire. More important, under the leadership of Jules Ferry, the moderate republicans of small towns and villages passed a series of laws between 1879 and 1886 establishing free compulsory elementary education for both girls and boys. At the same time, they greatly expanded the state system of public tax-supported schools. Thus France shared fully in the general expansion of public education that served as a critical nation-building tool throughout the Western world in the late nineteenth century.

In France most elementary and much secondary education had traditionally been in the parochial schools of the Catholic church, which had long been hostile to republics and to much of secular life. Free compulsory elementary education in France became secular republican education. The pledge of allegiance and the national anthem replaced the catechism and the Ave Maria. Militant young elementary teachers carried the ideology of patriotic republicanism into every corner of France. In their classes, they sought to win the loyalty of the young citizens to the republic so that France would never again vote en masse for dictators like Napoleon I and Napoleon III.

Although these educational reforms disturbed French Catholics, many of them rallied to the republic in the 1890s. The limited acceptance of the modern world by Pope Leo XIII (r. 1878–1903) eased tensions between church and state. Unfortunately, the Dreyfus affair changed all that.

Alfred Dreyfus, a Jewish captain in the French army, was falsely accused and convicted of treason. His family never doubted his innocence and fought unceasingly to reopen the case, enlisting the support of prominent republicans and intellectuals such as the novelist Émile Zola. In 1898 and 1899, the case split France apart. On one side was the army, which had manufactured evidence against Dreyfus, joined by anti-Semites and most of the Catholic establishment. On the other side stood the civil libertarians and most of the more radical republicans.

This battle, which eventually led to Dreyfus's being declared innocent, revived republican feeling against the church. Between 1901 and 1905, after centuries of close relations, the government severed all ties between the state and the Catholic church. The salaries of priests and bishops were no longer paid by the government, and all churches were given to local committees of lay Catholics.

Captain Alfred Dreyfus Leaving an 1899 reconsideration of his original court martial, Dreyfus receives an insulting "guard of dishonor" from soldiers whose backs are turned. Top army leaders were determined to brand Dreyfus as a traitor. *(Source: Bibliothèque Nationale, Paris)*

Catholic schools were put completely on their own financially, and in a short time they lost a third of their students. The state school system's power of indoctrination was greatly strengthened. In France, only the growing socialist movement, with its very different and thoroughly secular ideology, stood in opposition to patriotic, republican nationalism.

Great Britain and Ireland

Britain in the late nineteenth century has often been seen as a shining example of peaceful and successful political evolution. Germany was stuck with a manipulated parliament that gave an irresponsible emperor too much power. France had a quarrelsome parliament that gave its presidents too little power. Great Britain, in contrast, seemed to enjoy an effective two-party parliament that skillfully guided the country from classical liberalism to full-fledged democracy with hardly a misstep.

This view of Great Britain is not so much wrong as incomplete. After the right to vote was granted to males of the solid middle class in 1832, opinion leaders and politicians wrestled long and hard with the uncertainties of a further extension of the franchise. In his famous "Essay on Liberty," published in 1859, the philosopher John Stuart Mill (1806–1873), the leading heir to the Benthamite tradition (page 901), probed the problem of how to protect the rights of individuals and minorities in the emerging age of mass electoral participation. Mill pleaded eloquently for the practical and moral value inherent in safeguarding individual differences and unpopular opinions. In 1867 Prime Minister Benjamin Disraeli and the Conservatives extended the vote to all middle-class males and the best-paid workers in the Second Reform Bill. The son of a Jewish stockbroker, himself a novelist and urban dandy, the ever-fascinating Disraeli (1804–1881) was willing to risk this "leap in the dark" in order to gain new supporters. The Conservative party, he believed, needed to broaden its traditional base of aristocratic and landed support if it was to survive. After 1867 English political parties and electoral campaigns became more modern, and the "lower orders" appeared to vote as responsibly as their "betters." Hence in 1884 the Third Reform Bill gave the vote to almost every adult male.

While the House of Commons was drifting toward democracy, the House of Lords was content to slumber nobly. Between 1901 and 1910, however, that bastion of aristocratic conservatism tried to reassert itself. Acting as supreme court of the land, it ruled against labor unions in two important decisions. And after the Liberal party came to power in 1906, the Lords vetoed several measures passed by the Commons, including the so-called People's Budget. The Lords finally capitulated, as they had done in 1832, when the king threatened to create enough new peers to pass the new legislation.

Aristocratic conservatism yielded once and for all to popular democracy. The result was that extensive social welfare measures, slow to come to Great Britain, were passed in a spectacular rush between 1906 and 1914. During those years, the Liberal party, inspired by the fiery Welshman David Lloyd George (1863–1945), substantially raised taxes on the rich as part of the People's Budget. This income helped the government pay for national health insurance, unemployment benefits, old-age pensions, and a host of other social measures. The state was integrating the urban masses socially as well as politically.

This record of accomplishment was only part of the story, though. On the eve of the First World War, the ever-emotional, ever-unanswered question of Ireland brought Great Britain to the brink of civil war. In the 1840s, Ireland had been decimated by famine, which fueled an Irish revolutionary movement. Thereafter, the English slowly granted concessions, such as the abolition of the privileges of the Anglican church and rights for Irish peasants. The Liberal prime minister William Gladstone (1809–1898), who had proclaimed twenty years earlier that "my mission is to pacify Ireland," introduced bills to give Ireland self-government in 1886 and in 1893. They failed to pass. After two decades of relative quiet, Irish nationalists in the British Parliament saw their chance. They supported the Liberals in their battle for the People's Budget and received passage of a home-rule bill for Ireland in return.

Thus Ireland, the emerald isle, achieved self-government—but not quite, for Ireland is composed of two peoples. As much as the Irish Catholic majority in the southern counties wanted home rule, precisely that much did the Irish Protestants of the northern counties of Ulster come to oppose it. Motivated by the accumulated fears and hostilities of generations, the Protestants of Ulster refused to submerge themselves in a Catholic Ireland, just as Irish Catholics had refused to submit to a Protestant Britain.

The Ulsterites vowed to resist home rule in northern Ireland. By December 1913, they had raised 100,000 armed volunteers, and they were supported by much of English public opinion. Thus in 1914, the Liberals in the House of Lords introduced a compromise home-rule law that did not apply to the northern counties. This bill, which openly betrayed promises made to Irish nationalists, was rejected, and in September the original home-rule plan was passed but simultaneously suspended. The momentous Irish question was overtaken by cataclysmic world war in August 1914.

Irish developments illustrated once again the power of national feeling and national movements in the nineteenth century. Moreover, they were proof that European states, which traced their development far back in history, could not elicit greater loyalty unless they could capture and control that elemental current of national feeling. Thus, even though Great Britain had much going for it—power, Parliament, prosperity—none of these availed in the face of the conflicting nationalisms espoused by Catholics and Protestants in Northern Ireland.

Similarly, progressive Sweden was powerless to stop the growth of the Norwegian national movement, which culminated in Norway breaking away from Sweden and becoming a fully independent nation in 1905. One can also see how hopeless was the cause of the Ottoman Empire in Europe in the later nineteenth century. The Ottoman Empire was an old dynastic state without ethnic or linguistic unity. It was only a matter of time before the Serbs, Bulgarians, and Romanians would break away to form their own independent nation-states (see pages 1042–1043).

The Austro-Hungarian Empire

The dilemma of conflicting nationalisms in Ireland highlights how desperate the situation in the Austro-Hungarian Empire had become by the early twentieth century. In 1849 Magyar nationalism had driven Hungarian patriots to declare an independent Hungarian republic, which was savagely crushed by Russian and Austrian armies (see

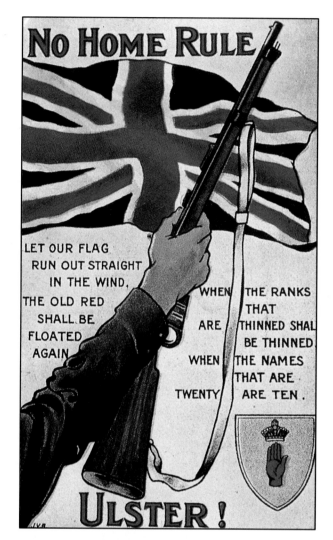

"No Home Rule"   Posters like this one helped to foment pro-British, anti-Catholic sentiment in the northern Irish counties of Ulster before the First World War. The rifle raised defiantly and the accompanying rhyme are a thinly veiled threat of armed rebellion and civil war. *(Source: Reproduced with kind permission of the Trustees of the Ulster Museum)*

pages 890–892). Throughout the 1850s, Hungary was ruled as a conquered territory, and Emperor Francis Joseph and his bureaucracy tried hard to centralize the state and Germanize the language and culture of the different nationalities.

Then, in the wake of defeat by Prussia in 1866, a weakened Austria was forced to strike a compromise and establish the so-called dual monarchy. The empire was divided in two, and the nationalistic Magyars gained virtual independence for Hungary. Henceforth each half of the empire agreed to

THE SPREAD OF NATIONALISM IN EUROPE, 1850–1914

1851	Louis Napoleon dismisses French National Assembly in coup d'état
1852–1870	Second Empire in France
1853–1856	Crimean War
1859	Mill, *Essay on Liberty*
1859–1870	Unification of Italy
1861	Abolition of serfdom in Russia
1862–1890	Bismarck's reign of power in German affairs
1864–1871	First Socialist International
1866	Prussia wins decisive victory in Austro-Prussian War
1866–1871	Unification of the German Empire
1867	Magyar nobility increases its power by restoring the constitution of 1848 in Hungary, thereby further dividing the Austro-Hungarian Empire
	Marx, *Capital*
	Second Reform Bill passed by British Parliament
1870–1871	Prussia wins decisive victory in Franco-Prussian War; William I proclaimed emperor of a united Germany
1871	Paris Commune
1871–1914	Third Republic in France
1878	Suppression of Social Democrats in Germany
1881	Assassination of Tsar Alexander II
1883–1889	Enactment of social security laws in Germany
1884	Third Reform Bill passed by British Parliament
1889–1914	Second Socialist International
1890	Repeal of anti-Social Democrat law in Germany
1892–1903	Witte directs modernization of Russian economy
1904–1905	Japan wins decisive victory in Russo-Japanese War
1905	Revolution in Russia: Tsar Nicholas II forced to issue the October Manifesto promising a popularly elected Duma
1906–1914	Liberal reform in Great Britain
1907–1912	Stolypin's agrarian reforms in Russia
1912	German Social Democratic party becomes largest party in the German Reichstag
1914	Irish Home Rule bill passed by British Parliament but immediately suspended with outbreak of First World War

deal with its own "barbarians"—its own minorities—as it saw fit. The two states were joined only by a shared monarch and common ministries for finance, defense, and foreign affairs. After 1867 the disintegrating force of competing nationalisms continued unabated, for both Austria and Hungary had several "Irelands" within their borders.

In Austria, ethnic Germans were only one-third of the population, and by the late 1890s many Germans saw their traditional dominance threatened by Czechs, Poles, and other Slavs. A particularly emotional and divisive issue in the Austrian parliament was the language used in government and elementary education at the local level. From 1900 to 1914, the parliament was so divided that ministries generally could not obtain a majority and ruled instead by decree. Efforts by both conservatives and socialists to defuse national antagonisms by stressing economic issues cutting across ethnic lines—which led to the introduction of universal male suffrage in 1907—proved largely unsuccessful.

One aspect of such national antagonisms was anti-Semitism, which was particularly virulent in Austria. After Jews obtained full legal equality in

1867, the Jewish populations of Austrian cities grew very rapidly, reaching 10 percent of the population of Vienna by 1900. Many Jewish businessmen were quite successful in banking and retail trade; and Jewish artists, intellectuals, and scientists, like the world-famous Sigmund Freud, played a major role in making Vienna a leading center of European culture and modern thought. When extremists charged the Jews with controlling the economy and corrupting German culture with alien ideas and ultramodern art, anxious Germans of all classes tended to listen. The popular mayor of Vienna from 1897 to 1910, Dr. Karl Lueger, combined anti-Semitic rhetoric with calls for "Christian socialism" and municipal ownership of basic services. Lueger appealed especially to the German lower middle class—and to an unsuccessful young artist named Adolf Hitler.

In Hungary, the Magyar nobility in 1867 restored the constitution of 1848 and used it to dominate both the Magyar peasantry and the minority populations until 1914. Only the wealthiest one-fourth of adult males had the right to vote, making parliament the creature of the Magyar elite. Laws promoting use of the Magyar (Hungarian) language in schools and government were rammed through and bitterly resented, especially by the Croatians and Romanians. While Magyar extremists campaigned loudly for total separation from Austria, the radical leaders of the subject nationalities dreamed of independence from Hungary. Unlike most major countries, which harnessed nationalism to strengthen the state after 1871, the Austro-Hungarian Empire was progressively weakened and destroyed by it.

MARXISM AND THE SOCIALIST MOVEMENT

Nationalism served, for better or worse, as a new unifying principle. But what about socialism? Did the rapid growth of socialist parties, which were generally Marxian parties dedicated to an international proletarian revolution, mean that national states had failed to gain the support of workers? Certainly, many prosperous and conservative citizens were greatly troubled by the socialist movement. And many historians have portrayed the years before 1914 as a time of increasing conflict between revolutionary socialism on the one hand and a nationalist alliance between conservative aristocracy and the prosperous middle class on the other. This question requires close examination.

The Socialist International

The growth of socialist parties after 1871 was phenomenal. Neither Bismarck's antisocialist laws nor his extensive social security system checked the growth of the German Social Democratic party, which espoused the Marxian ideology. By 1912 it had attracted millions of followers and was the largest party in the Reichstag. Socialist parties also grew in other countries, though nowhere else with quite such success. In 1883 Russian exiles in Switzerland founded a Russian Social Democratic party, which grew rapidly in the 1890s and thereafter, despite internal disputes. In France, various socialist parties re-emerged in the 1880s after the carnage of the Commune. In 1905 most of them were finally unified in a single, increasingly powerful Marxian party called the "French Section of the Workers International." Belgium and Austria-Hungary also had strong socialist parties of the Marxian persuasion.

As the name of the French party suggests, Marxian socialist parties were eventually linked together in an international organization. As early as 1848, Marx had laid out his intellectual system in the *Communist Manifesto* (see pages 875–876). He had declared that "the working men have no country," and he had urged proletarians of all nations to unite against their governments. Joining the flood of radicals and republicans who fled continental Europe for England and America after the revolutions of 1848, Marx settled in London. Poor and depressed, he lived on his meager earnings as a journalist and on the gifts of his friend Engels. Marx never stopped thinking of revolution. Digging deeply into economics and history, he concluded that revolution follows economic crisis and tried to prove it in *Critique of Political Economy* (1859) and his greatest theoretical work, *Capital* (1867).

The bookish Marx also excelled as a practical organizer. In 1864 he played an important role in founding the First International of socialists—the International Working Men's Association. In the following years, he battled successfully to control the organization and used its annual meetings as a means of spreading his realistic, "scientific" doctrines of inevitable socialist revolution. Then Marx enthusiastically embraced the passionate, vaguely radical patriotism of the Paris Commune and its terrible conflict with the French National Assembly as a giant step toward socialist revolution. This impetuous action frightened many of his early supporters, especially the more moderate British labor leaders. The First International collapsed.

Yet international proletarian solidarity remained an important objective for Marxists. In 1889, as the individual parties in different countries grew stronger, socialist leaders came together to form the Second International, which lasted until 1914. Although the International was only a federation of various national socialist parties, it had great psychological impact. Every three years,

delegates from the different parties met to interpret Marxian doctrines and plan coordinated action. May 1—May Day—was declared an annual international one-day strike, a day of marches and demonstrations. A permanent executive for the International was established. Many feared and many others rejoiced in the growing power of socialism and the Second International.

Unions and Revisionism

Was socialism really radical and revolutionary in these years? On the whole, it was not. Indeed, as socialist parties grew and attracted large numbers of members, they looked more and more toward gradual change and steady improvement for the working class, less and less toward revolution. The

Socialist Clubs helped spread Marxian doctrines among the working classes. There workers (and intellectuals) from different backgrounds debated the fine points and developed a sense of solidarity. *(Source: Bildarchiv Preussischer Kulturbesitz)*

mainstream of European socialists became militantly moderate—that is, they increasingly combined radical rhetoric with sober action.

Workers themselves were progressively less inclined to follow radical programs. There were several reasons for this reluctance. As workers gained the right to vote and to participate politically in the nation-state, their attention focused more on elections than on revolutions. And as workers won real, tangible benefits, this furthered the process. Workers were not immune to patriotic education and indoctrination during military service, however ardently socialist intellectuals might wish the contrary. Nor were workers a unified social group (see pages 910–914).

Perhaps most important of all, workers' standard of living rose substantially after 1850 as the promise of the Industrial Revolution was at least partially realized. In Great Britain, workers could buy almost twice as much with their wages in 1906 as in 1850, and most of the increase came after 1870. Workers experienced similar increases in most continental countries after 1850, though much less strikingly in late-developing Russia. Improvement in the standard of living was much more than merely a matter of higher wages. The quality of life improved dramatically in urban areas. For all these reasons, workers tended more and more to become militantly moderate: they demanded gains, but they were less likely to take to the barricades in pursuit of them.

The growth of labor unions reinforced this trend toward moderation. In the early stages of industrialization, modern unions were generally prohibited by law. A famous law of the French Revolution had declared all guilds and unions illegal in the name of "liberty" in 1791. In Great Britain, attempts by workers to unite were considered criminal conspiracies after 1799. Other countries had similar laws, and these obviously hampered union development. In France, for example, about two hundred workers were imprisoned each year between 1825 and 1847 for taking part in illegal combinations. Unions were considered subversive bodies, only to be hounded and crushed.

From this sad position workers struggled to escape. Great Britain led the way in 1824 and 1825, when unions won the right to exist but (generally) not the right to strike. After the collapse of Robert Owen's attempt to form one big union in the 1830s (see page 857), new and more practical kinds of unions appeared. Limited primarily to highly skilled workers such as machinists and carpenters, the "new model unions" avoided both radical politics and costly strikes. Instead, their sober, respectable leaders concentrated on winning better wages and hours for their members through collective bargaining and compromise. This approach helped pave the way to full acceptance in Britain in the 1870s, when unions won the right to strike without being held legally liable for the financial damage inflicted on employers. After 1890 unions for unskilled workers developed, and between 1901 and 1906, the legal position of British unions was further strengthened.

Germany was the most industrialized, socialized, and unionized continental country by 1914. German unions were not granted important rights until 1869, and until the antisocialist law was repealed in 1890, they were frequently harassed by the government as socialist fronts. Nor were socialist leaders particularly interested in union activity, believing as they did in the iron law of low wages and the need for political revolution. The result was that, as late as 1895, there were only about 270,000 union members in a male industrial workforce of nearly 8 million. Then, with German industrialization still storming ahead and almost all legal harassment eliminated, union membership skyrocketed to roughly 3 million in 1912.

This great expansion both reflected and influenced the changing character of German unions. Increasingly, unions in Germany focused on concrete bread-and-butter issues—wages, hours, working conditions—rather than on instilling pure socialist doctrine. Genuine collective bargaining, long opposed by socialist intellectuals as a "sellout," was officially recognized as desirable by the German Trade Union Congress in 1899. When employers proved unwilling to bargain, a series of strikes forced them to change their minds.

Between 1906 and 1913, successful collective bargaining was gaining a prominent place in German industrial relations. In 1913 alone, over ten thousand collective bargaining agreements affecting 1.25 million workers were signed. Further gradual improvement, not revolution, was becoming the primary objective of the German trade-union movement.

The German trade unions and their leaders were—in fact if not in name—thoroughgoing revisionists. Revisionism—that most awful of sins in the eyes of militant Marxists in the twentieth century—was an effort by various socialists to update Marxian doctrines to reflect the realities of the time. Thus the socialist Edward Bernstein argued in 1899 in his *Evolutionary Socialism* that Marx's predictions of ever-greater poverty for workers and ever-greater concentration of wealth in ever-fewer hands had been proved false. Therefore, Bernstein suggested, socialists should reform their doctrines and tactics. They should combine with other progressive forces to win gradual evolutionary gains for workers through legislation, unions, and further economic development. These views were formally denounced as heresy by the German Social Democratic party and later by the entire Second International. Nevertheless, the revisionist, gradualist approach continued to gain the tacit acceptance of many German socialists, particularly in the trade unions.

Moderation found followers elsewhere. In France, the great humanist and socialist leader Jean Jaurès formally repudiated revisionist doctrines in order to establish a unified socialist party, but he remained at heart a gradualist. Questions of revolutionary versus gradualist policies split Russian Marxists.

Socialist parties before 1914 had clear-cut national characteristics. Russians and socialists in the Austro-Hungarian Empire tended to be the most radical. The German party talked revolution and practiced reformism, greatly influenced by its enormous trade-union movement. The French party talked revolution and tried to practice it, unrestrained by a trade-union movement that was both very weak and very radical. In England, the socialist but non-Marxian Labour party, reflecting a well-established union movement, was formally committed to gradual reform. In Spain and Italy, Marxian socialism was very weak. There anarchism, seeking to smash the state rather than the bourgeoisie, dominated radical thought and action.

In short, socialist policies and doctrines varied from country to country. Socialism itself was to a large extent "nationalized" behind the imposing façade of international unity. This helps explain why, when war came in 1914, socialist leaders almost without exception supported their governments.

SUMMARY

From the mid-nineteenth century on, Western society became nationalistic as well as urban and industrial. Nation-states and strong-minded national leaders gradually enlisted widespread support and gave men and women a sense of belonging. Even socialism became increasingly national in orientation, gathering strength as a champion of working-class interests in domestic politics. Yet, while nationalism served to unite peoples, it also drove them apart. Though most obvious in Austria-Hungary and Ireland, this was in a real sense true for all of Western civilization. The universal national faith, which reduced social tensions within states, promoted a bitter, almost Darwinian competition between states and thus ominously threatened the progress and unity that it had helped to build.

NOTES

1. Quoted in G. Wright, *France in Modern Times* (Chicago: Rand McNally, 1960), p. 179.
2. Quoted in O. Pflanze, *Bismarck and the Development of Germany: The Period of Unification, 1815–1871* (Princeton, N.J.: Princeton University Press, 1963), p. 60.
3. Quoted in E. Eyck, *Bismarck and the German Empire* (New York: W. W. Norton, 1964), p. 59.
4. Quoted in H. Kohn, *The Mind of Germany: The Education of a Nation* (New York: Scribner, 1960), pp. 156–161.
5. Quoted in T. von Laue, *Sergei Witte and the Industrialization of Russia* (New York: Columbia University Press, 1963), p. 78.
6. Quoted in J. P. McKay, *Pioneers for Profit: Foreign Entrepreneurship and Russian Industrialization, 1885–1913* (Chicago: University of Chicago Press, 1970), p. 11.

SUGGESTED READING

The general works mentioned in the Suggested Reading for Chapter 27 treat the entire nineteenth century. In addition, G. Craig, *Germany, 1866–1945* (1980), and B. Moore, *Social Origins of Dictatorship and Democracy*

(1966), are outstanding. R. Anderson, *France, 1870–1914* (1977), provides a good introduction and has a useful blibliography.

Among specialized works of high quality, R. Williams, *Gaslight and Shadows* (1957), brings the world of Napoleon III vibrantly alive. Karl Marx's *The Eighteenth Brumaire of Louis Napoleon* is a famous contemporary denunciation of the coup d'état. E. Weber, *France, Fin de Siècle* (1986), and the engaging collective biography by R. Shattuck, *The Banquet Years* (1968), capture the spirit of artistic and intellectual Paris at the end of the century. E. Weber, *Peasants into Frenchmen* (1976), stresses the role of education and modern communications in the transformation of rural France after 1870. E. Thomas, *The Women Incendiaries* (1966), examines radical women in the Paris Commune. G. Chapman, *The Dreyfus Case: A Reassessment* (1955), and D. Johnson, *France and the Dreyfus Affair* (1967), are careful examinations of the famous case. In *Jean Barois,* Nobel Prize winner R. M. Du Gard accurately recreates in novel form the Dreyfus affair, and Émile Zola's novel *The Debacle* treats the Franco-Prussian War realistically.

D. M. Smith has written widely on Italy, and his *Garibaldi* (1956) and *Italy: A Modern History,* rev. ed. (1969), are recommended. P. Schroeder, *Austria, Great Britain and the Crimean War* (1972), is an outstanding and highly original diplomatic study. In addition to the important studies on Bismarck and Germany by Pflanze, Eyck, and Kohn cited in the Notes, F. Stern, *Gold and Iron* (1977), is a fascinating examination of relations between Bismarck and his financial adviser, the Jewish banker Bleichröder. L. Cecil, *Wilhelm II: Prince and Emperor, 1859–1900* (1989), probes the character and politics of Germany's ruler. G. Iggers, *The German Conception of History* (1968); K. D. Barkin, *The Controversy over German Industrialization, 1890–1902* (1970); and E. Spencer, *Management and Labor in Imperial Germany: Ruhr Industrialists as Employers* (1984), are valuable in-depth investigations. H. Glasser, ed., *The German Mind in the Nineteenth Century* (1981), is an outstanding anthology, as are R. E. Joeres and M. Maynes, eds., *German History in the Eighteenth and Nineteenth Centuries* (1986), and P. Mendès-Flohr, *The Jew in the Modern World: A Documentary History* (1980). C. Schorske, *Fin de Siècle Vienna: Politics and Culture* (1980), and P. Gay, *Freud, Jews, and Other Germans* (1978), are brilliant on aspects of modern culture. A. Sked, *The Decline and Fall of the Habsburg Empire, 1815–1918* (1989), and R. Kann, *The Multinational Empire,* 2 vols. (1950, 1964), probe the intricacies of the nationality problem in Austria-Hungary. S. Stavrianos has written extensively on southeastern Europe, including *The Balkans, 1815–1914* (1963).

In addition to the studies on Russian industrial development by von Laue and McKay cited in the Notes, W. Blackwell, *The Industrialization of Russia,* 2d ed. (1982), and A. Rieber, *Merchants and Entrepreneurs in Imperial Russia* (1982), are recommended. Among fine studies on Russian social development and modernization, H. Rogger, *Russia in the Age of Modernization and Revolution, 1881–1917* (1983), which has an extensive bibliography; T. Emmons, *The Russian Landed Gentry and the Peasant Emancipation of 1861* (1968); R. Zelnik, *Labor and Society in Tsarist Russia, 1855–1870* (1971); R. Johnson, *Peasant and Proletarian: The Working Class of Moscow at the End of the Nineteenth Century* (1979); and H. Troyat, *Daily Life in Russia Under the Last Tsar* (1962), are especially recommended. T. Friedgut, *Iuzovka and Revolution: Life and Work in Russia's Donbass, 1869–1924* (1989); R. Zelnik, *Labor and Society in Tsarist Russia, 1855–1870* (1971); and R. Johnson, *Peasant and Proletarian: The Working Class of Moscow at the End of the Nineteenth Century* (1979), skillfully treat different aspects of working-class life and politics. W. E. Mosse, *Alexander II and the Modernization of Russia* (1958), provides a good discussion of midcentury reforms. C. Black, ed., *The Transformation of Russian Society* (1960), offers a collection of essays on Russian modernization. I. Turgenev's great novel *Fathers and Sons* probes the age-old conflict of generations as well as nineteenth-century Russian revolutionary thought.

G. Dangerfield, *The Strange Death of Liberal England* (1961), brilliantly examines social tensions in Ireland as well as Englishwomen's struggle for the vote before 1914. W. Arnstein convincingly shows how the Victorian aristocracy survived and even flourished in nineteenth-century Britain in F. Jaher, ed., *The Rich, the Well-Born, and the Powerful* (1973), an interesting collection of essays on social elites in history. The theme of aristocratic strength and survival is expanded in A. Mayer's provocative *Persistence of the Old Regime: Europe to the Great War* (1981).

On late-nineteenth-century socialism, C. Schorske, *German Social Democracy, 1905–1917* (1955), is a modern classic. V. Lidtke, *The Outlawed Party* (1966), and J. Quataert, *Reluctant Feminists in German Social Democracy, 1885–1917* (1979), are also recommended for the study of German socialists. H. Goldberg, *The Life of Jean Jaurès* (1962), is a sympathetic account of the great French socialist leader. P. Stearns, who has written several books on European labor history, considers radical labor leaders in *Revolutionary Syndicalism and French Labor* (1971). D. Geary, ed., *Labour and Socialist Movements in Europe Before 1914* (1989), contains excellent studies on developments in different countries and has up-to-date bibliographies.

30

The World and the West

Flags of various countries flying in front of factories at Canton Harbor

While industrialization and nationalism were transforming urban life and Western society, Western society itself was reshaping the world. At the peak of its power and pride, the West entered the third and most dynamic phase of the aggressive expansion that began with the Crusades and continued with the great discoveries and the rise of seaborne colonial empires. An ever-growing stream of products, people, and ideas flowed out of Europe in the nineteenth century. Hardly any corner of the globe was left untouched. The most spectacular manifestations of Western expansion came in the late nineteenth century, when the leading European nations established or enlarged their far-flung political empires. The political annexation of territory in the 1880s—the "new imperialism," as it is often called by historians—was the capstone of a profound underlying economic and technological process.

- How and why did this many-sided, epoch-making expansion occur in the nineteenth century?
- What were some of its consequences for the West and for the rest of the world?

These are the questions examined in this chapter.

INDUSTRIALIZATION AND THE WORLD ECONOMY

The Industrial Revolution created, first in Great Britain and then in continental Europe and North America, a growing and tremendously dynamic economic system. In the course of the nineteenth century, that system was extended across the face of the earth. Some of the extension into non-Western areas was peaceful and beneficial for all concerned, for the West had many products and techniques desired by the rest of the world. If peaceful methods failed, however, Europeans did not stand on ceremony. They used their superior military power to force non-Western nations to open their doors to Western economic interests, and they did not worry when their aggression caused bitter resentment. In general, Westerners fashioned the global economic system so that the largest share of the ever-increasing gains from trade, technology, and migration flowed to the West and its propertied classes.

The Rise of Global Inequality

The Industrial Revolution in Europe marked a momentous turning point in world history. Indeed, only when Europe's economic breakthrough is placed in a world perspective can its revolutionary implications and consequences be fully appreciated. From a world perspective, the ultimate significance of the Industrial Revolution was that it allowed those regions of the globe that industrialized in the nineteenth century to increase their wealth and power enormously in comparison with those that did not. As a result, a gap between the industrializing regions—mainly Europe and North America—and the nonindustrializing regions—mainly Africa, Asia, and Latin America—opened up and grew steadily throughout the nineteenth century. This pattern of uneven global development became institutionalized, or built into the structure of the world economy. Thus evolved a "lopsided world," a world of rich lands and poor.

Historians have long been aware of this gap, but only recently have historical economists begun to chart its long-term evolution with some precision. Their findings are extremely revealing, although they contain a margin of error and other limitations as well. The findings of one such study are summarized in Figure 30.1. This figure compares the long-term evolution of average income per person in today's "developed" (or industrialized) regions—defined as western and eastern Europe, North America, and Japan—with that found in the "Third World," a term that is now widely used by international organizations and by scholars to group Africa, Asia, and Latin America into a single unit. To get these individual income figures, researchers estimate a country's gross national product (GNP) at different points in time, convert those estimates to some common currency, and divide by the total population.

Figure 30.1 highlights three main points. First, in 1750 the average standard of living was no higher in Europe as a whole than in the rest of the world. In 1750 Europe was still a poor agricultural society. Moreover, the average per person income in the wealthiest western European country (Great

Britain) was less than twice that in the poorest non-Western (or eastern European) land. By 1970, however, the average person in the wealthiest countries had an income fully twenty-five times as great as that received by the average person in the poorest countries of Africa and Asia.

Second, it was industrialization that opened the gap in average wealth and well-being between countries and regions. By 1830, Great Britain, the first industrial nation, had jumped well above the European average and was well in advance of its continental competitors. Great Britain's lead eventually narrowed, reflecting the industrialization of some other European countries and the United States in the course of the nineteenth century.

Finally, income per person stagnated in the Third World before 1913, in striking contrast to income per person in the industrializing regions. Only after 1945, in the era of political independence and decolonialization, did Third World countries finally make some real economic progress, beginning in their turn the critical process of industrialization.

These enormous income disparities are poignant indicators of equal disparities in food and clothing, health and education, life expectancy, and general material well-being. The rise of these disparities has generated a great deal of debate. One school of interpretation stresses that the West used science, technology, capitalist organization, and even its critical world view to create its wealth and greater physical well-being. Another school argues that the West used its political and economic power to steal much of its riches, continuing in the nineteenth (and twentieth) century the rapacious colonialism born of the era of expansion.

These issues are complex, and there are few simple answers. As noted in Chapter 26, the wealth-creating potential of technological improvement and more intensive capitalist organization was indeed great. At the same time, those breakthroughs rested, in part, on Great Britain having already used military power to dominate world trade and the Atlantic economy for its own great advantage. Great Britain, the United States, and the other Western powers continued to use force and the threat of force to tilt the expanding world economy in their favor in the nineteenth century. Wealth—unprecedented wealth—was indeed created, but the lion's share of that new wealth flowed to the West and to a tiny non-

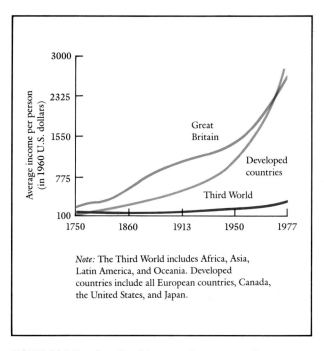

FIGURE 30.1 The Growth of Average Income per Person in the Third World, Developed Countries, and Great Britain, 1750–1970, in 1960 U.S. dollars and prices. *(Source: Data from P. Bairoch and M. Lévy-Leboyer, eds.,* Disparities in Economic Development Since the Industrial Revolution. *St. Martin's Press, New York, 1981, pp. 7–8, 10)*

Western elite of cooperative rulers, landowners, and big merchants.

Trade and Foreign Investment

Commerce between nations has always been a powerful stimulus to economic development. Never was this more true than in the nineteenth century, when world trade grew prodigiously. World trade grew modestly until about 1840, and then it took off. After a slowdown in the last years of the century, another surge lasted until the First World War. In 1913 the value of world trade was roughly $38 billion, or about *twenty-five* times what it had been in 1800. (This amount actually understates the growth, since average prices of both manufactured goods and raw materials were lower in 1913 than in 1800.) In a general way, the enormous increase in international commerce summed up the growth of an interlocking world economy, centered in and directed by Europe.

Great Britain played a key role in using trade to tie the world together economically. In 1815 Britain already had a colonial empire, for India, Canada, Australia, and other scattered areas remained British possessions after American independence. The technological breakthroughs of the Industrial Revolution allowed Britain to manufacture cotton textiles, iron, and other goods cheaply and to far outstrip domestic demand for such products. Thus British manufacturers sought export markets, first in Europe and then around the world.

Take the case of cotton textiles. India was by far the largest producer of cotton textiles in the seventeenth century, when the East India trading companies began exporting beautiful printed cloths to Europe to meet a rapidly growing demand. Worried European governments then passed mercantilist laws to limit these imports, which competed directly with domestic silk and woolen production. British merchants in the putting-out system searched for new techniques and patterns of organization that would enable them to compete with Indian cottons and lower-cost Indian labor. These efforts were highly successful in the late eighteenth century, as we saw in Chapter 26. By 1820 a revolutionized factory industry in Britain was exporting half of its production. Europe bought half of Britain's cotton-textile exports; India bought only 6 percent. Then, as European nations and the United States exercised sovereignty to erect protective tariff barriers and promote domestic industry, British cotton-textile manufacturers aggressively sought and found other foreign markets in non-Western areas. By 1850 India was buying 25 percent and Europe only 16 percent of a much larger total. As a British colony, India had no right to raise tariffs to protect its ancient cotton-textile industry. The Indian economy thus suffered a heavy blow, and thousands of Indian weavers lost their livelihoods.

Attaining undisputed world leadership in the revolutionized industries in the early nineteenth century, prosperous and powerful Britain also became the world's single best market after the repeal of the Corn Laws in 1846 (see page 885). A key argument in the battle against tariffs on imported grain had been that Britain had to buy from foreigners if foreigners were to obtain money to buy from Britain. Until 1914 Britain thus remained the world's emporium, where not only agricultural products and raw materials but also manufactured goods entered freely. Free access to the enormous market of Britain stimulated the development of mines and plantations in many non-Western areas.

The growth of trade was facilitated by the conquest of distance. The earliest railroad construction occurred in Europe (including Russia) and in America north of the Rio Grande; other parts of the globe saw the building of rail lines after 1860. By 1920 more than one-quarter of the world's railroads were in Latin America, Asia, Africa, and Australia. Wherever railroads were built, they drastically reduced transportation costs, opened new economic opportunities, and pulled people into a market economy. Moreover, in the areas of massive European settlement—North America and Australia—they were built in advance of the population and provided a means of settling the land.

The power of steam revolutionized transportation by sea as well as by land. In 1807 inhabitants of the Hudson Valley in New York saw the "Devil on the way to Albany in a saw-mill," as Robert Fulton's steamship *Clermont* traveled 150 miles upstream in thirty-two hours. Steam power, long used to drive paddle-wheelers on rivers, particularly in Russia and North America, finally began to supplant sails on the oceans of the world in the late 1860s. Lighter, stronger, cheap steel replaced iron, which had replaced wood. Screw propellers superseded paddle wheels, and mighty compound steam engines cut fuel consumption by half. Passenger and freight rates tumbled, and the intercontinental shipment of low-priced raw materials became feasible. In addition to the large passenger liners and freighters of the great shipping companies, there were innumerable independent tramp steamers searching endlessly for cargo around the world.

An account of an actual voyage by a typical tramp freighter highlights nineteenth-century developments in global trade. The ship left England in 1910, carrying rails and general freight to western Australia. From there, it carried lumber to Melbourne in southeastern Australia, where it took on harvester combines for Argentina. In Buenos Aires it loaded wheat for Calcutta, and in Calcutta it took on jute for New York. From New York it carried a variety of industrial products to Australia before returning to England with lead, wool, and wheat after a voyage of approximately

The Suez Canal   Completed in 1869, the hundred-mile canal cut in half the length of the journey between Europe and Asia. This picture from a popular weekly newspaper shows a line of ships passing through the canal on the opening day. *(Source: Giraudon/ Art Resource)*

72,000 miles to six continents in seventeen months.

The revolution in land and sea transportation helped European pioneers to open up vast new territories and to produce agricultural products and raw materials there for sale in European markets. Moreover, the development of refrigerated railway cars and, from the 1880s, refrigerator ships enabled first Argentina and then the United States, Australia, and New Zealand to ship mountains of chilled or frozen beef and mutton to European (mainly British) consumers. From Asia, Africa, and Latin America came not only the traditional tropical products—spices, tea, sugar, coffee—but new raw materials for industry, such as jute, rubber, cotton, and coconut oil.

Intercontinental trade was enormously facilitated by the Suez and Panama canals. Of great importance, too, was large and continuous investment in modern port facilities, which made loading and unloading cheaper, faster, and more dependable. Finally, transoceanic telegraph cables inaugurated rapid communication among the financial centers of the world. While a British tramp freighter steamed from Calcutta to New York, a broker in London was arranging, by telegram, for it to carry an American cargo to Australia. World commodity prices were also instantaneously conveyed by the same network of communication.

The growth of trade and the conquest of distance encouraged the expanding European economy to make massive foreign investments. Beginning about 1840, European capitalists started to invest large sums in foreign lands. They did not stop until the outbreak of the First World War in 1914. By that year, Europeans had invested more than $40 billion abroad. Great Britain, France, and Germany were the principal investing countries, although by 1913 the United States was emerging as a substantial foreign investor. The sums involved were enormous (Map 30.1). In the decade before 1914, Great Britain was investing 7 percent of its annual national income abroad, or slightly more than it was investing in its entire domestic economy. The great gap between rich and poor within Europe meant that the wealthy and moderately well-to-do could and did send great sums abroad in search of interest and dividends.

Most of the capital exported did not go to European colonies or protectorates in Asia and Africa. About three-quarters of total European investment went to other European countries, the United States and Canada, Australia and New Zealand, and Latin America. This was because

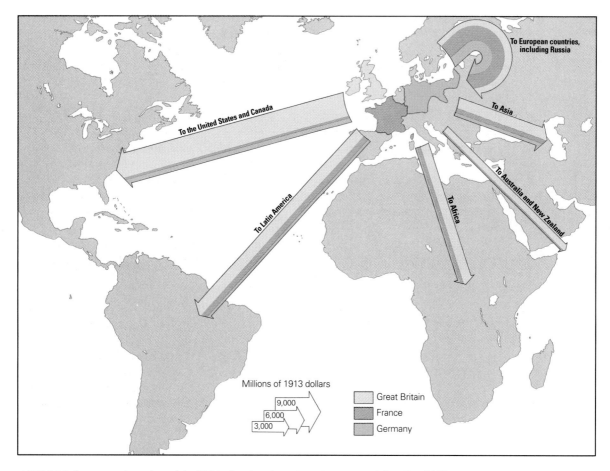

MAP 30.1 European Investment to 1914 Foreign investment grew rapidly after 1850, and Britain, France, and Germany were the major investing nations. Most European investment was not directed to the area seized by the "new imperialism."

Europe found many of its most profitable opportunities for investment in construction of the railroads, ports, and utilities that were necessary to settle and develop those almost-vacant lands. By loaning money for a railroad in Argentina or in Canada's prairie provinces, Europeans not only collected interest but also enabled settlers to buy European rails and locomotives, developed sources of cheap wheat, and opened still more territory for European settlement. Much of this investment—such as in American railroads, fully a third of whose capital in 1890 was European, or in Russian railroads, which drew heavily on loans from France—was peaceful and mutually beneficial. The victims were native American Indians and Australian aborigines, who were decimated by the diseases, liquor, and weapons of an aggressively expanding Western society.

The Opening of China and Japan

Europe's relatively peaceful development of robust offshoots in sparsely populated North America, Australia, and much of Latin America absorbed huge quantities of goods, investments, and migrants. From a Western point of view, that was perhaps the most important aspect of Europe's global thrust. Yet Europe's economic and cultural penetration of old, densely populated civilizations was also profoundly significant for the non-European peoples affected by it. With such civilizations Europeans also increased their trade and profit. Moreover, as had been the case ever since Vasco da Gama and the Spanish conquistadors, the expanding Western society was prepared to use force to attain its desires, if necessary. This was what happened in China and Japan, two crucial examples of the general pattern of intrusion into non-Western lands.

Traditional Chinese civilization was self-sufficient. For centuries China had sent more to Europe in the way of goods and inventions than it received, and this was still the case in the eighteenth century. Europeans and the English in particular had developed a taste for Chinese tea, but they had to pay for it with hard silver because China was supremely uninterested in European wares. Trade with Europe was carefully regulated by the Chinese imperial government—the Manchu Dynasty, which was more interested in isolating and controlling the strange "sea barbarians" than in pursuing commercial exchange. The imperial government refused to establish diplomatic relations with the "inferior" European states, and it required all foreign merchants to live in the southern city of Canton and to buy and sell only from the local merchant monopoly. Practices considered harmful to Chinese interests, such as the sale of opium and the export of silver from China, were strictly forbidden.

For years the little community of foreign merchants in Canton had to accept the Chinese system. By the 1820s, however, the dominant group, the British, was flexing its muscles. Moreover, in the smoking of opium—that "destructive and ensnaring vice" denounced by Chinese decrees—the British had found something that the Chinese really wanted. Grown legally in British-occupied India, opium was smuggled into China by means of fast ships and bribed officials. The more this rich trade developed, the greedier British merchants became and the more they resented the patriotic attempts of the Chinese government to stem the tide of drug addiction. By 1836 the aggressive goal of the British merchants in Canton was an independent British colony in China and "safe and unrestricted liberty" in trade. They pressured the British government to take decisive action and enlisted the support of British manufacturers with visions of vast Chinese markets to be opened.

At the same time, the Manchu government decided that the opium trade had to be stamped out. It was ruining the people and stripping the empire of its silver, which was going to British merchants to pay for the opium. The government began to prosecute Chinese drug dealers vigorously and in 1839 sent special envoy Lin Tse-hsü to Canton. Lin Tse-hsü ordered the foreign merchants to

East Meets West This painting gives a Japanese view of the first audience of the American Consul and his staff with the shogun, Japan's hereditary military governor, in 1859. The Americans appear strange and ill at ease. *(Source: Laurie Platt Winfrey, Inc.)*

obey China's laws, "for our great unified Manchu Empire regards itself as responsible for the habits and morals of its subjects and cannot rest content to see any of them become victims of a deadly poison."[1] The British merchants refused and were expelled, whereupon war soon broke out.

Using troops from India and in control of the seas, the British occupied several coastal cities and forced China to surrender. In the Treaty of Nanking in 1842, the imperial government was forced to cede the island of Hong Kong to Britain, pay an indemnity of $21 million, and open up five cities to foreign trade with low tariffs.

Thereafter the opium trade flourished, and Hong Kong rapidly became an Anglo-Chinese enclave. China continued to nurture illusions of superiority and isolation, however, and refused to accept foreign diplomats to Peking, the imperial capital. Finally, there was a second round of foreign attacks between 1856 and 1860, culminating in the occupation of Peking by seventeen thousand British and French troops and the intentional burning of the emperor's summer palace. Another round of harsh treaties gave European merchants and missionaries greater privileges and protection. Thus did Europeans use military aggression to blow a hole in the wall of Chinese seclusion. Blasting away at Chinese sovereignty as well, they forced the Chinese to accept trade and investment on unfavorable terms for the foreseeable future.

China's neighbor Japan had its own highly distinctive civilization and even less use for Westerners. European traders and missionaries first arrived in Japan in the sixteenth century. By 1640 Japan had reacted quite negatively to their presence. The government decided to seal off the country from all European influences, in order to preserve traditional Japanese culture and society. It ruthlessly persecuted Japanese Christians and expelled all but a few Dutch merchants, who were virtually imprisoned in a single port and rigidly controlled. When American and British whaling ships began to appear off Japanese coasts almost two hundred years later, the policy of exclusion was still in effect. An order of 1825 commanded Japanese officials to "drive away foreign vessels without second thought."[2]

Japan's unbending isolation seemed hostile and barbaric to the West, particularly to the United States. It complicated the practical problems of shipwrecked American sailors and the provisioning of whaling ships and China traders sailing in the eastern Pacific. It also thwarted the hope of trade and profit. Moreover, Americans shared the self-confidence and dynamism of expanding Western society. They had taken California from Mexico in 1848 and felt destined to play a great role in the Pacific. Americans convinced themselves that it was their duty to force the Japanese to share their ports and behave like a "civilized" nation.

After several unsuccessful American attempts to establish commercial relations with Japan, Commodore Matthew Perry steamed into Edo (now Tokyo) Bay in 1853 and demanded diplomatic negotiations with the emperor. Japan entered a grave crisis. Some Japanese warriors urged armed resistance, but senior officials realized how defenseless their cities were against naval bombardment. Shocked and humiliated, they reluctantly signed a treaty with the United States that opened two ports and permitted trade. Over the next five years, more treaties spelled out the rights and privileges of the Western nations and their merchants in Japan. Japan was "opened." What the British had done in China with war, the Americans had done in Japan with the threat of war.

Western Penetration of Egypt

Egypt's experience illustrates not only the explosive power of the expanding European economy and society but also their seductive appeal for some modernizing elites in non-Western lands. Of great importance in African and Middle Eastern history, the ancient land of the pharaohs had since 525 B.C. been ruled by a succession of foreigners, most recently by the Ottoman Turks. In 1798 French armies under young General Napoleon Bonaparte invaded the Egyptian part of the Ottoman Empire and occupied the territory for three years. Into the power vacuum left by the French withdrawal stepped an extraordinary Albanian-born Ottoman general, Muhammad Ali (1769–1849).

First appointed governor of Egypt by the Ottoman sultan, Muhammad Ali soon disposed of his political rivals. Impressed by Western military might, he set out to build his own state on the strength of a large, powerful army organized along European lines. He drafted for the first time the illiterate peasant masses of Egypt, and he hired

French and Italian army officers to train these raw recruits and their Ottoman officers. By the time of his death, Muhammad Ali had established a strong and virtually independent Egyptian state, to be ruled by his family on a hereditary basis within the Ottoman Empire.

Muhammad Ali's policies of modernization attracted large numbers of European fortune seekers to the banks of the Nile. As one Arab sheik of the Ottoman Empire remarked in the 1830s, "Englishmen are like ants; if one finds a bit of meat, hundreds follow."[3] The port city of Alexandria had more than fifty thousand Europeans by 1864, most of them Italians, Greeks, French, and English. Europeans served not only as army officers but also as engineers, doctors, high government officials, and policemen. Others found their "meat" in trade, finance, and shipping.

To pay for a modern army as well as for European services and manufactured goods, Muhammad Ali encouraged the development of commercial agriculture geared to the European market. This development had profound implications. Egyptian peasants had been poor but largely self-sufficient, growing food for their own consumption on state-owned lands allotted to them by tradition. Faced with the possibility of export agriculture, high-ranking officials and members of Muhammad Ali's family began carving large private landholdings out of the state domain. The new landlords made the peasants their tenants and forced them to grow cash crops like cotton for foreign markets. Borrowing money from European lenders at high rates, the landlords still made large profits, accumulated fortunes, and often lived like wealthy Europeans. The big landowners were "modernizing" agriculture, but to the detriment of peasant well-being.

These trends continued under Muhammad Ali's grandson Ismail, who in 1863 began his sixteen-year rule as Egypt's *khedive,* or "prince." Educated at France's leading military academy, Ismail was a Westernizing autocrat. He dreamed of using European technology and capital to accelerate Egyptian modernization and build a vast empire in northwest Africa. The large irrigation networks he promoted caused the further growth of large estates and commercial agriculture. Cotton production and exports to Europe boomed. Ismail also borrowed large sums to install modern communications, and with his support the Suez Canal

was completed by a French company in 1869. The Arabic of the masses rather than the Turkish of the conquerors became the official language, and young Egyptians educated in Europe helped spread new skills and new ideas in the bureaucracy. Cairo acquired modern boulevards, Western hotels, and an opera house. As Ismail proudly declared: "My country is no longer in Africa, we now form part of Europe."[4]

Yet Ismail was too impatient and too reckless. His projects were enormously expensive, and the sale of his stock in the Suez Canal to the British government did not relieve the situation. By 1876 Egypt owed foreign bondholders a colossal $450 million and could not pay the interest on its debt. Rather than let Egypt go bankrupt and repudiate its loans, as had some Latin American countries and U.S. state governments in the early nineteenth century, the governments of France and Great Britain intervened politically to protect the European bankers who held the Egyptian bonds. They forced Ismail to appoint French and British commissioners to oversee Egyptian finances, in order that the Egyptian debt would be paid in full. This was a momentous decision. It implied direct European political control and was a sharp break with the previous pattern of trade and investment. Throughout most of the nineteenth century, Europeans had used naked military might and political force primarily to make sure that non-Western lands would accept European trade and investment. Now Europeans were going to determine the state budget and effectively rule Egypt.

Foreign financial control evoked a violent nationalistic reaction among Egyptian religious leaders, young intellectuals, and army officers. In 1879, under the leadership of Colonel Ahmed Arabi, they formed the Egyptian Nationalist party. Continuing European pressure, which forced Ismail to abdicate in favor of his weak son Tewfiq (r. 1879–1892), resulted in bloody anti-European riots in Alexandria in 1882. A number of Europeans were killed, and Tewfiq and his court had to flee to British ships for safety. When the British fleet bombarded Alexandria, more riots swept the country, and Colonel Arabi declared that "an irreconcilable war existed between the Egyptians and the English." But a British expeditionary force decimated Arabi's forces and occupied Egypt.

The British said that their occupation was temporary, but British armies remained in Egypt until

Ellis Island in New York's harbor was the main entry point into the United States after 1892. For millions of immigrants the first frightening experience in the new land was being inspected and processed through its crowded "pens." *(Source: Culver Pictures)*

1956. They maintained the façade of the khedive's government as an autonomous province of the Ottoman Empire, but the khedive was a mere puppet. The British consul general Evelyn Baring, later Lord Cromer, ruled the country after 1883. Once a vocal opponent of involvement in Egypt, Baring was an authoritarian reformer who had come to believe that "without European interference and initiative reform is impossible here." Baring's rule did result in somewhat better conditions for peasants as well as tax reforms necessary to ensure revenues to pay foreign bondholders. But Egypt's

British rulers discouraged education because they feared it would lead to political unrest. Thus Cromer blocked all efforts to establish a university in Cairo until 1907 because, he said, it would only "manufacture demagoges."[5] Europeans knew what was best for Egyptians.

In Egypt, Baring and the British provided a new model for European expansion in densely populated lands. Such expansion was based on military force, political domination, and a self-justifying ideology of good administration. This model was to flourish until 1914. Thus did European industrialization lead to tremendous political as well as economic expansion throughout the world.

THE GREAT MIGRATION

Before considering European political empires, it is well to realize that a poignant human drama was part of the West's global expansion: literally millions of people picked up stakes and left their ancestral lands in the course of history's greatest migration. To millions of ordinary people, for whom the opening of China and the interest on the Egyptian debt had not the slightest significance, this great movement was the central experience in the saga of Western expansion. It was, in part, because of this great migration that the West's impact on the world in the nineteenth century was so powerful and many-sided.

The Pressure of Population

In the early eighteenth century, the growth of European population entered its third and decisive stage, which continued unabated until the twentieth century (see page 696). Birthrates eventually declined in the nineteenth century, but so did death rates, mainly because of the rising standard of living and secondarily because of the medical revolution. Thus the population of Europe (including Asiatic Russia) more than doubled, from approximately 188 million in 1800 to roughly 432 million in 1900.

These figures actually understate Europe's population explosion, for between 1815 and 1932 more than 60 million people left Europe. These migrants went primarily to the "areas of European settlement"—North and South America, Australia, New Zealand, and Siberia—where they contributed to a rapid growth of numbers. The population of North America (the United States and Canada) alone grew from 6 million to 81 million between 1800 and 1900 because of continuous immigration and the high fertility rates of North American women. Since population grew more slowly in Africa and Asia than in Europe, as Figure 30.2 shows, Europeans and people of European origin jumped from about 22 percent of the world's total to about 38 percent on the eve of the First World War.

The growing number of Europeans provided further impetus for Western expansion. It was a driving force behind emigration. As in the eighteenth century, the rapid increase in numbers put pressure on the land and led to land hunger and relative overpopulation in area after area. In most countries, migration increased twenty years after a rapid growth in population, as many children of the baby boom grew up, saw little available land and few opportunities, and migrated. This pattern was especially prevalent when rapid population increase predated extensive industrial development, which offered the best long-term hope of creating jobs within the country and reducing poverty. Thus millions of country folk went abroad, as well as to nearby cities, in search of work and economic opportunity.

Before looking at the people who migrated, let us consider three facts. First, the number of men and women who left Europe increased steadily until the First World War. As Figure 30.3 shows, more than 11 million left in the first decade of the twentieth century, over five times the number departing in the 1850s. The outflow of migrants was clearly an enduring characteristic of European society for the entire period.

Second, different countries had very different patterns of movement. As Figure 30.3 also shows, people left Britain and Ireland (which are not distinguished in the British figures) in large numbers from the 1840s on. This emigration reflected not only rural poverty but also the movement of skilled, industrial technicians and the preferences shown to British migrants in the British Empire. Ultimately, about one-third of all European migrants between 1840 and 1920 came from the British Isles. German migration was quite different. It grew irregularly after about 1830, reaching

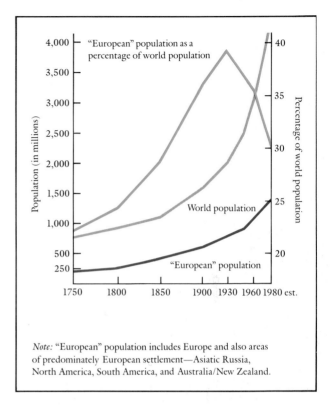

FIGURE 30.2 The Increase of European and World Populations, 1750–1980 *(Source: Data from W. Woodruff, Impact of Western Man: A Study of Europe's Role in the World Economy. St. Martin's Press, New York, 1967, p. 103; United Nations, Statistical Yearbook, 1982, 1985, pp. 2–3)*

a first peak in the early 1850s and another in the early 1880s. Thereafter it declined rapidly, for Germany's rapid industrialization was providing adequate jobs at home. This pattern contrasted sharply with that of Italy. More and more Italians left the country right up to 1914, reflecting severe problems in Italian villages and relatively slow industrial growth. In sum, migration patterns mirrored social and economic conditions in the various European countries and provinces.

Third, although the United States absorbed the largest number of European migrants, only slightly less than half went to the United States. Asiatic Russia, Canada, Argentina, Brazil, and Australia also attracted large numbers, as Figure 30.4 shows. Moreover, migrants accounted for a larger proportion of the total population in Argentina, Brazil, and Canada than in the United States. Between 1900 and 1910, for example, new

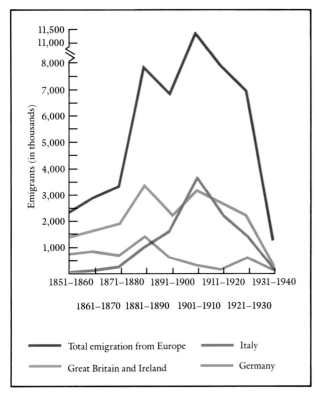

FIGURE 30.3 Emigration from Europe by Decades, 1851–1940 *(Source: Data from W. Woodruff,* Impact of Western Man: A Study of Europe's Role in the World Economy. *St. Martin's Press, New York, 1967, pp. 106–107 and references cited therein)*

arrivals represented 3 percent of Argentina's population each year, as opposed to only 1 percent for the United States. The common American assumption that European migration meant migration to the United States is quite inaccurate.

European Migrants

What kind of people left Europe, and what were their reasons for doing so? Most were poor people from rural areas, though seldom from the poorest classes. Indeed, the European migrant was most often a small peasant landowner or a village craftsman whose traditional way of life was threatened by too little land, estate agriculture, and cheap, factory-made goods. German peasants who left the Rhineland and southwestern Germany between 1830 and 1854, for example, felt trapped by

what Friedrich List (see page 851) called the "dwarf economy," with its tiny landholdings and declining craft industries. Selling out and moving to buy much cheaper land in the American Midwest became a common response.

Determined to maintain or improve their status, migrants were a great asset to the countries that received them. This was doubly so because the vast majority were young and very often unmarried. Fully two-thirds of those admitted to the United States were under thirty-one years of age, and 90 percent were under forty. They came in the prime of life and were ready to work hard in the new land, at least for a time.

Many Europeans, especially by the end of the nineteenth century, were truly migrants as opposed to immigrants—that is, they returned home after some time abroad. One in two migrants to Argentina, and probably one in three to the United States, eventually returned to their native land. The likelihood of repatriation varied greatly by nationality. Seven out of eight people who migrated from the Balkans to the United States in the late nineteenth century returned to their countries. At the other extreme, only one in ten from Ireland and only one in twenty among eastern European Jews returned to the country of origin.

Once again, the possibility of buying land in the old country was of central importance. Land in Ireland (as well as in England and Scotland) was tightly held by large, often absentee landowners, and little land was available for purchase. In Russia, Jews were left in relative peace until the assassination of Alexander II by non-Jewish terrorists in 1881 brought a new tsar and an official policy of pogroms and savage discrimination. Russia's 5 million Jews were already confined to the market towns and small cities of the so-called Pale of Settlement, where they worked as artisans and petty traders. Most land was held by non-Jews. When, therefore, Russian Jewish artisans began in the 1880s to escape both factory competition and oppression by migrating—a migration that eventually totaled 2 million people—it was basically a once-and-for-all departure. Non-Jewish migrants from Russia, who constituted a majority of those leaving the tsar's empire after 1905, had access to land and thus returned much more frequently to their peasant villages in central Russia, Poland, and the Ukraine.

The mass movement of Italians illustrates many of the characteristics of European migration. As late as the 1880s, three in every four Italians depended on agriculture. With the influx of cheap North American wheat, the long-standing problems of the Italian village became more acute. And since industry was not advancing fast enough to provide jobs for the rapidly growing population, many Italians began to leave their country for economic reasons. Most Italian migrants were not landless laborers from areas dominated by large estates; such people tended to stay in Italy and turned increasingly toward radical politics. Instead, most were small landowning peasants whose standard of living was falling because of rural overpopulation and agricultural depression. Migration provided them both an escape valve and a possible source of income to buy more land.

Many Italians went to the United States, but before 1900 more went to Argentina and Brazil. Indeed, two out of three migrants to those two developing countries came from Italy. Other Italians migrated to other European countries. France was a favorite destination. In 1911 the Italian-born population of France was roughly a third as large as that in the United States.

Ties of family and friendship played a crucial role in the movement of peoples. There are many examples of people from a given province or village settling together in rural enclaves or tight-knit urban neighborhoods thousands of miles away. Very often a strong individual—a businessman, a religious leader—would blaze the way and others would follow.

Many landless young European men and women were spurred to leave by a spirit of revolt and independence. In Sweden and in Norway, in Jewish Russia and in Italy, these young people felt frustrated by the small privileged classes, who often controlled both church and government and resisted demands for change and greater opportunity. Many a young Norwegian seconded the passionate cry of their national poet, Björnstjerne Björnson (1832–1910): "Forth will I! Forth! I will be crushed and consumed if I stay."[6]

Many young Jews wholeheartedly agreed with a spokesman of Kiev's Jewish community in 1882, who declared, "Our human dignity is being trampled upon, our wives and daughters are being dishonored, we are looted and pillaged: either we

get decent human rights or else let us go wherever our eyes may lead us."[7] Thus, for many, migration was a radical way to "get out from under." Migration slowed when the people won basic political and social reforms, such as the right to vote and social security.

FIGURE 30.4 Origin and Destination of European Emigrants, 1851–1960 *(Source: Data from W. Woodruff,* Impact of Western Man: A Study of Europe's Role in the World Economy. *St. Martin's Press, New York, 1967, pp. 108–109 and references cited therein)*

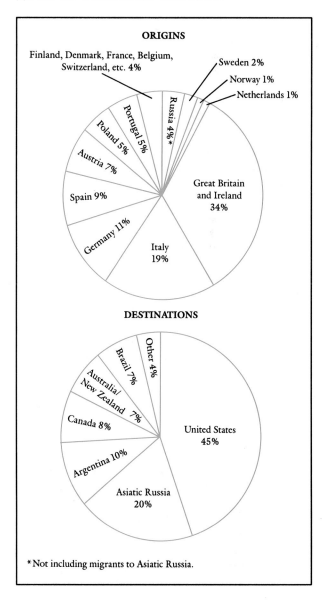

Asian Migrants

Not all migration was from Europe. A substantial number of Chinese, Japanese, Indians, and Filipinos—to name only four key groups—responded to rural hardship with temporary or permanent migration. At least 3 million Asians (as opposed to more than 60 million Europeans) moved abroad before 1920. Most went as indentured laborers to work under incredibly difficult conditions on the plantations or in the gold fields of Latin America, southern Asia, Africa, California, Hawaii, and Australia. White estate owners very often used Asians to replace or supplement blacks after the suppression of the slave trade.

In the 1840s, for example, there was a strong demand for field hands in Cuba, and the Spanish government actively recruited Chinese laborers. They came under eight-year contracts, were paid about twenty-five cents a day, and were fed potatoes and salted beef. Between 1853 and 1873, when such migration was stopped, more than 130,000 Chinese laborers went to Cuba. The majority spent their lives as virtual slaves. The great landlords of Peru also brought in more than 100,000 workers from China in the nineteenth century, and there were similar movements of Asians elsewhere.

Such migration from Asia would undoubtedly have grown to much greater proportions if planters and mine owners in search of cheap labor had had their way. But they did not. Asians fled the plantations and gold fields as soon as possible, seeking greater opportunities in trade and towns. There they came into conflict with other brown-skinned peoples—such as in Malaya and East Africa—and with white settlers in areas of European settlement.

These settlers demanded a halt to Asian migration. One Australian brutally summed up the typical view: "The Chinaman knows nothing about Caucasian civilization. It would be less objectionable to drive a flock of sheep to the poll than to allow Chinamen to vote. The sheep at all events would be harmless."[8] By the 1880s Americans and Australians were building "great white walls"—discriminatory laws designed to keep Asians out. Thus a final, crucial factor in the migrations before 1914 was the general policy of "whites only" in the rich open lands of possible permanent settlement. This, too, was part of Western dominance in the increasingly lopsided world. Largely successful in monopolizing the best overseas opportunities, Europeans and people of European ancestry reaped the main benefits from the great migration. By 1913 people in Australia, Canada, and the United States all had higher average incomes than people in Great Britain, still Europe's wealthiest nation.

WESTERN IMPERIALISM

The expansion of Western society reached its apex between about 1880 and 1914. In those years, the leading European nations not only continued to send massive streams of migrants, money, and manufactured goods around the world, but also rushed to create or enlarge vast political empires abroad. This political empire building contrasted sharply with the economic penetration of non-Western territories between 1816 and 1880, which had left a China or a Japan "opened" to European economic interests but still politically independent. By contrast, the empires of the late nineteenth century recalled the old European colonial empires of the seventeenth and eighteenth centuries and led contemporaries to speak of the "new imperialism."

Characterized by a frantic rush to plant the flag over as many people and as much territory as possible, the new imperialism had momentous consequences. It resulted in new tensions among competing European states, and it led to wars and rumors of war with non-European powers. The new imperialism was aimed primarily at Africa and Asia. It put millions of black, brown, and tan peoples directly under the rule of whites. How and why did whites come to rule these peoples?

The Scramble for Africa

The most spectacular manifestation of the new imperialism was the seizure of Africa, which broke sharply with previous patterns and fascinated contemporary Europeans and Americans.

As late as 1880, European nations controlled only 10 percent of the African continent, and their possessions were hardly increasing. The French had begun conquering Algeria in 1830, and within fifty years substantial numbers of French, Italian, and Spanish colonists had settled among the overwhelming Arab majority.

At the other end of the continent, in southern Africa, the British had taken possession of the Dutch settlements at Cape Town during the wars with Napoleon I. This takeover had led disgruntled Dutch cattlemen and farmers in 1835 to make their so-called Great Trek into the interior, where they fought the Zulu and Xhosa peoples for land. After 1853, while British colonies like Canada and Australia were beginning to evolve toward self-government, the Boers, or Afrikaners (as the descendants of the Dutch in the Cape Colony were beginning to call themselves), proclaimed their political independence and defended it against British armies. By 1880 Afrikaner and British settlers, who detested each other, had wrested control of much of the southern tip of Africa from the Zulu, Xhosa, and other African peoples.

European trading posts and forts dating back to the Age of Discovery and the slave trade dotted the coast of West Africa. The Portuguese proudly but ineffectively held their old possessions in Angola and Mozambique. Elsewhere, over the great mass of the continent, Europeans did not rule.

Between 1880 and 1900, the situation changed drastically. Britain, France, Germany, and Italy scrambled for African possessions as if their lives depended on them. By 1900 nearly the whole continent had been carved up and placed under European rule: only Ethiopia in northeast Africa and Liberia on the west African coast remained independent. Even the Afrikaner settler republics of southern Africa were conquered by the British in the bloody Boer War (1899–1902). In the years before 1914, the European powers tightened their control and established colonial governments to rule their gigantic empires (Map 30.2).

In the complexity of the European seizure of Africa, certain events and individuals stand out. Of enormous importance was the British occupation of Egypt, which established the new model of formal political control. There was also the role of Leopold II of Belgium (r. 1865–1909), an energetic, strong-willed monarch with a lust for distant territory. "The sea bathes our coast, the world lies before us," he had exclaimed in 1861. "Steam and electricity have annihilated distance, and all the non-appropriated lands on the surface of the globe can become the field of our operations and of our success."[9] By 1876 Leopold was focusing on central Africa. Subsequently he formed a financial syndicate under his personal control to send Henry Morton Stanley, a sensation-seeking journalist and part-time explorer, to the Congo basin. Stanley established trading stations, signed "treaties" with African chiefs, and planted Leopold's flag. Leopold's actions alarmed the French, who quickly sent out an expedition under Pierre de Brazza. In 1880 de Brazza signed a treaty of protection with the chief of the large Teke tribe and began to establish a French protectorate on the north bank of the Congo River.

Leopold's buccaneering intrusion into the Congo area raised the question of the political fate of black Africa—Africa south of the Sahara. By the time the British successfully invaded and occupied Egypt, the richest and most developed land in Africa in 1882, Europe had caught "African fever." There was a gold-rush mentality, and the race for territory was on.

To lay down some basic rules for this new and dangerous game of imperialist competition, Jules Ferry of France and Bismarck of Germany arranged an international conference on Africa in Berlin in 1884 and 1885. The conference established the principle that European claims to African territory had to rest on "effective occupation" in order to be recognized by other states. This principle was very important. It meant that Europeans would push relentlessly into interior regions from all sides and that no single European power would be able to claim the entire continent. The conference recognized Leopold's personal rule over a neutral Congo Free State and declared all of the Congo basin a free-trade zone. The conference also agreed to work to stop slavery and the slave trade in Africa.

The Berlin conference coincided with Germany's sudden emergence as an imperial power. Prior to about 1880, Bismarck, like many European leaders at the time, had seen little value in colonies. Colonies reminded him, he said, of a poor but proud nobleman who wore a fur coat when he could not afford a shirt underneath. Then, in 1884 and 1885, as political agitation for expansion increased, Bismarck did an abrupt about-face, and Germany established protectorates over a number of small African kingdoms and tribes in Togoland, Cameroons, German Southwest Africa, and later in German East Africa.

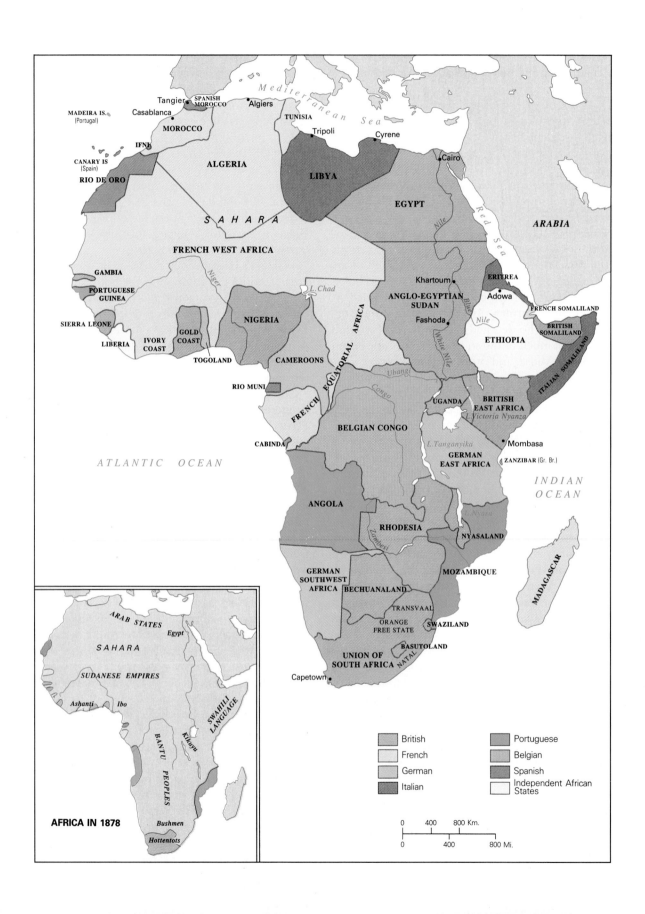

Mediterranean Sea

MADEIRA IS.
(Portugal)

Tangier •
SPANISH MOROCCO
Casablanca •
• Algiers

TUNISIA
Tripoli •
Cyrene •

IFNI

CANARY IS
(Spain)

MOROCCO

RIO DE ORO

ALGERIA

LIBYA

EGYPT

• Cairo

Red Sea

ARABIA

S A H A R A

Nile

FRENCH WEST AFRICA

GAMBIA

PORTUGUESE
GUINEA

Niger

L. Chad

Khartoum •

ERITREA

Adowa •

FRENCH SOMALILAND

SIERRA LEONE

NIGERIA

ANGLO-EGYPTIAN
SUDAN

Blue Nile

BRITISH
SOMALILAND

LIBERIA

IVORY
COAST

GOLD
COAST

White Nile

Fashoda •

ETHIOPIA

ITALIAN SOMALILAND

TOGOLAND

CAMEROONS

FRENCH EQUATORIAL AFRICA

Ubangi

RIO MUNI

Congo

UGANDA

BRITISH
EAST AFRICA

L. Victoria Nyanza

CABINDA

BELGIAN CONGO

L. Tanganyika

• Mombasa

ATLANTIC OCEAN

GERMAN
EAST AFRICA

ZANZIBAR (Gr. Br.)

INDIAN
OCEAN

ANGOLA

RHODESIA

Zambesi

L. Nyasa

NYASALAND

GERMAN
SOUTHWEST
AFRICA

BECHUANALAND

MOZAMBIQUE

MADAGASCAR

TRANSVAAL

ORANGE
FREE STATE

SWAZILAND

NATAL

BASUTOLAND

UNION OF
SOUTH AFRICA

Capetown •

ARAB STATES

Egypt

SAHARA

SUDANESE EMPIRES

Ashanti
Ibo

SWAHILI
LANGUAGE

BANTU
PEOPLES

Kikuyu

Bushmen

Hottentots

AFRICA IN 1878

British
French
German
Italian

Portuguese
Belgian
Spanish
Independent African
States

0   400   800 Km.

0   400   800 Mi.

Omdurman, 1898 European machine guns cut down the charging Muslim tribesmen again and again. "It was not a battle but an execution," said one witness. Thus the Sudan was conquered and one million square miles added to the British empire. *(Source: E. T. Archive)*

In acquiring colonies, Bismarck cooperated against the British with France's Jules Ferry, who was as ardent for empire as he was for education. With Bismarck's tacit approval, the French pressed vigorously southward from Algeria, eastward from their old forts on the Senegal coast, and northward from de Brazza's newly formed protectorate on the Congo River. The object of these three thrusts was Lake Chad, a malaria-infested swamp on the edge of the Sahara.

Meanwhile, the British began enlarging their west African enclaves and impatiently pushing northward from the Cape Colony and westward

MAP 30.2 The Partition of Africa European nations carved up Africa after 1880 and built vast political empires.

from the island of Zanzibar in the Indian Ocean. Their thrust southward from Egypt was blocked in the Sudan by an uprising of fiercely independent Muslims, who decimated a British force at Khartoum in 1885. The peoples of the Sudan maintained the Islamic state that they had established in 1881 in a revolt against foreign control of Egypt, and the British retreated to Cairo. Sudanese Muslims were deeply committed to Islam, and for them the struggle to preserve Islam and the struggle for freedom were one and the same thing.

The invaders bided their time, and in 1896 a British force under General Horatio H. Kitchener moved cautiously and more successfully up the Nile River, building a railroad to supply arms and reinforcements as it went. Finally, in 1898, these British troops met their foe at Omdurman, where

Sea of Okhotsk

Sakhalin

KARAFUTO (Jap. 1905)

AMUR DISTRICT (1858)

Khabarovsk (1858)

Vladivostok (1860)

Sea of Japan

Tokyo

JAPANESE EMPIRE

PACIFIC OCEAN

MANCHURIA

Harbin

KOREA (1905, 1910)

Mukden

Port Arthur (Rus. 1898, Jap. 1905)

Weihaiwei (Gr. Br. 1898)

East China Sea

Pescadores (Jap. 1895)

Formosa (Jap. 1895)

PHILIPPINE IS. (U.S.: from Spain 1898)

Ryukyu Is. (Jap.)

RUSSIAN EMPIRE

SIBERIA

L. Baikal

Lena

Chita

Irkutsk

OUTER MONGOLIA (Autonomous, Russian sphere 1912)

INNER MONGOLIA

Peking

Tientsin

Kiaochow (Ger. 1898)

Nanking

Shanghai (Gr. Br. 1842)

Hankow

Foochow

Amoy

Canton (Gr. Br. 1842)

Hong Kong (Gr. Br. 1842)

Macao (Port. 1557)

Kwangshowan (Fr. 1898)

Manila

South China Sea

BRITISH NORTH BORNEO (1888)

SARAWAK (1888)

Borneo

DUTCH EAST INDIES

New Guinea

Timor (Port. 1859) (Neth.)

Celebes

Yenisei

Ob

Irtysh

Tobolsk

Omsk

Trans-Siberian Railway

L. Balkhash (1854)

Tashkent (1864)

Aral Sea (1873)

SINKIANG

CHINA

Huang Ho

Yangtze

Chungking

TIBET

Lhasa

BHUTAN

BURMA (1852, 1885)

HIMALAYAS

NEPAL

Hanoi

SIAM

Bangkok

FRENCH INDOCHINA (1884, 1907)

Saigon

MALAY STATES (1800, 1824)

Singapore (Gr. Br. 1819)

Sumatra

Java

Rangoon

Bay of Bengal

Andaman Is. (Gr. Br.)

Merv (1884)

AFGHANISTAN

BALUCHISTAN (1883)

BRITISH SPHERE (1907)

KASHMIR (1846)

PUNJAB

Delhi

BRITISH INDIA

INDIA

Calcutta

Bombay

Yanaon (Fr.)

Madras

Pondichéry (Fr.)

Karikal (Fr.)

Ceylon

Diu (Port.)

Goa (Port.)

Karachi

Indus

Ganges

Arabian Sea

INDIAN OCEAN

Caspian Sea

Teheran

PERSIA

RUSSIAN SPHERE (1907)

Territories held by:

Great Britain
Netherlands
France
United States
Russia
Japan
Railroads

1000 Mi.

1000 Km.

500

500

0

0

brave Muslim tribesmen of the Sudan charged time and time again only to be cut down by the recently invented machine gun. For one smug participant, the young British officer Winston Churchill, it was "like a pantomime scene" in a play. "These extraordinary foreign figures . . . march up one by one from the darkness of Barbarism to the footlights of civilization . . . and their conquerors, taking their possessions, forget even their names. Nor will history record such trash." For another more somber English observer, "It was not a battle but an execution. The bodies were not in heaps . . . but they spread evenly over acres and acres."[10] In the end, eleven thousand Muslim tribesmen lay dead, and only twenty-eight Britons had been killed.

Continuing up the Nile after the battle of Omdurman, Kitchener's armies found that a small French force had already occupied the village of Fashoda. Locked in imperial competition ever since Britain had occupied Egypt, France had tried to beat the British to one of Africa's last unclaimed areas—the upper reaches of the Nile. The result was a serious diplomatic crisis and even the threat of war. Eventually, wracked by the Dreyfus affair (see page 949) and unwilling to fight, France backed down and withdrew its forces.

The reconquest of the Sudan exemplified some general characteristics of empire building in Africa. The fate of the Muslim force at Omdurman was usually inflicted on all native peoples who resisted European invaders: they were blown away by ruthless and vastly superior military force. But however much the Western powers lusted for territory and dominion around the world, they always had the sense to stop short of actually fighting each other for it. Imperial ambitions were not worth a great European war.

Imperialism in Asia

Although the conquest of Africa was more spectacular, Europeans also extended their political control in Asia. In 1815 the Dutch ruled little more than the island of Java in the East Indies. There-

MAP 30.3 Asia in 1914   India remained under British rule while China precariously preserved its political independence.

after they gradually brought almost all of the 3,000-mile archipelago under their political authority, though—in good imperialist fashion—they had to share some of the spoils with Britain and Germany. In the critical decade of the 1880s, the French under the leadership of Jules Ferry took Indochina. India, Japan, and China also experienced a profound imperialist impact (Map 30.3).

Two other great imperialist powers, Russia and the United States, also seized rich territories in Asia. Russia, whose history since the later Middle Ages had been marked by almost continuous expansion, moved steadily forward on two fronts throughout the nineteenth century. Russians conquered Muslim areas to the south in the Caucasus and in central Asia and also proceeded to nibble greedily on China's provinces in the Far East, especially in the 1890s.

The United States's great trophy was the Philippines, taken from Spain in 1898 after the Spanish-American War. When it quickly became clear that the Americans had no intention of granting self-rule, Philippine patriots rose against the United States in a war of independence. They were eventually defeated after thousands died in long, bitter fighting. Some Americans protested the taking of the Philippines, but they had no impact on government policy. Thus another big Western power joined the imperialist ranks in Asia.

Causes of the New Imperialism

Many factors contributed to the late nineteenth-century rush for territory and empire, which was in turn one aspect of Western society's generalized expansion in the age of industry and nationalism. Little wonder that controversies have raged over interpretation of the new imperialism, especially since authors of every persuasion have often exaggerated particular aspects in an attempt to prove their own theories. Yet despite complexity and controversy, basic causes are identifiable.

Economic motives played an important role in the extension of political empires, especially the British Empire. By the late 1870s, France, Germany, and the United States were industrializing rapidly behind rising tariff barriers. Great Britain was losing its early lead and facing increasingly tough competition in foreign markets. In this new economic situation, Britain came to value old possessions, such as India and Canada, more highly. The days when a leading free-trader like Richard Cobden could denounce the "bloodstained fetish of Empire" and statesman Benjamin Disraeli could call colonies a "millstone round our necks" came to an abrupt end. When continental powers began to grab unclaimed territory in the 1880s, the British followed suit immediately. They feared that France and Germany would seal off their empires with high tariffs and restrictions and that future economic opportunities would be lost forever.

Actually, the overall economic gains of the new imperialism proved limited before 1914. The new colonies were usually too poor to buy many manufactured goods, and they offered few immediately profitable investments. Nonetheless, even the poorest, most barren desert was jealously prized, and no territory was ever abandoned. Colonies became important for political and diplomatic reasons. Each leading country saw colonies as crucial to national security, military power, and international prestige. For instance, safeguarding the Suez Canal played a key role in the British occupation of Egypt, and protecting Egypt provided in turn a justification for the bloody reconquest of the Sudan. Military security was a major factor in the United States's decision to establish firm control over the Panama Canal Zone in 1903. Far-flung possessions guaranteed ever-growing navies the safe havens and the dependable coaling stations that they needed in time of crisis or war.

Many people in the West were convinced that colonies were essential to great nations. "There has never been a great power without great colonies," wrote one French publicist in 1877. "Every virile people has established colonial power," echoed the famous nationalist historian of Germany, Heinrich von Treitschke. "All great nations in the fullness of their strength have desired to set their mark upon barbarian lands and those who fail to participate in this great rivalry will play a pitiable role in time to come."[11]

Treitschke's harsh statement reflects not only the increasing aggressiveness of European nationalism after Bismarck's wars of German unification but also Social Darwinian theories of brutal competition between races. As one prominent English economist argued, the "strongest nation has always been conquering the weaker . . . and the strongest tend to be best." Thus European nations, which were seen as racially distinct parts of the dominant white race, had to seize colonies to show that they were strong and virile. Moreover, since racial struggle was nature's inescapable law, the conquest of inferior peoples was just. "The path of progress is strewn with the wreck . . . of inferior races," wrote one professor in 1900. "Yet these dead peoples are, in very truth, the stepping stones on which mankind has risen to the higher intellectual and deeper emotional life of today."[12] Social Darwinism and racial doctrines fostered imperial expansion.

Finally, certain special-interest groups in each country were powerful agents of expansion. Shipping companies wanted lucrative subsidies, and promoters wanted mining concessions. White settlers on dangerous, turbulent frontiers constantly demanded ever more land and greater protection. Missionaries and humanitarians wanted to spread religion and stop the slave trade. Explorers and adventurers sought knowledge and excitement. Military men and colonial officials, whose role has often been overlooked by writers on imperialism, foresaw rapid advancement and high-paid positions in growing empires. The actions of such groups and the determined individuals who led them thrust the course of empire forward.

Western society did not rest the case for empire solely on naked conquest and a Darwinian racial struggle, or on power politics and the need for naval bases on every ocean. In order to satisfy their consciences and answer their critics, imperialists developed additional arguments. A favorite idea was that Europeans could and should "civilize" nonwhites. According to this view, nonwhites would receive the benefits of modern economies, cities, advanced medicine, and higher standards of living; and eventually they might be ready for self-government and Western democracy. Thus the French spoke of their sacred "civilizing mission." Rudyard Kipling (1865–1936), who wrote masterfully of Anglo-Indian life and was perhaps the most influential writer of the 1890s, exhorted Europeans to unselfish service in distant lands:

Take up the White Man's Burden—
Send forth the best ye breed—
Go bind your sons to exile
To serve your captives' need,
To wait in heavy harness,
On fluttered folk and wild—
Your new-caught, sullen peoples
Half-devil and half-child.[13]

"The Administration of Justice"   In this 1895 illustration from a popular magazine, a Belgian official, flanked by native soldiers, settles a tribal dispute in the Congo State. This flattering view of Europe's "civilizing mission" suggests how imperial rule rested on more than just brute force. *(Source: Bettmann/Hulton)*

Many Americans accepted the ideology of the white man's burden. It was an important factor in the decision to rule rather than liberate the Philippines after the Spanish-American War. Like their European counterparts, these Americans believed that their civilization had reached unprecedented heights and that they had unique benefits to bestow on all "less-advanced" peoples. Another argument was that imperial government protected natives from tribal warfare as well as from the crudest forms of exploitation by white settlers and businessmen.

Some Westerners also sought the peace and stability of imperial rule in order to spread Christianity. In Africa, Catholic and Protestant missionaries competed with Islam south of the Sahara, seeking converts and building schools to spread the Gospel. Many Africans' first real contact with whites was in mission schools. As late as 1942, for example, 97 percent of Nigeria's small student population was in mission schools. Some peoples, like the Ibos in Nigeria, became highly Christianized.

Such occasional successes in black Africa contrasted with the general failure of missionary efforts in India, China, and the Islamic world. There, Christians often preached in vain to peoples with ancient, complex religious beliefs. Yet the number of Christian believers around the world did increase substantially in the nineteenth century, and missionary groups kept trying. Unfortunately, "many missionaries had drunk at the well of European racism," and this probably prevented them from doing better.[14]

Critics of Imperialism

The expansion of empire aroused sharp, even bitter, critics. A forceful attack came in 1902, after the unpopular Boer War, by the radical English

THE SPREAD OF WESTERN IMPERIALISM

1800–1913	World trade increases 25-fold
1816–1880	European economic penetration of non-Western countries
1835	Great Trek: Boers proclaim independence from Great Britain in the South African hinterland
1840s	European capitalists begin large-scale foreign investment
1842	Treaty of Nanking: Manchu government of China cedes Hong Kong to Great Britain
1846	Repeal of Corn Laws: Great Britain declares its strong support of free trade
1848	British defeat of last independent native state in India
1853	Perry's arrival in Tokyo: Japan opened to European influence
1857–1858	Great Rebellion in India
1858–1863	Anti-foreign reaction in Japan
1867	Meiji Restoration in Japan: adoption of Western reforms
1869	Completion of Suez Canal
1871	Abolition of feudal domains in Japan
1876	Ismail, khedive of Egypt, appoints British and French commissioners to oversee government finances
1880	Establishment of French protectorate on the northern bank of the Congo
1880–1900	European powers intensify their "scramble for Africa"
1882	British occupation of Egypt
1883	Formation of the Indian National Congress
1884–1885	International conference on Africa in Berlin: European powers require "effective occupation"; Germany acquires protectorates in Togo, Cameroon, South West Africa, and East Africa; Belgium acquires the Congo Free State
1890	Establishment of an authoritarian constitution in Japan
1893	France completes its acquisition of Indochina
1894	Sino-Japanese War: Japan acquires Formosa
1898	Battle of Omdurman: under Kitchener, British forces reconquer the Sudan Spanish-American War: United States acquires the Philippines "Hundred Days of Reform" in China
1899–1902	Boer War: British defeat Dutch settlers in South Africa
1900–1903	The Boxer Rebellion in China
1903	American occupation of the Panama Canal zone
1904–1905	Russo-Japanese War: Japan wins protectorate over Port Arthur in China
1910	Japanese annexation of Korea
1912	Fall of Manchu dynasty in China

economist J. A. Hobson (1858–1940) in his *Imperialism,* a work that influenced Lenin and others. Hobson contended that the rush to acquire colonies was due to the economic needs of unregulated capitalism, particularly the need of the rich to find profitable outlets for their surplus capital. Yet, Hobson argued, imperial possessions do not pay off economically for the country as a whole. Only unscrupulous special-interest groups profit from them, at the expense of both the European taxpayer and the natives. Moreover, the quest for empire diverts attention from domestic reform and closing the gap between rich and poor. These and similar arguments were not very persuasive. Most people then (and now) believed that imperialism was economically profitable for the homeland, and a broad and genuine enthusiasm for empire developed among the European masses.

Hobson and many other critics struck home, however, with their moral condemnation of whites imperiously ruling nonwhites. They rebelled against crude Social Darwinian thought. "O Evolution, what crimes are committed in thy name!" cried one foe. Another sardonically coined a new beatitude: "Blessed are the strong, for they shall prey on the weak."[15] Kipling and his kind were lampooned as racist bullies, whose rule rested on brutality, racial contempt, and the Maxim machine gun. Henri Labouchère, a member of Parliament and prominent spokesman for this position, mocked Kipling's famous poem:

Pile on the Brown Man's burden!
And if ye rouse his hate,
Meet his old-fashioned reasons
With Maxims up to date,
With shells and Dum-Dum bullets
A hundred times plain
The Brown Man's loss must never
Imply the White Man's gain.[16]

Similarly, in *Heart of Darkness*, the Polish-born novelist Joseph Conrad (1857–1924) castigated the "pure selfishness" of Europeans in "civilizing" Africa. The main character, once a liberal scholar, turns into a savage brute.

Critics charged Europeans with applying a degrading double standard and failing to live up to their own noble ideals. At home, Europeans had won or were winning representative government, individual liberties, and a certain equality of opportunity. In their empires, Europeans imposed military dictatorships on Africans and Asians, forced them to work involuntarily, almost like slaves, and discriminated against them shamelessly. Only by renouncing imperialism, critics insisted, and giving captive peoples the freedoms that Western society had struggled for since the French Revolution would Europeans be worthy of their traditions. Europeans who denounced the imperialist tide provided colonial peoples with a Western ideology of liberation.

RESPONSES TO WESTERN IMPERIALISM

To peoples in Africa and Asia, Western expansion represented a profoundly disruptive assault. Everywhere it threatened traditional ruling classes, traditional economies, and traditional ways of life. Christian missionaries and European secular ideologies attacked established beliefs and values. Non-Western peoples experienced a crisis of identity, a crisis made all the more painful by the power and arrogance of the white intruders.

The initial response of African and Asian rulers was to try to drive the unwelcome foreigners away.

This was the case in China, Japan, and the upper Sudan. Violent antiforeign reactions also exploded elsewhere again and again, but the superior military technology of the industrializing West almost invariably prevailed. Beaten in battle, many Africans and Asians concentrated on preserving their cultural traditions at all costs. Others found themselves forced to reconsider their initial hostility. Some (like Ismail of Egypt) concluded that the West was indeed superior in some ways and that it was therefore necessary to reform their societies and copy European achievements. Thus it is possible to think of responses to the Western impact as a spectrum, with "traditionalists" at one end, "Westernizers" or "modernizers" at the other, and many shades of opinion in between. Both before and after European domination, the struggle among these groups was often intense. With time, however, the modernizers tended to gain the upper hand.

When the power of both the traditionalists and the modernizers was thoroughly shattered by brute force, the great majority of Asians and Africans accepted imperial rule. Political participation in non-Western lands was historically limited to small elites, and the masses were accustomed to doing what their rulers told them to do. In these circumstances Europeans, clothed in power and convinced of their righteousness, governed smoothly and effectively. They received considerable support from both traditionalists (local chiefs, landowners, and non-Muslim religious leaders) and modernizers (the Western-educated merchants, professional classes, and civil servants).

Nevertheless, imperial rule was in many ways a hollow shell built on sand. Support for European rule among the conforming and accepting millions was shallow and weak. Thus the conforming masses followed with greater or lesser enthusiasm a few determined personalities who came to oppose the Europeans. Such leaders always arose, both when Europeans ruled directly and when they manipulated native governments, for at least two basic reasons.

First, the nonconformists—the eventual anti-imperialist leaders—developed a burning desire for human dignity. They came to feel that such dignity was incompatible with foreign rule—with its smirks and smiles, its paternalism and condescension. Second, potential leaders found in the West the ideologies and justification for their protest. They discovered liberalism with its credo of civil liberty and political self-determination. They echoed the demands of anti-imperialists in Europe and America that the West live up to its own ideals. More important, they found themselves attracted to modern nationalism, which asserted that every people had the right to control its own destiny. After 1917, anti-imperialist revolt would find another weapon in Lenin's version of Marxian socialism.

That the anti-imperialist search for dignity drew strength from Western culture is apparent in the development of three major Asian countries: India, Japan, and China.

Empire in India

India was the jewel of the British Empire, and no colonial area experienced a more profound British impact. Unlike Japan and China, which maintained a real or precarious independence, and unlike African territories, which were annexed by Europeans only at the end of the nineteenth century, India was ruled more or less absolutely by Britain for a very long time.

Arriving in India on the heels of the Portuguese in the seventeenth century, the British East India Company had conquered the last independent native state by 1848. The last "traditional" response to European rule—the attempt by the established ruling classes to drive the white man out by military force—was broken in India in 1857 and 1858. Those were the years of the Great Rebellion (which the British called a "mutiny"), when an insurrection by Muslim and Hindu mercenaries in the British army spread throughout northern and central India before it was finally crushed, primarily by loyal native troops from southern India. Thereafter Britain ruled India directly. India illustrates, therefore, for better and for worse, what generations of European domination could produce.

After 1858 India was ruled by the British Parliament in London and administered by a tiny, all-white civil service in India. In 1900 this elite consisted of fewer than 3,500 top officials, for a population of 300 million. The white elite, backed by white officers and native troops, was competent and maintained reasonably good authoritarian rule. Yet it practiced strict job discrimination and social segregation, and most of its members quite frankly considered the jumble of Indian peoples

and castes to be racially inferior. As Lord Kitchener, one of the most distinguished top military commanders of India, stated:

It is this consciousness of the inherent superiority of the European which has won for us India. However well educated and clever a native may be, and however brave he may prove himself, I believe that no rank we can bestow on him would cause him to be considered an equal of the British officer.[17]

When, for example, the British Parliament in 1883 was considering a major bill to allow Indian judges to try white Europeans in India, the British community rose in protest and defeated the measure. The idea that they might be judged by Indians was inconceivable to Europeans, for it was clear to the Europeans that the empire in India rested squarely on racial inequality.

In spite of (perhaps even because of) their strong feelings of racial and cultural superiority, the British acted energetically and introduced many desirable changes to India. Realizing that they needed well-educated Indians to serve as skilled subordinates in the government and army, the British established a modern system of progressive secondary education, in which all instruction was in English. Thus, through education and government service the British offered some Indians excellent opportunities for both economic and social advancement. High-caste Hindus were particularly quick to respond and emerged as skillful intermediaries between the British rulers and the Indian people—a new elite profoundly influenced by Western thought and culture.

This new bureaucratic elite played a crucial role in modern economic development, which was a second result of British rule. Irrigation projects for agriculture, the world's third largest railroad network for good communication, and large tea and jute plantations geared to the needs of the *international* economy were all developed. Unfortunately, the lot of the Indian masses improved little, for the increase in agricultural production was quite literally eaten up by population increase.

Finally, with a well-educated, English-speaking Indian bureaucracy and modern communications, the British created a unified, powerful state. They placed under the same general system of law and administration the different Hindu and Muslim peoples and the vanquished kingdoms of the entire subcontinent—groups that had fought each

The British in India   This photo suggests not only the incredible power and luxury of the British ruling class in India but also its confidence and self-satisfaction. As one British viceroy said, "We are all British gentlemen engaged in the magnificent work of governing an inferior race." *(Source: Bettmann/Hulton)*

other for centuries during the Middle Ages and had been repeatedly conquered by Muslim and Mongol invaders. It was as if Europe, with its many states and varieties of Christianity, had been conquered and united in a single great empire.

In spite of these achievements, the decisive reaction to European rule was the rise of nationalism among the Indian elite. No matter how Anglicized and necessary a member of the educated classes became, he or she could never become the white ruler's equal. The top jobs, the best clubs, the modern hotels, and even certain railroad compartments were sealed off to brown-skinned men and women. The peasant masses might accept such inequality as the latest version of age-old oppression, but the well-educated, English-speaking elite eventually could not. For the elite, racial discrimination meant not only injured pride but bitter injustice. It flagrantly contradicted the cherished Western concepts of human rights and equality. Moreover, it was based on dictatorship, no matter how benign.

By 1885, when educated Indians came together to found the predominantly Hindu Indian National Congress, demands were increasing for the equality and self-government that Britain enjoyed and had already granted white-settler colonies, such as Canada and Australia. By 1907, embold-

ened in part by Japan's success (see pages 983–985), the radicals in the Indian National Congress were calling for complete independence. Even the moderates were demanding home rule for India through an elected parliament. Although there were sharp divisions between Hindus and Muslims, Indians were finding an answer to the foreign challenge. The common heritage of British rule and Western ideals, along with the reform and revitalization of the Hindu religion, had created a genuine movement for national independence.

The Example of Japan

When Commodore Perry arrived in Japan in 1853 with his crude but effective gunboat diplomacy, Japan was a complex feudal society. At the top stood a figurehead emperor, but for more than two hundred years, real power had been in the hands of a hereditary military governor, the *shogun*. With the help of a warrior nobility known as *samurai*, the shogun governed a country of hard-working, productive peasants and city dwellers. Often poor and restless, the intensely proud samurai were deeply humiliated by the sudden American intrusion and the unequal treaties with Western countries. When foreign diplomats and merchants began to settle in Yokohama, radical samurai reacted with a wave of antiforeign terrorism and antigovernment assassinations between 1858 and 1863. The imperialist response was swift and unambiguous. An allied fleet of American, British, Dutch, and French warships bombarded and demolished key forts, which further weakened the power and prestige of the shogun's government. Then, in 1867, a coalition led by patriotic samurai seized control of the government with hardly any bloodshed and restored the power of the emperor. This was the Meiji Restoration, a great turning point in Japanese development.

The immediate, all-important goal of the new government was to meet the foreign threat. The battle cry of the Meiji reformers was "enrich the state and strengthen the armed forces." Yet how was this to be done? In an about-face that was one of history's most remarkable chapters, the young but well-trained, idealistic but flexible leaders of Meiji Japan dropped their antiforeign attacks. Convinced that Western civilization was indeed superior in its military and industrial aspects, they initiated from above a series of measures to reform Japan along modern lines. They were convinced that "Japan must be reborn with America its mother and France its father."[18] In the broadest sense, the Meiji leaders tried to harness the power inherent in Europe's dual revolution, in order to protect their country and catch up with the West.

Japanese Industrialization   The famous Tomioka silk reeling factory pioneered with mass-production techniques and women factory workers in the 1870s. The combination shown here of European technology with native dress symbolizes Japan's successful integration of Western practices into the traditional culture of its society. *(Source: Laurie Platt Winfrey, Inc.)*

In 1871 the new leaders abolished the old feudal structure of aristocratic, decentralized government and formed a strong, unified state. Following the example of the French Revolution, they dismantled the four-class legal system and declared social equality. They decreed freedom of movement in a country where traveling abroad had been a most serious crime. They created a free, competitive, government-stimulated economy. Japan began to build railroads and modern factories. Thus the new generation adopted many principles of a free, liberal society; and, as in Europe, such freedom resulted in a tremendously creative release of human energy.

Yet the overriding concern of Japan's political leadership was always a powerful state, and to achieve this, more than liberalism was borrowed from the West. A powerful modern navy was created, and the army was completely reorganized along French and German lines, with three-year military service for all males and a professional officer corps. This army of draftees effectively put down disturbances in the countryside, and in 1877 it was used to crush a major rebellion by feudal elements protesting the loss of their privileges. Japan also borrowed rapidly and adopted skillfully the West's science and modern technology, particularly in industry, medicine, and education. Many Japanese were encouraged to study abroad, and the government paid large salaries to attract foreign experts. These experts were always carefully controlled, though, and replaced by trained Japanese as soon as possible.

By 1890, when the new state was firmly established, the wholesale borrowing of the early restoration had given way to more selective emphasis on those things foreign that were in keeping with Japanese tradition. Following the model of the German Empire, Japan established an authoritarian constitution and rejected democracy. The power of the emperor and his ministers was vast, that of the legislature limited.

Japan successfully copied the imperialism of Western society. Expansion not only proved that Japan was strong; it also cemented the nation together in a great mission. Having "opened" Korea with the gunboat diplomacy of imperialism in 1876, Japan decisively defeated China in a war over Korea in 1894 and took Formosa. In the next years, Japan competed aggressively with the leading European powers for influence and territory in China, particularly Manchuria. There Japanese

and Russian imperialism met and collided. In 1904 Japan attacked Russia without warning, and at the end of a bloody war Japan emerged with a valuable foothold in China—Russia's former protectorate over Port Arthur (Map 30.4). By 1910, when it annexed Korea, Japan was a major imperial power, continuously expanding its influence in China.

Japan became the first non-Western country to use an ancient love of country to transform itself and thereby meet the many-sided challenge of Western expansion. Moreover, Japan demonstrated convincingly that a modern Asian nation could defeat and humble a great Western power. Many Chinese nationalists were fascinated by Japan's achievement. A group of patriots in French-ruled southern Vietnam sent Vietnamese students to Japan to learn the island empire's secret of success. Japan provided patriots in Asia and Africa with an inspiring example of national recovery and liberation.

Toward Revolution in China

In 1860 the 200-year-old Manchu Dynasty in China appeared on the verge of collapse. Efforts to repel the foreigners had failed, and rebellion and chaos wracked the country. Yet the government drew on its traditional strengths and made a surprising comeback that lasted more than thirty years.

Two factors were crucial in this reversal. First, the traditional ruling groups temporarily produced new, effective leadership. Loyal scholar-statesmen and generals quelled disturbances like the great Tai Ping Rebellion. A remarkable woman, the empress dowager Tzu Hsi, governed in the name of her young son and combined shrewd insight with vigorous action to revitalize the bureaucracy.

Second, destructive foreign aggression lessened, for the Europeans had achieved their primary goal of advantageous commercial and diplomatic relations. Indeed, some Europeans even contributed to the dynasty's recovery. A talented Irishman effectively reorganized China's customs office and increased the government tax receipts, and a sympathetic American diplomat represented China in foreign lands and helped strengthen the central government. Such efforts dovetailed with the dynasty's efforts to adopt some aspects of Western government and technology while maintaining traditional Chinese values and beliefs.

The parallel movement toward domestic reform and limited cooperation with the West collapsed under the blows of Japanese imperialism. The Sino-Japanese war of 1894–1895 and the subsequent harsh peace treaty revealed China's helplessness in the face of aggression, triggering a rush for foreign concessions and protectorates in China. At the height of foreign pressure in 1898, it appeared

that the Western powers and Japan might actually divide China among themselves, as they had recently divided Africa. Probably only the jealousy that each nation felt toward its imperial competitors saved China from partition, although the U. S. Open Door policy, which opposed formal annexation of Chinese territory, may have helped tip the balance. In any case, the tempo and the impact of foreign penetration greatly accelerated after 1894.

MAP 30.4 The Expansion and Modernization of Japan, 1868–1918   Japan was uniquely successful among Asian states in responding to the challenge of Western imperialism before 1914. Japan made great progress in building a modern economy and in creating a political empire beyond the home islands.

The Empress Dowager Tzu Hsi   drew on conservative forces, like the court eunuchs surrounding her here, to maintain her power. Three years after her death in 1908, a revolution broke out and forced the last Chinese emperor, a boy of six, to abdicate. *(Source: Courtesy of the Freer Gallery of Art, Smithsonian Institution, Washington, D.C.)*

So, too, did the intensity and radicalism of the Chinese reaction. Like the men of the Meiji Restoration, some modernizers saw salvation in Western institutions. In 1898 the government launched a desperate "hundred days of reform" in an attempt to meet the foreign challenge. Radical reformers like the revolutionary Sun Yat-sen (1866–1925), who came from the peasantry and was educated in Hawaii by Christian missionaries, sought to overthrow the dynasty altogether and establish a republic.

On the other side, some traditionalists turned back toward ancient practices, political conservatism, and fierce hatred of the "foreign devils." "Protect the country, destroy the foreigner" was their simple motto. Such conservative, antiforeign

patriots had often clashed with foreign missionaries, whom they charged with undermining reverence for ancestors and thereby threatening the Chinese family and the entire society. In the agony of defeat and unwanted reforms, secret societies like the Boxers rebelled. In northeastern China, more than two hundred foreign missionaries and several thousand Chinese Christians were killed. Once again, the imperialist response was swift and harsh. Peking was occupied and plundered by foreign armies. A heavy indemnity was imposed.

The years after the Boxer Rebellion (1900–1903) were even more troubled. Anarchy and foreign influence spread as the power and prestige of the Manchu Dynasty declined still further. Antiforeign, antigovernment revolutionary groups agitated and plotted. Finally, in 1912, a spontaneous uprising toppled the Manchu Dynasty. After thousands of years of emperors and empires, a loose coalition of revolutionaries proclaimed a Western-style republic and called for an elected parliament. The transformation of China under the impact of expanding Western society entered a new phase, and the end was not in sight.

SUMMARY

In the nineteenth century the industrializing West entered the third and most dynamic phase of its centuries-old intrusion into non-Western lands. In so doing, Western nations profitably subordinated those lands to their economic interests, sent forth millions of emigrants, and established political influence in Asia and vast political empires in Africa. The reasons for this culminating surge were many, but the economic thrust of robust industrial capitalism, an ever-growing lead in technology, and the competitive pressures of European nationalism were particularly important.

Western expansion had far-reaching consequences. For the first time in human history, the world became in many ways a single unit. Moreover, European expansion diffused the ideas and techniques of a highly developed civilization. Yet the West imposed inequality in commercial relations, and it relied on military might to conquer and rule. It treated non-Western peoples as racial inferiors.

Non-Western elites, often armed with Western doctrines, gradually responded to the Western challenge. They launched a national, anti-imperialist struggle for dignity, genuine independence, and modernization. This struggle would emerge as a central drama of world history after the great European civil war of 1914 to 1918, which reduced the West's technological advantage and shattered its self-confidence and complacent moral superiority.

NOTES

1. Quoted in A. Waley, *The Opium War Through Chinese Eyes* (New York: Macmillan, 1958), p. 29.

2. Quoted in J. W. Hall, *Japan, from Prehistory to Modern Times* (New York: Delacorte Press, 1970), p. 250.
3. Quoted in R. Hallett, *Africa to 1875* (Ann Arbor: University of Michigan Press, 1970), p. 109.
4. Quoted in Earl of Cromer, *Modern Egypt* (London: 1911), p. 48.
5. Quoted in G. Jensen, *Militant Islam* (New York: Harper & Row, 1979), p. 70.
6. Quoted in T. Blegen, *Norwegian Migration to America* (Northfield, Minn.: Norwegian-American Historical Association, 1940), 2.468
7. Quoted in I. Howe, *World of Our Fathers* (New York: Harcourt Brace Jovanovich, 1976), p. 25.
8. Quoted in C. A. Price, *The Great White Walls Are Built: Restrictive Immigration to North America and Australia, 1836–1888* (Canberra: Australian National University Press, 1974), p. 175.
9. Quoted in W. L. Langer, *European Alliances and Alignments, 1871–1890* (New York: Vintage Books, 1931), p. 290.
10. Quoted in J. Ellis, *The Social History of the Machine Gun* (New York: Pantheon Books, 1975), pp. 86, 101.
11. Quoted in G. H. Nadel and P. Curtis, eds., *Imperialism and Colonialism* (New York: Macmillan, 1964), p. 94.
12. Quoted in W. L. Langer, *The Diplomacy of Imperialism,* 2d ed. (New York: Knopf, 1951), pp. 86, 88.
13. Rudyard Kipling, *The Five Nations* (London: 1903), quoted by the permission of Mrs. George Bambridge, Methuen & Company, and Doubleday & Company, Inc.
14. E. H. Berman, "African Responses to Christian Mission Education," *African Studies Review* 17:3 (1974): 530.
15. Quoted in Langer, *Diplomacy of Imperialism,* p. 88.
16. Quoted in Ellis, pp. 99–100.
17. Quoted in K. M. Panikkar, *Asia and Western Dominance* (London: George Allen & Unwin, 1959), p. 116.
18. Quoted in Hall, p. 289.

SUGGESTED READING

General surveys of European expansion in a broad perspective include R. Betts, *Europe Overseas* (1968); A. Thornton, *Imperialism in the 20th Century* (1977); T. Smith, *The Patterns of Imperialism* (1981); and W. Woodruff, *Impact of Western Man* (1967), which has an extensive bibliography. D. K. Fieldhouse has also written two fine surveys, *Economics and Empire, 1830–1914* (1970), and *Colonialism, 1870–1945* (1981). G. Barraclough, *An Introduction to Contemporary History* (1964), argues powerfully that Western imperialism and the non-Western reaction to it have been crucial in world history since about 1890. J. A. Hobson's classic *Imperialism* (1902) is readily available, and the Marxist-Leninist case is effectively presented in V. G. Kieran, *Marxism and Imperialism* (1975). Two excellent anthologies on the problem of European expansion are G. Nadel and P. Curtis, eds., *Imperialism and Colonialism* (1964), and H. Wright, ed., The *"New Imperialism,"* rev. ed. (1975).

Britain's leading position in European imperialism is examined in a lively way by B. Porter, *The Lion's Share* (1976); J. Morris, *Pax Britannica* (1968); and D. Judd, *The Victorian Empire* (1970), a stunning pictorial history. B. Semmel has written widely on the intellectual foundations of English expansion, as in *The Rise of Free Trade Imperialism* (1970). J. Gallagher and R. Robinson, *Africa and the Victorians: The Climax of Imperialism* (1961), is an influential reassessment. H. Brunschwig, *French Colonialism, 1871–1914* (1966), and W. Baumgart, *Imperialism: The Idea and Reality of British and French Colonial Expansion* (1982), are well-balanced studies. A. Moorehead, *The White Nile* (1971), tells the fascinating story of the European exploration of the mysterious upper Nile. Volumes 5 and 6 of K. Latourette, *History of the Expansion of Christianity,* 7 vols. (1937–1945), examine the powerful impulse for missionary work in non-European areas. D. Headrick stresses Western technical superiority in *Tools of Empire: Technology and European Imperialism in the Nineteenth Century* (1981).

G. Perry, *The Middle East: Fourteen Islamic Centuries* (1983), concisely surveys nineteenth-century developments and provides up-to-date bibliographies. B. Lewis, *The Middle East and the West* (1963), is a standard older analysis of the impact of Western ideas on Middle Eastern thought, which may be compared with the more sympathetic view of G. Jansen, *Militant Islam* (1979). Hallett, cited in the Notes, and R. July, *A History of the African People* (1970), contain excellent introductions to Africa in the age of imperialism. D. Lamb, *The Africans* (1984), and J. D. Fage, *A History of Africa* (1978), are also recommended. B. Davidson, *The African Genius: An Introduction to African Social and Cultural History* (1969), imaginatively looks at Western expansion from an African point of view. A classic study of that same expansion from an Indian viewpoint is found in K. M. Panikkar, *Asia and Western Dominance: A Survey of the Vasco da Gama Epoch of Asian History* (1959). S. Wolpert, *A New History of India,* 2d ed. (1982), incorporates recent scholarship in a wide-ranging study that is highly recommended. On Africa and India, see also the Suggested Reading for Chapters 22, 23, and 33.

A. Waley, cited in the Notes, has written extensively and well on China. Valuable surveys of Chinese history include J. Spence, *The Search for Modern China* (1990), I. Hsü, *The Rise of Modern China,* 2d ed. (1975), and K. Latourette, *The Chinese: Their History and Culture,* rev. ed. (1964). All three have many suggestions for further reading. The most comprehensive scholarly work is the multivolume series edited by J. Fairbank and D. Twitchett, *The Cambridge History of China.* In addition to Hall, cited in the Notes, E. Reischauer's topical survey, *Japan: The Story of a Nation* (1981), is recommended. Excellent social studies include M. Hane, *Peasants, Rebels and Outcasts: The Underside of Modern Japan* (1982), and Y. Fukuzawa, *Autobiography* (1966), the personal account of a leading intellectual who witnessed the emergence of modern Japan. E. Sugimoto, *A Daughter of the Samurai* (1966), is another fascinating autobiography. E. Wolf, *Europe and the People Without History* (1982), considers the impact of imperialism on non-Western peoples with skill and compassion.

Two unusual and provocative studies on personal relations between European rulers and non-European subjects are D. Mannoni, *Prospero and Caliban: The Psychology of Colonialization* (1964), and F. Fanon, *The Wretched of the Earth* (1965), a bitter attack on white racism by a black psychologist active in the Algerian revolution. The Indian work by A. Nandy, *The Intimate Enemy: Loss and Recovery of Self Under Colonialism* (1983), is another stimulating psychological study, as is K. Ballhatchet, *Race, Sex and Class Under the Raj* (1980). Novels also bring the psychological and human dimensions of imperialism alive. H. Rider Haggard, *King Solomon's Mines,* portrays the powerful appeal of adventure in exotic lands, and Rudyard Kipling, the greatest writer of European expansion, is at his stirring best in *Kim* and *Soldiers Three.* Joseph Conrad unforgettably probes European motives in *Heart of Darkness,* and André Gide, in *The Immoralist,* closely examines European moral corruption in North Africa.

31

Nation Building in the Western Hemisphere and in Australia

Governor's Palace, Plaza de Armas, Lima, Peru

In the Western Hemisphere and in Australia, as in Europe, the nineteenth century was a period of nation building, geographic expansion, and industrial and commercial growth. Waves of emigrants moved from Europe and Asia to the Americas and to Australia. The millions who braved the oceans populated and built new nations also linked the Western Hemisphere and Australia with the rest of the globe.

The countries of North and South America became highly diverse ethnically and culturally, and the issue of race created serious tensions throughout the hemisphere. In the United States it helped to bring on the Civil War. In the late nineteenth and early twentieth centuries, European immigration directly affected the ways with which the United States and the Latin American nations coped with racial situations.

At the end of the eighteenth century, Canada and the countries of South America remained colonies. Their European mother countries looked on the democratic experiment of the infant United States with suspicion and scorn. The island continent of Australia, remote from Europe and economically undeveloped, served as a dumping ground for English criminals. By 1914 the Latin American states, Canada, and Australia were enjoying political independence and playing a crucial role in the world economy. The United States had become a colossus on which the Old World depended in the First World War.

- Why and how did the Spanish colonies of Latin America shake off European domination and develop into national states?

- What role did the concept of manifest destiny play in the evolution of the United States?

- How did slavery affect the black family in the United States?

- How did the Americas and Australia absorb new peoples, and what was the social impact of the immigrants?

- What geographical, economic, and political conditions shaped the development of Canada?

- What factors aided the economic growth of Australia?

These are among the questions that this chapter addresses.

LATIN AMERICA (1800–1929)

In 1800 the Spanish Empire in the Western Hemisphere stretched from the headwaters of the Mississippi River in present-day Minnesota to the tip of Cape Horn in the Antarctic (see Map 31.1). The Spanish crown claimed 7 million square miles, roughly one-third of the entire hemisphere. According to the Kentucky statesman Henry Clay (1777–1852), "Within this vast region, we behold the most sublime and interesting objects of creation: the loftiest mountains, the most majestic rivers in the world; the richest mines of precious metals, the choicest productions of the earth."[1] Spain believed that this great wealth existed for its benefit, and Spanish policies fostered bitterness and the desire for independence in the colonies.

Between 1806 and 1825 the Spanish colonies in Latin America were convulsed by upheavals that ultimately resulted in their separation from Spain. Some scholars regard these insurrections as wars of revolution; others call them wars of independence; still others consider them civil wars. All three characterizations contain elements of truth.

The Latin American wars were revolutions in the sense that the colonists revolted against the domination of Spain and fought for direct self-government. They were wars of independence in the sense that the colonies sought economic liberation and management of their own commercial affairs. They were civil wars in the sense that social and racial groups fought one another. The *Creoles*—people of Spanish descent born in America—resented the economic and political dominance of the *peninsulares,* as natives of Spain or Portugal were called. Peninsulares controlled the rich export-import trade, intercolonial trade, and the mining industries. At the same time *mestizos* of mixed Spanish and Indian background and *mulattos* of mixed Spanish and African heritage sought an end to their systematic subordination.

Between 1850 and the worldwide depression of 1929, the countries of Latin America developed into national states. The predominant factors in this evolution were the heritage of colonial exploitation, a neocolonial economic structure, massive immigration from Europe and Asia, and the fusion of Amerindian, Caucasian, African, and Asian peoples. The Latin American societies that emerged in the twentieth century can best be understood against this background.

The Origins of the Revolutions

Because of regional, geographic, and racial differences, the Latin American movements for independence took different forms in different places. Everywhere, however, they grew out of recent colonial economic grievances. By the late seventeenth century the Spanish colonies had achieved a high degree of economic diversity and independence. The mercantilist imperialism of the days of Cortés and Pizarro (see pages 568–575), which held that the colonies existed for Spain's financial benefit and should be economically dependent on Spain, had faded away. The colonies had become agriculturally and commercially self-sufficient producers of foodstuffs, wine, textiles, and consumer goods. What was not produced domestically was secured through trade between colonies. A healthy intercolonial trade had developed independent of Spain, despite formidable geographic obstacles and colonial policies designed to restrict it.

In Peru, for example, domestic agriculture supported the large mining settlements, and the colony did not have to import food. Craft workshops owned by the state or by private individuals produced consumer goods for the working class; what was not manufactured locally was bought from Mexico and transported by the Peruvian merchant marine. By 1700 Mexico and Peru were sending shrinking percentages of their revenues to Spain and retaining more for public works, defense, and administration. The colonies lived for themselves, not for Spain.

The reforms of the Spanish Bourbons radically reversed this economic independence. Spain's humiliating defeat in the War of the Spanish Succession prompted demands for sweeping reform of all of Spain's institutions, including colonial policies and practices (see page 617). To improve administrative efficiency, the enlightened monarch Charles III (r. 1759–1788) carved the region of modern Colombia, Venezuela, and Ecuador out of the vast viceroyalty of Peru; it became the new viceroyalty of New Granada with its capital at Bogotá. The Crown also created the viceroyalty of Rio de la Plata (present-day Argentina) with its capital at Buenos Aires (Map 31.1).

Far more momentous was Charles III's radical overhaul of colonial trade policies, to enable Spain to compete with Great Britain and Holland in the great eighteenth-century struggle for empire. The Spanish crown intended the colonies to serve as sources of raw materials and as markets for Spanish manufactured goods. Charles III's free-trade policies cut duties drastically for Spanish merchants. All Iberian ports, no longer just Cadiz, were allowed to trade with the colonies. In Latin America these actions stimulated the production of crops in demand in Europe: coffee in Venezuela; sugar in Cuba and throughout the Caribbean; hides, leather, and salted beef in the Rio de la Plata viceroyalty. In Mexico and Peru, production of silver climbed steadily in the last quarter of the century. The volume of Spain's trade with the colonies soared, possibly as much as 700 percent between 1778 and 1788.[2]

Colonial manufacturing, which had been growing steadily, suffered severely. Better-made and cheaper European goods drove colonial goods out of the marketplace. Colonial textiles, chinaware, and wine, for example, could not compete with cheap Spanish products. For one thing, Latin American free laborers were paid more than European workers in the eighteenth century; this helps explain the great numbers of immigrants to the colonies. Also, intercolonial transportation costs were higher than transatlantic costs. In Buenos Aires, for example, Spanish wines were actually cheaper than locally produced Mendoza wine. In the Rio de la Plata region, heavy export taxes and light import duties shattered the wine industry. When the wine merchants complained of "tyrannical taxes" and asked an end to the import of Spanish wines, the imperial government rejected their appeal.

Geographic obstacles also hampered the economic development of Latin America. Mountains, deserts, jungles, and inadequate natural harbors frustrated colonial efforts to promote economic integration.

Having made the colonies dependent on essential Spanish goods, however, Spain found that it could not keep the sea routes open. After 1789 the French Revolution and Napoleonic wars isolated Spain from Latin America. Foreign traders, especially from the United States, swarmed into Spanish-American ports. In 1796 the Madrid government lifted the restrictions against neutrals trading with the colonies, thus acknowledging Spain's inability to supply the colonies with needed goods and markets.[3] All these difficulties spelled disaster for colonial trade and industry.

At the end of the eighteenth century colonists also complained bitterly that only peninsulares

Disputed by Great Britain, Spain, and Russia

Effective frontier of Spanish settlement

ATLANTIC OCEAN

COAHUILA

VICEROYALTY OF NEW SPAIN

BAJIO LEÓN

Havana

Mexico City • • Veracruz

SAINT DOMINGUE (HAITI)

CUBA

JAMAICA

SANTO DOMINGO

PUERTO RICO

• Guatemala

Caribbean Sea

Caracas •

Suarez

Magdalena

• Bogotá

VICEROYALTY OF NEW GRANADA

GUIANA

Amazon

PACIFIC OCEAN

A N D E S

Lima •

VICEROYALTY OF PERU

VICEROYALTY OF BRAZIL

• Bahia

Spanish colonies

Viceroyalty of New Spain

Viceroyalty of New Granada

Viceroyalty of Peru

Audiencia of Chile

Viceroyalty of Rio de la Plata

Portuguese colony

Viceroyalty of Brazil

Disputed territory

Disputed by Great Britain, Spain, and Russia

Parana

São Paulo • • Rio de Janeiro

A N D E S

VICEROYALTY OF RIO DE LA PLATA

Santiago •

AUDIENCIA OF CHILE

Buenos Aires • • Montevideo

0   500   1000 Km.

0   500   1000 Mi.

ISLAS MALVINAS (FALKLAND ISLANDS)

Cape Horn

were appointed to the *audiencias*—the colonies' highest judicial bodies, which also served as councils to the viceroys—and to other positions in the colonial governments. According to the nineteenth-century Mexican statesman and historian Lucas Alamán (1792–1853),

this preference shown to Spaniards in political offices and ecclesiastical benefices has been the principal cause of the rivalry between the two classes; add to this the fact that Europeans possessed great wealth, which although it may have been the just reward of effort and industry, excited the envy of Americans and was considered as so much usurpation from them; consider that for all these reasons the Spaniards had obtained a decided preponderance over those born in the country; and it will not be difficult to explain the increasing jealousy and rivalry between the two groups which culminated in hatred and enmity.[4]

In the late seventeenth and early eighteenth centuries, large numbers of Creoles had been appointed to government positions, including the audiencias. Then, beginning in 1751, the Crown drastically reduced the appointments of Creoles, and the upper levels of colonial bureaucracies became overwhelmingly Spanish. Between 1730 and 1750, fully 53 percent of appointees to the audiencias had been Creoles; from 1751 to 1775, only 13 percent were Creoles.[5] This change in imperial policy provoked outrage. To the Creole elite of Spanish America, the world seemed "upside down."[6] Creoles hungered for political office and resented their successful Spanish rivals.

Madrid's tax reforms also aggravated discontent. In the 1770s and 1780s the Spanish crown needed income to finance imperial defense. Colonial ports had to be fortified and standing armies built. Like Great Britain, Spain believed its colonies should bear some of the costs of their own defense. Accordingly, Madrid raised the prices of tobacco and liquor and increased the *alcabala* (a sales tax of Arabic origin) on many items. Improved government administration made tax collection more efficient. Creole business and agricultural interests resented the Crown's monopoly of the tobacco industry and opposed new taxes.

As in the thirteen North American colonies a decade earlier, protest movements in Latin America claimed that the colonies were being taxed unconstitutionally. Merchants in Boston and Philadelphia had protested taxation without representation; the Spanish colonies, however, had no tradition of legislative approval of taxes. Creole mercantile leaders argued instead that the constitutional system was being violated because taxes were being imposed without consultation. They asserted that relations between imperial authorities and colonial interests stayed on an even keel through consultation and compromise and that when the Crown imposed taxes without consultation, it violated ancient constitutional practice.

North American ships calling at South American ports had introduced the subversive writings of Thomas Paine and Thomas Jefferson. The imperial government recognized the potential danger of the North American example. Although Spain had joined France on the side of the rebel colonies against Great Britain during the American Revolution, the Madrid government refused in 1783 to grant diplomatic recognition to the new United States. For decades the ideas of Voltaire, Rousseau, and Montesquieu had also trickled into Latin America. In 1794 the Colombian Antonio Nariño translated and published the French *Declaration of the Rights of Man and the Citizen*. Although Spanish authorities sentenced him to ten years in an African prison, Nariño lived to become the father of Colombian independence. By 1800 the Creole elite throughout Latin America was familiar with liberal Enlightenment political thought.[7] The Creoles assumed, however, that the "rights of man" were limited, and they did not share such rights with Indians and blacks.

Race in the Colonial Period

The racial complexion of Latin American societies is one of the most complicated in the world. Because few European women emigrated to the colonies, Spanish men had relations with Indian and African women. African men deprived of black women sought Indian women. The result was a population composed of every possible combination of Indian, Spanish, and African blood.

MAP 31.1 Latin America Before Independence Consider the factors that led to the boundaries of the various Spanish and Portuguese colonies in North and South America.

Diamond Mining in Brazil The discovery of gold and diamonds in Brazil in the seventeenth century increased the demand for slave labor. The English geologist John Mawe made this dramatic engraving of slaves washing for diamonds in the early nineteenth century. *(Source: Courtesy, Oliveira Lima Library, The Catholic University of America. Photo: Paul McKane, OSB)*

Spanish theories of racial purity rejected people of mixed blood, particularly those of African descent. A person's social status depended on the degree of European blood he or she possessed or appeared to possess. Peninsulares and Creoles reinforced their privileged status by showing contempt for people who were not white. As the great nineteenth-century German scientist Alexander von Humboldt put it, having spent five years traveling throughout South America, "Any white person, although he rides his horse barefoot, imagines himself to be of the nobility of the country."[8] Coupled with the Spaniard's aristocratic disdain for manual labor, a 300-year tradition had instilled in the minds of Latin Americans the notion that

dark skin and manual labor went together. Owners of mines, plantations, and factories had a vested interest in keeping blacks and Indians in servile positions. Racism and discrimination pervaded all the Latin American colonies.

In spite of the catastrophes that had befallen them in the sixteenth and seventeenth centuries, Indians still constituted the majority of the population of Latin America at the end of the colonial period. Demographers estimate that Indians accounted for between three-fifths and three-fourths of the total population. The colonies that became Peru and Bolivia had Indian majorities; the regions that became Argentina and Chile had European majorities. As the Indians declined in the seventeenth century, the Spanish grabbed Indian lands for wheat, corn, cattle, and sheep raising. Indians and black slaves toiled in the silver and gold mines of Mexico, Colombia, and Peru, in the wheat fields of Chile, in the humid, mosquito-ridden cane brakes of Mexico and the Caribbean, and in the diamond mines and coffee and sugar plantations of Brazil.

Nevertheless, nonwhites did experience some social mobility in the colonial period, certainly more than in North America. In Mexico, decreasing reliance on slaves led to a great increase in manumissions. Once freed, however, Negroes immediately became subject to the payment of a money tribute, as were the Indians. Freedmen also incurred the obligation of military service. A few mulattos rose in the army, some as high as the rank of colonel. The army and the church seem to have offered the greatest opportunities for social mobility. Many black slaves gained their freedom by fleeing to the jungles or mountains, where they established self-governing communities. Around the year 1800 Venezuela counted 24,000 fugitive slaves in a total population of 87,000.

Many Indians were still subject to the mita and repartimiento. The *mita,* a system of forced labor requiring all adult Indian males to work for part of each year in the silver mines, was thinly disguised slave labor; the silver mines were deathtraps. The law of *repartimiento* required Indians to buy goods solely from local *corregidores,* officials who collected taxes. The new taxes of the 1770s and 1780s fell particularly heavily on the Indians. When Indian opposition to these taxes and to oppressive conditions exploded into violence, Creoles organized the protest movements and assumed leadership of them.

The Comunero Revolution

In Peru in November 1779 the wealthy, well-educated mestizo Tupac Amaru (1742–1781), a descendant of the Inca kings, captured, tried, and executed the local corregidor. Tupac Amaru and his mostly Indian followers demanded the abolition of the alcabala tax and the mita and replacement of the corregidores with Indian governors. Proclaiming himself liberator of the people, Tupac Amaru waged a war of blood and fire against the Spanish governors. Violence swept the Peruvian highlands. Thousands lost their lives, and a vast amount of private property was destroyed. Poor communication among the rebel forces and the superior organization of the imperial armies enabled the Spanish to crush the revolt. Tupac Amaru, his family, and his captains were captured and savagely executed. Frightened colonial administrators, however, did grant some reforms. The Crown repealed the repartimiento, reduced the mita, and replaced the corregidores with a lighter system of intendants. The condition of the Indians temporarily improved.

News of the rebellion of Tupac Amaru trickled northward, where it helped stimulate revolution in the New Granada viceroyalty. Disorders occurred first at Socorro in modern Colombia (Map 31.2). Throughout the eighteenth century Socorro had prospered. Sugar cane, corn, and cattle flourished on its exceptionally fertile soil. Large cotton crops stimulated the production of textiles, mostly in a primitive cottage industry worked by women. Socorro's location on the Suarez River made it an agricultural and manufacturing center and an entrepôt for trade with the hinterland. Hard-working Spanish immigrants had prospered and often intermarried with the Indians.

When the viceroy published new taxes on tobacco and liquor and reorganized the alcabala, riots broke out in Socorro in March 1781 and spread to other towns. Representatives of peasants and artisan groups from many towns elected a *comun,* or central committee, to lead the insurrection. Each town elected its local comun and the captain of its militia. Known as the "Comunero Revolution," the insurrection in New Granada enjoyed broad-based support and good organization and appeared far more threatening to government authorities than had the uprising in Peru.

An Indian peasant army commanded by Creole captains marched on Bogotá. Government officials, lacking adequate military resources, sent a commission to play for time by negotiating with the comuneros. On June 4 the commission agreed to the rebels' terms: reduction of the alcabala and of the Indians' forced tribute, abolition of the new taxes on tobacco, and preference for Creoles over peninsulares in government positions. The joyful Indian army disbanded and went home. What they did not know was that the commission had already secretly disclaimed the agreement with the rebels on the grounds that it had been taken by force. Having succeeded in dispersing the Indians, the government at Bogotá won over the Creole leaders with promise of pardons and then moved in reserve troops who captured large numbers of rebels. When the last rebel holdout—that of José Antonio Galan—had been captured, a kangaroo court tried Galan and condemned him

to be taken out of jail, dragged and taken to the place of execution where he will be hung until dead, that his head be removed from his dead body, that the rest of his body be quartered, that his torso be committed to flames for which purpose a fire shall be lit in front of the platform. His head shall be sent to Guaduas, the scene of his scandalous insults, his right arm shall be displayed in the main square of Socorro, his left arm shall be displayed in the square of San Gil, his right leg shall be displayed in Charala his birthplace, and his left leg in the parish of Mogotes. All his descendants shall be declared infamous, all his property shall be confiscated by the royal treasury, his home shall be burnt, and the ground salted, so that in this fashion his infamous name may be forgotten.[9]

Thus ended the revolt of the comuneros in New Granada. They failed to win self-rule, but they forced the authorities to act in accordance with the spirit of the "unwritten constitution," whose guiding principle was consultation and compromise. Although the authorities used Galan's execution as a stick to kill social revolution, over the next twenty years they extended the carrot of government concern to promote colonial prosperity.

Independence

Napoleon Bonaparte lit the fuse of the Latin American powder keg. In 1808, as part of his effort to rule Europe, Napoleon deposed the Spanish king Ferdinand VII and placed his own brother

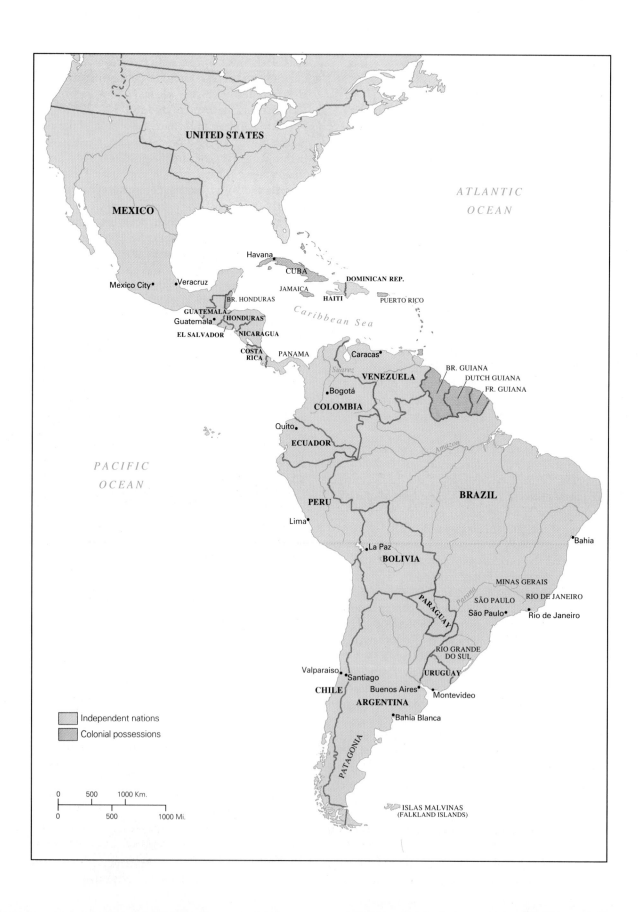

UNITED STATES

MEXICO

ATLANTIC
OCEAN

Mexico City● ●Veracruz

Havana●
CUBA
JAMAICA
BR. HONDURAS
GUATEMALA
Guatemala● HONDURAS●
EL SALVADOR NICARAGUA
COSTA
RICA PANAMA

DOMINICAN REP.
HAITI
PUERTO RICO
Caribbean Sea

Caracas●
Suarez
VENEZUELA

●Bogotá
COLOMBIA

Quito●
ECUADOR

BR. GUIANA
DUTCH GUIANA
FR. GUIANA

Amazon

PACIFIC
OCEAN

PERU

Lima●

●La Paz
BOLIVIA

BRAZIL

●Bahia

MINAS GERAIS

SÃO PAULO RIO DE JANEIRO
São Paulo●
PARAGUAY ●Rio de Janeiro
Parana
RÍO GRANDE
DO SUL

Valparaiso● ●Santiago
CHILE
Buenos Aires●
ARGENTINA

URUGUAY
●Montevideo

●Bahía Blanca

PATAGONIA

Independent nations
Colonial possessions

0   500   1000 Km.
0   500   1000 Mi.

ISLAS MALVINAS
(FALKLAND ISLANDS)

on the Spanish throne (see page 821). In Latin America the Creoles subsequently seized the opportunity. Since everything in Spanish America was done in the name of the king, the Creoles argued that the removal of the legitimate king shifted sovereignty to the people—that is, to themselves. In 1810 the small, wealthy Creole aristocracy used the removal of the Spanish king as justification for their seizure of political power and their preservation of that power.

Thus began the war for independence. An able scholar has described it as

a prolonged, confused, and in many ways contradictory movement. In Mexico it began as a popular social movement and ended many years later as a conservative uprising against a liberal Spanish constitution. In Venezuela it came to be a war unto the death; in other places it was a war between a small Creole minority and the Spanish authorities. It was not an organized movement with a central revolutionary directorate. It had no Continental Congress. . . . If there was no central direction, no centrally recognized leadership, likewise there was no formally accepted political doctrine.[10]

The Creoles who led the various movements for independence did not intend a radical redistribution of property or reconstruction of society; they merely rejected the authority of the Spanish crown.

In the final battle . . . the soldiers on the field came from Venezuela, Colombia, Ecuador, Peru, Argentina, and Chile, and among the officers there were Frenchmen and Englishmen who had opposed each other in the Napoleonic Wars. . . . The war stopped but did not officially end. There was no treaty of peace. There was no recognition of the new states. There was no definite agreement as to the form of government or even as to national boundaries. . . . In Latin America each separate area went its own way. Central America broke way from Mexico and then splintered into five separate nations. Uruguay, Paraguay, and Bolivia separated themselves from Argentina, Chile from Peru,

MAP 31.2 Latin America in 1830 What geographical factors have led to the relative political power of the United States and the Latin American nations?

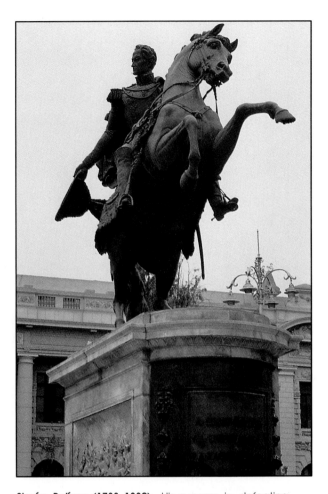

Simón Bolívar (1783–1830) His success in defeating Spanish armies earned him the title "the Liberator." President of Greater Colombia, Bolívar organized the government of Peru, created Bolivia, and dreamt of a United Spanish America. He is respected as the greatest Latin American hero. *(Source: Stuart Cohen/Comstock)*

and [Simón] Bolívar's attempt to federate the state of Greater Colombia (Venezuela, Colombia, and Ecuador) with Peru and Bolivia under a centralized government broke down.[11]

The great hero of the movement for independence was Simón Bolívar (1783–1830), who is considered the Latin American George Washington. A very able general, Bolívar's victories over the royalist armies won him the presidency of Greater Colombia in 1819. Bolívar dreamed of a continental union, and in 1826 he summoned a conference of the American republics at Panama. The meeting

Street Scene in Rio de Janeiro   Soldiers, planter-aristocrats, merchants, slaves, friars, and carriages thronged the cobblestone streets of the capital of Brazil. *(Source: Department of Rare Books, Cornell University Library)*

achieved little. Bolívar organized the government of Bolivia and became the head of the new state of Peru. The territories of Greater Colombia splintered apart, however, and a sadly disillusioned Bolívar went into exile, saying, "America is ungovernable. Those who served the revolution plowed the seas." The failure of pan-Americanism isolated individual countries, prevented collective action, and later paved the way for the political and economic intrusion of the United States and other powers.

Brazil's quest for independence from Portugal was unique: Brazil won its independence without violent upheaval. When Napoleon's troops entered Portugal, the royal family fled to Brazil and made Rio de Janeiro the capital of the Portuguese Empire. The new government immediately lifted the old mercantilist restrictions and opened Brazilian ports to the ships of all friendly nations. Under popular pressure, King Pedro I (r. 1822–1831),

proclaimed Brazil's independence in 1822 and published a constitution. Pedro's administration was wracked by factional disputes between Portuguese courtiers and Brazilian Creoles, a separatist movement in the Rio Grande do Sul region, and provincial revolts. His successor, Pedro II (r. 1831–1889), restored order and laid the foundations of the modern Brazilian state. His reign witnessed the expansion of the coffee industry, the beginnings of the rubber industry, and massive immigration.

The Consequences of Independence

The wars of independence ended around 1825. What effects did they have on Latin American societies? How were Latin American countries governed in the nineteenth century? What factors worked against the development of modern nations? Because the movements for independence differed in character and course in different regions and countries, generalizations about Mexico, the Caribbean islands, and South America are likely to be misleading. Significant changes did occur, however, throughout Latin America.

The newly independent nations did not achieve immediate political stability when the wars of independence ended. The Spanish crown had served as a unifying symbol, and its disappearance left a power vacuum. Civil disorder typically followed. The Creole leaders of the revolutions had no experience in government, and the wars had left a legacy of military, not civilian, leadership. Throughout the continent, idealistic but impractical leaders proclaimed republics—independent states governed by an assembly of representatives of the electorate. In practice, the generals ruled.

In Argentina, for example, Juan Manuel de Rosas (r. 1835–1852) assumed power amid widespread public disorder and ruled as dictator. In Mexico, liberals declared a federal republic, but incessant civil strife led to the rise of the dictator Antonio López de Santa Anna in the mid-nineteenth century. Likewise in Venezuela, strongmen, dictators, and petty aristocratic oligarchs governed from 1830 to 1892. Some countries suffered constant revolutions. In the course of the century Bolivia had sixty and Venezuela fifty-two. The rule of force prevailed almost everywhere. Enlightened dictatorship was the typical form of government.

The wars of liberation disrupted the economic life of most Latin American countries. The prosperity that many areas had achieved toward the end of the colonial period was destroyed. Mexico and Venezuela in particular lost large percentages of their populations and suffered great destruction of farmland and animals. Even areas that saw relatively little violence, such as Chile and New Granada, experienced a weakening of economic life. Armies were frequently recruited by force, and when the men were demobilized many did not return home. The consequent population dislocation hurt agriculture and mining. Guerrilla warfare disrupted trade and communications. Forced loans and the seizure of private property for military use ruined many people. In the 1820s Peru's economy staggered under the burden of supporting large armies. Isolated territories such as Paraguay and much of Central America suffered little damage, but most countries gained independence at the price of serious economic problems.

Brazil, which had a large slave population, did not free the slaves until 1888. Spain abolished slavery in its Cuban colony in a series of measures between 1870 and 1886; Cuba itself became independent in 1903, a consequence of the Spanish-American War. Elsewhere, however, independence accelerated the abolition of slavery. The destruction of agriculture in countries such as Mexico and Venezuela caused the collapse of the plantation system, and fugitive slaves could not be recaptured. Also, the royalists and patriot generals such as Bolívar offered slaves their freedom in exchange for military service. The result was that slaves constituted a large part of the military forces. Finally, most of the new independent states adopted republican constitutions declaring the legal equality of all men. For Indians and blacks, however, these noble words were meaningless, for the revolution brought about no redistribution of property. Nor could long-standing racist attitudes be eliminated by the stroke of a pen.

Although the edifice of racism persisted in the nineteenth century, Latin America experienced much more assimilation and offered Negroes greater economic and social mobility than did the United States. As a direct result of their heroic military service in the wars of independence, a substantial number of Negroes improved their social status. Some even attained the political heights: the Mexican revolutionary Vicente Guerrero, served as president of his country in 1829; Antonio Guzmán governed Venezuela as a benevolent dictator (r. 1870–1888); Ramón Castilla served as president of Peru (r. 1845–1851 and 1855–1862) and made great improvements in state financing.

What accounts for the relative racial permeability of Latin America in contrast with the severe segregation in the United States? As the Dutch scholar H. Hoetink points out, Latin American countries evolved a three-tiered socioracial structure, in contrast to the two-tiered racial edifice in the United States. Legally and socially, Latin American societies classified people as white, colored, or black, and marriages between whites and light-skinned colored people were commonly accepted. Legislative discrimination against colored people proved unenforceable. Thus light skin allowed for gradual assimilation into the middle and upper social echelons. In the United States, by contrast, anyone who was not "pure" white was classified as black.

Hoetink explains the problem partly in terms of the large population of poor whites in the United States: "Nowhere, but in the North American mainland, did the number of extremely poor whites always exceed the number of slaves. Nowhere, but in the U.S. South, were special police forces predominantly manned by poor whites."[12] Also, Latin American elites' definition of "whiteness" and perception of physical beauty seem to have been broader than those of the white majority in the United States.

Nevertheless, the advantages of assimilation did not (and do not) apply to dark-skinned people in Latin America. While substantial numbers of light-skinned colored people rose economically and socially, the great mass of dark-skinned blacks continued to experience all the consequences of systematic and insistent racism.

Neocolonialism

The leaders of the Latin American revolutions had hoped that their nations, once independent, would attract European and North American investment. Instead, political instability and the preoccupation of European and North American financiers with industrial expansion in their own countries discouraged investment. The advent of stable dictatorships, however, eventually paved the way for economic growth. After 1870 capital began to flow south and across the Atlantic. In Mexico, North American capital supported the production of hemp (used in the United States for grain harvesting), sugar, bananas, and rubber, frequently on American-owned plantations. British and American interests backed the development of tin, copper, and gold mining in Mexico. Oil drilling leaped forward, and by 1911 Mexico had taken third place among the world's oil producers. British financiers built Argentina's railroads, meatpacking industry, and utilities. British businessmen in Chile developed the copper and nitrate industries (nitrate is used in the production of pharmaceuticals and fertilizers); by 1890 the British controlled 70 percent of the nitrate industry. Likewise in Brazil, foreign capital—primarily British—flowed into coffee, cotton, and sugar production and manufacturing. In 1889 Brazil produced 56 percent of the world's coffee; by 1904 that figure had risen to 76 percent. When massive overproduction of coffee led to a sharp

drop in prices in 1906, a commission of British, American, German, and French bankers rescued the Brazilian government from near disaster.

The price paid for economic development by Latin America at the end of the nineteenth century was a new form of economic domination. Foreign investors acquired control of the railroads, mineral resources, and banking, and they made heavy inroads into real estate. British investments led all others, but beginning in 1898 the United States flexed its imperialistic muscles and sent gunboats and troops to defend its dollars in the Caribbean and Central America. By the turn of the century the Latin American nations were active participants in the international economic order, but foreigners controlled most of their industries.

Another distinctive feature of the neocolonial order was the cultivation of one crop. Each country's economy revolved around only one or two products: sugar in Cuba, nitrates and copper in Chile, meat in Argentina, coffee in Brazil. A sharp drop in the world market demand for a product could destroy the industry and with it the nation's economic structure. The outbreak of the First World War in 1914 drastically reduced exports of Latin American raw materials and imports of European manufactured goods, provoking general economic crisis.[13]

Throughout the eighteenth century the Spanish-owned *haciendas*—large landed estates— and plantations had continued to expand to meet the needs of commercial agriculture: wheat for the cities, corn for the Indians' consumption, sugar for export to Europe and North America. By means of purchase, forced removal of Indians, and outright seizure, the Spanish continued to take Indian land, as they had done in the seventeenth century. Some land was acquired merely to eliminate competition by depriving Indians of their fields, which were then left fallow.

The late nineteenth century witnessed ever greater concentrations of land in ever fewer hands. In places like the Valley of Mexico in southern Mexico, a few large haciendas controlled all the land. Under the dictatorship of General Porfirio Díaz, the Mexican government in 1883 passed a law allowing real estate companies (controlled by Díaz's political cronies) to survey public and "vacant" lands and to retain one-third of the land they surveyed. An 1894 law provided that land could be declared vacant if legal title to it could

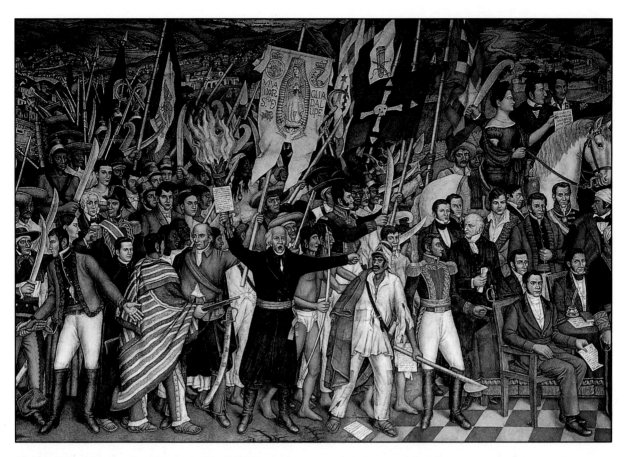

Mexico Today, Mexico Tomorrow   In this detail from a huge mural cycle completed for the National Palace of Mexico City, the naturalist painter Diego Rivera (1886–1957), in the style of traditional Mexican folk art, celebrates the triumph of creative labor in farming, mining, and industry, and denounces the evils of capitalism. A member of the Mexican Communist party, Rivera condemned through his art what he considered the oppression of both communism and fascism. *(Source: Robert Frerck/Odyssey)*

not be produced. Since few Indians had deeds to the land that their ancestors had worked for centuries, the door swung open to wholesale expropriation of small landowners and entire villages. Shrewd speculators tricked illiterate Indians into selling their lands for trifling sums. Thousands of litigants clogged the courts. Indians who dared armed resistance were crushed by government troops and carried off to virtual slave labor. Vast stretches of land came into the hands of private individuals—in one case, 12 million acres. Stripped of their lands, the Indians were a ready labor supply. They were mercilessly exploited. Debt peonage became common: landowners paid their laborers not in cash but in vouchers redeemable only at the company store, whose high prices and tricky bookkeeping kept the peons permanently in debt.

Some scholars maintain that the hacienda owners usually let their land lie fallow until it rose in value or attracted American investors. The lack of cultivation, they assert, kept the prices of corn and other crops artificially high. The owners themselves, supported by rents, passed indolent lives in extravagant luxury in Mexico City and other cities.

Other scholars argue that the haciendas were efficient enterprises whose owners sought to maximize profits on invested capital. The Sanchez Navarro family of northwestern Mexico, for instance, engaged in a wide variety of agricultural and commercial pursuits, exploiting their lands and resources as fully as possible. The Sanchez Navarros controlled 800,000 acres in 1821 and continued to acquire land; ultimately their *latifundio*—a

LATIN AMERICA, CA 1760–1900

1764–1780	Charles III of Spain's administrative and economic reforms
1781	Communero revolution in New Granada
1810–1825	Latin American wars of independence against Spain
1822	Proclamation by Portugal of Brazil's independence
1826	Call by Simón Bolívar for Panama Conference on Latin American union
1825–ca 1870	Political instability in most Latin American nations
ca 1870–1919	Latin American neocolonialism
1876–1911	Porfirio Diaz' control of Mexico
1888	Emancipation of slaves in Brazil; final abolition of slavery in Western Hemisphere
1880–1914	Massive immigration from Europe and Asia to Latin America
1898	Spanish American War; end of Spanish control over Cuba; transfer of Puerto Rico to United States

large landed estate—was about the size of West Virginia. Along with vast cattle ranches and sheep runs containing as many as 250,000 sheep, the Sanchez Navarros cultivated maize, wheat, and cotton. They invested heavily and profitably in silver mining and manufacturing and lent sizable sums at high interest. Although they brutally exploited their peons and practiced debt peonage, the Sanchez Navarros lived very modestly on their own estates rather than luxuriating in Mexico City. A final determination of whether the Sanchez Navarros were unique or representative of a type of magnate prevalent in the agricultural and business communities of nineteenth-century Mexico[14] must await further investigation.

The Impact of Immigration

In 1852 the Argentine political philosopher Juan Bautista Alberdi published *Bases and Points of Departure for Argentine Political Organization,* arguing that "to govern is to populate." Alberdi meant that the development of his country—and, by extension, all of Latin America—depended on immigration. Argentina had an adequate labor supply, but it was unevenly distributed throughout the country. Moreover, Alberdi maintained, Indians and blacks lacked basic skills, and it would take too long to train them. Therefore he pressed for massive immigration from the "advanced" countries of northern Europe and the United States. Alberdi's ideas won immediate acceptance and were even incorporated into the Argentine constitu-

tion, which declared that "the Federal government will encourage European immigration." Other Latin American countries adopted similar policies promoting immigration.[15]

European needs coincided perfectly with those of Latin America (see pages 938–940). After 1880, Ireland, Great Britain, Germany, Italy, Spain, and the central European nations experienced greater population growth than their labor markets could absorb. Meanwhile the growing industries of Europe needed South American raw materials and markets for their finished goods, and South American countries wanted European markets for their minerals, coffee, sugar, beef, and manufactured goods. Italian, Spanish, and Portuguese peoples poured into Latin America.

Immigration led to rapid urbanization, which meant Europeanization and industrialization. By 1900, Buenos Aires and Rio de Janeiro had populations of more than 500,000 people; Mexico City, Montevideo, Santiago, and Havana also experienced spectacular growth. Portuguese, Italian, French, Chinese, and Japanese immigrants gave an international flavor to the cities, and a more vigorous tempo replaced the somnolent Spanish atmosphere.

By 1914 Buenos Aires had emerged as one of the most cosmopolitan cities in the world. In less than half a century, the population of the city and its province had grown from 500,000 to 3.6 million. As Argentina's political capital, the city housed all its government bureaucracies and agencies. The meatpacking, food-processing, flour-milling, and wool industries were concentrated in

Buenos Aires. Half of all overseas tonnage passed through the city, which was also the heart of the nation's railroad network. The University of Buenos Aires was the intellectual hub of the nation. Elegant shops near the Plaza de Mayo catered to the expensive tastes of the elite upper classes, who constituted about 5 percent of the population.

Meanwhile the thousands of immigrants who toiled twelve hours a day, six days a week, on the docks and construction sites and in the meatpacking plants crowded into the city's *conventillos,* or tenements:

The one-room dwelling . . . served a family with two to five children or a group of four or five single men. At the door to each room stood a pile of wooden boxes. One generally held a basin for washing; another a charcoal brazier on which to cook the daily watery stew, or puchero; *and garbage accumulated in a third. Two or three iron cots, a pine table, a few wooden chairs, an old trunk, perhaps a sewing machine, and more boxes completed the furnishings. Light came from the open door and one window, from an oil or gas lamp, or occasionally from a bare electric light bulb. On the once-whitewashed walls were tacked pictures of popular heroes, generals, or kings torn from magazines, an image of the Madonna and a couple of saints, perhaps a faded photograph of family members in Europe. The women often eked out miserable incomes by taking in laundry and washing and drying it in the patios. Others ironed or sewed on a piecework basis. Some men worked here: in one corner a shoemaker might ply his trade, in another a man might bend over a small table repairing watches.*[16]

Domestic Scenes in Mid-Nineteenth-Century Rio The servants, lace tablecloth, and fancy dress of the mistress imply that this is a well-to-do household. The meal, consisting of meat, bread, fruit, and wine, seems to be eaten on imported china. *(Source: Courtesy, Oliveira Lima Library, The Catholic University of America. Photo: Paul McKane, OSB)*

Immigrants dreamed of rapid economic success in the New World, and there was in fact plenty of upward social mobility. The first generation almost always did manual labor, but its sons often advanced to upper blue-collar or white-collar jobs. The rare Genoese or Neapolitan immigrant whose labor and thrift made his son a millionaire quickly learned the meaning of assimilation: the son typically assumed the dress, style, and values of the Spanish elite. Hispanic attitudes toward class, manual labor, and egalitarianism prevailed, and the new immigrant rich imitated the Spanish nobility.[17]

Europeans gave an enormous boost to the development of industry and commerce. Italian and Spanish settlers in Argentina stimulated the expansion of the cattle industry and the development of the wheat and shoe industries. In Brazil, English investments facilitated the growth of the iron industry and the railroads. Swiss immigrants built the cheese business; Italians gained a leading role in the coffee industry; and the Japanese pioneered the development of the cotton industry. In Peru, the British controlled railroad construction, Italians became influential in banking and the restaurant business, and the French dominated jewelry, dressmaking, and pharmaceutical ventures. The arrival of millions of migrants changed the entire commercial structure of South America.

Immigration promoted further ethnic integration. The vast majority of migrants were unmarried males; seven out of ten people who landed in

Argentina between 1857 and 1924 were single males between thirteen and forty years old. Many of those who stayed sought out Indian or other low-status women. This kind of assimilation also occurred in Brazil, Mexico, Peru, and other South American countries. Male settlers from eastern Europe and women of all nationalities preferred to marry within their own ethnic groups. But men greatly outnumbered women, and a man who chose to marry usually had to marry an Indian.[18] Immigration, then, furthered the racial mixture of Europeans, Asians, and native South Americans.

For Latin America's sizable black population, immigration proved a calamity. Slavery had been technically abolished in Spanish America after independence and in Portuguese Brazil by 1888, but the economic and social status of the Negro population had scarcely changed. Accustomed to working the rural coffee plantations and the mines, blacks sometimes had little preparation for urban living. Many former slaves had skills, even for factory work, but racism explains the greater presence of immigrants in factories. In 1893, 71.2 percent of the working population of São Paulo was foreign-born. Anxious to adapt to America and to climb the economic ladder, immigrants quickly learned the traditional racial prejudices. Negro women usually found work as domestics, but employers excluded black males from good jobs. Racial prejudice kept the vast bulk of the South American black population in a wretched socioeconomic position until the Second World War.

Independence did little to change the basic social, economic, and political structure of Latin American countries. Although republican constitutions declared all men (but not women) equal under law, the elite continued to control status, wealth, and power almost everywhere as Creoles moved into positions formerly held by peninsulares. European and United States neocolonial support for steps to modernize the area's commerce and industry during the last half of the nineteenth century served to strengthen the position of the elite and allow it to use capitalistic values and ideals as a shield against demands for fundamental socioeconomic reforms. European styles in art, clothing, housing, and literature became highly popular, particularly among the elite, as they sought acceptance and approval by their economic masters. Meaningful structural change would await the revolutions and violent confrontations of the twentieth century.

THE UNITED STATES (1789–1929)

The victory of the North American colonies and the founding of the United States seemed to validate the Enlightenment idea that a better life on earth was possible (see pages 669–675). Americans carried over into the nineteenth and twentieth centuries an unbounded optimism about the future. The vastness of the land and its untapped resources reinforced that faith. The young nation, confident of its "manifest destiny," pushed relentlessly across the continent. Westward movement, however, threatened to extend black slavery, which generated increasing disagreement between the industrialized North and the agricultural South. The ensuing Civil War cost more American lives than any other war the nation was to fight. The victory of the North did not resolve the racial issue that had caused the war, but it did preserve the federal system.

The years between 1865 and 1917 witnessed the building of a new industrialized nation. Immigrants pursued the frontier to its end, provided the labor to exploit the country's mineral resources, turned small provincial towns into sophisticated centers of ethnic and cultural diversity, and built the railroads that tied the country together. However, the American economy absorbed immigrants faster than American society did. The ideology of manifest destiny lived on after the frontier closed and considerably affected relations between the United States and Latin America. In the First World War, American aid and American troops were the deciding factor in the Allied victory. After the war, "normalcy" and the façade of prosperity supported a persistent optimism. Only the Great Depression, beginning in 1929 and bringing enormous unemployment and terrible social problems, shook Americans' confidence in their potential and their future.

Manifest Destiny

In an 1845 issue of the *United States Magazine and Democratic Review*, editor John L. O'Sullivan boldly declared that foreign powers were trying to prevent American annexation of Texas in order to impede "the fulfillment of our manifest destiny to overspread the continent allotted by Providence for the free development of our yearly multiplying millions." O'Sullivan was articulating a sentiment prevalent in the United States since early in its history: that God had foreordained the nation to cover the entire continent. After a large-circulation newspaper picked up the phrase "manifest destiny," it was used on the floor of Congress and soon entered the language as a catchword for and justification of expansion. The concept of manifest destiny played an important role in some basic developments in American history: the settlement of peoples of diverse nationalities, the issue of slavery, the conflict over whether the United States was to remain agrarian or become a commercial and industrial society.

When George Washington took office in 1789, fewer than 4 million people inhabited the thirteen states on the eastern seaboard. By the time Abraham Lincoln became the sixteenth president in 1861, the United States stretched across the continent and had 31 million inhabitants.

During the colonial period, pioneers had pushed westward to the Appalachian Mountains. After independence, westward movement accelerated. The eastern states claimed all the land from the Atlantic to the Mississippi River, but two forces blocked immediate expansion. The Indians, trying to save their lands, allied with the British in Canada to prevent further American encroachment. However, the federal government, with an almost empty treasury, wanted revenue from land sales. In 1794 Britain agreed to evacuate border forts in the Northwest Territory and thereby end British support for the Indians. A similar treaty with Spain paved the way for southeastern expansion (Map 31.3).

Events in Europe and the Caribbean led to a massive increase in American territory. In 1800 Spain ceded the Louisiana Territory—the land between the Mississippi River and the Rocky Mountains—to France. Napoleon intended to use the Louisiana Territory to make France an imperial power in America, but a black revolution on the island of Hispaniola (present-day Haiti and Santa Domingo) upset his plans. Led by Toussaint L'Ouverture, Haiti's 500,000 slaves revolted against their 40,000 white owners. Napoleon quickly dispatched troops with orders to crush the revolt, seize New Orleans, and take possession of the Louisiana Territory. Alarmed, President Thomas Jefferson ordered the American minister in Paris, Robert Livingston, to negotiate to buy the Louisiana Territory.

When yellow fever and Haitian bullets carried off most of the French troops in Haiti, Napoleon relinquished his grandiose plans. He was planning war with Great Britain and realized that France's weakness at sea meant that Britain might be able to take Louisiana.

On the day Napoleon opened hostilities with England, his foreign minister Talleyrand casually asked Livingston, "What would you give us for the whole of Louisiana?" The astonished American proposed four million dollars. "Too low!" said Talleyrand. "Reflect and see me tomorrow." Less than three weeks later the deed of sale was signed. The United States paid only twelve million dollars for millions of acres of some of the world's richest farmland; the Louisiana Purchase was the greatest bargain in U.S. history.

Scarcely was the ink dry on the treaty when pressure rose for war with England. Repeated British attacks on American vessels on the high seas and British interference in American trade provided diplomatic justification for the War of 1812. Western settlers wanted further expansion. "War hawks" in the old Northwest Territory, Kentucky, Tennessee, and the southern frontier believed that a war with Britain would yield Canada, permanently end Indian troubles, and open up vast forest lands for settlement. The Treaty of Ghent (1814) ended the conflict, and the prewar boundaries were unchanged.

After the restoration of peace, settlers poured into the Northwest and the Gulf Plains (the region of Georgia, Alabama, and Mississippi). Congress sold land in lots of 160 acres at two dollars an acre; only eighty dollars was needed as down payment. Irish and German immigrants rapidly put the black earth of Indiana and Illinois under cultivation. Pioneers of American stock planted cotton in the lush delta of the Gulf Plains. Scandinavian and German settlers found the softly rolling hills of the Wisconsin country ideal for cattle.

Spain, preoccupied with rebellions in South America, sold the Florida territory to the United States government; and beginning in 1821, American settlers poured into the Mexican territory of Texas, whose soil proved excellent for the production of cotton and sugar. Contemptuous of the government of the Mexican president Santa Anna, Texans rebelled and proclaimed Texas an independent republic in 1836. Southern politicians, fearing that Texas would become a refuge for fugitive slaves, pressured President John Tyler to admit

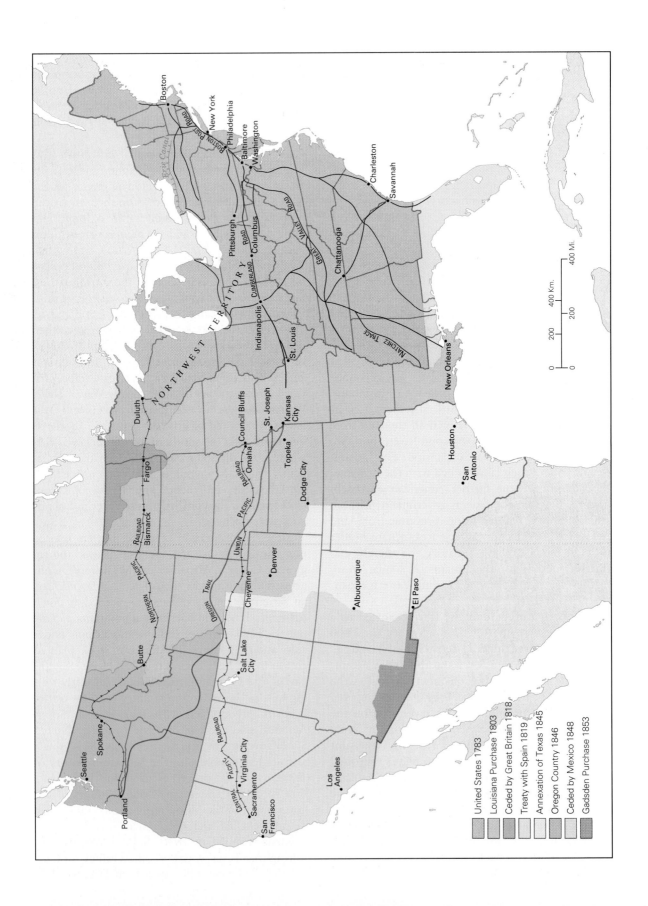

NORTHWEST TERRITORY

Boston
New York
Philadelphia
Baltimore
Washington
Charleston
Savannah
Pittsburgh
Columbus
Chattanooga
Indianapolis
St. Louis
New Orleans

BOSTON POST ROAD
Erie Canal
ROAD
CUMBERLAND
GREAT VALLEY ROAD
NATCHEZ TRACE

Duluth
Council Bluffs
St. Joseph
Kansas City
Topeka
Dodge City
Fargo
Bismarck
Omaha
Houston
San Antonio

Denver
Albuquerque
El Paso

Butte
Cheyenne
Salt Lake City

Spokane
Seattle
Virginia City
Sacramento
Portland
San Francisco
Los Angeles

NORTHERN PACIFIC RAILROAD
UNION PACIFIC RAILROAD
OREGON TRAIL
CENTRAL PACIFIC RAILROAD

400 Mi.
400 Km.
200
200
0
0

United States 1783
Louisiana Purchase 1803
Ceded by Great Britain 1818
Treaty with Spain 1819
Annexation of Texas 1845
Oregon Country 1846
Ceded by Mexico 1848
Gadsden Purchase 1853

Texas to the United States. A joint resolution of Congress, hastily signed by Tyler, did so in 1845.

The absorption of Texas's 267,339 square miles (France, by comparison, covers 211,200 square miles) whetted American appetites for the rest of the old Spanish Empire in North America. Some expansionists even dreamed of taking Cuba and Central America. President James Polk tried to buy California from Mexico, but the Mexicans harbored a grudge over the annexation of Texas and refused to do business.

Exploiting Mexico's political instability, Polk goaded Mexico into war. Mexico suffered total defeat and in the Treaty of Guadalupe Hidalgo (1848) surrendered its claims to Texas, yielded New Mexico and California, and recognized the Rio Grande as the international border. A treaty with Great Britain in 1846 had already recognized the American settlement in the Oregon territory. The continent had been acquired. The nation's "manifest destiny" was fulfilled. But what of the millions of Indians—the only native Americans—who inhabited this vast territory?

The Fate of the Indians

The Indians faithfully observed their treaties with the United States, but "white pioneers in the Northwest committed the most wanton and cruel murders of them, for which it was almost impossible to obtain a conviction from a pioneer jury."[19] Government officials frequently manipulated the Indians by gathering a few chiefs, plying them with cheap whiskey, and then inducing them to hand over their tribes' hunting grounds. By this method William Henry Harrison, superintendent of the Indians of the Northwest Territory and a future president, got the Native Americans to part with 48 million acres. He had the full backing of President Jefferson.

MAP 31.3 Territorial Growth of the United States The Cumberland Road between Cumberland, Maryland, and—by 1833—Columbus, Ohio, and the Erie Canal, which linked New York City and the Great Lakes region, carried thousands of easterners and immigrants to the Old Northwest and the frontier beyond. Transcontinental railroads subsequently made all the difference.

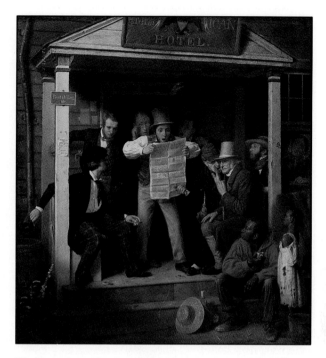

War News from Mexico, 1848 In this scene of everyday life, the front porch of the "American Hotel" represents a microcosm of American society. The man reading the newspaper bursts with excitement, as the well-dressed white men (and woman, partly hidden) eagerly listen to the news from the front. In showing the black child in a tattered dress while the seated black man drinks whiskey (a jug is half hidden under his hat) from a silver cup, Woodville makes a stereotypically racist statement. But Woodville did not witness such a scene: he painted this in Dusseldorf, Germany. (*Source: National Academy of Design*)

The policy of pushing the Indians westward across the Mississippi, which President James Monroe's administration had adopted early in the century, accelerated during Andrew Jackson's presidency (1829–1837). Thousands of Delawares, Shawnees, and Wyandots, tricked into moving from the Northwest Territory to reservations west of Missouri, died of cholera and measles during the journey. The survivors found themselves hopelessly in debt for supplies and farming equipment. The state of Georgia, meanwhile, was nibbling away at Cherokee lands, which were theoretically protected by treaty with the United States government. Then gold was discovered on the Cherokee lands, and a gold rush took place. A Vermont

Passage of the Choctaw   The Choctaw were the only Native Americans in the southeast whose economy rested on agriculture, and they were considered very competent farmers. But the United States government forced them to sell their lands and to move west of the Mississippi. The Choctaw and other tribes endured such sufferings on the journey west in the winter of 1831 that it became known as the "Trail of Tears." This painting romanticizes the event. *(Source: New Orleans Museum of Art: Gift of William E. Groves)*

missionary, the Reverend Samuel C. Worcester, carried the Indians' case to the Supreme Court. Chief Justice John Marshall ruled that the laws of Georgia had no force within the Cherokee territory and that white settlers and gold rustlers had to leave. President Jackson retorted, "John Marshall has made his decision. Now let him enforce it." The Creek, Cherokee, and other tribes were rounded up, expelled, and sent beyond the western boundaries of Missouri and Arkansas. They were guaranteed complete possession of their new reservations "as long as grass grows and water runs."[20] The shameful price of westward expansion was the dislocation and extermination of millions of Native Americans (Map 31.4).

Black Slavery in the South

Dutch traders brought the first black people as prisoners to Virginia in 1619 as one solution to the chronic shortage of labor in North America (white indentured servants who worked for a term of years was another solution). Black penal servitude became rooted in three regions: in the Chesapeake Bay area of Virginia and Maryland, where

MAP 31.4 Indian Cession of Lands to the United States   Forced removal of the Creek, Cherokee, and Chickasaw Indians led to the deaths of thousands on the Trail of Tears to reservations in Oklahoma, and to the destruction of their cultures.

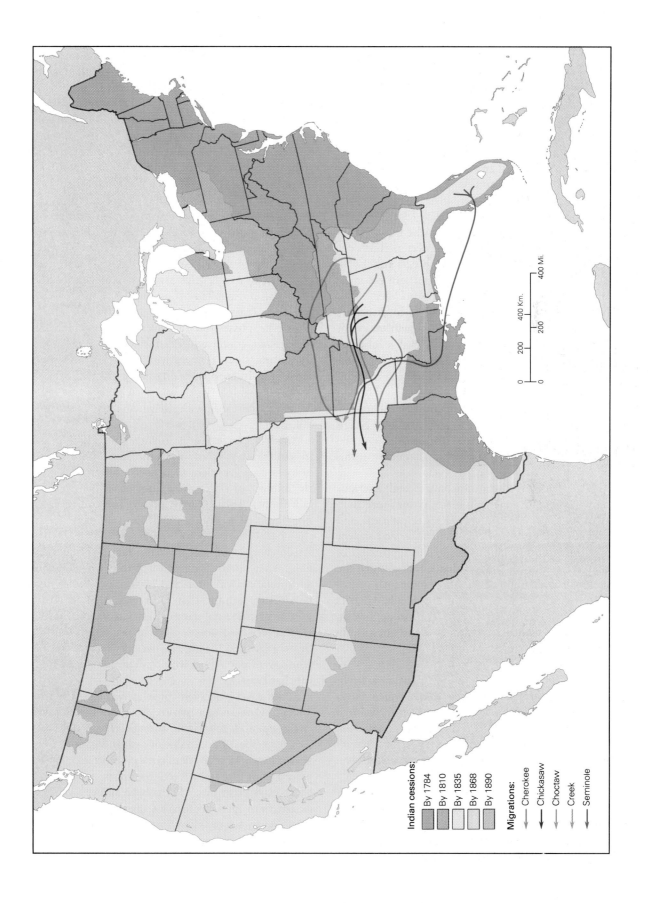

Indian cessions:

By 1784
By 1810
By 1835
By 1868
By 1890

Migrations:

Cherokee
Chickasaw
Choctaw
Creek
Seminole

400 Km.
400 Mi.

0   200   400
0   200

tobacco was the staple crop; in the coastal settlements of South Carolina and Georgia, where rice and indigo (a plant from which a blue dye is made) were raised; and in some of the northern colonies such as New York, where in the eighteenth century slaves and free blacks eventually totaled 15 percent of the population. The first black arrivals, however, were not slaves. In the seventeenth century, a system of racial servitude and discrimination did not exist. Some blacks themselves acquired property and indentured servants.

As rice cultivation expanded in the Carolinas in the early eighteenth century, however, planters demanded more laborers. Between 1720 and 1770, black prisoners poured into the southern colonies. In South Carolina they came to outnumber whites by almost two to one. White fears of black revolts pushed colonial legislatures to pass laws that established tight white control and blacks' legal position as slaves. Only in the decades 1730–1760 just before the publication of the Declaration of Independence did the slave system become enshrined in law. Economic demands led to the legal and social institutionalization of black slavery in North America. Racist arguments of blacks' supposed inferiority were used to justify that institutionalization.

Slavery and race relations have posed a serious dilemma for the American majority for more than two centuries. Powerful moral, legal, political, and sociological arguments have characterized slavery as a great evil, a violation of the central principle of the Declaration of Independence that all men are created equal. Eighteenth- and nineteenth-century Americans, however, could not decide whether the ringing words of the Declaration applied to blacks. One scholar recently posed the question in this way:

How did the slave-holding class, which was molded by the same forces that shaped the nation, which fought America's wars and helped inspire its Revolution, a class which boasted of its patriotism, its devotion to freedom, its adherence to the major tenets of liberalism—how did such a class justify its continuing commitment to slavery?[21]

The answer can be given in two words: *profit* and *status*.

The system of slavery involved many factors— the size of a plantation or farm and the number of slaves working it, the arability of the soil and the quantity of rainfall, the efficiency of plantation management, and individual initiative. Nevertheless, many slaveowners realized reasonable, sometimes handsome, profits in the decades before the Civil War. For white planters and farmers, slavery proved lucrative, and ownership of slaves was a status symbol as well as a means of social control. Slavery "was at the center of a well-established way of life to which [slaveowners] were accustomed and attached, and the disruption or demise of which they feared above all else."[22] Millions of whites, whether or not they owned many slaves, would have agreed with the South Carolina planter who wrote, "Slavery informs all our modes of life, all our habits of thought, lies at the basis of our social existence, and of our political faith." Since the possession of slaves brought financial profit *and* conferred social status and prestige, struggling small farmers had a material and psychological interest in maintaining black bondage. Slavery provided the means by which they might rise, and the floor beneath which they could not fall.

American society subsequently paid a high price in guilt and psychological conflict. Some slaveholders, like President George Washington, found the subject of slavery too uncomfortable even to talk about: "I shall frankly declare to you that I do not like even to think, much less talk of it."[23] In the half-century before the Civil War, most slaveowners were deeply religious. On the one hand, they taught their children to get rich by the accumulation of land and slaves; on the other hand, they taught that God would punish the greedy with eternal damnation. Slaveholders justified slavery by dismissing blacks as inferior, but religion preached that in the eyes of God black and white were equal and would ultimately be judged on that basis.

Some slaveowners felt completely trapped by the system. One master wrote, "I cannot just take them up and sell them though that would be clearly the best I could do for myself. I cannot free them. I cannot keep them with comfort. . . . What would I not give to be freed from responsibility for these poor creatures." Perhaps to an even greater extent than men, women of the planter class felt troubled by slavery. The South Carolina aristocrat Mary Boykin Chesnut confided to her diary in 1861:

The Cotton Pickers   Considered one of the most original American painters of the nineteenth century, Winslow Homer painted these sharecroppers on a visit to the South in 1876. The vastness of the field in that age before the invention of machines to pick the cotton suggests the enormity of the women's work. As their faces imply, Homer depicted black Americans as a psychologically complex people with beauty, strength, and dignity. *(Source: Winslow Homer,* The Cotton Pickers, *1876. Los Angeles County Museum of Art. Acquisition made possible through Museum Trustees)*

I wonder if it be a sin to think slavery a curse to any land. Sumner (the Massachusetts senator and abolitionist who bitterly denounced slavery in the U.S. Senate) said not one word of this hated institution which is not true. Men and women are punished when their masters and mistresses are brutes and not when they do wrong. . . . God forgive us, but ours is a monstrous system and wrong and iniquity. Perhaps the rest of the world is as bad—this only I see. Like the patriarchs of old our men live all in one house with their wives and their concubines, and the mulattoes one sees in every family exactly resemble the white children—and every lady tells you who is the father of all the mulatto children in everybody's household, but those in her own she seems to think drop from the clouds, or pretends so to think.[24]

Mary Chesnut believed that most white women of the South were abolitionists in their hearts. Although she enjoyed the attentions and services of her slaves, when Lincoln issued the Emancipation Proclamation she welcomed it with "an unholy joy."[25]

Westward Expansion and Civil War

Cotton was king in the mid-nineteenth century, and cotton carried slavery westward. It was westward expansion, not moral outrage, that brought the controversy over slavery to a head. As Congress created new territories, the question of whether slavery would be extended arose again and again (Map 31.5). For years elaborate compromises were worked out, but the North increasingly feared that the South was intent on controlling the nation. The South was afraid that free territories would harbor fugitive slaves. Issues of sectional political power became more and more heated.

In the 1850s the question of the further expansion of slavery agitated the nation. Perhaps no statesman better summarized the dilemma than Abraham Lincoln in a speech in 1854:

When they [southern proponents of expansion] remind us of their constitutional rights, I acknowledge them, not grudgingly, but fully, and fairly; and I would give them any legislation for the reclaiming of their fugitives, which should not, in its stringency, be more likely to carry a free man into slavery, than our ordinary criminal laws are to hang an innocent one. . . . But all this, to my judgment, furnishes no more excuse

for permitting slavery to go into our own free territory, than it would for reviving the African slave trade by law.

Slavery is founded in the selfishness of man's nature—opposition to it, in his love of justice. These principles are in eternal antagonism; and when brought into collision so fiercely, as slavery extension brings them, shocks, and throes, and convulsions must ceaselessly follow.[26]

Accepting the Republican party nomination for a seat in the United States Senate in 1858, Lincoln predicted the tragic events ahead:

A house divided against itself cannot stand.

I believe this government cannot endure, permanently half slave and half free.

I do not expect the Union to be dissolved—I do not expect the house to fall—but I do expect it will cease to be divided.

MAP 31.5 Slavery in the United States, 1860 The Confederacy waged a heroic struggle, but the North's industrial might and the waves of immigrants who fought in the Union army decided the war. Note the slave populations of such states as South Carolina and Mississippi, and consider how they influenced the later social and economic history of those regions.

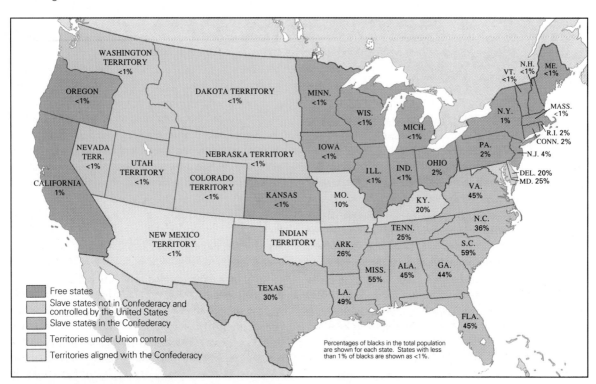

It will become all one thing, or all the other.

Either the opponents of slavery will arrest the further spread of it, and place it where the public mind shall rest in the belief that it is in the course of ultimate extinction; or its advocates will push it forward, till it shall become alike lawful in all the States, old as well as new—North as well as South.[27]

In this and every other speech that Lincoln made between 1854 and his election to the presidency in 1860, he argued against slavery less on moral or legal grounds than in terms of free labor's self-interest.

If slavery continued to expand, Lincoln insisted, it would become a nationwide institution. He appealed to both immigrants and native-born whites when he declared that slavery should be excluded from new territories so that they could be "an outlet for free white people everywhere, the world over—in which Hans, and Baptiste, and Patrick, and all other men from all the world, may find new homes and better their condition in life."[28] Free white workers, in other words, could not compete in the labor market against blacks; therefore, the territories should be kept open.

To protest Lincoln's victory in the election of 1860, South Carolina seceded from the Union in December 1860. Ten southern states soon followed South Carolina's example and formed the Confederacy. Its capital was at Richmond, Virginia.

The Civil War began in 1861. Lincoln fought it to preserve the Union and to maintain the free labor system; the abolition of slavery was a secondary outcome, which he in fact tried to avoid. When a Union general in the field declared the slaves of South Carolina and Georgia free, Lincoln overruled the order. He wanted to bring the seceding states back into the Union with their institutions intact. To many people it seemed absurd to fight the Confederacy, which depended on slavery to wage the war, without abolishing slavery. In the words of one historian, Lincoln wanted "to conduct the war for the preservation of *status quo,* which had produced the war."[29] Only after the war had dragged on and the slaughter had become frightful on both sides, only when it appeared that Great Britain might recognize the Confederacy, and only when it had been proved that the southern war effort benefited considerably from slave labor—only then did Lincoln, reluctantly, resolve on emancipation.

The Emancipation Proclamation became effective on January 1, 1863. It expressed no moral indignation. It freed slaves only in states and areas that were in rebellion against the United States. It preserved slavery in states that were loyal to the United States or under military jurisdiction. The London *Spectator* sneered, "The principle is not that a human being cannot justly own another, but that he cannot own him unless he is loyal to the United States."[30] The Emancipation Proclamation nevertheless spelled the doom of North American slavery. It transformed the Civil War from a political struggle to preserve the Union into a moral crusade for the liberty of all Americans.

European and English liberals greeted the proclamation with great joy. A gathering of working people in Manchester, England, wrote President Lincoln:

The erasure of that foul blot upon civilization and Christianity—chattel slavery—during your Presidency will cause the name of Abraham Lincoln to be honoured and revered by posterity. Accept our high admiration of your firmness in upholding the proclamation of freedom.[31]

As Lincoln acknowledged, this was a magnanimous statement, for the Civil War hurt working people in Manchester. In fact, it had a worldwide impact socially and economically.

Because the English and continental textile industries relied on raw American cotton, the Confederacy sought European help. In 1861, however, England had a 50 percent oversupply of fiber and cotton cloth. A huge crop, 23 billion pounds, shipped before the Union blockade of Confederate ports, filled British warehouses. By 1862, however, the picture in England had changed. Deprived of American cotton because of the blockade, the mills of Lancashire closed. Tens of thousands of workers were thrown out of work and nearly starved. Many emigrated to the United States. Between 1862 and 1864, efforts to alleviate the terrible suffering severely taxed the resources of the British government. English manufacturers were forced to find new suppliers. They found them in Egypt, India, and Brazil, where cotton production had been stimulated by the Union blockade of the South. The demands of English industry for Egyptian and Indian cotton played a significant role in the expansion of the English merchant marine fleet. Although England initially opposed construction of the Suez Canal, it later became a major shareholder. The canal was the swiftest route to Indian cotton.

The war also had important political consequences in Europe. In 1861 British and European opinion had divided along class lines. The upper classes sympathized with the American South; the commercial classes and working people sided with the North. The English people interpreted the northern victory as a triumph of the democratic experiment over aristocratic oligarchy. The Union success proved that popular government worked. Thus the United States gave a powerful stimulus to those in Britain and elsewhere who supported the cause of political democracy. When parliaments debated the extension of suffrage, the American example was frequently cited.

Military historians describe the American Civil War as the first modern war:

It was the first conflict in which the massive productive capacities of the Industrial Revolution were placed at the disposal of the military machine. It witnessed the first prominent use of mass production of goods to sustain mass armies, mass transportation on railroads, and telegraphic communication between different theaters and on the battlefield. It saw also the first use of such devices of the future as armored warships, breech-loading and repeating rifles, rifled artillery, land and sea mines, submarines, balloons, precursors of the machine gun, and trench warfare. . . . In its material manifestations alone, in its application of the resources of technology to the business of killing, the Civil War presaged the later world wars.[32]

In April 1865, the Confederate general Robert E. Lee surrendered his army at Appomattox Court House in Virginia, ending the war. Lincoln had called for "malice toward none and charity for all" in his second inaugural address in 1864 and planned a generous policy toward the defeated South. The bullet that killed him brought on a different kind of reconstruction, the central figure in which was the Negro.

During the period called "Reconstruction" (1865–1877), the vanquished South adjusted to a new social and economic order without slavery, and the eleven Confederate states rejoined the Union. Congress and the nation debated the political and social status of the Negro in the reconstructed South. The experience of slavery cast a deep and perhaps permanent mark in the collective memory of American blacks. Black people resented the abuse, the humiliation and subordination, the separation of families, the entire badge of servitude. For former slaves, Reconstruction represented an opportunity to exercise their new freedom, though southerners detested the very notion of social equality and northerners were ambivalent on the subject.

In practical terms, Reconstruction meant the reunion of black families separated before emancipation. Blacks wanted land to farm but, lacking cash, they soon accepted the sharecropping system: farmers paid landowners about half of a year's crops at harvest time in return for a cabin, food, mules, seed, and tools the rest of the year. Believing that education was the key to economic advancement, blacks flocked to country schools and to colleges supported by northern religious groups. Although the Fifteenth Amendment to the United States Constitution forbade states to deny anyone the vote "on account of race, color, or previous condition of servitude," whites used violence, terror, and, between 1880 and 1920, so-called Jim Crow laws to prevent blacks from voting and to enforce rigid racial segregation. Lacking strong northern support, blacks did not gain legal equality or suffrage in many parts of the old Confederacy until the 1960s. Racist assumptions and attitudes thwarted their legal, social, and economic advance.

In the construction of a black community, no institution played a larger role than the black Protestant churches. Local black churches provided hope to the oppressed, education to the illiterate when financially possible, and a forum for the spread of political ideas and platforms. During Reconstruction and ever since, black preachers, esteemed for their oratorical skill, organizational ability, and practical judgment, held important positions in black politics. In a racist and exploitative society, the black church gave support, security, and a sense of solidarity.

The Black Family

What impact did slavery have on the black family? Able scholars, both black and white, have long maintained that the enslavement of Africans in the eighteenth century led to the deterioration of the black family as a social unit in the nineteenth and twentieth centuries. As two authorities put it,

The Battle of Gettysburg, July 1–3, 1863   marked the high point of the Confederate advance and was the greatest battle of the war. This painting commemorates the climax on the third day, when Confederate General Robert E. Lee commanded Pickett's division to charge the Union center. Coming toward the viewer in the face of terrible fire, the brave Southerners have reached the first Union line. But General Hancock, shown with arm extended in the left foreground, is ordering the Northern counterattack that will decimate Pickett's troops and force the Confederates back into Virginia. *(Source: Photograph by Al Freni © 1985 Time-Life Books, Inc. Courtesy, The Seventh Regiment Fund, Inc.)*

"The most rudimentary type of family organization was not permitted to survive, to say nothing of the extensions of the family. The mother-child family, with the father either unknown, absent, or, if present, incapable of wielding influence, was the only type of family that could survive."[33] However, Herbert G. Gutman's authoritative *The Black Family in Slavery and Freedom, 1750–1925* has demonstrated that such theories are not supported by fact. In spite of the destructive effects of slavery, African-Americans established strong family units.

Most slave couples had long marriages. A study of the entire adult slave population of North Carolina in 1860 has shown that 25 percent of slave marriages lasted between ten and nineteen years, 20 percent lasted at least twenty years, and almost 10 percent endured thirty years or more. Most slave women spent their entire adult lives in settled unions with the same husband. Planters encouraged slave marriages, because, as one owner put it, "marriage adds to the comfort, happiness, and health of those entering upon it, besides insuring a greater increase." Large slave families advanced owners' economic interests, and planters rewarded slave women who had many children.[34]

Forcible separation due to the sale of one partner proved the greatest threat to the permanence of slave marriages. In spite of illiteracy, separated

The Oblate Sisters of Providence of Baltimore   In 1929 the Oblate Sisters of Providence, the oldest order of black nuns in the United States, gathered to celebrate a century of educational, missionary, and social work—operating orphanages, day care centers, schools, and homes for the elderly. Limited only by numbers, their work continues today. *(Source: The Oblate Sisters of Providence of Baltimore)*

spouses tried to remain in touch with one another. Once slavery had been abolished, separated couples went to enormous lengths to reunite their families. Evidence from all parts of the South reveals that this was the common pattern.

Women often had to resist the attentions of the slaveowners themselves; in addition, owners not infrequently supplied slave women with black men who had reputations for sexual prowess. Slave women, however, made choices: they tried to select their own husbands, rejecting—up to the point of risking being sold—mates chosen by their owners.

Historians of medicine know little about the birth-control methods used by slave couples. Considerable information survives, however, about abortion. In 1860 a Tennessee physician reported that slave women tried to abort by "medicine," "violent exercise," and other means. Cotton plants were "habitually and effectively resorted to by slaves of the South for producing abortion."[35]

Typically, slave women had their first child around the age of nineteen. The continual labor shortage in the South led slaveowners to encourage slaves to produce children. Owners urged teenage slaves to begin bearing children and to have more children soon thereafter. On the Good Hope plantation in South Carolina, for example, 80 percent of slave couples had at least four children. Almost all women had all their children by one husband, and most children grew to their teens in households with both parents present. Although premarital intercourse was common among slaves—though not as common as among young American adults during the 1970s—the weight of the evidence shows that women rarely engaged in extramarital sexual activity.

Settled slave marriages provided models for growing children. The pattern of stable black marriages lasted well into the present century. Research on black households in New York City in 1925 shows that 85 percent were headed by two parents.[36] The period since the Great Depression of 1929 has witnessed a general decline in the stability of American families, both white and black. Shifting values throughout American society, such as changed sexual attitudes and an enormous increase in the divorce rate, have increased the proportion of black families headed by one parent. In recent decades, the 1990 census shows, the difference between black and white wages has narrowed, but the total income of black households and white households has remained highly divergent because so many black households depend on the income of a single parent. The decline in family stability has proved an obstacle to black economic advancement.

Industrialization and Immigration

After the Civil War the United States underwent an industrial boom based on exploitation of the country's natural resources. The federal government turned over vast amounts of land and mineral resources to industry for development. In particular, the railroads—the foundation of industrial expansion—received 130 million acres. By 1900 the American railroad system was 193,000 miles long, connected every part of the nation, and represented 40 percent of the railroad mileage of the entire world. Immigrant workers built it.

The late nineteenth and early twentieth centuries witnessed the immigration of unprecedented numbers of Europeans and Asians to the United States (see page 969). Between 1860 and 1900, 14 million immigrants came, and during the peak years between 1900 and 1914, another 14 million passed through the U.S. Customs inspection station at Ellis Island in New York City. All sought a better life and higher standard of living.

The immigrants' ambitions precisely matched the labor needs of the times. Chinese, Scandinavian, and Irish immigrants laid 30,000 miles of railroad tracks between 1867 and 1873 and another 73,000 miles in the 1880s. Poles, Hungarians, Bohemians, and Italians poured into the coal and iron mines of western Pennsylvania and Appalachia. The steel magnate Andrew Carnegie recruited southern and eastern European immigrants for his smoking mills around Pittsburgh, Cleveland, and Gary, Indiana. At the Carnegie Steel Corporation (later USX), Slavs and Italians produced one-third of the world's total steel supply in 1900. John D. Rockefeller, whose Standard Oil Company earned tens of billions of dollars, employed thousands of Czechs, Poles, and other Slavs in his oil fields around the country. Lithua-

nians, Poles, Croats, Scandinavians, Irish, and Negroes entered the Chicago stockyards and built the meatpacking industry. Irish immigrants continued to operate the spinning frames and knitting machines of New England's textile mills. Industrial America developed on the sweat and brawn—the cheap labor—of its immigrant millions.

As industrial expansion transformed the eastern half of the United States, settlers conquered the trans-Mississippi West. Thousands of land-hungry farmers moved westward, where land was still only $1.25 an acre. In the final third of the nineteenth century, pioneers acquired 430 million acres and put 225 million of them under cultivation.

The West also held precious metals. The discovery of gold and silver in California, Colorado, Arizona, and Montana, and on the reservations of the Sioux Indians of South Dakota, precipitated huge rushes. Even before 1900, miners had extracted $1.24 billion in gold and $901 million in silver from western mines. Some miners left the West as soon as they had made their piles, but others settled down to farm and help their territories toward statehood. By 1912 the West had been won and the last frontier closed.

In the entire movement westward, women shared with men the long and dangerous journey and then the dawn-to-dusk, backbreaking work of carving a homestead out of the wilderness. Generally speaking, the frontier blurred sex roles: women commonly did the same agricultural work as men.[37] In addition, it fell to women to make a home out of crude log cabins that had no windows or doors or out of tarpaper shacks that had mud floors—if they were lucky; more frequently, settlers lacked even a roof over their heads. One "gently reared" bride of seventeen took one look at her mud roof and dirt floor and indignantly announced, "My father had a much better house for his hogs!" Lacking cookstoves, they had to prepare food over open fireplaces, using all kinds of substitutes for ingredients easily available back east. Before they could wash clothes, women had to make soap out of lye and carefully saved household ashes.

Considered the carriers of "high culture," women organized whatever educational, religious, musical, and recreational activities the frontier society possessed. Frontier women also had to defend their homes against prairie fires and Indian attacks. These burdens were accompanied by frequent pregnancies and, often, the need to give birth without medical help or even the support of other women. Many frontier women used such contraceptive devices as spermicides, condoms, and, after 1864, vaginal diaphragms. The death rate for infants and young children ran as high as 30 percent in the mid-nineteenth century. Even so, frontier women had large families.

As in South America, immigration led to rapid urbanization. In 1790 only 5.1 percent of Americans were living in centers of 2,500 or more people. By 1860 this figure had risen to 19.9 percent, and by 1900 almost 40 percent were living in cities. The overwhelming majority of the southern and eastern Europeans who came to North America at the turn of the century became urban industrial workers, their entire existence framed by the factory and the tenement. Newly uprooted from rural Europe, Italians, Greeks, Croats, Hungari-

ans, Czechs, Poles, Russians, and Jews contrasted sharply with their urban neighbors and with each other. Older residents saw only "a sea of strange faces, babbling in alien tongues and framed by freakish clothes. Walking through these multitudes now was really like a voyage round the globe."[38]

Between 1880 and 1920 industrial production soared. New inventions such as the steam engine, the dynamo (generator), and the electric light were given industrial and agricultural applications. Transcontinental railroads and innovations like the sewing machine and the assembly line made large-scale production possible. Large factories replaced small ones. Large factories could buy large machines, operate them at full capacity, and take advantage of railroad discount rates. In the automobile industry, for example, Henry Ford of De-

Chinese Laborers Chinese immigrant laborers, who laid thousands of miles of railroad track across the United States in the nineteenth century, played a major role in industrial expansion. (*Source: California State Railroad Museum, Southern Pacific Collection*)

troit set up assembly lines. Each worker working on the line performed only one task instead of assembling an entire car. In 1910 Ford sold 10,000 cars; in 1914, a year after he inaugurated the first moving assembly line, he sold 248,000 cars. Such developments changed the face of American society. Sewing machines made cheap, varied, mass-produced clothing available to city people in department stores and to country people through mail-order catalogs. The automobile increased opportunities for travel, general mobility, and change.

By the 1890s factory managers were stressing industrial efficiency and the importance of time. Management engineers wanted to produce more at lower cost. They aimed to reduce labor costs by eliminating unnecessary workers. As the quantity rather than the quality of goods produced became the measure of acceptability, workers' skills were less valued. As assembly-line workers more and more performed only monotonous and time-determined work, in effect they became interchangeable parts of the machines they operated.

Despite accelerated production, and perhaps because of overproduction, the national economy experienced repeated cycles of boom and bust in the late nineteenth century. Serious depressions in 1873, 1884, and 1893 slashed prices and threw many people out of work. Leading industrialists responded by establishing larger corporations and trusts. Trusts granted control of their stock to a board of trustees, which then managed the operation of all the companies owned by the trust. The legalization of trusts led to huge conglomerates, such as John D. Rockefeller's Standard Oil Company, which as a result of the merger of several smaller oil companies controlled 84 percent of the nation's oil in 1898. Standard Oil also controlled most American pipelines and was involved in natural gas production. Standard Oil monopolized the oil industry; J. P. Morgan's United States Steel, the iron and steel industries; and Swift & Co. of Chicago, the meat-processing industry.

Industrialization led to the creation of a vast class of salaried workers who depended totally on their employers for work. Corporate managers, however, were always preoccupied with cutting labor costs. Thus employers paid workers piecemeal for the number of articles produced, to encourage the use of the new machines; and managers hired more women and children and paid them much less than they paid men. Most women worked in the textile industry. Some earned as little as $1.56 for seventy hours of work, while men received $7 to $9 for the same work. Employers reduced wages, forcing workers to toil longer and harder to maintain a certain level of income. Owners fought in legislatures and courts against the installation of safety devices, so working conditions in mines and mills were frightful. In 1913, even after some safety measures had been taken, 25,000 people died in industrial accidents. Between 1900 and 1917, 72,000 railroad worker deaths occurred. Workers responded with strikes, violence, and, gradually, unionization.

Urbanization brought serious problems. In *How the Other Half Lives* (1890), Jacob Riis, a newspaper reporter and recent immigrant from Denmark, drew national attention to what he called "the foul core of New York's slums." His phrase "the other half" soon became a synonym for the urban poor. Riis estimated that 300,000 people inhabited a single square mile on New York's Lower East Side. Overcrowding, poor sanitation, and lack of health services caused frequent epidemics. The blight of slums increased crime, prostitution, alcoholism, and other drug-related addictions. Riis attacked the vicious economic exploitation of the poor.

New York City was not unique; slums and the social problems resulting from them existed in all large American cities. Reformers fought for slum clearance, but public apathy and vested economic interests delayed massive urban renewal until after the Second World War. In spite of all these industrial and urban difficulties, immigrants continued to come: the United States offered opportunity, upward social mobility, and a better life.

European and Asian immigrants aroused nativist sentiments—that is, intense hostility to their foreign and "un-American" looks, behavior, and loyalties—on the part of native-born Americans. Some of this antagonism sprang from the deep-rooted Anglo-Saxon racism of many Americans. Some grew out of old Protestant suspicions of Roman Catholicism, the faith of most of the new arrivals. A great deal of the dislike of the foreign-born sprang from fear of economic competition. To most Americans, the Chinese with their exotic looks and willingness to work for very little seemed the most dangerous. Increasingly violent agitation against Asians led to race riots in California and finally culminated in the Chinese Exclusion Act of 1882, which denied Chinese laborers entrance to the country.

Harlem Hellfighters Returning to New York in 1919 aboard the U.S.S. *Stockholm,* these black men of the famed U.S. 369th Division had fought in the bloody battle of the Meuse-Argonne during the First World War. The French government awarded 150 of them the coveted Croix de Guerre. *(Source: Springer/Bettmann Film Archive)*

Immigrants from Europe seized on white racism as a way of improving themselves in the job market: they could compensate for their immigrant status by claiming superiority to former slaves and their descendants. The arrival of thousands of Irish immigrants in the 1850s, followed by millions of Italians and Slavs between 1880 and 1914, aggravated an already bad situation. What the German scientist Alexander von Humboldt wrote about the attitude of peninsulares toward Creoles in Latin America in the early nineteenth century—"the lowest, least educated, and uncultivated European believes himself superior to the white born in the New World"[39]—precisely applies to the outlook of Irish, Italian, or Slavic immigrants to the United States at the turn of this century if one merely substitutes *black* for *white.* In

the eyes of all ethnic groups, the social status of blacks remained the lowest while that of immigrants rose. As the United States underwent expansion and industrialization in the course of the nineteenth century, blacks remained the worst off *because of immigration.*[40]

In the 1890s the nation experienced a severe economic depression. Faced with overproduction, the rich and politically powerful owners of mines, mills, and factories fought the organization of labor unions, laid off thousands, slashed wages, and ruthlessly exploited their workers. Workers in turn feared that immigrant labor would drive salaries lower. The frustrations provoked by pitifully low salaries in "good times," by unemployment during the depression, and by all the unresolved problems of industrial urban society boiled over into savage attacks on the foreign-born. One of the bloodiest incidents took place in western Pennsylvania in 1897, when about 150 unarmed Polish and Hungarian coal miners tried to persuade others to join their walkout. The mine owners convinced the local sheriff that the strike was illegal. As the strikers approached, the sheriff panicked and ordered his deputies to shoot. Twenty-one immigrants died and forty were wounded. The sheriff subsequently explained that the miners were only "infuriated foreigners . . . like wild beasts." Local people agreed that if the strikers had been American-born, no blood would have been shed.[41]

Pressure to restrict immigration varied with economic conditions: it slackened in times of relative prosperity and increased in periods of recession. After the First World War, labor leaders lobbied Congress for restrictions because they feared losing the wage gains achieved during the war. Some intellectuals argued that immigrants from southern and eastern Europe, with their unfamiliar cultural traditions, threatened to destroy American society. Italians were feared because of possible Cosa Nostra connections. Eastern Europeans were thought to have communist connections. In the 1920s Congress responded with laws that set severe quotas—2 percent of resident nationals as of the 1890 census—on immigration from southern and eastern Europe. The Japanese were completely excluded. These racist laws remained on the books until 1965.

CANADA: FROM FRENCH COLONY TO NATION

In 1608 the French explorer Samuel de Champlain (1567–1635) sailed down the St. Lawrence River and established a trading post on the site of present-day Quebec. Thus began the permanent colony of New France. The fur-trading monopolies subsequently granted to Champlain by the French crown attracted settlers, and Jesuit missionaries to the Indians further increased the French population. The British, however, vigorously challenged French control of the lucrative fur trade, and the long mid-eighteenth century global struggle for empire between the British and the French, known in North America as the "French and Indian Wars" because of Indian border warfare, tested French control (see pages

609–619). In 1759, on the Plains of Abraham, a field next to the city of Quebec, the English under General James Wolfe defeated the French under General Louis Montcalm. This battle ended the French Empire in North America. By the Treaty of Paris of 1763, France ceded Canada to Great Britain.

British Colony (1763–1839)

For the French Canadians, who in 1763 numbered about 90,000, the British conquest was a tragedy and the central event in their history. British governors replaced the French; English-speaking merchants from Britain and the thirteen American colonies to the south took over the colony's economic affairs. The Roman Catholic church remained and until about 1960 played a powerful role in the political and cultural, as well as religious, life of French Canadians. Most of the French Canadians engaged in agriculture, though a small merchant class sold furs and imported manufactured goods.

Intending to establish a permanent administration for Canada, in 1774 the British Parliament passed the Quebec Act. This law granted religious freedom to French Canadians and recognized French law in civil matters, but it denied Canadians a legislative assembly, a traditional feature of British colonial government. Parliament held that French Canadians had no experience in elective institutions; moreover, the example of the assemblies of the thirteen American colonies, which were then demanding more political power than the British wanted to grant, discouraged the establishment of a Canadian counterpart. Therefore, Parliament placed power in the hands of an appointed governor and an appointed council; the latter, however, was composed of French Canadians as well as English-speaking members. English Canadian businessmen protested that they were being denied a basic right of Englishmen—representation.

During the American Revolution, about 40,000 Americans demonstrated their loyalty to Great Britain and its empire by emigrating to Canada. These "loyalists" not only altered the French-English ratio in the population but also pressed for a representative assembly. In 1791 Parliament responded with the Constitution Act, which divided the province of Quebec at the Ottawa River into

Lower Canada (present-day Quebec, predominantly French and Catholic) and Upper Canada (present-day Ontario, primarily English and Protestant). The act also provided for an elective assembly in each of the two provinces. Because the assemblies' decisions could be vetoed by an appointed upper house or by the governor and his council, general discontent continued. Finally, in 1837, disputes over control of revenue, the judiciary, and the established churches erupted into open rebellion in both Upper and Lower Canada. The British government, fearful of a repetition of the American events of 1776, decided on a full investigation and appointed Lord Durham, a prominent liberal reformer, to make recommendations for reform. Lord Durham published his *Report on the Affairs of British North America,* later called the "Magna Carta" of British colonial administration, in 1839.

The Age of Confederation (1840–1905)

Lord Durham proposed the union of Upper and Lower Canada and the establishment in Canada of "responsible government," meaning that Canadians should manage their own local affairs through ministries responsible to their legislatures. The imperial government in London was to retain control over trade, foreign affairs, public lands, and the colonial constitution.

Accordingly, Parliament in 1840 passed the Union Act, which united Ontario and Quebec under one government composed of a governor, an appointed legislative council, and an elective assembly in which the two provinces had equal representation. The Union Act marks an important milestone toward confederation. When Lord Durham's son-in-law, Lord Elgin, was appointed governor in 1847, he made it clear that his cabinet (council) would be chosen from the party with the majority in the elected assembly; and, following the British model, the cabinet had to retain the support of that majority in order to stay in office.

The idea of a union or confederation of the other Canadian provinces persisted in the 1860s. During the American Civil War, English-American relations were severely strained, and "Canada found herself in the centre of the storm. The resulting fear of American aggression was a powerful factor in bringing confederation to completion."[42] Parliament's passage of the British North America Act in 1867 brought the Canadian constitution to its modern form. By the act the traditional British parliamentary system was adapted to the needs of the new North American nation. The provinces of New Brunswick and Nova Scotia joined Ontario and Quebec to form the Dominion of Canada. A governor-general, who represented the British crown and fulfilled ceremonial functions, governed through the Dominion cabinet, which, like the British cabinet, was composed of members selected from the lower house of the legislature, to which it was responsible.

Legislative power rested in a parliament of two houses: a Senate, whose members were appointed for life by the governor-general, and a House of Commons, whose members were elected by adult males. (Canadian women won the right to vote in national elections in 1917, shortly before women in the United States and Great Britain but after women in Australia.) In theory, the two houses had equal power, though money bills had to originate in the House of Commons; in practice, the Senate came to serve only as a deliberative check on hasty legislation and as a means of rewarding elder statesmen for their party services.

The Dominion cabinet received complete jurisdiction over internal affairs. Britain retained control over foreign policy. (In 1931 the British Statute of Westminster officially recognized Canadian autonomy in foreign affairs.) The constitution of 1982 abolished the power of the London Parliament to amend Canada's constitution and ended all appeals from the provinces to London. Because Quebec did not sign the 1982 document, however, federal-provincial relationships remain under study.

Believing that the American system of the division of powers between the states and the federal government left the states too strong and helped to bring on the Civil War, the framers of the Canadian constitution intended to create a powerful central government. Provincial legislatures, therefore, were assigned powers explicitly stated and applicable only to local conditions. With the implementation of the British North America Act, Canada attained "responsible government." John A. Macdonald (1815–1891), the strongest advocate of confederation, became the Dominion's first prime minister.

Macdonald vigorously pushed Canada's "manifest destiny" to absorb all the northern part of the continent. In 1869 his government purchased for

$1,500,000 the vast Northwest Territories of the Hudson Bay Company. From this territory the province of Manitoba emerged to become part of the Dominion in 1870. Fearful that the sparsely settled colony of British Columbia would join the United States, Macdonald lured British Columbia into the confederation with a subsidy to pay its debts and the promise of a transcontinental railroad to be completed between 1873 and 1883. Likewise, the debt-ridden little maritime province of Prince Edward Island was drawn into confederation with a large subsidy. In five short years, between 1868 and 1873, through Macdonald's imagination and drive, Canadian sovereignty stretched from coast to coast.

Believing that a transcontinental railroad was essential to Canada's survival as a nation, Macdonald declared that "until this great work is completed our Dominion is little more than a 'geographical expression.' We have as much interest in British Columbia as in Australia, and no more. The railroad, once finished, we become a great united country with a large interprovincial trade and a common interest."[43] On November 7, 1885, Macdonald received a telegram announcing that the first train from Montreal in Quebec was

Prospectors in the Klondike The discovery of gold in 1896 in the Canadian Klondike (in the Yukon Territory just east of the Alaskan border) drew thousands, including these hardy women prospectors. *(Source: Library of Congress)*

approaching the Pacific; traveling at 24 miles per hour, the train had made the coast-to-coast trip in a little over five days. The completion of the railroad led to the formation of two new prairie provinces, Alberta and Saskatchewan, which in 1905 entered the Dominion. (Only in 1949 did the island of Newfoundland renounce colonial status and join the Dominion.) The Canadian Pacific Railroad was Macdonald's greatest achievement.

Growth, Development, and National Maturity

Macdonald's hopes for large numbers of immigrants to people the thinly populated country did not immediately materialize. Between 1897 and 1912, however, 961,000 entered Canada from the British Isles, 594,000 from Europe, and 784,000 from the United States. Some immigrants went to work in the urban factories of Hamilton, Toronto, and Montreal. Most immigrants from continental Europe—Poles, Germans, Scandinavians, and Russians—flooded the Midwestern plains and soon transformed the prairies into one of the world's greatest grain-growing regions.

Because of Canada's small population, most of which in the early twentieth century was concentrated in Ontario and Quebec, the assimilation of the immigrants to the older English-Canadian culture occurred more slowly than in the "melting pot" of the United States. French Canadians remained the largest minority in the population. Distinctively different in language, law, and religion, and fiercely proud of their culture, they resisted assimilation. Since the 1950s, Italian and Hungarian immigration has contributed to the evolution of a more cosmopolitan culture.

Supported by population growth, Canada experienced an agricultural and industrial boom between 1891 and 1914. In those years wheat production rocketed from 2 million bushels per year to 150 million bushels. The discovery of gold, silver, copper, and nickel in northern Ontario led to the full exploitation of those mineral resources. British Columbia, Ontario, and Quebec produced large quantities of wood pulp, much of it sold to the United States. Canada's great rivers were harnessed to supply hydroelectric power for industrial and domestic use. Meanwhile the government erected tariffs to protect Canadian industry, estab-lished a national civil service, and built a sound banking system.

Canada's powerful support of the Allied cause in the First World War demonstrated its full maturity as a nation. In 1914 the British government still controlled the foreign policy of all parts of the empire. When Britain declared war on Germany, Canada unhesitatingly followed. More than 600,000 Canadian soldiers served with distinction in the army, some of them in the bloodiest battles in France; the 60,661 Canadians killed represent a greater loss than that experienced by the more populous United States. Canadian grain and food-stuffs supplied much of the food of the Allied troops, and Canadian metals were in demand for guns and shells. Canadian resentment, therefore, over lack of voice in the formulation of Allied war policies was understandable.

In 1917 the British government established the Imperial War Cabinet, a body composed of the chief British ministers and the prime ministers of the Dominions (Australia, Canada, New Zealand, and South Africa) to set policy. In 1918 Canada demanded and received—over the initial opposition of Britain, France, and the United States—the right to participate in the Versailles Peace Conference and in the League of Nations. Canada had become a respected and independent nation. Since 1939, Canada has been a member of the British Commonwealth of Nations.

AUSTRALIA: FROM PENAL COLONY TO NATION

In April 1770, James Cook, the English explorer, navigator, and captain of H.M.S. *Endeavor,* dropped anchor in a wide bay about ten miles south of the present city of Sydney on the coast of eastern Australia. Because the young botanist on board the ship, Joseph Banks, subsequently discovered 30,000 specimens of plant life in the bay, 1,600 of them unknown to European science, Captain Cook called the place Botany Bay. Totally unimpressed by the flat landscape and its few naked inhabitants—the Aborigines, or native people—Cook sailed north along the coast. Finally, the ship rounded Cape York Peninsula, the northernmost point of Australia. On August 21, on a rock later named Possession Island, Cook formally claimed the entire land south of where he stood for King George III, 16,000 miles away. Cook called the land "New South Wales." Australia (Map 31.6) became part of the British Empire.

The world's smallest continent, Australia is located southeast of Asia between the Pacific and Indian oceans. It is about half the size of Europe and almost as large as the United States (excluding Alaska and Hawaii). Three topographical zones roughly divide the continent. The Western Plateau, a vast desert and semidesert region, covers almost two-thirds. The Central Eastern Lowlands extend from the Gulf of Carpentaria in the north to western Victoria in the south. The Eastern Highlands are a complex belt of tablelands. Australia is one of the world's driest continents. It has a temperate climate and little intense cold.

The British Admiralty had sent Cook to chart the transit of the planet Venus across the sun—information that would help establish the earth's distance from the sun. Cook had completed the task at Tahiti in 1769. He had also been charged with finding or disproving the existence of "the

MAP 31.6 Australia The vast deserts in western Australia meant that cities and industries would develop mainly in the east. Australia's early geographical and cultural isolation bred a sense of inferiority. Air travel, the communications revolution, and the massive import of Japanese products and cheap American pop culture have changed that.

southern continent," a land first mentioned by the seventeenth-century Dutch explorer Abel Tasman. Scurvy, the common sailors' disease caused by vitamin C deficiency, and maritime ignorance of longitude had prevented Tasman and a series of eighteenth-century navigators from accurately charting the location of Australia.

When Cook arrived in Australia, about 300,000 Aborigines inhabited the continent. A peaceful and nomadic people who had emigrated from southern Asia millennia before, the Aborigines lived entirely by food gathering, fishing, and hunting. They had no domestic agriculture. Tribal customs governed their lives. Although they used spears and bows and arrows in hunting, they never practiced warfare as it was understood by more technologically advanced peoples such as the Aztecs of Mexico (see pages 571–572) or the Mandinke of West Africa (see pages 472–478). When white settlers arrived and occupied the Aborigines' lands, they never directed any concerted opposition to them. According to one Australian scholar, from 1788 to the present "Australian governments have been much more concerned with protecting the Aborigines than with fighting them."[44] Like the Indians of Central and South America, the Aborigines fell victim to the white peoples' diseases and to a spiritual malaise caused by the breakdown of their tribal life. Today, only about 45,000 pureblood Aborigines survive.

Penal Colony

The victory of the thirteen North American colonies in 1783 inadvertently contributed to the establishment of a colony in Australia five years later. Before 1775, the British government had shipped about one thousand convicts annually to Georgia. Crime in England was increasing in the 1770s and 1780s, and the transportation of felons "beyond the seas" seemed the answer to the problem of overcrowded prisons. Moreover, the establishment of a colony in Australia would provide a home for dispossessed loyalists who had fled America during the Revolution.

Some recent students of early Australian history deny those motivations. These scholars claim that other factors led to the founding of the colony: the British goal of checking French political and economic power in India, anxiety about the Dutch trading monopoly in the southwest Pacific, the

desire to set up strategic supply bases in the region, and the need to acquire pine trees and flax, which were essential for the construction of eighteenth-century ships and sails. But these arguments for the strategic potential of an Australian colony did not influence eighteenth-century British politicians. By the late 1760s French ships posed an insignificant threat to British interests. Moreover, Australia was thousands of miles away from the area of French and Dutch interests.

In England, the prisons were so full that old transport ships in southern naval ports were being used to house criminals, and pressure on the government to do something was intense. Finally, in August 1786, the British cabinet approved the establishment of a penal colony at Botany Bay to serve as "a remedy for the evils likely to result from the late alarming and numerous increase of felons in this country, and more particularly in the metropolis (London)."[45] The name "Botany Bay" became a byword for the forced and permanent exile of criminals. A competent but undistinguished semiretired navy officer, Captain Arthur Phillip, was appointed to lead the first expedition and to be governor of New South Wales. In May 1787 a fleet of eleven ships packed with one thousand felons and their jailers sailed for Australia. After an eight-month voyage it landed in Sydney Cove on January 28, 1788.

Mere survival in an alien world was the first challenge. Because the land at Botany Bay proved completely unsuited for agriculture and lacked decent water, Governor Phillip moved the colony ten miles north to Port Jackson, later called Sydney after the British Colonial Secretary Lord Thomas Sydney. Announcing that those who did not work would not eat, Phillip set the prisoners to planting seeds. Coming from the slums of London, the convicts knew nothing of agriculture, and some were too ill or old to work. The colony lacked draft animals and plows. The army and (after 1792) marine detachments sent to guard the prisoners considered it below their dignity to work the land. For years the colony of New South Wales tottered on the brink of starvation.

For the first thirty years, men far outnumbered women. Because the British government refused to allow wives to accompany their convict-husbands, prostitution flourished. Many women convicts, if not professional prostitutes when they left England, became such during the long voyage south. Army officers, government officials, and

Convicts Embarking for Botany Bay The English printmaker and caricaturist Thomas Rowlandson (1756–1827) sketched this scene with ink and watercolor wash. In the background the gibbet with hanging felons shows the legal alternative to transportation to Australia. *(Source: National Library of Australia)*

free immigrants chose favorite convicts as mistresses. The vast majority of children born in the colony were illegitimate. Officers and jailers, although descended from the middle and lower middle classes, tried to establish a colonial gentry and to impose the rigid class distinctions that they had known in England. Known as *exclusionists,* this self-appointed colonial gentry tried to exclude from polite society all freed or emancipated persons, called *emancipists*. Deep and bitter class feeling took root.

Economic Development

For eighty long years after 1787, Britain continued to transport convicts to New South Wales. Transportation rested on two premises: that criminals should be punished and that they should not be a financial burden on the state. Just as convicts

had been sold to planters in Georgia and Maryland before the revolt of the American colonies, so after 1787 the government maintained that convicts should build and strengthen the colonial economy of New South Wales.

Convicts became free when their sentences expired or were remitted, and few returned to England. Governor Phillip and his successors urged the Colonial Office to send free settlers. The Napoleonic war slowed emigration before 1815, but thereafter a steady stream of people relocated. The end of the European wars also released capital for potential investment. But investment in what? What was the economy of New South Wales to rest on? What commodity could be developed and exported to England?

Immigrants explored several economic enterprises. In the last decade of the eighteenth century, for example, sealing seemed a likely possibility. Sealing merchants hired aboriginal women to swim out to the seal rocks, lie down among the seals until their suspicions were dulled, and then at a signal rise up and club the seals to death. In 1815, a single ship carried 60,000 seal skins to London (a normal cargo contained at least 10,000 skins). Such destruction rapidly depleted the seals.

Credit for the development of the product that was to be Australia's staple commodity for export—wool—goes to John Macarthur (1767–1834), who first saw the economic potential of sheep farming in New South Wales. Granted a large tract of crown lands and assigned thirty convicts to work for him, Macarthur conducted experiments in the production of fine merino wool. In 1800 he sent sample fleeces to England to determine their quality. He also worked to change the government's penal view of New South Wales to a commercial one and to attract the financial support of British manufacturers.

The report of J. T. Bigge, an able lawyer sent out in 1819 to evaluate the colony, proved decisive. Persuaded by large landowners like Macarthur, Bigge reported that wool was the country's future staple. He recommended that convicts be removed from the temptations of towns and seaports and dispersed to work on the estates of men of capital. He also urged that British duties on colonial wool be suspended. The Colonial Office accepted this advice, and the pastoral economy of Australia, as the continent was beginning to be called, began.

Australia's temperate though capricious climate is ideally suited to sheep farming. Moreover, wool production requires much land and little labor—precisely the situation in Australia. In 1820 the sheep population was 120,000; by 1830 it reached a half-million. After 1820 the commercial importance of Australia exceeded its significance as a penal colony, and wool export steadily increased: From 75,400 pounds in 1821, to 2 million pounds in 1830, to 10 million pounds in 1839, to 24 million pounds in 1845.

Settlers also experimented with wheat farming. Soil deficiencies and the dry climate slowed early production, but farmers eventually developed a white-grained variety (in contrast to the red-grained variety grown in the Northern Hemisphere) planted during the Australian winter from May through July and harvested from September to January. By 1900 wheat proved Australia's second most valuable crop.

Population shortage remained a problem. In this area, the development of Australia owes some-

thing to the vision of Edward Gibbon Wakefield (1769–1862), a theorist of colonization. Between 1825 and 1850, 3 million people emigrated from Great Britain. In the quest for immigrants, Australia could not really compete with North America. The 12,000-mile journey to Australia cost between £20 and £25 and could take five weary months. By contrast, the trip to Canada or the United States cost only £5 and lasted just ten weeks. Wakefield proposed that Australian land be sold relatively cheaply and that proceeds from the sale be used to pay the passages of free laborers and mechanics. That eliminated the disadvantage of cost. Although over 2,500,000 British immigrants went to North America, 223,000 industrious English and Irish people chose Australia.

Population in the early nineteenth century concentrated on the eastern coast of the continent most of which remained unexplored. The growth of sheep farming stimulated exploration and led to the opening of the interior. In 1813 explorers discovered a route over the Blue Mountains. New settlements were made in Hobart, Tasmania, in 1813; in Queensland on the Brisbane River in 1824; and on the Swan River in Western Australia in 1829. Melbourne was established on Port Phillip Bay in 1835 and Adelaide on Gulf St. Vincent in 1836. These settlements served as the bases for further exploration and settlement. Population continued to grow with the arrival of more convicts (a total of 161,000 when the system was finally abolished in 1868). The Ripon Land Regulation Act of 1831, which provided land grants, attracted free settlers. By 1850 Australia had 500,000 inhabitants. The discovery of gold in Victoria in 1851 quadrupled that in a few years.

From Colony to Nation

On February 12, 1851, Edward Hargraves, an Australian-born prospector who had returned to Australia after unsuccessful digging in the California gold rush of 1849, discovered gold in a creek on the western slopes of the Blue Mountains. Hargraves gave the district the biblical name Ophir (Job 22:24), and the newspapers said the region was "one vast gold field." In July a miner found gold at Clunes, 100 miles west of Melbourne, and in September gold was found in what proved to be the richest field of all, Ballarat, just 75 miles west of Melbourne. Gold fever convulsed Australia. Although the government charged prospectors a very high license fee, men and women from all parts of the globe flocked to Australia to share in the fabulous wealth.

Besides the enormous population growth, what impact did the gold rush of 1851–1861 have on Australian society? Contemporaries agreed with explorer and politician W. C. Wentworth, who said that the gold rush opened a new era "which must in a very few years precipitate us from a colony to a nation."[46] Although recent scholars have disputed Wentworth, there is much truth to his viewpoint. The gold rush led to an enormous improvement in transportation within Australia. People customarily traveled by horseback and used two-wheel ox-drawn carts to bring wool from inland ranches to coastal cities. Gold prospectors ordinarily walked the 100-odd miles from Sydney or Melbourne to the gold fields. Then two newly arrived Americans, Freeman Cobb and James Rutherford, built sturdy four-wheel coaches capable of carrying heavy cargo and of negotiating the bush tracks. With stops to change horses, Cobb and Co. carried passengers and mail up to 80 miles

a day, a week's work for ox-drawn vehicles. By 1870 company coaches covered 28,000 miles per week. Railroad construction began in the 1870s, and between 1870 and 1890 9,000 miles of track were laid. Railroad construction, financed by British investors, stimulated agricultural growth.

The gold rush also provided the financial means for the promotion of education and culture. The 1850s witnessed the establishment of universities at Sydney and Melbourne and later at Adelaide and Hobart. Public libraries, museums, art galleries, and schools opened in the thirty years after 1851. In keeping with the overwhelmingly British ethnic origin of most immigrants to Australia, these institutions dispensed a distinctly British culture, though a remote and provincial version.

On the negative side, the large numbers of Asians in the gold fields—in Victoria in 1857 one adult male in seven was Chinese—sparked bitter racial prejudice. Scholars date the "white Australia policy" to the hostility, resentment, and fear that whites showed the Chinese.

Although Americans numbered only about 5,000 in Victoria and Asians 40,000, Americans

Sheepshearing Sheep farming was introduced early into Australia, and wool (with wheat and minerals) became the foundation of the nation's economy. The sheep were sheared in vast sheds like this one. *(Source: Tom Roberts,* Shearing the Rams, *1890. Reproduced by permission of the National Gallery of Victoria, Melbourne)*

with their California gold-rush experience, aggressive ways, and "democratic" frontier outlook, exercised an influence on Australian society far out of proportion to their numbers. "There was evidence to suggest that some Americans, bringing with them their pre–Civil War racist attitudes, had an appreciable influence on the growth of color prejudice in Australia."[47] On the Fourth of July in 1852, 1854, and 1857 (anniversaries of the American Declaration of Independence), anti-Chinese riots occurred in the gold fields of Victoria. After the gold-rush decade, public pressure for the exclusion of all colored peoples increased. Nevertheless, Asian peoples continued to arrive. Chinese and Japanese built the railroads and ran the market gardens near, and the shops in, the towns. Filipinos and Pacific Islanders did the hard work in the sugar-cane fields. Afghani and their camels controlled the carrying trade in some areas.

"Colored peoples" (as all nonwhites were called in Australia) adapted more easily than the British to the tropical climate and worked for lower wages. Thus they proved essential to the country's economic development in the nineteenth century. But fear that colored labor would lower living standards and undermine Australia's distinctly British culture triumphed. The Commonwealth Immigration Restriction Act of 1901 closed immigration to Asians and established the "white Australia policy." Australia achieved racial and cultural unity only at the price of Asian resentment at discrimination and the retardation of the economic development of the northern colonies, which desperately needed labor. The laws of 1901 remained on the books until the 1970s.

The gold rush had a considerable political impact. In 1850 the British Parliament had passed the Australian Colonies Government Act, which allowed the four most populous colonies—New South Wales, Tasmania, Victoria, and South Australia—to establish colonial legislatures, determine the franchise, and frame their own constitutions. The gold rush, vastly increasing population, accelerated the movement for self-government. Acknowledging this demand, the Colonial Secretary in London wrote that the gold discoveries "imparted new and unforeseen features to (Australia's) political and social condition." The British Parliament approved the constitutions of Victoria, New South Wales, South Australia, and Queensland. Western Australia's decision to remain a penal colony delayed responsible government there,

but by 1859 all other colonies were self-governing. The provincial parliament of South Australia was probably the most democratic in the world, since it was elected by universal manhood suffrage and by secret ballot. Other colonies soon adopted the secret ballot. In 1909 Australia became the first country in the world to adopt woman suffrage.

The government of Australia combines features of the British and American systems. In the later nineteenth century, pressure for continental federation culminated in meetings of the premiers (governors) of the colonies. They drafted a constitution that the British Parliament approved in the Commonwealth of Australia Constitution Act of 1900. The Commonwealth of Australia came into existence on January 1, 1901. From the Westminster model, Australia adopted the parliamentary form of government in which a cabinet is responsible to the House of Commons. From the American system, Australia took the concept of decentralized government whereby the states and the federal government share power. The states in Australia, as in the United States, retain considerable power, especially in local or domestic affairs.

Deep loyalty to the mother country led Australia to send 329,000 men and vast economic aid to Britain in the First World War. The issue of conscription, however, bitterly divided the country, partly along religious lines. About one-fourth of Australia's population was (and is) Irish and Roman Catholic. Although the Catholic population, like the dominant Anglican one, split over conscription, the powerful, influential, and long-lived Catholic archbishop of Melbourne, Daniel Mannix (r. 1917–1963) publically supported the Sinn Fein, the Irish nationalist (and later terrorist) movement. Mannix also denounced the English and the European war.

Twice submitted to public referendum, conscription twice failed. When the Australian poet Frank Wilmot wrote, "The fumes of ancient hells have invaded your spirit," he meant that English wrongs in Ireland had become part of Australian culture.

Australian troops fought valiantly in the Dardenelles campaign, where more than 10,000 died. During the long nightmare of trench warfare on the western front (see page 1045), Australian soldiers were brilliantly led by Sir John Monash, a Jewish Australian whose planning led to the Allied breakthrough and the ultimate defeat of Germany. With 213,850 casualties, however, the death toll proved so staggering that the war exerted a severely traumatic effect on Australian life and society. With the young men died the illusion that remote Australia could escape the problems and sins of the Old World. But the experience of the Great War drew the disparate colonies together; the war forged a sense of national identity among the states of Australia.

At the Paris Peace Conference in 1919, Australian delegates succeeded in excluding recognition of the principle of racial equality in the League of Nations Covenant. Australians did not want Asian immigrants. The treaties that followed the war allowed Australia a mandate over German New Guinea and the equatorial island of Nauru. Nauru had vast quantities of phosphates that Australian wheatfields needed as fertilizer. The former penal colony had become a colonial power.

cated culture and had been Christians for three centuries.

The notion of manifest destiny had swept the United States into the Caribbean and across the Pacific. Between 1900 and 1929 the United States intervened in Latin American affairs whenever it felt its economic interests were threatened. Americans secured control of the Panama Canal on their own terms, and in 1912 and 1926 U.S. Marines intervened in Nicaragua to bolster conservative governments. The result has been a bitter legacy of anti-American feeling throughout Latin America. Only with the launching of President Franklin D. Roosevelt's Good Neighbor Policy did relations between the United States and Latin America begin to improve.

Canada and Australia achieved political and economic maturity.

SUMMARY

In the later years of the nineteenth century, industrialization, expansion, and the assimilation of foreign peoples preoccupied the nations of the Western Hemisphere. Political instability slowed the development of most Latin American countries. A few reformers sought closer relations between North and South America, but little of significance was accomplished. In 1889, for example, a Pan-American Conference in Washington rejected a proposal to settle disputes among nations by arbitration.

A revolt in Cuba against incompetent Spanish administration had more far-reaching consequences. The American "yellow press" luridly described the horrors of the concentration camps where the Spanish incarcerated the rebels. When the battleship *Maine* was mysteriously blown up in Havana harbor, inflamed public opinion swept the United States into war. The Spanish-American War of 1898—the "splendid little war," as Secretary of State John Hay called it—lasted just ten weeks and resulted in the United States acquiring Cuba and the Philippine Islands. Denying any imperialistic ambitions in the Philippines, President William McKinley declared that the United States wanted only "to take them all and educate the Filipinos and uplift and civilize and Christianize them." McKinley, like most Americans, did not know that the Filipinos had an old and sophisti-

NOTES

1. Quoted in W. S. Robertson, *Rise of the Spanish American Republics* (New York: Free Press, 1965), p. 19.
2. See B. Keen and M. Wasserman, *A Short History of Latin America* (Boston: Houghton Mifflin, 1980), pp. 109–115.
3. J. Lynch, *The Spanish-American Revolutions, 1808–1826* (New York: Norton, 1973), pp. 13–14; Keen and Wasserman, pp. 145–146.
4. Quoted in Lynch, p. 18.
5. M. Burkholder and D. S. Chandler, *From Impotence to Authority: The Spanish Crown and the American Audiencias, 1687–1808* (Columbia, Mo.: University of Missouri Press, 1977), p. 145.
6. Ibid., p. 141.
7. Keen and Wasserman, p. 146.
8. Quoted in J. L. Phelan, *The People and the King: The Comunero Revolution in Colombia, 1781* (Madison, Wis.: University of Wisconsin Press, 1978), p. 62; see also L. B. Rout, *The African Experience in Spanish America* (New York: Cambridge University Press, 1977), p. 165.
9. Quoted in Phelan, pp. 206–207.
10. F. Tannenbaum, *Ten Keys to Latin America* (New York: Random House, 1962), pp. 69–71.
11. Ibid.
12. H. Hoetink, *Slavery and Race Relations in the Americas* (New York: Harper & Row, 1973), p. 14.
13. Keen and Wasserman, pp. 201–204.
14. See C. H. Harris, *A Mexican Family Empire: The Latifundio of the Sanchez Navarros, 1765–1867* (Austin:

University of Texas Press, 1975).

15. N. Sanchez-Albornoz, *The Population of Latin America: A History,* trans. W. A. R. Richardson (Berkeley: University of California Press, 1974), pp. 151–152.

16. J. R. Scobie, "Buenos Aires as a Commercial-Bureaucratic City, 1880–1910: Characteristics of a City's Orientation," *American Historical Review 77* (October 1972): 1046.

17. Ibid., p. 1064.

18. See M. Morner, ed., *Race and Class in Latin America. Part II: Immigration, Stratification, and Race Relations* (New York: Columbia University Press, 1971), pp. 73–122; Sanchez-Albornoz, pp. 160–167.

19. S. E. Morison, *The Oxford History of the American Peeople* (New York: Oxford University Press, 1965), pp. 380–381.

20. Ibid., pp. 446–452.

21. J. Oakes, *The Ruling Race: A History of American Slaveholders* (New York: Knopf, 1982), pp. x–xi.

22. See P. Parish, *Slavery: History and Historians* (New York: Harper & Row, 1989), pp. 45–46.

23. Quoted in Oakes, p. 120.

24. C. V. Woodward, ed., *Mary Chesnut's Civil War* (New Haven, Conn.: Yale University Press, 1981), p. 29.

25. Ibid., pp. xlix–l.

26. R. P. Basler, ed., *The Collected Works of Abraham Lincoln,* vol. II (New Brunswick, N.J.: Rutgers University Press, 1953), pp. 255–256, 271.

27. Ibid., pp. 461–462.

28. Quoted in R. Hofstadter, *The American Political Tradition* (New York: Random House, 1948), p. 114.

29. T. H. Williams, quoted in Hofstadter, pp. 128–129.

30. Quoted in Hofstadter, p. 132.

31. Quoted in Morison, p. 654.

32. T. H. Williams, *The History of American Wars: From Colonial Times to World War I* (New York: Alfred A. Knopf, 1981), p. 202.

33. A. Kardiner and L. Ovesey quoted in H. G. Gutman, *The Black Family in Slavery and Freedom, 1750–1925* (New York: Random House, 1977), p. xvii.

34. Quoted in R. W. Fogel and S. L. Engerman, *Time on the Cross: The Economics of American Negro Slavery* (Boston: Little, Brown, 1974), p. 84.

35. Ibid., pp. 81–82.

36. Gutman, p. xix.

37. S. L. Myres, *Westering Women and the Frontier Experience, 1800–1915* (Albuquerque: University of New Mexico Press, 1982), chaps. 6 and 7.

38. G. Barth, *City People: The Rise of Modern City Culture in the Nineteenth Century* (New York: Oxford University Press, 1980), p. 15.

39. Quoted in Lynch, p. 18.

40. Hoetink, p. 18.

41. Quoted in J. Higham, *Strangers in the Land: Patterns of American Nativism, 1860–1925* (New York: Atheneum, 1971), pp. 89–90.

42. Quoted in R. Cook, *Canada: A Modern Study* (Toronto: Clarke, Irwin, 1971), p. 89.

43. Quoted ibid., p. 127.

44. R. Ward, *Australia* (Englewood Cliffs, N.J.: Prentice-Hall, 1965, p. 21.

45. Quoted in R. Hughes, *The Fatal Shore* (New York: Knopf, 1987), p. 66.

46. Quoted in Ward, p. 60.

47. Ward, *op. cit.,* p. 59.

SUGGESTED READING

Perhaps the best introduction to the independence movements in Latin America is J. Lynch, *The Spanish-American Revolutions* (1973), which is soundly researched and includes a good bibliography. The most useful biographies of Simón Bolívar are those of G. Masur, *Simón Bolívar,* 2d ed. (1969), and J. J. Johnson and D. M. Ladd, *Simón Bolívar and Spanish American Independence, 1783–1830* (1968); the latter contains good selections of Bolívar's writings. For Brazil, see K. R. Maxwell, *Conflicts and Conspiracies: Brazil and Portugal, 1750–1808* (1973), and A. J. R. Russell-Wood, ed., *From Colony to Nation: Essays in the Independence of Brazil* (1975). A. P. Whitaker, *The United States and the Independence of Latin America, 1800–1830* (1941), remains the standard study of the role of the United States. The essays in E. Viotti da Costa, *The Brazilian Empire: Myths and Histories* (1985), are sound and penetrating.

J. Bazant, *A Concise History of Mexico* (1978), is a good starting point for the study of Mexican history, but M. C. Meyer and W. L. Sherman, *The Course of Mexican History* (1979), is the most thorough treatment. T. Halperin-Donghi, *The Aftermath of Revolution in Latin America* (1973), and C. C. Griffin, "Economic and Social Aspects of the Era of Spanish-American Independence," *Hispanic American Historical Review 29* (1949), provide important interpretations of the consequences of the revolutions.

The following studies offer good treatments of society and politics in Latin America in the nineteenth century: R. Graham and P. H. Smith, eds., *New Approaches to Latin American History* (1974); R. Roeder, *Juarez and His Mexico,* 2 vols. (1947), perhaps the best available work in English; H. S. Ferns, *Argentina* (1969); J. Kinsbruner, *Chile: A Historical Interpretation* (1973); A. J. Bauer, *Chilean Rural Society from the Spanish Conquest to 1930* (1975); E. B. Burns, *A History of Brazil* (1970); Robert Conrad, *The Destruction of Brazilian Slavery,*

1850–1888 (1973); and R. B. Toplin, *The Abolition of Slavery in Brazil* (1972). C. N. Degler, *Neither Black Nor White: Slavery and Race Relations in Brazil and the United States* (1971) remains the best comparative study of race in the two societies.

For social and economic developments and the triumph of neocolonialism, the following titles are useful: R. C. Conde, *The First Stages of Modernization in Spanish America* (1967); J. Bazant, *A Concise History of Mexico from Hidalgo to Cardenas, 1805–1940* (1978); R. Knowlton, *Church Property and the Mexican Reform, 1856–1910* (1976); R. D. Anderson, *Outcasts in Their Own Land: Mexican Industrial Workers, 1906–1911* (1976); J. Scobie, *Argentina: A City and a Nation,* 2d ed. (1971); M. J. Mamalakis, *The Growth and Structure of the Chilean Economy from Independence to Allende* (1976), which provides an excellent economic overview; A. G. Frank, *Capitalism and Underdevelopment in Latin America: Historical Studies of Chile and Brazil* (1969); D. Rock, *Politics in Argentina, 1890–1930: The Rise and Fall of Radicalism* (1975); R. Graham, *Britain and the Onset of Modernization in Brazil, 1850–1914* (1968).

The major themes in United States history have been extensively treated by many able scholars, and students will have no difficulty finding a wealth of material. J. M. Burns, *The Vineyard of Liberty* (1982), traces the origins and development of American society, politics, and culture, emphasizing the growth of liberty, from the 1780s to 1863; this work is a classic achievement. The standard study of manifest destiny remains F. Merk, *Manifest Destiny and Mission in American History: A Reinterpretation* (1963), but see also K. Jack Bauer, *The Mexican-American War, 1846–1848* (1976). In *The Only Land They Knew: The Tragic Story of the American Indians in the Old South* (1981), J. Leitch Wright recounts the interaction of Native Americans, Africans, and Europeans in the American South.

The best recent study of the pre–Civil War years is K. M. Stampp, *American in 1857: A Nation on the Brink* (1990). For slavery, see the elegant study by P. J. Parish cited in the Notes; Parish surveys an enormous body of scholarship. W. Jordan, *White over Black: American Attitudes Towards the Negro, 1550–1812* (1969), remains the best treatment of the relationship of racism to slavery; S. M. Elkins, *Slavery: A Problem in American Institutional and Intellectual Life,* 3d. rev. ed (1976), provides a good comparison of slavery in the United States and in Latin America. C. N. Degler, *Neither Black nor White: Slavery and Race Relations in Brazil and the United States* (1971), also treats the two continents. E. D. Genovese, *Roll, Jordan, Roll: The World the Slaves Made* (1974), gives the comprehensive Marxist treatment.

On black culture and black women and the family, see, in addition to Gutman's work cited in the Notes, J. Jones, *Labor of Love, Labor of Sorrow: Black Women,* *Work, and the Family from Slavery to the Present* (1985); C. Neverdon-Morton, *Afro-American Women of the South and the Advancement of the Race, 1895–1925* (1989); M. R. Malson et al., *Black Women in America: Social Science Perspectives* (1988), offers useful essays for classroom discussion. W. S. McFeely, *Frederick Douglass* (1991); and I. Berlin et al. eds., *Freedom: A Documentary History of Emancipation* (1990). For the powerful influence of the black church see E. Lincoln and C. H. Mamiya, *The Black Church in the African American Experience* (1990).

The literature on the Civil War and Reconstruction is mammoth. The following titles treat important aspects of them: D. Donald, ed., *Why the North Won the Civil War* (1977); J. H. Franklin, *Reconstruction* (1965); H. M. Hyman, *A More Perfect Union* (1973); and J. McPherson, *The Abolitionist Legacy* (1975). E. Foner, *Reconstruction: America's Unfinished Revolution, 1863–1877* (1988), has probably superseded previous works.

T. C. Cochrane, *Business in American Life* (1977); A. D. Chandler, *Strategy and Structure: Chapters in the History of American Industrial Enterprise* (1966); H. C. Livesay, *Andrew Carnegie and the Rise of Big Business* (1975); and D. F. Hawkes, *John D.: The Founding Father of the Rockefellers* (1980), are fine studies of industrialism and corporate growth in the late nineteenth century.

On the lives of Jews and other immigrants in American cities, see I. Howe's brilliant achievement, *World of Our Fathers* (1976), which is splendidly illustrated and contains a good bibliography, and S. S. Weinberg, *The World of Our Mothers: The Lives of Jewish Immigrant Women (1988).*

For developments in Canada, see, in addition to the highly readable sketch by R. Cook cited in the Notes, K. McNaught, *The Pelican History of Canada* (1976), a sound survey that emphasizes those cultural traits that are distinctly Canadian. For the Age of Confederation, J. M. S. Careless, *The Union of the Canadas, 1841–1857* (1967), offers a solid treatment by a distinguished scholar. D. G. Creighton, *John A. Macdonald,* 2 vols. (1952, 1955), is probably the best study of the great prime minister. The critical years of expansion and development are discussed in the full accounts of R. C. Brown and G. R. Cook, *Canada, 1896–1921* (1974), and R. Graham, *Canada, 1922–1939* (1979).

Perhaps the best starting point for the study of Australian history is the title by R. Hughes, cited in the Notes. M. Clark, *A Short History of Australia* (1987), is a highly readable general sketch, while C. M. H. Clark, *A History of Australia,* 6 vols. (1962–1987), is the standard political history. R. Terrill, *The Australians* (1987), offers an attractive appreciation of the Australian people and the society they made, from the first settlers to the present.

32

The Great Break:
War and Revolution

World War One trench warfare (John Nash, *Over the Top*)

In the summer of 1914 the nations of Europe went willingly to war. They believed they had no other choice. Moreover, both peoples and governments confidently expected a short war leading to a decisive victory. Such a war, they believed, would "clear the air," and European society would go on as before.

These expectations were almost totally mistaken. The First World War was long, indecisive, and tremendously destructive. To the shell-shocked generation of survivors, it was known simply as the "Great War": the war of unprecedented scope and intensity. From today's perspective it is clear that the First World War marked a great break in the course of world historical development. The war accelerated the growth of nationalism in Asia (see Chapter 33), and it consolidated the position of the United States as a global power. Yet the war's greatest impact was on Europe, the focus of this chapter. A noted British political scientist has gone so far as to say that even in victorious and relatively fortunate Great Britain, the First World War was *the* great turning point in government and society "as in everything else in modern British history. . . . There's a much greater difference between the Britain of 1914 and, say, 1920, than between the Britain of 1920 and today."[1]

That is a strong statement, but it contains much truth, for all of Europe as well as for Britain. It suggests three questions that this chapter tries to answer:

- What caused the Great War?

- How and why did war and revolution have such enormous and destructive consequences?

- How did the years of trauma and bloodshed form elements of modern life that people now accept and even cherish?

THE FIRST WORLD WAR

The First World War was so long and destructive because it involved all the Great Powers in Europe and because it spread to envelop several non-European states and peoples. Moreover, it quickly degenerated into a senseless military stalemate. Like two evenly matched boxers in a championship bout, each side tried to wear down its opponent. There was no referee to call a draw, only the blind hammering of a life-or-death struggle until one combatant fell prostrate.

The Bismarckian System of Alliances

In examining the complex origins of the First World War, one needs to begin with the Franco-Prussian War and the foundation of the German Empire, which opened a new era in international relations. France was decisively defeated in 1871 and forced to pay a large war indemnity and give up Alsace-Lorraine. In ten short years, from 1862 to 1871, Bismarck had made Prussia-Germany—traditionally the weakest of the Great Powers—the most powerful nation in Europe (see pages 937–940). Had Bismarck been a Napoleon I or a Hitler, for whom no gain was ever sufficient, continued expansion would no doubt sooner or later have raised a powerful coalition against the new German Empire. But he was not. As Bismarck never tired of repeating after 1871, Germany was a "satisfied" power. Germany had no territorial ambitions and only wanted peace in Europe.

But how was peace to be preserved? The most serious threat to peace came from the east, from Austria-Hungary and from Russia. Those two enormous multinational empires had many conflicting interests, particularly in the Balkans, where the Ottoman Empire—the "sick man of Europe"—was ebbing fast. There was a real threat that Germany might be dragged into a great war between the two rival empires. Bismarck's solution was a system of alliances (Figure 32.1) to restrain both Russia and Austria-Hungary, to prevent conflict between them, and to isolate a hostile France.

A first step was the creation in 1873 of the conservative Three Emperors' League, which linked the monarchs of Austria-Hungary, Germany, and Russia in an alliance against radical movements. In 1877 and 1878, when Russia's victories over the Ottoman Empire threatened the balance of Austrian and Russian interests in the Balkans and the balance of British and Russian interests in the Middle East, Bismarck played the role of sincere peacemaker. At the Congress of Berlin in 1878, he saw that Austria obtained the right to "occupy and

The Congress of Berlin, 1878   With the Austrian representative on his right and with other participants looking on, Bismarck the mediator symbolically seals the hard-won agreement by shaking hands with the chief Russian negotiator. The Great Powers often relied on such special conferences to settle their international disputes. *(Source: The Bettmann Archive)*

administer" the Ottoman provinces of Bosnia and Herzegovina to counterbalance Russian gains, while independent Balkan states were also carved from the disintegrating Ottoman Empire.

Bismarck's balancing efforts at the Congress of Berlin infuriated Russian nationalists. Their anger led Bismarck to conclude a defensive military alliance with Austria against Russia in 1879. Motivated by tensions with France, Italy joined Germany and Austria in 1882, thereby forming the Triple Alliance.

Bismarck continued to work for peace in eastern Europe, seeking to neutralize tensions between Austria-Hungary and Russia. In 1881 he capitalized on their mutual fears and cajoled them both into a secret alliance with Germany. This Alliance of the Three Emperors lasted until 1887. It established the principle of cooperation among all three powers in any further division of the Ottoman Empire, and each state pledged friendly neutrality in case one of the three found itself at war with a fourth power (except the Ottoman Empire).

Bismarck also maintained good relations with Britain and Italy, while cooperating with France in Africa but keeping France isolated in Europe. In 1887 Russia declined to renew the Alliance of the Three Emperors because of new tensions in the Balkans. Bismarck craftily substituted a Russian-German Reinsurance Treaty, by which both states promised neutrality if the other were attacked.

Bismarck's accomplishments in foreign policy after 1871 were great. For almost a generation, he maintained German leadership in international affairs, and he worked successfully for peace by managing conflicts and by restraining Austria-Hungary and Russia with defensive alliances.

The Rival Blocs

In 1890 the young, impetuous emperor William II (r. 1888–1941) dismissed Bismarck, in part because of the chancellor's friendly policy toward

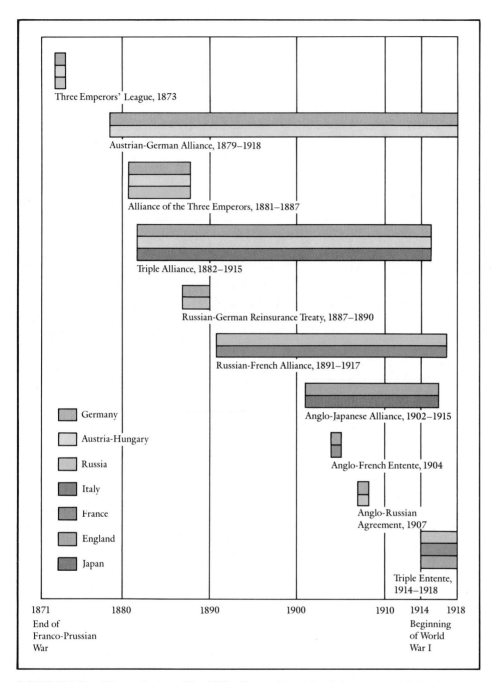

FIGURE 32.1 The Alliance System After 1871 Bismarck's subtle diplomacy maintained reasonably good relations among the eastern monarchies—Germany, Russia, and Austria-Hungary—and kept France isolated. The situation changed dramatically in 1891, when the Russian-French Alliance divided the Great Powers into two fairly equal military blocs.

Russia since the 1870s. William then adamantly refused to renew the Russian-German Reinsurance Treaty, in spite of Russian willingness to do so. This fateful departure in foreign affairs prompted long-isolated republican France to court absolutist Russia, offering loans, arms, and friendship. In both countries there were enthusiastic public demonstrations, and in St. Petersburg the autocratic Alexander III stood bareheaded on a French battleship while a band played the "Marseillaise," the hymn of the French Revolution. A preliminary agreement between the two countries was reached in 1891, and in early 1894 France and Russia became military allies. This alliance (see Figure 32.1) was to remain in effect as long as the Triple Alliance of Austria, Germany, and Italy: continental Europe was dangerously divided into two rival blocs.

The policy of Great Britain became increasingly crucial. Long content with "splendid isolation" and no permanent alliances, Britain after 1891 was Europe's only uncommitted Great Power. Could Britain afford to remain isolated, or would it feel compelled to take sides? Alliance with France or Russia certainly seemed highly unlikely. With its vast and rapidly expanding empire, Britain was often in serious conflict with these countries around the world in the heyday of imperialism.

Britain also squabbled with Germany, but many Germans and some Britons still believed that their statesmen would eventually formalize the "natural alliance" that they felt already united the advanced, racially related Germanic and Anglo-Saxon peoples. Such an understanding never materialized. Instead, the generally good relations that had prevailed between Prussia and Great Britain ever since the mid-eighteenth century, and certainly under Bismarck, gave way to a bitter Anglo-German rivalry.

There were several reasons for this tragic development. The hard-fought Boer War (1899–1902) between the British and the tiny Dutch republics of South Africa had a major impact on British policy. British statesmen saw that Britain was overextended around the world. The Boer War also brought into the open widespread anti-British feeling, as editorial writers in many nations denounced the latest manifestation of British imperialism. There was even talk of Germany, Austria, France, and Russia forming a grand alliance against the bloated but insatiable British Empire. Therefore British statesmen prudently set about shoring up their exposed position with alliances and agreements.

Britain improved its often-strained relations with the United States and in 1902 concluded a formal alliance with Japan (see Figure 32.1). Britain then responded favorably to the advances of France's skillful foreign minister, Théophile Delcassé, who wanted better relations with Britain and was willing to accept British rule in Egypt in return for British support of French plans to dominate Morocco. The resulting Anglo-French Entente of 1904 (see Figure 32.1) settled all outstanding colonial disputes between Britain and France.

Frustrated by Britain's turn toward France in 1904, Germany decided to test the strength of the entente and drive Britain and France apart. First Germany threatened and bullied France into dismissing Delcassé. However, rather than accept the typical territorial payoff of imperial competition—a slice of French jungle in Africa or a port in Morocco—in return for French primacy in Morocco, the Germans foolishly rattled their swords in 1905. Without presenting any precise or reasonable demands, the Germans insisted on an international conference in the Spanish city of Algeciras to examine all aspects of European influence in Morocco. Germany's crude bullying forced France and Britain closer together, and Germany left the Algeciras Conference of 1906 empty-handed and isolated (except for Austria-Hungary).

The result of the Moroccan crisis and the Algeciras Conference was something of a diplomatic revolution. Britain, France, Russia, and even the United States began to see Germany as a potential threat that might seek to dominate all Europe. At the same time, German leaders began to see sinister plots to "encircle" Germany and block its development as a world power. In 1907 Russia, battered by the disastrous war with Japan and the revolution of 1905, agreed to settle outstanding imperialist quarrels with Great Britain in Persia and in central Asia with a special Anglo-Russian Agreement (see Figure 32.1). As a result of that agreement, Germany's blustering paranoia increased and so did Britain's thinly disguised hostility.

Germany's decision to add a large, enormously expensive fleet of big-gun battleships to its already expanding navy also heightened tensions after 1907. German nationalists, led by the all-too-persuasive Admiral Alfred von Tirpitz, saw a large navy as the legitimate mark of a great world power. But British leaders like David Lloyd George saw it as a detestable military challenge, which forced them to spend the People's Budget on battleships rather than on social welfare. As Germany's rapid industrial growth allowed it to overcome Britain's early lead, economic rivalry also contributed to distrust and hostility between the two nations. Unscrupulous journalists and special-interest groups in both countries portrayed healthy competition in foreign trade and investment as a form of economic warfare.

In Britain and Germany, many educated shapers of public opinion and ordinary people were increasingly locked in a fateful love-hate relationship with the two countries. Proud nationalists in both countries simultaneously admired and feared the power and accomplishments of their nearly equal rival. In 1909 the mass-circulation London *Daily Mail* hysterically informed its readers in a series of reports that "Germany is deliberately preparing to destroy the British Empire."[2] By then, Britain was psychologically, if not officially, in the Franco-Russian camp. The leading nations of Europe were divided into two hostile blocs, both ill prepared to deal with upheaval on Europe's southeastern frontier.

The Outbreak of War

In the early years of the twentieth century, war in the Balkans was as inevitable as anything can be in human history. The reason was simple: nationalism was destroying the multinational Ottoman Empire and threatening to break up the Austro-Hungarian Empire. The only questions were what kinds of wars would occur and where they would lead.

Greece had long before led the struggle for national liberation, winning its independence in 1832. In 1875 widespread nationalist rebellion in the Ottoman Empire's European possessions resulted in Turkish repression, Russian intervention, and Great Power tensions. Bismarck helped resolve this crisis at the 1878 Congress of Berlin, which worked out the partial division of Ottoman holdings in Europe. Austria-Hungary obtained the right to "occupy and administer" Bosnia and Herzegovina. Serbia and Romania won complete independence, and a part of Bulgaria won local autonomy. The Ottoman Empire retained important

Balkan holdings, for Austria-Hungary and Russia each feared the other's domination of totally independent states in the area (Map 32.1).

After 1878 the siren call of imperialism lured European energies, particularly Russian energies, away from the Balkans. This division helped preserve the fragile balance of interests in southeastern Europe. By 1903, however, nationalism in the Balkans was on the rise once again. Serbia led the way, becoming openly hostile toward both Austria-Hungary and the Ottoman Empire. The Serbs, a Slavic people, looked to Slavic Russia for support of their national aspirations. To block Serbian expansion and to take advantage of Russia's weakness after the revolution of 1905, Austria in 1908 formally annexed Bosnia and Herzegovina with their predominantly Serbian populations. The kingdom of Serbia erupted in rage but could do nothing without Russian support.

Then in 1912, in the First Balkan War, Serbia turned southward. With Greece and Bulgaria it took Macedonia from the Ottoman Empire and then quarreled with its ally Bulgaria over the spoils of victory—a dispute that led in 1913 to the Second Balkan War. Austria intervened in 1913 and forced Serbia to give up Albania. After centuries, nationalism had finally destroyed the Ottoman Empire in Europe (Map 32.2). This sudden but long-awaited event elated the Balkan nationalists and dismayed the leaders of multinational Austria-Hungary. The former hoped and the latter feared that Austria might be next to be broken apart.

Within this tense context, Archduke Francis Ferdinand, heir to the Austrian and Hungarian thrones, and his wife Sophie were assassinated by Bosnian revolutionaries on June 28, 1914, during a state visit to the Bosnian capital of Sarajevo. The assassins were closely connected to the ultranationalist Serbian society The Black Hand. This revolutionary group was secretly supported by members of the Serbian government and was dedicated to uniting all Serbians in a single state. Although the leaders of Austria-Hungary did not and could not know all the details of Serbia's involvement in the assassination plot, they concluded after some hesitation that Serbia had to be severely punished once and for all. After a month of maneuvering, on July 23 Austria-Hungary presented Serbia with an unconditional ultimatum.

The Serbian government had just forty-eight hours in which to agree to cease all subversion in Austria and all anti-Austrian propaganda in

MAP 32.1 The Balkans After the Congress of Berlin, 1878 The Ottoman Empire suffered large territorial losses but remained a power in the Balkans.

MAP 32.2 The Balkans in 1914 Ethnic boundaries did not follow political boundaries, and Serbian national aspirations threatened Austria-Hungary.

Serbia. Moreover, a thorough investigation of all aspects of the assassination at Sarajevo was to be undertaken in Serbia by a joint commission of Serbian and Austrian officials. These demands amounted to control of the Serbian state. When Serbia replied moderately but evasively, Austria began to mobilize and then declared war on Serbia on July 28. Thus a desperate multinational Austria-Hungary deliberately chose war in a last-ditch attempt to stem the rising tide of hostile nationalism. The "Third Balkan War" had begun.

Of prime importance in Austria-Hungary's fateful decision was Germany's unconditional support. Emperor William II and his chancellor, Theobald von Bethmann-Hollweg (Bismarck had resigned in 1890), gave Austria-Hungary a "blank check" and urged aggressive measures in early July even

though they realized that war between Austria and Russia was the most probable result. They knew that Russian pan-Slavs saw Russia not only as the protector but also as the eventual liberator of southern Slavs. As one pan-Slav had said much earlier, "Austria can hold her part of the Slavonian mass as long as Turkey holds hers and vice versa."[3] At the very least a resurgent Russia could not stand by, as in the Bosnian crisis, and simply watch the Serbs be crushed. Yet Bethmann-Hollweg apparently hoped that while Russia (and therefore France) went to war, Great Britain would remain neutral, unwilling to fight over "Russian aggression" in the distant Balkans. After all, Britain had only "friendly understandings" with France and Russia on colonial questions and had no alliance with either power.

In fact, the diplomatic situation was already out of control. Military plans and timetables began to dictate policy. Russia, a vast country, would require much longer to mobilize its armies than Germany and Austria-Hungary. On July 28, as Austrian armies bombarded Belgrade, Tsar Nicholas II ordered a partial mobilization against Austria-Hungary. Almost immediately he found that this was impossible. All the complicated mobilization plans of the Russian general staff had assumed a war with both Austria and Germany: Russia could not mobilize against one without mobilizing against the other. On July 29, therefore, Russia ordered full mobilization and in effect declared general war.

The same tragic subordination of political considerations to military strategy descended on Germany. The German general staff had also thought only in terms of a two-front war. The German plan for war called for knocking out France first with a lightning attack through neutral Belgium before turning on Russia.

On August 2, 1914, General Helmuth von Moltke, "acting under a dictate of self-preservation," demanded that Belgium permit German armies to pass through its territory. Belgium, whose neutrality was solemnly guaranteed by all the great states including Prussia, refused. Germany attacked. Thus Germany's terrible, politically disastrous response to a war in the Balkans was an all-out invasion of France by way of the plains of neutral Belgium on August 3. In the face of this act of aggression, Great Britain declared war on Germany the following day. The First World War had begun.

Reflections on the Origins of the War

Although few events in history have aroused such interest and controversy as the coming of the First World War, the question of immediate causes and responsibilities can be answered with considerable certainty. Austria-Hungary deliberately started the "Third Balkan War." A war for the right to survive was Austria-Hungary's desperate, if understandable, response to the aggressive, yet also understandable, revolutionary drive of Serbian nationalists to unify their people in a single state. In spite of Russian intervention in the quarrel, it was clear from the beginning of the crisis that Germany not only pushed and goaded Austria-Hungary but was

also responsible for turning a little war into the Great War by means of its sledgehammer attack on Belgium and France. Why was this so?

After Bismarck's resignation in 1890, German leaders lost control of the international system. They felt increasingly that Germany's status as a world power was declining while that of Britain, France, Russia, and the United States was growing. Indeed, the powers of what officially became in August 1914 the Triple Entente (see Figure 32.1)—Great Britain, France, and Russia—were checking Germany's vague but real aspirations as well as working to strangle Austria-Hungary, Germany's only real ally. Germany's aggression in 1914 reflected the failure of all European statesmen, not just German leaders, to incorporate Bismarck's mighty empire permanently and peacefully into the international system.

There were other underlying causes. The new overseas expansion—imperialism—did not play a direct role, since the European powers always settled their colonial conflicts peacefully. Yet the easy imperialist victories did contribute to a general European overconfidence and reinforced national rivalries. In this respect imperialism was influential.

The triumph of nationalism was a crucial underlying precondition of the Great War. Nationalism—in the form of Serbian aspirations and the grandiose pan-German versus pan-Slavic racism of some fanatics—was at the heart of the Balkan wars. Nationalism drove the spiraling arms race. More generally, the aristocracy and middle classes arrived at nationalistic compromises while ordinary people looked toward increasingly responsive states for psychological and material well-being (see pages 945–953).

Broad popular commitment to "my country right or wrong" weakened groups that thought in terms of international communities and consequences. Thus the big international bankers, who were frightened by the prospect of war in July 1914, and the extreme-left socialists, who believed that the enemy was at home and not abroad, were equally out of step with national feeling.

Finally, the wealthy governing classes underestimated the risk of war in 1914. They had forgotten that great wars and great social revolutions very often go together in history. Metternich's alliance of conservative forces in support of international peace and the domestic status quo had become only a distant memory.

The First Battle of the Marne

When the Germans invaded Belgium in August 1914, they and everyone else believed that the war would be short, for urban society rested on the food and raw materials of the world economy: "The boys will be home by Christmas." The Belgian army heroically defended its homeland, however, and fell back in good order to join a rapidly landed British army corps near the Franco-Belgian border. This action complicated Germany's plan of concentrating its armies on the right wing and boldly capturing Paris in a vast encircling movement. By the end of August dead-tired German soldiers were advancing along an enormous front in the scorching summer heat. The neatly designed prewar plan to surround Paris from the north and west had been thrown into confusion.

French armies totaling 1 million, reinforced by more than 100,000 British troops, had retreated in orderly fashion before Germany's 1.5 million men in the field. Under the leadership of the steel-nerved General Joseph Joffre, the French attacked a gap in the German line at the Battle of the Marne on September 6. For three days, France threw everything into the attack. At one point, the French government desperately requisitioned all the taxis of Paris to rush reserves to the troops at the front. Finally, the Germans fell back. Paris and France had been miraculously saved.

Stalemate and Slaughter

The attempts of French and British armies to turn the German retreat into a rout were unsuccessful, and so were moves by both sides to outflank each other in northern France. As a result, both sides began to dig trenches to protect themselves from machine-gun fire. By November 1914, an unbroken line of trenches extended from the Belgian ports through northern France past the fortress of Verdun and on to the Swiss frontier.

In the face of this unexpected stalemate, slaughter on the western front began in earnest. Troops on both sides dug in behind rows of trenches, mines, and barbed wire. For weeks ceaseless shelling by heavy artillery supposedly "softened up" the enemy in a given area (and also signaled the coming attack). Then young draftees and their junior officers went "over the top" of the trenches in frontal attacks on the enemy's line.

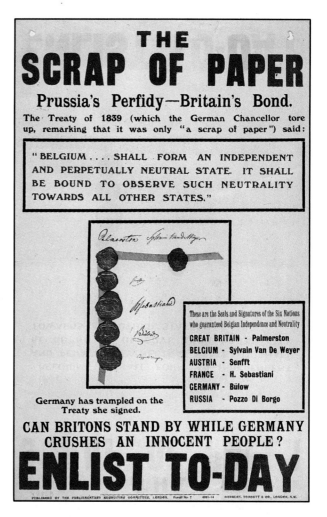

This British Poster shows the signature page of the 1839 treaty guaranteeing the neutrality of Belgium. When German armies invaded Belgium in 1914, Chancellor Bethmann-Hollweg cynically dismissed the treaty as a "scrap of paper"—a perfect line for anti-German propaganda. (*Source: By courtesy of the Trustees of the Imperial War Museum*)

The cost in lives was staggering, the gains in territory minuscule. The massive French and British offensives during 1915 never gained more than three miles of blood-soaked earth from the enemy. In the Battle of the Somme in the summer of 1916, the British and French gained an insignificant 125 square miles at the cost of 600,000 dead or wounded, while the Germans lost half a million men. That same year, the unsuccessful German campaign against Verdun cost 700,000 lives on both sides. The British poet Siegfried Sassoon

Preparing the Attack   The great offenses of the First World War required the mobilization of men and material on an unprecedented scale. This photo shows American troops moving up. *(Source: U.S. Army Signal Corps)*

(1886–1967) wrote of the Somme offensive: "I am staring at a sunlit picture of Hell."

Terrible 1917 saw General Robert Nivelle's French army almost destroyed in a grand spring attack at Champagne, while at Passchendaele in the fall, the British traded 400,000 casualties for fifty square miles of Belgian Flanders. The hero of Erich Maria Remarque's great novel *All Quiet on the Western Front* (1929) describes one such attack:

We see men living with their skulls blown open; we see soldiers run with their two feet cut off. Still the little piece of convulsed earth in which we lie is held. We have yielded no more than a few hundred yards of it as a prize to the enemy. But on every yard there lies a dead man.

Such was war on the western front.

The war of the trenches shattered an entire generation of young men. Millions who could have provided political creativity and leadership after the war were forever missing. Moreover, those who lived through the holocaust were maimed, shell-shocked, embittered, and profoundly disillusioned. The young soldiers went to war believing in the world of their leaders and elders, the pre-1914 world of order, progress, and patriotism. Then, in Remarque's words, the "first bombardment showed us our mistake, and under it the world as they had taught it to us broke in pieces." For many, the sacrifice and comradeship of the battlefield became life's crucial experience, an experience that "soft" civilians could never understand. A chasm opened up between veterans and civilians, making the difficult postwar reconstruction all the more difficult.

The Widening War

On the eastern front, slaughter did not degenerate into suicidal trench warfare. With the outbreak of the war, the "Russian steamroller" immediately moved into eastern Germany. Very badly damaged by the Germans under Generals Paul von Hindenburg and Erich Ludendorff at the battles of Tannenberg and the Masurian Lakes in August and September 1914, Russia never threatened Germany again. On the Austrian front, enormous armies seesawed back and forth, suffering enormous losses. Austro-Hungarian armies were repulsed twice by little Serbia in bitter fighting. But with the help of German forces, they reversed the Russian advances of 1914 and forced the Russians to retreat deep into their own territory in the eastern campaign of 1915. A staggering 2.5 million Russians were killed, wounded, or taken prisoner that year.

These changing tides of victory and hopes of territorial gains brought neutral countries into the war (Map 32.3). In Europe Italy, a member of the Triple Alliance since 1882, had declared its neutrality in 1914 on the grounds that Austria had launched a war of aggression. Then, in May 1915, Italy joined the Triple Entente of Great Britain, France, and Russia in return for promises of Austrian territory. Bulgaria also declared its neutrality in 1914. But after the Ottoman Empire joined in October 1914 with Austria and Germany, now known as the Central Powers, Bulgaria weighed enticing promises from all sides. In September 1915 it decided to follow the Ottoman Empire's lead in order to settle old scores with Serbia. Bulgarian and German armies were successful, and

The Fruits of War   The extent of carnage, the emotional damage, and the physical destruction were equally unprecedented. Once great cathedrals standing in ruin symbolized the disaster. *(Source: UPI/Bettmann Newsphotos)*

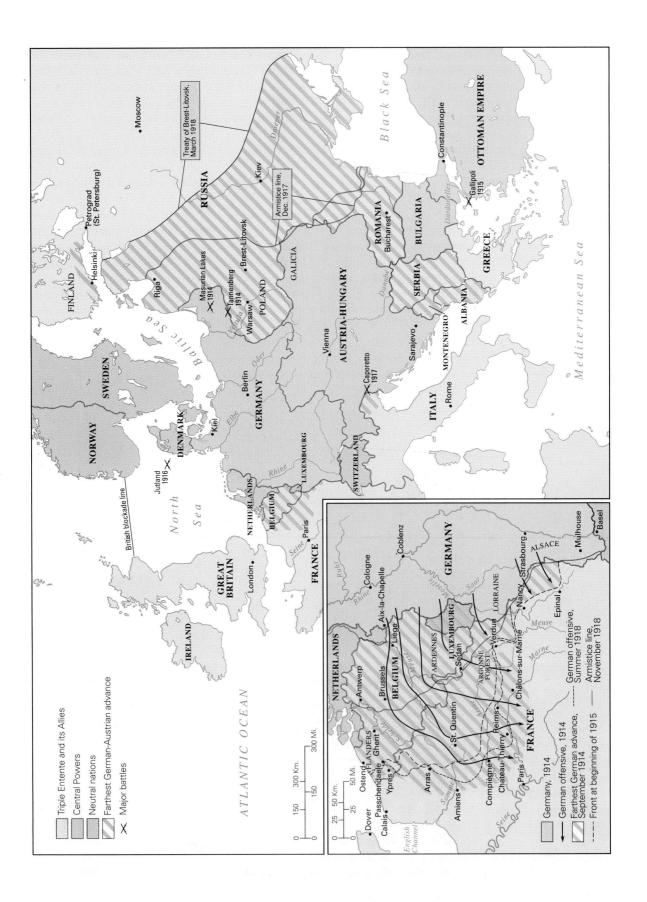

Main map labels

ATLANTIC OCEAN

IRELAND

GREAT BRITAIN
London

North Sea

NORWAY

SWEDEN

DENMARK
Kiel

Jutland 1916 ✕

British blockade line

Baltic Sea

FINLAND
Helsinki

Petrograd (St. Petersburg)

Moscow

RUSSIA

Dnieper

Treaty of Brest-Litovsk, March 1918

Armistice line, Dec. 1917

Black Sea

Kiev

Riga

Masurian Lakes 1914 ✕

Vistula

Tannenberg 1914 ✕

Brest-Litovsk

POLAND

Warsaw

GALICIA

Oder

Berlin

GERMANY

Elbe

Rhine

NETHERLANDS

BELGIUM

LUXEMBOURG

Paris

Seine

FRANCE

SWITZERLAND

Vienna

AUSTRIA-HUNGARY

Caporetto 1917 ✕

ITALY

Rome

Sarajevo

SERBIA

MONTENEGRO

ALBANIA

BULGARIA

ROMANIA

Bucharest

Danube

GREECE

Constantinople

Dardanelles

OTTOMAN EMPIRE

Gallipoli 1915 ✕

Mediterranean Sea

Legend

Triple Entente and its Allies

Central Powers

Neutral nations

Farthest German-Austrian advance

✕ Major battles

Scale: 0   150   300 Km.
0   150   300 Mi.

Inset map labels

English Channel

Dover

Calais

Ostend

Passchendaele

Ypres

FLANDERS

Ghent

Antwerp

Brussels

BELGIUM

Liège

Aix-la-Chapelle

Cologne

Coblenz

Ruhr

Rhine

GERMANY

Moselle

NETHERLANDS

ARDENNES

LUXEMBOURG

Sedan

ARGONNE FOREST

Verdun

LORRAINE

Saar

Nancy

Strasbourg

ALSACE

Mulhouse

Basel

Epinal

Meuse

Châlons-sur-Marne

Marne

Reims

Château-Thierry

Compiègne

St. Quentin

Somme

Arras

Amiens

Paris

Seine

FRANCE

Inset legend

Germany, 1914

German offensive, 1914

Farthest German advance, September 1914

Front at beginning of 1915

German offensive, Summer 1918

Armistice line, November 1918

Scale: 0   25   50 Km.
0   25   50 Mi.

the Central Powers occupied all of the Balkans, with the exception of Greece.

The entry of the Ottoman Turks carried the war into the Middle East, a momentous development. Heavy fighting with Russia saw bloody battle lines seesawing back and forth. In 1915 British forces tried to take the Dardanelles and Constantinople from Turkey, but they were badly defeated. The British were more successful at inciting Arab nationalists against their Turkish overlords. An enigmatic British colonel, soon known to millions as Lawrence of Arabia, helped lead the Arab revolt in early 1917. In 1918 British armies totally smashed the old Ottoman state, drawing primarily on imperial forces from Egypt, India, Australia, and New Zealand. Thus war brought revolutionary change to the Middle East (see pages 1075–1079).

War also spread to some parts of East Asia and Africa. Instead of revolting as the Germans hoped, the colonial subjects of the British and French supported their foreign masters, providing critical supplies and fighting in armies in Europe and in the Ottoman Empire. They also helped local British and French commanders seize Germany's colonies around the globe. The Japanese, allied in Asia with the British since 1902, similarly used the war to grab German outposts in the Pacific Ocean and on the Chinese mainland, infuriating Chinese patriots and heightening long-standing tensions between the two countries.

Another crucial development in the expanding conflict came in April 1917, when the United States declared war on Germany. American intervention grew out of the war at sea, sympathy for the entente, and the increasing desperation of total war. At the beginning of the war, Britain and France had established a total naval blockade to strangle the Central Powers and prevent deliveries of food and raw materials. No neutral ship could sail to Germany with any cargo. The blockade irked Americans, but effective propaganda over German atrocities in occupied Belgium and lush profits from selling war supplies to Britain and France blunted American indignation.

MAP 32.3 The First World War in Europe The trench war on the western front was concentrated in Belgium and northern France. The war in the east encompassed an enormous territory.

Moreover, in early 1915 Germany launched a counter-blockade using the murderously effective submarine, a new weapon that violated traditional niceties of fair warning under international law. In May 1915, after sinking about ninety ships in the British war zone, a German submarine sank the British passenger liner *Lusitania,* which was carrying arms and munitions as well as passengers. More than a thousand lives, among them 139 Americans, were lost. President Woodrow Wilson protested vigorously, forcing Germany to relax its submarine warfare for almost two years; the alternative would have been almost certain U.S. entry into the war.

Early in 1917, the German military command—confident that improved submarines could starve its island enemy, Britain, into submission before the United States could come to Britain's rescue—resumed unrestricted submarine warfare. Like the invasion of Belgium, this was a reckless gamble. British shipping losses reached staggering proportions, though by late 1917 naval strategists came up with the inevitable effective response: the convoy system for safe transatlantic shipping. In the meantime, President Wilson had told a sympathetic Congress and people that the "German submarine warfare against commerce is a warfare against mankind." Thus the last uncommitted great nation, as fresh and enthusiastic as Europe had been in 1914, entered the world war in April 1917, almost three years after it had begun. Eventually the United States was to tip the balance in favor of the Triple Entente and its allies.

THE HOME FRONT

The widening Great War had significant economic, social, and political repercussions for the people on the home front. The people behind the lines were tremendously involved in the titanic struggle. War's impact on them was no less massive than on the men crouched in the trenches.

Mobilizing for Total War

In August 1914 most people in Europe greeted the outbreak of hostilities enthusiastically. The masses in every country believed that their nation was in the right and defending itself from aggression. With the exception of a few extreme left-wingers, even socialists supported the war. Tough standby plans to imprison socialist leaders and break general strikes protesting the war proved quite unnecessary in 1914. Everywhere patriotic support of the masses and the working class contributed to national unity and an energetic war effort.

By mid-October generals and politicians began to realize that more than patriotism would be needed to win the war, whose end was not in sight. Each country experienced a relentless, desperate demand for men and weapons. Countless shortages quickly developed. In each European country economic life and organization had to change and change fast to keep the war machine from sputtering to a stop. And change they did.

In each country a government of national unity began to plan and control economic and social life in order to wage "total war." Free-market capitalism was abandoned, at least "for the duration." Instead, government planning boards established priorities and decided what was to be produced and consumed. Rationing, price and wage controls, and even restrictions on workers' freedom of movement were imposed by government. Only through such regimentation could a country make the greatest possible military effort. Thus, though there were national variations, the great nations all moved toward planned economies commanded by the established political leadership.

The economy of total war blurred the old distinction between soldiers on the battlefield and civilians at home. The war was a war of whole peoples and entire populations, and the loser would be the society that cracked first. Interestingly enough, the ability of governments to manage and control highly complicated economies strengthened the cause of socialism. With the First World War, socialism became for the first time a realistic economic blueprint rather than a utopian program.

Germany illustrates the general trend. It also went furthest in developing a planned economy to wage total war. As soon as war began, Walter Rathenau, the talented, foresighted Jewish industrialist in charge of Germany's largest electrical company, convinced the government to set up a War Raw Materials Board to ration and distribute raw materials. Under Rathenau's direction, every useful material from foreign oil to barnyard manure

was inventoried and rationed. Moreover, the board launched spectacularly successful attempts to produce substitutes, such as synthetic rubber and synthetic nitrates, which were essential to the German war machine.

Food was also rationed in accordance with physical need. Men and women doing hard manual work were given extra rations. During the last two years of the war, only children and expectant mothers received milk rations. At the same time, Germany failed to tax the war profits of private firms heavily enough. This failure contributed to massive deficit financing, inflation, the growth of a black market, and the eventual re-emergence of class conflict.

Following the terrible battles of Verdun and the Somme in 1916, the military leaders Hindenburg and Ludendorff became the real rulers of Germany, and they decreed the ultimate mobilization for total war. Germany, said Hindenburg, could win only "if all the treasures of our soil that agriculture and industry can produce are used exclusively for the conduct of War. . . . All other considerations must come second."[4] This goal, they believed, required that every German man, woman, and child be drafted into the service of the war. Thus, in December 1916, the military leaders rammed through the parliament the Auxiliary Service Law, which required all males between seventeen and sixty to work only at jobs considered critical to the war effort.

Although women and children were not specifically mentioned, this forced-labor law was also aimed at them. Many women already worked in war factories, mines, and steel mills, where they labored like men at the heaviest and most dangerous jobs. With the passage of the Auxiliary Service Law, many more women followed. Children were organized by their teachers into garbage brigades to collect every scrap of useful material: grease strained from dishwater, coffee grounds, waste paper, tin cans, metal door knockers, bottles, rags, hair, bones, and so forth, as well as acorns, chestnuts, pine cones, and rotting leaves. Potatoes gave way to turnips, and people averaged little more than a thousand calories a day. Thus in Germany total war led to the establishment of history's first "totalitarian" society, and war production increased while some people literally starved to death.

Great Britain mobilized for total war less rapidly and less completely than Germany, for it could im-

Waging Total War A British war plant strains to meet the insatiable demand for trench-smashing heavy artillery shells. Quite typically, many of these defense workers are women. *(Source: By courtesy of the Trustees of the Imperial War Museum)*

port materials from its empire and from the United States. By 1915, however, a serious shortage of shells led to the establishment of a Ministry of Munitions under David Lloyd George. The ministry organized private industry to produce for the war, controlled profits, allocated labor, fixed wage rates, and settled labor disputes. By December 1916, when Lloyd George became prime minister, the British economy was largely planned and regulated. More than two hundred factories and 90 percent of all imports were bought and allocated directly by the state. Subsequently, even food was strictly rationed. War production continued to soar. Great Britain followed successfully in Germany's footsteps.

The Social Impact

The social impact of total war was no less profound than the economic impact, though again there were important national variations. The millions of men at the front and the insatiable needs of the military created a tremendous demand for workers. Jobs were available for everyone. This situation had seldom if ever been seen before 1914, when unemployment and poverty had been facts of urban life. The exceptional demand for labor brought about momentous changes.

One such change was greater power and prestige for labor unions. Having proved their loyalty in August 1914, labor unions became an indispensable partner of government and private industry in the planned war economies. Unions cooperated with war governments on work rules, wages, and production schedules in return for real participation in important decisions. This entry of labor leaders and unions into policy-making councils paralleled the entry of socialist leaders into the war governments.

The role of women changed dramatically. In every country, large numbers of women left home and domestic service to work in industry, transportation, and offices. By 1917 women formed fully 43 percent of the labor force in Russia. Moreover, women became highly visible—not only as munitions workers but as bank tellers, mail carriers, even police officers.

At first, the male-dominated unions were hostile to women moving into new occupations, believing that their presence would lower wages and change work rules. But government pressure and the principle of equal pay for equal work (at least until the end of the war) overcame these objections. Women also served as nurses and doctors at the front. In general, the war greatly expanded the range of women's activities and changed attitudes toward them. As a direct result of women's many-sided war effort, Britain, Germany, and Austria granted women the right to vote immediately after the war. Women also showed a growing spirit of independence during the war as they started to bob their hair, shorten their skirts, and smoke in public.

War also promoted social equality, blurring class distinctions and lessening the gap between rich and poor. This blurring was most apparent in Great Britain, where wartime hardship was never extreme. In fact, the bottom third of the population generally lived better than ever before, for the poorest gained most from the severe shortage of labor. The English writer Robert Roberts recalled how his parents' tiny grocery store in the slums of Manchester thrived as never before during the war, when people who had scrimped to buy bread and soup bones were able to afford fancy cakes and thick steaks. In continental countries greater equality was reflected in full employment, ration-

Wartime Propaganda was skillful and effective. The poster on the left spurred men to volunteer for military service before the draft was introduced in Britain in 1916. The poster on the right appeals to patriotism and the love of family as it urges the French to buy another batch of war bonds. *(Source: By courtesy of the Trustees of the Imperial War Museum)*

ing according to physical need, and a sharing of hardship. There, too, society became more uniform and more egalitarian, in spite of some war profiteering.

Death itself had no respect for traditional social distinctions. It savagely decimated the young aristocratic officers who led the charge, and it fell heavily on the mass of drafted peasants and unskilled workers who followed. Yet death often spared the aristocrats of labor, the skilled workers and foremen. Their lives were too valuable to squander at the front, for they were needed to train and direct the newly recruited women and older unskilled men laboring valiantly in war plants at home.

Growing Political Tensions

During the first two years of war, most soldiers and civilians supported their governments. Even in Austria-Hungary—the most vulnerable of the belligerents, with its competing nationalities—loyalty to the state and monarchy remained astonishingly strong through 1916. Belief in a just cause, patriotic nationalism, the planned economy, and a sharing of burdens united peoples behind their various national leaders. Furthermore, each government did its best to control public opinion to bolster morale. Newspapers, letters, and public addresses were rigorously censored. Good news was overstated; bad news was repressed or distorted.

Each government used both crude and subtle propaganda to maintain popular support. German propaganda hysterically pictured black soldiers from France's African empire raping German women, and German atrocities in Belgium and elsewhere were ceaselessly recounted and exaggerated by the French and British. Patriotic posters and slogans, slanted news, and biased editorials inflamed national hatreds and helped sustain superhuman efforts.

By the spring of 1916, however, people were beginning to crack under the strain of total war. In April 1916, Irish nationalists in Dublin tried to take advantage of this situation and rose up against British rule in their Easter Rebellion. A week of bitter fighting passed before the rebels were crushed and their leaders executed. Strikes and protest marches over inadequate food began to flare up on every home front. Soldiers' morale began to decline. Italian troops mutinied. Numerous French units refused to fight after General Nivelle's disastrous offensive of May 1917. A rising tide of war-weariness and defeatism also swept France's civilian population before Georges Clemenceau emerged as a ruthless and effective wartime leader in November 1917. Clemenceau established a virtual dictatorship, pouncing on strikers and jailing without trial journalists and politicians who dared to suggest a compromise peace with Germany.

The strains were worse for the Central Powers. In October 1916, the chief minister of Austria was assassinated by a young socialist crying, "Down with Absolutism! We want peace!"[5] The following month, when the feeble old Emperor Francis Joseph died sixty-eight years after his mother Sophia had pushed him onto the throne in 1848 (see page 891), a symbol of unity disappeared. In spite of absolute censorship, political dissatisfaction and conflicts among nationalities grew. In April 1917, Austria's chief minister summed up the situation in the gloomiest possible terms. The country and army were exhausted. Another winter of war would bring revolution and disintegration, he predicted. The allied blockade kept tightening; people were starving.

The strain of total war and of the Auxiliary Service Law was also evident in Germany. In the winter of 1916 to 1917, Germany's military position appeared increasingly desperate. Stalemates and losses in the west were matched by temporary Russian advances in the east. Thus the military insisted on the all-or-nothing gamble of unrestricted submarine warfare when the Entente refused in December 1916 to consider peace on terms favorable to the Central Powers.

Also, the national political unity of the first two years of war was collapsing as the social conflict of prewar Germany re-emerged. A growing minority of socialists in the parliament began to vote against war credits, calling for a compromise "peace without annexations or reparations." In July 1917, a coalition of socialists and Catholics passed a resolution in the parliament to that effect. Such a peace was unthinkable for conservatives and military leaders. So also was the surge in revolutionary agitation and strikes by war-weary workers that occurred in early 1917. When the bread ration was further reduced in April, more than 200,000 workers struck and demonstrated for a week in Berlin, returning to work only under the threat of prison and military discipline. Thus militaristic Germany, like its ally Austria-Hungary (and its enemy France), was beginning to crack in 1917. Yet it was Russia that collapsed first and saved the Central Powers, for a time.

THE RUSSIAN REVOLUTION

The Russian Revolution of 1917 was one of modern history's most momentous events. Directly related to the growing tensions of the First World War, its significance went far beyond the wartime agonies of a single European nation. The Russian Revolution opened a new era. For some it was Marx's socialist vision come true; for others, it was the triumph of dictatorship. To all, it presented a radically new prototype of state and society.

The Fall of Imperial Russia

Like its allies and its enemies, Russia embraced war with patriotic enthusiasm in 1914. At the Winter Palace, while throngs of people knelt and sang "God Save the Tsar," Tsar Nicholas II (r. 1894–1917) repeated the oath that Alexander I had made in 1812 and vowed never to make peace as long as the enemy stood on Russian soil. Russia's lower house, the Duma, voted war credits. Conservatives anticipated expansion in the Balkans, while liberals and most socialists believed alliance with Britain and France would bring democratic reforms. For a moment, Russia was united.

Soon, however, the strains of war began to take their toll. Unprecedented artillery barrages used up Russia's supplies of shells and ammunition, and better-equipped German armies inflicted terrible losses. For a time in 1915, substantial numbers of Russian soldiers were sent to the front without rifles; they were told to find their arms among the dead. There were 2 million Russian casualties in 1915 alone. Morale declined among soldiers and civilians. Nonetheless, Russia's battered peasant army did not collapse but continued to fight courageously until early 1917.

Under the shock of defeat, Russia moved toward full mobilization on the home front. The Duma and organs of local government took the lead, setting up special committees to coordinate defense, industry, transportation, and agriculture. These efforts improved the military situation, and Rus-

sian factories produced more than twice as many shells in 1916 as in 1915. Yet there were many failures, and Russia mobilized less effectively for total war than the other warring nations.

The great problem was leadership. Under the constitution resulting from the revolution of 1905 (see pages 944–945), the tsar had retained complete control over the bureaucracy and the army. Legislation proposed by the Duma, which was weighted in favor of the wealthy and conservative classes, was subject to the tsar's veto. Moreover, Nicholas II fervently wished to maintain the sacred inheritance of supreme royal power, which with the Orthodox church was for him the key to Russia's greatness. A kindly, slightly stupid man, Nicholas failed to form a close partnership with his citizens in order to fight the war more effectively. He relied instead on the old bureaucratic apparatus, distrusting the moderate Duma, rejecting popular involvement, and resisting calls to share power.

As a result, the Duma, the educated middle classes, and the masses became increasingly critical of the tsar's leadership. Following Nicholas's belated dismissal of the incompetent minister of war, demands for more democratic and responsive government exploded in the Duma in the summer of 1915. In September, parties ranging from conservative to moderate socialist formed the Progressive Bloc, which called for a completely new government responsible to the Duma instead of to the tsar. In answer, Nicholas temporarily adjourned the Duma and announced that he was traveling to the front in order to lead and rally Russia's armies.

His departure was a fatal turning point. With the tsar in the field with the troops, control of the government was taken over by the hysterical empress, Tsarina Alexandra, and a debauched adventurer, the monk Rasputin. A minor German princess and granddaughter of England's Queen Victoria, Nicholas's wife was a devoted mother with a sick child, a strong-willed woman with a hatred of parliaments. Having constantly urged her husband to rule absolutely, Alexandra tried to do so herself in his absence. She seated and unseated the top ministers. Her most trusted adviser was "our Friend Grigori," an uneducated Siberian preacher who was appropriately nicknamed Rasputin—the "Degenerate."

Rasputin began his career with a sect noted for mixing sexual orgies with religious ecstasies, and his influence rested on mysterious healing powers.

Alexis, Alexandra's fifth child and heir to the throne, suffered from a rare disease, hemophilia. The tiniest cut meant uncontrollable bleeding, terrible pain, and possible death. Medical science could do nothing. Only Rasputin could miraculously stop the bleeding, perhaps through hypnosis. The empress's faith in Rasputin was limitless. "Believe more in our Friend," she wrote her husband in 1916. "He lives for you and Russia." In this atmosphere of unreality, the government slid steadily toward revolution.

In a desperate attempt to right the situation and end unfounded rumors that Rasputin was the empress's lover, three members of the high aristocracy murdered Rasputin in December 1916. The empress went into semipermanent shock, her mind haunted by the dead man's prophecy: "If I die or you desert me, in six months you will lose your son

and your throne."[6] Food shortages in the cities worsened, morale declined. On March 8, women in Petrograd (formerly St. Petersburg) calling for bread started riots, which spontaneously spread to the factories and throughout the city. From the front the tsar ordered the troops to restore order, but discipline broke down and the soldiers joined the revolutionary crowd. The Duma responded by declaring a provisional government on March 12, 1917. Three days later, Nicholas abdicated without protest.

The Provisional Government

The March revolution was the result of an unplanned uprising of hungry, angry people in the capital, but it was joyfully accepted throughout the

Mass Demonstrations in Petrograd in June 1917 showed a surge of working-class support for the Bolsheviks. In this photo a few banners of the Mensheviks and other moderate socialists are drowned in a sea of Bolshevik slogans. *(Source: Sovfoto)*

country. The patriotic upper and middle classes rejoiced at the prospect of a more determined and effective war effort, while workers happily anticipated better wages and more food. All classes and political parties called for liberty and democracy. They were not disappointed. As Lenin said, Russia became the freest country in the world. After generations of arbitrary authoritarianism, the provisional government quickly established equality before the law; freedom of religion, speech, and assembly; the right of unions to organize and strike; and the rest of the classic liberal program.

Yet both the liberal and the moderate socialist leaders of the provisional government rejected social revolution. The reorganized government formed in May 1917, which included the fiery agrarian socialist Alexander Kerensky, refused to confiscate large landholdings and give them to peasants, fearing that such drastic action in the countryside would only complete the disintegration of Russia's peasant army. For the patriotic Kerensky, as for other moderate socialists, the continuation of war was still the all-important national duty. There would be plenty of time for land reform later, and thus all the government's efforts were directed toward a last offensive in July. Human suffering and war-weariness grew, sapping the limited strength of the provisional government.

From its first day, the provisional government had to share power with a formidable rival—the Petrograd Soviet (or council) of Workers' and Soldiers' Deputies. Modeled on the revolutionary soviets of 1905, the Petrograd Soviet was a huge, fluctuating mass meeting of two to three thousand workers, soldiers, and socialist intellectuals. Seeing itself as a true grass-roots revolutionary democracy, this counter- or half-government suspiciously watched the provisional government and issued its own radical orders, further weakening the provisional government. The most famous of these orders was Army Order No. 1, issued to all Russian military forces as the provisional government was forming.

Order No. 1 stripped officers of their authority and placed power in the hands of elected committees of common soldiers. Designed to protect the revolution from some counter-revolutionary Bonaparte on horseback, Army Order No. 1 instead led to a total collapse of army discipline. Many an officer was hanged for his sins. Meanwhile, following the foolhardy summer offensive,

masses of peasant soldiers began "voting with their feet," to use Lenin's graphic phrase. They began returning to their villages to help their families get a share of the land, land that peasants were simply seizing as they settled old scores in a great agrarian upheaval. All across the country, liberty was turning into anarchy in the summer of 1917. It was an unparalleled opportunity for the most radical and most talented of Russia's many socialist leaders, Vladimir Ilyich Lenin (1870–1924).

Lenin and the Bolshevik Revolution

Lenin's whole life was dedicated to the cause of revolution. He was born into the middle class and at seventeen became an implacable enemy of imperial Russia when his older brother was executed for plotting to kill the tsar in 1887. As a law student he began searching for a revolutionary faith. He found it in Marxian socialism, which began to win converts among radical intellectuals as industrialization surged forward in Russia in the 1890s. Exiled to Siberia for three years because of socialist agitation, Lenin studied Marxist doctrines with religious intensity. After his release, he joined fellow believers in western Europe. There Lenin lived for seventeen years and developed his own revolutionary interpretations of the body of Marxian thought.

Three interrelated ideas were central for Lenin. First, turning to the early fire-breathing Marx of 1848 and the *Communist Manifesto* for inspiration, Lenin stressed that capitalism could be destroyed only by violent revolution. He tirelessly denounced all revisionist theories of a peaceful evolution to socialism as betraying Marx's message of unending class conflict. Lenin's second, more original, idea was that under certain conditions a socialist revolution was possible even in a relatively backward country like Russia. Though capitalism was not fully developed there and the industrial working class was small, the peasants were poor and thus potential revolutionaries.

Lenin believed that at a given moment revolution was determined more by human leadership than by vast historical laws. Thus came Lenin's third basic idea: the necessity of a highly disciplined workers' party, strictly controlled by a dedicated elite of intellectuals and full-time revolutionaries like Lenin himself. Unlike ordinary workers and trade-union officials, this elite would never be seduced by short-term gains. It would not stop until revolution brought it to power.

Lenin's theories and methods did not go unchallenged by other Russian Marxists. At the meetings of the Russian Social Democratic Labor party in London in 1903, matters came to a head. Lenin demanded a small, disciplined, elitist party; his opponents wanted a more democratic party with mass membership. The Russian party of Marxian socialism promptly split into two factions. Lenin's camp was called Bolsheviks, or "Majority group"; his opponents were Mensheviks, or "Minority group." Lenin's majority did not last, but Lenin did not care. He kept the fine-sounding name Bolshevik and developed the party he wanted: tough, disciplined, revolutionary.

Unlike most socialists, Lenin did not rally round the national flag in 1914. Observing events from neutral Switzerland, he saw the war as a product of imperialistic rivalries and a marvelous opportunity for class war and socialist upheaval. The March revolution was, Lenin felt, a step in that direction. Since propaganda and internal subversion were accepted weapons of total war, the German government graciously provided the impatient Lenin, his wife, and about twenty trusted colleagues with safe passage across Germany and back into Russia in April 1917. The Germans hoped that Lenin would undermine the sagging war effort of the world's freest society. They were not disappointed.

Arriving triumphantly at Petrograd's Finland Station on April 3, Lenin attacked at once. To the great astonishment of the local Bolsheviks, he rejected all cooperation with the "bourgeois" provisional government of the liberals and moderate socialists. His slogans were radical in the extreme: "All power to the Soviets." "All land to the peasants." "Stop the war now." Never a slave to Marxist determinism, the brilliant but not unduly intellectual Lenin was a superb tactician. The moment was now.

Yet Lenin almost overplayed his hand. An attempt by the Bolsheviks to seize power in July collapsed, and Lenin fled and went into hiding. He was charged with being a German agent, and indeed he and the Bolsheviks were getting money from Germany.[7] But no matter. Intrigue between Kerensky, who became prime minister in July, and his commander in chief General Lavr Kornilov, a popular war hero "with the heart of a lion and the brains of a sheep," resulted in Kornilov's leading a feeble attack against the provisional government in

Valdimir Lenin   Dramatically displaying both his burning determination and his skill as a revolutionary orator, Lenin addresses the victorious May Day celebration of 1918 in Moscow's Red Square. *(Source: Culver Pictures)*

September. In the face of this rightist "counterrevolutionary" threat, the Bolsheviks were rearmed and redeemed. Kornilov's forces disintegrated, but Kerensky lost all credit with the army, the only force that might have saved him and democratic government in Russia.

Trotsky and the Seizure of Power

Throughout the summer, the Bolsheviks had appealed very effectively to the workers and soldiers of Petrograd, markedly increasing their popular support. Party membership had soared from

THE RUSSIAN REVOLUTION

1914	Russia enthusiastically enters the First World War
1915	Two million Russian casualties
	Progressive Bloc calls for a new government responsible to the Duma rather than to the tsar
	Tsar Nicholas adjourns the Duma and departs for the front; control of the government falls to Alexandra and Rasputin
December 1916	Murder of Rasputin
March 8, 1917	Bread riots in Petrograd (St. Petersburg)
March 12, 1917	Duma declares a provisional government
March 15, 1917	Tsar Nicholas abdicates without protest
April 3, 1917	Lenin returns from exile and denounces the provisional government
May 1917	Reorganized provisional government, including Kerensky, continues the war
	Petrograd Soviet issues Army Order no. 1, granting military power to committees of common soldiers
Summer 1917	Agrarian upheavals: peasants seize estates, peasant soldiers desert the army to participate
October 1917	Bolsheviks gain a majority in the Petrograd Soviet
November 6, 1917	Bolsheviks seize power; Lenin heads the new "provisional workers' and peasants' government"
November 1917	Lenin ratifies peasant seizure of land and worker control of factories; all banks nationalized
January 1918	Lenin permanently disbands the Constituent Assembly
February 1918	Lenin convinces the Bolshevik Central Committee to accept a humiliating peace with Germany in order to pursue the revolution
March 1918	Treaty of Brest-Litovsk: Russia loses one-third of its population
	Trotsky as war commissar begins to rebuild the Russian army
	Government moves from Petrograd to Moscow
1918–1920	Great Civil War
Summer 1918	Eighteen competing regional governments; White armies oppose the Bolshevik revolution
1919	White armies on the offensive but divided politically; they receive little benefit from Allied intervention
1920	Lenin and Red armies victorious, retaking Belorussia and the Ukraine

50,000 to 240,000, and in October the Bolsheviks gained a fragile majority in the Petrograd Soviet. Moreover, Lenin had found a strong right arm—Leon Trotsky, the second most important person in the Russian Revolution.

A spellbinding revolutionary orator and independent radical Marxist, Trotsky (1877–1940) supported Lenin wholeheartedly in 1917. It was he who brilliantly executed the Bolshevik seizure of power. Painting a vivid but untruthful picture of German and counter-revolutionary plots, Trotsky first convinced the Petrograd Soviet to form a special Military-Revolutionary Committee

in October and make him its leader. Military power in the capital passed into Bolshevik hands. Trotsky's second master stroke was to insist that the Bolsheviks reduce opposition to their coup by taking power in the name, not of the Bolsheviks, but of the more popular and democratic soviets, which were meeting in Petrograd from all over Russia in early November. On the night of November 6, militants from Trotsky's committee joined with trusty Bolshevik soldiers to seize government buildings and pounce on members of the provisional government. Then on to the congress of soviets! There a Bolshevik majority—roughly

390 of 650 turbulent delegates—declared that all power had passed to the soviets and named Lenin head of the new government.

The Bolsheviks came to power for three key reasons. First, by late 1917 democracy had given way to anarchy: power was there for those who would take it. Second, in Lenin and Trotsky the Bolsheviks had an utterly determined and truly superior leadership, which both the tsarist government and the provisional government lacked. Third, in 1917 the Bolsheviks succeeded in appealing to many soldiers and urban workers, people who were exhausted by war and eager for socialism. With time, many workers would become bitterly disappointed, but for the moment they had good reason to believe that they had won what they wanted.

Dictatorship and Civil War

History is full of short-lived coups and unsuccessful revolutions. The truly monumental accomplishment of Lenin, Trotsky, and the rest of the Bolsheviks was not taking power but keeping it. In the next four years, the Bolsheviks went on to conquer the chaos they had helped to create, and they began to build their kind of socialist society. How was this done?

Lenin had the genius to profit from developments over which he and the Bolsheviks had no control. Since summer, a peasant revolution had been sweeping across Russia as the tillers of the soil invaded and divided among themselves the great and not-so-great estates of the landlords and the church. Peasant seizure of the land—a Russian 1789—was not very Marxist, but it was quite unstoppable in 1917. Thus Lenin's first law, which supposedly gave land to the peasants, actually merely approved what peasants were already doing. Urban workers' great demand in November was direct control of individual factories by local workers' committees. This, too, Lenin ratified with a decree in November.

Unlike many of his colleagues, Lenin acknowledged that Russia had lost the war with Germany, that the Russian army had ceased to exist, and that the only realistic goal was peace at any price. The price was very high. Germany demanded in December 1917 that the Soviet government give up all its western territories. These areas were inhabited by Poles, Finns, Lithuanians, and other non-

Russians—all those peoples who had been conquered by the tsars over three centuries and put into the "prisonhouse of nationalities," as Lenin had earlier called the Russian Empire.

At first, Lenin's fellow Bolsheviks would not accept such great territorial losses. But when German armies resumed their unopposed march into Russia in February 1918, Lenin had his way in a very close vote in the Central Committee of the party. In the words of a noted American scholar, "Not even his greatest enemy can deny that at this moment Lenin towered like a giant over his Bolshevik colleagues."[8] A third of old Russia's population was sliced away by the German meat ax in the Treaty of Brest-Litovsk in March 1918. With peace, Lenin escaped the certain disaster of continued war and could uncompromisingly pursue his goal of absolute political power for the Bolsheviks—now renamed Communists—within Russia.

In November 1917, the Bolsheviks had proclaimed their regime only a "provisional workers' and peasants' government," promising that a freely elected Constituent Assembly would draw up a new constitution. But the freest elections in Russia's history—both before and after 1917—produced a stunning setback for the Bolsheviks, who won less than one-fourth of the elected delegates. The Socialist Revolutionaries—the peasants' party—had a clear majority. The Constituent Assembly met for only one day, on January 18, 1918. It was then permanently disbanded by Bolshevik soldiers acting under Lenin's orders. Thus, even before the peace with Germany, Lenin was forming a one-party government.

The dissolution of the democratically elected Constituent Assembly helped feed the flames of civil war. People who had risen up for self-rule in November saw that once again they were getting dictatorship from the capital. For the next three years, "Long live the democratic soviets; down with the Bolsheviks" was to be a popular slogan. The officers of the old army took the lead in organizing the "White" opposition to the Bolsheviks in southern Russia and the Ukraine, in Siberia, and to the west of Petrograd. The Whites came from many social groups and were united only by their hatred of the Bolsheviks—the Reds.

By the summer of 1918, fully eighteen self-proclaimed regional governments—several of which represented minority nationalities—competed with Lenin's Bolsheviks in Moscow. By the end of the year, White armies were on the attack.

In October 1919, it appeared that they might triumph as they closed in on Lenin's government from three sides. Yet they did not. By the spring of 1920, the White armies had been almost completely defeated, and the Bolshevik Red Army had retaken Belorussia and the Ukraine. The following year, the Communists also reconquered the independent nationalist governments of the Caucasus. The civil war was over; Lenin had won.

Lenin and the Bolsheviks won for several reasons. Strategically, they controlled the center while the Whites were always on the fringes and disunited. Moreover, the poorly defined political program of the Whites was vaguely conservative, and it did not unite all the foes of the Bolsheviks under a progressive, democratic banner. Most important, the Communists quickly developed a better army, an army for which the divided Whites were no match.

Once again, Trotsky's leadership was decisive. The Bolsheviks had preached democracy in the army and had elected officers in 1917. But beginning in March 1918, Trotsky as war commissar re-established the draft and drastic discipline for the newly formed Red Army. Soldiers deserting or disobeying an order were summarily shot. Moreover, Trotsky made effective use of former tsarist army officers, who were actively recruited and given unprecedented powers of discipline over their troops. In short, Trotsky formed a disciplined and effective fighting force.

The Bolsheviks also mobilized the home front. Establishing "war communism"—the application of the total-war concept to a civil conflict—they seized grain from peasants, introduced rationing, nationalized all banks and industry, and required everyone to work. These measures served to maintain labor discipline and to keep the Red Army supplied.

"Revolutionary terror" also contributed to the Communist victory. The old tsarist secret police was re-established as the Cheka, which hunted down and executed thousands of real or supposed foes, like the tsar's family and other "class enemies." Moreover, people were shot or threatened with being shot for minor nonpolitical failures. The Cheka sowed fear, and fear silenced opposition.

Finally, foreign military intervention in the civil war ended up helping the Communists. After Lenin made peace with Germany, the Allies (the Americans, British, and Japanese) sent troops to Archangel and Vladivostok to prevent war matériel that they had sent the provisional government from being captured by the Germans. After the Soviet government nationalized all foreign-owned factories without compensation and refused to pay all of Russia's foreign debts, Western governments and particularly France began to support White armies. Yet these efforts were small and halfhearted. In 1919 Western peoples were sick of war, and few Western politicians believed in a military crusade against the Bolsheviks. Thus Allied intervention in the civil war did not aid the Whites effectively, though it did permit the Communists to appeal to the patriotic nationalism of ethnic Russians, which was particularly strong among former tsarist army officers. Allied intervention was both too little and too much.

The Russian Revolution and the Bolshevik triumph was, then, one of the reasons the First World War was such a great turning point in modern history. A radically new government, based on socialism and one-party dictatorship, came to power in a great European state, maintained power, and encouraged worldwide revolution. Although halfhearted constitutional monarchy in Russia was undoubtedly headed for some kind of political crisis before 1914, it is hard to imagine the triumph of the most radical proponents of change and reform except in a situation of total collapse. That was precisely what happened to Russia in the First World War.

THE PEACE SETTLEMENT

Victory over revolutionary Russia boosted sagging German morale, and in the spring of 1918 the Germans launched their last major attack against France. Yet this offensive failed like those before it. With breathtaking rapidity, the United States, Great Britain, and France decisively defeated Germany militarily. Bulgaria also collapsed. Austria-Hungary and the Ottoman Empire broke apart and ceased to exist. The guns of world war finally fell silent. Then, as civil war spread in Russia and as chaos engulfed much of eastern Europe and the Middle East, the victorious Western Allies came together in Paris to establish a lasting peace.

Expectations were high; optimism was almost unlimited. The Allies labored intensively and soon worked out terms for peace with Germany and for the creation of the peace-keeping League of Nations. Nevertheless, the hopes of peoples and politicians were soon disappointed, for the peace settlement of 1919 turned out to be a terrible failure. Rather than creating conditions for peace, it sowed the seeds of another war. Surely this was the ultimate tragedy of the Great War, a war that left 10 million dead and another 20 million wounded. How did it happen? Why was the peace settlement unsuccessful?

The End of the War

In early 1917, the strain of total war was showing everywhere. After the Russian Revolution in March, there were major strikes in Germany. In July a coalition of moderates passed a "peace resolution" in the German parliament, calling for peace without territorial annexations. To counter this moderation born of war-weariness, the German military established a virtual dictatorship. The military also aggressively exploited the collapse of Russian armies after the Bolshevik Revolution. Advancing almost unopposed on the eastern front in early 1918, the German high command won great concessions from Lenin in the Treaty of Brest-Litovsk in March 1918.

With victory in the east quieting German moderates, General Ludendorff and company fell on France once more in the spring offensive of 1918. For a time, German armies pushed forward, coming within thirty-five miles of Paris. But Ludendorff's exhausted, overextended forces never broke through. They were decisively stopped in July at the second Battle of the Marne, where 140,000 fresh American soldiers saw action. Adding 2 million men in arms to the war effort by August, the late but massive American intervention decisively tipped the scales in favor of Allied victory.

By September, British, French, and American armies were advancing steadily on all fronts, and a panicky General Ludendorff realized that Germany had lost the war. Yet he insolently insisted that moderate politicians shoulder the shame of defeat, and on October 4, the emperor formed a new, more liberal German government to sue for peace. As negotiations over an armistice dragged on, an angry and frustrated German people finally rose up. On November 3, sailors in Kiel mutinied, and throughout northern Germany, soldiers and workers began to establish revolutionary councils on the Russian soviet model. The same day, Austria-Hungary surrendered to the Allies and began breaking apart. Revolution broke out in Germany, and masses of workers demonstrated for peace in Berlin. With army discipline collapsing, the emperor was forced to abdicate and fled to Holland. Socialist leaders in Berlin proclaimed a German republic on November 9 and simultaneously agreed to tough Allied terms of surrender. The armistice went into effect November 11, 1918. The war was over.

Revolution in Germany

Military defeat brought political revolution to Germany and Austria-Hungary, as it had to Russia and the old Ottoman Empire (see pages 1078–

Rosa Luxemburg A brilliant writer and a leader in the German Social Democratic party, Luxemburg scorned moderate socialism and stressed the revolutionary character of Marxism. Murdered by army officers in 1919, she was canonized by the faithful as a communist saint. *(Source: Courtesy, Centralne Archiwum KCPZPR, Warsaw, Poland)*

1081). In Austria-Hungary, the revolution was primarily nationalistic and republican in character. Having started the war to preserve an antinationalist dynastic state, the Habsburg Empire had perished in the attempt. In its place, independent Austrian, Hungarian, and Czechoslovakian republics were proclaimed, while a greatly expanded Serbian monarchy united the south Slavs and took the name of Yugoslavia. The prospect of firmly establishing the new national states overrode class considerations for most people in east central Europe.

The German Revolution of November 1918 resembled the Russian Revolution of March 1917. In both cases, a genuine popular uprising toppled an authoritarian monarchy and established a liberal provisional republic. In both countries, liberals and moderate socialists took control of the central government while workers' and soldiers' councils formed a counter-government. In Germany, however, the moderate socialists won and the Lenin-like radical revolutionaries in the councils lost. In communist terms, the liberal, republican revolution in Germany in 1918 was only half a revolution: it was a bourgeois political revolution without a communist second installment; it was Russia without Lenin's Bolshevik triumph.

There were several reasons for the German outcome. The great majority of Marxian socialist leaders in the Social Democratic party were, as before the war, really pink and not red. They wanted to establish real political democracy and civil liberties, and they favored the gradual elimination of capitalism. They were also German nationalists, appalled by the prospect of civil war and revolutionary terror. Moreover, there was much less popular support among workers and soldiers for the extreme radicals than in Russia. Nor did the German peasantry, which already had most of the land, at least in western Germany, provide the elemental force that has driven all great modern revolutions, from the French to the Chinese.

Of crucial importance also was the fact that the moderate German Social Democrats, unlike Kerensky and company, accepted defeat and ended the war the day they took power. This act ended the decline in morale among soldiers and prevented the regular army with its conservative officer corps from disintegrating. When radicals, led by Karl Liebknecht and Rosa Luxemburg and their supporters in the councils, tried to seize control of the government in Berlin in January, the moderate socialists called on the army to crush the uprising. Liebknecht and Luxemburg were arrested and then brutally murdered by army leaders. In reaction, the radicals in the Social Democratic party broke away in anger and formed a pro-Lenin German Communist party shortly thereafter. Finally, even if the moderate socialists had followed Liebknecht and Luxemburg on the Leninist path, it is very unlikely that they would have succeeded. Civil war in Germany would certainly have followed, and the Allies, who were already occupying western Germany according to the terms of the armistice, would have marched on to Berlin and ruled Germany directly. Historians have often been unduly hard on Germany's moderate socialists.

The Treaty of Versailles

The peace conference on Germany opened in Paris in January 1919 with seventy delegates representing twenty-seven victorious nations. There were great expectations. A young British diplomat later wrote that the victors "were convinced that they would never commit the blunders and iniquities of the Congress of Vienna of 1815." Then the "misguided, reactionary, pathetic aristocrats" had cynically shuffled populations; now "we believed in nationalism, we believed in the self-determination of peoples." Indeed, "we were journeying to Paris . . . to found a new order in Europe. We were preparing not Peace only, but Eternal Peace."[9] The general optimism and idealism had been greatly strengthened by President Wilson's January 1918 peace proposal, the Fourteen Points, which stressed national self-determination and the rights of small countries.

The real powers at the conference were the United States, Great Britain, and France, for defeated Germany was not allowed to participate and Russia was locked in civil war and did not attend. Italy was considered part of the Big Four, but its role was quite secondary. Almost immediately the three great allies began to quarrel. President Wilson, who was wildly cheered by European crowds as the spokesman for a new idealistic and democratic international cooperation, was almost obsessed with creating a League of Nations. Wilson insisted that this question come first, for he believed that only a permanent international organization could protect member states from aggres-

The Treaty of Versailles   was signed in the magnificent Hall of MIrrors, part of the vast palace that Louis XIV had built to celebrate his glory. The Allies did not allow Germany to participate in the negotiation of the treaty. *(Source: National Archives, Washington)*

sion and avert future wars. Wilson had his way, although Lloyd George of Great Britain and especially Clemenceau of France were unenthusiastic. They were primarily concerned with punishing Germany.

Playing on British nationalism, Lloyd George had already won a smashing electoral victory in December on the popular platform of making Germany pay for the war. "We shall," he promised, "squeeze the orange until the pips squeak." Personally inclined to make a somewhat moderate peace with Germany, Lloyd George was to a considerable extent a captive of demands for a total victory worthy of the sacrifices of total war against a totally depraved enemy. As Rudyard Kipling summed up the general British feeling at the end of the war, the Germans were "a people with the heart of beasts."[10]

France's Georges Clemenceau, "the Tiger" who had broken wartime defeatism and led his country to victory, wholeheartedly agreed. Like most French people, Clemenceau wanted old-fashioned revenge. But he also wanted lasting security for

France. This, he believed, required the creation of a buffer state between France and Germany, the permanent demilitarization of Germany, and vast German reparations. He feared that sooner or later Germany with its 60 million people would attack France with its 40 million, unless the Germans were permanently weakened. Moreover, France had no English Channel (or Atlantic Ocean) as a reassuring barrier against German aggression. Wilson, supported by Lloyd George, would hear none of it. Clemenceau's demands seemed vindictive, violating morality and the principle of national self-determination. By April the conference was deadlocked on the German question, and Wilson packed his bags to go home.

Clemenceau's obsession with security reflected his anxiety about France's long-term weakness. In the end, convinced that France should not break with its allies because France could not afford to face Germany alone in the future, he agreed to a compromise. He gave up the French demand for a Rhineland buffer state in return for a formal defensive alliance with the United States and Great

Britain. Under the terms of this alliance, both Wilson and Lloyd George promised that their countries would come to France's aid in the event of a German attack. Thus Clemenceau appeared to win his goal of French security, as Wilson had won his of a permanent international organization. The Allies moved quickly to finish the peace settlement, believing that necessary adjustments would later be possible within the dual framework of a strong Western alliance and the League of Nations (Map 32.4).

The Treaty of Versailles between the Allies and Germany was the key to the settlement, and the terms were not unreasonable as a first step toward re-establishing international order. Germany's colonies were given to France, Britain, and Japan as League of Nations mandates. Germany's territorial losses within Europe were minor, thanks to Wilson. Alsace-Lorraine was returned to France. Parts of Germany inhabited primarily by Poles were ceded to the new Polish state, in keeping with the principle of national self-determination. Predominantly German Danzig was also placed within the Polish tariff lines, but as a self-governing city under League of Nations protection. Germany had to limit its army to 100,000 men and agree to build no military fortifications in the Rhineland.

More harshly, the Allies declared that Germany (with Austria) was responsible for the war and had therefore to pay reparations equal to all civilian damages caused by the war. This unfortunate and much-criticized clause expressed inescapable popular demands for German blood, but the actual figure was not set and there was the clear possibility that reparations might be set at a reasonable level in the future, when tempers had cooled.

When presented with the treaty, the German government protested vigorously. But there was no alternative, especially in that Germany was still starving because the Allies had not yet lifted their naval blockade. On June 28, 1919, German representatives of the ruling moderate Social Democrats and the Catholic party signed the treaty in the Sun King's Hall of Mirrors at Versailles, where Bismarck's empire had been joyously proclaimed almost fifty years before.

Separate peace treaties were concluded with the other defeated powers—Austria, Hungary, Bulgaria, and Turkey (the successor to the Ottoman Empire). For the most part, these treaties merely ratified the existing situation in east central Europe following the breakup of the Austro-Hungarian Empire. Like Austria, Hungary was a particularly big loser, as its "captive" nationalities (and some interspersed Hungarians) were ceded to Romania, Czechoslovakia, Poland, and Yugoslavia. Italy got some Austrian territory. The Ottoman Empire was broken up. France received control of Lebanon and Syria. Britain took Iraq and Palestine, which was to include a Jewish national homeland first promised by Britain in 1917. Officially League of Nations mandates, these acquisitions of the Western powers were one of the more imperialistic elements of the peace settlement. Another was mandating Germany's holdings in China to Japan. The age of Western imperialism lived on (see pages 1072–1075). National self-determination remained a reality only for Europeans and their offspring.

American Rejection of the Versailles Treaty

The rapidly concluded peace settlement of early 1919 was not perfect, but within the context of war-shattered Europe it was an acceptable beginning. The principle of national self-determination, which had played such a large role in starting the war, was accepted and served as an organizing framework. Germany had been punished but not dismembered. A new world organization complemented a traditional defensive alliance of satisfied powers. The remaining problems could be solved in the future. The Allied leaders had seen speed as essential because they detested Lenin and feared that his Bolshevik Revolution might spread. They realized that their best answer to Lenin's unending calls for worldwide upheaval was peace and tranquillity for war-weary peoples.

There were, however, two great interrelated obstacles to such peace: Germany and the United States. Plagued by communist uprisings, reactionary plots, and popular disillusionment with losing the war at the last minute, Germany's moderate socialists and their liberal and Catholic supporters faced an enormous challenge. Like French republicans after 1871, they needed time (and luck) if they were to establish firmly a peaceful and democratic republic. Progress in this direction required understanding yet firm treatment of Germany by the victorious Western Allies, and particularly by the United States.

MAP 32.4 Shattered Empires and Territorial Changes After the First World War   The Great War brought tremendous changes in eastern Europe. New nations were established, and a dangerous power vacuum was created between Germany and Soviet Russia.

However, the United States Senate and, to a lesser extent, the American people rejected President Wilson's handiwork. Republican senators led by Henry Cabot Lodge refused to ratify the Treaty of Versailles without changes in the articles creating the League of Nations. The key issue was the league's power—more apparent than real—to require member states to take collective action against aggression.

Lodge and others believed that this requirement gave away Congress's constitutional right to declare war. No doubt Wilson would have been wise to accept some reservations. But, in failing health, Wilson with narrow-minded self-righteousness rejected all attempts at compromise. He instructed loyal Democratic senators to vote against any reservations whatsoever to the Treaty of Versailles. In doing so, Wilson assured that the treaty was never ratified by the United States in any form and that the United States never joined the League of Nations. Moreover, the Senate refused to ratify Wilson's defensive alliance with France and Great Britain. America turned its back on Europe.

Perhaps understandable in the light of American traditions and the volatility of mass politics, the Wilson-Lodge fiasco and the newfound gospel of isolationism nevertheless represented a tragic renunciation of America's responsibility. Using America's action as an excuse, Great Britain, too, refused to ratify its defensive alliance with France. Bitterly betrayed by its allies, France stood alone. Very shortly, France was to take actions against Germany that would feed the fires of German resentment and seriously undermine democratic forces in the new German republic. The great hopes of early 1919 were turning to ashes by the end of the year. The Western alliance had collapsed, and a grandiose plan for permanent peace had given way to a fragile truce. For this and for what came later, the United States must share a large part of the guilt.

SUMMARY

Why did the First World War have such revolutionary consequences? Why was it such a great break with the past? The Great War was, first of all, a war of committed peoples. In France, Britain, and Germany in particular, governments drew on genuine popular support. This support reflected not only the diplomatic origins of the war but also the way western European society had been effectively unified under the nationalist banner in the later nineteenth century. The relentlessness of total war helps explain why so many died, why so many were crippled physically and psychologically, and why Western civilization would in so many ways never be the same again. More concretely, the war swept away monarchs and multinational empires. National self-determination apparently triumphed, not only in Austria-Hungary but in much of Russia's western borderlands as well. Except in Ireland and parts of Soviet Russia, the revolutionary dream of national unity, born of the French Revolution, had finally come true.

Two other revolutions were products of the war. In Russia, the Bolsheviks established a radical regime, smashed existing capitalist institutions, and stayed in power with a new kind of authoritarian rule. Whether the new Russian regime was truly Marxian or socialist was questionable, but it indisputably posed a powerful, ongoing revolutionary challenge in Europe and its colonial empires.

More subtle, but quite universal in its impact, was an administrative revolution. This revolution, born of the need to mobilize entire societies and economies for total war, greatly increased the power of government. And after the guns grew still, government planning and wholesale involvement in economic and social life did not disappear in Europe. Liberal market capitalism and a well-integrated world economy were among the casualties of the administrative revolution, and greater social equality was everywhere one of its results. Thus, even in European countries where a communist takeover never came close to occurring, society still experienced a great revolution.

Finally, the "war to end war" did not bring peace but only a fragile truce. In the West the Allies failed to maintain their wartime solidarity. Germany remained unrepentant and would soon have more grievances to nurse. Moreover, the victory of national self-determination in eastern Europe created a power vacuum between a still-powerful Germany and a potentially mighty communist Russia. A vast area lay open to military aggression from two sides.

NOTES

1. M. Beloff, *U.S. News & World Report,* March 8, 1976, p. 53.
2. Quoted in J. Remak, *The Origins of World War I* (New York: Holt, Rinehart & Winston, 1967), p. 84.
3. Quoted in W. E. Mosse, *Alexander II and the Modernization of Russia* (New York: Collier Books, 1962), pp. 125–126.
4. Quoted in F. P. Chambers, *The War Behind the War, 1914–1918* (London: Faber & Faber, 1939), p. 168.
5. Quoted in R. O. Paxton, *Europe in the Twentieth Century* (New York: Harcourt Brace Jovanovich, 1975), p. 109.

6. Quoted in Chambers, pp. 302, 304.
7. A. B. Ulam, *The Bolsheviks* (New York: Collier Books, 1968), p. 349.
8. Ibid., p. 405.
9. H. Nicolson, *Peacemaking 1919* (New York: Grosset & Dunlap Universal Library, 1965), pp. 8, 31–32.
10. Quoted ibid., p. 24.

SUGGESTED READING

O. Hale, *The Great Illusion, 1900–1914* (1971), is a thorough account of the prewar era. Both J. Remak, *The Origins of World War I* (1967), and L. Lafore, *The Long Fuse* (1971), are highly recommended studies of the causes of the First World War. A. J. P. Taylor, *The Struggle for Mastery in Europe, 1848–1919* (1954), is an outstanding survey of diplomatic developments with an exhaustive bibliography. V. Steiner, *Britain and the Origins of the First World War* (1978), and G. Kennan, *The Decline of Bismarck's European Order: Franco-Russian Relations, 1875–1890* (1979), are also major contributions. K. Jarausch, *The Enigmatic Chancellor* (1973), is an important study on Bethmann-Hollweg and German policy in 1914. C. Falls, *The Great War* (1961), is the best brief introduction to military aspects of the war. B. Tuchman, *The Guns of August* (1962), is a marvelous account of the dramatic first month of the war and the beginning of military stalemate. G. Ritter provides an able study in *The Schlieffen Plan* (1958). J. Winter, *The Experience of World War I* (1988), is a strikingly illustrated history of the war, and A. Horne, *The Price of Glory: Verdun 1916* (1979), is a moving account of the famous siege. J. Ellis, *Eye-Deep in Hell* (1976), is a vivid account of trench warfare. Vera Brittain's *Testament of Youth*, the moving autobiography of a nurse in wartime, shows lives buffeted by new ideas and personal tragedies.

F. L. Carsten, *War Against War* (1982), considers radical movements in Britain and Germany. The best single volume on the home fronts is still F. Chambers, *The War Behind the War, 1914–1918* (1939). Chambers drew heavily on the many fine books on the social and economic impact of the war in different countries published by the Carnegie Endowment for International Peace under the general editorship of J. T. Shotwell. A. Marwick, *The Deluge* (1970), is a lively account of war and society in Britain. G. Feldman, *Army, Industry, and Labor in Germany, 1914–1918* (1966), shows the impact of total war and military dictatorship on Germany. Three excellent collections of essays, R. Wall and J. Winter, eds., *The Upheaval of War: Family, Work, and Welfare in Europe, 1914–1918* (1988), J. Roth, ed., *World War I* (1967), and R. Albrecht-Carrié, ed., *The Meaning of the First World War* (1965), deftly probe the enormous consequences of the war for people and society. The debate over Germany's guilt and aggression, which has been reopened in recent years, may be best approached through G. Feldman, ed., *German Imperialism, 1914–1918* (1972), and A. Hillgruber, *Germany and the Two World Wars* (1981). M. Fainsod, *International Socialism and the World War* (1935), ably discusses the splits between radical and moderate socialists during the conflict. In addition to Erich Maria Remarque's great novel *All Quiet on the Western Front,* Henri Barbusse's *Under Fire* (1917) and Jules Romain's *Verdun* (1939) are highly recommended for their fictional yet realistic recreations of the war. P. Fussell, *The Great War and Modern Memory* (1975), probes all the powerful literature inspired by the war.

R. Suny and A. Adams, eds., *The Russian Revolution and Bolshevik Victory,* 3d ed. (1990), presents a wide range of old and new interpretations. A. Ulam's work cited in the Notes, which focuses on Lenin, is a masterful introduction to the Russian Revolution: S. Fitzpatrick, *The Russian Revolution* (1982), provides a provocative reconsideration. B. Wolfe, *Three Who Made a Revolution* (1955), a collective biography of Lenin, Trotsky, and Stalin, and R. Conquest, *V. I. Lenin* (1972), are recommended. Leon Trotsky himself wrote the colorful and exciting *History of the Russian Revolution* (1932), which may be compared with the classic eyewitness account of the young, pro-Bolshevik American John Reed, *Ten Days That Shook the World* (1919). R. Daniels, *Red October* (1969), provides a clear account of the Bolshevik seizure of power, and R. Pipes, *The Formation of the Soviet Union* (1968), is recommended for its excellent treatment of the nationality problem during the revolution. D. Koenker, W. Rosenberg, and R. Suny, eds., *Party, State and Society in the Russian Civil War* (1989), probes the social foundation of Bolshevik victory. A. Wildman, *The End of the Russian Imperial Army* (1980), is a fine account of the soldiers' revolt, and G. Leggett, *The Cheka: Lenin's Secret Police* (1981), shows revolutionary terror in action. Boris Pasternak's justly celebrated *Doctor Zhivago* is a great historical novel of the revolutionary era. R. Massie, *Nicholas and Alexandra* (1971), is a moving popular biography of Russia's last royal family and the terrible health problem of the heir to the throne. H. Nicolson's study listed in the Notes captures the spirit of the Versailles settlement. T. Bailey, *Woodrow Wilson and the Lost Peace* (1963), and W. Widenor, *Henry Cabot Lodge and the Search for an American Foreign Policy* (1981), are also highly recommended. A. Mayer provocatively stresses the influence of domestic social tensions and widespread fear of further communist revolt in *The Politics and Diplomacy of Peacemaking* (1969).

PERIOD (CA 1700–1920)	AFRICA AND THE MIDDLE EAST	THE AMERICAS
1700	Approximately 11,000,000 slaves shipped from Africa, ca 1450–1850 Dutch found Cape Colony, 1657 Rise of the Ashanti, West Africa, ca 1700 Decline of the Safavid Empire under Nadir Shah, 1737–1747	Spain's defeat in War of the Spanish Succession, 1701–1714, prompts trade reform, leading to colonial dependence on Spanish goods, 18th century
1750	Sultan Selim III establishes first diplomatic relations between Ottoman Empire and Europe, introduces administrative and military reforms, 1761–1808 British seize Cape town, 1795 Napoleon's campaign in Egypt, 1798	"French and Indian wars," 1756–1763 Quebec Act, 1774 American Revolution, 1775–1783 Comunero revolution, New Granada, 1781
1800	Muhammad Ali founds dynasty in Egypt, 1805–1848 Slavery abolished in British Empire, 1807 Peak year of African transatlantic slave trade, 1820 European capitalists begin large-scale investment in Africa, 1840s	Latin American wars of independence from Spain, 1806–1825 Brazil wins independence from Portugal, 1822 Monroe Doctrine, 1823 Political instability in most Latin American countries, 1825–1870 Mexican War, 1846–1848
1850	Crimean War, 1853–1856 Suez Canal opens, 1869 Europeans intensify "scramble for Africa," 1880–1900 Battle of Omdurman, 1898 Boer War, 1899–1902	American Civil War, 1861–1865 British North America Act, 1867, for Canada Porfirio Diaz controls Mexico, 1876–1911 U.S. practices "dollar diplomacy" in Latin America, 1890–1920s Spanish-American War, 1898; U.S. gains Philippines
1900	Union of South Africa formed, 1910 French annex Morocco, 1912 Ottoman Empire enters World War One on Germany's side Treaty of Sèvres dissolves Ottoman Empire, 1919; Mustafa Kemal mounts nationalist struggle in Turkey	Massive immigration from Europe and Asia to the Americas, 1880–1914 Mexican Revolution, 1910 Panama Canal opens, 1914 U.S. enters World War One, 1917 Mexico adopts constitution, 1917

EAST ASIA	INDIA AND SOUTHEAST ASIA	EUROPE
Tokugawa Regime in Japan, characterized by political stability and economic growth, 1600–1867 Manchus establish Ch'ing Dynasty, 1644–1911 Height of Ch'ing Dynasty under Emperor Ch'ien-lung, 1736–1799	Mughal power contested by Hindus and Muslims, 18th century Persian invaders defeat Mughal army, loot Delhi, 1739 French and British fight for control of India, 1740–1763	Growth of absolutism in central and eastern Europe, ca 1680–1790 The Enlightenment, ca 1680–1800 Development of Cabinet system in England, 1714–1742 Height of land enclosure in England, ca 1760–1810
Maximum extent of Ch'ing Empire, 1759	Battle of Plassey, 1757 Treaty of Paris, 1763; French colonies to Britain Cook in Australia, 1768–1771; first British prisoners to Australia, 1788 East India Act, 1784	Englishman James Watt produces first steam engine, 1769 Louis XVI of France, 1774–1792 Outbreak of French Revolution, 1789 National Convention declares France a republic, 1792
Java War, 1825–1830 Anglo-Chinese Opium War, 1839–1842 Treaty of Nanking, 1842: Manchus surrender Hong Kong to British	British found Singapore, 1819 British defeat last independent native state in India, 1848	Napoleonic Empire, 1804–1814 Congress of Vienna, 1814–1815 European economic penetration of non-Western countries, ca 1816–1880 Greece wins independence from Ottoman Empire, 1829 Revolutions in France, Prussia, Italy, and Austria, 1848–1849
Taiping Rebellion, 1850–1864 Perry's arrival opens Japan to U.S. and Europe, 1853 Meiji Restoration in Japan, 1867 Adoption of constitution in Japan, 1890 Sino-Japanese War, 1894–1895 "Hundred Days of Reform" in China, 1898	Great Rebellion in India, 1857–1858 French seize Saigon, 1859 Indian National Congress formed, 1885 French acquire Indochina, 1893	Second and Third Empires in France, 1852–1914 Unification of Italy, 1859–1870 Otto von Bismarck's reign of power in German affairs, 1862–1890 Franco-Prussian War, 1870–1871; foundation of the German Empire Parliamentary Reform Bill, Great Britain, 1867 Second Socialist International, 1889–1914
Boxer Rebellion in China, 1900–1903 Russian-Japanese War, 1904–1905 Chinese Revolution; fall of Ch'ing Dynasty, 1911 Chinese Republic, 1912–1949	Commonwealth of Australia, 1900 Muslim League formed, 1906 Radicals make first calls for Indian independence, 1907 Amritsar Massacre in India, 1919 Intensification of Indian nationalism, 1919–1947	Revolution in Russia; Tsar Nicholas II forced to issue October Manifesto, 1905 Triple Entente (Britain, Russia, France), 1914–1918 World War One, 1914–1918 Treaty of Versailles, 1919

33

Nationalism in Asia, 1914–1939

Turks celebrating victory at Smyrna, October 1922

From Asia's perspective the First World War was largely a European civil war that shattered the united front of Western imperialism and convulsed prewar relationships throughout Asia. Most crucially, the war speeded the development of modern nationalism in Asia. Before 1914, the nationalist gospel of anti-imperialist political freedom and racial equality had already won converts among Asia's Westernized, educated elites. In the 1920s and 1930s it increasingly won the souls of the masses. As in Europe in the nineteenth century, nationalism in Asia betwen 1914 and 1939 became a mass movement with potentially awesome power.

There were at least three reasons for the upsurge of nationalism in Asia. First and foremost, nationalism provided the most effective means of organizing the anti-imperialist resistance both to direct foreign rule and to indirect Western domination. Second, nationalism called for fundamental changes and challenged old political practices and beliefs. Thus modernizers used it as a weapon in their ongoing contest for influence and power with conservative traditionalists. Modernizers also used nationalism as a conduit to spread other values, like industrialization, or the European secular world view with its faith in science, critical thinking, and progress. Third, nationalism spread because it gave both leaders and followers a vision of a shining future for a rejuvenated people. Thus nationalism provided an ideology to ennoble the sacrifices that the struggle for rejuvenation would require.

The spread of nationalism also had its dark side. As in Europe (see page 873), nationalists in Asia developed a strong sense of "we" and "they." "They" were often the enemy—the oppressor. White-skinned European imperialists were just such a "they," and nationalist feeling generated the power to destroy European empires and successfully challenge widespread foreign economic domination. But, as in Europe, nationalism in Asia also stimulated bitter conflicts and wars between peoples, in two different ways. First, it stimulated conflicts between relatively homogeneous peoples in large states, rallying, for example, Chinese against Japanese and vice versa. Second, nationalism often heightened tensions between ethnic (or religious) groups within states, especially states with a variety of peoples, like British India or the Ottoman Empire. Such states had been formed by authoritarian rulers and their armies and bureaucracies, very much like the Austrian or Russian empires before 1914. When their rigid rule declined or snapped, increasingly self-conscious and nationalistic peoples might easily quarrel, seeking to divide the existing state or to dominate the enemy "they" within its borders.

Although modern nationalism has everywhere exhibited certain shared characteristics, it has never been monolithic. In Asia especially, the range of historical experience has been enormous, and the new and often narrow ideology of nationalism was grafted onto old, rich, and complex civilizations. Between the outbreak of the First and Second World Wars each Asian country developed a distinctive national movement, rooted in its unique culture and history. Each nation's people created its own national reawakening, which renovated thought and culture as well as politics and economics.

- How did modern nationalism—the dominant force in most of the world in the twentieth century—develop in Asia between the First and Second World Wars?

- How did national movements arise in different countries, and how did some of these parallel movements come into brutal conflict?

These are the questions that this chapter seeks to answer.

THE FIRST WORLD WAR AND WESTERN IMPERIALISM

Every Asian national movement shared in a burning desire for genuine freedom from foreign imperialism. The First World War had a profound effect on these aspirations by altering relations between Asia and Europe.

In the words of a distinguished Indian historian, "the Great War of 1914–1918 was from the Asian point of view a civil war within the European community of nations."[1] For four years Asians watched the haughty bearers of the "white man's burden" vilifying and destroying each other. Far from

Delegates to the Peace Conference of 1919   Standing in the foreground is Prince Faisal, third son of King Hussein of Hejaz and frustrated spokesman for the Arab cause at Versailles. The British officer T. E. Lawrence—popularly known as Lawrence of Arabia—is second from the right in the middle row. *(Source: Imperial War Museum)*

standing united and supremely self-confident in an apparently unbeatable imperialistic phalanx, the Western nations were clawing at each other in total disarray. The impact of this spectacle was enormous. Japan's defeat of imperial Russia in 1904 (see page 944) had shown that an Asian power could beat a European great power; now for the first time Asians saw the entire West as divided and vulnerable.

In the East Asian countries of China and Japan few people particularly cared who won the vicious family quarrel in distant Europe. In India and French Indochina enthusiasm was also limited, but the impact of the war was unavoidably greater. The British and the French were driven by the harsh logic of total war to draft their colonial subjects into the conflict. They uprooted hundreds of thousands of Asians to fight the Germans and the Ottoman Turks. This too had major consequences. An Indian or Vietnamese soldier who fought in France and came in contact there with democratic and republican ideas was likely to be less willing to accept foreign rule when he returned home.

The British and the French also made rash promises to gain the support of colonial peoples during the war. British leaders promised Jewish nationalists in Europe a homeland in Palestine even as they promised Arab nationalists independence from the Ottoman Empire. In India the British were forced in 1917 to announce a new policy of self-governing institutions in order to counteract Indian popular unrest fanned by wartime inflation and heavy taxation. After the war the nationalist genie that the colonial powers had called on refused to slip meekly back into the bottle.

The war aims of President Wilson also raised the hopes of peoples under imperial rule. In January 1918 Wilson proposed to make peace on the basis of his Fourteen Points (see page 1062), whose key idea was national self-determination for the peoples of Europe and of the Ottoman Empire. Wilson also proposed that in all colonial questions "the interests of native populations be given equal weight with the desires of European governments." Wilson's program seemed to call for national self-rule, preservation of the rights of weak nations, and international justice. This subversive message was broadcast around the world by American propagandists in 1918 and 1919. It had enormous appeal for educated Asians, fueling their hopes of freedom and dignity.

Military service and Wilsonian self-determination also fired the hopes of some Africans and some visionary American black supporters of African freedom. The First World War, however, had less impact on European imperialism in black Africa—Africa south of the Sahara—than in Asia and the Arab world. Because the European conquest of black Africa was not completed until 1900, Africans outside of certain coastal areas had not experienced foreign domination long enough for nationalist movements to develop. Moreover, European rulers customarily grouped many tribes and peoples into a single administrative unit, and ethnic diversity slowed the development of a common national loyalty. For black Africa, the Great Depression and the Second World War were to prove much more influential in the growth of nationalist movements (see pages 1237–1238).

Once the Allies had won the war, they tried to shift gears and re-establish or increase their political and economic domination in Asia and Africa. Although fatally weakened, Western imperialism remained very much alive in 1918. Part of the reason for its survival was that President Wilson was certainly no revolutionary. At the Versailles Peace Conference he proved willing to compromise on colonial questions in order to achieve some of his European goals and the creation of the League of Nations. Also, Allied statesmen and ordinary French and British citizens quite rightly believed that their colonial empires had contributed to

their ultimate victory over the Central Powers. They were in no mood to give up such valuable possessions voluntarily. Finally and very importantly, the victors remained convinced of the superiority of their civilization. They believed that their rule was best for colonial peoples. A few "discontented" Asian or African intellectuals might agitate for self-rule; but Europeans in general, and colonial officials in particular, believed that the humble masses were grateful for the law and order brought by the white man's administration. If pressed, Europeans said that such administration was preparing colonial subjects for eventual self-rule, but only in the distant future.

The compromise at Versailles between Wilson's vague, moralistic idealism and the European preoccupation with "good administration" was the establishment of a system of League of Nations mandates over Germany's former colonies and the old Ottoman Empire. Article 22 of the League of Nations Covenant, which was part of the Treaty of Versailles, assigned territories "inhabited by peoples incapable of governing themselves" to various "developed nations." "The well-being and development of such peoples" was declared "a sacred trust of civilization." A Permanent Mandates Commission was created to oversee the developed nations' fulfillment of their international responsibility; most of the members of the Permanent Mandates Commission came from European countries that had colonies. Thus the League elaborated a new principle, development toward the eventual goal of self-government, but left its implementation to the colonial powers themselves.

The mandates system clearly demonstrated that Europe was determined to maintain its imperial power and influence. It is no wonder that patriots throughout Asia were bitterly disappointed after the First World War. They saw France, Great Britain, and other nations—industrialized Japan was the only Asian state to obtain mandates—grabbing Germany's colonies as spoils of war and extending the existing system of colonial protectorates in Muslim North Africa into the territories of the old Ottoman Empire. Yet Asian patriots were not about to give up. They preached the nationalist creed and struggled to build mass movements capable of achieving freedom and independence.

In this struggle they were encouraged and sometimes inspired by Soviet communism. Immediately after seizing power in 1917, Lenin and his fellow Bolsheviks declared that the Asian peoples conquered by the tsars, now inhabitants of the Soviet Union, were complete equals of the Russians with a right to their own development. (In actuality this equality hardly existed, but the propaganda was effective nonetheless.) The Communists also denounced European and American imperialism and pledged to support revolutionary movements in all colonial countries, even when they were primarily movements of national independence led by "middle-class" intellectuals instead of by revolutionary workers. Foreign political and economic exploitation was the immediate enemy, they said, and socialist revolution could wait until after Western imperialism had been defeated.

The example, ideology, and support of Russian Communists exerted a powerful influence in the 1920s and 1930s, particularly in China and French Indochina. Middle-class nationalists were strengthened in their battle with foreign rule, and the ranks of communist nationalists also swelled. A nationalistic young Vietnamese man, who had pleaded the cause of Vietnamese independence unsuccessfully at the Versailles Peace Conference, described his feelings when he read Lenin's statement on national self-determination for colonial peoples, adopted by the Communist Third International in 1920:

These resolutions filled me with great emotion, enthusiasm, and faith. They helped me see the problem clearly. My joy was so great I began to cry. Alone in my room I wrote the following words, as if I were addressing a great crowd: "My dear compatriots, so miserable and oppressed, here is what we need. Here is the path to our liberation." [2]

The young nationalist was Ho Chi Minh (1890–1969), who was to fight a lifetime to create an independent, communist Vietnam.

The appeal of nationalism in Asia was not confined to territories under direct European rule, like French Indochina and League of Nations mandates. The extraordinary growth of international trade after 1850 had drawn millions of peasants and shopkeepers throughout Asia into the Western-dominated world economy, disrupting local markets and often creating hostility toward European businessmen. Moreover, Europe and the United States had forced even the most solid Asian states, China and Japan, to accept unequal

treaties and humiliating limitations on their sovereignty. Thus the nationalist promise of genuine economic independence and true political equality with the West appealed as powerfully in old but weak states like China as in colonial territories like British India.

Finally, as in Russia after the Crimean War or in Japan after the Meiji Restoration, the nationalist creed went hand in hand with acceptance of modernization by the educated elites. Modernization promised changes that would enable old societies to compete effectively with the world's leading nations.

THE MIDDLE EAST

The most flagrant attempt to expand the scope of Western imperialism occurred in what is usually called the Middle East, but which is perhaps more accurately termed West Asia—that vast expanse that stretches eastward from the Suez Canal and Turkey's Mediterranean shores across the Tigris-Euphrates Valley and the Iranian Plateau to the Arabian Sea and the Indus Valley. There the British and the French successfully encouraged an Arab revolt in 1916 and destroyed the Ottoman Empire. The conquering Europeans then sought to replace the Turks as principal rulers throughout the region, even in Turkey itself. Turkish, Arab, and Iranian nationalists, as well as Jewish nationalists arriving from Europe, reacted violently. They struggled to win dignity and nationhood, and as the Europeans were forced to make concessions, they sometimes came into sharp conflict with each other, most notably in Palestine.

The First World War and the Arab Revolt

The Ottoman Empire, like neighboring Egypt (see pages 966–968), had long been subject to European pressure and had also adopted European military and educational reforms in the 1820s and 1830s. In the late nineteenth century, however, the Ottoman Empire became increasingly weak and autocratic. The combination of declining international stature and domestic tyranny eventually led to an upsurge of revolutionary activity among idealistic exiles and nationalistic young army officers who wanted to seize power and save the Ottoman state. These fervent patriots, the so-called Young Turks, succeeded in the revolution of 1908, and subsequently they were determined to hold the remnants of the vast multiethnic empire together. Defeated by Bulgaria, Serbia, and Greece in the Balkan War of 1912, stripped of practically all territory in Europe, the Young Turks redoubled their efforts in Asia. The most important of their Asian possessions were Syria—consisting of modern-day Lebanon, Syria, Israel, and Jordan—and Iraq. The Ottoman Turks also claimed the Arabian peninsula but exercised only a loose control there.

For centuries the largely Arabic populations of Syria and Iraq had been tied to their Ottoman rulers by their common faith in Islam (though there were Christian Arabs as well). Yet beneath the surface, ethnic and linguistic tensions simmered between Turks and Arabs, who were as different as Chinese and Japanese or French and Germans. As early as 1883, a Frenchman who had traveled widely in the Arab provinces claimed:

Everywhere I came upon the same abiding and universal sentiment: hatred of the Turks. The notion of concerted action to throw off the detested yoke is gradually shaping itself. . . . An Arab movement, newly-risen, is looming in the distance; a race hitherto downtrodden will presently claim its due place in the destinies of Islam.[3]

Europeans like this French traveler often encouraged Arabs in the Ottoman Empire to see their situation in nationalistic terms. Nationalism was part of the Western world view and it undermined the all-encompassing nature of Islam, the traditional defense against European expansion in West Africa and North Africa. Arab nationalism appealed particularly to the Ottoman Empire's sizable minority of Arab Christians, who were most numerous in the province of Syria and who were increasingly attracted by French power and culture.

The actions of the Young Turks after 1908 made the embryonic "Arab movement" a reality. Although some Turkish reformers argued for an Ottoman liberalism that would give equal political rights to all ethnic and religious groups within the empire, the majority successfully insisted on a narrow Turkish nationalism. They further centralized the Ottoman Empire and extended the sway of the Turkish language, culture, and race. In 1909 the Turkish government brutally slaughtered thousands of Armenian Christians, a prelude to the wholesale destruction of more than a million Armenians during the heavy fighting with Russia in the First World War. Meanwhile the Arab revolt gathered strength. By 1914 the great majority of Arab leaders believed that armed conflict with their Turkish masters was inevitable.

In close contact with Europeans for centuries, the Turks willingly joined forces with Germany and Austria-Hungary in late 1914. The Young Turks were pro-German because Germans had helped reform Ottoman armies before the war and had built important railroads, like the one to Baghdad. Alliance with Germany permitted the Turks to renounce immediately the limitations on Ottoman sovereignty that the Europeans had imposed in the nineteenth century, and it offered the prospect of settling old scores with Russia, the historic enemy.

The Young Turks' fatal decision to side with the Central Powers pulled the entire Middle East into the European civil war and made it truly a world conflict. While Russia attacked the Ottomans in the Caucasus, the British had to protect Egypt and the Suez Canal, the life line to India. Thus Arab leaders opposed to Ottoman rule suddenly found an unexpected ally in Great Britain. The foremost Arab leader was Hussein Ibn-Ali (1856–1931), a direct descendant of the prophet Muhammad through the house of Quraysh. As the *sharif*, or chief magistrate of Mecca, the most holy city in the Muslim world, Hussein governed much of the Ottoman Empire's territory along the Red Sea, an area known as the Hejaz. Basically anti-Turkish, Hussein refused to second the Turkish sultan's call for a holy war against the Triple Entente. His refusal pleased the British, who feared that such calls would trigger a Muslim revolt in India.

In 1915 Hussein managed to win vague British commitments for an independent Arab kingdom. The British attempt to take the Dardanelles and capture Constantinople in 1915 failed miserably, and Britain (and Russia) badly needed a new ally on the Ottoman front. Thus in 1916 Hussein revolted against the Turks, proclaiming himself king of the Arabs. Hussein joined forces with the British under T. E. Lawrence, who in 1917 led Arab tribesmen and Indian soldiers in a highly successful guerrilla war against the Turks on the Arabian peninsula. In September 1918, British armies and their Arab allies smashed into Syria. This offensive culminated in the triumphal entry of Hussein's son Faisal into Damascus.

Similar victories were eventually scored in the Ottoman province of Iraq. Britain had established a protectorate over the emirate of Kuwait in 1899, and from there British troops occupied the southern Iraqi city of Basra in 1914. Moving up the Tigris-Euphrates Valley, British armies from India and armed forces from Australia and New Zealand were repulsed by Ottoman forces at Kut el Amara in 1916, but they smashed through to capture Baghdad in 1917. Throughout Syria and Iraq there was wild Arab rejoicing. Many patriots expected a large, unified Arab state to rise from the dust of the Ottoman collapse.

Within two years, however, many Arab nationalists felt bitterly betrayed by Great Britain and its allies. The issues involved are complex, controversial, and highly emotional, but it is undeniable that this bitterness left an enduring legacy of hatred toward the West. Part of the reason for the Arabs's bitterness was that Britain and France had signed secret wartime treaties to divide and rule the old Ottoman Empire. In the Sykes-Picot Agreement of 1916, Britain and France had secretly agreed that France would receive modern-day Lebanon, Syria, and much of southern Turkey and Britain would receive Palestine, Jordan, and Iraq. The Sykes-Picot treaties, drawn up to reinforce Allied determination to fight on, contradicted British (and later Wilsonian) promises concerning Arab independence after the war. When Britain and France set about implementing these secret plans, Arab nationalists felt cheated and betrayed.

A related source of Arab bitterness was Britain's wartime commitment to a Jewish homeland in Palestine. The famous Balfour Declaration of November 1917, made by the Britsh foreign secretary Arthur Balfour, declared:

His Majesty's Government views with favor the establishment in Palestine of a National Home for the Jewish People, and will use their best endeavors to facilitate the achievement of this object, it being clearly understood that nothing shall be done which may prejudice the civil and religious rights of existing non-Jewish communities in Palestine, or the rights and political status enjoyed by Jews in any other country.

As careful reading reveals, the Balfour Declaration made contradictory promises to European Jews and Middle Eastern Arabs. It has been a subject of passionate debate ever since 1917.

Some British Cabinet members apparently believed such a declaration would appeal to German, Austrian, and American Jews and thus help the British war effort. Others sincerely supported the Zionist vision of a Jewish homeland. These supporters also believed that such a homeland would be grateful to Britain and help maintain British control of the Suez Canal. In any event, Arabs were dismayed. In 1914 Jews accounted for about 11 percent of the predominantly Arab population in the three Ottoman administrative units that would subsequently be lumped together by the British to form Palestine. A "National Home for the Jewish People" implied to the Arabs—and to the Zionist Jews as well—the establishment of some kind of Jewish state that would be incompatible with majority rule. Also, a state founded on religious and ethnic exclusivity was out of keeping with both Islamic and Ottoman tradition, which had historically been more tolerant of religious diversity and minorities than had the Christian monarchs or nation-states in Europe.

Despite strong French objections, Hussein's son Faisal (1885–1933) was allowed to attend the Paris Peace Conference. The Allies, however, made clear that he represented only the recently proclaimed kingdom of Hejaz, not all Arabs. Faisal invoked Wilson's idea of self-determination, but despite Wilson's lukewarm support Faisal's effort to secure an independent state embracing all Arabs came to nothing. The independence of the kingdom of Hejaz was confirmed, but in return Faisal was forced to accept Franco-British demands for mandates in Syria, Iraq, and Palestine. (The Saudis had attacked Hussein in 1916 and they conquered his kingdom of Hejaz in 1924–1925, incorporating it with the Nejd in 1932 to form Saudi Arabia.) The British mandate in Palestine formally incorporated the Balfour Declaration and its commitment to a Jewish national home. On his return to Syria, Faisal's followers repudiated the agreement he had reluctantly accepted. In March 1920 they met as the Syrian National Congress and proclaimed Syria independent with Faisal as king. A similar congress declared Iraq an independent kingdom.

Western reaction to events in Syria and Iraq was swift and decisive. France and Britain convened the League of Nations to approve the mandates they wanted. Then a French army stationed in Lebanon attacked Syria, taking Damascus in July

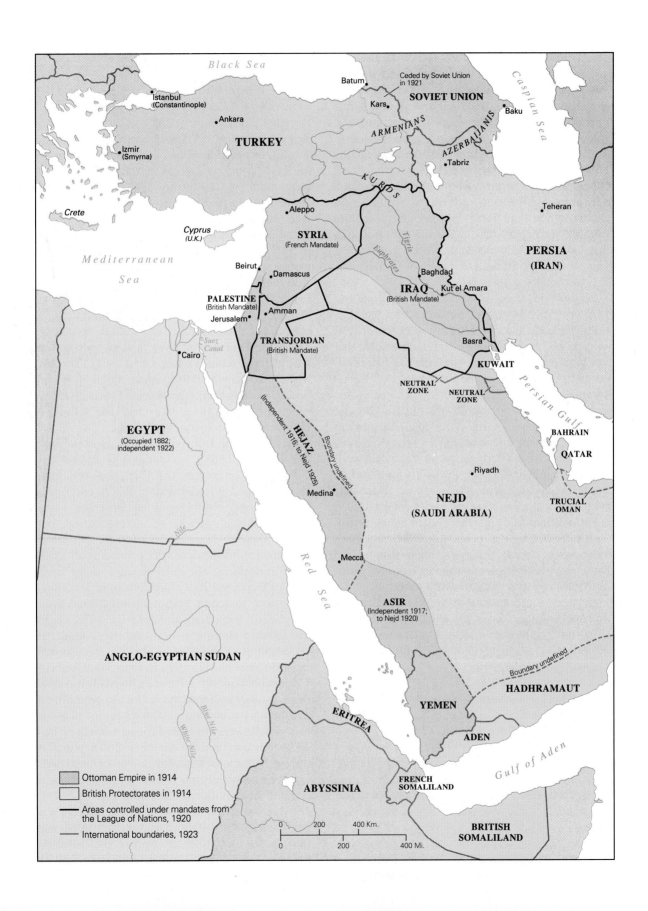

Black Sea

Istanbul
(Constantinople)

Batum
Kars

Ceded by Soviet Union
in 1921

SOVIET UNION

Baku

Caspian Sea

Ankara

ARMENIANS

AZERBAIJANIS

TURKEY

Izmir
(Smyrna)

Tabriz

KURDS

Teheran

Crete

Aleppo

Cyprus
(U.K.)

SYRIA
(French Mandate)

Euphrates

Tigris

Baghdad

PERSIA
(IRAN)

Mediterranean
Sea

Beirut

Damascus

IRAQ
(British Mandate)

Kut el Amara

PALESTINE
(British Mandate)

Amman

Jerusalem

Suez
Canal

Cairo

TRANSJORDAN
(British Mandate)

Basra

KUWAIT

NEUTRAL
ZONE

NEUTRAL
ZONE

Persian Gulf

BAHRAIN

QATAR

EGYPT
(Occupied 1882;
independent 1922)

HEJAZ
(Independent 1916; to Nejd 1925)

Boundary undefined

Medina

Riyadh

NEJD
(SAUDI ARABIA)

TRUCIAL
OMAN

Nile

Red Sea

Mecca

ASIR
(Independent 1917;
to Nejd 1920)

Boundary undefined

ANGLO-EGYPTIAN SUDAN

HADHRAMAUT

Blue Nile

White Nile

ERITREA

YEMEN

ADEN

Gulf of Aden

FRENCH
SOMALILAND

ABYSSINIA

Ottoman Empire in 1914

British Protectorates in 1914

Areas controlled under mandates from
the League of Nations, 1920

International boundaries, 1923

0   200   400 Km.

0   200   400 Mi.

BRITISH
SOMALILAND

1920. Faisal fled and the French took over. Meanwhile the British put down an uprising in Iraq with bloody fighting and established military rule there. Western imperialism appeared to have replaced Turkish rule in the Middle East (Map 33.1).

The Turkish Revolution

In November 1918 the Allied fleet entered Constantinople, the Ottoman capital. A young English official vividly described the strange and pathetic situation he encountered:

I found the Ottoman Empire utterly smashed, her vast territories stripped into pieces, and her conquered populations blinded and bewildered by their sudden release. The Turks were worn out, dead-tired, and without bitterness awaited their fate. . . The debris of the old order waited to be constructed into a new system.[4]

The Allies' "new system" was blatant imperialism, and it proved harsher for the defeated Turks than for the "liberated" Arabs. A treaty forced on the helpless sultan dismembered Turkey and reduced it to a puppet state. Great Britain and France occupied parts of Turkey, and Italy and Greece claimed shares as well. There was a sizable Greek minority in western Turkey, and Greek nationalists cherished the "Great Idea" of incorporating this territory into a modern Greek empire modeled on long-dead Christian Byzantium. In 1919 a Greek army carried by British ships landed on the Turkish coast at Smyrna. The sultan ordered his exhausted troops not to resist, and Greek

Mustafa Kemal explains his radical reform of the written language. Impeccably elegant European dress symbolizes Kemal's conception of a modernized Turkey. *(Source: Historical Pictures Service, Chicago)*

MAP 33.1 The Partition of the Ottoman Empire, 1914–1923 The decline of the mighty Ottoman Empire had begun in 1699, when the Habsburgs conquered Hungary, and it had accelerated after 1805, when Egypt became virtually independent. By 1914 the Ottoman Turks had been pushed out of the Balkans and their Arab provinces were on the edge of revolt; that revolt erupted in the First World War and contributed greatly to the Ottomans' defeat. When the Allies then attempted to implement their plans, including independence for the Armenian people, Mustafa Kemal arose to forge in battle the modern Turkish state.

armies advanced into the interior. Turkey seemed finished.

But Turkey produced a great leader and revived to become an inspiration to the entire Middle East. Mustafa Kemal (1881–1938), the father of modern Turkey, was a military man. The son of a petty government official and sympathetic to the Young Turk movement, Kemal had distinguished himself in the Great War by directing the successful defense of the Dardanelles against British attack, the most famous Turkish victory of the war. Back in Constantinople after the armistice, Mustafa Kemal watched with anguish the Allies' aggression and the sultan's cowardice. In early 1919 he moved to central Turkey and began working to unify the Turkish resistance.

The sultan, bowing to Allied pressure, initially denounced Kemal, but the cause of national liberation proved more powerful. The catalyst was the Greek invasion and attempted annexation of much of western Turkey. A young woman who was to play a major role in the Turkish revolution described feelings she shared with countless others:

After I learned about the details of the Smyrna occupation by Greek armies, I hardly opened my mouth on any subject except when it concerned the sacred struggle. . . . I suddenly ceased to exist as an individual. I worked, wrote and lived as a unit of that magnificent national madness.[5]

Refusing to acknowledge the Allied dismemberment of their country, the Turks battled on through 1920 despite staggering defeats. The next year the Greeks, egged on by the British, advanced almost to Ankara, the nationalist stronghold in central Anatolia. There Mustafa Kemal's forces took the offensive and won a great victory. The Greeks and their British allies sued for peace. After long negotiations, the resulting Treaty of Lausanne (1923) solemnly abolished the hated Capitulations imposed by European powers in the nineteenth century to give their citizens special privileges in the Ottoman Empire, and recognized the territorial integrity of a truly independent Turkey. Turkey lost only its former Arab provinces.

Mustafa Kemal, a nationalist without religious faith, believed that Turkey should modernize and secularize along Western lines. His first moves were political. Drawing on his prestige as a war hero, Kemal called on the somewhat reluctant National Assembly to depose the sultan and establish a republic. He had himself elected president and moved the capital from cosmopolitan Constantinople (soon to be renamed Istanbul) to Ankara in the Turkish heartland. Kemal savagely crushed the demands for independence of ethnic minorities like the Armenians and the Kurds, but he realistically abandoned all thought of winning back lost Arab territories. He focused instead on internal affairs, creating a one-party system—partly inspired by the Bolshevik example—to work his will.

The most radical of Kemal's changes pertained to religion and culture. For centuries, most of the intellectual and social activities of believers had been sternly regulated by Islamic religious authorities, in keeping with the Sacred Law. Profoundly influenced by the example of western Europe, Mustafa Kemal set out, like the philosophes of the Enlightenment, to limit the place of religion and religious leaders in daily affairs. Like Russia's Peter the Great, he employed dictatorial measures rather than reason to reach his goal. Kemal and his followers simply decreed a revolutionary separation of church and state. Religious courts were abolished, replaced by a completely new legal system based on European law codes. Religious schools gave way to state schools that taught such secular subjects as science, mathematics, and social sciences.

To dramatize the break with the past, Mustafa Kemal struck down many entrenched patterns of behavior. Women, traditionally secluded and dominated by males in Islamic society, received the right to vote. Marriage was now governed by civil law on a European model, rather than by the Islamic code. Women were allowed to seek divorces, and no longer could a wealthy man take a second, third, or fourth wife, as under Islamic law. Men were forbidden to wear the tall red fez as headgear; government employees were ordered to wear business suits and felt hats, erasing the visible differences between Muslims and "infidel" Europeans. The old Arabic script was replaced with a new Turkish alphabet based on Roman letters; it made the written language closer to the spoken vernacular. The new alphabet isolated Turks from their historical heritage and literature, as the radical reformers probably hoped it would. The simpler, more phonetic alphabet facilitated massive government efforts to spread basic literacy after 1928. Finally, in 1935, family names on the European model were introduced. The National Assembly granted Mustafa Kemal the surname Atatürk, which means "father of the Turks."

By the time of his death in 1938, Atatürk and his supporters had consolidated their revolution. Government-sponsored industrialization was fostering urban growth and new attitudes. Turks no longer considered business and science beneath their dignity. Nevertheless, poverty persisted in rural areas, as did some religious discontent among devout Muslims. After the Second World War, this religious discontent caused Turkish governments to modify some of Atatürk's most radical reforms in a conservative direction. But like the

Japanese after the Meiji Restoration, the Turkish people had rallied around the nationalist banner to repulse European imperialism and were building a modern secular nation-state.

Iran and Afghanistan

In Persia (renamed Iran in 1935), strong-arm efforts to build a unified modern nation ultimately proved less successful than in Turkey.

The late nineteenth century had been a sorry period in Iran's long and sometimes glorious history. Iran was subject to extreme foreign pressure: the Russians were pressing relentlessly from the north, and the British were pushing upward from India and the Persian Gulf. Like China in a similar predicament at the same time, Iran managed to play the Great Powers against each other to maintain a precarious independence. However, the spectacle of the shah granting economic privileges to foreigners alienated native merchants. An inspired religious leader, Jamal al-Din al-Afghani (1838–1897), began to preach government reform as a means of reviving Islamic civilization. In 1906 a nationalistic coalition of merchants, religious leaders, and intellectuals revolted. The despotic shah was forced to grant a constitution and establish a national assembly, the *Majlis*. Nationalist hopes ran high.

Yet the Iranian revolution of 1906 was doomed to failure, largely because of European imperialism. Without consulting Iran, Britain and Russia in 1907 simply divided the country into spheres of influence. Britain's sphere ran along the Persian Gulf; the Russian sphere encompassed the whole northern half of Iran. Thereafter Russia intervened constantly. It blocked reforms, occupied cities, and completely dominated the country by 1912. When Russian power temporarily collapsed in the Bolshevik Revolution, British armies rushed into the power vacuum. By bribing corrupt Iranians liberally, Great Britain in 1919 negotiated a treaty allowing the installation of British "advisers" in every department of the government. The Majlis refused to ratify the treaty, which confirmed Iranians' worst suspicions about Britain and the West.

That blatant attempt to make Iran a British satellite was a key event in the development of Iranian nationalism. It aroused the national spirit. In 1921 reaction against the British brought to power a military dictator, Reza Shah Pahlavi (1877–1944), who proclaimed himself shah in 1925 and ruled until 1941.

Inspired throughout his reign by the example of Turkey's Mustafa Kemal, the patriotic, religiously indifferent Reza Shah had three basic goals: to build a modern nation, to free Iran from foreign domination, and to rule with an iron fist. The challenge was enormous. Iran was a vast, backward country of deserts, mountain barriers, and rudimentary communications. Most of the rural population was poor and illiterate, and among the Persian majority were sizable ethnic minorities with their own aspirations. Furthermore, Iran's powerful religious leaders hated Western (Christian) domination but were no less opposed to a more secular, less Islamic society.

To realize his vision of a strong Iran, the energetic shah created a modern army, built railroads, and encouraged commerce and industry. He won control over ethnic minorities such as the Kurds in the north and Arab tribesmen on the border with Iraq. He withdrew many of the privileges granted to foreigners and raised taxes on the powerful Anglo-Persian Oil Company, which had been founded in 1909 to exploit the first great oil strike in the Middle East. Yet Reza Shah was ultimately less successful than Atatürk. Because the European-educated elite in Iran was smaller than in Turkey, the idea of re-creating Persian greatness on the basis of a secularized society attracted fewer determined supporters. Many powerful religious leaders turned against him. Reza Shah became increasingly brutal, greedy, and tyrannical, murdering his enemies and lining his pockets. His support of Hitler's Nazi Germany also exposed Iran's tenuous and fragile independence to the impact of European conflicts.

Afghanistan, meanwhile, was nominally independent in the nineteenth century, but the British imposed political restrictions and constantly meddled in the country. In 1919 the new, violently anti-British amir Amanullah (1892–1960) declared a holy war on the British government in India and won complete independence for the first time. Amanullah then decreed revolutionary reforms designed to hurl his primitive country into the twentieth century. The result was tribal and religious revolt, civil war, and retreat from reform. Islam remained both religion and law. A powerful but primitive patriotism had enabled Afghanistan to win political independence from the West, but modest efforts to build a modern society met little success.

The Arab States and Palestine

The establishment of French and British mandates at gunpoint forced Arab nationalists to seek independence by gradual means after 1920. Arab nationalists were indirectly aided by Western taxpayers, who wanted cheap—that is, peaceful—empires. As a result, Arabs won considerable control over local affairs in the mandated states, except Palestine, though the mandates remained European satellites in international and economic affairs.

The wily British chose Faisal, whom the French had so recently deposed in Syria, as king of Iraq. Faisal obligingly signed an alliance giving British advisers broad behind-the-scenes control. The king also accepted British ownership of Iraq's oil fields, thereby giving the West a stranglehold on the Iraqi economy. Given the limitations imposed on him, Faisal (r. 1921–1933) proved an able ruler, gaining the support of his people and encouraging moderate reforms. In 1932 he secured Iraqi independence at the price of a long-term military alliance with Great Britain.

Egypt, occupied by Great Britain ever since 1882 (see page 967) and a British protectorate since 1914, pursued a similar path. Following intense nationalist agitation after the Great War, Great Britain in 1922 proclaimed Egypt formally independent but continued to occupy the country militarily. In 1936, the British agreed to a treaty restricting their troops to their big bases in the Suez Canal Zone.

The French were less compromising in Syria. They practiced a policy of divide-and-rule, carving out a second mandate in Lebanon and generally playing off ethnic and religious minorities against each other. Lebanon eventually became a republic, dominated by a very slender Christian majority and under French protection. Arab nationalists in Syria finally won promises of Syrian independence in 1936 in return for a treaty of friendship with France.

In short, the Arab states gradually freed themselves from Western political mandates but not from the Western military threat or from pervasive Western influence. Of great importance, large Arab landowners and urban merchants increased their wealth and political power after 1918, and they often supported the Western hegemony from which they benefited greatly. Western control over the newly discovered oil fields by foreign companies helped to convince radical nationalists that economic independence and genuine freedom had not yet been achieved. The struggle against the West had to continue, they believed.

Relations between the Arabs and the West were complicated by the tense situation in the British mandate of Palestine, and that situation deteriorated in the interwar years. Both Arabs and Jews denounced the British, who tried unsuccessfully to compromise with both sides. The anger of Arab nationalists, however, was aimed primarily at Jewish settlers. The key issue was Jewish migration from Europe to Palestine.

A small Jewish community had survived in Palestine ever since the destruction of Jerusalem and the dispersal of the Jews in Roman times. But Jewish nationalism, known as "Zionism," was a recent phenomenon of European origin. The Dreyfus affair (see page 949) and anti-Jewish riots in Russia had convinced a cultured Austrian journalist named Theodore Herzl (1860–1904) that even nonreligious Jews would never be fully accepted in Europe. He believed that only the re-creation of a Jewish state, preferably but not necessarily in Palestine, could guarantee Jews dignity and security. Under Herzl's leadership, the Zionist movement encouraged Jews from all over the world to settle in the Palestine region on lands purchased by Jewish philanthropists with the approval of the relatively tolerant Ottoman rulers. Some Jewish idealists from Russia and central Europe were attracted to Palestine by the Zionist vision, but until 1921 the great majority of Jewish emigrants preferred the United States.

After the First World War the situation changed radically. An isolationist United States drastically limited immigration from eastern Europe, where war and revolution had caused chaos and kindled anti-Semitism. Moreover, the British began honoring the Balfour Declaration despite Arab protests. Thus the number of Jewish immigrants to Palestine from turbulent Europe grew rapidly. The first surge came in the early 1920s. The second came in the 1930s, when German and Polish per-

The Founding of Tel-Aviv, 1908 This rare photo shows Jewish settlers coming together to found Tel-Aviv as a new city on the outskirts of the old port of Jaffa. Tel-Aviv grew modestly at first, but its population surged in the 1930s after Hitler came to power and many European Jews sought refuge in Palestine. *(Source: Zionist Archives and Library)*

secution created a mass of Jewish refugees. By 1939 the Jewish population of Palestine had increased almost fivefold over 1914 and accounted for about 30 percent of all inhabitants.

Jewish settlers in Palestine faced formidable economic and political difficulties. Much of the land purchased by the Jewish National Fund was productive. But many of the sellers of such land were wealthy absentee Arab landowners, the kind who had profited from the rise of commercial agriculture in Egypt and other parts of the Ottoman Empire and who had little interest in the welfare of their Arab tenants (see page 967). When the new Jewish owners subsequently replaced those age-old Arab tenants with Jewish settlers, Arab farmers and intellectuals burned with a sense of injustice. Moreover, most Jewish immigrants came from ur-

ban backgrounds and preferred to establish new cities like Tel Aviv or to live in existing towns, where they competed with the Arabs. The land issue combined with economic and cultural friction to harden Arab protest into hatred. Anti-Jewish riots and even massacres ensued.

The British gradually responded to Arab pressure and tried to slow Jewish immigration. This effort satisfied neither Jews nor Arabs, and by 1938 the two communities were engaged in an undeclared civil war. On the eve of the Second World War, the frustrated British proposed an independent Palestine as well as a cap of 75,000 additional Jewish immigrants. This low number would permanently limit the Jews to being only about one-third of Palestine's total population. Zionists felt themselves in grave danger.

THE MIDDLE EAST, 1914–1939

1914	Ottoman Empire enters First World War on Germany's side
1916	Allies agree secretly to partition Ottoman Empire
1916–1917	Arab revolt against Turkish rule grows
November 1917	Balfour Declaration pledges British support for a Jewish homeland in Palestine
October 1918	Arabs and British triumph as Ottoman Empire collapses
1919	Treaty of Versailles divides old Ottoman Empire into League of Nations mandates
1919	Mustafa Kemal mounts nationalist struggle against foreign occupation
1920	Faisal proclaimed king of Syria but quickly deposed by the French, who establish their mandate in Syria
Early 1920s	Tide of Jewish immigration surges into British mandate of Palestine
1923	Treaty of Lausanne recognizes independent Turkey; Mustafa Kemal begins to secularize Turkish society
1925	Reza Shah takes power in Iran and rules to 1941
1932	Iraq gains political independence in return for long-term military alliance with Great Britain
1936	Syrian nationalists sign treaty of friendship with France in return for promises of independence
late 1930s	Tensions mount between Arabs and Jews in Palestine

In the face of adversity, Jewish settlers from many different countries gradually succeeded in forging a cohesive community. Hebrew, which for centuries had been used only in religious worship, was revived as a living language to bind the Jews in Palestine together. Despite its slow beginnings, rural development achieved often spectacular results. The key unit of agricultural organization was the *kibbutz,* a collective farm on which each member shared equally in the work, rewards, and defense of the farm. Men and women labored side by side; a nursery cared for the children and a common dining hall served meals. Some cooperative farms turned arid grazing land into citrus groves and irrigated gardens. An egalitarian socialist ideology also characterized industry, which grew rapidly and was owned largely by the Jewish trade unions. By 1939 a new but old nation was emerging in the Middle East.

TOWARD SELF-RULE IN INDIA

The national movement in British India grew out of two interconnected cultures, Hindu and Muslim, which came to see themselves as fundamentally different in rising to challenge British rule. Nowhere has the power of modern nationalism, both to unify and to divide, been more strikingly demonstrated than in India.

Promises and Repression (1914–1919)

Indian nationalism had emerged in the late nineteenth century (see page 983), and when the First World War began, the British feared revolt. Instead, somewhat like Europe's equally mistrusted socialist workers, Indians supported the war effort. About 1.2 million Indian soldiers and laborers volunteered for duty and served in Europe, Africa, and the Middle East. The British government in India and the native Indian princes sent large supplies of food, money, and ammunition. In return, the British opened more good government jobs to Indians and made other minor concessions.

As the war in distant Europe ground on, however, inflation, high taxes, food shortages, and a terrible influenza epidemic created widespread suffering and discontent. The prewar nationalist movement revived, stronger than ever, and the moderate and radical wings of the Indian National Congress joined forces. Moreover, in 1916 the

Hindus leading the Congress party hammered out an alliance—the Lucknow Pact—with India's Muslim League. Founded in 1906 to uphold Muslim interests, the league had grown out of fears arising from the fact that under British rule the once-dominant Muslim minority had fallen behind the Hindu majority, especially in the Western education necessary to secure good jobs in the government. The Lucknow Pact forged a powerful united front of Hindus and Muslims and called for putting India on equal footing with self-governing white British dominions like Canada, Australia, and New Zealand.

The British response was contradictory. On the one hand, the secretary of state for India made the unprecedented announcement in August 1917 that British policy in India called for the "gradual development of self-governing institutions and the progressive realization of responsible government." The means of achieving this great step forward were spelled out in late 1919 in the Government of India Act, which established a dual administration: part Indian and elected, part British and authoritarian. Such noncontroversial activities as agriculture, health, and education were transferred from British to Indian officials who were accountable to elected provincial assemblies. More sensitive matters like taxes, police, and the courts remained solely in British hands.

The positive impact of this reform, so typical of the British tradition of gradual political change, was seriously undermined by old-fashioned authoritarian rule. Despite the unanimous opposition of the elected Indian members, the British in 1919 rammed the repressive Rowlatt Acts through India's Imperial Legislative Council. These acts indefinitely extended wartime "emergency measures" designed to curb unrest and root out "conspiracy." The result was a wave of rioting across India.

Under these tense conditions an unsuspecting crowd of some ten thousand gathered to celebrate

Toward Self Rule   A British and an Indian official oversee efforts to lift an injured camel out of a canal, symbolizing the new policy of joint administration in 1919. Although the Amritsar Massacre undermined Indian faith in British promises, joint administration was a major step toward independence. *(Source: By permission of the British Library)*

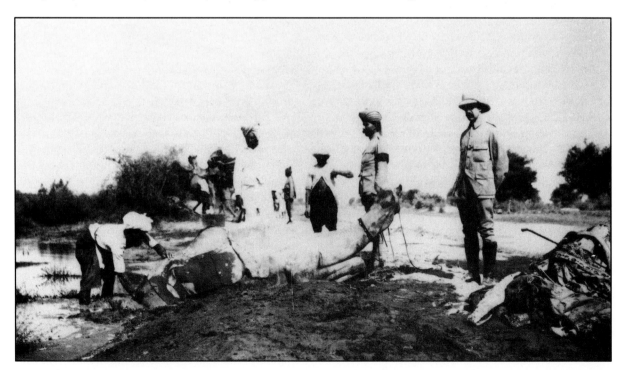

a Hindu religious festival in an enclosed square in Amritsar, a city in the northern province of Punjab. The local English commander, General Reginald Dyer, had, unknown to the crowd, banned all public meetings that very day. Dyer marched his native Gurkha troops onto the field and, without warning, ordered them to fire. The soldiers kept firing into the unarmed mass at point-blank range until the ammunition ran out. A total of 1,650 rounds were fired, killing 379 and wounding 1,137; nine of every ten rounds claimed a victim. The Amritsar Massacre shattered wartime hopes in a frenzy of postwar reaction. India seemed to stand on the verge of more violence and repression and, sooner or later, terrorism and guerrilla war. That India took a different path to national liberation was due largely to Mohandas "Mahatma" Gandhi (1869–1948), who became the most fascinating and influential Indian since Ashoka (see pages 81–83).

Hindu Society and Mahatma Gandhi

By the time of Gandhi's birth in 1869, the Indian subcontinent was firmly controlled by the British. Part of the country was directly ruled by British (and subordinate Indian) officials, ultimately answerable to the British Parliament in London. These areas included Bengal and its teeming capital of Calcutta in eastern India, Bombay and its hinterland in western India, the Punjab in the northwest, and Madras on the southeast coast. So-called protected states were more sheltered from European ideas and from the world economy. There many of the old ways remained intact. The native prince—usually known as the *maharaja*—remained the titular ruler, though he was bound to the British by unequal treaties and had to accept the "advice" of the British resident assigned to his court.

It was in just such a tiny backwater protected state that Gandhi grew up. His father was a member of the merchant caste—*gandhi* means "grocer" in the Gujarati language. The Indian caste system has always been more flexible and dynamic than unsympathetic Westerners have wanted to believe, and for six generations the heads of Gandhi's family had served as hereditary prime ministers in various minuscule realms on the Kathiawar peninsula, north of Bombay on the Arabian Sea.

The extended (or joint) family, which had for generations been the most important unit of Indian society, powerfully influenced young Gandhi. Gandhi's father was the well-to-do head of the clan, which included five brothers and their wives, children, and children's children. The big three-story ancestral home swarmed with relatives. A whole community crowded into the labyrinth of tiny rooms and spilled out into the open courtyards. There the entire extended family celebrated holidays and Hindu festivals. There the prime minister routinely entertained a score of dinner guests each day. In such a communal atmosphere, patience, kindness, and a good-natured love of people were essential virtues; the aggressive, solitary individualism so prized in Europe and North America would have threatened group harmony. So it was for Gandhi.

In the Hindu family the woman is subordinate but respected. She is "worshipped as a mother, venerated as a wife, loved as a sister, but not much regarded as a woman. Woman as woman is the handmaid of man; her duty is to worship her husband, to bear and rear his children."[6] Every Hindu girl married young, often before puberty; her husband was chosen by her parents. The young bride moved into her father-in-law's house, where, according to one famous Indian nationalist, it was "the common rule for intercourse to take place on that very night when she has the first menstruation. . . This custom has been practiced for at least 2500 years."[7]

Marriage was a sacrament that could not be dissolved by divorce or even by death. Widows were forbidden by custom to remarry and, until the British abolished the practice in 1829, a dutiful wife from a high-ranking caste was expected to throw herself on her husband's funeral pyre and join him immediately in the world beyond. More generally, a woman's fate was linked to that of the family, in which she was the trusted guardian of orthodox Hindu values.

Gandhi's mother was the ideal Hindu housewife. Married as a young illiterate girl to a forty-two-year-old man whose first wives had died without male children, Putali Ba bore three boys and a girl. According to Gandhi, his ever-cheerful mother was "the first to rise and the last to go to bed . . . and she never made any distinction between her own children and other children in the family."[8] Very devoted but undogmatic in relig-

The March to the Sea Gandhi repeatedly used nonviolent resistance to challenge British rule and mobilize the Indian masses. Here he leads his supporters in the famous march to the sea in 1929. *(Source: Press Association Limited)*

ious matters, Putali Ba fasted regularly and exercised a strong influence on her precocious son. Gandhi was married at thirteen to a local girl who became his lifelong companion.

After his father's death, Gandhi decided to study law in England. No member of his subcaste had ever done so, and the local elders declared Gandhi an outcaste, claiming that Hindu practices would not be possible in alien England. Gandhi disagreed. To win over his wife and anxious mother, he swore that he would not touch meat, women, or wine in the foreign land. Gandhi kept his word and became a zealous vegetarian, refusing even to eat eggs because they were potential living creatures. After passing the English bar, he returned to India. But his practice in Bombay failed, and in 1893 he decided to try his luck as a lawyer for wealthy Indian merchants in South Africa. It was a momentous decision.

The Roots of Militant Nonviolence

Soon after arriving in South Africa, the elegant young lawyer in Western dress took a business trip by train. A white man entered Gandhi's first-class compartment, took one look, and called the conductor. Gandhi was ordered to ride in the baggage car. When he protested, a policeman threw him off the train. Years later Gandhi recalled this experience as a critical turning point in his life. He had refused to bow to naked racial injustice.

As Gandhi's law practice flourished, he began to examine the plight of Indians in South Africa.

After the British abolished black slavery in the empire, plantation owners in South Africa and elsewhere had developed a "new system of slavery"[9]: they imported desperately poor Indians as indentured laborers on five-year renewable contracts. When some thrifty, hard-working Indians completed their terms and remained in South Africa as free persons and economic competitors, the Dutch and British settlers passed brutally discriminatory laws. The law books called Indians "semi-barbarous Asiatics," and some towns even prohibited Indians from walking on the sidewalks. Poor Indians had to work on white-owned plantations or return to India; rich Indians lost the vote. Gandhi undertook the legal defense of his countrymen, infuriating the whites. In 1896 a hysterical mob almost lynched the "coolie lawyer."

Meanwhile Gandhi was searching for a spiritual theory of social action. Identifying with South Africa's black majority as well as with his own countrymen, he meditated on the Hindu pursuit of spiritual strength through fasting, sexual abstinence, devotion to duty, and reincarnation. He also studied Christian teachings. Gradually Gandhi developed and articulated a weapon for the weak that he called "Satyagraha." *Satya* in Hindu means "spiritual truth," which equals love; *agraha* is "strength" or "force." Gandhi conceived of Satyagraha, loosely translated as "Soul Force," as a means of striving for truth and social justice through love, suffering, and conversion of the oppressor. Its tactic is courageous nonviolent resistance. Satyagraha owed a good deal to the Christian Gospels, for Christ's call to "love your enemies" touched Gandhi to the core.

As the undisputed leader of South Africa's Indians before the First World War, Gandhi put his philosophy into action. When the white government of South Africa severely restricted Asians' immigration and internal freedom of movement, he led a campaign of mass resistance. Thousands of Indian men and women marched across forbidden borders and peacefully withstood beatings, arrest, and imprisonment.

The struggle was hard and the odds long, but Gandhi never wavered. He remarked to a friend at the time, "Men say I am a saint losing myself in politics. The fact is I am a politician trying my hardest to be a saint."[10] In 1914, South Africa's exasperated whites agreed to many of the Indians' demands. A law was passed abolishing discriminatory taxes on Indian traders, recognizing the legality of non-Christian marriages, and permitting the continued immigration of free Indians. Satyagraha—militant nonviolence in pursuit of social justice—had proved itself a powerful force in Gandhi's hands.

Gandhi Leads the Way

In 1915 Gandhi returned to India. His reputation had preceded him: the masses hailed him as a "Mahatma," or "Great Soul"—a Hindu title of veneration for a man of great knowledge and humanity—and the name stuck. Feeling his way into Indian affairs, Gandhi, dressed in peasant garb, crisscrossed India on third-class trains, listening to common folk and talking to Congress party leaders. Moved by the wretched misery of the very poor, he led some sharecroppers against British landowners and organized a strike of textile workers in his native Gujarat. But it was the aftermath of the Amritsar Massacre that catapulted Gandhi to leadership of the national movement in India.

Drawing on his South African experience, Gandhi in 1920 launched a national campaign of nonviolent resistance to British rule. Denouncing British injustice, he urged his countrymen to boycott British goods, jobs, and honors. He returned medals that he had won in South Africa and told peasants not to pay taxes or buy heavily taxed liquor. Gandhi electrified the people.

The result was nothing less than a revolution in Indian politics. The nationalist movement had previously touched only the tiny, prosperous, Western-educated elite. Now both the illiterate masses of village India and the educated classes heard a voice that seemed to be in harmony with their profoundest values. Even Gandhi's renunciation of sex—with his wife's consent—accorded with a popular Hindu belief attributing special power to those who do not squander their life force in sexual intercourse. Gandhi's call for militant nonviolence was particularly appealing to the masses of Hindus who were not members of the warrior caste or the so-called military races and who were traditionally passive and nonviolent. The British had regarded ordinary Hindus as cowards. Gandhi told them that they could be courageous and even morally superior:

Formerly, when people wanted to fight with one another, they measured between them their bodily strength; now it is possible to take away thousands of lives by one man working behind a gun from a hill. . . .

What do you think? Wherein is courage required—in blowing others to pieces from behind a cannon, or with a smiling face to approach a cannon and be blown to pieces? Who is the true warrior—he who keeps death always as a bosom-friend, or he who controls the death of others? Believe me that a man devoid of courage and manhood can never be a passive resister.[11]

Gandhi made Congress into a mass political party, welcoming members from every ethnic group and cooperating closely with the Muslim minority.

In 1922, some Indian resisters turned to violence. A mob murdered twenty-two policemen and savage riots broke out. Gandhi abruptly called off his campaign. Arrested for fomenting rebellion, Gandhi told the British judge that he had committed "a Himalayan blunder to believe that India had accepted nonviolence."[12] Released from prison after two years, Gandhi set up a commune, established a national newspaper, and set out to reform Indian society and improve the lot of the poor. He welcomed the outcaste untouchables into his fellowship. He worked to help child widows, promote cottage industry, and end the use of alcohol. For Gandhi, moral improvement, social progress, and the national movement always went hand in hand.

The resistance campaign of 1920–1922 left the British severely shaken. Although moderate Indians had participated effectively in the system of dual government, the commission formed by the British in 1927 to consider further steps toward self-rule included no Indian members. Indian resentment was intense. In 1929, the radical nationalists, led by the able and aristocratic Jawaharlal Nehru (1889–1964), pushed through the National Congress a resolution calling for virtual independence within a year. The British predictably stiffened, and Indian radicals talked of a bloody showdown.

In this tense situation Gandhi masterfully reasserted his leadership. To satisfy the extremists, he took a hard line toward the British, but he controlled the extremists by insisting on nonviolent methods. He then organized another massive resistance campaign, this time against the hated salt tax, which affected every Indian family. Gandhi himself led 50,000 people in a spectacular march to the sea to make salt without paying a

The Flag of the Indian National Congress flies over this mass political meeting. Gandhi believed that India had to revive its handicraft industry and he chose the Indian spinning wheel—placed in the center of the party's flag—as a symbol of national rejuvenation. *(Source: Wide World Photos)*

tax, in defiance of the law. A Western journalist described their reception:

Suddenly, at a word of command, scores of native policemen rushed upon the advancing marchers and rained blows on their heads. . . . No one of the marchers even raised an arm to fend off the blows. They went down like ten-pins. From where I stood I heard the whack of the clubs on unprotected skulls. . . . Those struck down fell sprawling, unconscious or writhing with fractured skulls or broken shoulders. . . . The survivors, without breaking ranks, silently and doggedly marched on until struck down.[13]

Over the next few months 60,000 protesters, including Gandhi, went to jail, but this time there was very little rioting. Finally, in 1931, the frustrated, unnerved British released Gandhi from jail and sat down to negotiate with him, as an equal, over self-rule for India. There were many complications, including the determined opposition of diehard imperialists like Winston Churchill. But in 1935 the negotiations resulted in a new constitution, which greatly strengthened India's parliamentary representative institutions. It was virtually a blueprint for independence.

Gandhi inspired people far beyond India's borders. Martin Luther King, Jr., was later to be deeply influenced by his tactic and philosophy of nonviolent social action. Gandhi did much to transform the elitist nationalism of Indian intellectuals into a mighty mass movement with social as well as political concerns. Above all, Gandhi nurtured national identity and self-respect. As Nehru summed it up, Gandhi "instilled courage and manhood in India's people; . . . courage is the one sure foundation of character, he had said; without courage there is no morality, no religion, no love."[14]

Despite his best efforts, Gandhi failed to heal a widening split between Hindus and Muslims. The development of an Indian nationalism based largely on Hindu symbols and customs increasingly disturbed the Muslim minority. Tempers mounted and atrocities were committed by both sides. By the late 1930s the leaders of the Muslim League were calling for the creation of a Muslim nation in British India, a "Pakistan" or "land of the pure." As in Palestine, the rise of conflicting nationalisms in India was to lead to tragedy (see page 1083).

TURMOIL IN EAST ASIA

Because of the efforts of the Meiji reformers, nationalism and modernization were well developed in Japan by 1914. Not only was Japan capable of competing politically and economically with the world's leading nations, but it had already begun building its own empire and proclaiming its special mission in Asia. China lagged far behind, but after 1912 the pace of nationalist development there began to quicken.

In the 1920s the Chinese nationalist movement managed to win a large measure of political independence from the imperialist West and promoted extensive modernization. But these achievements were soon undermined by internal conflict and war with an expanding Japan. Nationalism also flourished elsewhere in Asia, scoring a major victory in the Philippine Islands.

The Rise of Nationalist China

The revolution of 1911–1912, which overthrew the Manchu Dynasty (see page 987), opened an era of unprecedented change for Chinese society. Before the revolution, many progressive Chinese had realized that fundamental technological and political reforms were necessary to save the Chinese state and to meet the many-sided Western challenge. Most had hoped, however, to preserve the traditional core of Chinese civilization and culture. The fall of the 2,000-year-old dynastic system shattered such hopes. If the emperor himself was no longer sacred, what was? Everything was open to question and to alteration.

The central figure in the revolution was a crafty old military man, Yüan Shih-k'ai (1859–1916). Called out of retirement to save the dynasty, Yüan betrayed the Manchus and convinced the revolutionaries that he was a Chinese Bismarck who could unite the country peacefully and prevent foreign intervention. Once elected president of the republic, however, Yüan concentrated on building his own power. He quarreled with parliament and with Sun Yat-sen (see page 987), the inspiring revolutionary leader who had built the Kuomintang, or Nationalist party. Once again Yüan was a betrayer. In 1914, he used military force to dissolve China's parliament and ruled as a dictator. China's first modern revolution had failed.

The extent of the failure became apparent only after Yüan's death in 1916. The central government in Peking almost disintegrated. For more than a decade power resided in a multitude of local military leaders, the so-called warlords. Most warlords were men of strong, flamboyant personality, capable of building armies by preying on the peasantry and of winning legal recognition from Peking. None of them proved able to establish either a new dynasty or a modern state. Their wars, taxes, and corruption created only terrible suffering.

Foreign imperialism intensified the agony of warlordism. Although China declared its neutrality in 1914, Japan used the Great War in Europe as an opportunity to seize Germany's holdings on the Shantung Peninsula and in 1915 forced China to accept Japanese control of Shantung and southern Manchuria (see Map 30.4, page 986). Japan's expansion angered China's growing middle class and enraged China's young patriots. On May 4, 1919, five thousand students in Peking exploded against the decision of the Versailles Peace Conference to leave the Shantung Peninsula in Japanese hands. This famous incident launched the "May Fourth Movement," which opposed both foreign domination and warlord government.

The May Fourth Movement and the anti-imperialism of Bolshevik Russia renewed the hopes of Chinese nationalists. Struggling for a foothold in southern China, Sun Yat-sen (1866–1925) decided in 1923 to ally his Nationalist party with the Communist Third International and the newly formed Chinese Communist party. The result was the first of many so-called national liberation fronts, in keeping with Lenin's blueprint for (temporarily) uniting all anticonservative, anti-imperialist forces in a common revolutionary struggle. In an effort to develop a disciplined party apparatus and a well-indoctrinated party army, Sun reorganized the Nationalist party along Bolshevik lines.

Sun, however, was no Communist. In his *Three Principles of the People,* elaborating on the official Nationalist party ideology—nationalism, democracy, and people's livelihood—nationalism remained of prime importance:

For the most part the four hundred million people of China can be spoken of as completely Han Chinese. With common habits and customs, we are completely of one race. But in the world today what position do

Civil War in China Chiang Kai-shek's move to purge his Communist allies in 1927 marked the beginning of a long bitter conflict. Here dead combatants lie on a main street in Canton, where in December 1927 a Communist uprising established an independent commune that was soon crushed. *(Source: BBC Hulton/The Bettmann Archive)*

we occupy? Compared to the other peoples of the world we have the greatest population and our civilization is four thousand years old; we should be advancing in the front rank with the nations of Europe and America. But the Chinese people have only family and clan solidarity, they do not have national spirit. Therefore even though we have four hundred million people gathered together in one China, in reality they are just a heap of loose sand. Today we are the poorest and weakest nation in the world, and occupy the lowest position in international affairs. Other men are the carving knife and serving dish; we are the fish and the meat. Our position at this time is most perilous. If we do not earnestly espouse nationalism and weld together our four hundred million people into a strong nation, there is a danger of China's being lost and our people being destroyed. If we wish to avert this catastrophe, we must espouse nationalism and bring this national spirit to the salvation of the country.[15]

Democracy, on the other hand, had a less exalted meaning. Sun equated it with firm rule by the Nationalists, who would promote the people's livelihood through land reform and welfare measures. Sun was in some ways a traditional Chinese rebel and reformer who wanted to re-establish order and protect the peasants.

Sun's plan was to use the Nationalist party's revolutionary army to crush the warlords and reunite China under a strong central government. When Sun unexpectedly died in 1925, this task was assumed by Chiang Kai-shek (1887–1975), the young Japanese-educated director of the party's army training school. In 1926 and 1927, Chiang led enthusiastic Nationalist armies in a highly successful attack on warlord governments in central and northern China. Preceded by teams of party propagandists, the well-disciplined Nationalist armies were welcomed by the people. In a series of complicated moves, the Nationalists consolidated their rule in 1928 and established a new capital at Nanking. Foreign states recognized the Nanking government, and superficial observers believed China to be truly reunified.

In fact, national unification was only skin-deep. China remained a vast agricultural country plagued by foreign concessions, regional differences, and a lack of modern communications. Moreover, Japan was opposed to a China strong enough to challenge Japan's stranglehold on Manchuria. Finally, the uneasy alliance between the Nationalist party and the Chinese Communist party had turned into a bitter, deadly rivalry. Justifiably fearful of Communist subversion of the Nationalist government and encouraged by his military success and by wealthy Chinese capitalists, Chiang decided in April 1927 to liquidate his left-wing "allies" in a bloody purge. Secret agents raided Communist cells without warning, and soldiers gunned down suspects on sight. Chinese Communists went into hiding and vowed revenge.

China's Intellectual Revolution

Nationalism was the most powerful idea in China between 1911 and 1929, but it was only one aspect of a highly complex intellectual revolution that hammered at traditional Chinese thought and practice, advocated cultural renaissance, and led China into the modern world. Two other currents in that intellectual revolution, generally known as the "New Culture Movement," were significant.

The New Culture Movement was founded by young Western-oriented intellectuals in Peking during the May Fourth era. These intellectuals fiercely attacked China's ancient Confucian ethics, which subordinated subjects to rulers, sons to fathers, and wives to husbands. Confucius had lived in a distant feudal age, they said; his teachings were totally inappropriate to modern life. In such widely read magazines as *New Youth* and *New Tide*, the modernists provocatively advocated new and anti-Confucian virtues: individualism, democratic equality, and the critical scientific method. They also promoted the use of simple, understandable written language, a language freed from classical scholarship and literary conventions, as a means to clear thinking and mass education. China, they said, needed a whole new culture, a radically different world view.

The most influential of these intellectuals championing liberalism was Hu Shih (1891–1962). Educated on a scholarship in the United States, Hu had studied with the educational philosopher John Dewey, whose thoroughly American pragmatism stressed compromise and practical problem solving. A master at tearing down old beliefs, the mature Hu Shih envisioned a vague and uninspiring future. The liberation and reconstruction of China was possible, he said, but it would have to occur gradually, "bit by bit, drop by drop." Hu personified the limitations of the Western liberal tradition in China.

The other major current growing out of the New Culture Movement was Marxian socialism. It too was Western in origin, "scientific" in approach, and materialist in its denial of religious belief and Confucian family ethics. But while liberalism and individualism reflected the bewildering range of Western thought since the Enlightenment, Marxian socialism offered Chinese intellectuals the certainty of a single all-encompassing creed. As one young Communist exclaimed:

I am now able to impose order on all the ideas which I could not reconcile; I have found the key to all the problems which appeared to me self-contradictory and insoluble.[16]

Marxism was undeniably Western and therefore modern. But it also provided a means of criticizing Western dominance, thereby salving Chinese pride: China's pitiful weakness was due to rapacious foreign capitalistic imperialism. Also Marxism, as modified by Lenin and applied by the Bolsheviks, appeared to get results. For Chinese believers, it promised salvation soon. Chinese Communists could and did interpret Marxism-Leninism to appeal to the masses—the peasants.

Mao Tse-tung (1893–1976) in particular recognized quickly the enormous revolutionary potential of the Chinese peasantry, impoverished and oppressed by parasitic landlords. A member of a prosperous, hard-working peasant family, Mao converted to Marxian socialism in 1918 while employed as an assistant librarian at Peking University and began his revolutionary career as an urban labor organizer. In 1925 protest strikes by Chinese textile workers against their Japanese employers unexpectedly spread from the big coastal cities to rural China, prompting Mao to reconsider the peasants. Investigating the rapid growth of radical peasant associations in Hunan province, Mao argued passionately in a 1927 report that

the force of the peasantry is like that of the raging winds and driving rain. It is rapidly increasing in violence. No force can stand in its way. The peasantry will tear apart all nets which bind it and hasten along the road to liberation. They will bury beneath them all forces of imperialism, militarism, corrupt officialdom, village bosses and evil gentry. Every revolutionary party, every revolutionary comrade will be subjected to their scrutiny and be accepted or rejected by them.[17]

Mao Tse-tung Adapting Marxian theory to Chinese reality, Mao concentrated on the revolutionary potential of the peasantry. Here the forty-year-old Mao is preaching his gospel to representatives of poor peasants in southern China in 1933. *(Source: Wide World Photos)*

The task of Communists was to harness the peasant hurricane and use its elemental force to destroy the existing order and take power. Mao's first experiment in peasant revolt—the Autumn Harvest Uprising of September 1927—was no more successful than the abortive insurrections of urban workers launched by his more orthodox comrades. But Mao learned quickly. He advocated equal distribution of land and broke up his forces into small guerrilla groups. After 1928 he and his supporters built up a self-governing Communist soviet, centered at Juichin in southeastern China, and dug in against Nationalist attacks.

The Changing Chinese Family

For many generations, Confucian reverence for the family and family ties helped stabilize traditional Chinese society and gave life meaning. The

A Manchu Family   The women of a large, rich Manchu family pose for a solemn group portrait. Coming out of Manchuria and ruling China until 1912, the Manchus sought to preserve a separate cultural identity. Unlike Chinese women, Manchu women did not bind their feet. *(Source: Popperfoto)*

Confucian principle of subordination suffused family life—subordination of the individual to the group, of the young to the old, of the wife to the husband. Given in marriage by her parents at an early age, the wife owed unquestioning obedience to her husband and mother-in-law. Wealthy husbands customarily took additional wives or purchased concubines from poor families, but for women divorce and running away were almost unthinkable. Women of all ages were commonly sold, and they lacked all property rights.

A Daughter of Han, a rare autobiography of a Chinese woman, as told to an American friend, offers an unforgettable glimpse of Chinese family life. Born in 1867 to poor parents in a northern city, Lao T'ai T'ai lived it all. Her foot-binding was delayed to age nine, "since I loved so much to run and play." When the bandages were finally drawn tight, "my feet hurt so much that for two years I had to crawl on my knees."[18] Her arranged marriage at fourteen was a disaster: her husband

was a drug addict—"in those days everyone took opium to some extent"—who grabbed everything to pay for his habit. "There was no freedom then for women," and she endured her situation until her husband sold their four-year-old daughter to buy opium. Taking her remaining baby daughter, Lao T'ai T'ai fled. She became a beggar, a cook in wealthy households, and a peddler of luxury goods to wealthy cooped-up women.

The two unshakable values that buoyed her were a tough, fatalistic acceptance—"Only fortune that comes of itself will come. There is no use to seek for it"—and devotion to her family. Lao T'ai T'ai eventually returned home to her husband, who was "good" in those years, "but I did not miss him when he died. I had my newborn son and I was happy. My house was established. . . . Truly all my life I spent thinking of my family." Her lifelong devotion was reciprocated by her faithful son and granddaughter, who cared for her well in old age.

EAST ASIA, 1911–1939

1911–1912	Revolution in China overthrows Manchu dynasty and establishes republic
1915	Japan seizes German holdings in China and expands into southern Manchuria
May 4, 1919	Demonstration by Chinese students against Versailles peace conference and Japan sparks broad nationalist movement
1920s	New Cultural Movement challenges traditional Chinese values
1922	Japan signs naval agreement with Western powers
1923	Sun Yat-sen allies the Nationalist Party with Chinese Communists
	Kita Ikki advocates ultranationalism in Japan
1925–1928	Chiang Kai-shek, leader of the Nationalist Party, attacks warlord government and seeks to unify China
1927	Chiang Kai-shek purges his Communist allies
	Mao Tse-tung recognizes the revolutionary potential of the Chinese peasantry
1930–1934	Nationalists campaign continually against the Chinese Communists
1931	Mukden Incident leads to Japanese occupation of Manchuria
1932	Japan proclaims Manchuria an independent state
1934	Mao Tse-tung leads Communists on Long March to new base in northwestern China
	The Philippines gain self-governing commonwealth status from United States
1936	Japan allies with Germany in anti-Communist pact
1937	Japanese militarists launch general attack on China

Lao T'ai T'ai's remarkable life history encompasses both old and new Chinese attitudes toward the family. Her son moved to the city, prospered, and had only one wife. Her granddaughter eventually became a college teacher, an anti-Japanese patriot, and a determined foe of arranged marriages, admirably personifying the trend toward greater freedom and equality for Chinese women after 1911. Foot-binding was outlawed and gradually died out unlamented. Marriage for love became increasingly common, and unprecedented educational and economic opportunities opened up for women. Polygamy declined. In the short space of three generations, rising nationalism and the intellectual revolution accomplished monumental changes in Chinese family life.

From Liberalism to Ultranationalism in Japan

The efforts of the Meiji reformers (see page 983) to build a powerful nationalistic state and resist Western imperialism were spectacularly successful and deeply impressive to Japan's fellow Asians. The Japanese, alone among non-Western peoples, had mastered modern industrial technology by 1910 and fought victorious wars against both China and Russia. The First World War brought more triumphs. Japan easily seized Germany's Asian holdings and held on to most of them as League of Nations mandates. The Japanese economy expanded enormously. Profits soared as Japan won new markets that wartime Europe could no longer supply.

In the early 1920s Japan seemed to make further progress on all fronts. Most Japanese nationalists believed that Japan had a semidivine mission to enlighten and protect Asia, but some were convinced that they could achieve their goal peacefully. In 1922, Japan signed a naval arms limitation treaty with the Western powers and returned some of its control over the Shantung Peninsula to China. These conciliatory moves reduced tensions in East Asia. At home, Japan seemed headed toward genuine democracy. The electorate expanded twelvefold between 1918 and 1925 as all males over twenty-five won the vote. Two-party competition was intense, and cabinet ministers were made responsible to the lower house. Japanese living standards were the highest in Asia. Literacy was universal.

Japan's remarkable rise, however, was accompanied by serious problems. Japan had a rapidly growing population, but natural resources were scarce. As early as the 1920s Japan was exporting manufactured goods in order to pay for imports of food and essential raw materials. Deeply enmeshed in world trade, Japan was vulnerable to every boom and bust. These conditions reinforced the widespread belief that colonies and foreign expansion were matters of life and death for Japan.

Also, rapid industrial development had created an imbalanced "dualistic" economy. The modern sector consisted of a handful of giant conglomerate firms, the *zaibatsu,* or "financial combine." A zaibatsu firm like Mitsubishi employed thousands of workers and owned banks, mines, steel mills, cotton factories, shipyards, and trading companies, all of which were closely interrelated. Zaibatsu firms had enormous economic power and dominated the other sector of the economy, which

Little Samurai Proud to wear the battle dress of Japan's feudal warriors, a group of boys imitate their leader in a patriotic procession on Empire Day in 1934. The values of Japanese nationalism are being passed to the next generation. *(Source: UPI/Bettmann Newsphotos)*

consisted of an unorganized multitude of peasant farmers and craftsmen. The result was financial oligarchy, corruption of government officials, and a weak middle class.

Behind the façade of party politics, the old and new elites—the emperor, high government officials, big businessmen, and military leaders—were jockeying savagely for the real power. Cohesive leadership, which had played such an important role in Japan's modernization by the Meiji reformers, had ceased to exist.

By far the most serious challenge to peaceful progress, however, was fanatical nationalism. As in Europe, ultranationalism first emerged in Japan in the late nineteenth century but did not flower fully until the First World War and the 1930s. Though often vague, Japan's ultranationalists shared several fundamental beliefs.

The ultranationalists were violently anti-Western. They rejected democracy, big business, and Marxian socialism, which they blamed for destroying the older, superior Japanese practices that they wanted to restore. Reviving old myths, they stressed the emperor's godlike qualities and the samurai warrior's code of honor and obedience. Despising party politics, they assassinated moderate leaders and plotted armed uprisings to achieve their goals. Above all else, the ultranationalists preached foreign expansion. Like Western imperialists with their "white man's burden," Japanese ultranationalists thought theirs was a noble mission. "Asia for the Asians" was their self-satisfied rallying cry. As the famous ultranationalist Kita Ikki wrote in 1923:

Our seven hundred million brothers in China and India have no other path to independence than that offered by our guidance and protection. . . . The noble Greece of Asian culture must complete her national reorganization on the basis of her own national polity. At the same time, let her lift the virtuous banner of an Asian league and take the leadership in a world federation which must come.[19]

The ultranationalists were noisy and violent in the 1920s, but it took the Great Depression of the 1930s to tip the scales decisively in their favor. The worldwide depression hit Japan like a tidal wave in 1930. Exports and wages collapsed; unemployment and raw suffering soared. Starving peasants ate the bark off trees and sold their daughters to brothels. The ultranationalists blamed the system, and people listened.

Japan Against China

Among those who listened with particular care were young Japanese army officers in Manchuria. This underpopulated, resource-rich province of northeastern China, controlled by the Japanese army since its victory over Russia in 1905, seemed a particularly valuable asset in the depression. Many junior Japanese officers in Manchuria came from the peasantry and were distressed by the stories of rural suffering they heard from home. They also knew that the budget and prestige of the Japanese army had declined in the prosperous 1920s.

Most worrisome of all to the young officers was the rise of Chinese nationalism. This new political force challenged the control that Japan exercised over Manchuria through Chinese warlord puppets. In response, junior Japanese officers in Manchuria, in cooperation with top generals in Tokyo, secretly manufactured an excuse for aggression in late 1931. They blew up some tracks on a Japanese-owned railroad near the city of Mukden and then quickly occupied all of Manchuria in "self-defense."

In 1932 Japan proclaimed Manchuria an independent state with a Manchu puppet as emperor. When the League of Nations condemned its aggression in Manchuria, Japan resigned in protest. Politics in Japan became increasingly chaotic. The army, though reporting directly to the emperor of Japan, was clearly an independent force subject to no outside control.

For China, the Japanese conquest of Manchuria was disastrous. After unifying most of China in 1928, the Nationalist government had won from the Western powers the right to set tariffs and other marks of sovereignty. The government had also begun to expand higher education, build railroads, and improve the banking system. Japanese aggression in Manchuria drew attention away from these modernizing efforts, which in any event had been none too vigorous. The Nationalist government promoted a massive boycott of Japanese goods but lost interest in social reform.

Above all, the Nationalist government after 1931 completely neglected land reform and the grinding poverty of the Chinese peasants. As in

The Japanese Army in Manchuria Consolidating their hold on China's rich northern province, these Japanese troops are occupying the strategic city of Hailar near the border with the Soviet Union. The Japanese seizure of Manchuria in 1931 was disastrous for China, a prelude to Japan's general attack in 1937. *(Source: Wide World Photos)*

many poor agricultural societies, Chinese peasants paid roughly half of their crops to their landlords as rent. Ownership of land was very unequal. One careful study estimated that fully half of the land was owned by a mere 4 percent of the families, usually absentee landlords living in cities. Poor peasants and farm laborers—70 percent of the rural population—owned only one-sixth of the land.

Peasants were heavily in debt and chronically underfed. Eggs and meat accounted for only 2 percent of the food consumed by poor and middle-income peasants. A contemporary Chinese economist spelled out the revolutionary implications: "It seems clear that the land problem in China today is as acute as that of eighteenth-century France or nineteenth-century Russia."[20] Mao Tse-tung certainly agreed.

Having abandoned land reform, partly because they themselves were often landowners, the Nationalists under Chiang Kai-shek devoted their energies between 1930 and 1934 to five great campaigns of encirclement and extermination against the Communists' rural power base in southeastern China. In 1934 they closed in for the kill, only to miss again. In one of the most incred-

MAP 33.2 The Chinese Communist Movement and the War with Japan, 1927–1938 After urban uprisings ordered by Stalin failed in 1927, Mao Tse-tung succeeded in forming a self-governing Communist soviet in mountainous southern China. Relentless Nationalist attacks between 1930 and 1934 finally forced the Long March to Yenan, where the Communists were well positioned for guerrilla war against the Japanese.

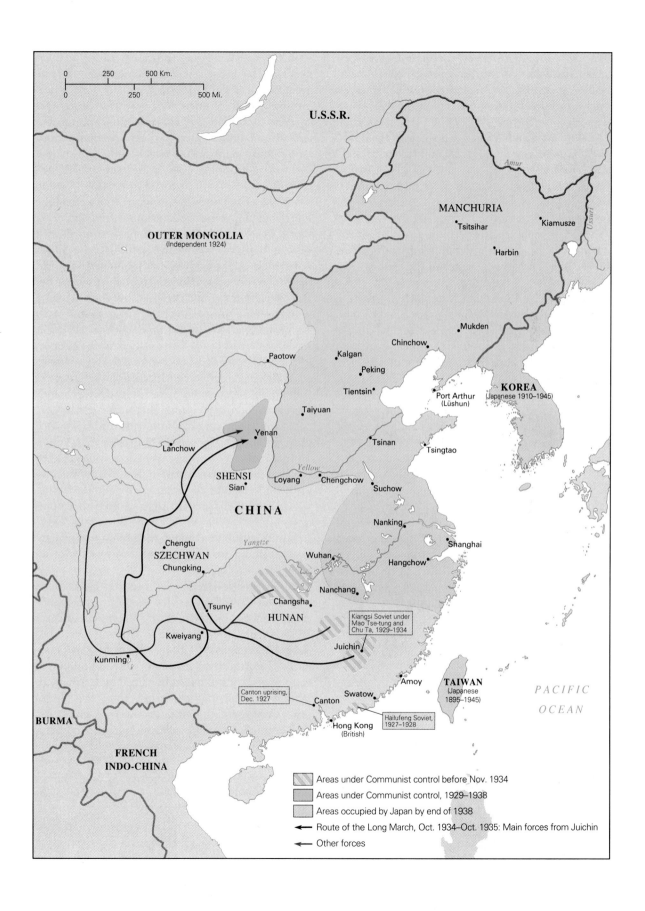

0 | 250 | 500 Km.

0 | 250 | 500 Mi.

U.S.S.R.

MANCHURIA

Tsitsihar

Kiamusze

Harbin

OUTER MONGOLIA
(Independent 1924)

Amur

Ussuri

Mukden

Chinchow

Paotow

Kalgan

Peking

KOREA
(Japanese 1910–1945)

Tientsin

Taiyuan

Port Arthur
(Lüshun)

Lanchow

Yenan

Tsinan

Tsingtao

SHENSI

Sian

Loyang

Chengchow

Yellow

Suchow

CHINA

Chengtu

Yangtze

Nanking

Shanghai

SZECHWAN

Wuhan

Hangchow

Chungking

Nanchang

Tsunyi

Changsha

Kweiyang

HUNAN

Kiangsi Soviet under
Mao Tse-tung and
Chu Ta, 1929–1934

Kunming

Juichin

TAIWAN
(Japanese
1895–1945)

Amoy

*PACIFIC
OCEAN*

Canton uprising,
Dec. 1927

Swatow

BURMA

Canton

Hailufeng Soviet,
1927–1928

Hong Kong
(British)

**FRENCH
INDO-CHINA**

Areas under Communist control before Nov. 1934

Areas under Communist control, 1929–1938

Areas occupied by Japan by end of 1938

Route of the Long March, Oct. 1934–Oct. 1935: Main forces from Juichin

Other forces

ible sagas of modern times, the main Communist army broke out of the Nationalist encirclement, beat off attacks, and marched 6,000 miles in twelve months to a remote region on the northwestern border (Map 33.2). Of the estimated 100,000 men and women who began the Long March, only from 8,000 to 10,000 reached the final destination. There Mao Tse-tung built up his forces once again, established a new territorial base, and won the support of local peasants by undertaking land reform.

Mao Tse-tung and his Communists gradually emerged as the more determined nationalists. Once again, the decisive factor in the eyes of ordinary Chinese was Japanese aggression. In 1937, the Japanese military and the ultranationalists were in command and decided to use a minor incident near Peking as a pretext for a general attack. The Nationalist government, which had just formed a united front with the Communists in response to the demands of Chinese patriots, fought hard but could not halt the Japanese.

By late 1938, Japanese armies occupied sizable portions of coastal China (see Map 33.2). The Nationalists and the Communists had retreated to the interior, both refusing to accept defeat. The determination of the Communist guerrillas equaled that of the Nationalists, and their political skill proved superior. In 1939, as Europe (and the United States) edged toward the Second World War, the undeclared war between China and Japan bogged down in a savage stalemate. The bloody clash on the mainland provided a spectacular example of conflicting nationalism, convulsing China and preparing for Communist victory.

Southeast Asia

The tide of nationalism was also rising in Southeast Asia. Like their counterparts in India, China, and Japan, nationalists in Southeast Asia urgently wanted genuine political independence and freedom from foreign rule. In both French Indochina and the Dutch East Indies, local nationalists were inspired by events elsewhere in Asia. Japan's rise to the status of Great Power, the struggle of Gandhi and the Congress party in India, and China's unification under the Nationalists all encouraged Vietnamese and Indonesian patriots to press their own demands. In both cases they ran up against an imperialist stone wall.

In the words of one historian, "Indochina was governed by Frenchmen for Frenchmen, and the great liberal slogans of liberty, equality, and fraternity were not considered to be export goods for overseas dominions."[21] This uncompromising attitude stimulated the growth of an equally stubborn Communist opposition, which emerged despite ruthless repression as the dominant anti-French force.

In the East Indies—modern Indonesia—the Dutch made some concessions after the First World War, establishing a people's council with very limited lawmaking power. But in the 1930s the Dutch cracked down hard, jailing all the important nationalist leaders. Like the French, the Dutch were determined to hold on.

In the Philippines, however, a mature and well-established nationalist movement achieved greater success. As in colonial Latin America, the Spanish in the Philippines had been indefatigable missionaries. By the late nineteenth century 80 percent of the Filipino population was Catholic. Filipinos shared a common cultural heritage as well as a common racial origin. Education, especially for girls, was quite advanced for Southeast Asia, and in 1843 a higher percentage of people could read in the Philippines than in Spain itself. Economic development helped to create a Westernized elite, which turned first to reform and then to revolution in the 1890s. As in Egypt or Turkey, long-standing intimate contact with Western civilization created a strong nationalist movement at an early date.

Filipino nationalists were bitterly disillusioned when the United States, having taken the Philippines from Spain in the Spanish-American War of 1898, ruthlessly beat down a patriotic revolt and denied the universal Filipino desire for independence. The Americans claimed that the Philippines were not ready and might be seized by Germany or Britain. As the imperialist power in the Philippines, the United States encouraged education and promoted capitalistic economic development. As in British India, an elected legislature was given some real powers. In 1919 President Wilson even promised eventual independence, though subsequent Republican administrations saw it as a distant goal.

As in India and French Indochina, demands for independence grew. One important contributing factor was American racial attitudes. Americans treated Filipinos as inferiors and introduced segre-

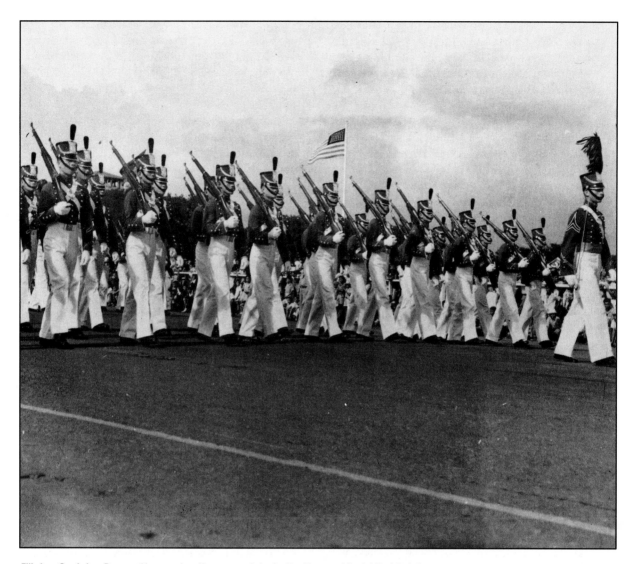

Filipino Cadets Dressed in smart uniforms modeled after those of their West Point counterparts in the United States, these future officers of the Philippine army march with flawless precision. They are passing the reviewing stand in a 1937 parade celebrating American promises of political independence for the Philippines. *(Source: UPI/Bettmann Newsphotos)*

gationist practices borrowed from the American South. American racism made passionate nationalists of many Filipinos.

However, it was the Great Depression that had the most radical impact on the Philippines. As the United States collapsed economically, the Philippines suddenly appeared to be a liability rather than an asset. American farm groups lobbied for protection from cheap Filipino sugar. To protect American jobs, labor unions demanded an end to Filipino immigration. In 1934 Congress made the

Philippines a self-governing commonwealth and scheduled independence for 1944. Sugar imports were reduced, and immigration was limited to only fifty Filipinos per year.

Like Britain and France in the Middle East, the United States was determined to hold on to its big military bases in the Philippines as it permitted increased local self-government and promised eventual political independence. The continued presence of U.S. fleets and armies was denounced by some Filipino nationalists. Others were less certain that the American presence was the immediate problem. Japan was fighting in China and expanding economically into the Philippines and throughout Southeast Asia. By 1939, a new threat to Filipino independence appeared to come from Asia itself.

SUMMARY

The Asian revolt against the West began before the First World War. But only after 1914 did Asian nationalist movements broaden their bases and become capable of challenging Western domination effectively. These mass movements sought human dignity as well as political freedom. Generally speaking, Asian nationalists favored modernization and adopted Western techniques and ideas even as they rejected Western rule. Everywhere Asian nationalists had to fight long and hard, though their struggle gained momentum from the relative decline of European power and confidence, the encouragement of the Soviet Union, and American calls for self-determination.

Asia's nationalist movements arose out of separate historical experiences and distinct cultures. This chapter surveys the variations on the common theme of nationalism in Turkey, the Arab world, India, China, Japan, and the Philippines. This diversity helps explain why Asian peoples became defensive in their relations with one another while rising against Western rule. Like earlier nationalists in Europe, Asian nationalists developed a strong sense of "we" and "they"; "they" included other Asians as well as Europeans. Nationalism meant freedom, modernization, and cultural renaissance, but it nonetheless proved a mixed blessing.

NOTES

1. K. M. Panikkar, *Asia and Western Dominance: A Survey of the Vasco da Gama Epoch of Asian History* (London: George Allen & Unwin, 1959), p. 197.
2. Quoted in Henri Grimal, *La Décolonisation, 1919–1965* (Paris: Armand Colin, 1965), p. 100.
3. Quoted in Peter Mansfield, *The Ottoman Empire and Its Successors* (New York: St. Martin's Press, 1973), p. 18.
4. Harold Armstrong, *Turkey in Travail: The Birth of a New Nation* (London: John Lane, 1925), p. 75.
5. Quoted in Lord Kinross, *Atatürk: A Biography of Mustafa Kemal, Father of Modern Turkey* (New York: Morrow, 1965), p. 181.
6. Percival Spear, *India, Pakistan, and the West,* 3d ed. (Oxford: Oxford University Press, 1958), p. 67.
7. Quoted in Erik Erikson, *Gandhi's Truth: On the Origins of Militant Nonviolence* (New York: Norton, 1969), p. 225.
8. Ibid., p. 105.
9. Hugh Tinker, *A New System of Slavery: The Export of Indian Labour Overseas, 1830–1920* (London: Oxford University Press, 1974).
10. Quoted in Louis Fischer, *Gandhi: His Life and Message for the World* (New York: New American Library, 1954), p. 35.
11. Quoted in Erikson, p. 225.
12. Quoted in Woodbridge Bingham, Hilary Conroy, and Fran Iklé, *A History of Asia,* vol. 1, 2d ed. (Boston: Allyn and Bacon, 1974), p. 447.
13. Webb Miller, *I Found No Peace: The Journal of a Foreign Correspondent* (New York: Simon and Schuster, 1936), p. 193.
14. Quoted in Lloyd Rudolph and Susanne Rudolph, *The Modernity of Tradition: Political Development in India* (Chicago: University of Chicago Press, 1967), p. 248.
15. Quoted in William Theodore deBary, Wing-tsit Chan, and Burton Watson, *Sources of Chinese Tradition* (New York: Columbia University Press, 1964), pp. 768–769.
16. Quoted in John F. Fairbank, Edwin O. Reischauer, and Albert M. Craig, *East Asia: Tradition and Transformation* (Boston: Houghton Mifflin, 1973), p. 774.
17. Quoted in Benjamin I. Schwartz, *Chinese Communism and the Rise of Mao* (Cambridge, Mass.: Harvard University Press, 1951), p. 74.
18. Ida Pruitt, *A Daughter of Han: The Autobiography of a Chinese Working Woman* (New Haven, Conn.: Yale University Press, 1945), p. 22. Other quotations are taken, in order, from pages 83, 71, 182, 166, and 235.
19. Quoted in William Theodore deBary, Ryusaku Tsunoda, and Donald Keene, *Sources of Japanese Tradition,* vol. 2 (New York: Columbia University Press, 1958), p. 269.
20. Quoted in Olga Lang, *Chinese Family and Society* (New Haven, Conn.: Yale University Press, 1946), p. 70.
21. Quoted in Woodbridge Bingham, Hilary Conroy, and Fran Iklé, *A History of Asia,* vol. 2, 2d ed. (Boston: Allyn and Bacon, 1974), p. 480.

SUGGESTED READING

All of the works cited in the Notes are highly recommended. Two important general studies of nationalism and independence movements are H. Kohn, *The Age of Nationalism: The First Era of Global History* (1962), and R. Emerson, *From Empire to Nation: The Rise to Self-Assertion of Asian and African Peoples* (1960). These may be compared with the provocative works of E. Kedourie, *Nationalism in Asia and Africa* (1970) and *England and the Middle East: The Destruction of the Ottoman Empire, 1914–1921* (1956), and with a justly famous global history of the twentieth century by G. Barraclough, *An Introduction to Contemporary History* (1975). Two fine studies of the Middle East are G. Lenczowski, *The Middle East in World Affairs,* 4th ed. (1980), and S. N. Fisher, *The Middle East: A History,* 3d ed. (1979), both of which have detailed bibliographies. On Turkey, in addition to Lord Kinross's Atatürk (1965), see B. Lewis, *The Emergence of Modern Turkey* (1961), and D. Kushner, *The Rise of Turkish Nationalism, 1876–1908* (1977). Peter Mansfield, *The Arab World: A Comprehensive History* (1976), and S. G. Haim, ed., *Arab Nationalism: An Anthology* (1964), provide engaging general coverage and important source materials. W. Lacqueur, *A History of Zionism* (1972), and A. Eban, *My People* (1968), discuss the Jewish homeland in Palestine. The Arab viewpoint is presented by G. Antonius, *The Arab Awakening: The Story of the Arab National Movement* (1946). R. Cottam, *Nationalism in Iran*, rev. ed. (1979), complements the classic study of D. Wilbur, *Iran: Past and Present,* 9th ed. (1981).

The historical literature on modern India is very rich. S. Wolpert, *A New History of India,* 2d ed. (1982), is an excellent introduction, with up-to-date scholarship and detailed suggestions for further reading. Also see the handsomely illustrated volume by F. Watson, *A Concise History of India* (1975). In addition to the biographies of Gandhi by Erikson and Fischer cited in the Notes, J. Brown, *Gandhi's Rise to Power: Indian Politics, 1915–1922* (1972), and L. Gordon, *Bengal: The Nationalist Movement, 1876–1970* (1974), are major studies. Developments in the Muslim community are considered by P. Hardy, *The Muslims of British India* (1972); B. Metcalf, *Islamic Revival in British India: Deoband,*

1860–1900 (1982); and F. Robinson, *Atlas of the Islamic World Since 1500* (1982), a beautifully illustrated survey encompassing far more than India.

Studies of China in the twentieth century are also very numerous. J. Spence, *The Search for Modern China* (1990), and I. Hsü, *The Rise of Modern China,* 4th ed. (1990), are comprehensive studies with extensive bibliographies, which may be supplemented by the documentary collection of F. Schurmann and O. Schell, eds., *Republican China: Nationalism, War and the Rise of Communism, 1911–1949* (1967). J. Spence, *The Gate of Heavenly Peace: The Chinese and Their Revolution, 1895–1980* (1981), skillfully focuses on leading literary figures. T. Chow, *The May Fourth Movement: Intellectual Revolution in Modern China* (1960), examines a critical time period. Other important studies of China in this period include R. Hofheinz, Jr., *The Broken Wave: The Chinese Communist Peasant Movement, 1922–1928* (1977); S. Schram, *Mao Tse-tung* (1966); H. Schriffrin, *Sun Yat-sen and the Origins of the Chinese Revolution* (1970); and L. Eastman, *The Abortive Revolution: China Under Nationalist Rule, 1927–1937* (1974). P. Ebrey, ed., *Chinese Civilization and Society: A Sourcebook* (1981), complements the classic studies of the Chinese family by Lang and Pruitt, which may be compared with M. J. Levy, *The Family Revolution in Modern China* (1949). E. Reischauer, *Japan: The Story of a Nation,* rev. ed. (1970), and P. Duus, *The Rise of Modern Japan* (1976), are excellent interpretations of the recent history of the island nation. W. Lockwood, *The Economic Development of Japan, 1868–1938* (1954), and R. Storry, *The Double Patriots: A Story of Japanese Nationalism* (1973), are valuable specialized works. M. Hane, *Peasants, Rebels, and Outcasts: The Underside of Modern Japan* (1982), sees few benefits for the poor before 1945. S. Garon, *The State and Labor in Modern Japan* (1988), skillfully analyzes the history of Japanese labor relations. Two edited collections, J. Morley, *The China Quagmire* (1983), and R. Myers and M. Peattie, *The Japanese Colonial Expansion, 1895–1945* (1984), probe Japan's imperial expansion. For Southeast Asia, see D. G. E. Hall, *A History of South-east Asia,* 4th ed. (1981); J. Pluvier, *South-East Asia from Colonialism to Independence* (1974); and the Suggested Reading for Chapter 37. Two more recommended works are M. Osborne, *Southeast Asia: An Illustrated History,* expanded ed. (1988), and D. R. Sardesa, *Southeast Past and Present,* 2d ed. (1989).

34

The Age of Anxiety in the West

Isaac Soyer, *Employment Agency*, 1937

When Allied diplomats met in Paris in early 1919 with their optimistic plans for building a lasting peace, most people looked forward to happier times. They hoped that life would return to normal after the terrible trauma of total war. They hoped that once again life would make sense in the familiar prewar terms of peace, prosperity, and progress. These hopes were in vain. The Great Break—the First World War and the Russian Revolution—had mangled too many things beyond repair. Life would no longer fit neatly into the old molds or former routines.

Instead, great numbers of men and women in the West felt themselves increasingly adrift in a strange, uncertain, and uncontrollable world. They saw themselves living in an age of anxiety, an age of continuous crisis, which lasted until at least the early 1950s. In almost every area of human experience, people went searching for ways to put meaning back into life.

- What did the doubts and searching mean for Western thought, art, and culture?
- How did political leaders try to re-establish real peace and prosperity between 1919 and 1939?
- Why did those leaders fail?

These questions are explored in this chapter.

UNCERTAINTY IN MODERN THOUGHT

Before the Great War, a complex revolution in thought and ideas was under way in Western society, but only small, unusual groups were aware of it. After the war, new and upsetting ideas began to spread widely. People in the West began to question and even abandon many cherished values and beliefs that had guided Western society since the eighteenth-century Enlightenment and the nineteenth-century triumph of industrial development, scientific advances, and evolutionary thought.

Before 1914 most people in the West still believed in progress, reason, and the rights of the individual. Progress seemed to be a daily reality, apparent in rising standards of living, the taming of

the cities, and steady increases in popular education. Such developments encouraged a comforting belief in the logical universe of Newtonian physics, as well as faith in the ability of a rational human mind to understand that universe through intellectual investigation. Just as there seemed to be laws of science, so there seemed to be laws of society that rational human beings could discover and then wisely act on. The rights of the individual were not taken for granted and were actually increasing. Well-established rights were gradually spreading to women and workers, and new "social rights" like old-age pensions were emerging. In short, before the Great War, most Europeans and North Americans had a moderately optimistic view of the world, and with good reason.

Since the 1880s, however, a small band of serious thinkers and creative writers had been attacking these well-worn optimistic ideas. These critics rejected the general faith in progress and the power of the rational human mind. Their views were greatly strengthened by the experience of history's most destructive war. The First World War suggested to many that human beings were a pack of violent, irrational animals quite capable of tearing individuals and their rights to shreds. Pessimism and a general crisis of the mind increased as a growing chorus of thinkers, creative writers, and scientists echoed and enlarged on the themes first expressed between 1880 and 1914. After the war, people did not know what to think. Their disorientation was particularly acute in the 1930s, when the rapid rise of harsh dictatorships and the Great Depression transformed old certainties into bitter illusions.

No one expressed this state of uncertainty better than the French poet and critic Paul Valéry (1871–1945) in the early 1920s. Speaking of the "crisis of the mind," Valéry noted that Europe was looking at its future with dark foreboding:

The storm has died away, and still we are restless, uneasy, as if the storm were about to break. Almost all the affairs of men remain in a terrible uncertainty. We think of what has disappeared, and we are almost destroyed by what has been destroyed; we do not know what will be born, and we fear the future, not without reason. . . . Doubt and disorder are in us and with us. There is no thinking man, however shrewd or learned he may be, who can hope to dominate this anxiety, to escape from this impression of darkness.[1]

"The War, as I Saw It" This was the title of a series of grotesque drawings that appeared in 1920 in *Simplicissimus,* Germany's leading satirical magazine. Nothing shows better the terrible impact of World War One than this profoundly disturbing example of expressionist art. *(Source: Caroline Buckler)*

In the midst of economic, political, and social disruptions Valéry saw the "cruelly injured mind," besieged by doubts and suffering from anxieties. This was the general intellectual crisis of the twentieth century—a crisis that touched almost every field of thought. The implications of new ideas and discoveries in philosophy, physics, psychology, and literature disturbed thinking men and women everywhere in the West.

Modern Philosophy

Among those thinkers in the late nineteenth century who challenged the belief in progress and the general faith in the rational human mind, the German philosopher Friedrich Nietzsche (1844–1900) was particularly influential. Nietzsche believed that Western civilization had lost its creativity and decayed into mediocrity. Christianity's "slave morality" had glorified weakness and humility. Furthermore, human beings in the West had overstressed rational thinking at the expense of passion and emotion. Nietzsche viewed the pillars of conventional morality—reason, democracy, progress, respectability—as outworn social and psychological constructs whose influence was suffocating creativity. The only hope of revival was for a few superior individuals to free themselves from the humdrum thinking of the masses and embrace life passionately. Such individuals would become true heroes, supermen capable of leading the dumb herd of inferior men and women. Nietzsche also condemned both political democracy and greater social equality.

The growing dissatisfaction with established ideas before 1914 was apparent in other important thinkers. In the 1890s, the French philosophy professor Henri Bergson (1859–1941) convinced many young people through his writing that immediate experience and intuition are as important as rational and scientific thinking for understanding reality. Indeed, according to Bergson, a religious experience or a mystical poem is often more accessible to human comprehension than a scientific law or a mathematical equation.

Another thinker who agreed about the limits of rational thinking was the French socialist Georges Sorel (1847–1922). Sorel frankly characterized Marxian socialism as an inspiring but unprovable religion rather than a rational scientific truth. Socialism would come to power, he believed, through a great, violent strike of all working people that would miraculously shatter capitalist society. Sorel rejected democracy and believed that the masses of the new socialist society would have to be tightly controlled by a small revolutionary elite.

The First World War accelerated the revolt against established certainties in philosophy, but that revolt went in two very different directions. In English-speaking countries, the main development was the acceptance of logical empiricism (or logical positivism) in university circles. In continental countries, where esoteric and remote logical empiricism has never won many converts, the primary development in philosophy was existentialism.

Logical empiricism was truly revolutionary. It quite simply rejected most of the concerns of traditional philosophy—from the existence of God to the meaning of happiness—as nonsense and hot air. This outlook began primarily with the Aus-

trian philosopher Ludwig Wittgenstein (1889–1951), who later emigrated to England, where he trained numerous disciples.

Wittgenstein argued in his pugnacious *Tractatus Logico-Philosophicus (Essay on Logical Philosophy)* in 1922 that philosophy is only the logical clarification of thoughts and therefore it becomes the study of language, which expresses thoughts. The great philosophical issues of the ages—God, freedom, morality, and so on—are quite literally senseless, a great waste of time, for statements about them can be neither tested by scientific experiments nor demonstrated by the logic of mathematics. Statements about such matters reflect only the personal preferences of a given individual. As Wittgenstein put it in the famous last sentence of his work, "Of what one cannot speak, of that one must keep silent." Logical empiricism, which has remained dominant in England and the United States to this day, drastically reduced the scope of philosophical inquiry. Anxious people could find few if any answers in this direction.

Highly diverse and even contradictory, existential thinkers were loosely united in a courageous search for moral values in a world of terror and uncertainty. Theirs were true voices of the age of anxiety.

Most existential thinkers in the twentieth century have been atheists. Like Nietzsche, who had already proclaimed that "God is dead," they did not believe that a supreme being had established humanity's fundamental nature and given life its meaning. In the words of the famous French existentialist Jean-Paul Sartre (1905–1980), human beings simply exist: "They turn up, appear on the scene." Only after they "turn up" do they seek to define themselves. Honest human beings are terribly alone, for there is no God to help them. They are hounded by despair and the meaninglessness of life. The crisis of the existential thinker epitomized the modern intellectual crisis: the shattering of traditional beliefs in God, reason, and progress.

Existentialists did recognize that human beings, unless they kill themselves, must act. Indeed, in the words of Sartre, "man is condemned to be free." There is, therefore, the possibility—indeed, the necessity—of giving meaning to life through actions, of defining oneself through choices. To do so, individuals must become "engaged" and choose their own actions courageously, consistently, and in full awareness of their inescapable responsibility for their own behavior. In the end, existentialists argued, human beings can overcome the absurdity that existentialists saw in life.

Modern existentialism developed first in Germany in the 1920s, when the philosophers Martin Heidegger (1889–1976) and Karl Jaspers (1883–1969) found a sympathetic audience among disillusioned postwar university students. But it was in France during the years immediately after the Second World War that existentialism came of age. The terrible conditions of that war reinforced the existential view of life and the existential approach to it. On the one hand, the armies of the German dictator Adolf Hitler had conquered most of Europe and unleashed a hideous reign of barbarism. On the other, men and women had more than ever to define themselves by their actions. Specifically, each individual had to choose whether to join the Resistance against Hitler or to accept and even abet tyranny. The writings of Sartre, who along with Albert Camus (1913–1960) was the leading French existentialist, became enormously influential. Sartre, active in the Resistance, and his colleagues offered a powerful answer to profound moral issues and the contemporary crisis.

The Revival of Christianity

In intellectual circles, Christianity and religion in general had been on the defensive since the Enlightenment and especially during the late nineteenth century. But in the aftermath of the Great Break, the loss of faith in human reason and in continual progress led to renewed interest in the Christian view of the world. A number of thinkers and theologians began to revitalize the fundamentals of Christianity. They had a powerful impact on society. Sometimes described as "Christian existentialists" because they shared the loneliness and despair of atheistic existentialists, they revived the tradition of Saint Augustine. They stressed human beings' sinful nature, the need for faith, and the mystery of God's forgiveness.

This development was a break with the late nineteenth century. In the years before 1914, some theologians, especially Protestant theologians, had felt the need to interpret Christian doctrine and the Bible so that they did not seem to contradict science, evolution, and common sense. Christ was therefore seen primarily as the greatest

moral teacher, and the "supernatural" aspects of his divinity were strenuously played down. An important if extreme example of this tendency was the young Albert Schweitzer's *Quest of the Historical Jesus* (1906). A theologian and later a famous medical missionary and musician of note, Schweitzer (1875–1965) argued that Christ while on earth was a completely natural man whose teachings had been only temporary rules to prepare himself and his disciples for the end of the world, which they were erroneously expecting. In short, some modern theologians were embarrassed by the miraculous, unscientific aspects of Christianity and turned away from them.

The revival of fundamental Christian belief after the Great War was fed by rediscovery of the work of the nineteenth-century Danish religious philosopher Sören Kierkegaard (1813–1855), whose ideas became extremely influential. Kierkegaard had rejected formalistic religion and denounced the worldliness of the Danish Lutheran church. He had eventually resolved his personal anguish over his own imperfect nature by making a total religious commitment to a remote and majestic God.

Similar ideas were brilliantly developed by the Swiss Protestant theologian Karl Barth (1886–1968), whose many influential writings after 1920 sought to re-create the religious intensity of the Reformation. For Barth, the basic fact about human beings was that they are imperfect, sinful creatures whose reason and will are hopelessly flawed. Religious truth is therefore made known to human beings only through God's grace. People have to accept God's word and the supernatural revelation of Jesus Christ with awe, trust, and obedience. Lowly mortals should not expect to "reason out" God and his ways.

Among Catholics, the leading existential Christian thinker was Gabriel Marcel (1887–1973). Born into a cultivated French family, where his atheistic father was "gratefully aware of all that . . . art owed to Catholicism but regarded Catholic thought itself as obsolete and tainted with absurd superstitions,"[2] Marcel found in the Catholic church an answer to what he called the postwar "broken world." Catholicism and religious belief provided the hope, humanity, honesty, and piety for which he hungered.

After 1914 religion became much more relevant and meaningful to thinking people, and many illustrious individuals turned to religion between about 1920 and 1950. The poets T. S. Eliot and W. H. Auden, the novelists Evelyn Waugh and Aldous Huxley, the historian Arnold Toynbee, the Oxford professor C. S. Lewis, the psychoanalyst Karl Stern, and the physicist Max Planck were all either converted to religion or attracted to it for the first time. Religion, often of a despairing, existential variety, was one meaningful answer to terror and anxiety. In the words of another famous Roman Catholic convert, English novelist Graham Greene, "One began to believe in heaven because one believed in hell."[3]

The New Physics

Ever since the Scientific Revolution of the seventeenth century, scientific advances and their implications have greatly influenced the beliefs of thinking people. By the late nineteenth century, science was one of the main pillars supporting Western society's optimistic and rationalistic view of the world. The Darwinian concept of evolution had been accepted and assimilated in most intellectual circles. Progressive minds believed that science, unlike religion and philosophical speculation, was based on hard facts and controlled experiments. Science seemed to have achieved an unerring and almost completed picture of reality. Unchanging natural laws seemed to determine physical processes and permit useful solutions to more and more problems. All this was comforting, especially to people who were no longer committed to traditional religious beliefs. And all this was challenged by the new physics.

An important first step toward the new physics was the discovery at the end of the century that atoms were not like hard, permanent little billiard balls. They were actually composed of many far-smaller, fast-moving particles, such as electrons and protons. The Polish-born physicist Marie Curie (1867–1934) and her French husband discovered that radium constantly emits subatomic particles and thus does not have a constant atomic weight. Building on this and other work in radiation, the German physicist Max Planck (1858–1947) showed in 1900 that subatomic energy is emitted in uneven little spurts, which Planck called "quanta," and not in a steady stream as previously believed. Planck's discovery called into question the old sharp distinction between matter and energy; the implication was that matter and

energy might be different forms of the same thing. The old view of atoms as the stable, basic building blocks of nature, with a different kind of unbreakable atom for each of the ninety-two chemical elements, was badly shaken.

In 1905 the German-born Jewish genius Albert Einstein (1879–1955) went further than the Curies and Planck in challenging Newtonian physics. His theory of special relativity postulated that time and space are not absolute. The closed framework of Newtonian physics was quite limited compared to that of Einsteinian physics, which unified an apparently infinite universe with the incredibly small, fast-moving subatomic world. Moreover, Einstein's theory stated clearly that matter and energy are interchangeable and that all matter contains enormous levels of potential energy.

The 1920s opened the "heroic age of physics," in the apt words of one of its leading pioneers, Ernest Rutherford (1871–1937). Breakthrough followed breakthrough. In 1919 Rutherford showed that the atom could be split. By 1944 seven subatomic particles had been identified, of which the most important was the neutron. The neutron's capacity to pass through other atoms allowed for even more intense experimental bombardment of matter, leading to chain reactions of unbelievable force—and to the atomic bomb.

Although few nonscientists understood the revolution in physics, the implications of the new theories and discoveries, as presented by newspapers and popular writers, were disturbing to millions of men and women in the 1920s and 1930s. The new universe was strange and troubling. It lacked any absolute objective reality. Everything was "relative"—that is, dependent on the observer's frame of reference. Moreover, the universe was uncertain and undetermined, without stable building blocks. Instead of Newton's dependable, rational laws, there seemed to be only tendencies and probabilities in an extraordinarily complex and uncertain universe. And that universe, described by abstract mathematical symbols, seemed to have little to do with human experience and human problems.

Freudian Psychology

With physics presenting an uncertain universe so unrelated to ordinary human experience, questions about the power and potential of the human mind assumed special significance. The findings and speculations of the leading psychologist, Sigmund Freud (see page 921), were particularly disturbing.

Before Freud, poets and mystics had probed the unconscious and irrational aspects of human behavior. But most professional, "scientific" psychologists assumed that a single, unified conscious mind processed sense experiences in a rational and logical way. Human behavior in turn was the result of rational calculation—of "thinking"—by the conscious mind. Basing his insights on the analysis of dreams and of hysteria, Freud developed a very different view of the human psyche beginning in the late 1880s.

According to Freud (1856–1939), human behavior is basically irrational. The key to understanding the mind is the primitive, irrational unconscious, which Freud called the *id*. The unconscious is driven by sexual, aggressive, and pleasure-seeking desires and is locked in a constant battle with the other parts of the mind: the rationalizing conscious (the *ego*), which mediates what a person can do, and ingrained moral values (the *superego*), which tell what a person should do. Human behavior is a product of fragile compromise between instinctual drives and the controls of rational thinking and moral values. Since the instinctual drives are extremely powerful, the ever-present danger for individuals and whole societies is that unacknowledged drives will overwhelm the control mechanisms in a violent, distorted way. Yet Freud also agreed with Nietzsche that these mechanisms of rational thinking and

Munch: The Dance of Life Like his contemporary Sigmund Freud, the expressionist painter Edvard Munch studied the turmoil and fragility of human thought and action. Solitary figures struggling with fear and uncertainty dominate his work. Here the girl in white represents innocence, the tense woman in black stands for mourning and rejection and the woman in red evokes the joy of passing pleasure. *(Source: © Nasjonalgalleriet, Oslo. Photo: Jacques Lathion)*

traditional moral values can be too strong. They can repress sexual desires too effectively, crippling individuals and entire peoples with guilt and neurotic fears.

Freudian psychology and clinical psychiatry had become an international movement by 1910, but only after 1918 did they receive popular attention, especially in the Protestant countries of northern Europe and in the United States. Many opponents and even some enthusiasts interpreted Freud as saying that the first requirement for mental health is an uninhibited sex life. Thus, after the First World War, the popular interpretation of Freud reflected and encouraged growing sexual experimentation, particularly among middle-class

Virginia Woolf Her novels captured sensations like impressionist paintings, and her home attracted a circle of artists and writers known as the Bloomsbury Group. Many of Woolf's essays dealt with women's issues and urged greater opportunity for women's creativity. *(Source: © Gisèle Freund/Photo Researchers)*

women. For more serious students, the psychology of Freud and his followers drastically undermined the old, easy optimism about the rational and progressive nature of the human mind.

Twentieth-Century Literature

Literature articulated the general intellectual climate of pessimism, relativism, and alienation. Novelists developed new techniques to express new realities. The great nineteenth-century novelists had typically written as all-knowing narrators, describing realistic characters and their relationship to an understandable if sometimes harsh society. In the twentieth century, most major writers adopted the limited, often confused viewpoint of a single individual. Like Freud, these novelists focused their attention on the complexity and irrationality of the human mind, where feelings, memories, and desires are forever scrambled.

Serious novelists also used the stream-of-consciousness technique to explore the psyche. The novel *Jacob's Room* (1922), by Virginia Woolf (1882–1941), is a series of internal monologues in which ideas and emotions from different periods of time bubble up as randomly as from a patient on a psychoanalyst's couch. William Faulkner (1897–1962), perhaps America's greatest twentieth-century novelist, used the same technique in *The Sound and the Fury* (1929), much of whose intense drama is confusedly seen through the eyes of an idiot. The most famous stream-of-consciousness novel—and surely the most disturbing novel of its generation—is *Ulysses,* which the Irish novelist James Joyce (1882–1941) published in 1922. Into *Ulysses's* account of an ordinary day in the life of an ordinary man, Joyce weaves an extended ironic parallel between his hero's aimless wanderings through the streets and pubs of Dublin and the adventures of Homer's hero Ulysses on his way home from Troy. Abandoning conventional grammar and blending foreign words, puns, bits of knowledge, and scraps of memory together in bewildering confusion, Joyce intended the language of *Ulysses* to mirror modern life itself: a gigantic riddle waiting to be unraveled.

As creative writers turned their attention from society to the individual and from realism to psychological relativity, they rejected the idea of progress. Some even described "anti-utopias," nightmare visions of things to come. In 1918 an obscure German high school teacher named Oswald Spengler (1880–1936) published *The Decline of the West,* which quickly became an international sensation. According to Spengler, every culture experiences a life cycle of growth and decline. Western civilization, in Spengler's opinion, was in its old age, and death was approaching in the form of conquest by the yellow race. T. S. Eliot (1888–1965), in his famous poem *The Waste Land* (1922), depicted a world of growing desolation, although after his conversion to Anglo-Catholicism in 1927, Eliot came to hope cautiously for humanity's salvation. No such hope appeared in the work of Franz Kafka (1883–1924), whose novels *The Trial* and *The Castle,* as well as several of his greatest short stories, portray helpless individuals crushed by inexplicably hostile forces. The German-Jewish Kafka died young, at forty-one, and so did not see the world of his nightmares materialize in the Nazi state.

MODERN ART AND CULTURE

Throughout the twentieth century, there has been considerable unity in the arts. The "modernism" of the immediate prewar years and the 1920s is still strikingly modern. Manifestations of modernism in art, architecture, and music have of course been highly varied, just as in physics, psychology, and philosophy; yet there are resemblances, for artists, scientists, and original thinkers partake of the same culture. Creative artists rejected old forms and old values. Modernism in art and music meant constant experimentation and a search for new kinds of expression. And though many people find the modern visions of the arts strange, disturbing, and even ugly, the twentieth century, so dismal in many respects, will probably stand as one of Western civilization's great artistic eras.

Architecture and Design

Modernism in the arts was loosely unified by a revolution in architecture. The architectural revolution not only gave the other arts striking new settings, it intended nothing less than to transform the physical framework of the urban society according to a new principle: functionalism. Believing that buildings, like industrial products, should be useful and "functional"—that is, they should serve, as well as possible, the purpose for which they were made—some architects and designers worked with engineers, town planners, and even sanitation experts. Moreover, they threw away useless ornamentation and found beauty and esthetic pleasure in the clean lines of practical constructions and efficient machinery.

The United States, with its rapid urban growth and lack of rigid building traditions, pioneered in the new architecture. In the 1890s the Chicago school of architects, led by Louis H. Sullivan (1856–1924), used cheap steel, reinforced concrete, and electric elevators to build skyscrapers and office buildings lacking almost any exterior ornamentation. In the first decade of the twentieth century, Sullivan's student Frank Lloyd Wright (1869–1959) built a series of radically new and truly modern houses featuring low lines, open interiors, and mass-produced building materials. Europeans were inspired by these and other American examples of functional construction such as the massive, unadorned grain elevators of the Midwest.

Around 1905, when the first really modern buildings were going up in Europe, architectural leadership shifted to the German-speaking countries and remained there until Hitler took power in 1933. In 1911 the twenty-eight-year-old Walter Gropius (1883–1969) broke sharply with the past in his design of the Fagus shoe factory at Alfeld, Germany. A clean, light, elegant building of glass and iron, Gropius's new factory represented a jump right into the middle of the century.

After the First World War, the new German republic gave Gropius the authority to merge the schools of fine and applied arts at Weimar into a single, interdisciplinary school, the Bauhaus. In spite of intense criticism from conservative politicians and university professors, the Bauhaus brought together many leading modern architects, artists, designers, and theatrical innovators, who worked as an effective, inspired team. Throwing out traditional teaching methods, they combined the study of fine art, such as painting and sculpture, with the study of applied art in the crafts of printing, weaving, and furniture making. Throughout the 1920s, the Bauhaus, with its stress on functionalism and good design for everyday life, attracted enthusiastic students from all over the world. It had a great and continuing impact.

Another leader in the modern or "international" style was Ludwig Mies van der Rohe (1886–1969), who followed Gropius as director of the Bauhaus in 1930 and emigrated to the United States in 1937. His classic Lake Shore Apartments in Chicago, built between 1948 and 1951, symbolize the triumph of steel-frame and glass-wall modern architecture, which grew out of Sullivan's skyscrapers and German functionalism in the great building boom after the Second World War.

Modern Painting

Modern painting grew out of a revolt against French impressionism. The impressionism of such French painters as Claude Monet (1840–1926),

Frank Lloyd Wright: The "Falling Water" House   Often considered Wright's masterpiece, Falling Water combines modern architectural concepts with close attention to a spectacular site. Anchored to a high rock ledge by means of reinforced concrete, the house soars out over a cascading waterfall at Bear Run in western Pennsylvania. Built in 1937 for a Pittsburgh businessman, Falling Water is now open to the public and attracts 70,000 visitors each year. *(Source: Western Pennsylvania Conservancy/Art Resource)*

Picasso: Guernica In this rich, complex work a shrieking woman falls from a burning house on the far right. On the left a woman holds a dead child, while toward the center are fragments of a warrior and a screaming horse pierced by a spear. Picasso has used only the mournful colors of black, white, gray, and dark blue. *(Source: Museo del Prado, Madrid. Pablo Picasso, Guernica (1937, May–early June). Oil on canvas. © SPADEM, Paris/VAGA, New York, 1982)*

Pierre Auguste Renoir (1841–1919), and Camille Pissarro (1830–1903) was, in part, a kind of super-realism. Leaving exact copying of objects to photography, these artists sought to capture the momentary overall feeling, or impression, of light falling on a real-life scene before their eyes. By 1890, when impressionism was finally established, a few artists known as "postimpressionists," or "expressionists," were already striking out in new directions. After 1905 art took on the abstract, nonrepresentational character that it generally retains today.

Though individualistic in their styles, postimpressionists were united in their desire to know and depict worlds other than the visible world of fact. Like the early nineteenth-century romantics, they wanted to portray unseen, inner worlds of emotion and imagination. Like modern novelists, they wanted to express a complicated psychological view of reality as well as an overwhelming emotional intensity. In *The Starry Night* (1889), for example, the great Dutch expressionist Vincent van Gogh (1853–1890) painted the vision of his mind's eye. Flaming cypress trees, exploding stars, and a cometlike Milky Way swirl together in one great cosmic rhythm.

Fascination with form, as opposed to light, was characteristic of postimpressionism and expressionism. Paul Cézanne (1839–1906), who had a profound influence on twentieth-century painting, was particularly committed to form and ordered design. He told a young painter, "You must see in nature the cylinder, the sphere, and the cone."[4] As Cézanne's later work became increasingly abstract and nonrepresentational, it also moved away from the traditional three-dimensional perspective toward the two-dimensional plane, which has characterized so much of modern art. The expressionism of a group of painters led by Henri Matisse (1869–1954) was so extreme that an exhibition of their work in Paris in 1905 prompted shocked critics to call them *les fauves*— "the wild beasts." Matisse and his followers were primarily concerned not with real objects but with the arrangement of color, line, and form as an end in itself.

In 1907 a young Spaniard in Paris, Pablo Picasso (1881–1973), founded another movement: cubism. Cubism concentrated on a complex geometry of zigzagging lines and sharp-angled, overlapping planes. About three years later came the ultimate stage in the development of abstract, nonrepresentational art. Artists such as the Russian-born Wassily Kandinsky (1866–1944) turned away from nature completely. "The observer," said Kandinsky, "must learn to look at [my] pictures . . . as form and color combinations . . . as a representation of mood and not as a representation of objects."[5] On the eve of the First World War, extreme expressionism and abstract painting were developing rapidly not only in Paris but also in Russia and Germany. Modern art had become international.

In the 1920s and 1930s, the artistic movements of the prewar years were extended and consolidated. The most notable new developments were dadaism and surrealism. Dadaism attacked all accepted standards of art and behavior, delighting in outrageous conduct. Its name, from the French word *dada,* meaning "hobbyhorse," is deliberately silly. A famous example of dadaism was a reproduction of Leonardo da Vinci's *Mona Lisa* in which the famous woman with the mysterious smile sports a mustache and is ridiculed with an obscene inscription. After 1924 many dadaists were attracted to surrealism, which became very influential in art in the late 1920s and 1930s. Surrealism was inspired to a great extent by Freudian psychology. Surrealists painted a fantastic world of wild dreams and complex symbols where watches melted and giant metronomes beat time in precisely drawn but impossible alien landscapes.

Refusing to depict ordinary visual reality, surrealist painters made powerful statements about the age of anxiety. Picasso's 26-foot-long mural *Guernica* (1937) masterfully unites several powerful strands in twentieth-century art. Inspired by the Spanish Civil War (see page 1157), the painting commemorates the bombing of the ancient Spanish town of Guernica by fascist planes, an attack that took the lives of a thousand people—one out of every eight inhabitants—in a single night of terror. Combining the free distortion of expressionism, the overlapping planes of cubism, and the surrealist fascination with grotesque subject matter, *Guernica* is what Picasso meant it to be: an unforgettable attack on brutality and darkness.

Modern Music

Developments in modern music were strikingly parallel to those in painting. Composers, too, were attracted by the emotional intensity of ex-pressionism. The ballet *The Rite of Spring* by Igor Stravinsky (1882–1971) practically caused a riot when it was first performed in Paris in 1913 by Sergei Diaghilev's famous Russian dance company. The combination of pulsating, barbaric rhythms from the orchestra pit and an earthy representation of lovemaking by the dancers on the stage seemed a shocking, almost pornographic enactment of a primitive fertility rite.

After the experience of the First World War, when irrationality and violence seemed to pervade the human experience, expressionism in opera and ballet flourished. One of the most famous and powerful examples is the opera *Wozzeck* by Alban Berg (1885–1935), first performed in Berlin in 1925. Blending a half-sung, half-spoken kind of dialogue with harsh, atonal music, *Wozzeck* is a gruesome tale of a soldier driven by Kafka-like inner terrors.

Some composers turned their backs on long-established musical conventions. As abstract painters arranged lines and color but did not draw identifiable objects, so modern composers arranged sounds without creating recognizable harmonies. Led by the Viennese composer Arnold Schönberg (1874–1951), they abandoned traditional harmony and tonality. The musical notes in a given piece were no longer united and organized by a key; instead they were independent and unrelated. Schönberg's twelve-tone music of the 1920s arranged all twelve notes of the scale in an abstract, mathematical pattern, or "tone row." This pattern sounded like no pattern at all to the ordinary listener and could be detected only by a highly trained eye studying the musical score. Accustomed to the harmonies of classical and romantic music, audiences generally resisted modern atonal music. Only after the Second World War did it begin to win acceptance.

Movies and Radio

Until after the Second World War at the earliest, those revolutionary changes in art and music appealed mainly to a minority of "highbrows" and not to the general public. That public was primarily and enthusiastically wrapped up in movies and radio. The long-declining traditional arts and amusements of people in villages and small towns almost vanished and were replaced by standardized, commercial entertainment.

Moving pictures were first shown as a popular novelty in naughty peepshows—"What the Butler Saw"—and penny arcades in the 1890s, especially in Paris. The first movie houses date from an experiment in Los Angeles in 1902. They quickly attracted large audiences and led to the production of short, silent action films like the eight-minute *Great Train Robbery* of 1903. American directors and business people then set up "movie factories," at first in the New York area and after 1910 in Los Angeles. These factories churned out two short films each week. On the eve of the First World War, full-length feature films were suggesting the screen's vast possibilities.

During the First World War the United States became the dominant force in the rapidly expanding silent-film industry. In the 1920s, Mack Sennett (1884–1960) and his zany Keystone Cops specialized in short, slapstick comedies noted for frantic automobile chases, custard-pie battles, and gorgeous bathing beauties. Screen stars such as Mary Pickford and Lillian Gish, and Douglas Fairbanks and Rudolph Valentino became household names, with their own "fan clubs." Yet Charlie Chaplin (1889–1978), a funny little Englishman working in Hollywood, was unquestionably the king of the "silver screen" in the 1920s. In his enormously popular role as a lonely tramp, complete with baggy trousers, battered derby, and an awkward, shuffling walk, Chaplin symbolized the "gay spirit of laughter in a cruel, crazy world."[6] Chaplin also demonstrated that, in the hands of a genius, the new medium could combine mass entertainment and artistic accomplishment.

The early 1920s were also the great age of German films. Protected and developed during the war, the large German studios excelled in bizarre expressionist dramas. Unfortunately, their period of creativity was short-lived. By 1926 American money was drawing the leading German talents to Hollywood and consolidating America's international domination. Film making was big business, and European theater owners were forced to book whole blocks of American films to get the few pictures they really wanted. This system put European producers at a great disadvantage until "talkies" permitted a revival of national film industries in the 1930s, particularly in France.

Whether foreign or domestic, motion pictures became the main entertainment of the masses until after the Second World War. In Great Britain one in every four adults went to the movies twice a week in the late 1930s, and two in five went at least once a week. Continental countries had similar figures. The greatest appeal of motion pictures was that they offered ordinary people a temporary escape from the hard realities of everyday life. For an hour or two a moviegoer could flee the world of international tensions, uncertainty, unemployment, and personal frustrations. The appeal of escapist entertainment was especially strong during the Great Depression. Millions flocked to musical comedies featuring glittering stars such as Ginger Rogers and Fred Astaire and to the fanciful cartoons of Mickey Mouse and his friends.

Radio became possible with the transatlantic "wireless" communication of Guglielmo Marconi (1874–1937) in 1901 and the development of the vacuum tube in 1904, which permitted the transmission of speech and music. But only after 1920 did every major Western country establish national broadcasting networks. In the United States, such networks were privately owned and were financed by advertising. In Great Britain, Parliament set up an independent, high-minded public corporation, the British Broadcasting Corporation (BBC), which was supported by licensing fees. Elsewhere in Europe, the typical pattern was direct control by the government. Whatever the institutional framework, radio became popular and influential. By the late 1930s, more than three out of every four households in both democratic Great Britain and dictatorial Germany had at least one cheap, mass-produced radio. Other European countries were not far behind.

Radio in unscrupulous hands was particularly well suited for political propaganda. Dictators like Mussolini and Hitler controlled the airwaves and could reach enormous national audiences with their frequent, dramatic speeches. In democratic countries, politicians such as President Franklin Roosevelt and Prime Minister Stanley Baldwin effectively used informal "fireside chats" to bolster their support.

Motion pictures also became powerful tools of indoctrination, especially in countries with dictatorial regimes. Lenin himself encouraged the development of Soviet film making, believing that the new medium was essential to the social and ideological transformation of the country. Beginning in the mid-1920s, a series of epic films, the most famous of which were directed by Sergei Eisenstein (1898–1948), brilliantly dramatized the communist view of Russian history.

In Germany, Hitler turned to a young and immensely talented woman film maker, Leni Riefenstahl (b. 1902), for a masterpiece of documentary propaganda, *The Triumph of the Will,* based on the Nazi party rally at Nuremberg in 1934. Riefenstahl combined stunning aerial photography, joyful crowds welcoming Hitler, and mass processions of young Nazi fanatics. Her film was a brilliant and all-too-powerful documentary of Germany's "Nazi rebirth."

THE SEARCH FOR PEACE AND POLITICAL STABILITY

The Versailles settlement had established a shaky truce, not a solid peace. Within the general context of intellectual crisis and revolutionary artistic experimentation, politicians and national leaders struggled to create a stable international order.

The pursuit of real and lasting peace proved difficult. Germany hated the Treaty of Versailles. France was fearful and isolated. Britain was undependable, and the United States had turned its back on European problems. Eastern Europe was in ferment, and no one could predict the future of communist Russia. Moreover, the international economic situation was poor and greatly complicated by war debts and disrupted patterns of trade. Yet for a time, from 1925 to late 1929, it appeared that peace and stability were within reach. When the subsequent collapse of the 1930s mocked these hopes, the disillusionment of liberals in the democracies was intensified.

Germany and the Western Powers

Germany was the key to lasting peace. Only under the pressure of the Allies' naval blockade and threat to extend their military occupation from the Rhineland to the rest of the country had Germany's new republican government signed the Treaty of Versailles in June 1919. To Germans of all political parties, the treaty represented a harsh, dictated peace to be revised or repudiated as soon as possible. The treaty neither broke nor reduced Germany, which was potentially still the strongest country in Europe. Thus the treaty fell between

two stools: it was too harsh for a peace of reconciliation, too soft for a peace of conquest.

Moreover, with ominous implications for the future, France and Great Britain did not see eye to eye on Germany. By the end of 1919, France wanted to stress the harsh elements in the Treaty of Versailles. Most of the war in the west had been fought on French soil, and much of rich, industrialized northern France had been devastated. The expected costs of reconstruction were staggering; like Great Britain, France during the war had borrowed large sums from the United States, which had to be repaid. Thus French politicians believed that massive reparations from Germany were a vital economic necessity; and if the Germans had to suffer to make the payments, the French would not be overly concerned. Having compromised with President Wilson only to be betrayed by America's failure to ratify the treaty, many French leaders saw strict implementation of all provisions of the Treaty of Versailles as France's last best hope. Large reparation payments could hold Germany down indefinitely, and France would realize its goal of security.

The British soon felt differently. Prewar Germany had been Great Britain's second-best market in the entire world, and after the war a healthy, prosperous Germany appeared to be essential to the British economy. Indeed, many English people agreed with the analysis of the young English economist John Maynard Keynes (1883–1946), who eloquently denounced the Treaty of Versailles in his *Economic Consequences of the Peace* (1919). According to Keynes's interpretation, astronomical reparations and harsh economic measures would indeed reduce Germany to the position of an impoverished second-rate power, but such impoverishment would increase economic hardship in all countries. Only a complete revision of the foolish treaty could save Germany—and Europe. Keynes's attack exploded like a bombshell and became very influential. It stirred deep guilt feelings about Germany in the English-speaking world, feelings that often paralyzed English and American leaders in their relations with Germany and its leaders between the First and Second World Wars.

The British were also suspicious of France's army—momentarily the largest in Europe—and France's foreign policy. Ever since 1890, France had looked to Russia as a powerful ally against Germany. But with Russia hostile and communist, and with Britain and the United States unwilling to make any firm commitments, France turned to the newly formed states of eastern Europe for diplomatic support. In 1921 France signed a mutual defense pact with Poland and associated itself closely with the so-called Little Entente, an alliance that joined Czechoslovakia, Romania, and Yugoslavia against defeated and bitter Hungary. The British and the French were also on cool terms because of conflicts relating to their League of Nations mandates in the Middle East.

While French and British leaders drifted in different directions, the Allied reparations commission completed its work. In April 1921 it announced that Germany had to pay the enormous sum of 132 billion gold marks ($33 billion) in annual installments of 2.5 billion gold marks. Facing possible occupation of more of its territory, the young German republic, which had been founded in Weimar but moved back to Berlin, made its first payment in 1921. Then in 1922, wracked by rapid inflation and political assassinations, and motivated by hostility and arrogance as well, the Weimar Republic announced its inability to pay more. It proposed a moratorium on reparations for three years, with the clear implication that thereafter reparations would either be drastically reduced or eliminated entirely.

The British were willing to accept this offer, but the French were not. Led by their tough-minded, legalistic prime minister, Raymond Poincaré (1860–1934), they decided that they either had to call Germany's bluff or see the entire peace settlement dissolve to France's great disadvantage. So, despite strong British protests, France and its ally Belgium decided to pursue a firm policy. In early January 1923, French and Belgian armies began to occupy the Ruhr district, the heartland of industrial Germany, creating the most serious international crisis of the 1920s.

The Occupation of the Ruhr

The strategy of Poincaré and his French supporters was simple. Since Germany would not pay reparations in hard currency or gold, France and Belgium would collect reparations in kind—coal, steel, and machinery. If forcible collection proved impossible, France would occupy Germany and force it to accept the Treaty of Versailles.

"Hands Off the Ruhr" The French occupation of the Ruhr to collect reparations payments raised a storm of patriotic protest, including this anti-French poster of 1923. *(Source: Internationaal Instituut voor Sociale Geschiedenis)*

Strengthened by a wave of patriotism, the German government ordered the people of the Ruhr to stop working and start resisting—passively—the French occupation. The coal mines and steel mills of the Ruhr grew silent, leaving 10 percent of Germany's total population in need of relief. The French answer to passive resistance was to seal off not only the Ruhr but the entire Rhineland from the rest of Germany, letting in only enough food to prevent starvation. The French also revived plans for a separate state in the Rhineland.

By the summer of 1923, France and Germany were engaged in a tremendous test of wills. As the

German government had anticipated, French armies could not collect reparations from striking workers at gunpoint. But French occupation was indeed paralyzing Germany and its economy, for the Ruhr district normally produced 80 percent of Germany's steel and coal. Moreover, the occupation of the Ruhr turned rapid German inflation into runaway inflation. Faced with the need to support the striking Ruhr workers and their employers, the German government began to print money to pay its bills. Prices soared. People went to the store with a big bag of paper money and returned home with only a handful of groceries. German money rapidly lost all value, and so did anything else with a stated fixed value.

Runaway inflation brought about a social revolution. The accumulated savings of many retired and middle-class people were wiped out. The old middle-class virtues of thrift, caution, and self-reliance were cruelly mocked by catastrophic inflation. People told themselves that nothing had real value anymore, not even money. The German middle and lower middle classes, feeling cheated, burned with resentment. Many hated and blamed the Western governments, their own government, big business, the Jews, the workers, the communists for their misfortune. They were psychologically prepared to follow radical leaders in a crisis.

In August 1923, as the mark fell and political unrest grew throughout Germany, Gustav Stresemann (1878–1929) assumed leadership of the government. Stresemann adopted a compromising attitude. He called off passive resistance in the Ruhr and in October agreed in principle to pay reparations, but he asked for a re-examination of Germany's ability to pay. Poincaré accepted. His hard line was becoming increasingly unpopular with French citizens, and it was hated in Britain and the United States. Moreover, occupation was dreadfully expensive, and France's own currency was beginning to lose value on foreign exchange markets.

More generally, in both Germany and France, power was finally passing to the moderates, who realized that continued confrontation was a destructive, no-win situation. Thus, after five long years of hostility and tension culminating in a kind of undeclared war in the Ruhr in 1923, Germany and France decided to give compromise and cooperation a try. The British, and even the Americans, were willing to help. The first step was a reasonable compromise on the reparations question.

Hope in Foreign Affairs (1924–1929)

The reparations commission appointed an international committee of financial experts headed by an American banker, Charles G. Dawes, to re-examine reparations from a broad perspective. The committee made a series of recommendations known as the "Dawes Plan" (1924), and the plan was accepted by France, Germany, and Britain. German reparations were reduced and placed on a sliding scale, like an income tax, whereby yearly payments depended on the level of German economic prosperity. The Dawes Plan also recommended large loans to Germany, loans that could come only from the United States. These loans were to help Stresemann's government put its new currency on a firm basis and promote German recovery. In short, Germany would get private loans from the United States and pay reparations to France and Britain, thus enabling those countries to repay the large sums they owed the United States.

This circular flow of international payments was complicated and risky. For a time, though, it worked. The German republic experienced a spectacular economic recovery. By 1929 Germany's wealth and income were 50 percent greater than in 1913. With prosperity and large, continuous inflows of American capital, Germany easily paid about $1.3 billion in reparations in 1927 and 1928, enabling France and Britain to pay the United States. In 1929 the "Young Plan," named after an American businessman, further reduced German reparations and formalized the link between German reparations and French-British debts to the United States. In this way the Americans, who did not have armies but who did have money, belatedly played a part in the general economic settlement, which though far from ideal facilitated the worldwide recovery of the late 1920s.

The economic settlement was matched by a political settlement. In 1925 the leaders of Europe signed a number of agreements at Locarno, Switzerland. Stresemann, who guided Germany's foreign policy until his death in 1929, had suggested a treaty with France's conciliatory Aristide Briand (1862–1932), who had returned to office in 1924 after French voters rejected the bellicose Poincaré. By this treaty Germany and France solemnly pledged to accept their common border, and both Britain and Italy agreed to fight either country if it invaded the other. Stresemann also agreed to settle boundary disputes with Poland and Czechoslovakia by peaceful means, and France promised those countries military aid if they were attacked by Germany. For their efforts Stresemann and Briand shared the Nobel Peace Prize in 1926. The effect of the treaties of Locarno was far-reaching. For years, a "spirit of Locarno" gave Europeans a sense of growing security and stability in international affairs.

Hopes were strengthened by other developments. In 1926 Germany joined the League of Nations, where Stresemann continued his peace offensive. In 1928 fifteen countries signed the Kellogg-Briand Pact, which "condemned and renounced war as an instrument of national policy." The signing states agreed to settle international disputes peacefully. Often seen as idealistic nonsense because it made no provisions for action in case war actually occurred, the pact was nevertheless a hopeful step. It grew out of a suggestion by Briand that France and the United States renounce the possibility of war between their two countries. Briand was gently and subtly trying to draw the United States back into involvement with Europe. When Secretary of State Frank B. Kellogg (1856–1937) proposed a multinational pact, Briand appeared close to success. Thus the cautious optimism of the late 1920s also rested on the hope that the United States would accept its responsibilities as a great world power and consequently contribute to European stability.

Hope in Democratic Government

Domestic politics also offered reason to hope. During the occupation of the Ruhr and the great inflation, republican government in Germany had appeared on the verge of collapse. In 1923 Communists momentarily entered provincial governments, and in November an obscure nobody named Adolf Hitler leaped on a table in a beer hall in Munich and proclaimed a "national socialist revolution." But Hitler's early plot was poorly

The Fruits of Germany's Inflation   In the end, currency had value only as waste paper. Here bank notes are being purchased by the bail for paper mills, along with old rags (*Lumpen*) and bones (*Knochen*). (*Source: Archiv für Kunst u. Geschichte*)

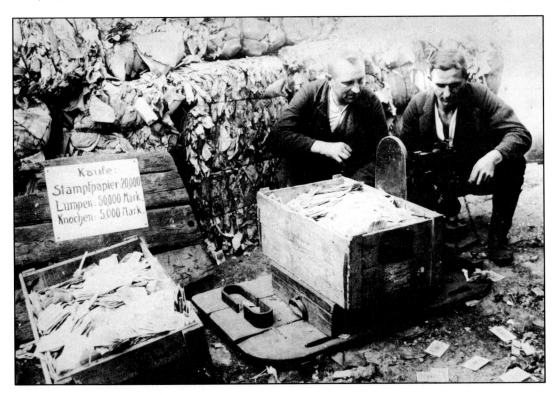

organized and easily crushed, and Hitler was sentenced to prison, where he outlined his theories and program in *Mein Kampf (My Struggle)*. Throughout the 1920s, Hitler's National Socialist party attracted support only from a few fanatical anti-Semites, ultranationalists, and disgruntled former servicemen. In 1928 his party had an insignificant twelve seats in the national parliament. Indeed, after 1923 democracy seemed to take root in Weimar Germany. A new currency was established, and the economy boomed.

The moderate businessmen who tended to dominate the various German coalition governments were convinced that economic prosperity demanded good relations with the Western powers, and they supported parliamentary government at home. Stresemann himself was a man of this class, and he was the key figure in every government until his death in 1929. Elections were held regularly, and republican democracy appeared to have growing support among a majority of Germans.

There were, however, sharp political divisions in the country. Many unrepentant nationalists and monarchists populated the right and the army. Germany's Communists were noisy and active on the left. The Communists, directed from Moscow, reserved their greatest hatred and sharpest barbs for their cousins the Social Democrats, whom they endlessly accused of betraying the revolution. The working classes were divided politically, but most supported the nonrevolutionary but socialist Social Democrats.

The situation in France had numerous similarities to that in Germany. Communists and Socialists battled for the support of the workers. After 1924 the democratically elected government rested mainly in the hands of coalitions of moderates, and business interests were well represented. France's great accomplishment was the rapid rebuilding of its war-torn northern region. The expense of this undertaking led, however, to a large deficit and substantial inflation. By early 1926 the franc had fallen to 10 percent of its prewar value, causing a severe crisis. Poincaré was recalled to office, and Briand became minister for foreign affairs. The Poincaré government proceeded to slash spending and raise taxes, restoring confidence in the economy. The franc was "saved," stabilized at about one-fifth of its prewar value. Good times prevailed until 1930.

Despite its political shortcomings, France attracted artists and writers from all over the world

in the 1920s. Much of the intellectual and artistic ferment of the times flourished in Paris. More generally, France appealed to foreigners and the French as a harmonious combination of small businesses and family farms, of bold innovation and solid traditions.

Britain, too, faced challenges after 1920. The wartime trend toward greater social equality continued, however, helping to maintain social harmony. The great problem was unemployment. Many of Britain's best markets had been lost during the war. In June 1921 almost 2.2 million people—23 percent of the labor force—were out of work, and throughout the 1920s unemployment hovered around 12 percent. Yet the state provided unemployment benefits of equal size to all those who were without jobs and supplemented those payments with subsidized housing, medical aid, and increased old-age pensions. These and other measures kept living standards from seriously declining, defused class tensions, and pointed the way toward the welfare state that Britain established after the Second World War.

Relative social harmony was accompanied by the rise of the Labour party as a determined champion of the working classes and of greater social equality. Committed to the kind of moderate, "revisionist" socialism that had emerged before the First World War (see pages 954–956), the Labour party replaced the Liberal party as the main opposition to the Conservatives. The new prominence of the Labour party reflected the decline of old liberal ideals of competitive capitalism, limited government control, and individual responsibility. In 1924 and 1929, the Labour party under Ramsay MacDonald (1866–1937) governed the country with the support of the smaller Liberal party. Yet Labour moved toward socialism gradually and democratically, so that the middle classes were not overly frightened as the working classes won new benefits.

The Conservatives under Stanley Baldwin (1867–1947) showed the same compromising spirit on social issues. The last line of Baldwin's greatest speech in March 1925 summarized his international and domestic programs: "Give us peace in our time, O Lord." Thus, in spite of such conflicts as the 1926 strike by hard-pressed coal miners, which ended in an unsuccessful general strike, social unrest in Britain was limited in the 1920s and in the 1930s as well. In 1922 Britain granted southern, Catholic Ireland full autonomy

An American in Paris   The young Josephine Baker suddenly became a star when she brought an exotic African eroticism to French music halls in 1925. American blacks and Africans had a powerful impact on entertainment in Europe in the 1920s and 1930s. *(Source: Bettmann/Hulton)*

after a bitter guerrilla war, thus removing another source of prewar friction. In summary, developments in both international relations and in the domestic politics of the leading democracies gave cause for cautious optimism in the late 1920s.

THE GREAT DEPRESSION (1929–1939)

Like the Great War, the Great Depression must be spelled with capital letters. Economic depression was nothing new. Economic hard times occurred throughout the nineteenth century with predict-

able regularity, as they recur in the form of recessions and slumps to this day. What was new about this depression was its severity and duration. It struck with ever-greater intensity from 1929 to 1933, and recovery was uneven and slow. Moreover, the Great Depression was truly global in scope.

The social and political consequences of prolonged economic collapse were enormous all around the world. Subsequent military expansion in Japan has already been described (see page 1097), and later chapters examine a similarly powerful impact on Latin America and Africa. In Europe and the United States, the depression shat-

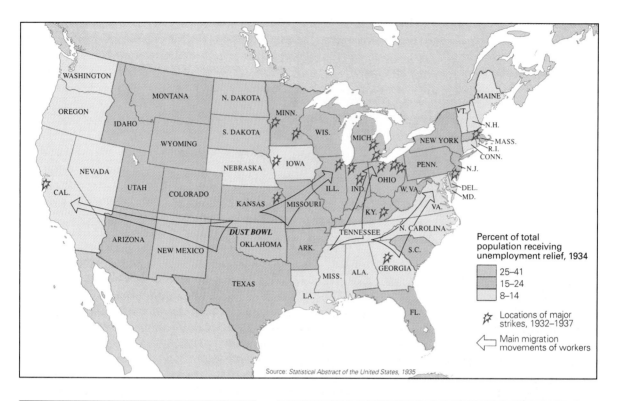

Source: *Statistical Abstract of the United States, 1935*

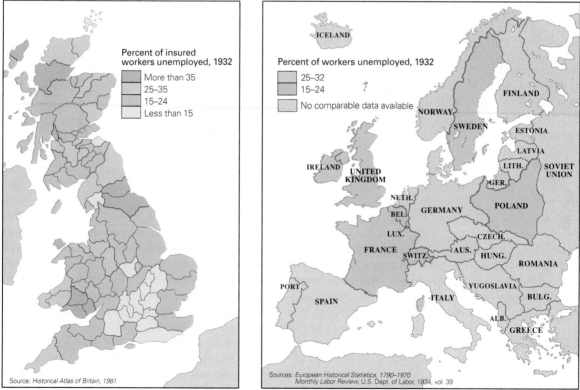

Percent of insured
workers unemployed, 1932

- More than 35
- 25–35
- 15–24
- Less than 15

Source: *Historical Atlas of Britain, 1981*

Percent of workers unemployed, 1932

- 25–32
- 15–24
- No comparable data available

Sources: *European Historical Statistics, 1790–1970*
Monthly Labor Review, U.S. Dept. of Labor, 1934, vol. 39

Percent of total
population receiving
unemployment relief, 1934

- 25–41
- 15–24
- 8–14

☆ Locations of major
strikes, 1932–1937

⇐ Main migration
movements of workers

MAP 34.1 The Great Depression in the United States, Britain, and Europe National and
regional differences were substantial. Germany, industrial northern Britain, and the
American Middle West were particularly hard-hit.

tered the fragile optimism of political leaders in the late 1920s. Mass unemployment made insecurity a reality for millions of ordinary people, who had paid little attention to the intellectual crisis or to new directions in art and ideas (Map 34.1). In desperation, people looked for leaders who would "do something." They were willing to support radical attempts to deal with the crisis by both democratic leaders and dictators.

The Economic Crisis

There is no agreement among historians and economists about why the Great Depression was so deep and lasted so long. Thus it is best to trace the course of the great collapse before trying to identify what caused it.

Though economic activity was already declining moderately in many countries by early 1929, the crash of the stock market in the United States in October of that year really started the Great Depression. The American stock market boom, which had seen stock prices double between early 1928 and September 1929, was built on borrowed money. Many wealthy investors, speculators, and people of modest means had bought stocks by paying only a small fraction of the total purchase price and borrowing the remainder of the purchase price from their stockbrokers. Such buying "on margin" was extremely dangerous. When prices started falling, the hard-pressed margin buyers either had to put up more money, which was often impossible, or sell their shares to pay their brokers. Thus thousands of people started selling all at once. The result was a financial panic. Countless investors and speculators were wiped out in a matter of days or weeks.

The general economic consequences were swift and severe. Stripped of their wealth and confidence, battered investors and their fellow citizens started buying fewer goods. Production began to slow down, and unemployment began to rise. Soon the entire American economy was caught in a vicious, spiraling decline.

The financial panic in the United States triggered a worldwide financial crisis, and that crisis resulted in a drastic decline in production in country after country. Throughout the 1920s American bankers and investors had lent large amounts of capital not only to Germany but to many other countries. Many of these loans were short-term,

and once panic broke, New York bankers began recalling them. Gold reserves thus began to flow out of European countries, particularly Germany and Austria, toward the United States. It became very hard for European business people to borrow money, and the panicky public began to withdraw its savings from the banks. These banking problems eventually led to the crash of the largest bank in Austria in 1931 and then to general financial chaos. The recall of private loans by American bankers also accelerated the collapse in world prices, as business people around the world dumped industrial goods and agricultural commodities in a frantic attempt to get cash to pay what they owed.

The financial crisis led to a general crisis of production: between 1929 and 1933, world output of goods fell by an estimated 38 percent. As this happened, each country turned inward and tried to go it alone. In 1931, for example, Britain went off the gold standard, refusing to convert bank notes into gold, and reduced the value of its money. Britain's goal was to make its goods cheaper and therefore more salable in the world market. But because more than twenty nations, including the United States in 1934, also went off the gold standard, no country gained a real advantage. Similarly, country after country followed the example of the United States when it raised protective tariffs to their highest levels ever in 1930 and tried to seal off shrinking national markets for American producers only. Within this context of fragmented and destructive economic nationalism, recovery finally began in 1933.

Although opinions differ, two factors probably best explain the relentless slide to the bottom from 1929 to early 1933. First, the international economy lacked leadership able to maintain stability when the crisis came. Specifically, as a noted American economic historian concludes, the seriously weakened British, the traditional leaders of the world economy, "couldn't and the United States wouldn't" stabilize the international economic system in 1929.[7] The United States, which had momentarily played a positive role after the occupation of the Ruhr, cut back its international lending and erected high tariffs.

The second factor was poor national economic policy in almost every country. Governments generally cut their budgets and reduced spending when they should have run large deficits in an attempt to stimulate their economies. Since the Second World War, such a "counter-cyclical policy," advocated by John Maynard Keynes, has become a well-established weapon against depression. But in the 1930s Keynes's prescription was generally regarded with horror by orthodox economists.

Mass Unemployment

The need for large-scale government spending was tied to mass unemployment. As the financial crisis led to cuts in production, workers lost their jobs and had little money to buy goods. This led to still more cuts in production and still more unemploy-

Middle-Class Unemployment An English office worker's unusual sandwich board poignantly summarizes the bitter despair of the unemployed in the 1930s. *(Source: Bettmann/Hulton)*

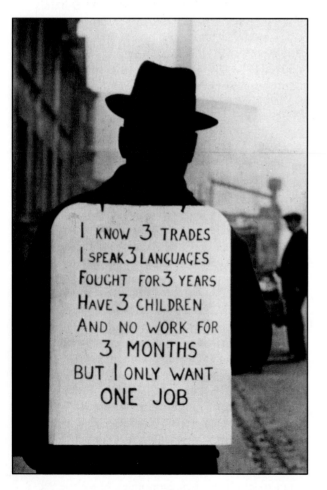

ment, until millions were out of work. In Britain, unemployment had averaged 12 percent in the 1920s; between 1930 and 1935, it averaged more than 18 percent. Far worse was the case of the United States, where unemployment had averaged only 5 percent in the 1920s. In 1932 unemployment soared to about one-third of the entire U.S. labor force: fourteen million people were out of work (see Map 34.1). Only by pumping new money into the economy could the government increase demand and break the vicious cycle of decline.

Along with its economic effects, mass unemployment posed a great social problem that mere numbers cannot adequately express. Millions of people lost their spirit and dignity in an apparently hopeless search for work. Homes and ways of life were disrupted in millions of personal tragedies. Young people postponed marriages they could not afford, and birthrates fell sharply. There was an increase in suicide and mental illness. Poverty or the threat of poverty became a grinding reality. In 1932 the workers of Manchester, England, appealed to their city officials—a typical appeal echoed throughout the Western world:

We tell you that thousands of people . . . are in desperate straits. We tell you that men, women, and children are going hungry. . . . We tell you that great numbers are being rendered distraught through the stress and worry of trying to exist without work. . . .

If you do not do this—if you do not provide useful work for the unemployed—what, we ask, is your alternative? Do not imagine that this colossal tragedy of unemployment is going on endlessly without some fateful catastrophe. Hungry men are angry men.[8]

Mass unemployment was a terrible time bomb preparing to explode.

The New Deal in the United States

Of all the major industrial countries, only Germany was harder hit by the Great Depression, or reacted more radically to it, than the United States. Depression was so traumatic in the United States because the 1920s had been a period of complacent prosperity. The Great Depression and the response to it marked a major turning point in American history.

President Herbert Hoover (1874–1964) and his administration initially reacted to the stock market crash and economic decline with dogged optimism and limited action. In May 1930 Hoover told a group of business and farm leaders, "I am convinced that we have now passed the worst and with continued unity of effort we shall rapidly recover." When, however, the full force of the financial crisis struck Europe in the summer of 1931 and boomeranged back to the United States, people's worst fears became reality. Banks failed; unemployment soared. In 1932 industrial production fell to about 50 percent of its level in 1929. In these tragic circumstances Franklin Delano Roosevelt (1882–1945), an inspiring wheelchair aristocrat previously crippled by polio, won a landslide electoral victory with grand but vague promises of a "New Deal for the forgotten man."

Roosevelt's basic goal was to reform capitalism in order to preserve it. In his words, "A frank examination of the profit system in the spring of 1933 showed it to be in collapse; but substantially everybody in the United States, in public office and out of public office, from the very rich to the very poor, was as determined as was my Administration to save it."[9] Roosevelt rejected socialism and government ownership of industry in 1933. To right the situation, he chose forceful government intervention in the economy.

In this choice, Roosevelt and his advisers were greatly influenced by America's experience in the First World War. During the wartime emergency, the American economy had been thoroughly planned and regulated. Roosevelt and his "brain trust" of advisers adopted similar policies to restore prosperity and reduce social inequality. Roosevelt was flexible, pragmatic, and willing to experiment. Government intervention and experimentation were combined in some of the New Deal's most significant measures.

The most ambitious attempt to control and plan the economy was the National Recovery Administration (NRA), established by Congress right after Roosevelt took office. The key idea behind the NRA was to reduce competition and fix prices and wages for everyone's benefit. This goal required government, business, and labor to hammer out detailed regulations for each industry. Along with this kind of national planning in the private sector of the economy, the government believed it could sponsor enough public works projects to assure recovery. Because the NRA broke with the cherished American tradition of free competition and aroused conflicts among business people, consumers, and bureaucrats, it did not work well. By the time the NRA was declared unconstitutional in 1935, Roosevelt and the New Deal were already moving away from government efforts to plan and control the entire economy.

Instead, Roosevelt and his advisers attacked the key problem of mass unemployment directly. The federal government accepted the responsibility of employing directly as many people as financially possible, something Hoover had consistently rejected. Thus, when it became clear in late 1933 that the initial program of public works was too small, new agencies were created to undertake a vast range of projects.

The most famous of these agencies is the Works Progress Administration (WPA), set up in 1935. At its peak in late 1938, this government agency employed more than three million individuals. One-fifth of the entire labor force worked for the WPA at some point in the 1930s. To this day, thousands of public buildings, bridges, and highways built by the WPA stand as monuments to energetic government efforts to provide people with meaningful work. The WPA was enormously popular in a nation long schooled in self-reliance and the work ethic. The hope of a job with the government helped check the threat of social revolution in the United States.

Other social measures aimed in the same direction. Following the path blazed by Germany's Bismarck in the 1880s, the U.S. government in 1935 established a national social security system, with old-age pensions and unemployment benefits, to protect many workers against some of life's uncertainties. The National Labor Relations Act of 1935 gave union organizers the green light by declaring collective bargaining to be the policy of the United States. Following some bitter strikes, such as the sit-down strike at General Motors in early 1937, union membership more than doubled, from four million in 1935 to nine million in 1940. In general, between 1935 and 1938 government rulings and social reforms chipped away at the privileges of the wealthy and tried to help ordinary people.

Yet, despite its undeniable accomplishments in social reform, the New Deal was only partly successful as a response to the Great Depression. At

President Roosevelt used his famous "fireside chats" to explain his changing policies and to reassure the American people that the New Deal initiatives were working. This photo captures Roosevelt's forceful personality and contagious confidence, which he conveyed over the air waves. *(Source: Brown Brothers)*

the height of the recovery, in May 1937, seven million workers were still unemployed. The economic situation then worsened seriously in the recession of 1937 and 1938. Production fell sharply, and although unemployment never again reached the fifteen million mark of 1933, it hit eleven million in 1938 and was still a staggering ten million when war broke out in Europe in September 1939.

The New Deal never did pull the United States out of the depression. This failure frustrated Americans then, and it is still puzzling today. Perhaps, as some have claimed, Roosevelt should have used his enormous popularity and prestige in 1933 to nationalize the banks, the railroads, and some heavy industry, so that national economic planning could have been successful. On the other hand, Roosevelt's sharp attack on big business and the wealthy after 1935 had popular appeal but also damaged business confidence and made the great

capitalists uncooperative. Given the low level of profit and the underutilization of many factories, however, it is questionable whether business would have behaved much differently even if the New Deal had catered to it.

Finally, it is often argued that the New Deal did not put enough money into the economy through deficit financing. Like his predecessors in the White House, Roosevelt was attached to the ideal of the balanced budget. His largest deficit was only $4.4 billion in 1936. Compare this figure with deficits of $21.5 billion in 1942 and $57.4 billion in 1943, when the nation was prosperously engaged in total war and unemployment had vanished. By 1945 many economists concluded that the New Deal's deficit-financed public works had been too small a step in the right direction. These Keynesian views were to be very influential in economic policy in Europe and America after the Second World War.

The Scandinavian Response to Depression

Of all the Western democracies, the Scandinavian countries under Socialist leadership responded most successfully to the challenge of the Great Depression. Having grown steadily in number in the late nineteenth century, the Socialists became the largest political party in Sweden and then in Norway after the First World War. In the 1920s they passed important social reform legislation for both peasants and workers, gained practical administrative experience, and developed a unique kind of socialism. Flexible and nonrevolutionary, Scandinavian socialism grew out of a strong tradition of cooperative community action. Even before 1900, Scandinavian agricultural cooperatives had shown how individual peasant families could join together for everyone's benefit. Labor leaders and capitalists were also inclined to work together.

When the economic crisis struck in 1929, Socialist governments in Scandinavia built on this pattern of cooperative social action. Sweden in particular pioneered in the use of large-scale deficits to finance public works and thereby maintain production and employment. Scandinavian governments also increased social welfare benefits, from old-age pensions and unemployment insurance to subsidized housing and maternity allowances. All this spending required a large bureaucracy and high taxes, first on the rich and then on practically everyone. Yet both private and cooperative enterprise thrived, as did democracy. Some observers saw Scandinavia's welfare socialism as an appealing "middle way" between sick capitalism and cruel communism or fascism.

Recovery and Reform in Britain and France

In Britain, MacDonald's Labour government and then, after 1931, the Conservative-dominated coalition government followed orthodox economic theory. The budget was balanced, but unemployed workers received barely enough welfare to live. Despite government lethargy, the economy recovered considerably after 1932. By 1937 total production was about 20 percent higher than in 1929. In fact, for Britain the years after 1932 were actually somewhat better than the 1920s had been, quite the opposite of the situation in the United States and France.

This good, but by no means brilliant, performance reflected the gradual reorientation of the British economy. After going off the gold standard in 1931 and establishing protective tariffs in 1932, Britain concentrated increasingly on the national rather than the international market. The old export industries of the Industrial Revolution, such as textiles and coal, continued to decline, but new industries like automobiles and electrical appliances grew in response to British demand at home. Moreover, low interest rates encouraged a housing boom. By the end of the decade there were highly visible differences between the old, depressed industrial areas of the north and the new, growing areas of the south. These developments encouraged Britain to look inward and avoid unpleasant foreign questions.

Because France was relatively less industrialized and more isolated from the world economy, the Great Depression came later there. But once it hit France, it stayed and stayed. Decline was steady until 1935, and the short-lived recovery never brought production or employment back up to predepression levels. Economic stagnation both reflected and heightened an ongoing political crisis. There was no stability in government. As before 1914, the French parliament was made up of many political parties that could never cooperate for very long. In 1933, for example, five coalition cabinets formed and fell in rapid succession.

The French lost the underlying unity that had made government instability bearable before 1914. Fascist-type organizations agitated against parliamentary democracy and looked to Mussolini's Italy and Hitler's Germany for inspiration. In February 1934, French fascists and semifascists rioted and threatened to overturn the republic. At the same time, the Communist party and many workers opposed to the existing system were looking to Stalin's Russia for guidance. The vital center of moderate republicanism was sapped from both sides.

Frightened by the growing strength of the fascists at home and abroad, the Communists, the Socialists, and the Radicals formed an alliance—the Popular Front—for the national elections of May 1936. Their clear victory reflected the trend toward polarization. The number of Communists in the parliament jumped dramatically from 10 to 72, while the Socialists, led by Léon Blum (1872-1950), became the strongest party in

France with 146 seats. The really quite moderate Radicals slipped badly, and the conservatives lost ground to the semifascists.

In the next few months, Blum's Popular Front government made the first and only real attempt to deal with the social and economic problems of the 1930s in France. Inspired by Roosevelt's New Deal, the Popular Front encouraged the union movement and launched a far-reaching program of social reform, complete with paid vacations and a forty-hour workweek. Popular with workers and the lower middle class, these measures were quickly sabotaged by rapid inflation and cries of revolution from fascists and frightened conservatives. Wealthy people sneaked their money out of the country, labor unrest grew, and France entered a severe financial crisis. Blum was forced to announce a "breathing spell" in social reform.

The fires of political dissension were also fanned by civil war in Spain. The Communists demanded that France support the Spanish republicans, while many French conservatives would gladly have joined Hitler and Mussolini in aiding the attack of Spanish fascists. Extremism grew, and France itself was within sight of civil war. Blum was forced to resign in June 1937, and the Popular Front quickly collapsed. An anxious and divided France drifted aimlessly once again, preoccupied by Hitler and German rearmament.

SUMMARY

After the First World War, Western society entered a complex and difficult era—truly an age of anxiety. Intellectual life underwent a crisis marked by pessimism, uncertainty, and fascination with irrational forces. Ceaseless experimentation and rejection of old forms characterized art and music while motion pictures and radio provided a new, standardized entertainment for the masses. Previously avant-garde intellectual and artistic developments, along with the insecure state of mind they expressed, gained wider currency.

Politics and economics were similarly disrupted. In the 1920s political leaders groped to create an enduring peace and rebuild the prewar prosperity, and for a brief period late in the decade they seemed to succeed. Then the Great Depression shattered the fragile stability. Uncertainty re-

turned with redoubled force in the 1930s. The international economy collapsed, and unemployment struck millions. The democracies turned inward as they sought to cope with massive domestic problems and widespread disillusionment. Generally speaking, they were not very successful. The old liberal ideals of individual rights and responsibilities, elected government, and economic freedom seemed ineffective and outmoded, even when they managed to survive. And in many countries they were abandoned completely.

NOTES

1. P. Valéry, *Variety,* trans. M. Cowley (New York: Harcourt, Brace, 1927), pp. 27–28.
2. G. Marcel, as quoted in S. Hughes, *The Obstructed Path: French Social Thought in the Years of Desperation, 1930–1960* (New York: Harper & Row, 1967), p. 82.
3. G. Greene, *Another Mexico* (New York: Viking Press, 1939), p. 3.
4. Quoted in A. H. Barr, Jr., *What Is Modern Painting?* 9th ed. (New York: Museum of Modern Art, 1966), p. 27.
5. Ibid., p. 25.
6. R. Graves and A. Hodge, *The Long Week End: A Social History of Great Britain, 1918–1939* (New York: Macmillan, 1941), p. 131.
7. C. P. Kindleberger, *The World in Depression, 1929–1939* (Berkeley: University of California Press, 1973), p. 292.
8. Quoted in S. B. Clough et al., eds., *Economic History of Europe: Twentieth Century* (New York: Harper & Row, 1968), pp. 243–245.
9. Quoted in D. Dillard, *Economic Development of the North Atlantic Community* (Englewood Cliffs, N.J.: Prentice-Hall, 1967), p. 591.

SUGGESTED READING

Among general works, E. Wiskemann, *Europe of the Dictators, 1919–1945* (1966), and R. Sontag, *A Broken World, 1919–1939* (1971), are particularly recommended. The latter has an excellent bibliography. A. Bullock, ed., *The Twentieth Century* (1971), is a lavish visual feast combined with penetrating essays on major developments since 1900. Two excellent accounts of contemporary history—one with a liberal and the other with a conservative point of view—are R. Paxton, *Europe in the Twentieth Century* (1975), and P. Johnson, *Modern Times: The World from the Twenties to the Eighties* (1983). Crucial changes in thought before and after the First World War are discussed in three rewarding intellectual histories: G. Masur, *Prophets of Yesterday* (1961); H. S. Hughes, *Consciousness and Society* (1956); and M. Biddiss, *Age of the Masses: Ideas and Society Since 1870* (1977). R. Stromberg, *European Intellectual History Since 1789,* 4th ed. (1986), and F. Baumer, *Modern European Thought: Continuity and Change in Ideas, 1600–1950* (1970), are recommended general surveys.

J. Rewalds, *The History of Impressionism,* rev. ed. (1961), and *Post-Impressionism* (1956) are excellent, as is the work by Barr cited in the Notes. P. Collaer, *A History of Modern Music* (1961), and H. R. Hitchcock, *Architecture: Nineteenth and Twentieth Centuries* (1958), are good introductions. T. Wolfe, *From Bauhaus to Our House* (1981), is a lively critique of modern architecture. L. Barnett, *The Universe and Dr. Einstein* (1952), is a fascinating study of the new physics. A. Storr, *Freud* (1989), and P. Rieff, *Freud* (1956), consider the man and how his theories have stood the test of time. M. White, ed., *The Age of Analysis* (1955), opens up basic questions of twentieth-century psychology and philosophy. H. Liebersohn, *Fate and Utopia in German Sociology* (1988), analyzes developments in German social science, and P. Gay, *Weimar Culture* (1970), is a brilliant exploration of the many-sided artistic renaissance in Germany in the 1920s. M. Marrus, ed., *Emergence of Leisure* (1974), is a pioneering inquiry into an important aspect of mass culture. H. Daniels-Rops, *A Fight for God,* 2 vols. (1966), is a sympathetic history of the Catholic church between 1870 and 1939.

G. Ambrosius and W. Hibbard, *A Social and Economic History of Twentieth-Century Europe* (1989), provides a good survey; C. Maier, *Recasting Bourgeois Europe* (1975), is an ambitious comparative study of social classes and conflicts in France, Germany, and Italy after the First World War. P. Fritzsche, *Rehearsals for Fascism: Populism and Political Mobilization in Weimar Germany* (1990); R. Wohl, *The Generation of 1914* (1979); R. Kuisel, *Capital and State in Modern France: Renovation and Economic Management* (1982); and W. McDougall, *France's Rhineland Diplomacy, 1914–1924* (1978), are four more important studies on aspects of the postwar challenge. M. Childs, *Sweden: The Middle Way* (1961), applauds Sweden's efforts at social reform. W. Neuman, *The Balance of Power in the Interwar Years, 1919–1939* (1968), perceptively examines international politics after the Locarno treaties of 1925. In addition to the contemporary works discussed in the text, the crisis of the interwar period comes alive in R. Crossman, ed., *The God That Failed* (1950), in which famous Western writers tell why they were attracted to and later repelled by communism; J. Ortega y Gasset's renowned *The Revolt of the Masses* (1932); and F. A. Hayek's *The Road to Serfdom* (1944), a famous warning of the dangers to democratic freedoms.

In addition to Kindleberger's excellent study of the Great Depression cited in the Notes, there is J. K. Galbraith's very lively and understandable account of the stock market collapse, *The Great Crash* (1955). J. Garraty, *Unemployment in History* (1978), is noteworthy, though novels best portray the human tragedy of economic decline. Winifred Holtby, *South Riding* (1936), and Walter Greenwood, *Love on the Dole* (1933), are moving stories of the Great Depression in England; Hans Fallada, *Little Man, What Now?* (1932), is the classic counterpart for Germany. Also highly recommended as commentaries on English life between the wars are Robert Graves, *Goodbye to All That,* rev. ed. (1957), and George Orwell, *The Road to Wigan Pier* (1972). Among French novelists, André Gide painstakingly examines the French middle class and its values in *The Counterfeiters,* and Albert Camus, the greatest of the existential novelists, is at his unforgettable best in *The Stranger* and *The Plague.*

35

Dictatorships and the Second World War

Adolf Hitler at Bueckeberg (Westphalia)

The era of anxiety and economic depression was also a time of growing strength for political dictatorship. Popularly elected governments and basic civil liberties declined drastically in Europe. On the eve of the Second World War, liberal democratic government survived only in Great Britain, France, the Low Countries, the Scandinavian nations, and neutral Switzerland. Elsewhere in Europe, various kinds of "strong men" ruled. Dictatorship seemed the wave of the future. Thus the decline in liberal political institutions and the intellectual crisis were related elements in the general crisis of European civilization.

The era of dictatorship is a highly disturbing chapter in the history of Western civilization. The key development was not simply the resurgence of dictatorship but the rise of a new kind of tyranny—the modern totalitarian state. Modern totalitarianism reached its fullest realization in Communist Russia and Nazi Germany in the 1930s. Stalin and Hitler mobilized their peoples for enormous undertakings and ruled with unprecedented severity. Hitler's mobilization was ultimately directed toward racial aggression and territorial expansion, and his ruthless attack on Poland in 1939 started the Second World War.

Nazi armies were defeated by a great coalition, and people today want to believe that the era of totalitarian dictatorship was a terrible accident, that Stalin's slave labor camps and Hitler's gas chambers "can't happen again." Yet the cruel truth is that terrible atrocities continue to plague the world: the Khmer Rouge inflicted genocide on people in Kampuchea in recent times; civil wars in the Horn of Africa have brought horrible man-made famines, and there are many other examples. Thus it is vital to understand Europe's tragic era of totalitarian dictatorship in order to guard against a recurrence.

- What was the nature of the twentieth-century totalitarian state?

- How did totalitarianism affect ordinary people?

- How did the rise of totalitarian states result in another world war?

These are the questions that this chapter seeks to answer.

AUTHORITARIAN AND TOTALITARIAN STATES

The modern totalitarian state differed from the old-fashioned authoritarian state. Completely rejecting liberal values and drawing on the experience of total war, the modern totalitarian state exercised much greater control over the masses and mobilized them for constant action. The nature of this control may be examined by comparing the old and new forms of dictatorship in a general way, before entering the strange worlds of Stalin's Russia and Hitler's Germany.

Conservative Authoritarianism

The traditional form of antidemocratic government in European history has been conservative authoritarianism. Like Catherine the Great in Russia and Metternich in Austria, the leaders of such governments have tried to prevent major changes that would undermine the existing social order. To do so, they have relied on obedient bureaucracies, vigilant police departments, and trustworthy armies. Popular participation in government has been forbidden or else severely limited to such natural allies as landlords, bureaucrats, and high church officials. Liberals, democrats, and socialists have been persecuted as radicals, often finding themselves in jail or exile.

Yet old-fashioned authoritarian governments were limited in their power and in their objectives. Lacking modern technology and communications, they did not have the power to control many aspects of their subjects' lives. Nor did they wish to do so. Preoccupied with the goal of mere survival, these governments largely limited their demands to taxes, army recruits, and passive acceptance. As long as the people did not try to change the system, they often had considerable personal independence.

After the First World War, this kind of authoritarian government revived, especially in the less developed eastern part of Europe. There, the parliamentary regimes that had been founded on the wreckage of empires in 1918 fell one by one. By early 1938 only economically and socially advanced Czechoslovakia remained true to liberal political ideals. Conservative dictators also took over in Spain and Portugal.

There were several reasons for this development. These nations lacked a strong tradition of self-government, with its necessary restraint and compromise. Moreover, many of these new states were torn by ethnic conflicts that threatened their very existence. Dictatorship appealed to nationalists and military leaders as a way to repress such tensions and preserve national unity. Large landowners and the church were still powerful forces in these largely agrarian areas, and they often looked to dictators to save them from progressive land reform or communist agrarian upheaval. So did some members of the middle class, which was small and weak in eastern Europe. Finally, though some kind of democracy managed to stagger through the 1920s in Austria, Bulgaria, Romania, Greece, Estonia, and Latvia, the Great Depression delivered the final blow in those countries in 1936.

Although some of the authoritarian regimes adopted certain Hitlerian and fascist characteristics in the 1930s, their general aims were not totalitarian. They were concerned more with maintaining the status quo than with forcing society into rapid change or war. This tradition lives on, especially in some of the military dictatorships that ruled in Latin America until quite recently.

Hungary was a good example of conservative authoritarianism. In the chaos of collapse in 1919, Béla Kun formed a Lenin-style government, but communism in Hungary was soon crushed by foreign troops, large landowners, and hostile peasants. Thereafter, a combination of great and medium-size landowners instituted a semi-authoritarian regime, which maintained the status quo in the 1920s. Hungary had a parliament, but

Nazi Mass Rally, 1936 This picture captures the spirit of modern totalitarianism. The uniformed members of the Nazi party have willingly merged themselves into a single force and await the command of the godlike leader. *(Source: Wide World Photos)*

elections were carefully controlled. The peasants did not have the right to vote, and an upper house representing the landed aristocracy was re-established. There was no land reform, no major social change. In the 1930s the Hungarian government remained conservative and nationalistic. Increasingly, it was opposed by a Nazi-like fascist movement, the Arrow Cross, which demanded radical reform and totalitarian measures.

Another example of conservative authoritarianism was newly independent Poland, where democratic government was overturned in 1926 when General Joseph Pilsudski established a military dictatorship. Sandwiched between Russia and Germany, Poland was torn by bitter party politics. Pilsudski silenced opposition and tried to build a strong state. His principal supporters were the army, major industrialists, and dedicated nationalists.

In Yugoslavia, King Alexander (r. 1921–1934) proclaimed a centralized dictatorship in 1929 to prevent ethnic rivalries among Serbs, Croats, and Slovenes from tearing the country apart. An old-style authoritarian, Alexander crushed democracy, jailed separatists, and ruled through the bureaucracy.

Another example of conservative authoritarianism was Portugal, at the westernmost end of the European peninsula. Constantly shaken by military coups and uprisings after a republican revolution in 1910, very poor and backward Portugal finally got a strong dictator in Antonio de Oliveira Salazar in 1932. A devout Catholic, Salazar gave the church the strongest possible position in the country while controlling the press and outlawing most political activity. Yet there was no attempt to mobilize the masses or to accomplish great projects. The traditional society was firmly maintained, and that was enough.

Modern Totalitarianism

Both modern totalitarianism and conservative authoritarianism are dictatorships, but they differ. They may be thought of as two distinct types of political organization that in practice sometimes share certain elements.

Modern totalitarianism burst on the scene with the revolutionary total-war effort of 1914 to 1918. The Great War called forth a tendency to subordinate all institutions and all classes to one supreme objective: victory. Nothing, absolutely nothing, had equal value. People were called to make ever-greater sacrifices, and their personal freedom was constantly reduced by ever-greater government control. As the outstanding French thinker Elie Halévy put it in 1936, the varieties of modern totalitarian tyranny—fascism, Nazism, and communism—may be thought of as "feuding brothers" with a common father, the nature of modern war.[1]

The crucial experience of the First World War was carried further by Lenin and the Bolsheviks during the Russian civil war. Lenin showed how a dedicated minority could make a total effort and achieve victory over a less determined majority. Lenin also demonstrated how institutions and human rights might be subordinated to the needs of a single group—the Communist party—and its leader, Lenin. Thus Lenin provided a model for single-party dictatorship, and he inspired imitators.

Building on its immediate origins in the First World War and the Russian civil war, modern totalitarianism reached maturity in the 1930s in Stalinist Russia and Nazi Germany. Both had several fundamental characteristics of modern totalitarianism.

Armed with modern technology and communications, the true totalitarian state began as a dictatorship exercising complete political power, but it did not stop there. Increasingly, the state took over and tried to control just as completely the economic, social, intellectual, and cultural aspects of life. Although such unlimited control could not be fully realized, individuals' freedom of action was greatly reduced. Deviation from the norm even in art or family behavior could become a crime. In theory, nothing was politically neutral; nothing was outside the scope of the state.

This grandiose vision of total state control broke decisively not only with conservative authoritarianism but also with nineteenth-century liberalism and democracy. Indeed, totalitarianism was a radical revolt against liberalism. Liberalism sought to limit the power of the state and protect the sacred rights of the individual. Moreover, liberals stood for rationality, harmony, peaceful progress, and a strong middle class. All of that disgusted totalitarians as sentimental slop. They believed in will power, preached conflict, and worshiped violence.

They believed that the individual was infinitely less valuable than the state and that there were no lasting rights, only temporary rewards for loyal and effective service. Only a single powerful leader and a single party, both unrestrained by law or tradition, determined the destiny of the totalitarian state.

Unlike old-fashioned authoritarianism, modern totalitarianism was based not on an elite but on the masses. As in the First World War, the totalitarian state sought and sometimes won the support and even the love of ordinary people. Modern totalitarianism built on politically alert masses, on people who had already become engaged in the political process, most notably through commitment to nationalism and socialism. Its character as a mass movement gave totalitarianism much of its elemental force.

The final shared characteristic of real totalitarian states was their boundless dynamism. The totalitarian society was a fully mobilized society, a society moving toward some goal. It was never content merely to survive, like an old-fashioned military dictatorship or a decaying democracy. Paradoxically, totalitarian regimes never reached their goals. Or, more precisely, as soon as one goal was achieved at the cost of enormous sacrifice, another arose at the leader's command to take its place. Thus totalitarianism was in the end a permanent revolution, an unfinished revolution, in which rapid, profound change imposed from on high went on forever.

Vicious Anti-Semitism was visible in all European countries before World War One. This 1898 French cartoon shows the Jewish banker Rothschild worshiping gold and exploiting the whole world. Jews were also denounced as revolutionary socialists intent upon destroying private property and the middle class. *(Source: Historical Pictures Service, Chicago)*

Totalitarianism of the Left and the Right

The two most developed totalitarian states—Stalin's Communist Russia and Hitler's Nazi Germany—shared all the central characteristics of totalitarianism. But although those regimes may seem more alike than not, there were at least two major differences between them.

Communism as practiced in Soviet Russia grew out of Marxian socialism. Nazism in Germany grew out of extreme nationalism and racism. This distinction meant that private property and the middle class received very different treatment in the two states. In Soviet Russia, the socialist program of the radical left was realized: all large holdings of private property were taken over by the state, and the middle class lost its wealth and

status. In Germany, big landowners and industrialists on the conservative right were sharply criticized but managed to maintain their private wealth. This difference in property and class relations has led some scholars to speak of "totalitarianism of the left"—Stalinist Russia—and "totalitarianism of the right"—Nazi Germany.

More important were the differing possibilities for regeneration. Socialism, with its concern for social justice and human progress, is linked to the living core of Western civilization and the Judeo-Christian tradition. Stalin's communism was an ugly perversion of socialism, but even in its darkest moments it had the potential for reforming itself and creating a more humane society. But Nazism had no such potential. Based on the phobias of anticapitalism, anti-Semitism, and racism, its elements could be found in many a European city before the First World War. Totally negative and devoid of even perverted truth, it promised only destruction and never rebirth.

STALIN'S RUSSIA

Lenin established the basic outlines of a modern totalitarian dictatorship in Russia after the Bolshevik Revolution and during the civil war. Joseph Stalin (1879–1953) finished the job. A master of political infighting, Stalin cautiously consolidated his power and eliminated his enemies in the mid-1920s. Then in 1928, as undisputed leader of the ruling Communist party, he launched the first five-year plan—the "revolution from above," as he so aptly termed it.

The five-year plans were extremely ambitious. Often incorrectly considered a mere set of economic measures to speed up Soviet Russia's industrial development, the five-year plans actually marked the beginning of a renewed attempt to mobilize and transform Soviet society along socialist lines. The goal was to create a new way of life and to generate new attitudes and new loyalties. The means that Stalin and the small Communist party elite chose were constant propaganda, enormous sacrifice, and unlimited violence and state control. In this way the Soviet Union in the 1930s became a dynamic, modern totalitarian state.

Lenin and Stalin in 1922   Lenin re-established limited economic freedom throughout Russia in 1921, but he ran the country and the Communist party in an increasingly authoritarian way. Stalin carried the process much further and eventually built a regime based on harsh dictatorship. *(Source: Sovfoto)*

From Lenin to Stalin

By spring 1921 Lenin and the Bolsheviks had won the civil war, but they ruled a shattered and devastated land. Many farms were in ruins, and food supplies were exhausted. In southern Russia, drought combined with the ravages of war to produce the worst famine in generations. By 1920, according to the government, from 50 to 90 percent of the population in seventeen provinces was starving. Industrial production also broke down completely. In 1921, for example, output of steel and cotton textiles was only about 4 percent of what it had been in 1913. The revolutionary Trotsky later wrote that the "collapse of the productive forces surpassed anything of the kind history had ever seen. The country, and the government with it, were at the very edge of the abyss."[2] The Bolsheviks had destroyed the economy as well as their foes.

In the face of economic disintegration and rioting by peasants and workers, as well as an open rebellion by previously pro-Bolshevik sailors at Kronstadt—a rebellion that had to be quelled with machine guns—the tough but ever-flexible Lenin changed course. In March 1921 he announced the New Economic Policy (NEP), which re-established limited economic freedom in an attempt to rebuild agriculture and industry. During the civil war, the Communists had simply seized grain without payment. Lenin in 1921 substituted a grain tax on the country's peasant producers, who were permitted to sell their surpluses in free markets. Peasants were also encouraged to buy as many goods as they could afford from private traders and small handicraft manufacturers, groups that were now allowed to reappear. Heavy industry, railroads, and banks, however, remained wholly nationalized. Thus NEP saw only a limited restoration of capitalism.

Lenin's New Economic Policy was shrewd and successful, from two points of view. Politically, it was a necessary but temporary compromise with Russia's overwhelming peasant majority. Flushed with victory after their revolutionary gains of 1917, the peasants would have fought to hold onto their land. With fond hopes of immediate worldwide revolution fading by 1921, Lenin realized that his government was not strong enough to take it from them. As he had accepted Germany's harsh terms at Brest-Litovsk in 1918, Lenin made a deal with the only force capable of overturning his government.

Economically, NEP brought rapid recovery. In 1926 industrial output had surpassed the level of 1913, and Russian peasants were producing almost as much grain as before the war. Counting shorter hours and increased social benefits, workers were living somewhat better than they had in the past.

As the economy recovered and the government partially relaxed its censorship and repression, an intense struggle for power began in the inner circles of the Communist party, for Lenin had left no chosen successor when he died in 1924. The principal contenders were the stolid Stalin and the flamboyant Trotsky.

The son of a shoemaker, Joseph Dzhugashvili—later known as "Stalin"—studied for the priesthood but was expelled from his theological seminary, probably for rude rebelliousness. By 1903 he had joined the Bolsheviks. In the years before the First World War, he engaged in many revolutionary activities in the Transcaucasian area of southern Russia, including a daring bank robbery to get money for the Bolsheviks. This raid gained Lenin's attention and approval. Ethnically a Georgian and not a Russian, Stalin in his early writings focused on the oppression of minority peoples in the Russian Empire. Stalin was a good organizer but a poor speaker and writer, with no experience outside of Russia.

Leon Trotsky, a great and inspiring leader who had planned the 1917 takeover (see page 1058) and then created the victorious Red Army, appeared to have all the advantages. Yet it was Stalin who succeeded Lenin. Stalin won because he was more effective at gaining the all-important support of the party, the only genuine source of power in the one-party state. Rising to general secretary of the party's Central Committee just before Lenin's first stroke in 1922, Stalin used his office to win friends and allies with jobs and promises. Stalin also won recognition as commissar of nationalities, a key position in which he governed many of Russia's minorities.

The "practical" Stalin also won because he appeared better able than the brilliant Trotsky to relate Marxist teaching to Russian realities in the 1920s. First, as commissar of nationalities, he built on Lenin's idea of granting minority groups a certain degree of freedom in culture and language while maintaining rigorous political control through carefully selected local Communists. Stalin could loudly claim, therefore, to have found a way to solve the ancient problem of ethnic demands for independence in the multinational state. And of course he did.

Second, Stalin developed a theory of "socialism in one country," which was more appealing to the majority of Communists than Trotsky's doctrine of "permanent revolution." Stalin argued that Russia had the ability to build socialism on its own. Trotsky maintained that socialism in Russia could succeed only if revolution occurred quickly throughout Europe. To many Communists, Trotsky's views seemed to sell Russia short and to promise risky conflicts with capitalist countries by recklessly encouraging revolutionary movements around the world. Stalin's willingness to break with NEP and push socialism at home appealed to young militants. In short, Stalin's theory of socialism in one country provided many in the party with a glimmer of hope in the midst of the capitalist-appearing NEP, which they had come to detest.

With cunning skill Stalin gradually achieved absolute power between 1922 and 1927. First, he allied with Trotsky's personal enemies to crush Trotsky, who was expelled from the Soviet Union in 1929 and eventually was murdered in Mexico in 1940, undoubtedly on Stalin's order. Stalin then aligned with the moderates, who wanted to go slow at home, to suppress Trotsky's radical followers. Finally, having defeated all the radicals, he turned against his allies, the moderates, and destroyed them as well. Stalin's final triumph came at the Party Congress of December 1927, which condemned all "deviation from the general party line" formulated by Stalin. The dictator was then ready to launch his "revolution from above"—the real Russian revolution for millions of ordinary citizens.

The Five-Year Plans

The Party Congress of 1927, which ratified Stalin's seizure of power, marked the end of the New Economic Policy and the beginning of the era of socialist five-year plans. The first five-year plan had staggering economic objectives. In just five years, total industrial output was to increase by 250 percent. Heavy industry, the preferred sector, was to grow even faster; steel production, for example, was to jump almost 300 percent. Agricultural production was slated to increase by 150 percent, and one-fifth of Russia's peasants were scheduled to give up their private plots and join socialist collective farms. In spite of warnings from moderate Communists that these goals were unrealistic, Stalin raised them higher as the plan got under way. By 1930 a whirlwind of economic and social change was sweeping the country.

Stalin unleashed his "second revolution" for a variety of interrelated reasons. There were, first of all, ideological considerations. Like Lenin, Stalin and his militant supporters were deeply committed to socialism as they understood it. Since the country had recovered economically and their rule was secure, they burned to stamp out NEP's private traders, independent artisans, and few well-to-do peasants. Purely economic motivations were also important. Although the economy had recovered, it seemed to have stalled in 1927 and 1928. A new socialist offensive seemed necessary if industry and agriculture were to grow rapidly.

Political considerations were most important. Internationally, there was the old problem, remaining from prerevolutionary times, of catching up with the advanced and presumably hostile capitalist nations of the West. Stalin said in 1931, when he pressed for ever-greater speed and sacrifice: "We are fifty or a hundred years behind the advanced countries. We must make good this distance in ten years. Either we do it, or we shall go under."[3]

Domestically, there was what Communist writers of the 1920s called the "cursed problem"—the problem of the Russian peasants. For centuries, Russian peasants had wanted to own the land, and finally they had it. Sooner or later, the Communists reasoned, the peasants would become conservative little capitalists and pose a threat to the regime. Thus Stalin decided on a preventive war against the peasantry in order to bring it under the absolute control of the state.

That war was *collectivization*—the forcible consolidation of individual peasant farms into large, state-controlled enterprises. Beginning in 1929, peasants all over the Soviet Union were ordered to give up their land and animals and to become members of collective farms, although they continued to live in their own homes. As for the *kulaks*, the better-off peasants, Stalin instructed party workers to "liquidate them as a class." Stripped of their land and livestock, the kulaks

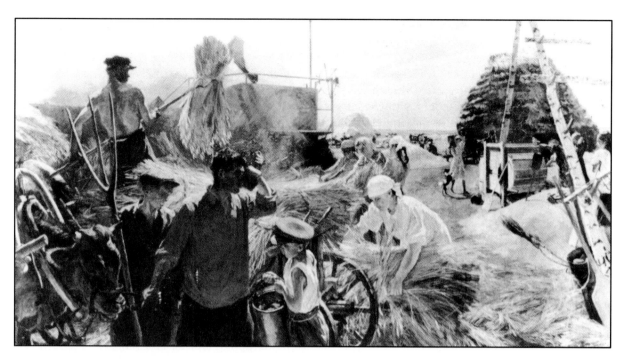

Plastov: Collective Farm Threshing   This example of socialist realism portrays the results of collectivization in positive terms, but the propaganda message does not seem heavy-handed. These peasants have become employees of a large collective farm and are threshing its wheat crop. Socialist realism was expected to depict—and to glorify—the achievements of the New Soviet society. *(Source: Kiev State Museum of Russian Art)*

were generally not even permitted to join the collective farms. Many starved or were deported to forced-labor camps for "re-education."

Since almost all peasants were in fact poor, the term *kulak* soon meant any peasant who opposed the new system. Whole villages were often attacked. One conscience-stricken colonel in the secret police confessed to a foreign journalist: "I am an old Bolshevik. I worked in the underground against the Tsar and then I fought in the Civil War. Did I do all that in order that I should now surround villages with machineguns and order my men to fire indiscriminately into crowds of peasants? Oh, no, no!"[4]

Forced collectivization of the peasants led to economic and human disaster. Large numbers of peasants slaughtered their animals and burned their crops in sullen, hopeless protest. Between 1929 and 1933, the number of horses, cattle, sheep, and goats in the Soviet Union fell by at least half. Nor were the state-controlled collective farms more productive. The output of grain barely increased between 1928 and 1938, when it was almost identical to that of 1913. Communist economists had expected collectivized agriculture to pay for new factories. Instead, the state had to invest heavily in agriculture, building thousands of tractors to replace slaughtered draft horses. Collectivized agriculture was unable to make any substantial financial contribution to Soviet industrial development in the first five-year plan. The human dimension of the tragedy was shocking. Collectivization created man-made famine in 1932 and 1933, and many perished. Indeed, Stalin confided to Churchill at Yalta in 1945 that ten million people had died in the course of collectivization.

Yet collectivization was a political victory of sorts. By the end of 1932, fully 60 percent of Russian peasant families had been herded onto collective farms; by 1938, 93 percent. Regimented and indoctrinated as employees of an all-powerful state, the peasants were no longer even a potential political threat to Stalin and the Communist party. Moreover, the state was assured of grain for bread for urban workers, who were much more important politically than the peasants. Collective farmers had to meet their grain quotas first and worry about feeding themselves second. Many collectivized peasants drew much of their own food from tiny, grudgingly tolerated garden plots that they worked in their off hours. No wonder some peasants joked, with that grim humor peculiar to the totalitarian society, that the initials then used by the Communist party actually stood for "The Second Serfdom, That of the Bolsheviks."

The industrial side of the five-year plans was more successful—indeed, quite spectacular. The output of industry doubled in the first five-year plan and doubled again in the second. Soviet industry produced about four times as much in 1937 as it had in 1928. No other major country had ever achieved such rapid industrial growth. Heavy industry led the way; consumer industry grew quite slowly. Steel production—a near-obsession with Stalin, whose name fittingly meant "man of steel" in Russian—increased roughly 500 percent between 1928 and 1937. A new heavy industrial complex was built almost from scratch in western Siberia. Industrial growth also went hand in hand with urban development. Cities rose where nomadic tribes had grazed their flocks. More than twenty-five million people migrated to cities during the 1930s.

The great industrialization drive, concentrated between 1928 and 1937, was an awe-inspiring achievement purchased at enormous sacrifice. The sudden creation of dozens of new factories required a great increase in investment and a sharp decrease in consumption. Few nations had ever invested more than one-sixth of their yearly net national income. Soviet planners decreed that more than one-third of net income go for investment. This meant that only two-thirds of everything being produced could be consumed by the people and the increasingly voracious military. The money was collected from the people by means of heavy, hidden sales taxes.

There was, therefore, no improvement in the average standard of living. Indeed, the most careful studies show that the average nonfarm wage apparently purchased only about half as many goods in 1932 as in 1928. After 1932 real wages rose slowly, so that in 1937 workers could buy about 60 percent of what they had bought in 1928. Thus rapid industrial development went with an unprecedented decline in the standard of living for ordinary people.

Two other factors contributed importantly to rapid industrialization: firm labor discipline and foreign engineers. Between 1930 and 1932, trade unions lost most of their power. The government could assign workers to any job anywhere in the country, and individuals could not move without the permission of the police. When factory managers needed more hands, they called on their counterparts on the collective farms, who sent them millions of "unneeded" peasants over the years.

Foreign engineers were hired to plan and construct many of the new factories. Highly skilled American engineers, hungry for work in the depression years, were particularly important until newly trained Soviet experts began to replace them after 1932. The gigantic mills of the new Siberian steel industry were modeled on America's best. Those modern mills were eloquent testimony to the ability of Stalin's planners to harness even the skill and technology of capitalist countries to promote the surge of socialist industry.

Life in Stalinist Society

The aim of Stalin's five-year plans was to create a new kind of society and human personality, as well as a strong industrial economy and a powerful army. Stalin and his helpers were good Marxian economic determinists. Once everything was owned by the state, they believed, a socialist society and a new kind of human being would inevitably emerge. They were by no means totally successful, but they did build a new society, whose broad outlines existed to the early 1980s. For the people, life in Stalinist society had both good and bad aspects.

The most frightening aspect of Stalinist society was brutal, unrestrained police terrorism. First directed primarily against the peasants after 1929, terror was increasingly turned on leading Communists, powerful administrators, and ordinary people for no apparent reason. As one Soviet woman later recalled, "We all trembled because there was no way of getting out of it. Even a Communist himself can be caught. To avoid trouble became an exception."[5] A climate of fear fell on the land.

In the early 1930s, the top members of the party and government were Stalin's obedient servants, but there was some grumbling in the party. At a small gathering in November 1932, even Stalin's wife complained bitterly about the misery of the people. Stalin showered her with insults, and she died that same night, apparently by her own hand. In late 1934 Stalin's number-two man, Sergei Kirov, was suddenly and mysteriously murdered. Although Stalin himself probably ordered Kirov's murder, he used the incident to launch a reign of terror.

In August 1936 sixteen prominent old Bolsheviks confessed to all manner of plots against Stalin in spectacular public trials in Moscow. Then, in 1937, lesser party officials and newer henchmen were arrested. In addition to party members, union officials, managers, intellectuals, army officers, and countless ordinary citizens were struck down. Local units of the secret police were even ordered to arrest a certain percentage of the people in their districts. In all, at least eight million people were probably arrested, and millions never returned from prisons and forced-labor camps.

Stalin's mass purges were truly baffling, and many explanations have been given for them. Possibly Stalin believed that the old Communists, like the peasants under NEP, were a potential threat to be wiped out in a preventive attack. Yet why did leading Communists confess to crimes they could not possibly have committed? Their lives had been devoted to the party and the socialist revolution. In the words of the German novelist Arthur Koestler, they probably confessed "in order to do a last service to the Party," the party they loved even when it was wrong. Some of them were subjected to torture and brainwashing. It has been argued that the purges indicate that Stalin was sadistic or insane, for his blood bath greatly weakened the government and the army. Others see the terror as an aspect of the fully developed totalitarian state, which must by its nature always be fighting real or imaginary enemies. At the least, the mass purges were a message to the people: no one was secure. Everyone had to serve the party and its leader with redoubled devotion.

Another aspect of life in the 1930s was constant propaganda and indoctrination. Party activists lectured workers in factories and peasants on collective farms, and newspapers, films, and radio broadcasts endlessly recounted socialist achievements and capitalist plots. Art and literature became highly political. Whereas the 1920s had seen considerable experimentation in modern art and theater, the intellectual elite were ordered by Stalin to become "engineers of human minds." Writers and artists who could effectively combine genuine creativity and political propaganda became the darlings of the regime. They often lived better than top members of the political elite. It became increasingly important for the successful writer and artist to glorify Russian nationalism. History was rewritten so that early tsars like Ivan the Terrible and Peter the Great became worthy forerunners of the greatest Russian leader—Stalin.

Stalin seldom appeared in public, but his presence was everywhere—in portraits, statues, books, and quotations from his "sacred" writings. Although the government persecuted religion and turned churches into "museums of atheism," the state had both an earthly religion and a high priest—Marxian socialism and Joseph Stalin.

Life was hard in Stalin's Soviet Russia. The standard of living declined substantially in the 1930s. The masses of people lived primarily on black bread and wore old, shabby clothing. There were constant shortages in the stores, although very heavily taxed vodka was always readily available. A shortage of housing was a particularly serious problem. Millions were moving into the cities, but the government built few new apartments. In 1940 there were approximately 4 people per room in every urban dwelling, as opposed to 2.7 per room in 1926. A relatively lucky family received one room for all its members and shared both a kitchen and a toilet with others on the floor. Less fortunate workers, kulaks, and class enemies built scrap-lumber shacks or underground dugouts in shanty-towns.

Life was hard, but not hopeless. Idealism and ideology appealed to many Russians, who saw themselves heroically building the world's first socialist society while capitalism crumbled in the West. This optimistic belief in the future of Soviet Russia also attracted many disillusioned Western liberals to communism in the 1930s.

On a more practical level, Soviet workers did receive some important social benefits, such as old-age pensions, free medical services, free education, and day-care centers for children. Unemployment was almost unknown. Finally, there was the possibility of personal advancement.

The keys to improving one's position were specialized skills and technical education. Rapid industrialization required massive numbers of trained experts, such as skilled workers, engineers, and plant managers. Thus the state provided tremendous incentives to those who could serve its needs. It paid the mass of unskilled workers and

Adult Education   Illiteracy, especially among women, was a serious problem after the Russian Revolution. This early photo shows how adults successfully learned to read and write throughout the Soviet Union. *(Source: Sovfoto)*

collective farmers very low wages, but it dangled high salaries and many special privileges before its growing technical and managerial elite. This elite joined with the political and artistic elites in a new upper class, whose members were rich, powerful, and insecure, especially during the purges. Yet the possible gains of moving up outweighed the risks. Millions struggled bravely in universities, institutes, and night schools for the all-important specialized education. One young man summed it up: "In Soviet Russia there is no capital except education. If a person does not want to become a collective farmer or just a cleaning woman, the only means you have to get something is through education."[6]

Women in Soviet Russia

Women's lives were radically altered by Stalinist society. Marxists had traditionally believed that both capitalism and the middle-class husband ex-

ploited women. The Russian Revolution of 1917 immediately proclaimed complete equality of rights for women. In the 1920s divorce and abortion were made very easy, and women were urged to work outside the home and liberate themselves sexually. A prominent and influential Bolshevik feminist, Alexandra Kollontai, went so far as to declare that the sexual act had no more significance than "drinking a glass of water." This observation drew a sharp rebuke from the rather prudish Lenin, who said that "no sane man would lie down to drink from a puddle in the gutter or even drink from a dirty glass."[7] After Stalin came to power, sexual and familial liberation was played down, and the most lasting changes for women involved work and education.

The changes were truly revolutionary. Young women were constantly told that they must be fully equal to men, that they could and should do anything men could do. Russian peasant women had long experienced the equality of backbreaking physical labor in the countryside, and they continued to enjoy that equality on collective farms. With the advent of the five-year plans, millions of women also began to toil in factories and in heavy construction, building dams, roads, and steel mills in summer heat and winter frost. Yet most of the opportunities open to men through education were also opened to women. Determined women pursued their studies and entered the ranks of the better-paid specialists in industry and science. Medicine practically became a woman's profession. By 1950, 75 percent of all doctors in Soviet Russia were women.

Thus Stalinist society gave women great opportunities but demanded great sacrifices as well. The vast majority of women simply had to work outside the home. Wages were so low that it was almost impossible for a family or couple to live on only the husband's earnings. Moreover, the full-time working woman had a heavy burden of household tasks in her off hours, for most Soviet men in the 1930s still considered the home and the children the woman's responsibility. Finally, rapid change and economic hardship led to many broken families, creating further physical, emotional, and mental strains for women. In any event, the often-neglected human resource of women was ruthlessly mobilized in Stalinist society. This, too, was an aspect of the Soviet totalitarian state.

MUSSOLINI'S ITALY

Like all the other emerging dictators, Mussolini hated liberalism, and he destroyed it in Italy. Mussolini and his supporters were the first to call themselves "fascists"—revolutionaries determined to create a certain kind of totalitarian state. As Mussolini's famous slogan of 1926 put it, "Everything in the state, nothing outside the state, nothing against the state." But Mussolini in power, unlike Stalin and Hitler, did not create a real totalitarian state. His dictatorship was rather an instructive hybrid, a halfway house between conservative authoritarianism and modern totalitarianism.

The Seizure of Power

Before the First World War, Italy was a liberal state moving gradually toward democracy. But there were serious problems. Much of the Italian population was still poor, and class differences were extreme. Many peasants were more attached to their villages and local interests than to the national state. Moreover, the papacy and many devout Catholics, as well as the socialists, were strongly opposed to the heirs of Cavour and Garibaldi, middle-class lawyers and politicians who ran the country largely for their own benefit. Relations between church and state were often tense.

The war worsened the political situation. Having fought on the side of the Allies almost exclusively for purposes of territorial expansion, Italian nationalists were bitterly disappointed with Italy's modest gains at Versailles. Workers and peasants also felt cheated: to win their support during the war, the government had promised social and land reform, which it did not deliver after the war.

Encouraged by the Russian Revolution of 1917, radical workers and peasants began occupying factories and seizing land in 1920. These actions scared and radicalized the property-owning classes. The Italian middle classes were already in an ugly mood, having suffered from inflation during the war. Moreover, after the war, the pope lifted his ban on participation by Catholics in Italian politics, and a strong Catholic party quickly emerged. Thus by 1922 almost all the major groups in Italian society were opposed—though for different reasons—to the liberal parliamentary government.

Into these crosscurrents of unrest and frustration stepped the blustering, bullying Benito Mussolini (1883–1945). Son of a village schoolteacher and a poor blacksmith, Mussolini began his political career as a Socialist leader and radical newspaper editor before the First World War. In 1914, powerfully influenced by antiliberal cults of violent action, the young Mussolini urged that Italy join the Allies, a stand for which he was expelled from the Italian Socialist party by its antiwar majority. Later Mussolini fought at the front and was wounded in 1917. Returning home, he began organizing bitter war veterans like himself into a band of Fascists—from the Italian word for "a union of forces."

At first, Mussolini's program was a radical combination of nationalist and socialist demands, including territorial expansion, benefits for workers, and land reform for peasants. As such, it competed with the better-organized Socialist party and failed to get off the ground. When Mussolini saw that his violent verbal assaults on the rival Social-ists won him growing support from the frightened middle classes, he shifted gears in 1920. In thought and action, Mussolini was a striking ex-ample of the turbulence of the age of anxiety.

Mussolini and his growing private army of Black Shirts began to grow violent. Typically, a band of Fascist toughs would roar off in trucks at night and swoop down on a few isolated Socialist organ-izers, beating them up and force-feeding them al-most deadly doses of castor oil. Few people were killed, but Socialist newspapers, union halls, and local Socialist party headquarters were destroyed. Mussolini's toughs pushed Communists and So-cialists out of the city governments of northern Italy.

Mussolini, a skillful politician, refused to be-come a puppet of frightened conservatives and capitalists. He allowed his followers to convince themselves that they were not just opposing the "reds" but were making a real revolution of their own. Many believed that they were not only de-stroying parliamentary government but forming a strong, dynamic movement that would help the little people against the established interests.

With the government breaking down in 1922, largely because of the chaos created by his direct-action bands, Mussolini stepped forward as the savior of order and property. Striking a con-servative note in his speeches and gaining the sympathetic neutrality of army leaders, Musso-lini demanded the resignation of the existing gov-ernment and his own appointment by the king. In October 1922, to force matters, a large group of Fascists marched on Rome to threaten the king and force him to call on Mussolini. The threat worked. Victor Emmanuel III (r. 1900–1946), who had no love for the old liberal politicians, asked Mussolini to form a new cabinet. Thus, after widespread violence and a threat of armed upris-ing, Mussolini seized power "legally." He was im-mediately granted dictatorial authority for one year by the king and the parliament.

The Regime in Action

Mussolini became dictator on the strength of Italians' rejection of parliamentary government, coupled with fears of Russian-style revolution. Yet what he intended to do with his power was by no means clear until 1924. Some of his dedicated sup-porters pressed for a "second revolution." Musso-lini's ministers, however, included old conserva-tives, moderates, and even two reform-minded Socialists. A new electoral law was passed giving two-thirds of the representatives in the parliament to the party that won the most votes, a change that allowed the Fascists and their allies to win an overwhelming majority in 1924. Shortly thereaf-ter, five of Mussolini's Fascist thugs kidnapped and murdered Giacomo Matteotti, the leader of the Socialists in the parliament. In the face of this outrage, the opposition demanded that Musso-lini's armed squads be dissolved and all violence be banned.

Although he may or may not have ordered Mat-teotti's murder, Mussolini stood at the crossroads of a severe political crisis. After some hesitation, he charged forward. Declaring his desire to "make the nation Fascist," he imposed a series of repres-sive measures. Freedom of the press was abolished, elections were fixed, and the government ruled by decree. Mussolini arrested his political opponents, disbanded all independent labor unions, and put dedicated Fascists in control of Italy's schools. Moreover, he created a Fascist youth movement, Fascist labor unions, and many other Fascist or-ganizations. By the end of 1926, Italy was a one-party dictatorship under Mussolini's unques-tioned leadership.

Yet Mussolini did not complete the establish-ment of a modern totalitarian state. His Fascist party never became all-powerful. It never de-stroyed the old power structure, as the Com-munists did in Soviet Russia, or succeeded in dominating it, as the Nazis did in Germany. Mem-bership in the Fascist party was more a sign of an Italian's respectability than a commitment to radi-cal change. Interested primarily in personal power, Mussolini was content to compromise with the old conservative classes that controlled the army, the economy, and the state. He never tried to purge these classes or even move very vigorously against them. He controlled and propagandized labor but left big business to regulate itself, profitably and securely. There was no land reform.

Mussolini also came to draw on the support of the Catholic church. In the Lateran Agreement of 1929, he recognized the Vatican as a tiny inde-pendent state, and he agreed to give the church heavy financial support. The pope expressed his satisfaction and urged Italians to support Musso-lini's government.

Nothing better illustrates Mussolini's unwillingness to harness everyone and everything for dynamic action than his treatment of women. He abolished divorce and told women to stay at home and produce children. To promote that goal, he decreed a special tax on bachelors in 1934. In 1938 women were limited by law to a maximum of 10 percent of the better-paying jobs in industry and government. Italian women, as women, appear not to have changed their attitudes or behavior in any important way under Fascist rule.

It is also noteworthy that Mussolini's government did not persecute Jews until late in the Second World War, when Italy was under Nazi control. Nor did Mussolini establish a truly ruthless police state. Only twenty-three political prisoners were condemned to death between 1926 and 1944. In spite of much pompous posing by the

Mussolini loved to swagger and bully. Here in his office he instinctively strikes his favorite theatrical pose, even as he discusses with its painter a less aggressive portrait of himself. *(Source: Courtesy, Gabriele Stocchi, Rome)*

chauvinist leader and in spite of mass meetings, salutes, and a certain copying of Hitler's aggression in foreign policy after 1933, Mussolini's Italy was undemocratic but never really totalitarian.

HITLER'S GERMANY

The most frightening totalitarian state was Nazi Germany. A product of Hitler's evil genius as well as of Germany's social and political situation and the general attack on liberalism and rationality in the age of anxiety, Nazi Germany emerged rapidly after Hitler came to power in 1933. The Nazis quickly smashed or took over most independent organizations, mobilized the economy, and began brutally persecuting the Jewish population. From the start, all major decisions were in the hands of the aggressive dictator Adolf Hitler.

The Roots of Nazism

Nazism grew out of many complex developments, of which the most influential were extreme nationalism and racism. These two ideas captured the mind of the young Hitler, and it was he who dominated Nazism for as long as it lasted.

Born the fourth child of a successful Austrian customs official and an indulgent mother, Adolf Hitler (1889–1945) spent his childhood happily in small towns in Austria. A good student in grade school, Hitler did poorly on reaching high school and dropped out at age fourteen after the death of his father. After four years of unfocused loafing, Hitler finally left for Vienna to become an artist. Denied admission to the Imperial Academy of Fine Arts because he lacked talent, the dejected Hitler stayed on in Vienna. There he lived a comfortable, lazy life on his generous orphan's pension and found most of the perverted beliefs that guided his life.

In Vienna Hitler soaked up extreme German nationalism, which was particularly strong there. Austro-German nationalists, as if to compensate for their declining position in the Austro-Hungarian Empire, believed Germans to be a superior people and the natural rulers of central Europe. They often advocated union with Germany and violent expulsion of "inferior" peoples as the means of maintaining German domination of the Austro-Hungarian Empire.

Hitler was deeply impressed by Vienna's mayor, Karl Lueger, whom he called the "mightiest mayor of all times." Lueger claimed to be a "Christian socialist." With the help of the Catholic trade unions, he had succeeded in winning the support of the little people of Vienna for an attack on capitalism and liberalism, which he held responsible for un-Christian behavior and excessive individualism. A master of mass politics in the urban world, Lueger showed Hitler the enormous potential of anticapitalist and antiliberal propaganda.

From Lueger and others, Hitler eagerly absorbed virulent anti-Semitism, racism, and hatred of Slavs. He was particularly inspired by the racist ravings of a former monk named Lanz von Liebenfels. Preaching the crudest, most exaggerated distortions of the Darwinian theory of survival, Liebenfels stressed the superiority of Germanic races, the inevitability of racial conflict, and the inferiority of the Jews. Liebenfels even anticipated the breeding and extermination policies of the Nazi state. He claimed that the master race had to multiply its numbers by means of polygamy and breeding stations, while it systematically sterilized and liquidated inferior races. Anti-Semitism and racism became Hitler's most passionate convictions, his explanation for everything. He believed that inferior races—the Slavs and the Jews in particular—were responsible for Austria's woes. The Jews, he claimed, directed an international conspiracy of finance capitalism and Marxian socialism against German culture, German unity, and the German race. Hitler's belief was totally irrational, but he never doubted it.

Although he moved to Munich in 1913 to avoid being drafted in the Austrian army, the lonely Hitler greeted the outbreak of the First World War as a salvation. He later wrote in his autobiography, *Mein Kampf,* that, "overcome by passionate enthusiasm, I fell to my knees and thanked heaven out of an overflowing heart." The struggle and discipline of war gave life meaning, and Hitler served bravely as a dispatch carrier on the western front.

When Germany was suddenly defeated in 1918, Hitler's world was shattered. Not only was he a fanatical nationalist, but war was his reason for living. Convinced that Jews and Marxists had "stabbed Germany in the back," he vowed to fight on. And in the bitterness and uncertainty of postwar Germany, his wild speeches began to attract attention.

In late 1919 Hitler joined the German Workers' party, a tiny extremist group in Munich. In addition to denouncing Jews, Marxists, and democrats, the German Workers' party promised unity under a uniquely German "national socialism," which would abolish the injustices of capitalism and create a mighty "people's community." By 1921 Hitler had gained absolute control of this small but growing party. Moreover, Hitler was already a master of mass propaganda and political showmanship. Party members sported badges and uniforms, gave victory salutes, and marched like robots through the streets of Munich. But Hitler's most effective tool was the mass rally, a kind of political revival meeting. Songs, slogans, and demonstrations built up the tension until Hitler finally arrived. He then often worked his audience into a frenzy with wild, demagogic attacks on the Versailles Treaty, the Jews, the war profiteers, and Germany's Weimar Republic.

Party membership multiplied tenfold after early 1922. In late 1923, when the Weimar Republic seemed on the verge of collapse, Hitler decided on an armed uprising in Munich. Inspired by Mussolini's recent easy victory, Hitler had found an ally in General Ludendorff of First World War fame. After Hitler had overthrown the Bavarian government, Ludendorff was supposed to march on Berlin with Hitler's support. The plot was poorly organized, however, and it was crushed by the police, backed up by the army, in less than a day. Hitler was arrested, tried, and sentenced to five years in prison. He had failed for the moment. But Nazism had been born, and it did not die.

Hitler's Road to Power

At his trial, Hitler violently denounced the Weimar Republic and skillfully presented his own program. In doing so, he gained enormous publicity and attention. Moreover, he learned from his unsuccessful revolt. Hitler concluded that he had to undermine rather than overthrow the government, that he had to use its tolerant democratic framework to intimidate the opposition and come to power through electoral competition. He forced his more violent supporters to accept his new strategy. Finally, Hitler used his brief prison

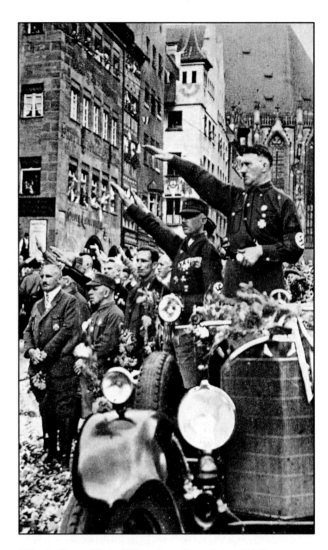

Hitler in Opposition   Hitler returns the salute of his Brown Shirts in this photograph from the third party day rally in Nuremberg in 1927. The Brown Shirts formed a private army within the Nazi movement, and their uniforms, marches, salutes, and vandalism helped keep Hitler in the public eye in the 1920s. *(Source: Courtesy, Bison Books, London)*

term—he was released in less than a year—to dictate *Mein Kampf*. There he expounded on his basic themes: "race," with the stress on anti-Semitism; "living space," with a sweeping vision of war and conquered territory; and the leader-dictator (the *Führer*) with unlimited, arbitary power. Hitler's followers had their bible.

In the years of prosperity and relative stability between 1924 and 1929, Hitler concentrated on building his National Socialist German Workers' party, or Nazi party. By 1928 the party had a hundred thousand highly disciplined members under Hitler's absolute control. To appeal to the middle classes, Hitler de-emphasized the anticapitalist elements of national socialism and vowed to fight Bolshevism.

The Nazis were still a small splinter group in 1928, when they received only 2.6 percent of the vote in the general elections and twelve Nazis won seats in the parliament. There the Nazi deputies pursued the legal strategy of using democracy to destroy democracy. As Hitler's talented future minister of propaganda Joseph Goebbels (1897–1945) explained in 1928 in the party newspaper, "We become Reichstag deputies in order to paralyze the spirit of Weimar with its own aid. . . . We come as enemies! As the wolf breaks into the sheepfold, so we come."[8]

In 1929 the Great Depression began striking down economic prosperity, one of the barriers that had kept the wolf at bay. Unemployment jumped from 1.3 million in 1929 to 5 million in 1930; that year Germany had almost as many unemployed as all the other countries of Europe combined. Industrial production fell by one-half between 1929 and 1932. By the end of 1932, an incredible 43 percent of the labor force was unemployed, and it was estimated that only one in every three union members was working full-time. No factor contributed more to Hitler's success than the economic crisis. Never very interested in economics before, Hitler began promising German voters economic as well as political and military salvation.

Hitler focused his promises on the middle and lower middle class—small business people, office workers, artisans, and peasants. Already disillusioned by the great inflation of 1923, these people were seized by panic as bankruptcies increased, unemployment soared, and the dreaded Communists made dramatic election gains. The middle and lower middle classes deserted the conservative and moderate parties for the Nazis in great numbers.

The Nazis also appealed strongly to German youth. Indeed, in some ways the Nazi movement was a mass movement of young Germans. Hitler himself was only forty in 1929, and he and most of his top aides were much younger than other leading German politicians. "National Socialism is the organized will of the youth," proclaimed the official Nazi slogan, and the battle cry of Gregor

Strasser, a leading Nazi organizer, was "Make way, you old ones."[9] In 1931 almost 40 percent of Nazi party members were under thirty, compared with 20 percent of Social Democrats. Two-thirds of Nazi members were under forty. National recovery, exciting and rapid change, and personal advancement: these were the appeals of Nazism to millions of German youths.

In the election of 1930, the Nazis won 6.5 million votes and 107 seats, which made them second in strength only to the Social Democrats, the moderate socialists. The economic situation continued to deteriorate, and Hitler kept promising that he would bring recovery. In 1932 the Nazi vote leaped to 14.5 million, and the Nazis became the largest party in the Reichstag.

Another reason Hitler came to power was the breakdown of democratic government as early as May 1930. Unable to gain support of a majority in the Reichstag, Chancellor Heinrich Brüning convinced the president, the aging war hero General Hindenburg, to authorize rule by decree. The Weimar Republic's constitution permitted such rule in emergency situations, but the rather authoritarian, self-righteous Brüning intended to use it indefinitely. Moreover, Brüning was determined to overcome the economic crisis by cutting back government spending and ruthlessly forcing down prices and wages. Brüning's ultra-orthodox policies not only intensified the economic collapse in Germany, they also convinced the lower middle classes that the country's republican leaders were stupid and corrupt. These classes were pleased rather than dismayed by Hitler's attacks on the republican system. After President Hindenburg forced Brüning to resign in May 1932, the new government headed by Franz von Papen continued to rule by decree.

The continuation of the struggle between the Social Democrats and Communists, right up until the moment Hitler took power, was another aspect of the breakdown of democratic government. The Communists foolishly refused to cooperate with the Social Democrats, even though the two parties together outnumbered the Nazis in the Reichstag, even after the elections of 1932. German Communists (and the complacent Stalin) were blinded by their ideology and their hatred of the Socialists. They were certain that Hitler's rise represented the last agonies of monopoly capitalism and that a communist revolution would quickly follow his taking power. The Socialist leaders pleaded, even at the Russian embassy, for at least a temporary alliance with the Communists to block Hitler, but to no avail. Perhaps the Weimar Republic was already too far gone, but this disunity on the left was undoubtedly another nail in its coffin.

Finally, there was Hitler's skill as a politician. A master of mass propaganda and psychology, he had written in *Mein Kampf* that the masses were the "driving force of the most important changes in this world" and were themselves driven by hysterical fanaticism and not by knowledge. To arouse such hysterical fanaticism, he believed that all propaganda had to be limited to a few simple, endlessly repeated slogans. Thus, in the terrible economic and political crisis, he harangued vast audiences with passionate, irrational oratory. Men moaned and women cried, seized by emotion. And many uncertain individuals, surrounded by thousands of entranced listeners, found security and a sense of belonging.

At the same time, Hitler excelled at dirty, back-room politics. That, in fact, brought him to power. In 1932 he cleverly succeeded in gaining the support of key people in the army and big business. These people thought that they could use Hitler for their own advantage, to get increased military spending, fat contracts, and tough measures against workers. Conservative and nationalistic politicians like Papen thought similarly. They thus accepted Hitler's demand to join the government only if he became chancellor. There would be only two other National Socialists and nine solid Conservatives as ministers, and in such a coalition government, they reasoned, Hitler could be used and controlled. On January 30, 1933, Hitler was legally appointed chancellor by Hindenburg.

The Nazi State and Society

Hitler moved rapidly and skillfully to establish an unshakable dictatorship. His first step was to continue using terror and threats to gain more power while maintaining legal appearances. He immediately called for new elections and applied the enormous power of the government to restrict his opponents. In the midst of a violent electoral campaign, the Reichstag building was partly destroyed by fire. Although the Nazis themselves may have set the fire, Hitler screamed that the Communist party was responsible. On the strength of this accusation, he convinced President Hindenburg to sign dictatorial emergency acts that practically abolished freedom of speech and assembly, in addition to most personal liberties.

When the Nazis won only 44 percent of the vote in the elections, Hitler immediately outlawed the Communist party and arrested its parliamentary representatives. Then, on March 23, 1933, the Nazis pushed through the Reichstag the so-called Enabling Act, which gave Hitler absolute dictatorial power for four years. Only the Social Democrats voted against this bill, for Hitler had successfully blackmailed the Center party by threatening to attack the Catholic church.

Armed with the Enabling Act, Hitler and the Nazis moved to smash or control all independent organizations. Meanwhile, Hitler and his propagandists constantly proclaimed that their revolution was legal and constitutional. This deceitful stress on legality, coupled with the divide-and-conquer technique, disarmed the opposition until it was too late for effective resistance.

The systematic subjugation of independent organizations and the creation of a totalitarian state had massive repercussions. The Social Democratic and Center parties were soon dissolved, and Germany became a one-party state. Only the Nazi party was legal. Elections were farces. The Reichstag was jokingly referred to as the most expensive glee club in the country, for its only function was to sing hymns of praise to the Führer. Hitler and the Nazis took over the government bureaucracy intact, installing many Nazis in top positions. At the same time, they created a series of overlapping Nazi party organizations, responsible solely to Hitler. Thus Hitler had both an established bureaucracy for normal business and a private, personal "party government" for special duties.

In the economic sphere, strikes were forbidden and labor unions were abolished, replaced by a Nazi Labor Front. Professional people—doctors and lawyers, teachers and engineers—also saw their previously independent organizations swallowed up in Nazi associations. Nor did the Nazis neglect cultural and intellectual life. Publishing houses were put under Nazi control, and universities and writers were quickly brought into line. Democratic, socialist, and Jewish literature was put on ever-growing blacklists. Passionate students and pitiful professors burned forbidden books in public squares. Modern art and architecture were ruthlessly prohibited. Life became violently anti-intellectual. As Hitler's cynical minister of propaganda, Joseph Goebbels, put it, "When I hear the word 'culture' I reach for my gun."[10] By 1934 a totalitarian state characterized by frightening dynamism and obedience to Hitler was already largely in place.

By 1934 only the army retained independence, and Hitler moved brutally and skillfully to establish his control there, too. He realized that the army, as well as big business, was suspicious of the Nazi storm troopers (the S.A.), the quasi-military band of three million toughs in brown shirts who had fought Communists and beaten up Jews before the Nazis took power. These unruly storm troopers expected top positions in the army and even talked of a "second revolution" against capi-

talism. Needing the support of the army and big business, Hitler decided that the S.A. leaders had to be eliminated. On the night of June 30, 1934, he struck.

Hitler's elite personal guard—the S.S.—arrested and shot without trial roughly a thousand S.A. leaders and assorted political enemies. While his propagandists spread lies about S.A. conspiracies, the army leaders and President Hindenburg responded to the purge with congratulatory telegrams. Shortly thereafter, the army leaders swore a binding oath of "unquestioning obedience . . . to the Leader of the German State and People, Adolf Hitler." The purge of the S.A. was another decisive step toward unlimited totalitarian terror. The S.S., the elite guard that had loyally murdered the S.A. leaders, grew rapidly. Under its methodical, inhu-

"Hitler, Our Last Hope"   So reads the vary effective Nazi campaign poster, which is attracting attention with its gaunt and haggard faces. By 1932 almost half of all Germans, like these in Berlin, had come to agree. *(Source: Bildarchiv Preussischer Kulturbesitz. Photo: Herbert Hoffman, 1932)*

man leader, Heinrich Himmler (1900–1945), the S.S. joined with the political police, the *Gestapo,* to expand its network of special courts and concentration camps. Nobody was safe.

From the beginning, the Jews were a special object of Nazi persecution. By the end of 1934, most Jewish lawyers, doctors, professors, civil servants, and musicians had lost their jobs and the right to practice their professions. In 1935 the infamous Nuremberg Laws classified as Jewish anyone having one or more Jewish grandparents and deprived Jews of all rights of citizenship. By 1938 roughly one-fourth of Germany's half-million Jews had emigrated, sacrificing almost all their property in order to leave Germany.

Following the assassination of a German diplomat in Paris by a young Jewish boy trying desperately to strike out at persecution, the attack on the Jews accelerated. A well-organized wave of violence destroyed homes, synagogues, and businesses, after which German Jews were rounded up and made to pay for the damage. It became very difficult for Jews to leave Germany. Some Germans privately opposed these outrages, but most went along or looked the other way. Although this lack of response partly reflected the individual's helplessness in the totalitarian state, it was also a sign of the strong popular support that Hitler's government enjoyed.

Hitler's Popularity

Hitler had promised the masses economic recovery—"work and bread"—and he delivered. Breaking with Brüning's do-nothing policies, Hitler immediately launched a large public works program to pull Germany out of the depression. Work began on superhighways, offices, gigantic sports stadiums, and public housing. In 1936, as Germany rearmed rapidly, government spending began to concentrate on the military. The result was that unemployment dropped steadily, from six million in January 1933 to about one million in late 1936. By 1938 there was a shortage of workers, and women eventually took many jobs previously denied them by the antifeminist Nazis. Thus everyone had work, and between 1932 and 1938 the standard of living for the average employed worker rose more than 20 percent. The profits of business also increased. For millions of people, economic recovery was tangible evidence in their daily lives

that the excitement and dynamism of Nazi rule were based on more than show.

For the masses of ordinary German citizens, who were not Jews, Slavs, Gypsies, Jehovah's Witnesses, or Communists, Hitler's government meant greater equality and exceptional opportunities. It must be remembered that in 1933 the position of the traditional German elites—the landed aristocracy, the wealthy capitalists, and the well-educated professional classes—was still very strong. Barriers between classes were generally high. Hitler's rule introduced vast changes in this pattern. For example, stiff educational requirements, which favored the well-to-do, were greatly relaxed. The new Nazi elite was composed largely of young and poorly educated dropouts, rootless lower-middle-class people like Hitler, who rose to the top with breathtaking speed.

More generally, the Nazis, like the Russian Communists, tolerated privilege and wealth only as long as they served the needs of the party. Big business was constantly ordered around, to the point that "probably never in peacetime has an ostensibly capitalist economy been directed as non- and even anti-capitalistically as the German economy between 1933 and 1939."[11] Hitler brought about a kind of social revolution, which was enthusiastically embraced by millions of modest middle-class and lower-middle-class people and even by many workers.

Hitler's extreme nationalism, which had helped him gain power, continued to appeal to Germans after 1933. Ever since the wars against Napoleon, many Germans had believed in a special mission for a superior German nation. The successes of Bismarck had furthered such feelings, and near-victory in the Great World War made nationalists eager for renewed expansion in the 1920s. Thus, when Hitler went from one foreign triumph to another (see pages 1158–1159) and a great German empire seemed within reach, the majority of the population was delighted and praised the Führer's actions.

By no means all Germans supported Hitler, however, and a number of German groups actively resisted him after 1933. Tens of thousands of political enemies were imprisoned, and thousands were executed. Opponents of the Nazis pursued various goals, and under totalitarian conditions they were never unified, a fact that helps account for their ultimate lack of success. In the first years of Hitler's rule, the principal resisters were the

EVENTS LEADING TO WORLD WAR TWO

1919	Treaty of Versailles
	J. M. Keynes, *Economic Consequences of the Peace*
1919–1920	U.S. Senate rejects the Treaty of Versailles
1921	Germany is billed $35 billion in reparations
1922	Mussolini seizes power in Italy
	Germany proposes a moratorium on reparations
January 1923	France and Belgium occupy the Ruhr
	Germany orders passive resistance to the occupation
October 1923	Stresemann agrees to reparations with re-examination of Germany's ability to pay
1924	Dawes Plan: German reparations reduced and put on a sliding scale; large U.S. loans to Germany recommended to promote German recovery; occupation of the Ruhr ends
	Adolf Hitler, *Mein Kampf*
1924–1929	Spectacular German economic recovery; circular flow of international funds enables sizable reparations payments
1925	Treaties of Locarno promote European security and stability
1926	Germany joins the League of Nations
1928	Kellogg-Briand Pact renounces war as an instrument of international affairs
1929	Young Plan further reduces German reparations
	Crash of U.S. stock market
1929–1933	Depths of the Great Depression
1931	Japan invades Manchuria
1932	Nazis become the largest party in the Reichstag
January 1933	Hitler appointed chancellor
March 1933	Reichstag passes the Enabling Act, granting Hitler absolute dictatorial power
October 1933	Germany withdraws from the League of Nations
July 1934	Nazis murder Austrian chancellor
March 1935	Hitler announces German rearmament
June 1935	Anglo-German naval agreement
October 1935	Mussolini invades Ethiopia and receives Hitler's support
1935	Nuremburg Laws deprive Jews of all rights of citizenship
March 1936	German armies move unopposed into the demilitarized Rhineland
July 1936	Outbreak of civil war in Spain
1937	Japan invades China
	Rome-Berlin Axis
March 1938	Germany annexes Austria
September 1938	Munich Conference: Britain and France agree to German seizure of the Sudetenland from Czechoslovakia
March 1939	Germany occupies the rest of Czechoslovakia; the end of appeasement in Britain
August 1939	Russo-German nonaggression pact
September 1, 1939	Germany invades Poland
September 3, 1939	Britain and France declare war on Germany

Communists and the Social Democrats in the trade unions. But the expansion of the S.S. system of terror after 1935 smashed most of these leftists. A second group of opponents arose in the Catholic and Protestant churches. However, their efforts were directed primarily at preserving genuine religious life, not at overthrowing Hitler. Finally, in 1938 (and again in 1942 to 1944), some high-ranking army officers, who feared the consequences of Hitler's reckless aggression, plotted against him, unsuccessfully.

NAZI EXPANSION AND THE SECOND WORLD WAR

Although economic recovery and increased opportunities for social advancement won Hitler support, they were only by-products of Nazi totalitarianism. The guiding concepts of Nazism remained space and race—the territorial expansion of the superior German race. As Germany regained its economic strength and as independent organizations were brought under control, Hitler formed alliances with other dictators and began expanding. German expansion was facilitated by the uncertain, divided, pacific Western democracies, which tried to buy off Hitler to avoid war.

Yet war inevitably broke out, in both the West and the East, for Hitler's ambitions were essentially unlimited. On both war fronts the Nazi soldiers scored enormous successes until late 1942, establishing a horrifyingly vast empire of death and destruction. Hitler's reckless aggression also raised a mighty coalition determined to smash the Nazi order. Led by Britain, the United States, and the Soviet Union, the "Grand Alliance"—to use Winston Churchill's favorite term—functioned quite effectively in military terms. By the summer of 1943, the tide of battle had turned. Two years later, Germany and its allies lay in ruins, utterly defeated. Thus the terrible Nazi empire proved short-lived.

Aggression and Appeasement (1933–1939)

Hitler's tactics in international politics after 1933 strikingly resembled those he used in domestic politics between 1924 and 1933. When Hitler was weak, he righteously proclaimed that he intended to overturn the "unjust system" established by the treaties of Versailles and Locarno—but only by legal means. As he grew stronger, and as other leaders showed their willingness to compromise, he increased his demands and finally began attacking his independent neighbors (Map 35.1).

Hitler realized that his aggressive policies had to be carefully camouflaged at first, for Germany's army was limited by the Treaty of Versailles to only a hundred thousand men. As he told a group of army commanders in February 1933, the early stages of his policy of "conquest of new living space in the East and its ruthless Germanization" had serious dangers. If France had real leaders, Hitler said, it would "not give us time but attack us, presumably with its eastern satellites."[12] To avoid such threats to his plans, Hitler loudly proclaimed his peaceful intentions to all the world. Nevertheless, he felt strong enough to walk out of a sixty-nation disarmament conference and withdraw from the League of Nations in October 1933. Stresemann's policy of peaceful cooperation was dead; the Nazi determination to rearm was out in the open.

Following this action, which met with widespread approval at home, Hitler moved to incorporate independent Austria into a Greater Germany. Austrian Nazis climaxed an attempted overthrow by murdering the Austrian chancellor in July 1934. They were unable to take power, however, because a worried Mussolini, who had initially greeted Hitler as a fascist little brother, massed his troops on the Brenner Pass and threatened to fight. When, in March 1935, Hitler established a general military draft and declared the "unequal" disarmament clauses of the Treaty of Versailles null and void, other countries appeared to understand the danger. With France taking the lead, Italy and Great Britain protested strongly and warned against future aggressive actions.

Yet the emerging united front against Hitler quickly collapsed. Of crucial importance, Britain adopted a policy of appeasement, granting Hitler everything he could reasonably want (and more) in order to avoid war. The first step was an Anglo-German naval agreement in June 1935, which broke Germany's isolation. The second step came in March 1936, when Hitler suddenly marched his armies into the demilitarized Rhineland, brazenly violating the treaties of Versailles and Locarno. This was the last good chance to stop the Nazis, for Hitler had ordered his troops

MAP 35.1 The Growth of Nazi Germany, 1933–1939 Until March 1939, Hitler brought ethnic Germans into the Nazi state; then he turned on the Slavic peoples, whom he had always hated.

to retreat if France resisted militarily. But an uncertain France would not move without British support, and the occupation of German soil by German armies seemed right and just to Britain. Its strategic position greatly improved, Germany had handed France a tremendous psychological defeat.

British appeasement, which practically dictated French policy, lasted far into 1939. It was motivated by British feelings of guilt toward Germany and the pacifism of a population still horrified by the memory of the First World War. Like many Germans, British political leaders seriously underestimated Hitler. They believed that they could use him to stop Russian communism. A leading member of Britain's government personally told Hitler in November 1937 that it was his conviction that Hitler "not only had accomplished great things in Germany itself, but that through the total destruction of Communism in his own country . . . Germany rightly had to be considered as a Western bulwark against Communism."[13] Such rigid anticommunist feelings made an alliance between the Western powers and Stalin very unlikely.

As Britain and France opted for appeasement and Russia watched all developments suspiciously, Hitler found powerful allies. In 1935 the bombastic Mussolini decided that imperial expansion was needed to revitalize fascism. From Italian colonies on the east coast of Africa he attacked the independent African kingdom of Ethiopia. The Western powers and the League of Nations piously condemned Italian aggression—a posture that angered Mussolini—without saving Ethiopia from defeat. Hitler, who had secretly supplied Ethiopia with arms to heat up the conflict, supported Italy energetically and thereby overcame Mussolini's lingering doubts about the Nazis. The result in 1936 was an agreement on close cooperation between Italy and Germany, the so-called Rome-Berlin Axis. Japan, which had been expanding into Manchuria since 1931, soon joined the alliance between Italy and Germany.

At the same time, Germany and Italy intervened in the long, complicated Spanish Civil War, where their support eventually helped General Francisco Franco's fascist movement defeat republican Spain. Spain's only official aid came from Soviet Russia, for public opinion in Britain and especially in France was hopelessly divided on the Spanish question.

By late 1937, as he was proclaiming his peaceful intentions to the British and their gullible prime minister, Neville Chamberlain (1869–1940), Hitler told his generals his real plans. His "unshakable decision" was to crush Austria and Czechoslovakia at the earliest possible moment, as the first step in his long-contemplated drive to the east for "living space." By threatening Austria with invasion, Hitler forced the Austrian chancellor in March 1938 to put local Nazis in control of the government. The next day, German armies moved in unopposed, and Austria became two more provinces of Greater Germany (see Map 35.1).

Simultaneously, Hitler began demanding that the pro-Nazi, German-speaking minority of western Czechoslovakia—the Sudetenland—be turned over to Germany. Yet democratic Czechoslovakia

Cartoonist David Low's biting criticism of appeasing leaders appeared shortly after Hitler remilitarized the Rhineland. Appeasement also appealed to millions of ordinary citizens, who wanted to avoid at any cost another great war. *(Source: Cartoon by David Low. Reproduced by permission of* London Evening Standard/Solo*)*

was prepared to defend itself. Moreover, France had been Czechoslovakia's ally since 1924; and if France fought, Soviet Russia was pledged to help. As war appeared inevitable—for Hitler had already told the leader of the Sudeten Germans that "we must always ask so much we cannot be satisfied"—appeasement triumphed again. In September 1938 Chamberlain flew to Germany three times in fourteen days. In these negotiations, to which Russia was deliberately not invited, Chamberlain and the French agreed with Hitler that the Sudetenland should be ceded to Germany immediately. Returning to London from the Munich Conference, Chamberlain told cheering crowds that he had secured "peace with honor . . . peace for our time." Sold out by the Western powers, Czechoslovakia gave in.

Confirmed once again in his opinion of the Western democracies as weak and racially degenerate, Hitler accelerated his aggression. In a shocking violation of his solemn assurances that the Sudetenland was his last territorial demand, Hitler's armies occupied the Czech lands in March 1939, and Slovakia became a puppet state. The effect on Western public opinion was electrifying. For the first time, there was no possible rationale of self-determination for Nazi aggression, since Hitler was seizing Czechs and Slovaks as captive peoples. Thus, when Hitler used the question of German minorities in Danzig as a pretext to confront Poland, a suddenly militant Chamberlain declared that Britain and France would fight if Hitler attacked his eastern neighbor. Hitler did not take these warnings seriously and decided to press on.

In an about-face that stunned the world, Hitler offered and Stalin signed a ten-year Nazi-Soviet nonaggression pact in August 1939, whereby each dictator promised to remain neutral if the other became involved in war. Even more startling was the attached secret protocol, which ruthlessly divided eastern Europe into German and Russian zones, "in the event of a political territorial reorganization." Although this top-secret protocol sealing the destruction of Poland and the Baltic states became known only after the war, the nonaggression pact itself was enough to make Britain and France cry treachery, for they too had been negotiating with Stalin. But Stalin had remained distrustful of Western intentions. Moreover, Britain and France had offered him military risk without gain; Hitler had offered territorial gain without risk. For Hitler, everything was set. He told his

generals on the day of the nonaggression pact: "My only fear is that at the last moment some dirty dog will come up with a mediation plan." On September 1, 1939, German armies and warplanes smashed into Poland from three sides. Two days later, finally true to their word, Britain and France declared war on Germany. The Second World War had begun.

Hitler's Empire (1939–1942)

Using planes, tanks, and trucks in the first example of the *blitzkrieg,* or "lightning war," Hitler's armies crushed Poland in four weeks. While Soviet Russia quickly took its part of the booty—the eastern half of Poland and the Baltic states of Lithuania, Estonia, and Latvia—French and British armies dug in in the west. They expected another war of attrition and economic blockade.

In spring 1940 the lightning war struck again. After occupying Denmark, Norway, and Holland, German motorized columns broke through southern Belgium, split the Franco-British forces, and trapped the entire British army on the beaches of Dunkirk. By heroic efforts the British withdrew their troops but not their equipment.

France was taken by the Nazis. The aging marshal Henri-Philippe Pétain (1856–1951) formed a new French government—the so-called Vichy government—to accept defeat, and German armies occupied most of France. By July 1940 Hitler ruled practically all of western continental Europe; Italy was an ally, and the Soviet Union was a friendly neutral. Only Britain, led by the uncompromising Winston Churchill (1874–1965), remained unconquered. Churchill proved to be one of history's greatest wartime leaders, rallying his fellow citizens with stirring speeches, infectious confidence, and bulldog determination.

Germany sought to gain control of the air, the necessary first step for an amphibious invasion of Britain. In the Battle of Britain, up to a thousand German planes attacked British airfields and key factories in a single day, dueling with British defenders high in the skies. Losses were heavy on both sides. Then in September Hitler angrily and foolishly changed his strategy, turning from military objectives to indiscriminate bombing of British cities in an attempt to break British morale. British factories increased production of their excellent fighter planes; anti-aircraft defense improved with the help of radar; and the heavily bombed people of London defiantly dug in. In September through October 1940, Britain was beating Germany three to one in the air war. There was no possibility of immediate German invasion of Britain.

In these circumstances, the most reasonable German strategy would have been to attack Britain through the eastern Mediterranean, taking Egypt and the Suez Canal and pinching off Britain's supply of oil. Mussolini's early defeats in Greece had drawn Hitler into the Balkans, where Germany quickly conquered Greece and Yugoslavia while forcing Hungary, Romania, and Bulgaria into alliances with Germany by April 1941. These successes reinforced the logic of a thrust into the eastern Mediterranean. But Hitler was not a reasonable person. His lifetime obsession with a vast eastern European empire for the so-called master race irrationally dictated policy. By late 1940 he had already decided on his next move, and in June 1941 German armies suddenly attacked the Soviet Union along a vast front. With Britain still unconquered, Hitler's decision was a wild, irrational gamble, epitomizing the violent, unlimited ambitions of modern totalitarianism.

Faithfully fulfilling all his obligations under the Nazi-Soviet Pact and even ignoring warnings of impending invasion, Stalin was caught off guard. Nazi armies moved like lightning across the Russian steppe. By October 1941 Leningrad was practically surrounded, Moscow besieged, and most of the Ukraine conquered; yet the Russians did not collapse. When a severe winter struck German armies outfitted in summer uniforms, the invaders were stopped.

While Hitler's armies dramatically expanded the war in Europe, his Japanese allies did the same in Asia. Engaged in a general but undeclared war against China since 1937 (see pages 1097–1100), Japan's rulers had increasingly come into diplomatic conflict with the Pacific Basin's other great power, the United States. When the Japanese occupied French Indochina in July 1941, the United States retaliated by cutting off sales of vital rubber, scrap iron, oil, and aviation fuel. Tension mounted further, and on December 7, 1941, Japan attacked the U.S. naval base at Pearl Harbor in Hawaii. Hitler immediately declared war on the United States even though his treaty obligations with Japan did not require him to initiate this course of action.

As Japanese forces advanced swiftly into Southeast Asia after the crippling surprise attack at Pearl Harbor, Hitler and his European allies continued the two-front war against the Soviet Union and Great Britain. Not until late 1942 did the Nazis suffer their first major defeats. In the meantime, Hitler ruled a vast European empire stretching from the outskirts of Moscow to the English Channel. Hitler and the top Nazi leadership began building their "New Order," and they continued their efforts until their final collapse in 1945. In doing so, they showed what Nazi victory would have meant (Map 35.2).

Hitler's New Order was based firmly on the guiding principle of Nazi totalitarianism: racial imperialism. Within this New Order, the Nordic peoples—the Dutch, the Norwegians, and the Danes—received preferential treatment, for they were racially related to the Germans. The French, an "inferior" Latin people, occupied the middle position. They were heavily taxed to support the Nazi war effort but were tolerated as a race. Once Nazi reverses began to mount in late 1942, however, all the occupied territories of western and northern Europe were exploited with increasing intensity. Material shortages and both mental and physical suffering afflicted millions of people.

Slavs in the conquered territories to the east were treated with harsh hatred as "subhumans." At the height of his success in 1941 to 1942, Hitler painted for his intimate circle the fantastic details of a vast eastern colonial empire, where the Poles, Ukrainians, and Russians would be enslaved and forced to die out while Germanic peasants resettled their abandoned lands. Himmler and the elite corps of S.S. volunteers struggled loyally, sometimes against the German army, to implement part of this general program even before victory was secured. In parts of Poland, the S.S. arrested and evacuated Polish peasants to create a German "mass settlement space." Polish workers and Russian prisoners of war were transported to Germany, where they did most of the heavy labor and were systematically worked to death. The conditions of Russian slave labor in Germany were so harsh that four out of five Russian prisoners did not survive the war.

Finally, Jews were condemned to extermination, along with Gypsies, Jehovah's Witnesses, and captured Communists. By 1939 German Jews had lost all their civil rights, and after the fall of Warsaw the Nazis began deporting them to Poland. There

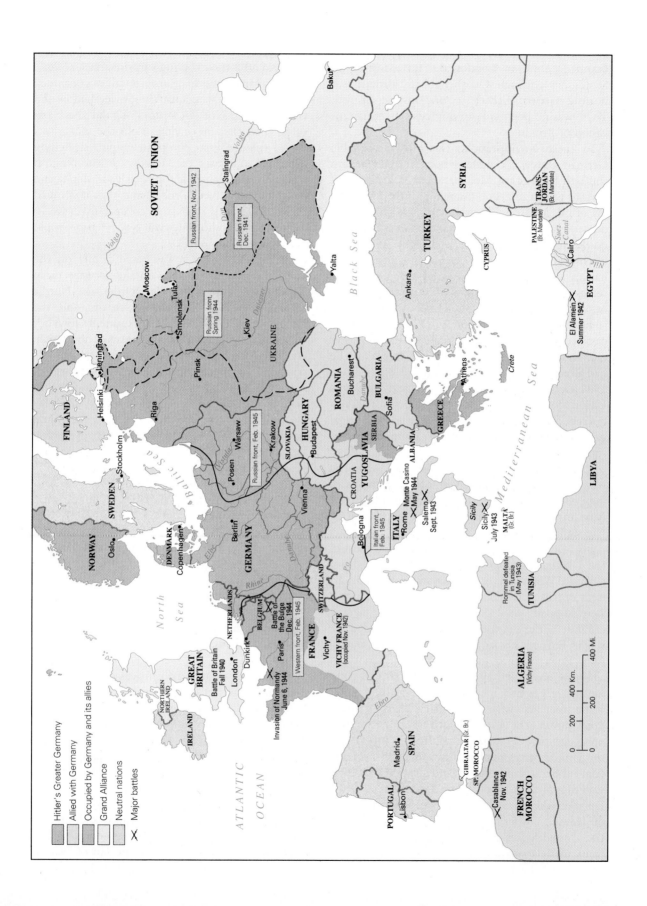

they and Jews from all over Europe were concentrated in ghettos, compelled to wear the Jewish star, and turned into slave laborers. But by 1941 Himmler's S.S. was carrying out the "final solution of the Jewish question"—the murder of every single Jew. All over Hitler's empire, Jews were arrested, packed like cattle onto freight trains, and dispatched to extermination camps.

There the victims were taken by force or deception to "shower rooms," which were actually gas chambers. These gas chambers, first perfected in the quiet, efficient execution of seventy thousand mentally ill Germans between 1938 and 1941, permitted rapid, hideous, and thoroughly bureaucratized mass murder. For fifteen to twenty minutes came the terrible screams and gasping sobs of men, women, and children choking to death on poison gas. Then, only silence. Special camp workers quickly tore the victims' gold teeth from their jaws and cut off their hair for use as chair stuffing. The bodies were then cremated or sometimes boiled for oil to make soap; the bones were crushed to produce fertilizers. At Auschwitz, the most infamous of the Nazi death factories, as many as twelve thousand human beings were slaughtered each day. On the turbulent Russian front, the S.S. death squads forced the Jewish population to dig giant pits, which became mass graves as the victims were lined up on the edge and cut down by machine guns. The extermination of European Jews was the ultimate monstrosity of Nazi racism and racial imperialism. By 1945 six million Jews had been murdered.

The Grand Alliance

While the Nazis built their savage empire, the Allies faced the hard fact that chance, rather than choice, had brought them together. Stalin had been cooperating fully with Hitler between August 1939 and June 1941, and only the Japanese attack on Pearl Harbor in December 1941 and Hitler's immediate declaration of war had over-

whelmed powerful isolationism in the United States. The Allies' first task was to try to overcome their mutual suspicions and build an unshakable alliance on the quicksand of accident. By means of three interrelated policies they succeeded.

First, President Franklin Delano Roosevelt (1882–1945) accepted Churchill's contention that the United States should concentrate first on defeating Hitler. Only after victory in Europe would the United States turn toward the Pacific for an all-out attack on Japan, the lesser threat. Therefore, the United States promised and sent large amounts of military aid to Britain and Russia, and American and British forces in each combat zone were tightly integrated under a single commander. America's policy of "Europe first" helped solidify the anti-Hitler coalition.

Second, within the European framework, the Americans and the British put immediate military needs first. They consistently postponed tough political questions relating to the eventual peace settlement and thereby avoided, until after the war, conflicts that might have split the alliance.

Third, to further encourage mutual trust, the Allies adopted the principle of the "unconditional surrender" of Germany and Japan. The policy of unconditional surrender cemented the Grand Alliance because it denied Hitler any hope of dividing his foes. It probably also discouraged Germans and Japanese who might have tried to overthrow their dictators in order to make a compromise peace. Of great importance for the postwar shape of Europe, it meant that Russian and Anglo-American armies would almost certainly come together to divide all of Germany, and most of the Continent, among themselves.

The military resources of the Grand Alliance were awesome. The strengths of the United States were its mighty industry, its large population, and its national unity. Even before the attack on Pearl Harbor, President Roosevelt had called America the "arsenal of democracy" and given military aid to Britain and Russia. Now the United States geared up rapidly for all-out war production and drew heavily on a generally cooperative Latin America for resources. It not only equipped its own armies but eventually gave its allies about $50 billion of arms and equipment. Britain received by far the most, but about one-fifth of the total went to Russia in the form of badly needed trucks, planes, and munitions.

Map 35.2 The Second World War in Europe The map shows the extent of Hitler's empire at its height, before the battle of Stalingrad in late 1942, and the subsequent advances of the Allies until Germany surrendered on May 7, 1945.

Prelude to Murder This photo captures the terrible inhumanity of Nazi racism. Frightened and bewildered families from the soon-to-be destroyed Warsaw ghetto are being forced out of their homes by German soldiers for deportation to concentration camps. There they face murder in the gas chambers. *(Source: Roger-Viollet)*

Too strong to lose and too weak to win when it stood alone, Britain, too, continued to make a great contribution. The British economy was totally and effectively mobilized, and the sharing of burdens through rationing and heavy taxes on war profits maintained social harmony. Moreover, as 1942 wore on, Britain could increasingly draw on the enormous physical and human resources of its empire and the United States. By early 1943 the Americans and the British combined small aircraft carriers with radar-guided bombers to rid the Atlantic of German submarines. Britain, the impregnable floating fortress, became a gigantic frontline staging area for the decisive blow to the heart of Germany.

As for Soviet Russia, so great was its strength that it might have defeated Germany without Western help. In the face of the German advance,

whole factories and populations were successfully evacuated to eastern Russia and Siberia. There, war production was reorganized and expanded, and the Red Army was increasingly well supplied. The Red Army was also well led, for a new generation of talented military leaders quickly arose to replace those so recently purged. Most important of all, Stalin drew on the massive support and heroic determination of the Soviet people. Broad-based Russian nationalism, as opposed to narrow communist ideology, became the powerful unifying force in what was appropriately called the "Great Patriotic War of the Fatherland."

Finally, the United States, Britain, and Soviet Russia were not alone. They had the resources of much of the world at their command. And, to a greater or lesser extent, they were aided by a growing resistance movement against the Nazis throughout Europe, even in Germany. Thus, although Ukrainian peasants often welcomed the Germans as liberators, the barbaric occupation policies of the Nazis quickly drove them to join and support behind-the-lines guerrilla forces. More generally, after Russia was invaded in June 1941, Communists throughout Europe took the lead in the underground Resistance, joined by a growing number of patriots and Christians. Anti-Nazi leaders from occupied countries established governments-in-exile in London, like that of the "Free French" under the intensely proud General Charles de Gaulle (1890–1970). These governments gathered valuable secret information from Resistance fighters and even organized armies to help defeat Hitler.

The Tide of Battle

Barely halted at the gates of Moscow and Leningrad in 1941, the Germans renewed their Russian offensive in July 1942. This time they drove toward the southern city of Stalingrad in an attempt to cripple communications and seize the crucial oil fields of Baku (see Map 35.2). Reaching Stalingrad, the Germans slowly occupied most of the ruined city in a month of incredibly savage house-to-house fighting.

Then, in November 1942, Soviet armies counterattacked. They rolled over Romanian and Italian troops to the north and south of Stalingrad, quickly closing the trap and surrounding the entire German Sixth Army of 300,000 men. The surrounded Germans were systematically destroyed, until by the end of January 1943 only 123,000 soldiers were left to surrender. Hitler, who refused to allow a retreat, suffered a catastrophic defeat. In the summer of 1943, the larger, better-equipped Soviet armies took the offensive and began moving forward.

In late 1942 the tide also turned in the Pacific and in North Africa. By late spring 1942, Japan had established a great empire in East Asia (Map 35.3). Unlike the Nazis, the Japanese made clever appeals to local nationalists, who sometimes saw Japan and its so-called Greater Asian Co-prosperity Sphere as potent allies against Western domination.

Then, in the Battle of the Coral Sea in May 1942, Allied naval and air power stopped the Japanese advance and also relieved Australia from the

threat of invasion. This victory was followed by the Battle of Midway Island, in which American pilots sank all four of the attacking Japanese aircraft carriers and established American naval superiority in the Pacific. In August 1942, American marines attacked Guadalcanal in the Solomon Islands. Badly hampered by the policy of "Europe first"—only 15 percent of Allied resources were going to fight the war in the Pacific in early 1943—the Americans, under General Douglas MacArthur and Admiral Chester Nimitz, and the Australians nevertheless began "island hopping"

Mobilizing the Soviet People Joining the historic Russian warrior and the young Soviet soldier in the common cause, this poster portrays the defense of the nation as a sacred mission and illustrates the way Soviet leaders successfully appealed to Russian nationalism during the war. (*Source: Library of Congress*)

toward Japan. Japanese forces were on the defensive.

In North Africa, the war had been seesawing back and forth since 1940. In May 1942, combined German and Italian armies, under the brilliant General Erwin Rommel, attacked British-occupied Egypt and the Suez Canal for the second time. After a rapid advance, they were defeated by British forces at the Battle of El Alamein, only seventy miles from Alexandria (see Map 35.2). In Oc-

tober the British counterattacked in Egypt, and almost immediately thereafter an Anglo-American force landed in Morocco and Algeria. These French possessions, which were under the control of Pétain's Vichy French government, quickly went over to the side of the Allies.

Having driven the Axis powers from North Africa by the spring of 1943, Allied forces maintained the initiative by invading Sicily and then mainland Italy. Mussolini was deposed by a

MAP 35.3 The Second World War in the Pacific   Japanese forces overran an enormous territory in 1942, which the Allies slowly recaptured in a long bitter struggle. As this map shows, Japan still held a large Asian empire in August 1945, when the unprecedented devastation of atomic warfare suddenly forced it to surrender.

The City of Nagasaki A second atomic bomb struck Nagasaki on August 9, 1945, three days after the first giant fireball incinerated Hiroshima. Approximately 75,000 Japanese were killed or injured at Nagasaki. In this grim photo, taken about a month after the attack, a Japanese survivor pushes his bicycle along a path cleared through the ruins. *(Source: UPI/Bettmann Newsphotos)*

war-weary people, and the new Italian government publicly accepted unconditional surrender in September 1943. Italy, it seemed, was liberated. Yet Mussolini was rescued by German commandos in a daring raid and put at the head of a puppet government. German armies seized the city of Rome and all of northern Italy. Fighting continued in Italy.

Indeed, bitter fighting continued in Europe for almost two years. Germany, less fully mobilized for war than Britain in 1941, applied itself to total war in 1942 and enlisted millions of prisoners of war and slave laborers from all across occupied Europe in that effort. Between early 1942 and July 1944, German war production actually tripled. Although British and American bombing raids killed many German civilians, they were surprisingly ineffective from a military point of view. Also, German resistance against Hitler failed. After an un-

successful attempt on Hitler's life in July 1944, thousands of Germans were brutally liquidated by S.S. fanatics. Terrorized at home and frightened by the prospect of unconditional surrender, the Germans fought on with suicidal stoicism.

On June 6, 1944, American and British forces under General Dwight Eisenhower landed on the beaches of Normandy in history's greatest naval invasion. Having tricked the Germans into believing that the attack would come near the Belgian border, the Allies secured a foothold on the coast of Normandy (see Map 35.2). In a hundred dramatic days, more than two million men and almost a half-million vehicles pushed inland and broke through German lines. Rejecting proposals to strike straight at Berlin in a massive attack, Eisenhower moved forward cautiously on a broad front. Not until March 1945 did American troops cross the Rhine and enter Germany.

The Russians, who had been advancing steadily since July 1943, reached the outskirts of Warsaw by August 1944. For the next six months they moved southward into Romania, Hungary, and Yugoslavia. In January 1945, Red armies again moved westward through Poland, and on April 26 they met American forces on the Elbe River. The Allies had closed their vise on Nazi Germany and overrun Europe. As Soviet forces fought their way into Berlin, Hitler committed suicide in his bunker, and on May 7 the remaining German commanders capitulated.

Three months later, the United States dropped atomic bombs on Hiroshima and Nagasaki in Japan (see Map 35.3). Mass bombing of cities and civilians, one of the terrible new practices of the Second World War, had ended in the final nightmare—unprecedented human destruction in a single blinding flash. The Japanese surrendered. The Second World War, which had claimed the lives of more than fifty million soldiers and civilians, was over.

also won enthusiastic supporters by offering tough, ruthless people from modest backgrounds enormous rewards for loyal and effective service. Thus these totalitarian dictatorships rested on considerable genuine popular support, as well as on police terror. This combination gave them their awesome power and dynamism. That dynamism, however, was channeled in quite different directions. Stalin and the Communist party aimed at building their kind of socialism and the new socialist personality at home. Hitler and the Nazi elite aimed at unlimited territorial and racial aggression on behalf of a master race; domestic recovery was only a means to that end.

Unlimited Nazi aggression made war inevitable, first with the western European democracies, then with Germany's totalitarian neighbor, and finally with the United States. Plunging Europe into the ultimate nightmare, unlimited aggression unwittingly forged a mighty coalition that smashed the racist Nazi empire and its leader. In the words of the ancient Greeks, he whom the gods would destroy, they first make mad.

SUMMARY

The Second World War marked the climax of the tremendous practical and spiritual maladies of the age of anxiety, which led in many lands to the rise of dictatorships. Many of these dictatorships were variations on conservative authoritarianism, but there was also a fateful innovation—the modern totalitarian regime, most fully developed in Communist Russia and Nazi Germany. The totalitarian regimes utterly rejected the liberalism of the nineteenth century. Inspired by the lessons of total war and Lenin's one-party rule, they tried to subordinate everything to the state. Although some areas of life escaped them, state control increased to a staggering, unprecedented degree. The totalitarian regimes trampled on basic human rights with unrestrained brutality and police terror. Moreover, these regimes were armed with the weapons of modern technology, rendering opposition almost impossible.

Both Communist Russia and Nazi Germany tried to gain the willing support of their populations. Monopolizing the means of expression and communication, they claimed to represent the masses and to be building new, more equal societies. Many people believed them. Both regimes

NOTES

1. E. Halévy, *The Era of Tyrannies* (Garden City, N.Y.: Doubleday, 1965), pp. 265–316, esp. p. 300.
2. Quoted in P. C. Roberts, " 'War Communism': A Re-Examination," *Slavic Review* 29 (June 1970): 25.
3. Quoted in A. G. Mazour, *Soviet Economic Development: Operation Outstrip, 1921–1965* (Princeton, N.J.: Van Nostrand, 1967), p. 130.
4. Quoted in I. Deutscher, *Stalin: A Political Biography,* 2d ed. (New York: Oxford University Press, 1967), p. 325.
5. Quoted in H. K. Geiger, *The Family in Soviet Russia* (Cambridge, Mass.: Harvard University Press, 1968), p. 123.
6. Ibid., p. 156.
7. Quoted in B. Rosenthal, "Women in the Russian Revolution and After," in *Becoming Visible: Women in European History,* ed. R. Bridenthal and C. Koonz (Boston: Houghton Mifflin, 1976), p. 383.
8. Quoted in K. D. Bracher, "The Technique of the National Socialist Seizure of Power," in T. Eschenburg et al., *The Path to Dictatorship, 1918–1933* (Garden City, N.Y.: Doubleday, 1966), p. 117.
9. Quoted in K. D. Bracher, *The German Dictatorship: The Orgins, Structure and Effects of National Socialism* (New York: Praeger, 1970), pp. 146–147.

10. Quoted in R. Stromberg, *An Intellectual History of Modern Europe* (New York: Appleton-Century-Crofts, 1966), p. 393.

11. D. Schoenbaum, *Hitler's Social Revolution: Class and Status in Nazi Germany, 1933–1939* (Garden City, N.Y.: Doubleday, 1967), p. 114.

12. Quoted in Bracher, p. 289.

13. Ibid., p. 306.

SUGGESTED READING

The historical literature on totalitarian dictatorships is rich and fascinating. H. Arendt, *The Origins of Totalitarianism* (1951), is a challenging interpretation. E. Weber, *Varieties of Fascism* (1964), stresses the radical social aspirations of fascist movements all across Europe. F. L. Carsten, *The Rise of Fascism,* rev. ed. (1982), and W. Laqueur, ed., *Fascism* (1976), are also recommended.

R. Stites, *The Women's Liberation Movement in Russia: Feminism, Nihilism, and Bolshevism, 1860–1930* (1978); S. Fitzpatrick, *Cultural Revolution in Russia, 1928–1931* (1978); and the works by Geiger and Deutscher cited in the Notes are all highly recommended, as is Deutscher's sympathetic three-volume study of Trotsky. S. Cohen, *Bukharin and the Bolshevik Revolution* (1973), examines the leading spokesman of moderate communism, who was destroyed by Stalin. R. Conquest, *The Great Terror* (1968), is an excellent account of Stalin's purges of the 1930s. A. Solzhenitsyn, *The Gulag Archipelago* (1964), passionately condemns Soviet police terror, which Solzhenitsyn tracks back to Lenin. A. Koestler, *Darkness at Noon* (1956), is a famous fictional account of Stalin's trials of the Old Bolsheviks. R. Medvedev, *Let History Judge* (1972), is a penetrating and highly recommended history of Stalinism by a Russian dissident. R. Conquest, *The Harvest of Sorrow* (1986), recounts authoritatively Soviet collectivization and the man-made famine. Three other remarkable books are J. Scott, *Behind the Urals* (1942, 1973), an eyewitness account of an American steelworker in Russia in the 1930s; S. Alliluyeva, *Twenty Letters to a Friend* (1967), the amazing reflections of Stalin's daughter, who chose twice to live in the United States before returning home; and M. Fainsod, *Smolensk Under Soviet Rule* (1958), a unique study based on Communist records captured first by the Germans and then by the Americans.

A. De Grand, *Italian Fascism: Its Origins and Development,* 2d ed. (1989), and E. R. Tannebaum, *The Fascist Experience* (1972), are excellent studies of Italy under Mussolini. I. Silone, *Bread and Wine* (1937), is a moving novel by a famous opponent of dictatorship in Italy. Two excellent books on Spain are H. Thomas, *The Spanish Civil War* (1961), and E. Malefakis, *Agrarian Reform and Peasant Revolution in Spain* (1970). In the area of foreign relations, G. Kennan, *Russia and the West Under Lenin and Stalin* (1961), is justly famous, while A. L. Rowse, *Appeasement* (1961), powerfully denounces the policies of the appeasers. R. Paxton, *Vichy France* (1973), tells a controversial story extremely well, and J. Lukac, *The Last European War* (1976), skillfully—and infuriatingly—argues that victory by Hitler could have saved Europe from both Russian and American domination.

On Germany, F. Stern, *The Politics of Cultural Despair* (1963), and G. Mosse, *The Crisis of German Ideology* (1964), are excellent complementary studies on the origins of Nazism. The best single work on Hitler's Germany is Bracher's *The German Dictatorship,* cited in the Notes; W. Shirer, *The Rise and Fall of the Third Reich* (1960), is the best-selling account of an American journalist who experienced Nazi Germany firsthand. J. Fest, *Hitler* (1974), and A. Bullock, *Hitler* (1953), are engrossing biographies of the Führer. In addition to *Mein Kampf, Hitler's Secret Conversations, 1941–1944* (1953), reveals the dictator's wild dreams and beliefs. Among countless special studies, E. Kogon, *The Theory and Practice of Hell* (1958), is a chilling examination of the concentration camps; M. Mayer, *They Thought They Were Free* (1955), probes the minds of ten ordinary Nazis and why they believed Hitler was their liberator; and A. Speer, *Inside the Third Reich* (1970), contains the fascinating recollections of Hitler's wizard of the armaments industry. G. Mosse, *Toward the Final Solution* (1978), is a powerful history of European racism. A. Mayer, *Why Did the Heavens Not Darken? The "Final Solution" in History* (1989), and L. Dawidowicz, *The War Against the Jews, 1933–1945* (1975), are moving accounts of the Holocaust. Jørgen Haestrup, *Europe Ablaze* (1978), is a monumental account of wartime resistance movements throughout Europe, and *The Diary of Anne Frank* is a remarkable personal account of a young Jewish girl in hiding during the Nazi occupation of Holland.

J. Campbell's *The Experience of World War II* (1989) is attractively illustrated and captures the drama of global conflict. G. Wright, *The Ordeal of Total War, 1939–1945* (1968), is the best comprehensive study on the Second World War. B. H. Liddell Hart, *The History of the Second World War* (1971), is an overview of military developments. Three dramatic studies of special aspects of the war are A. Dallin, *German Rule in Russia, 1941–1945* (1957), which analyzes the effects of Nazi occupation policies on the Soviet population; L. Collins and D. La Pierre, *Is Paris Burning?* (1965), a best-selling account of the liberation of Paris and Hitler's plans to destroy the city; and J. Toland, *The Last Hundred Days* (1966), a lively account of the end of the war.

36

Recovery and Crisis in Europe and the Americas

An East German border guard at the Berlin Wall in the 1960s

The total defeat of the Nazis and their allies laid the basis for one of Western civilization's most remarkable recoveries. A battered western Europe dug itself out from under the rubble and fashioned a great renaissance in the postwar era. The Western Hemisphere, with its strong European heritage, also made exemplary progress. And the Soviet Union became more humane and less totalitarian after Stalin's death. Yet there was also a tragic setback. Dictatorship settled over eastern Europe, and the Grand Alliance against Hitler gave way to an apparently endless cold war, in which conflict between East and West threatened world peace.

Sometime during the late 1960s or early 1970s, the postwar era of recovery came to an end. Postwar certainties like domestic political stability and social harmony evaporated, and several countries experienced major crises. Moreover, the almost automatic economic improvement of the postwar years was abruptly replaced by serious economic difficulties, which lasted throughout most of the 1970s and 1980s. Of critical importance, this pattern in the industrialized nations of a generation of progress followed by a generation of crisis was shared by much of the world, as the next two chapters show. Thus the knitting together of the peoples and regions of this small planet has been accelerated by similar historical experiences in recent times.

- What were the causes of the cold war?
- How and why, in spite of the sad division of Europe into two hostile camps, did western Europe recover so successfully from the ravages of war and Nazism?
- To what extent did communist eastern Europe and the Americas experience a similar recovery?
- Why, after a generation, did the economy shift into reverse gear, and what were some of the social consequences of the reversal?
- How did political crisis strike many countries from the late 1960s onward?
- Why did a reform movement eventually triumph in eastern Europe in 1989 and bring an end to the cold war?

These are the questions that this chapter seeks to answer.

THE COLD WAR (1942–1953)

In 1945 triumphant American and Russian soldiers came together and embraced on the banks of the Elbe River in the heart of vanquished Germany. At home, in the United States and in the Soviet Union, the soldiers' loved ones erupted in joyous celebration. Yet victory was flawed. The Allies could not cooperate politically in peacemaking. Motivated by different goals and hounded by misunderstandings, the United States and the Soviet Union soon found themselves at loggerheads. By the end of 1947, Europe was rigidly divided. It was West versus East in a cold war that eventually was waged around the world.

The Origins of the Cold War

The most powerful allies in the wartime coalition—the Soviet Union and the United States—began to quarrel almost as soon as the unifying threat of Nazi Germany disappeared. The hostility between the Eastern and Western superpowers was a tragic disappointment for millions of people, but it was not really so surprising. It was the sad but logical outgrowth of military developments, wartime agreements, and long-standing political and ideological differences.

In the early phases of the Second World War, the Americans and the British made military victory their highest priority. They consistently avoided discussion of Stalin's war aims and the shape of the eventual peace settlement. This policy was evident in December 1941 and again in May 1942, when Stalin asked the United States and Britain to agree to the Soviet Union's moving its western border of 1938 farther west at the expense of Poland, in effect ratifying the gains that Stalin had made from his deal with Hitler in 1939.

Stalin's request ran counter to the moralistic Anglo-American Atlantic Charter of August 1941. In good Wilsonian fashion, the Atlantic Charter had called for peace without territorial expansion or secret agreements and for free elections and self-determination for all liberated nations. In this spirit, the British and Americans declined to promise Polish territory to Stalin. He received only a military alliance and no postwar commitments. Yet the United States and Britain did not

The Big Three In 1945 a triumphant Winston Churchill, an ailing Franklin Roosevelt, and a determined Joseph Stalin met at Yalta in southern Russia to plan for peace. Cooperation soon gave way to bitter hostility. *(Source: F.D.R. Library)*

try to take advantage of the Soviet Union's precarious position in 1942, because they feared that hard bargaining would anger Stalin and encourage him to consider making a separate peace with Hitler. They focused instead on the policy of unconditional surrender to solidify the alliance.

By late 1943, as Allied armies scored major victories, specific issues related to the shape of the postwar world could no longer be postponed. The conference that Stalin, Roosevelt, and Churchill held in the Iranian capital of Teheran in November 1943 thus proved of crucial importance in determining subsequent events. There, the "Big Three" jovially reaffirmed their determination to crush Germany and searched for the appropriate military strategy. Churchill, fearful of the military

dangers of a direct attack and anxious to protect Britain's political interests in the eastern Mediterranean, argued that American and British forces should follow up their North African and Italian campaigns with an indirect attack on Germany through the Balkans. Roosevelt, however, agreed with Stalin that an American-British frontal assault through France would be better. This agreement was part of Roosevelt's general effort to meet Stalin's wartime demands whenever possible, and it had momentous political implications. It meant that the Soviet and the American-British armies would come together in defeated Germany along a north-south line and that only Soviet troops would liberate eastern Europe. Thus the basic shape of postwar Europe was emerging even as the fighting continued. Real differences over questions like Poland were carefully ignored.

When the Big Three met again in February 1945 at Yalta on the Black Sea in southern Russia, advancing Soviet armies were within a hundred miles of Berlin. The Red Army had occupied not only Poland but also Bulgaria, Romania, Hungary, part of Yugoslavia, and much of Czechoslovakia. The temporarily stalled American-British forces had yet to cross the Rhine into Germany. Moreover, the United States was far from defeating Japan. Indeed, it was believed that the invasion and occupation of Japan would cost a million American casualties—an estimate that contributed to the subsequent decision to drop atomic bombs in order to save American lives. In short, the Soviet Union's position was strong and America's weak.

There was little the increasingly sick and apprehensive Roosevelt could do but double his bet on Stalin's peaceful intentions. It was agreed at Yalta that Germany would be divided into zones of occupation and would pay heavy reparations to the Soviet Union in the form of agricultural and industrial goods, though many details remained unsettled. At American insistence, Stalin agreed to declare war on Japan after Germany was defeated. He also agreed to join the proposed United Nations, which the Americans believed would help preserve peace after the war; it was founded in April 1945 in San Francisco.

For Poland and eastern Europe—"that Pandora's Box of infinite troubles," according to American Secretary of State Cordell Hull—the Big Three struggled to reach an ambiguous compromise at Yalta: eastern European governments were to be freely elected but pro-Russian. As Churchill put it at the time, "The Poles will have their future in their own hands, with the single limitation that they must honestly follow in harmony with their allies, a policy friendly to Russia."[1]

The Yalta compromise over eastern Europe broke down almost immediately. Even before the Yalta Conference, Bulgaria and Poland were controlled by communists who arrived home with the Red Army. Minor concessions to noncommunist groups thereafter did not change this situation. Elsewhere in eastern Europe, pro-Soviet "coalition" governments of several parties were formed, but the key ministerial posts were reserved for Moscow-trained communists.

At the postwar Potsdam Conference of July 1945, the long-ignored differences over eastern Europe finally surged to the fore. The compromising Roosevelt had died and been succeeded by the more determined President Harry Truman, who demanded immediate free elections throughout eastern Europe. Stalin refused pointblank. "A freely elected government in any of these East European countries would be anti-Soviet," he admitted simply, "and that we cannot allow."[2]

Here, then, is the key to the much-debated origins of the cold war. American ideals, pumped up by the crusade against Hitler, and American politics, heavily influenced by millions of voters from eastern Europe, demanded free elections in Soviet-occupied eastern Europe. Stalin, who had lived through two enormously destructive German invasions, wanted absolute military security from Germany and its potential Eastern allies, once and for all. Suspicious by nature, he believed that only communist states could be truly dependable allies, and he realized that free elections would result in independent and possibly hostile governments on his western border. Moreover, by the middle of 1945 there was no way short of war that the United States and its Western allies could determine developments in eastern Europe, and war was out of the question. Stalin was bound to have his way.

West Versus East

The American response to Stalin's exaggerated conception of security was to "get tough." In May 1945 Truman abruptly cut off all aid to Russia. In October he declared that the United States would never recognize any government established by force against the free will of its people. In March 1946 former British prime minister Churchill ominously informed an American audience that an "iron curtain" had fallen across the Continent, dividing Germany and all of Europe into two antagonistic camps. Emotional, moralistic denunciations of Stalin and communist Russia emerged as part of American political life. Yet the United States also responded to the popular desire to "bring the boys home" and demobilized with great speed. When the war against Japan ended in September 1945, there were 12 million Americans in the armed forces; by 1947 there were only 1.5

million, as opposed to 6 million for the Soviet Union. Some historians have argued that American leaders believed that the atomic bomb gave the United States all the power it needed; but "getting tough" really meant "talking tough."

Stalin's agents quickly reheated what they viewed as the "ideological struggle against capitalist imperialism." The large, well-organized Communist parties of France and Italy obediently started to uncover American plots to take over Europe and challenged their own governments with violent criticisms and large strikes. The Soviet Union also put pressure on Iran and Turkey, and while Greek communists battled Greek royalists, another bitter civil war raged in China. By the spring of 1947, it appeared to many Americans that Stalin wanted much more than just puppet regimes in Soviet-occupied eastern Europe. He seemed determined to export communism by subversion throughout Europe and around the world.

The United States responded to this challenge with the Truman Doctrine, which was aimed at "containing" communism in areas already occupied by the Red Army. Truman told Congress in March 1947: "I believe it must be the policy of the United States to support free people who are resisting attempted subjugation by armed minorities or by outside pressure." To begin, Truman asked Congress for military aid to Greece and Turkey. Then, in June, Secretary of State George C. Marshall offered Europe economic aid—the Marshall Plan—to help it rebuild.

Stalin refused Marshall Plan assistance for all of eastern Europe. He purged the last remaining

The Berlin Air Lift   Standing in the rubble of their bombed-out city, a German crowd in the American sector awaits the arrival of a U.S. transport plane flying in over the Soviet blockade in 1948. The crisis over Berlin was a dramatic indication of growing tensions among the Allies, which resulted in the division of Europe into two hostile camps. *(Source: Walter Sanders, LIFE MAGAZINE © Time Inc.)*

noncommunist elements from the coalition governments of eastern Europe and established Soviet-style, one-party communist dictatorships. The seizure of power in Czechoslovakia in February 1948 was particularly brutal and antidemocratic, and it greatly strengthened Western fears of limitless communist expansion, beginning with Germany. Thus, when Stalin blocked all traffic through the Soviet zone of Germany to Berlin, the former capital, which the occupying powers had also divided into sectors at the end of the war, the Western Allies acted firmly but not provocatively. Hundreds of planes began flying over the Soviet roadblocks around the clock, supplying provisions to the people of West Berlin and thwarting Soviet efforts to swallow up the West Berliners. After 324 days the Soviets backed down: containment seemed to work. In 1949, therefore, the United States formed an anti-Soviet military alliance of Western governments: the North Atlantic Treaty Organization (NATO). Stalin countered by tightening his hold on his satellites, later united in the Warsaw Pact. Europe was divided into two hostile blocs.

In late 1949 the communists triumphed in China, frightening and angering many Americans, some of whom saw an all-powerful worldwide communist conspiracy extending even into the upper reaches of the American government. When the Russian-backed communist forces of northern Korea invaded southern Korea in 1950, President Truman acted swiftly. American-led United Nations armies intervened. The cold war had spread around the world and become very hot.

The rapid descent from victorious Grand Alliance to bitter cold war was intimately connected with the tragic fate of eastern Europe. After 1932, when the eastern European power vacuum invited Nazi racist imperialism, the appeasing Western democracies mistakenly did nothing. They did, however, have one telling insight: how, they asked themselves, could they unite with Stalin to stop Hitler without giving Stalin great gains on his western borders? After Hitler's invasion of the Soviet Union, the Western powers preferred to ignore this question and hope for the best. But when Stalin later began to claim the spoils of victory, the United States began to protest and professed outrage. This belated opposition quite possibly encouraged even more aggressive measures by the always-suspicious Stalin, and it helped explode the quarrel over eastern Europe into a global confrontation. This Soviet-American confrontation became institutionalized, and it lasted for decades despite intermittent periods of relaxation. Only when the Soviet Union's policy toward eastern Europe changed dramatically in the 1980s was the original cause of the conflict removed and the long cold war apparently brought to an end (see pages 1194–1200).

THE WESTERN EUROPEAN RENAISSANCE

As the cold war divided Europe into two blocs, the future appeared bleak on both sides of the iron curtain. Economic conditions were the worst in generations. Politically, Europe was weak and divided, a battleground for cold war ambitions. Moreover, European empires were crumbling in the face of nationalism in Asia and Africa. Yet Europe recovered, and the Western nations led the way. In less than a generation, western Europe achieved unprecedented economic prosperity and peaceful social transformation. Moreover, western Europe began moving toward genuine unity and regained much of its traditional prominence in world affairs. It was an amazing rebirth—a true renaissance.

The Postwar Challenge

After the war, economic conditions in western Europe were terrible. Simply finding enough to eat was a real problem. Runaway inflation and black markets testified to severe shortages and hardship. The bread ration in Paris in 1946 was little more than it had been in 1942 under the Nazi occupation. Many people believed that Europe was quite simply finished. The prominent British historian Arnold Toynbee felt that, at best, western Europeans might seek to civilize the crude but powerful Americans, somewhat as the ancient Greeks had civilized their Roman conquerors.

Suffering was most intense in defeated Germany. The major territorial change of the war had moved the Soviet Union's border far to the west. Poland was in turn compensated for this loss to the Soviets with land taken from Germany (Map 36.1). To solidify these changes in boundaries,

MAP 36.1 Europe After the Second World War Both the Soviet Union and Poland took land from Germany, which the Allies partitioned into occupation zones. Those zones subsequently formed the basis of the east and the west German states, as the iron curtain fell to divide both Germany and Europe.

Postwar Reconstruction   The Hamburg apartments on the left were bombed-out shells in 1945, along with 300,000 other housing units in the city. Yet by 1951 these same apartments were replaced, or ingeniously rebuilt (right). In half of the shells, crushed rubble mixed with concrete was poured to provide missing walls and to achieve a quick and economical rehabilitation. *(Source: National Archives, Washington)*

thirteen million people were driven from their homes in eastern Germany (and other countries in eastern Europe) and forced to resettle in a greatly reduced Germany. The Russians were also seizing factories and equipment as reparations, even tearing up railroad tracks and sending the rails to the Soviet Union.

In 1945 and 1946, conditions were not much better in the Western zones, for the Western Allies also treated the German population with great severity at first. By February 1946 the average daily diet of a German in the Ruhr had been reduced to two slices of bread, a pat of margarine, a spoonful of porridge, and two small potatoes. Countless Germans sold prized possessions to American soldiers to buy food. By the spring of 1947, refugee-clogged, hungry, prostrate Germany was on the verge of total collapse and threatening to drag down the rest of Europe.

Yet western Europe was not finished. The Nazi occupation and the war had discredited old ideas and old leaders. All over Europe, many people were willing to change and experiment in hopes of building a new and better Europe out of the rubble. New groups and new leaders were coming to the fore to guide these aspirations. Progressive Catholics and revitalized Catholic political parties—the Christian Democrats—were particularly influential.

In Italy, the Christian Democrats emerged as the leading party in the first postwar elections in 1946, and in early 1948 they won an absolute majority in the parliament in a landslide victory. Their very able leader was Alcide De Gasperi, a courageous antifascist and former Vatican librarian, firmly committed to political democracy, economic reconstruction, and moderate social reform. In France, too, the Catholic party provided some of the best postwar leaders, like Robert Schuman. This was particularly true after January 1946, when General Charles de Gaulle, the inspiring wartime leader of the Free French, resigned after having re-established the free and democratic Fourth Republic. As Germany was partitioned by the cold war, a radically purified Federal Republic of Germany (as West Germany was officially known) found new and able leadership among its Catholics. In 1949 Konrad Adenauer, the former mayor of Cologne and a long-time anti-Nazi, began his long, highly successful democratic rule; the Christian Democrats became West Germany's majority party for a generation. In providing effective leadership for their respective countries, the Christian Democrats were inspired and united by a common Christian and European heritage. They steadfastly rejected totalitarianism and narrow nationalism and placed their faith in democracy and cooperation.

THE WESTERN EUROPEAN RENAISSANCE

The Socialists and the Communists, active in the Resistance against Hitler, also emerged from the war with increased power and prestige, especially in France and Italy. They, too, provided fresh leadership and pushed for social change and economic reform with considerable success. In the immediate postwar years, welfare measures such as family allowances, health insurance, and increased public housing were enacted throughout much of Europe. In Italy social benefits from the state came to equal a large part of the average worker's wages. In France large banks, insurance companies, public utilities, coal mines, and the Renault auto company were nationalized by the government. Britain followed the same trend. The voters threw out Churchill and the Conservatives in 1945, and the socialist Labour party under Clement Attlee moved toward establishment of a "welfare state." Many industries were nationalized, and the government provided each citizen with free medical service and taxed the middle and upper classes more heavily. Thus, all across Europe, social reform complemented political transformation, creating solid foundations for a great European renaissance.

The United States also supplied strong and creative leadership. Frightened by fears of Soviet expansion, the United States provided western Europe with both massive economic aid and ongoing military protection. Economic aid was channeled through the Marshall Plan. Between early 1948 and late 1952, the United States furnished foreign countries roughly $22.5 billion, of which seven-eighths was in the form of outright gifts rather than loans. Military security was provided through NATO, established as a regional alliance for self-defense and featuring American troops stationed permanently in Europe and the American nuclear umbrella. Thus the United States assumed its international responsibilities after the Second World War, exercising the leadership it had shunned after 1919.

Economic "Miracles"

As Marshall Plan aid poured in, the battered economies of western Europe began to turn the corner in 1948. The outbreak of the Korean War in 1950 further stimulated economic activity, and Europe entered a period of rapid economic progress that lasted into the late 1960s. By 1963 western Europe was producing more than two-and-one-half times as much as it had produced before the war. Never before had the European economy grown so fast, and it was a time of loudly proclaimed economic "miracles."

There were many reasons for western Europe's brilliant economic performance. American aid helped the process get off to a fast start. Moreover, economic growth became a basic objective of all western European governments, for leaders and voters were determined to avoid a return to the dangerous and demoralizing stagnation of the 1930s. Thus governments generally accepted Keynesian economics (see page 1126) and sought to stimulate their economies. Some also adopted a number of imaginative strategies. Those in Germany and France were particularly successful and influential.

Under Minister of Economy Ludwig Erhard, a roly-poly, cigar-smoking former professor, postwar West Germany broke decisively with the straitjacketed Nazi economy. Erhard bet on the free-market economy while maintaining the extensive social welfare network inherited from the Hitler era. He and his teachers believed not only that capitalism was more efficient but also that political and social freedom could thrive only if there were real economic freedom. Erhard's first step was to reform the currency and abolish rationing and price controls in 1948. He boldly declared, "The only ration coupon is the Mark."[3] By the late 1950s, West Germany had a prospering economy and full employment, a strong currency and stable prices. West Germany success renewed respect for free-market capitalism and encouraged freer trade among other European nations.

The French innovation was a new kind of planning. Under the guidance of Jean Monnet, an economic pragmatist and apostle of European unity, a planning commission set ambitious but flexible goals for the French economy. It used Marshall Plan aid money and the nationalized banks to funnel money into key industries, several of which were state owned. It also encouraged private enterprise to "think big," and the often-cautious French business community responded. Thus France combined flexible planning and a "mixed" state and private economy to achieve the most rapid economic development in its long history.

Other factors also contributed to western Europe's economic boom. In most countries there were many people ready to work hard for low wages and the hope of a better future. Expanding industries in those countries thus had a great asset to draw on. Moreover, although many consumer products had been invented or perfected since the late 1920s, during the depression and war few Europeans had been able to buy them. In 1945 the electric refrigerator, the washing machine, and the automobile were rare luxuries. There was a great potential demand, which the economic system moved to satisfy.

Finally, ever since 1919 the nations of Europe had suffered from high tariffs and small national markets. In the postwar era, European countries junked many of these economic barriers and gradually created a large unified market known as the "Common Market." This historic action, which certainly stimulated the economy, was part of a larger search for European unity.

Toward European Unity

Western Europe's political recovery was spectacular in the generation after 1945. Republics were re-established in France, West Germany, and Italy. Constitutional monarchs were restored in Belgium, Holland, and Norway. Democratic governments, often within the framework of multiparty politics and shifting parliamentary coalitions, took root again and thrived. National self-determination was accompanied by civil liberties and individual freedom. All of this was an extraordinary achievement.

So also was the still-continuing march toward a united Europe. The Christian Democrats with their shared Catholic heritage were particularly committed to "building Europe," and other groups shared their dedication. Many Europeans believed that narrow, exaggerated nationalism had been a fundamental cause of both world wars and that only through unity could European conflict be avoided in the future. Many western Europeans also realized how weak their countries were in comparison with the United States and the Soviet Union, the two superpowers that had divided Europe from outside and made it into a cold war battleground. Thus the cold war encouraged some visionaries to seek a new "European nation," a superpower capable of controlling western Europe's destiny and reasserting its influence in world affairs.

The close cooperation among European states required by the Marshall Plan led to the creation of both the Organization of European Economic Cooperation (OEEC) and the Council of Europe in 1948. European federalists hoped that the Council of Europe would quickly evolve into a true European parliament with sovereign rights, but this did not happen. Britain, with its empire and its "special relationship" with the United States, consistently opposed giving any real political power—any sovereignty—to the council. Many old-fashioned continental nationalists and communists felt similarly. The Council of Europe became little more than a multinational debating society.

Frustrated in the direct political approach, European federalists turned toward economics as a way of working toward genuine unity. Two far-seeing French statesmen, the planner Jean Monnet and Foreign Minister Robert Schuman, courageously took the lead in 1950. The Schuman Plan called for a special international organization to control and integrate all European steel and coal production. West Germany, Italy, Belgium, the Netherlands, and Luxembourg accepted the French idea in 1952; the British would have none of it. The immediate economic goal—a single competitive market without national tariffs or quotas—was rapidly realized. The more far-reaching political goal was to bind the six-member nations so closely together economically that war among them would become unthinkable and virtually impossible. This brilliant strategy did much to reduce tragic old rivalries, particularly that of France and Germany.

The Coal and Steel Community encouraged further technical and economic cooperation among "the Six." In 1957 the same six nations signed the Treaty of Rome, which created the European Economic Community, generally known as the "Common Market" (Map 36.2). The first goal of the treaty was a gradual reduction of all tariffs among the Six in order to create a single market almost as

MAP 36.2 European Alliance Systems After the cold war divided Europe into two hostile military alliances, six Western European countries formed the Common Market in 1957. The Common Market grew later to include most of Western Europe. The Communist states organized their own economic association—COMECON.

Date is year independence was achieved.
Shading indicates former ruler.

Great Britain	Belgium
France	Portugal
Netherlands	United States
Italy	

JAPAN

NORTH KOREA 1948
SOUTH KOREA 1948
From Japan

PACIFIC OCEAN

PHILIPPINES 1946

BRUNEI 1984
From Great Britain

INDONESIA 1949

NORTH VIETNAM 1954
Unified 1974

SOUTH VIETNAM 1954

CAMBODIA 1954

MALAYSIA 1963

SINGAPORE 1965

LAOS 1949

MYANMAR (BURMA) 1947

PAKISTAN 1947, BANGLADESH 1973

SRI LANKA (CEYLON) 1948

INDIA 1947

PAKISTAN 1947

INDIAN OCEAN

MAURITIUS 1968
From Great Britain

UNITED ARAB EMIRATES 1971

QATAR 1971

BAHRAIN 1971

KUWAIT 1961

JORDAN 1946

P.D.R. OF YEMEN 1967
Unified with Yemen 1990

YEMEN

SOMALIA 1960

DJIBOUTI 1977

MADAGASCAR 1960

GREAT BRITAIN

NETHERLANDS

BELGIUM

FRANCE

ITALY

PORTUGAL

SPAIN

CYPRUS 1960

ISRAEL 1948

MALTA 1964
From Great Britain

LIBYA 1951

TUNISIA 1957

ALGERIA 1962

MOROCCO 1956

WESTERN SAHARA (MOROCCO) 1975
From Spain

MAURITANIA 1960

MALI 1960

NIGER 1960

CHAD 1960

SUDAN 1956

UGANDA 1962

KENYA 1963

CENTRAL AFRICAN REPUBLIC 1960

ZAIRE 1960

RWANDA 1962

BURUNDI 1962

TANZANIA 1964

MALAWI 1964

CAMEROON 1960

NIGERIA 1960

BENIN 1960

BURKINA FASO 1960

GHANA 1957

TOGO 1957

CÔTE D'IVOIRE 1960

GUINEA 1958

SENEGAL 1960

GAMBIA 1965

GUINEA-BISSAU 1974

SIERRA LEONE 1961

LIBERIA 1820s

EQUATORIAL GUINEA 1968 From Spain

GABON 1960

CONGO 1960

ANGOLA 1975

ZAMBIA 1964

ZIMBABWE 1980

MOZAMBIQUE 1974

NAMIBIA 1990

BOTSWANA 1966

SWAZILAND 1968

LESOTHO 1966

SOUTH AFRICA (Republic 1961)

ATLANTIC OCEAN

0	500	1000	1500 Km.
0	500	1000	1500 Mi.

large as that of the United States. Other goals included the free movement of capital and labor and common economic policies and institutions. The Common Market was a great success. Tariffs were rapidly reduced, and companies and regions specialized in what they did best.

The development of the Common Market fired imaginations and encouraged hopes of rapid progress toward political as well as economic union. In the 1960s, however, these hopes were frustrated by a resurgence of more traditional nationalism. Once again, France took the lead. Mired in a bitter colonial war in Algeria, the French turned in 1958 to General de Gaulle, who established the Fifth French Republic and ruled as its president until 1969. The last of the bigger-than-life wartime leaders, de Gaulle was at heart a romantic nationalist dedicated to reasserting France's greatness and glory. Resolving the Algerian conflict, he labored to re-create a powerful, truly independent France. Viewing the United States as the main threat to genuine French (and European) independence, he withdrew all French military forces from the "American-controlled" NATO command as France developed its own nuclear weapons. Within the Common Market, de Gaulle twice vetoed the application of the pro-American British, who were having second thoughts and wanted to join. More generally, he refused to permit the scheduled advent of majority rule within the Common Market, and he forced his partners to accept many of his views. Thus, throughout the 1960s the Common Market thrived economically but remained a union of sovereign states.

Decolonization

The postwar era saw the total collapse of European political empires. Between 1947 and 1962 almost every colonial territory gained formal independence: Europe's long overseas expansion was dramatically reversed. Future generations will almost certainly see this rolling back of Western expansion as one of world history's truly great turning points (Map 36.3).

The most basic cause of imperial collapse—what Europeans called "decolonization"—was the rising demand of Asian and African peoples for national self-determination, racial equality, and personal dignity. This demand spread from intellectuals to the masses in virtually every colonial territory after the First World War. As a result, colonial empires had already been shaken by 1939 and the way was prepared for the eventual triumph of independence movements (see pages 1238–1243). Yet decolonization also involved the imperial powers, and looking at the process from their perspective helps explain why independence came so quickly and why a kind of neocolonialism subsequently took its place in some areas.

European empires had been based on an enormous power differential between the rulers and the ruled, a difference that had declined almost to the vanishing point by 1945. Not only was western Europe poor and battered immediately after the war, but Japan had demonstrated for a second time that whites were not invincible. With its political power and moral authority in tatters, Europe could either submit to decolonization or enter into risky wars of reconquest.

Most Europeans regarded their empires very differently after 1945 than before 1914, or even before 1939. Empire had rested on self-confidence and self-righteousness; Europeans had believed their superiority to be not only technical and military but spiritual and moral as well. The horrors of the Second World War destroyed such complacent arrogance and gave opponents of imperialism much greater influence in Europe. After 1945 many Europeans were willing to let go of their colonies more or less voluntarily and to concentrate on rebuilding at home.

Indian independence played a key role in decolonization. When the Labour party came to power in Great Britain in 1945, it was determined to leave India. British socialists had always opposed imperialism, and the heavy cost of governing India had become an intolerable burden. Empire in India ended in 1947, and most Asian colonies achieved independence shortly thereafter. Although the French obstinately tried to re-establish colonial rule in Indochina, they were defeated in 1954, and two independent Vietnamese states

MAP 36.3 The New States in Africa and Asia Divided primarily along religious lines into two states, British India led the way to political independence in 1947. Most African territories achieved statehood by the mid-1960s, as European empires passed away, unlamented.

came into being. The French also fought a long, dirty war to keep Algeria French, but Algeria won its independence in 1962 (see Map 36.3).

In much of Africa south of the Sahara, decolonization proceeded much more smoothly. Beginning in 1957, Britain's colonies achieved independence with little or no bloodshed and then entered a very loose association with Britain as members of the British Commonwealth of Nations. In 1958 the clever de Gaulle offered the leaders of French black Africa the choice of a total break with France or immediate independence within a kind of French commonwealth. All but one of the new states chose association with France. African leaders did so because they identified with French culture and because they wanted aid from France. The French, buoyed up by economic growth and political recovery, were eager to help—provided their former colonies would accept close ties with France on French terms. As in the past, the French and their Common Market partners, who helped foot the bill, saw themselves as continuing their civilizing mission in black Africa. More importantly, they saw in Africa untapped markets for their industrial goods, raw materials for their factories, outlets for profitable investment, and good temporary jobs for their engineers and teachers. The British acted somewhat similarly, especially after they finally joined the Common Market in 1973.

As a result, western European countries actually managed to increase their economic and cultural ties with their former African colonies in the 1960s and 1970s. Above all, they used the lure of special trading privileges with the Common Market and heavy investment in French- and English-language education to enhance a powerful Western presence in the new African states. This situation led a variety of leaders and scholars to charge that western Europe (and the United States) had imposed a system of neocolonialism on the former colonies. According to this view, *neocolonialism* was a system designed to perpetuate Western economic domination and undermine the promise of political independence, thereby extending to Africa (and much of Asia) the neocolonial subordination that the United States had established in Latin America after the political revolutions of the early nineteenth century (see pages 992–1004). At the very least, enduring influence in black Africa testified to western Europe's resurgent economic and political power in international relations.

The Changing Class Structure

Rapid economic growth, combined with scientific and technological progress, went a long way toward creating a new society in Europe after the Second World War. European society became more mobile and more democratic. Old class barriers relaxed, and class distinctions became fuzzier.

Changes in the structure of the middle class were particularly influential in the general drift toward a less rigid class structure. In the nineteenth and early twentieth centuries, the model for the middle class had been the independent, self-employed individual who owned a business or practiced a liberal profession like law or medicine. Ownership of property—usually inherited property—and strong family ties had often been the keys to wealth and standing within the middle class. After 1945, this pattern declined drastically in western Europe. A new breed of managers and experts replaced traditional property owners as the leaders of the middle class. Ability to serve the needs of a big organization largely replaced inherited property and family connections in determining an individual's social position in the middle and upper middle class. At the same time, the middle class grew massively and became harder to define.

There were several reasons for these developments. Rapid industrial and technological expansion created in large corporations and government agencies a powerful demand for technologists and managers, of whom only a few at best could come from the old property-owning families. Moreover, the old propertied middle class lost control of many family-owned businesses. Even very wealthy families had to call on the general investing public for capital, and many small businesses (including family farms) simply passed out of existence as their former owners joined the ranks of salaried employees.

Top managers and ranking civil servants therefore represented the model for a new middle class of salaried specialists. Well paid and highly trained, often with backgrounds in engineering or accounting, these experts increasingly came from all social classes, even the working class. Pragmatic and realistic, they were primarily concerned with efficiency and practical solutions to concrete problems. Everywhere successful managers and technocrats passed on the opportunity for all-important advanced education to their children, but only in rare instances could they pass on the positions they had attained. Thus the new middle class, which was based largely on specialized skills and high levels of education, was more open, democratic, and insecure than the old propertied middle class.

The structure of the lower classes also became more flexible and open. There was a mass exodus from farms and the countryside, as one of the most traditional and least mobile groups in European society drastically declined. Meanwhile, because of rapid technological change, the industrial working class ceased to expand, and job opportunities for white-collar and service employees grew rapidly. Such employees bore a greater resemblance to the new middle class of salaried specialists than to industrial workers, who were also better educated and more specialized.

While the demands of growing economies and big bureaucracies were breaking down rigid class divisions, European governments were reducing class tensions with a series of social security reforms. Many of these reforms—like increased unemployment benefits and more extensive old-age pensions—simply strengthened social security measures first pioneered in Bismarck's Germany before the First World War. Other programs were new.

Britain's Labour government took the lead immediately after 1945 in establishing a comprehensive national health system; other European governments followed the British example. Depending on the system, patients either received completely free medical care or paid only a small portion of the total cost.

Most countries also introduced family allowances—direct government grants to parents to help them raise their children. These allowances helped many poor families make ends meet. Most European governments also gave maternity grants and built inexpensive public housing for low-income families and individuals. These and other social reforms provided a humane floor of well-being, below which few individuals could fall in the advanced countries of northern and western Europe. Reforms also promoted greater equality

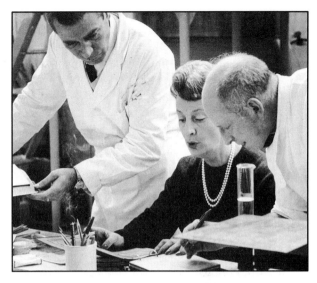

A Modern Manager Despite considerable discrimination, women were increasingly found in the expanding middle class of salaried experts after World War Two, working in business, science, and technology. *(Source: Niépce-Rapho/Photo Researchers)*

because they were expensive and were paid for in part by higher taxes on the rich.

The rising standard of living and the spread of standardized consumer goods also worked to level Western society. In the mid-nineteenth century, food and drink cost roughly two-thirds of the average family's income in western and northern Europe. By the mid-1960s, they took only about one-third to two-fifths of that family's income, and more money was available for consumer goods.

The European automobile industry expanded phenomenally. Automobile ownership was commonplace far down the social scale in the United States by the mid-1920s, but only the rich could generally afford cars in Europe before the Second World War. In 1948 there were only five million cars in western Europe. By 1957 the number of cars had increased to fifteen million, and by 1965 it had tripled again to forty-four million as car ownership was democratized and came within the range of better-paid workers.

Europeans took great pleasure in the products of the "gadget revolution" as well. Like Americans, Europeans filled their houses and apartments with washing machines, vacuum cleaners, refrigerators, dishwashers, radios, TVs, and stereos. The purchase of these and other consumer goods was greatly facilitated by installment purchasing, which allowed people to buy on credit. Before the Second World War, Europeans had rarely bought "on time." But with the expansion of social security safeguards, reducing the need to accumulate savings for hard times, ordinary people were increasingly willing to take on debt. This change had far-reaching consequences.

The most astonishing leisure-time development in the consumer society was the blossoming of mass travel and tourism. Before the Second World War, travel for pleasure and relaxation remained a rather aristocratic pastime. Most people had neither the time nor the money for it. But with month-long paid vacations required by law in most European countries, and widespread automobile ownership, beaches and ski resorts came within the reach of the middle class and many workers. By the late 1960s packaged tours with cheap group flights and bargain hotel accommodations had made even distant lands easily accessible. One-fifth of West Germany's population traveled abroad each year. A French company grew rich building imitation Tahitian paradises around the world. At Swedish nudist colonies on secluded West African beaches, office workers from Stockholm fleetingly worshiped the sun in the middle of the long northern winter. Truly, consumerism had come of age.

Political Upheaval in the Late 1960s

For twenty years after 1945, most Europeans were preoccupied with the possibilities of economic progress and consumerism. The more democratic

Student Protest in Paris These rock-throwing students in the Latin Quarter of Paris are trying to force education reforms or even to topple de Gaulle's government. Throughout May 1968 students clashed repeatedly with France's tough riot police in bloody street fighting. (*Source: Bruno Barbey/Magnum*)

class structure also helped to reduce social tension, and ideological conflict went out of style. In the late 1960s, however, sharp criticism and social conflicts re-emerged, heralding a new era of uncertainty and crisis.

Much of the criticism came from radical students. They rejected the materialism of their parents and claimed that the postwar society was repressive and badly flawed. With their counterparts in North America, they argued that the Vietnam War (see pages 1201–1202) proved that Western civilization was immoral and imperialistic.

The very rapid expansion of European higher education had created problems as well as opportunities for students. Classes were badly overcrowded, and competition for grades was intense. "Practical" areas of study were added to the curriculum, but they were added less quickly than many students wanted. Thus many students felt that they were not getting the kind of education they needed for jobs in the modern economy and that universities as well as society needed fundamental, even revolutionary reforms.

Tensions came to a head in the late 1960s and early 1970s. Following in the footsteps of their American counterparts, European university students rose to challenge their university administrations and even their governments. The most far-reaching of these revolts occurred in France in 1968. Students occupied university buildings, clashed violently with police, and appealed to France's industrial workers for help. A general strike then spread across France in May 1968, and it seemed certain that President de Gaulle's Fifth Republic would collapse. De Gaulle, however, stiffened, moving troops toward Paris and calling for new elections. Thoroughly frightened by the protest-turned-upheaval and fearful that a successful revolution could lead only to an eventual communist takeover, the masses of France voted for a return to law and order. de Gaulle and his party scored the biggest electoral victory in modern French history, and the mini-revolution collapsed. Yet the proud de Gaulle and the confident, though old-fashioned, nationalism that he represented had been cruelly mocked. In 1969, tired and discouraged, he resigned over a minor issue, and within a year he was dead.

The international student revolution of the late 1960s was announcing the end of an era. The social stability and material progress of the postwar years were giving away to conflict and crisis.

The Troubled Economy in Recent Times

The reappearance of economic crisis in the 1970s brought the most serious problems for the average person. The postwar international monetary system, which had proved instrumental in the unprecedented postwar boom, was based on the American dollar. Because foreign governments could exchange dollars for gold at $35 an ounce, the dollar was considered to be "as good as gold." The United States proceeded to make needed dollars readily available to the rest of the world—so readily that by early 1971 it had only $11 billion in gold left, and Europe had accumulated 50 billion American dollars as claims against that gold. Foreigners then panicked and raced to exchange their dollars for gold. President Richard Nixon was forced to stop the sale of American gold, and the value of the dollar declined against many European currencies. Fixed rates of exchange were abandoned, and great uncertainty replaced postwar predictability in international trade and finance.

Even more damaging was the dramatic reversal in the price and availability of energy. The great postwar boom was fueled by cheap oil, especially in western Europe. Cheap oil from the Middle East permitted energy-intensive industries—automobiles, chemicals, and electric power—to expand rapidly and lead other sectors of the economy forward. By 1971, the Arab-led Organization of Petroleum Exporting Countries (OPEC) had watched the price of crude oil decline consistently compared with the price of manufactured goods. OPEC decided to reverse that trend by presenting a united front against the oil companies. The stage was set for a revolution in energy prices during the fourth Arab-Israeli war in October 1973 (see page 1232). In the course of a year crude oil prices quadrupled. It was widely realized that the rapid price rise was economically destructive, but the world's big powers did nothing. The Soviet Union was a great oil exporter and benefited directly. A cautious western Europe looked to the United States for leadership, but the United States was immobilized, its attention absorbed by the Watergate crisis in politics (see page 1202). Without the benefit of organization, therefore, governments, companies, and individuals had no other choice than to deal piecemeal with the so-called oil shock—a "shock" that really turned out to be an earthquake.

Saudi Riches   Saudi Arabia has enormous oil reserves, making it one of the most influential members of the Organization of Petroleum Exporting Countries and giving it one of the world's highest per capita incomes. Oil has also made rich men of Prince Fahd and King Khalid, shown here. *(Source: Robert Azzi/Woodfin Camp & Associates)*

Coming on the heels of upheaval in the international monetary system, the revolution in energy prices plunged the world into its worst economic decline since the 1930s. The energy-intensive industries that had driven the economy up in the 1950s and 1960s now dragged it down. Unemployment rose. Productivity and living standards declined.

By 1976 a modest recovery was in progress, but when Iranian oil production collapsed during Iran's fundamentalist Islamic revolution (see page 1232), the price of crude oil doubled again in 1979 and the world economy succumbed to its second oil shock. Unemployment and inflation rose dramatically before another uneven recovery began in 1982. In the summer of 1985, the unemployment rate in western Europe rose to its highest levels since the Great Depression. Fully nineteen million people were unemployed. Although unemployment declined in the late 1980s, large numbers of people remained out of work.

Anxious observers, recalling the disastrous consequences of the Great Depression, worried that democratic government and steps toward European unity would be destroyed by social conflicts and economic nationalism. But, on the whole, the welfare system fashioned in the postwar era prevented mass suffering and social unrest. Extended benefits for the unemployed, pensions for the aged, free medical care for the needy, surplus food and special allowances for parents with children—all these and a host of lesser supports did their part. The socially responsive national state undoubtedly contributed to the preservation of political stability and democracy in the face of economic disorder that might have been the cause of revolution and dictatorship in earlier times.

Nor did the Common Market disintegrate in the face of severe economic dislocation. Indeed, it continued to exert a powerful attraction on nonmembers. In 1973, Denmark and Iceland, in addition to Britain, finally joined. In 1977, Greece, Portugal, and Spain applied for membership. The negotiations were long and difficult, especially for Spain. Spain was a big low-cost producer of wine, olive oil, and fresh fruit, which French and Italian farmers feared would come flooding into Common Market countries and drive them out of business. In the end, subsidies to injured farmers and special transition rules for agricultural products achieved a characteristic Common Market compromise. Greece joined in 1981, Portugal and Spain in 1986.

After de Gaulle's death, the nations of the Common Market cooperated more closely in many international undertakings and negotiations. The Common Market decided in 1977, for example, to go ahead with plans for a nuclear breeder reactor to produce electric power, and it tried to develop a common policy on peace in the Middle East, terrorism, and economic negotiations with Third World countries. The movement toward European unity stayed alive. The Common Market countries eventually set 1992 as the year for the attainment of total economic and social integration, and new projects and discussions on the prospects of greater political unity filled the media as the 1990s opened. Some Europeans even believed that the transformation of eastern Europe (see pages 1196–1200) opened the way to genuine unity in the not-so-distant future. This admittedly optimistic vision suggested that western Europe had weathered the storms of the 1970s and 1980s, which contrasted so sharply with the clear sailing of the 1950s and 1960s.

SOVIET EASTERN EUROPE

While western Europe surged ahead economically after the Second World War and regained political independence as American influence gradually waned, eastern Europe followed a different path. The Soviet Union first tightened its grip on the "liberated" nations of eastern Europe under Stalin and then refused to let go. Thus postwar economic recovery in eastern Europe proceeded along Soviet lines, and political and social developments were strongly influenced by changes in the Soviet Union. These changes went forward at a slow and uneven pace, and they appeared to almost halt after Leonid Brezhnev came to power and crushed a socialist reform movement in Czechoslovakia in 1968.

Yet beneath the apparent stagnation of the Brezhnev years Soviet society experienced a major transformation. This transformation encouraged new political thinking in the Soviet Union and in turn enabled the long-frustrated reform movement to triumph spectacularly in eastern Europe in the unexpected revolution of 1989. Thus one must look primarily at the Soviet Union in order to understand the history of eastern European peoples since 1945.

Stalin's Last Years

The unwillingness of the United States to accept Stalin's control of territories occupied by the triumphant Red Army was at least partly responsible for the outbreak and institutionalization of the cold war. Americans, however, were not the only ones who felt betrayed by Stalin's postwar actions.

The Great Patriotic War of the Fatherland had fostered Russian nationalism and a relaxation of totalitarian terror. It also produced a rare but real unity between Soviet rulers and most Russian people. When an American correspondent asked a distinguished sixty-year-old Jewish scientist, who had decided to leave Russia for Israel in 1972, what had been the best period in Russian history, he received a startling answer: the Second World War. The scientist explained: "At that time we all felt closer to our government than at any other time in our lives. It was not their country then, but our country. . . . It was not their war, but our war."[4] Having made such a heroic war effort, the vast majority of the Soviet people hoped in 1945 that a grateful party and government would grant greater freedom and democracy. Such hopes were soon crushed.

Even before the war ended, Stalin was moving his country back toward rigid dictatorship. As early as 1944, the leading members of the Communist party were being given a new motivating slogan: "The war on Fascism ends, the war on capitalism begins."[5] By early 1946, Stalin was publicly singing the old tune that war was inevitable as long as capitalism existed. Stalin's new foreign foe in the West provided an excuse for re-establishing totalitarian measures, for the totalitarian state cannot live without enemies.

One of Stalin's first postwar goals was to repress the millions of Soviet citizens who were living outside Soviet borders when the war ended. Many had been captured by the Nazis; others were ordinary civilians who had been living abroad. Many were opposed to Stalin; some had fought for the Germans. Determined to hush up the fact that large numbers of Soviet citizens hated his regime so much that they had willingly supported the Germans and refused to go home, Stalin demanded that all these "traitors" be given back to him. At Yalta, Roosevelt and Churchill agreed, and roughly 2 million people were delivered to Stalin against their will. Most were immediately arrested and sent to forced-labor camps, where about 50 percent perished. The revival of many forced-labor camps, which had accounted for roughly one-sixth of all new construction in the Soviet Union before the war, was further stimulated by large-scale purges of many people who had never left the Soviet Union, particularly in 1945 and 1946.

Culture and art were also purged. Violent campaigns led by Stalin's trusted henchman Andrei Zhdanov reimposed rigid anti-Western ideological conformity. Zhdanov denounced many artists, including the composers Sergei Prokofiev and Dimitri Shostakovich and the outstanding film director Sergei Eisenstein. The great poet Anna Akhmatova was condemned as "a harlot and nun who mixes harlotry and prayer" and, like many others, driven out of the writers' union. This expulsion practically ensured that her work would not be published. In 1949 Stalin launched a savage verbal attack on Soviet Jews, accusing them of being pro-Western and antisocialist.

In the political realm, Stalin reasserted the Communist party's complete control of the government and his absolute mastery of the party. Five-year plans were reintroduced to cope with the enormous task of economic reconstruction. Once again, heavy and military industry were given top priority, and consumer goods, housing, and still-collectivized agriculture were neglected. Everyday life was very hard: in 1952 the wages of ordinary people still bought 25 to 40 percent less than in 1928. In short, it was the 1930s all over again in

the Soviet Union, although police terror was less intense.

Stalin's prime postwar innovation was to export the Stalinist system to the countries of eastern Europe. The Communist parties of eastern Europe had established one-party states by 1948, thanks to the help of the Red Army and the Russian secret police. Rigid ideological indoctrination, attacks on religion, and a lack of civil liberties were soon facts of life. Industry was nationalized, and the middle class was stripped of its possessions. Economic life was then faithfully recast in the Stalinist mold. Forced industrialization, with five-year plans and a stress on heavy industry, lurched forward without regard for human costs. For the sake of ideological uniformity, agriculture had to be collectivized; this process went much faster in Bulgaria and Czechoslovakia than in Hungary and Poland.

Only Josip Tito (1892–1980), the popular resistance leader and Communist chief of Yugoslavia, was able to resist Soviet domination successfully. Tito openly broke with Stalin in 1948, and since there was no Russian army in Yugoslavia, he got away with it. Tito's successful proclamation of Communist independence led the infuriated and humiliated Stalin to purge the Communist parties of eastern Europe. Popular Communist leaders who, like Tito, had led the resistance against Germany, were made to star in reruns of the great show trials of the 1930s (see page 1143). Thus did history repeat itself as Stalin sought to create absolutely obedient instruments of domination in eastern Europe.

Reform and De-Stalinization

In 1953 the aging Stalin finally died, and the totalitarian system that he had built began to change. Even as Stalin's heirs struggled for power, they realized that reforms were necessary. There was widespread fear and hatred of Stalin's political terrorism, and even Stalin's secret-police chief, Lavrenti Beria, publicly favored relaxing controls in an unsuccessful attempt to seize power. Beria was arrested and shot, but the power of the secret police was curbed and many of the forced-labor camps were gradually closed. Change was also necessary for economic reasons. Agriculture was in bad shape, and shortages of consumer goods were

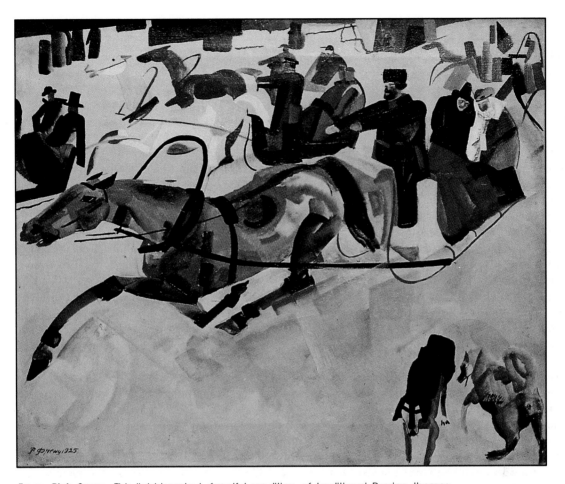

Frenz: Pink Snow This light-hearted, fanciful rendition of traditional Russian themes hardly seems a threat to the Stalinist state. Yet it failed to conform to the official style of socialist realism and thus was suppressed with a host of other works during Zhdanov's brutal cultural purge. *(Source: Sovfoto)*

discouraging hard work and initiative. Moreover, Stalin's belligerent foreign policy had led directly to a strong Western alliance, which isolated and contained the Soviet Union.

On the question of just how much change should be permitted, the Communist leadership was badly split. Conservatives wanted to make as few changes as possible. Reformers, who were led by Nikita Khrushchev, argued for major innovations. Khrushchev (1894–1971), who had joined the party as an uneducated coal miner in 1918 at twenty-four and had risen steadily to a high-level position in the 1930s, was emerging as the new ruler by 1955.

To strengthen his position and that of his fellow reformers within the party, Khrushchev launched an all-out attack on Stalin and his crimes at a closed session of the Twentieth Party Congress in 1956. In gory detail he described to the startled Communist delegates how Stalin had tortured and murdered thousands of loyal Communists, how he had trusted Hitler completely and bungled the country's defense, and how he had "supported the glorification of his own person with all conceivable methods." Khrushchev's "secret speech" was read to Communist party meetings throughout the country and it strengthened the reform movement.

The liberalization—or "de-Stalinization," as it was called in the West—of the Soviet Union was genuine. The Communist party jealously maintained its monopoly on political power, but

Khrushchev shook up the party and brought in new members. The economy was made more responsive to the needs of the people as some resources were shifted from heavy industry and the military toward consumer goods and agriculture. Stalinist controls over workers were relaxed. The Soviet Union's very low standard of living finally began to improve and continued to rise throughout the booming 1960s. By 1970 Soviet citizens were able to buy twice as much food, three times as much clothing, and twelve times as many appliances as in 1950.

De-Stalinization created great ferment among writers and intellectuals who hungered for cultural freedom. The poet Boris Pasternak (1890–1960) finished his great novel *Doctor Zhivago* in 1956. Published in the West but not in Russia, *Doctor Zhivago* is both a literary masterpiece and a powerful challenge to communism. It tells the story of a prerevolutionary intellectual who rejects the violence and brutality of the revolution of 1917 and the Stalinist years. Even as he is destroyed, he triumphs because of his humanity and Christian spirit. Pasternak was denounced—but he was not shot. Other talented writers followed Pasternak's lead, and courageous editors let the sparks fly.

The writer Alexander Solzhenitsyn (b. 1918) created a sensation when his *One Day in the Life of Ivan Denisovich* was published in the Soviet Union in 1962. Solzhenitsyn's novel portrays in grim detail life in a Stalinist concentration camp—a life to which Solzhenitsyn himself had been unjustly condemned—and is a damning indictment of the Stalinist past.

Khrushchev also de-Stalinized Soviet foreign policy. "Peaceful coexistence" with capitalism was possible, he argued, and great wars were not inevitable. Khrushchev made positive concessions, agreeing in 1955 to real independence for a neutral Austria after ten long years of Allied occupation. Thus there was considerable relaxation of cold war tensions between 1955 and 1957. At the same time, Khrushchev began wooing the new nations of Asia and Africa—even if they were not communist—with promises and aid.

De-Stalinization stimulated rebelliousness in the eastern European satellites. Having suffered in silence under Stalin, Communist reformers and the masses were quickly emboldened to seek much greater liberty and national independence. Poland took the lead in March 1956: riots there resulted

in the release of more than nine thousand political prisoners, including the previously purged leader Wladyslaw Gomulka. Taking charge of the government, Gomulka skillfully managed to win greater autonomy for Poland while calming anti-Soviet feeling.

Hungary experienced a real and tragic revolution. Led by students and workers—the classic urban revolutionaries—the people of Budapest installed a liberal Communist reformer as their new chief in October 1956. Soviet troops were forced to leave the country. The new government promised free elections and renounced Hungary's military alliance with Moscow. As in 1849, the Russian leaders answered by invading Hungary with a large army and crushing, once again, a national, democratic revolution.

Fighting was bitter until the end, for the Hungarians hoped that the United States would fulfill its earlier propaganda promises and come to their aid. When this did not occur because of American unwillingness to risk a general war, most people in eastern Europe concluded that their only hope was to strive for small domestic gains while following Russia obediently in foreign affairs. This cautious approach produced some results, and east Europeans could hope for still greater freedom in the future.

Brezhnev and Stagnation

By late 1962, opposition in party circles to Khrushchev's policies was strong, and within two years Khrushchev fell in a bloodless palace revolution. Under Leonid Brezhnev (1906–1982), the Soviet Union began a period of stagnation and limited "re-Stalinization." The basic reason for this development was that Khrushchev's Communist colleagues saw de-Stalinization as a dangerous, two-sided threat. How could Khrushchev denounce the dead dictator without eventually denouncing and perhaps even arresting his still-powerful henchmen? In a heated secret debate in 1957, when the conservatives had tried without success to depose the menacing reformer, Khrushchev had pointed at two of Stalin's most devoted followers, Molotov and Kaganovich, and exclaimed: "Your hands are stained with the blood of our party leaders and of innumerable innocent Bolsheviks!" "So are yours!" Molotov and Kaganovich shouted back at him. "Yes, so are mine," Khrushchev replied. "I admit this. But during the purges I was merely carrying out your order. . . . I was not responsible. You were."[6] Moreover, the widening campaign of de-Stalinization posed a clear threat to the dictatorial authority of the party. It was producing growing, perhaps uncontrollable, criticism of the whole communist system. The party had to tighten up while there was still time. It was clear that Khrushchev had to go.

Another reason for conservative opposition was that Khrushchev's policy toward the West was erratic and ultimately unsuccessful. In 1958 he ordered the Western allies to evacuate West Berlin within six months. In response, the allies reaffirmed their unity, and Khrushchev backed down. Then in 1961, as relations with communist China deteriorated dramatically, Khrushchev ordered the East Germans to build a wall between East and West Berlin, thereby sealing off West Berlin in clear violation of existing access agree-ments between the Great Powers. The recently elected U.S. president, John F. Kennedy, acqui-esced to the construction of the Berlin Wall. Emboldened and seeing a chance to change the balance of military power decisively, Khrushchev ordered missiles with nuclear warheads installed in Fidel Castro's communist Cuba in 1962. President Kennedy countered with a naval blockade of Cuba. After a tense diplomatic crisis, Khrushchev agreed to remove the Soviet missiles in return for American pledges not to disturb Castro's regime. Khrushchev looked like a bumbling buffoon; his influence, already slipping, declined rapidly after the Cuban fiasco.

After Brezhnev and his supporters took over in 1964, they started talking quietly of Stalin's "good points" and ignoring his crimes. This informed Soviet citizens that further liberalization could not be expected at home. Russian leaders, determined never to suffer Khrushchev's humiliation in the face of American nuclear superiority,

The End of Reform In August 1968 Soviet tanks rumbled into Prague to extinguish Czechoslovakian efforts to build a humane socialism. Here people watch the massive invasion from the sidewalks, knowing full well the suicidal danger of armed resistance. *(Source: Joseph Koudelka PP/Magnum)*

also launched a massive arms buildup. Yet Brezhnev and company proceeded cautiously in the mid-1960s.

In the wake of Khrushchev's reforms, the 1960s brought modest liberalization and more consumer goods to eastern Europe, as well as somewhat greater national autonomy, especially in Poland and Romania. In January 1968, the reform elements in the Czechoslovak Communist party gained a majority and voted out the long-time Stalinist leader in favor of Alexander Dubček (b. 1921), whose new government launched dramatic reforms.

Educated in Moscow, Dubček was a dedicated Communist. But he and his allies believed that they could reconcile genuine socialism with personal freedom and internal party democracy. Thus local decision making by trade unions, managers, and consumers replaced rigid bureaucratic planning. Censorship was relaxed, and the reform program proved enormously popular.

Although Dubček remembered the lesson of the Hungarian revolution and constantly proclaimed his loyalty to the Warsaw Pact, the determination of the Czech reformers to build what they called "socialism with a human face" created an acute political crisis in eastern Europe. Frightened hard-line Communists, especially in Poland and East Germany, knew full well that they lacked popular support. Moreover, the Soviet Union feared that a liberalized Czechoslovakia would eventually be drawn to neutralism or even to the democratic West. Thus the East bloc countries launched a concerted campaign of intimidation against the Czech leaders, and in August 1968, 500,000 Russian and allied eastern European troops suddenly occupied Czechoslovakia. The Czechs made no attempt to resist militarily, and the arrested Czech leaders were flown to Moscow, where they surrendered to Soviet demands. Gradually but inexorably, the reform program was abandoned and its supporters were removed from office. Thus the Czechoslovak experiment in humanizing communism was aborted.

Shortly after the invasion of Czechoslovakia, Brezhnev declared the so-called Brezhnev Doctrine, according to which the Soviet Union and its allies had the right to intervene in any socialist country whenever they saw the need. The occupation of Czechoslovakia and the ensuing Brezhnev Doctrine raised a storm of protest but did not seriously alter ongoing Western efforts to achieve better relations with the East bloc countries. The reason was simple. The West considered Czechoslovakia to be part of the Soviet sphere of influence, and it believed that change in eastern Europe could only continue to follow developments in the Soviet Union.

The 1968 invasion of Czechoslovakia was the crucial event of the Brezhnev era, which really lasted beyond the aging leader's death in 1982 until the emergence in 1985 of Mikhail Gorbachev. The invasion demonstrated unmistakably the intense conservatism of the Soviet Union's predominately Russian leaders and the determination of the ruling elite to maintain the status quo in the Soviet bloc. That determination resulted in further re-Stalinization of the Soviet Union, though with collective rather than personal dictatorship and without uncontrolled terror. Thus 1968, like 1848, was a fatal year in European history. It brought revolution and repression in both Czechoslovakia and France, and it marked the end of an era for the entire continent.

The compromise inherent in limited re-Stalinization seemed to suit the Soviet leaders and a majority of the Soviet people, and the Soviet Union appeared quite stable in the 1970s and early 1980s. A rising standard of living for ordinary people contributed to stability, although the economic difficulties of the 1970s markedly slowed the rate of improvement, and long lines and innumerable shortages persisted. The enduring differences between the life of the elite and the life of ordinary people also reinforced the system. In order to gain access to special, well-stocked stores, attend special schools, and travel abroad, ambitious individuals still had tremendous incentive to do as the state wished.

Another source of stability was that ordinary citizens in the Russian heartland remained more intensely nationalistic than almost any other people in the world. Party leaders successfully identified themselves with this patriotism, stressing their role in saving the motherland during the Second World War and protecting it now from foreign foes, including eastern European "counter-revolutionaries." Moreover, the politically dominant Great Russians, who are concentrated in central Russia and in Siberia—formally designated the Russian Federation—and who held through the Communist party the commanding leadership

MAP 36.4 Soviet Peoples Encompassing one-sixth of the earth's land mass, the enormous Soviet Union contained many ethnic groups and fifteen separate republics. The Great Russians dominated the Communist party and the entire country, but they represented less than half of the total population. As Mikhail Gorbachev's reforms undermined the pervasive control of the Communist party, nationalists in the various republics called increasingly for genuine autonomy and even independence.

positions in the non-Russian republics, constitute only half of the total Soviet population. The Great Russian leaders generally feared that greater freedom and open political competition might result in demands for autonomy and even independence, not only by eastern European nationalities but by non-Russian nationalities within the Soviet Union itself (Map 36.4). Thus Western-style liberalism and democracy appeared as alien and divisive political philosophies that would undermine Russia's power and achievements.

The strength of the government was expressed in the re-Stalinization of culture and art. Free ex-

pression and open protest disappeared. Modest acts of open nonconformity and protest were severely punished—but with sophisticated, cunning methods. Most frequently, dissidents were blacklisted and thus rendered unable to find a decent job, for the government was the only employer. This fate was enough to keep most in line. The more determined but unrenowned protesters were quietly imprisoned in jails or mental institutions. Celebrated nonconformists such as Solzhenitsyn were permanently expelled from the country. Thus the worst aspects of Stalin's totalitarianism were eliminated, but a self-perpetuating Communist elite maintained its monopoly on the instruments of power.

Yet beneath the immobility of political life in the Brezhnev era, the Soviet Union experienced profound changes. As a perceptive British journalist put it in 1986, "The country went through a

Newly Elected President Mikhail Gorbachev vowed in his acceptance speech before the Supreme Soviet, the U.S.S.R.'s parliament, to assume "all responsibility" for the success or failure of perestroika. Previous parliaments were no more than tools of the Communist party, but this one has actively debated and frequently opposed government programs. *(Source: Vlastimir Shone/ Gamma-Liaison)*

social revolution while Brezhnev slept."[7] Three aspects of this revolution, which was appreciated by few Western observers at the time, were particularly significant.

First, the growth of the urban population, which had raced forward at breakneck speed in the Stalin years, continued rapidly in the 1960s and 1970s. In 1985 two-thirds of all Soviet citizens lived in cities, and one-fourth lived in big cities (see Map 36.4). Of great significance, this expanding urban population lost its old peasant ways. As a result, it acquired more education, better job skills, and greater sophistication.

Second, the number of highly trained scientists, managers, and specialists expanded prodigiously, jumping fourfold between 1960 and 1985. Thus the class of well-educated, pragmatic, and self-confident experts, which played such an important role in restructuring industrial societies after the Second World War (see pages 1182–1183), developed rapidly in the Soviet Union.

Finally, education and freedom for experts in their special areas helped foster the growth of Soviet public opinion. Educated people read, discussed, and formed definite ideas about social questions. Developing definite ideas on such things as environmental pollution or urban transportation, educated urban people increasingly saw themselves as worthy of having a voice in society's decisions, even its political decisions. This, too, was part of the quiet transformation that set the stage for the dramatic reforms of the Gorbachev era.

The Gorbachev Era

Fundamental change in Russian history has often come in short, intensive spurts, which contrast vividly with long periods of immobility. Four of these spurts were the ambitious "Westernization" of Peter the Great in the early eighteenth century (see pages 637–639), the great reforms connected with the freeing of the serfs in the mid-nineteenth century (pages 942–943), the Russian Revolution of 1917 (pages 1054–1060), and Stalin's wrenching "revolution from above" in the 1930s (pages 1138–1142). To this select list of decisive transformations must be added the era of fundamental reforms launched by Mikhail Gorbachev in 1985. Gorbachev's reforms have already had a profound impact, and they have permitted democracy and national self-determination to triumph spectacularly in the old satellite empire.

The Soviet Union's Communist elite seemed secure in the early 1980s, as far as any challenge from below was concerned. The long-established system of administrative controls continued to stretch downward from the central ministries and state committees to provincial cities and from there to factories, neighborhoods, and villages. At each level of this massive state bureaucracy, the overlapping hierarchy of the Communist party, with its 17.5 million members, continued to watch over all decisions and manipulate every aspect of national life. Organized opposition was impossible, and average people simply left politics to the bosses.

The massive state and party bureaucracy was a mixed blessing. It safeguarded the elite, but it promoted apathy in the masses. Discouraging personal initiative and economic efficiency, it was ill suited to secure the effective cooperation of the rapidly growing class of well-educated urban experts. Therefore, when the ailing Brezhnev finally died in 1982, his successor introduced modest reforms to improve economic performance and to combat worker absenteeism and high-level corruption. Little came of these efforts, but they combined with a worsening economic situation to set the stage for the emergence in 1985 of Mikhail Gorbachev (b. 1931), the most vigorous Soviet leader since Stalin.

Gorbachev was smart, charming, and tough. As long-time Soviet foreign minister Andrei Gromyko reportedly said, "This man has a nice smile, but he has got iron teeth."[8] In his first year in office, Gorbachev attacked corruption and incompetence in the upper reaches of the bureaucracy, and he consolidated his power by packing the top level of the party with his supporters. He attacked alcoholism and drunkenness, which were deadly scourges of Soviet society. More basically, he elaborated a series of reform policies designed to revive and even remake the vast Soviet Union.

The first set of reform policies was designed to transform and restructure the economy, which was falling ever further behind the economy of the West and failing to provide for the very real needs of the Soviet population. To accomplish this economic restructuring—this *perestroika*—Gorbachev and his supporters permitted freer prices, more independence for state enterprises, and the setting up of profit-seeking private cooperatives to pro-

vide personal services. These reforms initially produced some improvements, but shortages then grew as the economy stalled at an intermediate point between central planning and free-market mechanisms. By 1990 Gorbachev's timid economic initiatives had met with very little success, eroding his support and that of the Communist party.

Gorbachev's bold and far-reaching campaign "to tell it like it is" was much more successful. Very popular in a country where censorship, dull uniformity, and outright lies had long characterized public discourse, the newfound openness—the *glasnost*—of the government and the media marked an astonishing break with the past. A disaster like the Chernobyl nuclear-reactor accident, which devastated part of the Ukraine and showered Europe with radioactive fallout, was investigated and reported with honesty and painstaking thoroughness. The works of long-banned and vilified Russian émigré writers sold millions of copies in new editions, and denunciations of Stalin and his terror became standard fare in plays and movies. Openness in government pronouncements led rather quickly to something approaching free speech and free expression, a veritable cultural revolution.

Democratization was the third element of Gorbachev's reform. Beginning as an attack on corruption in the Communist party and as an attempt to bring the class of educated experts into the decision-making process, it led to the first free elections in the Soviet Union since 1917. Gorbachev and the party remained in control, but a minority of critical independents were elected in April 1989 to a revitalized Congress of People's Deputies. Many top-ranking Communists who ran unopposed saw themselves defeated as a majority of angry voters struck their names from the ballot. Millions of Soviets then watched the new congress for hours on television as Gorbachev and his ministers saw their proposals debated and even rejected.

Democratization also encouraged demands for greater autonomy by non-Russian minorities—demands that certainly went beyond what Gorbachev had envisaged. In April 1989 troops with sharpened shovels charged into a rally of Georgian separatists in Tbilisi and left twenty dead. But whereas China's Communist leaders brutally massacred similar prodemocracy demonstrators in Beijing (Peking) in June 1989 and reimposed rigid authoritarian rule, Gorbachev drew back from

MAP 36.5 Democratic Movements in Eastern Europe, 1989 With Gorbachev's repudiation of the Brezhnev Doctrine, the desire for freedom and democracy spread throughout eastern Europe. Countries that had been satellites in the orbit of the Soviet Union began to set themselves free to establish their own place in the universe of free nations.

repression. Thus nationalist demands continued to grow in the non-Russian Soviet republics, an unexpected consequence of democratization.

Finally, the Soviet leader brought "new political thinking" to the field of foreign affairs—and he acted on it. He withdrew Soviet troops from Afghanistan (see page 1203), encouraged reform movements in Poland and Hungary, and sought to reduce East-West tensions. Of enormous historical importance, Gorbachev pledged to respect the political choices of the peoples of eastern Europe, and he thereby repudiated the Brezhnev Doctrine, which had proclaimed the right of the Soviet Union and its allies to intervene at will in eastern Europe. By 1989 it seemed that if Gorbachev held to his word, the tragic Soviet occupation of eastern Europe might wither away, taking the long cold war with it.

The Revolutions of 1989

Instead, history accelerated, and 1989 brought a series of largely peaceful revolutions throughout eastern Europe (Map 36.5). These revolutions overturned existing communist regimes and led to the formation of provisional governments dedicated to democratic elections, human rights, and national rejuvenation. The face of eastern Europe changed dramatically, almost overnight.

Solidarity and the Polish people led the way. Poland was an unruly satellite from the beginning, and Stalin said that introducing communism to Poland was like putting a saddle on a cow. Efforts to saddle the cow—really a spirited stallion—had led to widespread riots in 1956. As a result, the Polish Communists dropped efforts to impose Soviet-style collectivization on the peasants and to break the Roman Catholic church. With an independent agriculture and a vigorous church, the Communists failed to monopolize society.

They also failed to manage the economy effectively, and bureaucratic incompetence coupled with worldwide recession put the economy into a nose dive by the mid-1970s. Then the "Polish miracle" occurred: Cardinal Karol Wojtyla, archbishop of Cracow, was elected pope and in June 1979 he returned to his native land to preach the love of Christ and country and the "inalienable rights of man." Pope John Paul II electrified the Polish nation, and the economic crisis became a spiritual crisis as well.

In August 1980, scattered strikes snowballed into a working-class revolt. Led by a feisty electrician and devout Catholic named Lech Walesa, the workers organized a free and democratic trade union that they called "Solidarity." Solidarity became the union of the nation, and cultural and intellectual freedom blossomed in Poland. But Solidarity did not try to take power in 1981. History, the Brezhnev Doctrine, and virulent attacks from communist neighbors all seemed to guarantee the intervention of the Red Army and a terrible blood bath if Solidarity directly challenged the Communist monopoly of political power with a general strike. Then, as economic hardship increased, grassroots radicalism and frustration mounted: a hunger-march banner proclaimed that "A hungry nation can eat its rulers."[9] With an eye on Western public opinion, the Polish Communist leadership shrewdly denounced Solidarity for promoting economic collapse and provoking Soviet invasion. The

The Rise of Solidarity   This photograph shows the determination and mass action that allowed Polish workers to triumph in August 1980. Backed by a crowd of enthusiastic supporters, leader Lech Walesa announces the historic Gdansk Agreement to striking workers at the main gate of the Lenin Shipyards. *(Source: Jean Gaumy/Magnum)*

Communist leader General Wojciech Jaruzelski suddenly proclaimed martial law in December 1981, arresting Solidarity's leaders and "saving" the nation.

Outlawed and driven underground, Solidarity fought successfully to maintain its organization and to voice the aspirations of the Polish masses. Thus popular support for outlawed Solidarity remained strong and deep under martial law in the 1980s, preparing the way for its resurgence at the end of the decade.

By 1988 widespread labor unrest, raging inflation, and the outlawed Solidarity's refusal to cooperate with the military government had brought Poland to the brink of economic collapse. Profiting from Gorbachev's tolerant attitude and skillfully mobilizing its forces, Solidarity pressured Poland's frustrated Communist leaders into another round of negotiations that might work out a sharing of power to resolve the political stalemate and the economic depression. The subsequent agreement legalized Solidarity again and declared that a large minority of representatives to the Polish parliament would be chosen by free elections in June 1989. The Communist party was still guaranteed a majority, but Solidarity won every single contested seat in an overwhelming victory. On July 4, 1989, Solidarity members jubilantly entered the 460-member Polish parliament, the first freely elected opposition in a communist country. A month later the editor of Solidarity's weekly newspaper was sworn in as the first noncommunist leader in eastern Europe since Stalin had used Soviet armies to impose his system there after the Second World War.

Hungary followed Poland. Hungary's Communist boss, János Kádár, had permitted liberalization of the rigid planned economy after the 1956 upris-

Celebrating on the Berlin Wall In a year filled with powerful images, none was more dramatic or more hopeful than the opening of the Berlin Wall, symbol of the harsh division between Eastern and Western Europe. *(Source: Tom Haley/SIPA-PRESS)*

ing, in exchange for political obedience and continued Communist control. In May 1988, in an effort to hang on to power by granting modest political concessions, the party replaced Kádár with a reform Communist. But growing popular resistance rejected piecemeal progress, forcing the Communist party to renounce one-party rule and schedule free elections for early 1990. Welcoming Western investment and moving rapidly toward multiparty democracy, Hungarians gleefully tore down the barbed-wire "iron curtain" that separated Hungary and Austria and opened their border to East German refugees.

As thousands of dissatisfied East Germans began pouring into Hungary, before going on to immediate resettlement in thriving West Germany, growing economic dislocation and huge candlelight demonstrations brought revolution in East Berlin. The Berlin Wall was opened, and people danced for joy atop that grim symbol of the prison state. East Germany's aging Communist leaders were swept aside and in some cases arrested. General elections were scheduled for March 1990. Subsequently, a conservative-liberal "Alliance for Germany," which was closely tied to West German Chancellor Helmut Kohl's Christian Democrats, defeated the East German Social Democrats (the Communists ignominiously fell to minor-party status). The Alliance for Germany quickly negotiated an economic union on favorable terms with Chancellor Kohl, and in July 1990 a historic agreement between Kohl and Gorbachev removed the last obstacles to German unification, which came in October 1990. Communism also died in Czechoslovakia in December 1989, in an almost good-humored ousting of Communist bosses in ten short days.

Only in Romania was revolution violent and bloody. There the iron-fisted Communist dictator, Nicolae Ceauşescu, had long combined Stalinist brutality with stubborn independence from Moscow. Faced with mass protests, Ceauşescu, alone among eastern European bosses, ordered his ruthless security forces to slaughter thousands, thereby sparking a classic armed uprising. After Ceauşescu's forces were defeated, the tyrant and his wife were captured and executed by a military court. A coalition government emerged from the fighting, although the legacy of Ceauşescu's oppression left a troubled country with an uncertain political future.

In Bucharest's Palace Square, cranes remove the statue of Lenin that dominated the square during the dictatorship of Nicolae Ceauşescu. Despite Ceauşescu's vow that democratic reform would come to Romania "when pears grow on poplar trees," citizens joined in a mass revolt to topple the despot and his oppressive regime. *(Source: BI/Gamma-Liaison)*

As the 1990s began, the revolutionary changes that Gorbachev had permitted, and even encouraged, had triumphed in all but two eastern European states: tiny Albania and the vast Soviet Union itself. The great question then became whether the Soviet Union would follow its former satellites, and whether reform communism would give way there to a popular anticommunist revolution. Near civil war between Armenians and Azerbaijanis in the Caucasus, assertions of independence in the Baltic states, including Lithuania's bold declaration of national sovereignty, and growing dissatisfaction among the Great Russian masses were all parts of a fluid, unstable political situation (see Map 36.4). Increasingly, the reform-minded Gorbachev stood as a besieged moderate.

As competing Russian politicians called for an end to communist rule and as nationalists demanded independence in the non-Russian republics of the Soviet Union, the Communist old guard also challenged Gorbachev. Defeated at the Communist party congress in July 1990, a gang of desperate hardliners tried to seize control of the government in August 1991. But the attempted coup collapsed in the face of massive popular resistance. Gorbachev was rescued and returned to power. An anticommunist revolution swept Russia. Although uncertainties abounded, it seemed clear that the peoples of the once-unified Soviet Union were making great progress toward personal freedom, national self-determination, and political democracy, a most surprising development in full accord with the noblest traditions of Western society.

THE WESTERN HEMISPHERE

One way to think of what historians used to call the "New World" is as a vigorous offshoot of Western civilization, an offshoot that has gradually developed its own characteristics while retaining European roots. From this perspective can be seen many illuminating parallels and divergences in the histories of Europe and the Americas. After the Second World War, the Western Hemisphere experienced a many-faceted recovery, somewhat similar to that of Europe though it began earlier, especially in Latin America. And when the postwar era drew to a close, the countries of the New World began to experience their own crises.

Postwar Prosperity in the United States

The Second World War cured the depression in the United States and brought about the greatest boom in American history. Unemployment practically vanished and personal income doubled as the well-being of Americans increased dramatically. Despite fears that peace would bring renewed depression, conversion to a peacetime economy went smoothly. The U.S. economy then proceeded to advance fairly steadily for a long generation.

Prosperity helps explain why postwar domestic politics consisted largely of modest adjustments to the status quo until the 1960s. Truman's upset victory in 1948 demonstrated that Americans had no interest in undoing Roosevelt's social and economic reforms. The Congress proceeded to increase social security benefits, subsidize middle- and lower-class housing, and raise the minimum wage. These and other liberal measures consolidated the New Deal. In 1952 the Republican party and the voters turned to General Dwight D. Eisenhower (1890–1969), a national hero and self-described moderate.

The federal government's only major new undertaking during the Eisenhower years (1952–1960) was the interstate highway system, a suitable symbol of the basic satisfaction of the vast majority. Some Americans feared that the United States was becoming a "blocked society," obsessed with stability and incapable of wholesome change. This feeling contributed in 1960 to the election of the young John F. Kennedy (1917–1963), who promised to "get the country moving again." President Kennedy captured the popular imagination, revitalized the old Roosevelt coalition, and modestly expanded existing liberal legislation before he was struck down by an assassin's bullet in 1963.

The Civil Rights Revolution

Belatedly and reluctantly, complacent postwar America experienced a genuine social revolution: after a long struggle, blacks (and their white supporters) threw off a deeply entrenched system of segregation, discrimination, and repression. This civil rights movement advanced on several fronts. Eloquent lawyers from the National Association for the Advancement of Colored People (NAACP) challenged school segregation in the courts. In 1954 they won a landmark decision in the Supreme Court: "separate educational facilities are inherently unequal." Blacks effectively challenged institutionalized inequality with bus boycotts, sit-ins, and demonstrations. As civil rights leader Martin Luther King, Jr. (1929–1968), told the white power structure, "We will not hate you, but we will not obey your evil laws."[10]

In key northern states blacks used their growing political power to gain the support of the liberal wing of the Democratic party. A liberal landslide

The March on Washington in August 1963 marked a dramatic climax in the civil rights struggle. More than 200,000 people gathered at the Lincoln Memorial to hear the young Martin Luther King, Jr., deliver his greatest address, his "I have a dream" speech. *(Source: Francis Miller, LIFE MAGAZINE © Time Warner Inc.)*

elected Lyndon Johnson (1908–1973) president in 1964. The Civil Rights Act of 1964 categorically prohibited discrimination in public services and on the job. In the follow-up Voting Rights Act of 1965, the federal government firmly guaranteed all blacks the right to vote. By the 1970s, substantial numbers of blacks had been elected to public and private office throughout the southern states, proof positive that dramatic changes had occurred in American race relations.

Blacks enthusiastically supported new social legislation in the mid-1960s. President Johnson solemnly declared "unconditional war on poverty." Congress and the administration created a host of antipoverty projects, such as a domestic peace corps, free preschools for poor children, and community-action programs. Although these programs were directed to all poor Americans—the majority of whom were white—they were also intended to increase economic equality for blacks.

Thus the United States promoted in the mid-1960s the kind of fundamental social reform that western Europe had embraced immediately after the Second World War. The United States became more of a welfare state, as government spending for social benefits rose dramatically and approached European levels.

The Vietnam Trauma and Beyond

President Johnson wanted to go down in history as a master reformer and a healer of old wounds. Instead he opened new ones with the Vietnam War.

American involvement in Vietnam had its origins in the cold war and the ideology of containment (see page 1174). From the late 1940s on, most Americans and their leaders viewed the world in terms of a constant struggle to stop the spread of communism. As Europe began to revive and

China established a communist government in 1949, efforts to contain communism shifted to Asia. The bloody Korean War (1950–1953) ended in stalemate, but the United States did succeed in preventing a communist government in South Korea. After the defeat of the French in Indochina in 1954, the Eisenhower administration refused to sign the Geneva accords that temporarily divided the country into two zones pending national unification by means of free elections. President Eisenhower then acquiesced in the refusal of the anticommunist South Vietnamese government to accept the verdict of elections and provided it with military aid. President Kennedy greatly increased the number of American "military advisers" to sixteen thousand and had the existing South Vietnamese leader deposed in 1963 when he refused to follow American directives.

After successfully depicting his opponent, Barry Goldwater, as a trigger-happy extremist in a nuclear age and resoundingly winning the 1964 election on a peace platform, President Johnson greatly expanded the American role in the Vietnam conflict. As Johnson explained to his ambassador in Saigon, "I am not going to lose Vietnam. I am not going to be the President who saw Southeast Asia go the way China went."[11] American strategy was to "escalate" the war sufficiently to break the will of the North Vietnamese and their southern allies without resorting to "overkill" that might risk war with the entire communist bloc. Thus South Vietnam received massive military aid; American forces in the South gradually grew to a half-million men; and the United States bombed North Vietnam with ever-greater intensity. But there was no invasion of the North, nor did the United States dare to interrupt the seaborne shipment of military supplies from the Soviet Union to the North. In the end, the American strategy of savage but limited warfare backfired. It was the Americans themselves who grew weary and the American leadership that cracked.

The undeclared war in Vietnam, fought nightly on American television, eventually divided the United States in a great political battle. Initial support was strong, but by 1967 a growing number of critics denounced the war as an immoral and unsuccessful intrusion into a complex and distant civil war. There were major protests, often led by college students. Criticism reached a crescendo after the Vietcong "Tet Offensive" in January 1968.

This, the communists' first major attack with conventional weapons on major cities, failed militarily but showed that the communist forces in South Vietnam were still strong. U.S. critics of the Vietnam War interpreted the bloody battle as proof that a Vietcong victory was inevitable. America's leaders lost heart. In 1968, after an ambiguous defeat in the New Hampshire primary, President Johnson called for negotiations with North Vietnam and announced that he would not stand for re-election.

Elected by a razor-slim margin in 1968, President Richard Nixon (b. 1913) sought to gradually disengage America from Vietnam and the accompanying national crisis. Intensifying the continuous bombardment of the enemy while simultaneously pursuing peace talks with the North Vietnamese, Nixon cut American forces in Vietnam from 550,000 to 24,000 in four years. The cost of the war dropped dramatically. Moreover, President Nixon launched a flank attack in diplomacy. He journeyed to China in 1972 and reached a spectacular if limited reconciliation with the People's Republic of China. This reconciliation took advantage of China's growing fears of the Soviet Union and undermined North Vietnam's position. In January 1973, fortified by the overwhelming endorsement of the voters in his 1972 electoral triumph, President Nixon and Secretary of State Henry Kissinger finally reached a peace agreement with North Vietnam. The agreement allowed remaining American forces to complete their withdrawal, and the United States reserved the right to resume bombing if the accords were broken. South Vietnamese forces seemed to hold their own, and the storm of crisis in the United States seemed past.

On the contrary, the country reaped the Watergate whirlwind. Like some other recent American presidents, Nixon authorized spying activities that went beyond the law. Going further than his predecessors, Nixon authorized special units to use various illegal means to stop the leaking of government documents to the press. One such group broke into the Democratic party headquarters in Washington's Watergate complex in June 1972 and was promptly arrested. Nixon and many of his assistants then tried to hush up the bungled job, but the media and the machinery of congressional investigation eventually exposed the administration's web of lies and lawbreaking. In 1974 a beleaguered Nixon was forced to resign in disgrace.

The consequences of renewed political crisis flowing from the Watergate affair were profound. First, Watergate resulted in a major shift of power away from the presidency toward Congress, especially in foreign affairs. Therefore, as American aid to South Vietnam diminished in 1973 and as an emboldened North Vietnam launched a general invasion against South Vietnamese armies in early 1974, first President Nixon and then his successor, President Gerald Ford (b. 1913), stood by because Congress refused to permit any American military response. After more than thirty-five years of battle, the Vietnamese communists unified their country in 1975 as a fledgling totalitarian state—a second consequence of the U.S. crisis. Third, in the wake of Watergate, the belated fall of South Vietnam—generally seen as a disastrous American military defeat—shook America's postwar pride and confidence. The Vietnam aftermath left the United States divided and uncertain about its proper role in world affairs. The postwar belief in worldwide containment of communism was seriously damaged, but no alternative concept generated general support in the 1970s.

One possibility was the policy of *détente*, or progressive relaxation of cold war tensions. Nixon's phased withdrawal from Vietnam was part of détente, which reached its apogee when all European nations (except isolationist Albania), the United States, and Canada signed the Final Act of the Helsinki Conference in 1975. Thirty-five nations agreed that Europe's existing political frontiers could not be changed by force, and they solemnly accepted numerous provisions guaranteeing the human rights and political freedoms of their citizens.

Optimistic hopes for détente in international relations gradually faded in the later 1970s. Brezhnev's Soviet Union ignored the human rights provisions of the Helsinki agreement, and East-West political competition remained very much alive outside Europe. Many Americans became convinced that the Soviet Union was taking advantage of détente, steadily building up its military might and pushing for political gains in Africa, Asia, and Latin America. The Soviet invasion of Afghanistan in December 1979, which was designed to save an increasingly unpopular Marxist regime, was especially alarming. Many Americans feared that the oil-rich states of the Persian Gulf would be next, and they looked again to the Atlantic alliance and military might to contain communist expansion.

President Jimmy Carter (b. 1924), elected in 1976, tried to lead the Atlantic alliance beyond verbal condemnation, but among the European allies only Great Britain supported the American policy of economic sanctions. The alliance showed the same lack of concerted action when Solidarity rose in Poland. Some observers concluded that the alliance had lost the will to think and act decisively in dealings with the Soviet bloc.

In fact, the Atlantic alliance, formed in the late 1940s to prevent further Soviet expansion in

Nixon in China, 1972 Shown here toasting U.S.–China friendship with Chinese Premier Chou En-lai in Peking in February 1972, President Nixon took advantage of Chinese fears of the Soviet Union to establish good relations with Asia's Communist giant. Arriving after twenty-five years of mutual hostility, reconciliation with China was Nixon's finest achievement. *(Source: John Dominis,* LIFE MAGAZINE © *Time Inc. 1972)*

Diego Rivera (1886–1957) was one of the great and committed painters of the Mexican Revolution. Rivera believed that art should reflect the "new order of things" and inspire the common people—the workers and the peasants. One of Rivera's many wall paintings, this vibrant central mural in the National Palace in Mexico City, depicts a brutal Spanish conquest and a liberating revolution. *(Source: Robert Frerck/Odyssey Productions)*

Europe, endured and remained true to its original purpose in the 1980s. The U.S. military build-up launched by Jimmy Carter in his last years in office was greatly accelerated by President Ronald Reagan (b. 1911), who was swept into office in 1980 by a wave of patriotism following an agonizing hostage crisis in Iran (see page 1233). The new American leadership acted as if the military balance had tipped in favor of the Soviet Union. Increasing defense spending enormously and starving social welfare programs, the Reagan administration concentrated especially on nuclear arms and an expanded navy as keys to American power in the post-Vietnam age. European governments reluctantly agreed to help strengthen NATO forces and to allow medium-range nuclear warheads on their soil.

Thus the Atlantic alliance bent, but it did not break in the 1980s. In doing so, the United States and its Western allies gave indirect support to on-going efforts to liberalize authoritarian communist eastern Europe and probably helped convince Mikhail Gorbachev that endless cold war conflict was foolish and dangerous.

Economic Nationalism in Latin America

Although the countries of Latin America share a Spanish-Portuguese heritage, their striking differences make it difficult to generalize meaningfully about modern Latin American history. Yet a growing economic nationalism seems unmistakable. As the early nineteenth century saw Spanish and Portuguese colonies win wars of political independence, so has recent history been an ongoing quest for genuine economic independence through local control and industrialization.

To understand the rise of economic nationalism, one must remember that Latin American countries developed as producers of foodstuffs and raw materials that were exported to Europe and the United States in return for manufactured goods and capital investment. This exchange brought considerable economic development but exacted a heavy price: neocolonialism (see pages 1002–1004). Latin America became very dependent on foreign markets, products, and investments. Industry did not develop, and large landowners tied to production for the world market profited most from economic development and thus enhanced their social and political power.

The old international division of labor was finally destroyed by the Great Depression. Prices and exports of Latin American commodities collapsed as Europe and the United States drastically reduced their purchases and raised tariffs to protect domestic products. With their foreign sales plummeting, Latin American countries could not buy the industrial goods that they needed from abroad.

Latin America suffered the full force of the global depression. Especially in the largest Latin American countries—Argentina, Brazil, Chile, and Mexico—the result was a profound shift toward economic nationalism after 1930. The most popularly based governments worked to reduce foreign influence and gain control of their own economies and natural resources. They energetically promoted national industry by means of high tariffs, government grants, and even state enterprise. They favored the lower middle and urban working classes with social benefits and higher wages in order to increase their purchasing power and gain their support. These efforts at recovery gathered speed during the Second World War and were fairly successful. By the late 1940s, the factories of Argentina, Brazil, and Chile could generally satisfy domestic consumer demand for the products of light industry. In the 1950s, some countries began moving into heavy industry. Economic nationalism and the rise of industry are particularly striking in the two largest and most influential countries, Mexico and Brazil, which together account for half of the population of Latin America.

Mexico Overthrowing the elitist, upper-class rule of the tyrant Porfirio Díaz, the spasmodic, often-chaotic Mexican Revolution of 1910 culminated in 1917 in a new constitution. This radical nationalistic document called for universal suffrage, massive land reform, benefits for labor, and strict control of foreign capital. Actual progress was quite modest until 1934, when a charismatic young Indian from a poor family, Lazaro Cárdenas, became president and dramatically revived the languishing revolution. Under Cárdenas, many large estates were divided up among small farmers or returned undivided to Indian communities.

Meanwhile, state-supported Mexican businessmen built many small factories to meet domestic needs. The government also championed the cause of industrial workers. In 1938, when Mexican workers became locked in a bitter dispute with

British and American oil companies, Cárdenas nationalized the petroleum industry—to the amazement of a world unaccustomed to such bold action. Finally, the 1930s saw the flowering of a distinctive Mexican culture, which proudly embraced its long-despised Indian past and gloried in the modern national revolution.

In 1940 the official, semi-authoritarian party that has governed Mexico continuously since the revolution selected the first of a series of more moderate presidents. These presidents used the full power of the state to promote industrialization through a judicious mixture of public, private, and even foreign enterprise. Following the postwar trend in Europe and the United States, the Mexican economy grew rapidly, at about 6 percent per year from the early 1940s to the late 1960s. However, in Mexico, unlike Europe and the United States, the upper and middle classes reaped the lion's share of the benefits.

Brazil After the fall of Brazil's monarchy in 1889 (see page 1000), politics was dominated by the coffee barons and by regional rivalries. These rivalries and deteriorating economic conditions allowed a military revolt led by Getulio Vargas, governor of one of Brazil's largest states, to seize control of the federal government in 1930. Vargas, who proved to be a consummate politician, fragmented the opposition and established a mild dictatorship that lasted until 1945. His rule was generally popular, combining effective economic nationalism and moderate social reform.

Vargas decisively tipped the balance of political power away from the Brazilian states to the ever-expanding federal government, which became a truly national government for the first time. Vargas and his allies also set out to industrialize Brazil and gain economic independence. While the national coffee board used mountains of surplus coffee beans to fire railroad locomotives, the government supported Brazilian manufacturers with high tariffs, generous loans, and labor peace. This pro-business policy did not prevent new social legislation: workers received shorter hours, pensions, health and accident insurance, paid vacations, and other benefits. Finally, Vargas shrewdly upheld the nationalist cause in his relations with the giant to the north. Brazil was modernizing rapidly.

Modernization continued for the next fifteen years. The economy boomed. Presidential politics was re-established, though the military kept a watchful eye for extremism among the civilian politicians. Economic nationalism was especially vigorous under the flamboyant President Juscelino Kubitschek. Between 1956 and 1960, the government borrowed heavily from international bankers to promote industry and built the new capital of Brasília in the midst of a wilderness. Kubitschek's slogan was "Fifty Years' Progress in Five," and he meant it.

The Brazilian and Mexican formula of national economic development, varying degrees of electoral competition, and social reform was shared by some other Latin American countries, notably Argentina and Chile. By the late 1950s, optimism was widespread, though cautious. Economic and social progress seemed to be bringing less violent, more democratic politics to the region. These expectations were shaken by the Cuban Revolution.

The Cuban Revolution

Although many aspects of the Cuban Revolution are obscured by controversy, certain background conditions are clear. First, achieving nominal independence in 1898 as a result of the Spanish-American War, Cuba was for many years virtually an American protectorate. The Cuban constitution gave the United States the legal right to intervene in Cuban affairs, a right that was frequently exercised until President Franklin Roosevelt renounced it in 1934. Second, and partly because the American army had often been the real power on the island, Cuba's political institutions were weak and Cuban politicians were extraordinarily corrupt. Third, Cuba was one of Latin America's most prosperous countries by the 1950s, but its sugar-and-tourist economy was completely dependent on the United States. Finally, the enormous differences between rich and poor in Cuba were typical of Latin America. But Cuba also had a strong Communist party, and that was highly unusual.

Fidel Castro (b. 1927), a magnetic leader with the gift of oratory, managed to unify all opposition elements in a revolutionary front, and his guerrilla forces triumphed in late 1958. Castro had promised a "real" revolution, and it soon became clear that "real" meant "communist." Wealthy Cubans fled to Miami, and the middle class began to follow. Cuban relations with the Eisenhower administration deteriorated rapidly. Thus, in April 1961, the newly elected U.S. president, John Kennedy, went ahead with a pre-existing CIA plan to use Cuban exiles to topple Castro. But the Kennedy administration abandoned the exiles as soon as they were put ashore at the Bay of Pigs, and the exiles were quickly captured.

The Bay of Pigs invasion—a triumph for Castro and a humiliating fiasco for the United States—had significant consequences. It freed Castro to build his version of a communist society. Political life in Cuba featured "anti-imperialism," an alliance with the Soviet bloc, the dictatorship of the party, and a Castro cult. Revolutionary enthusiasm was genuine among party activists, much of Cuba's youth, and some of the masses some of the time. Prisons and emigration silenced opposition. The economy was characterized by state ownership, collective farms, and Soviet trade and aid. Early efforts to industrialize ran aground, and sugar production continued to dominate the economy. Socially, the Castro regime pursued equality and the creation of a new socialist personality. In short, revolutionary totalitarianism came to the Americas.

The failure of the United States to derail Castro probably encouraged Khrushchev to start putting nuclear missiles in Cuba and in turn led directly to the most serious East-West crisis since the Korean War. The Soviets backed down (see page 1191), but Castro's survival had major consequences for Latin America. Above all, it heightened both hopes and fears that similar revolutions could spread throughout the region. In the United States, Castro aroused cold war fears of communism in Latin America. Using the Organization of American States to isolate Cuba, the United States in 1961 pledged $10 billion in aid over ten years to a new hemispheric "Alliance for Progress." The Alliance was intended to promote long-term economic development and social reform, which American liberals assumed would immunize the rest of Latin America from the Cuban disease.

Authoritarianism and Democracy in Latin America

U.S. aid contributed modestly to continued Latin American economic development in the 1960s, although population growth canceled out two-thirds of the increase on a per capita basis. Demo-cratic social reforms—the other half of the Alliance for Progress formula—proceeded slowly, however. Instead, the era following the Cuban Revolution saw increasing conflict between leftist movements and ruling elites contending for power. In most countries the elites and their military allies won the struggle, imposing a new kind of conservative authoritarianism as their collective response to the social and economic crisis. By the late 1970s, only four Latin American countries—Costa Rica, Venezuela, Colombia, and Mexico—retained some measure of democratic government. Brazil, Argentina, and Chile represented the general trend.

Influential Brazil led the way. Intense political competition in the early 1960s prompted President João Goulart to swing to the left to gain fresh support. Castroism appeared to spread in the impoverished northeast, and mass meetings of leftists were answered by huge demonstrations of conservatives. Meanwhile Goulart called for radical change, proposing that the great landed estates be broken up and that Brazil's many illiterates receive the right to vote. When Goulart and his followers appeared ready to use force to implement their program, army leaders took over in 1964. The right-wing military government banned political parties and ruled by decree. Industrialization and urbanization went forward under military rule, but the gap between rich and poor widened as well.

In Argentina, the military had intervened in 1955 to oust the dictatorial populist and economic nationalist Juan Perón, but it had restored elected government. Then, worried by a Peronist revival and heartened by the Brazilian example, the army took control in 1966 and again in 1976 after a brief civilian interlude. Each military takeover was followed by an escalation of repression, and culturally and economically advanced Argentina became a brutal military dictatorship.

If events in Argentina were discouraging, those in Chile were tragic. Chile has a population of predominantly European origin and a long tradition of democracy and moderate reform. Thus when Salvador Allende, a doctor and the Marxist head of a coalition of Communists, Socialists, and Radicals, won a plurality of 36 percent of the vote in fair elections in 1970, he was duly elected president by the Congress. Allende completed the nationalization of the American-owned copper companies—the great majority of Chileans had already

Return to Democracy in Argentina   Elected president in 1983 after seven years of increasingly brutal military rule, Raul Alfonsín stands with sash and rod—the symbols of authority—to swear the presidential oath of office in Buenos Aires. Alfonsín's inauguration gave rise to great popular rejoicing. *(Source: Urraca/Sygma)*

embraced economic nationalism—and proceeded to socialize private industry, accelerate the breakup of landed estates, and radicalize the poor.

Marxism in action evoked a powerful backlash in Chile. The middle class struck back, and by 1973 Chile seemed headed for civil war. Then, with widespread conservative support and strong U.S. backing, the traditionally impartial army struck in a well-organized coup. Allende died, probably murdered, and thousands of his supporters were arrested, or worse. As in Argentina, the military imposed a harsh despotism.

The revival of antidemocratic authoritarianism in Latin America challenged not only the Marxist and socialist program but most liberal and moderate reform as well. Thus military governments, supported by Washington and local big business, effectively defended private capital and halted or reversed radical change. Yet some observers noted that the new military governments grew out of political crises that threatened national unity as well as the upper classes. In such circumstances, the politically conscious officer corps saw the military as the only institution capable of preventing chaos. Moreover, the new authoritarians were determined modernizers. Eager to catch up with the more advanced countries, they were often deeply committed to nationalism, industrialization, technology, and some modest social progress. They even promised free elections in the future.

That time came in the 1980s, when another democratic wave gained momentum throughout

Latin America. In South America the three Andean nations—Peru, Bolivia, and Ecuador—led the way with the re-establishment of elected governments, all of which were committed in varying degrees to genuine social reform. In Argentina, the military government gradually lost almost all popular support because of its "dirty war" against its own citizens, in which it imprisoned, tortured, and murdered thousands whom it arbitrarily accused of opposing the regime. In 1982, in a desperate gamble to rally the people around the nationalist flag, Argentina's military rulers sent nine thousand troops to seize the Falkland (or Malvinas) Islands (see Map 31.2, page 998) from Great Britain. But the British, led by the "iron lady," Prime Minister Margaret Thatcher, retook the islands in a brief war, routing Argentina's poorly led troops and forcing its humiliated generals to schedule national elections. Elected by an overwhelming majority in 1983, President Raul Alfonsín prosecuted former military rulers for their crimes, reformed the currency, and appeared to lay solid foundations for liberty and political democracy.

In 1985, the Brazilian military also turned over power to an elected government, thereby completing a peaceful transition begun in the late 1970s. Relatively successful in its industrialization effort, Brazil's military government had proved unable (or unwilling) to improve the social and economic position of the masses. After twenty-one years of rule, and with even Brazil's richest families calling for reforms to forestall social upheaval, the military leaders were ready to let civilian politicians have a try. Chile also turned from harsh military dictatorship to elected government. Thus Latin America entered the second half of the 1980s with 94 percent of its population living under civilian and constitutional regimes, and a major turn toward democracy and civil liberty appeared under way.

The most dramatic developments in Central America occurred in Nicaragua. In 1979, a broad coalition of liberals, socialists, and Marxist revolutionaries drove long-time dictator Anastasio Somoza from power. The Somoza family had relied on solid U.S. support in its four-decade dictatorship, and the new Sandinista government viewed the United States as an oppressive imperialist power. The new leaders wanted genuine political and economic independence from the United States, as well as throughgoing land reform, some state ownership of industry, and friendly ties with communist countries.

These policies infuriated the Reagan administration, which applied economic sanctions and tried everything short of sending American soldiers to overturn the Sandinista government. The Nicaraguan economy collapsed, and the popularity of the Sandinista government eventually declined. Then, after a decade of rule, the Sandinistas accepted free elections and stepped down when they were defeated by a coalition led by a winsome Violetta Chamorro.

Thus, as the 1990s opened, almost all of Latin America lived under civilian and constitutional governments seeking to mobilize the broad-based support that seemed necessary to deal effectively with the region's enduring economic and social problems.

SUMMARY

The postwar recovery of western Europe and the Americas was a memorable achievement in the long, uneven course of Western civilization. The transition from imperialism to decolonization proceeded rapidly, surprisingly smoothly, and without serious damage to western Europe. Genuine political democracy gained unprecedented strength in the West, and economic progress and social reforms improved the lives of ordinary citizens.

Postwar developments in eastern Europe displayed both similarities to and differences from developments in western Europe and the Americas. Perhaps the biggest difference was that Stalin imposed harsh one-party rule in the lands occupied by his armies, which was a critical factor in the onset of the long and bitter cold war. Nevertheless, the Soviet Union became more liberal and less dictatorial under Khrushchev, and the standard of living in the Soviet Union improved markedly in the 1950s and 1960s.

In the late 1960s and early 1970s, Europe and the Americas entered a new and turbulent time of crisis. Many nations, from France to Czechoslovakia and from Argentina to the United States, experienced major political difficulties, as social conflicts and ideological battles divided peoples and shook governments. Beginning with the oil shocks of the 1970s, severe economic problems added to the turmoil. Yet in western Europe and North America the welfare system held firm, and both democracy and the movement toward European unity successfully passed through the storm. Elsewhere the response to political and economic crisis sent many countries veering off toward repression, as the communist system in eastern Europe was tightened up in the Brezhnev years and a new kind of conservative authoritarianism arose in most of Latin America. Then, in the 1980s, both regions turned back toward free elections and civil liberties, most spectacularly so in the east European revolution of 1989. As the 1990s opened, differences in political organization and human rights were less pronounced in a reuniting Western civilization than at any time since the fateful opening of the First World War.

NOTES

1. Quoted in N. Graebner, *Cold War Diplomacy, 1945–1960* (Princeton, N.J.: Van Nostrand, 1962), p. 17.
2. Ibid.
3. Quoted in J. Hennessy, *Economic "Miracles"* (London: André Deutsch, 1964), p. 5.
4. Quoted in H. Smith, *The Russians* (New York: Quadrangle/New York Times, 1976), p. 303.
5. Quoted in D. Treadgold, *Twentieth Century Russia,* 5th ed. (Boston: Houghton Mifflin, 1981), p. 442.
6. Quoted in I. Deutscher, in *Soviet Society,* ed. A. Inkeles and K. Geiger (Boston: Houghton Mifflin, 1961), p. 41.
7. M. Walker, *The Waking Giant: Gorbachev's Russia* (New York: Pantheon Books, 1987), p. 175.
8. Quoted in *Time,* January 6, 1986, p. 66.
9. T. G. Ash, *The Polish Revolution: Solidarity* (New York: Scribner's, 1983), p. 186.
10. Quoted in S. E. Morison et al., *A Concise History of the American Republic* (New York: Oxford University Press, 1977), p. 697.
11. Ibid., p. 735.

SUGGESTED READING

An excellent way to approach wartime diplomacy is through the accounts of the statesmen involved. Great leaders and matchless stylists, both Winston Churchill and Charles de Gaulle have written histories of the war in the form of memoirs. Other interesting memoirs are those of Harry Truman (1958); Dwight Eisenhower, *Crusade in Europe* (1948); and Dean Acheson, *Present at the Creation* (1969), a beautifully written defense of American foreign policy in the early cold war. W. A. Williams, *The Tragedy of American Diplomacy* (1962), and W. La Feber, *America, Russia, and the Cold War* (1967), claim, on the contrary, that the United States was primarily responsible for the conflict with the Soviet Union. Two other important studies focusing on American policy are J. Gaddis, *The United States and the Origins of the Cold War* (1972), and D. Yergin, *Shattered Peace: The Origins of the Cold War and the National Security Council* (1977). A. Fontaine, a French journalist, provides a balanced general approach in his *History of the Cold War,* 2 vols. (1968). V. Mastny's thorough investigation of Stalin's war aims, *Russia's Road to the Cold War* (1979), is also recommended.

R. Mayne, *The Recovery of Europe, 1945–1973,* rev. ed. (1973), and N. Luxenburg, *Europe Since World War II,* rev. ed. (1979), are recommended general surveys, as are two other important works: W. Laqueur, *Europe Since Hitler,* rev. ed. (1982), and P. Johnson, *Modern Times: The World from the Twenties to the Eighties* (1983). T. White, *Fire in the Ashes* (1953), is a vivid view of European resurgence and Marshall Plan aid by an outstanding journalist. I. and D. Unger, *Postwar America: The United States Since 1945* (1989), and W. Leuchtenberg, *In the Shadow of FDR: From Harry Truman to Ronald Reagan,* rev. ed. (1989), discuss developments in the United States. Postwar economic and technological developments are analyzed in G. Ambrosius and W. Hibbard, *A Social and Economic History of Twentieth-Century Europe* (1989). A. Shonfield, *Modern Capitalism* (1965), provides an engaging, optimistic assessment of the growing importance of government investment and planning in European economic life. The culture and politics of protest are provocatively analyzed in H. Hughes, *Sophisticated Rebels: The Political Culture of European Dissent, 1968–1987* (1988), and W. Hampton, *Guerrilla Minstrels: John Lennon, Joe Hill, Woody Guthrie, Bob Dylan* (1986). Two outstanding works on France are J. Ardagh, *The New French Revolution* (1969), which puts the momentous social changes since 1945 in human terms, and D. L. Hanley et al., eds., *France: Politics and Society Since 1945* (1979). On Germany, H. Turner, *The Two Germanies Since 1945: East and West* (1987), and R. Dahrendorf, *Society and Democracy in Germany* (1971), are recommended. The spiritual dimension of West German recovery is probed by G. Grass in his world-famous novel *The Tin Drum* (1963); W. Laqueur, *The Germans* (1985), is a recent journalistic report by a well-known historian. A. Marwick, *British Society Since 1945* (1982), is good on postwar developments; P. Jenkins, *Mrs. Thatcher's Revolu-*

tion: The End of the Socialist Era (1988), is a provocative critique. Two outstanding books on the Vietnam War are N. Sheehan, *A Bright and Shining Lie: John Paul Vann and America in Vietnam* (1988), and A. Short, *The Origins of the Vietnam War* (1989).

H. Seton-Watson, *The East European Revolution* (1965), is a good history of the communization of eastern Europe, and S. Fischer-Galati, ed., *Eastern Europe in the Sixties* (1963), discusses major developments. P. Zinner, *Revolution in Hungary* (1962), is excellent on the tragic events of 1956. I. Svitak, *The Czechoslovak Experiment, 1968–1969* (1971), and Z. Zeman, *Prague Spring* (1969), are good on Czechoslovakia. T. Ash, *The Polish Revolution: Solidarity* (1983), is the best book on the subject, and M. Kaufman, *Mad Dreams, Saving Graces: Poland, a Nation in Conspiracy* (1989), is recommended. Z. Brzezinski, *The Soviet Bloc: Unity and Conflict* (1967), and J. Hough and M. Fainsod, *How the Soviet Union Is Governed* (1978), are important general studies. A. Amalrik, *Will the Soviet Union Survive Until 1984?* (1970), is a fascinating critique of Soviet history, and A. Lee, *Russian Journal* (1981), is a moving personal account of a young American woman. H. Smith has writ-

ten two outstanding journalistic reports on the Soviet Union under Brezhnev and Gorbachev, *The Russians* (1976) and *The New Russians* (1990). Gorbachev's reforms are perceptively examined by Walker, *The Waking Giant,* cited in the Notes, and M. Lewin, *The Gorbachev Phenomenon: A Historical Interpretation* (1988).

R. von Albertini, *Decolonialization* (1971), is a good history of the decline and fall of European empires, a theme also considered in T. Vadney, *The World Since 1945* (1988), and H. van der Wee, *Prosperity and Upheaval: The World Economy, 1945–1980* (1986). Two excellent general studies on Latin America are J. E. Fagg, *Latin America: A General History,* 3d ed. (1977), and R. J. Shafer, *A History of Latin America* (1978). Both contain detailed suggestions for further reading. E. Burns, *A History of Brazil* (1970); M. Meyer and W. Sherman, *The Course of Mexican History* (1979); and B. Loveman, *Chile: The Legacy of Hispanic Capitalism* (1979), are recommended studies of developments in three leading nations. W. La Feber, *Inevitable Revolutions: The United States in Central America* (1983), is an important, quite critical assessment of U.S. support of neocolonial patterns in Central America.

37

Asia and Africa in the Contemporary World

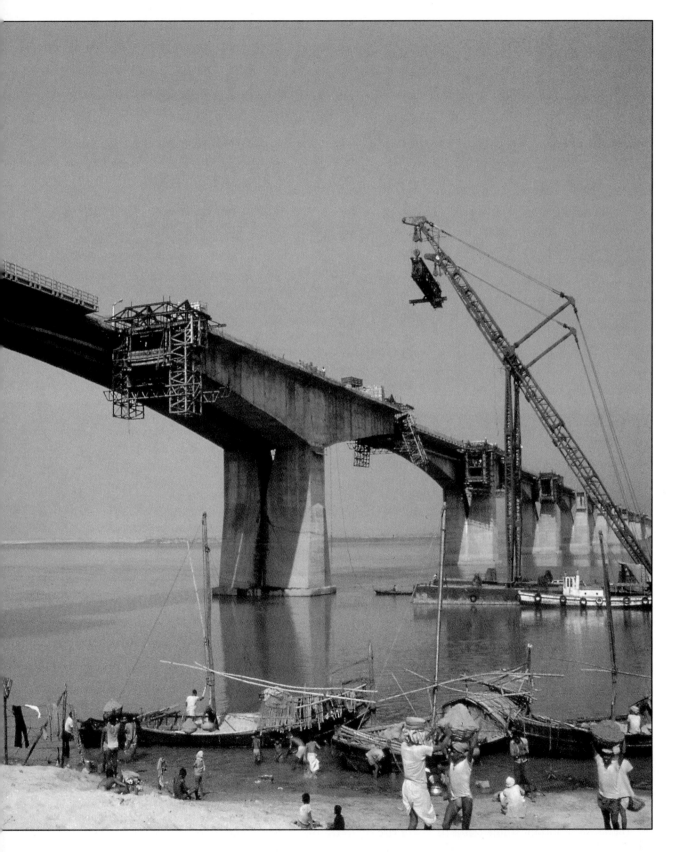

Construction of Asia's longest river bridge, spanning the River Ganges in India

When future historians look back at our era, they are likely to be particularly struck by the epoch-making resurgence of Asia and Africa after the Second World War. They will try to explain the astonishingly rapid rise of new or radically reorganized Asian and African countries and their increasingly prominent role in world affairs.

- How did Asian and African countries reassert or establish their political independence in the postwar era?
- How in the postindependence world did leading states face up to the enormous challenges of nation building, challenges that were all the more difficult after the 1960s?

These are the questions that this chapter seeks to answer.

THE RESURGENCE OF EAST ASIA

In 1945 Japan and China, the two great powers of East Asia, lay exhausted and devastated. Japanese aggression had sown extreme misery in China and reaped an atomic whirlwind at Hiroshima and Nagasaki. The future looked bleak. Yet both nations recovered even more spectacularly than western Europe. In the course of recovery the two countries, closely linked since the 1890s, went their separate ways. As China under Mao Tse-tung (Mao Zedong) transformed itself into a strong, self-confident communist state, Japan under American occupation turned from military expansion to democracy and extraordinarily successful economic development. Not until the 1970s did the reborn giants begin moving somewhat closer together.

The Communist Victory in China

There were many reasons for the triumph of communism in China. As a noted historian has forcefully argued, however, "Japanese aggression was . . . the most important single factor in Mao's rise to power."[1] When Japanese armies advanced rapidly in 1938 (see page 1100), the Nationalist government of Chiang Kai-shek (Jiang Jieshi) moved its capital to Chungking, deep in the Chinese interior. The Japanese then occupied an area five hundred miles wide in northern and central China, and the war settled into stalemate in 1939. These wartime conditions enabled the Communists, aided by their uneasy "united front" alliance with the Nationalists, to build up their strength in guerrilla bases in the countryside behind Japanese lines. Mao Tse-tung, at the peak of his creative powers, avoided pitched battles and concentrated on winning peasant support and forming a broad anti-Japanese coalition. By reducing rents, enticing intellectuals, and spreading propaganda, Mao and the Communists emerged in peasant eyes as the true patriots, the genuine nationalists. And the promise of radical redistribution of the land strongly reinforced their appeal to poor peasants and landless laborers.

Meanwhile, the long war with Japan was exhausting the established government and its supporters. American generals were never satisfied with China's war effort, but in fact fully half of Japan's overseas armies were pinned down in China in 1945. Chiang Kai-shek's Nationalists had mobilized 14 million men, and a staggering 3 million Chinese soldiers had been killed or wounded. The war created massive Chinese deficits and runaway inflation, hurting morale and ruining lives.

When Japan suddenly collapsed in August 1945, Communists and Nationalists both rushed to seize evacuated territory. Heavy fighting broke out in Manchuria. The United States, which had steadfastly supported the Nationalists during the Second World War, tried unsuccessfully to work out a political compromise, but civil war resumed in earnest in April 1946. At first Chiang Kai-shek's more numerous Nationalists had the upper hand. Soon the better-led, more determined Communists rallied, and by 1948 the demoralized Nationalist forces were disintegrating. The following year Chiang Kai-shek and a million mainland Chinese fled to the island of Taiwan, and in October 1949 Mao Tse-tung proclaimed the People's Republic of China.

Within three years the Communists had succeeded in consolidating their rule. The Communist government seized the holdings of landlords and rich peasants—10 percent of the farm population had owned between 70 and 80 percent of the land—and distributed it to 300 million poor peasants and landless laborers. This revolutionary land reform was extremely popular. Although the Chinese Communists soon began pushing the development of socialist collectives, they did so less brutally than had the Soviets in the 1930s and retained genuine support in the countryside.

Meanwhile, the Communists were dealing harshly with their foes. Mao admitted in 1957 that 800,000 "class enemies" had been summarily liquidated between 1949 and 1954; the true figure is probably much higher. By means of mass arrests, forced-labor camps, and, more generally, re-education through relentless propaganda and self-criticism sessions, all visible opposition from the old ruling groups was destroyed.

Finally, Mao and the Communists reunited China's 550 million inhabitants in a strong centralized state. They laid claim to a new "Mandate of Heaven" and demonstrated that China was once again a great power. This was the real significance of China's participation in the Korean War. In 1950, when the American-led United Nations forces in Korea crossed the 38th parallel and appeared to threaten China's industrial base in Manchuria, the Chinese attacked, advanced swiftly, and fought the Americans to a bloody standstill on the Korean peninsula. This struggle against "American imperialism" mobilized the masses, and military success increased Chinese self-confidence.

Mao's China

Asserting Chinese power and prestige in the armed conflict with the United States, Mao and the party looked to the Soviet Union for inspiration in the early 1950s. Along with the gradual collectivization of agriculture, China adopted a typical Soviet five-year plan to develop large factories and heavy industry rapidly. Many Chinese plants were built by Russian specialists; Soviet economic aid was also considerable. The first five-year plan was successful, as were associated efforts to redirect higher education away from the liberal arts toward science and engineering.

A People's Court tries a case as local villagers follow the proceedings intently. The man on his knees is accused of selling a young girl living in his household, an old practice that has become a serious crime in revolutionary China. *(Source: Popperfoto)*

People remained very poor, but undeniable economic growth followed on the Communists' social revolution.

In the cultural and intellectual realms too, the Chinese followed the Soviet example. Basic civil and political rights, which had been seriously curtailed by the Nationalists, were simply abolished. Temples and churches were closed; all religion was persecuted. Freedom of the press died, and the government went to incredible lengths to control information. A Soviet-style puritanism took hold. To the astonishment of "old China hands," the Communists quickly eradicated the long-standing scourges of prostitution and drug abuse, which they had long regarded as humiliating marks of exploitation and national decline. More generally, the Communists enthusiastically promoted Soviet-Marxian ideas concerning women and the family. Full equality and freedom from housework and child care became primary goals. Work in fields and factories was hailed as a proud badge of women's liberation rather than a shameful sign of poverty. It became rather easy for a woman to get a divorce, although premarital chastity remained the accepted norm.

By the mid-1950s, the People's Republic of China seemed to be firmly set on the Marxist-Leninist course of development previously perfected in the Soviet Union. In 1958, however, China began to go its own way. Mao had always stressed revolutionary free will and peasant equality. Now he proclaimed a spectacular acceleration of development, a "Great Leap Forward" in which soaring industrial growth was to be based on small-scale backyard workshops run by peasants living in gigantic self-contained communes. Creating an authentic new socialist personality that rejected individualism and traditional family values was a second goal. In extreme cases, commune members ate in common dining halls, nurseries cared for children, and fiery crusaders preached the evils of family ties.

The intended great leap past the Soviets to socialist utopia—true communism—produced an economic disaster in the countryside, for frantic efforts with primitive technology often resulted only in chaos. By 1960, only China's efficient rationing system was preventing starvation. But when Khrushchev criticized Chinese policy, Mao condemned Khrushchev and his Russian colleagues as detestable "modern revisionists"—capi-

talists and cowards unwilling to risk a world war that would bring communist revolution in the United States. The Russians abruptly cut off economic aid and withdrew their scientists who were helping China build an atomic bomb. A mood of fear and hostility developed in both countries in the 1960s as the communist world split apart.

Mao lost influence in the party after the fiasco of the Great Leap Forward and the Sino-Soviet split, but in 1965 the old revolutionary staged a dramatic comeback. Apprehensive that China was becoming bureaucratic, capitalistic, and "revisionist" like the Soviet Union, Mao launched what he called the "Great Proletarian Cultural Revolution." Its objective was to purge the party of time-serving bureaucrats and to recapture the revolutionary fervor and social equality of the Long March and his guerrilla struggle (see page 1100). The army and the nation's young people, especially students, responded enthusiastically. Encouraged by Mao to organize themselves into radical cadres called "Red Guards," young people denounced their teachers and practiced rebellion in the name of revolution. One Red Guard manifesto, "Long Live the Revolutionary Rebel Spirit of the Proletariat," exulted:

Revolution is rebellion, and rebellion is the soul of Mao Tse-tung's thought. Daring to think, to speak, to act, to break through, and to make revolution—in a word, daring to rebel—is the most fundamental and most precious quality of proletarian revolutionaries; it is fundamental to the Party spirit of the Party of the proletariat! . . .

You say we are too arrogant? "Arrogant" is just what we want to be. Chairman Mao says, "And those in high positions we counted as no more than the dust." We are bent on striking down not only the reactionaries in our school, but the reactionaries all over the world. Revolutionaries take it as their task to transform the world. How can we not be "arrogant"?[2]

The Red Guards also sought to forge a new socialist spirit by purging China of all traces of "feudal" and "bourgeois" culture and thought. Some ancient monuments and works of art were destroyed. Party officials, professors, and intellectuals were exiled to remote villages to purify themselves with the heavy labor of the peasant masses and to rekindle a burning devotion to the semidivine Chairman Mao. The Red Guards attracted enor-

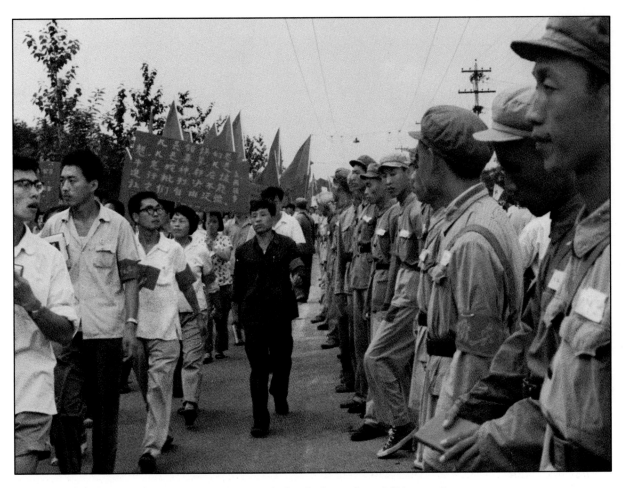

Chinese Red Guards march in a political demonstration before a line of Chinese soldiers. This photo captures the youth and determination of the Red Guards, who are carrying the "Little Red Book," the world-renowned collection of Chairman Mao's slogans and revolutionary teachings. *(Source: Wide World Photos)*

mous worldwide attention. Many observers were appalled, but China's young revolutionaries inspired radical admirers around the world and served as an extreme model for the student rebellions of the late 1960s.

The Limits of Reform

Mao and the Red Guards succeeded in mobilizing the masses, shaking up the party, and creating greater social equality. But the Cultural Revolution also created growing chaos and a general crisis of confidence, especially in the cities. Intellectuals, technicians, and purged party officials saw

themselves as victims of senseless persecution. Fighting back, they launched a counterattack on the radicals and regained much of their influence by 1969. Thus China shifted to the right at the same time that Europe and the United States did. This shift in China, coupled with actual fighting between China and the Soviet Union on the northern border in 1969 and not-so-secret Soviet talk of atomic attack, opened the door to a limited but lasting reconciliation between China and the United States in 1972.

The moderates were led by Deng Xiaoping (b. 1904), a long-time member of the Communist elite who had been branded a dangerous agent of capitalism during the Cultural Revolution. After

China's Peasants benefitted the most from Deng's reforms and the subsequent economic progress. Still clad in the blue cotton jackets of the Maoist era, these peasants are purchasing more expensive synthetic fabrics, which they will sew into brightly colored dresses and fancy shirts. *(Source: Camera Press)*

Mao's death in 1976, Deng and his supporters initiated a series of new policies, embodied in the ongoing campaign of the "Four Modernizations"—agriculture, industry, science and technology, and national defense. The campaign to modernize had a profound effect on China's people, and Deng proudly called it China's "second revolution."

China's 800 million peasants experienced the greatest and most beneficial change from this "second revolution"—a fact that at first glance may seem surprising. The support of the peasantry had played a major role in the Communist victory. After 1949, land reform and rationing undoubtedly improved the diet of poor peasants. Subsequently, literacy campaigns taught rural people how to read, and "barefoot doctors"—local peasants trained to do simple diagnosis and treatment—brought modern medicine to the countryside. The Communists also promoted handicraft industries to provide rural employment. Neverthe-

less, rigid collectivized agriculture had failed to provide either the peasants or the country with adequate food, as Chinese documents published in the 1980s made clear. Levels of agricultural production and per capita food consumption were no higher in the mid-1970s than in the mid-1950s, and only slightly higher than in 1937, before the war with Japan.

Determined to prevent a return to Maoist extremism as well as to modernize the economy, Deng and the reformers looked to the peasants as natural allies. Their answer to the stalemate in agricultural production was to let China's peasants farm the land in small family units rather than in large collectives. Peasants were encouraged to produce what they could produce best and "dare to be rich." Peasants responded enthusiastically, increasing food production by more than 50 percent in just six years after 1978. As a result of this achievement, both rural and urban Chinese finally gained enough calories and protein for normal life and growth, although the grain-dominated diet remained monotonous.

The successful use of free markets and family responsibility in agriculture encouraged further economic experimentation. Foreign capitalists were allowed to open factories in southern China, and they successfully exported Chinese products around the world. The private enterprise of Chinese citizens was also permitted in cities. Snack shops, beauty parlors, and a host of small businesses sprang up, along with rock music and a rage for English lessons. As signs of liberalization abounded, the Chinese economy bucked the world trend and grew rapidly at an annual rate of almost 10 percent between 1978 and 1987. The level of per capita income more than doubled in these years.

Yet the extent of change must not be exaggerated. Industry remained largely state owned and centrally planned; only 3 percent of the urban workforce was employed by private enterprise in 1986. Cultural change was limited, and the party maintained its strict control of the media. Above all, under Deng's leadership the Communist party zealously preserved its monopoly of political power.

Dictatorial rule in the midst of economic liberalization helps explain why the worldwide movement for greater democracy and political freedom in the late 1980s also took root in China. Chinese university students led the movement, organizing large demonstrations and calling for genuine political reform in late 1986. The government responded by banning all demonstrations and gradually halting the trend toward a freer economy. Inflation then soared to more than 30 percent a year, and in 1988 consumers cleared the shelves in a buying panic.

The economic reversal and the conviction that Chinese society was becoming more corrupt and unjust led China's idealistic university students to renew their demonstrations in April 1989. The students evoked tremendous popular support, and more than a million people streamed into Beijing's central Tiananmen Square on May 17 in support of their demands. The old men gathered around Deng and then declared martial law and ordered the army to clear the students. Incredibly, masses of courageous Chinese citizens using only their bodies and voices as weapons peacefully

blocked the soldiers' entry into the city for two weeks. But after ominous threats from the government gradually reduced the number of protesting students to less than 10,000, the hesitant army finally struck. In the early hours of June 4, 1989, tanks rolled into Tiananmen Square. At least 700 students died as a wave of repression, arrests, and executions descended on China.

China's Communist leaders claimed that they had saved the country from a counter-revolutionary plot to destroy socialism. In fact, they had temporarily saved the Communist monopoly of power and showed the limits of permissible reform. Like so many leading Chinese in modern times, Deng and his circle were most interested in making China strong, and they still saw authoritarian rule as the means to that goal.

Japan's American Revolution

After Japan's surrender in August 1945, American occupation forces began landing in the Tokyo-Yokohama area. Riding through what had been the heart of industrial Japan, the combat-hardened veterans saw an eerie sight. Where mighty mills and factories had once hummed with activity, only smokestacks and giant steel safes remained standing amid miles of rubble and debris. The empty landscape manifested Japan's state of mind as the nation lay helpless before its conqueror.

Japan, like Nazi Germany, was formally occupied by all the Allies, but real power resided in American hands. The commander was General Douglas MacArthur (1880–1964), the five-star hero of the Pacific, who with his advisers exercised almost absolute authority.

MacArthur and the Americans had a revolutionary plan for defeated Japan. Convinced that militaristic, antidemocratic forces were responsible for Japanese aggression and had to be destroyed, they introduced fundamental reforms designed to make Japan a free, democratic society along American lines. The Americans believed in their mission and in the obvious superiority of their civilization. The exhausted, demoralized Japanese, who had feared a worse fate, accepted passively. Long-suppressed liberal leaders emerged to offer crucial support and help carry the reforms forward.

Japan's sweeping American revolution began with demilitarization and a systematic purge.

Twenty-five top government leaders and army officers were tried and convicted as war criminals by a special international tribunal; other courts sentenced hundreds to death and sent thousands to prison. Over 220,000 politicians, businessmen, and army officers were declared ineligible for office.

Many Americans also wanted to try Emperor Hirohito (r. 1926–1989) as a war criminal, but MacArthur wisely decided to let him reign as a useful figurehead. According to the American-dictated constitution of 1946, the emperor was "the symbol of the State and of the people with whom resides sovereign power." The new constitution made the government fully responsible to the Diet, whose members were popularly elected by all adults. A bill of rights granted basic civil liberties and freed all political prisoners, including Communists. The constitution also abolished forever all Japanese armed forces. Japan's resurrected liberals enthusiastically supported this American move to destroy militarism.

The American occupation left Japan's powerful bureaucracy largely intact and used it to implement the fundamental social and economic reforms that were rammed through the Japanese Diet. Many had a New Deal flavor. The occupation promoted the Japanese labor movement, and the number of union workers increased fifteenfold in three years. The occupation also introduced American-style antitrust laws. The gigantic zaibatsu firms (see page 1096) were broken up into many separate companies in order to encourage competition and economic democracy. The American reformers proudly "emancipated" Japanese women, granting them equality before the law.

The occupation also imposed truly revolutionary land reform. MacArthur, often seen in the United States as a rigid conservative, pressured the Japanese Diet into buying up the land owned by absentee landlords and selling it to peasants on very generous terms. This reform strengthened the small, independent peasant, who became a staunch defender of postwar democracy.

The United States's efforts to remake Japan in its own image were powerful but short-lived. By 1948, when the United States began to look at the world through a cold war lens, occupation policy shifted gears. The Japanese later referred to this about-face as "the reverse course." As China went decisively communist, American leaders began to

see Japan as a potential ally, not as an object of social reform. The American command began purging leftists and rehabilitating prewar nationalists, many of whom joined the Liberal Democratic party, which became increasingly conservative and emerged as the dominant political organization in postwar Japan. The United States ended the occupation in 1952. Under the treaty terms, Japan regained independence and the United States retained its vast military complex in Japan. In actuality, Japan became a military protectorate, a special ally shielded, and restricted, by America's nuclear capability.

"Japan, Inc."

Restricted to satellite status in world politics, the Japanese people applied their exceptional creative powers to rebuilding their country. Japan's economic recovery, like Germany's, proceeded painfully slowly immediately after the war. At the time of the Korean War, however, the economy took off and grew with spectacular speed for a whole generation. Between 1950 and 1970 the real growth rate of Japan's economy—adjusted for inflation—averaged a breathtaking 10 percent a year—almost three times that of the United States. Even after the shock of much higher energy prices in 1973, the petroleum-poor Japanese did considerably better than most other peoples. In 1986 average per capita income in Japan exceeded that in the United States for the first time. As recently as 1965, the average Japanese had earned only one-fourth of the average American's income.

Japan's emergence as an economic superpower fascinated some outsiders and troubled others. While Asians and Africans looked to Japan for the secrets of successful modernization, some Americans and Europeans whipped up quick recipes for copying Japanese success. Some of Japan's Asian neighbors again feared Japanese exploitation. And in the 1970s and 1980s, some Americans and Europeans bitterly accused "Japan, Inc." of an unholy alliance between government and business. Industries and workers hurt by "unfair" Japanese competition called on their governments for aggressive countermeasures.

Many of the ingredients in western Europe's recovery also operated in Japan. American aid, cheap labor, and freer international trade all helped spark the process. As in western Europe, the government concentrated its energies on economic development. Japanese businessmen recognized the opportunity to replace their bombed-out plants with the latest, most efficient technology.

Japan's astonishing economic surge also seems to have had deep roots in Japanese history, culture, and national character. Restricted by geography to mountainous islands, Japan was for centuries safely isolated from invaders. By the time American and European pressure forced open its gates in the mid-nineteenth century, Japan was politically unified and culturally homogeneous. Agriculture, education, and material well-being were advanced even by European standards. Moreover, Japanese society put the needs of the group before those of the individual. When the Meiji reformers redefined Japan's primary task as catching up with the West, they had the support of a sophisticated and disciplined people. Japan's modernization, even including a full share of aggressive imperialism, was extremely rapid.

By the end of the American occupation, this tight-knit, group-centered society had reassessed its future and worked out a new national consensus. Japan's new task was to build its economy and compete efficiently in world markets. Improved living standards emerged as a related goal after the initial successes of the 1950s. The ambitious "double-your-income" target for the 1960s was ultimately surpassed by 50 percent.

Government and big business shared leading roles in the drama of economic growth. As during the Meiji Restoration (see page 984), capable, respected bureaucrats directed and aided the efforts of cooperative business leaders. The government decided which industries were important, then made loans and encouraged mergers to create powerful firms in those industries. The antitrust policy introduced by the American occupation, based on the very un-Japanese values of individualism and unrestrained competition, was scrapped.

Big business was valued and respected because it served the national goal and mirrored Japanese society. Big companies, and to a lesser extent small ones, traditionally hired workers for life immediately after they finished school. Employees were never fired and seldom laid off, and in return they were loyal and obedient. To an extent difficult for a Westerner to imagine, the business firm in Japan was a big, well-disciplined family. The workday be-

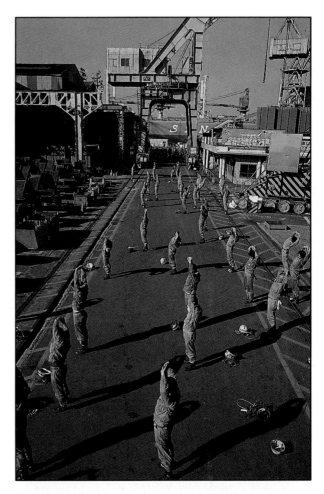

Company Spirit Japanese workers at this big shipping firm shout and sing in unison as they go through their morning exercise routine. Such practices encourage group solidarity in Japan, where the success of the group is placed above the success of the individual. *(Source: Paolo Koch/Photo Researchers, Inc.)*

gan with the company song. Employees' social lives also revolved around the company. Wages were based on age. (Discrimination against women remained severe: wages and job security were strikingly inferior.) Most unions became moderate, agreeable company unions. The social and economic distance between salaried managers and workers was slight and often breached. *Efficiency, quality,* and *quantity* were the watchwords. Management was quick to retrain employees, secure in the knowledge that they would not take their valuable new skills elsewhere. These factors, not "unfair" competition, were most important in accounting for Japan's economic success.

Japanese society, with its inescapable stress on cooperation and compromise, has proved well adapted to the challenges of modern industrial urban civilization. For example, Japan alone among industrial nations has experienced a marked decrease in crime over the last generation. In the 1970s and 1980s the Japanese addressed themselves effectively to such previously neglected problems as serious industrial pollution and their limited energy resources. Highly dependent on imported resources and foreign sales, Japan groped for a new role in world politics. Closer relations with China, increased loans to Southeast Asia, and tough trade negotiations with the United States were all features of that ongoing effort.

NEW NATIONS IN SOUTH ASIA AND THE MUSLIM WORLD

South Asia and the Muslim world have transformed themselves no less spectacularly than China and Japan. The national independence movements, which had been powerful mass campaigns since the 1930s, triumphed decisively over weakened and demoralized European imperialism after the Second World War. Between 1947 and 1962, as decolonization gathered irresistible strength, virtually every colonial territory won its political freedom. The complete reversal of the long process of European expansion was a turning point in world history.

The newly independent nations of South Asia and the revitalized states of the Muslim world exhibited many variations on the dominant themes of national renaissance and modernization, especially as the struggle for political independence receded into the past.

The Indian Subcontinent

After the First World War, Mahatma Gandhi and the Indian Congress party developed the philosophy of militant nonviolence to oppose British rule of India and to lessen oppression of the Indian poor by the Indian rich (see pages 1087–1090). By 1929 Gandhi had succeeded in transforming the Congress party from a narrow, middle-class party into a mass independence movement. Gradually and grudgingly, Britain's rulers introduced reforms culminating in limited self-government in 1937.

The Second World War accelerated the drive toward independence but also pointed it in a new direction. Congress party leaders, humiliated that Great Britain had declared war against Germany on India's behalf without consulting them, resigned their posts in the Indian government and demanded self-rule as the immediate price of political cooperation. In 1942, Gandhi called on the British to "Quit India" and threatened another civil disobedience campaign. He and the other Congress leaders were quickly arrested and jailed for the virtual duration of the war. As a result, India's wartime support for hard-pressed Britain was substantial but not always enthusiastic. Meanwhile, the Congress party's prime political rival skillfully seized the opportunity to increase its influence.

That rival was the Muslim League, led by the brilliant, elegant English-educated lawyer Muhammad Ali Jinnah (1876–1948). Jinnah and the other leaders of the Muslim League feared Hindu domination of an independent Indian state led by the Congress party. Asserting in nationalist terms the right of Muslim areas to separate from the Hindu majority, Jinnah described the Muslims of India as

a nation of a hundred million, and what is more, we are a nation with our distinct culture and civilization, language, literature, arts, and architecture . . . laws and moral codes, customs and special aptitudes and ambitions. In short, we have our own distinctive outlook on life and of life.[3]

Jinnah told 100,000 listeners at the Muslim League's Lahore Conference in March 1940,

If the British Government is really in earnest and sincere to secure the peace and happiness of the people of the subcontinent, the only course open to us all is to allow the major nations separate homelands by dividing India into autonomous national states.[4]

The Muslim League's insistence on the division of India appalled Gandhi. He regarded Jinnah's two-nation theory as simply untrue and as promising the victory of hate over love. Gandhi's argument was most accurate when applied to the Bengali Muslims of northeastern India's Ganges River basin. Their language, dress, racial appearance, food, and social customs were virtually identical to those of Bengali Hindus; only in religion did the two groups differ. The passionate debate between Jinnah and Gandhi continued unabated during the war as millions argued whether India was one nation or two. By 1945 the subcontinent was intellectually and emotionally divided, though still momentarily held together by British rule.

When Britain's Labour government agreed to speedy independence for India after 1945, conflicting Hindu and Muslim nationalisms and religious hatred became obstacles leading to murderous clashes between the two communities in 1946. In a last attempt to preserve the subcontinent's political unity, the British proposed a federal constitution providing for extensive provincial—and thus religious and cultural—autonomy. When after some hesitation Jinnah and the Muslim League would accept nothing less than an independent Pakistan, India's last viceroy—war hero Lord Louis Mountbatten (1900–1979), Queen Victoria's great-grandson—proposed partition. Both sides accepted. At the stroke of midnight on August 14, 1947, one-fifth of humanity gained political independence. As the sumptuous, horse-drawn coach of the last viceroy pulled away from the final ceremony, endless cries of "Long live Mountbatten!" rose from the tremendous crowds—ringing testimony to India's residue of good feeling toward its vanquished conquerors and their splendidly peaceful departure.

Yet independence through partition was to bring tragedy. In the weeks after independence, communal strife exploded into an orgy of massacres and mass expulsions. Perhaps 100,000 Hindus and Muslims were slaughtered, and an estimated 5 million refugees from both communities fled in opposite directions to escape being hacked to death by frenzied mobs.

This wave of violence was a bitter potion for Congress leaders, who were completely powerless to stop it. "What is there to celebrate?" exclaimed Gandhi. "I see nothing but rivers of blood."[5] In January 1948, announcing yet another fast to protest Hindu persecution of Muslims in the Indian capital of New Delhi and to restore "heart friendship" between the two communities, Gandhi was gunned down by a Hindu fanatic. As the Mahatma's death tragically testifies, the constructive and liberating forces of modern nationalism have frequently deteriorated into blind hatred.

After the ordeal of independence, relations between India and Pakistan—both members of the British Commonwealth—remained tense. Fighting over the disputed area of Kashmir continued until 1949 and broke out again in 1965–1966 and 1971. Mutual hostility remains deeply ingrained to this day (Map 37.1).

Pakistan Like many newly independent states, Pakistan eventually adopted an authoritarian government in 1958. Unlike most, Pakistan failed to preserve its exceptionally fragile unity, which proved to be the unworkable dream of its Muslim League leaders.

Pakistan's western and eastern provinces were separated by more than a thousand miles of Indian territory, as well as by language, ethnic background, and social custom. They shared only the Muslim faith that had temporarily brought them together against the Hindus. The Bengalis of East Pakistan constituted a majority of the population of Pakistan as a whole but were neglected by the central government, which remained in the hands of West Pakistan's elite after Jinnah's death. In essence, East Pakistan remained a colony of West Pakistan.

Tensions gradually came to a head in the late 1960s. Bengali leaders calling for virtual independence were charged with treason, and martial law was proclaimed in East Pakistan. In 1971 the Bengalis revolted. Despite savage repression—10 million Muslim Bengalis fled temporarily to India, which provided some military aid—the Bengalis won their independence as the new nation of Bangladesh in 1973. The world's eighth most populous country, Bangladesh remains one of its poorest.

India India was ruled for a generation after 1947 by Jawaharlal Nehru (1889–1964) and the Congress party, which introduced major social reforms. Hindu women and even young girls were granted legal equality, which included the right to vote, to seek a divorce, and to marry outside their caste. The constitution also abolished the untouchable caste and, in an effort to compensate for

MAP 37.1 The Partition of British India, 1947   Violence and fighting were most intense where there were large Hindu and Muslim minorities—in Kashmir, Punjab, and Bengal. The tragic result of partition, which has occurred repeatedly throughout the world in the twentieth century, was a forced exchange of populations and greater homogeneity on both sides of the border.

centuries of the most profound discrimination, established "ex-untouchable" quotas for university scholarships and government jobs. In practice, attitudes toward women and untouchables evolved slowly—especially in the villages, where 85 percent of the people lived.

The Congress leadership tried with modest success to develop the country economically by means of democratic socialism. But population growth of about 2.4 percent per year ate up much of the increase in output, and halfhearted government efforts to promote birth control met with indifference or hostility. Intense poverty remained the lot of most people and encouraged widespread corruption within the bureaucracy.

The Congress party maintained a moralizing neutrality in the cold war and sought to group India and other newly independent states in Asia and Africa into a "third force" of "nonaligned" nations. This effort culminated in the Afro-Asian Conference in Bandung, Indonesia, in 1955.

Nehru's daughter, Indira Gandhi (1917–1984), became prime minister in 1966. Mrs. Gandhi (whose deceased husband was no relation to Mahatma Gandhi) dominated Indian political life for a generation with a combination of charm, tact, and toughness. As it became clear that population growth was frustrating efforts to improve living standards, Mrs. Gandhi's government stepped up measures to promote family planning. Bus posters featuring smiling youngsters proclaimed that "A Happy Family Is a Small Family,"

and doctors and nurses promoted intra-uterine loop rings for women and condoms and surgical vasectomy for men. Most Indian males rejected vasectomy for both psychological and religious reasons. As a doctor in a market town explained to a Western journalist:

They have mostly heard of family planning around here by now, but they are afraid. They are afraid that the sterilizing operation will destroy their male power and make them docile, like castrated animals. Mostly, they are afraid of interfering with God's will.[6]

In the face of such reluctance—and in an effort to clamp down on widespread corruption at all levels of government—Mrs. Gandhi in 1975 subverted parliamentary democracy and proclaimed a state of emergency. Attacking dishonest officials, black marketeers, and tax evaders, she also threw the weight of the government behind a heavy-handed

Indian Refugees Independence and partition brought a wave of bloodshed that sent millions of Hindus and Muslims fleeing for their lives in opposite directions. Here desperate Muslims seek precious space atop a train that will carry them to safety in Pakistan. *(Source: Wide World Photos)*

campaign of mass sterilization to reduce population growth. In some areas, poor men with very large families were rounded up and made to accept a few cents' payment to submit to a simple, almost painless irreversible vasectomy. Everywhere the pressure was intense, and 7 million men were sterilized in 1976.

Many Indian and foreign observers believed that Mrs. Gandhi's emergency measures marked the end of the parliamentary democracy and Western liberties introduced in the last phase of British rule. But Mrs. Gandhi—true to the British tradition—called for free elections, in which she suffered a spectacular defeat, largely because of the vastly unpopular sterilization campaign and her subversion of democracy. But her successors fell to fighting among themselves, and in 1980 Mrs. Gandhi won an equally stunning electoral victory.

Her defeat and re-election undoubtedly strengthened India's democratic tradition.

Mrs. Gandhi's last years in office were plagued by another old political problem, one that cost her her life. Democratic India remained a patchwork of religions, languages, and peoples. This enduring diversity threatened to divide the country along ethnic or religious lines, as conflicting national aspirations had earlier torn British India into two and then three different states. Several peoples developed a strong ethnic consciousness and made political demands, most notably the 15 million Sikhs of the Punjab in northern India.

The Sikhs have their own religion—a blend of Islam and Hinduism—and a distinctive culture, including a warrior tradition and the wearing of elegantly coiled turbans. Industrious and cohesive, most Sikhs wanted (and still want) greater auton-

Sikh Patriots With the domes of the majestic Golden Temple rising behind them, a mass of Sikhs gather to protest the Indian army's bloody assault on their most holy shrine. The vast majority of Sikhs want greater autonomy at the least. Sikh radicals seek an independent state. *(Source: Bartholomew/Gamma-Liaison)*

ASIA SINCE 1945

1945	Japan surrenders
	Civil war begins in China
1946	Japan receives democratic constitution
	The Philippines gain independence
1947	Communal strife follows independence for India and Pakistan
1948	Civil war between Arabs and Jews in Palestine
1949	Korean War begins
	Mao Tse-tung (Mao Zedong) proclaims the People's Republic of China
	Indonesia under Sukarno wins independence from the Dutch
1950	China enters Korean War
	Japan begins long period of rapid economic growth
1951	Iran tries unsuccessfully to nationalize the Anglo-Iranian Oil Company
1952	American occupation of Japan officially ends
1954	Vietnamese nationalists defeat the French at Dien Bien Phu
1955	First Afro-Asian Conference of non-aligned nations meets at Bandung, Indonesia
1958	Mao Tse-tung announces the Great Leap Forward
1960	Open split between China and the Soviet Union emerges
1965	The Great Proletarian Cultural Revolution begins in China
	Growing American involvement in the Vietnamese civil war
1966	Indira Gandhi becomes Prime Minister of India
1972	President Nixon's visit to China signals improved Sino-American relations
1975	War in Vietnam ends with Communist victory
1976	China pursues modernization after Mao's death
1979	Revolution topples the shah of Iran
1984	Growth of Sikh nationalism in India
1986	Democratic movement in the Philippines brings Corazon Aquino to power
1989	Chinese government uses the army to crush student demonstrations

omy for the Punjab. By 1984, some radicals were fighting for an independent homeland—a Sikh national state. In retaliation, Mrs. Gandhi tightened control in the Punjab and ordered the army to storm the Sikhs' sacred Golden Temple at Amritsar. Six hundred died in the assault. Five months later, two of Mrs. Gandhi's Sikh bodyguards—she prided herself on their loyalty—cut her down with machine-gun fire in her own garden. Violence followed as Hindu mobs slaughtered over a thousand Sikhs throughout India.

Elected prime minister by a landslide sympathy vote, one of Mrs. Gandhi's sons, Rajiv Gandhi (1944–1991), showed considerable skill at effecting a limited reconciliation with a majority of the Sikh population. But slow economic growth, government corruption, and Rajiv Gandhi's lack of warmth gradually undermined his support. In 1989, he was voted out of office, and a fragile coalition of opposition took power. Despite poverty and ethnic tensions, India remained committed to free elections and representative government.

Southeast Asia

The rest of southeast Asia gained independence quickly after 1945, but the attainment of stable political democracy proved a more difficult goal.

Sri Lanka and Malaya Ceylon, renamed Sri Lanka in 1972, quickly and smoothly gained freedom from Britain in 1948. Malaya, however, encountered serious problems not unlike those of British India. The native Malays, an Islamic agricultural people, feared and disliked the Chinese,

President Corazón Aquino Shown here with her infectious smile and dignity, Corazón Aquino led the democratic movement to power in the Philippines and she enjoyed tremendous popular support. For millions of Filipinos she was simply "Cory"—their trusted friend. *(Source: Wide World Photos)*

who had come to the Malaya Peninsula as poor migrant workers in the nineteenth century and stayed on to dominate the urban economy. The Malays having pressured the British into giving them the dominant voice in a multi-ethnic federation of Malayan territories, local Chinese communists launched an all-out guerrilla war in 1948. They were eventually defeated by the British and the Malays, and Malaya became self-governing in 1957 and independent in 1961. Yet two peoples soon meant two nations. In 1965, the largely Chinese city of Singapore was pushed out of the Malayan-dominated Federation of Malaysia. Ethnic tension continued to erupt periodically in Malaysia, which still retained a large Chinese minority. The independent city-state of Singapore prospered on the hard work and inventiveness of its largely Chinese population.

The Philippine Islands The Philippine Islands (see Map 37.2) suffered greatly under Japanese occupation during the Second World War. After the war the United States extended economic aid while retaining its large military bases, and it fol-lowed through on its earlier promises by granting the Philippines independence in 1946. As in Malaya, communist guerrillas tried unsuccessfully to seize power. The Philippines pursued American-style two-party competition until 1965, when President Ferdinand Marcos (1917–1989) subverted the constitution and ruled as a dictator. Abolishing martial law in 1981 but retaining most of his power, Marcos faced growing opposition as the economy crumbled and land-hungry communist guerrillas made striking gains in the countryside. Led by a courageous Corazón Aquino (b. 1933), whose politician husband had been murdered, probably by Marcos supporters, the opposition won a spectacular electoral victory in 1986 and forced Marcos to take refuge in Hawaii, where he subsequently died.

As president, Mrs. Aquino negotiated a cease-fire with the communist rebels and beat off several attempted takeovers by dissident army officers. But a tiny elite continued to dominate the country, and the gap between rich and poor remained huge. The question of whether U.S. military bases in the Philippines should be closed after September 1991, when their lease came up for renewal, became a passionate and divisive issue. After four turbulent years in office, President Aquino and the Filipino people still faced the tremendous challenge of reconciliation and genuine reform.

Indonesia The Netherlands East Indies, having successfully resisted stubborn Dutch efforts at reconquest, emerged in 1949 as independent Indonesia under the nationalist leader Achmed Sukarno (1901–1970). The populous new nation encompassed a variety of peoples, islands, and religions (Islam was predominant; see Map 37.2). Beginning in 1957, Sukarno tried to forge unity by means of his so-called guided democracy. He rejected parliamentary democracy as politically divisive and claimed to replicate at the national level the traditional deliberation and consensus of the Indonesian village. For a time the authoritarian, anti-Western Sukarno seemed to be under the sway of well-organized Indonesian communists, who murdered and mutilated the seven leading army generals whom they had kidnapped as part of an unsuccessful uprising in 1965. The army immediately retaliated, systematically slaughtering a half-million or more Indonesian communists, radicals, and noncommunist Chinese. Sukarno was forced to resign, and Muslim generals ruled thereafter without any pretense of free and open political competition.

Vietnam, Laos, and Cambodia The most bitterly destructive fighting occurred in French Indochina. The French tried to reimpose imperial rule there after the communist and nationalist guerrilla leader Ho Chi Minh (1890–1969) declared an independent republic in 1945. In spite of considerable aid from the United States, the French were decisively defeated in 1954 in the battle of Dien Bien Phu. At the subsequent international peace conference, French Indochina gained independence. Laos and Cambodia (later known as Kampuchea) became separate states; Vietnam was "temporarily" divided into two hostile sections at the 17th parallel pending elections to select a single unified government within two years (see Map 36.3).

The elections were never held, and the civil war that soon broke out between the two Vietnamese governments, one communist and one anticommunist, became a very hot cold war conflict in the

1960s. The United States invested tremendous military effort but fought its Vietnam War as a deeply divided country (see pages 1201–1205). The tough, dedicated communists eventually proved victorious in 1975. Thus events in Vietnam roughly recapitulated those in China, but in a long, drawn-out fashion: after a bitter civil war worsened by cold war hatreds, the communists succeeded in creating a unified Marxist nation.

The Muslim World

Throughout the vast arc of predominantly Islamic lands that stretches from Indonesia in Southeast Asia to Senegal in West Africa (Map 37.2), change and bewildering internal conflict prevailed after 1945. But everywhere nationalism remained the predominant political force. Although anti-Western and hospitable to radical social reform, nationalism in the Muslim world remained consistently true to Islam and generally anticommunist. Cold war conflicts and enormous oil resources enhanced the region's global standing.

In the Arab countries of North Africa and the Middle East, with their shared but highly differentiated language and culture, nationalism wore two faces. The idealistic, unrealized side focused on the pan-Arab dream, the dream of uniting all Arabs in a single nation that would be strong enough to resist the West and achieve genuine independence. Like German or Italian nationalists in the mid-nineteenth century, pan-Arabs believed that Arabs formed a single people and that they were destined to have their own nation state. This pan-Arab vision contributed to political and economic alliances like the Arab League, but no Arab Bismarck appeared and the vision foundered on intense regional, ideological, and personal rivalries. Thus the practical, down-to-earth side of Arab nationalism focused largely on nation building *within* the particular states that supplanted former League of Nations mandates and European colonies.

Palestine and Israel Before the Second World War, Arab nationalists were loosely united in their opposition to the colonial powers and to Jewish migration to Palestine. The French gave up their League of Nations mandates in Syria and Lebanon in 1945, having been forced by popular uprisings

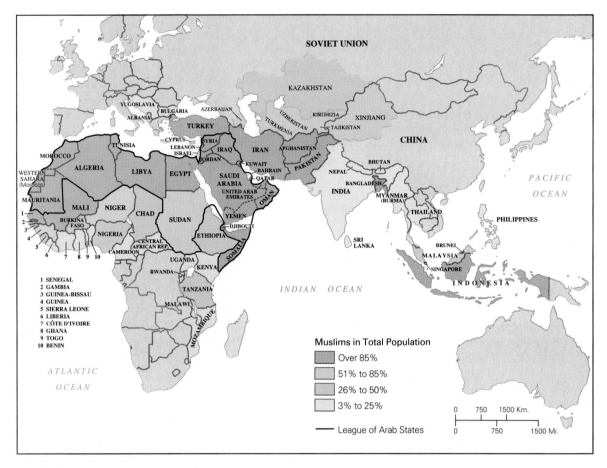

MAP 37.2 Modern Islam, ca 1990 Although the Islamic heartland remains the Middle East and North Africa, Islam is growing steadily in black Africa and is the faith of heavily populated Indonesia.

and British-American pressure to follow the British example. Attention then focused even more sharply on British-mandated Palestine. The situation was volatile. The Jews' demand that the British permit all survivors of Hitler's death camps to settle in Palestine was strenuously opposed by the Palestinian Arabs and the seven independent states of the newly founded Arab League (Egypt, Iraq, Jordan, Lebanon, Saudi Arabia, Syria, and Yemen). Murder and terrorism flourished, nurtured by bitterly conflicting Arab and Jewish nationalisms.

The British—their occupation policies in Palestine condemned by Arabs and Jews, by Russians and Americans—announced in 1947 their intention to withdraw from Palestine in 1948. The insoluble problem was dumped in the lap of the United Nations. In November 1947 the United Nations General Assembly passed a nonbinding

resolution supporting a plan to partition Palestine into two separate states—one Arab and one Jewish (Map 37.3). The Jews accepted but the Arabs rejected partition of Palestine.

By early 1948 an undeclared civil war was raging in Palestine. The departing British looked on impartially. When the British mandate officially ended on May 14, 1948, the Jews proclaimed the state of Israel. Arab countries immediately launched an attack on the new Jewish state. Fighting for their lives, the Israelis drove off the invaders and conquered more territory. Roughly 900,000 Arab refugees—the exact number is disputed—fled or were expelled from old Palestine. This war left an enormous legacy of Arab bitterness toward Israel and its political allies, Great Britain and the United States, and it led to the creation of the Palestine Liberation Organization, a

Legend:

- Israel after Arab invasion and War of Independence, 1948
- Occupied by Israel in Six-Day War, 1967
- Maximum occupation by Israel, 1982
- Arab nations
- Oil fields
- Suez Canal

Main map labels:

Mediterranean Sea

Beirut
Sidon
LEBANON
Tyre
Acre
Haifa
Sea of Galilee
Beirut-Damascus highway
Damascus
Mt. Hermon
SYRIA
GOLAN HEIGHTS

Tulkarm
Nablus
Tel Aviv
WEST BANK
ISRAEL
Jericho
Jerusalem
Amman
JORDAN
Ashqelon
Gaza
Hebron
Dead Sea
Beersheba
Rabba

Port Said
Israeli occupation line during Suez crisis, 1956
Israeli occupation line after Six-Day War, 1967
El Arish
El Qantara
Ismailia
Auja
NEGEV
Line of Israeli withdrawal from Sinai Peninsula, 1975
Great Bitter Lake
Cairo
SINAI PENINSULA
Memphis
Suez
El Shatt
Cease-fire line after Yom Kippur War, 1973
Israeli withdrawal from Sinai Peninsula completed, 1981
Elat
Aqaba
EGYPT
Nile
Abu Zenima
Gulf of Suez
Mt. Sinai
Gulf of Aqaba
SAUDI ARABIA
Nabq
Strait of Tiran
Sharm el Sheikh
Red Sea

0   50   100 Km.
0   50   100 Mi.

Inset map:

British Mandate of Palestine, 1920–1948
U.N. Partition Plan, Nov. 1947
- Proposed Jewish state
- Proposed Arab state
- International Zone

LEBANON
SYRIA
Acre
Haifa
Tulkarm
Tel Aviv
Nablus
Jaffa
Jericho
Jerusalem
Gaza
Hebron
Dead Sea
Beersheba
Mediterranean Sea
PALESTINE
EGYPT
NEGEV
TRANSJORDAN
SINAI PENINSULA

0   50 Km.
0   50 Mi.

MAP 37.3 Palestine, Israel, and the Middle East, 1947–1990 Since the British mandate expired on May 14, 1948, there have been five major wars and innumerable armed clashes in what was formerly Palestine. After winning the War of Independence in 1948, Israel achieved spectacular victories in 1967 in the Six-Day War, occupying the Sinai Peninsula, the Golan Heights, and the West Bank. The Yom Kippur War of 1973 eventually led to the Israeli evacuation of the Sinai and peace with Egypt, but there has been no agreement on the West Bank.

loose union of Palestinian refugee groups opposed to Israel.

Egypt   The humiliation of defeat triggered a nationalist revolution in Egypt, where a young army colonel named Gamal Abdel Nasser (1918–1970) drove out the corrupt and pro-Western king Farouk in 1952. A gifted politician and the unchallenged leader of the largest Arab state, Nasser enjoyed powerful influence in the Middle East and throughout Asia and Africa. Perhaps his most successful and widely imitated move was radical land reform: large estates along the Nile were nationalized and divided up among peasants without violence or drastic declines in production. Nasser, who preached the gospel of neutralism in the cold war and jailed Egyptian communists, turned for aid to the Soviet Union to demonstrate Egypt's

A Leader and His People   Millions of ordinary Egyptians were fanatically devoted to Gamal Abdel Nasser. Here he is mobbed by ecstatic supporters at the Cairo railroad station two days after an unsuccessful attempt on his life in 1954. *(Source: Popperfoto)*

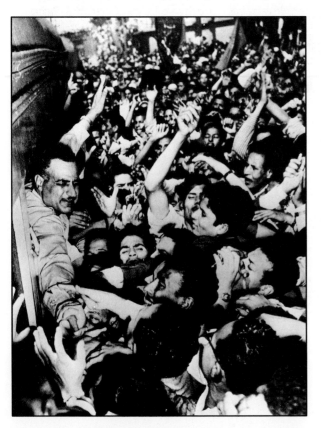

independence of the West. Relations with Israel and the West worsened, and in 1956 the United States abruptly canceled its offer to finance a giant new dam on the Nile, intended to promote economic development.

Nasser retaliated by immediately nationalizing the Suez Canal Company, the last remaining vestige and symbol of European power in the Middle East. Outraged, the British and French joined forces with the Israelis and successfully invaded Egypt. That action was to be the last gasp of imperial power in the Middle East in the 1950s. The Americans, suddenly moralistic, reversed course and sided with the Soviets—who were at that very moment crushing the Hungarian revolution—to force the British, French, and Israelis to withdraw from Egypt. This great victory for Nasser encouraged anti-Western radicalism, hopes of pan-Arab political unity, and a vague "Arab socialism." In Iraq radicals overthrew a conservative pro-Western government. In the aftermath of Suez, Egypt merged—temporarily—with Syria.

Yet the Arab world remained deeply divided. The only shared goals were opposition to Israel—war recurred in 1967 and in 1973—and support for the right of Palestinian refugees to return to their homeland. In late 1977, after more than a generation of bitter Arab-Israeli conflict, President Anwar Sadat of Egypt tried another tack: a stunningly unexpected official visit to Israel, where his meeting with Israeli Prime Minister Menachim Begin was watched on television by millions around the world. Sadat's visit led to direct negotiations between Israel and Egypt, which were effectively mediated by U.S. President Jimmy Carter, and a historic if limited peace settlement. Each country gained: Egypt got back the Sinai Peninsula, which Israel had taken in the 1967 Six-Day War (see Map 37.3), and Israel obtained peace and normal relations with Egypt. Sadat's initiative was denounced as treason by other Arab leaders, who continued to support the Palestine Liberation Organization against Israel.

After Sadat was assassinated by Islamic fundamentalists in 1981, Egypt's relations with the Begin government deteriorated badly over the question of ever-increasing Israeli settlement on the West Bank—the area west of the Jordan River inhabited by Palestinian Arabs but taken by Israel from Jordan during the 1967 war and occupied by Israel ever since. Yet Egypt quietly stood by when

Israeli troops occupied southern Lebanon in 1982 in an attempt to destroy the Palestine Liberation Organization. Israel's subsequent withdrawal from Lebanon helped preserve the fragile peace between the former enemies.

Algeria In the French colony of Algeria, Arab nationalism was emboldened by Nasser's great triumph—and by the defeat of the French in Indochina. Neighboring Tunisia and Morocco (see Map 37.2), both more recently colonized and sparsely settled by Europeans than Algeria, had won independence from France in 1956. But Algeria's large European population—1 million French-speaking Europeans lived among 8 million Muslims—considered Algeria home and an integral part of France. When nationalism stirred Algerian Muslims to revolt, they found themselves confronting a solid block of European settlers determined to defend their privileged position.

It was this determination that made the ensuing Algerian war so bitter and bloody. In 1958 a military coup in Algeria, resulting from the fears of the European settlers that a disillusioned, anticolonial majority of French voters would sell them out, brought General de Gaulle back to power in France. Contrary to expectations, de Gaulle accepted the principle of self-determination for Algeria in 1959, and in a national referendum the vast majority of the French population agreed. In 1962, after more than a century of French conquest, Algeria became an independent Arab state. The European population quickly fled.

Turkey, Iran, and Iraq The recent history of the non-Arab states of Turkey and Iran and the Arab state of Iraq (see Map 37.2) testify to the diversity of national development in the Muslim world. That history also dramatically illustrates the intense competition between rival states.

Turkey remained basically true to Atatürk's vision of a thoroughly modernized, secularized, Europeanized state (see page 1080). Islam played a less influential role in daily life and thought there than in other Middle Eastern countries, and Turkey joined NATO to protect itself from possible Soviet aggression.

Iran tried again to follow Turkey's example, as it had before 1939 (see page 1081). Once again, its success was limited. The new shah—Muhammad Reza Pahlavi (r. 1941–1979), the son of Reza Shah Pahlavi—angered Iranian nationalists by courting Western powers and Western oil companies in the course of freeing his country from Soviet influence after the war. In 1951, however, the shah accepted the effort of the Iranian Majlis and the fiery Prime Minister Muhammad Mossaddeq to nationalize the British-owned Anglo-Iranian Oil Company. In retaliation an effective Western boycott of Iranian oil plunged the economy into chaos. Refusing to compromise or be dismissed, Mossaddeq forced the shah to flee to Europe in 1953. But Mossaddeq's victory was short-lived, for the shah was quickly restored to his throne by loyal army officers and with the help of the American CIA.

The shah set out to build a powerful modern nation to ensure his rule. Iran's gigantic oil revenues provided the necessary cash. The shah undermined the power bases of the traditional politicians—large landowners and religious leaders—by means of land reform, secular education, and increased power for the central government. Modernization surged forward, but at the price of ancient values, widespread corruption, and harsh dictatorship. The result was a violent reaction against secular values: an Islamic revolution in 1978 led by religious leaders grouped around the spellbinding Ayatollah Ruholla Khomeini. After the shah fled Iran in 1979, radicals seized fifty-two American diplomats and imprisoned them for a year as they consolidated their power.

Iran's radical Islamic republic frightened its neighbors. Iraq, especially, feared that Iran—a nation of Shi'ite Muslims (see page 274)—would succeed in getting Iraq's Shi'ite majority to revolt against its Sunnite leaders. Thus in September 1980, Iraq's president Saddam Hussein (b. 1937) launched a surprise attack, expecting his well-equipped armies to defeat an increasingly chaotic Iran. Instead, Iraqi aggression galvanized the Iranian revolutionaries in a fanatical determination to defend their homeland and punish Iraq's leader. Iranians and Iraqis—Persians and Arabs—clashed in one of the bloodiest wars in modern times, a savage stalemate that killed hundreds of thousands of soldiers before finally grinding to a halt in 1988.

Emerging from the eight-year war with a big tough army and a sizable arsenal of weapons from Western countries and the Soviet bloc, Iraq's strong man set out to make himself the leader of a revitalized and radicalized Arab world. Eyeing the great oil wealth of his tiny southern neighbor, Saddam Hussein's forces suddenly overran Kuwait in August 1990 and proclaimed its annexation to Iraq. To Saddam's surprise, his aggression brought a vigorous international response (see page 1287). In early 1991 his troops were chased out of Kuwait by an American led, U.N.-sanctioned military coalition, after American planes had first destroyed most of Iraq's infrastructure with the heaviest bombing since the Second World War. The American troops, accompanied by small British, French, and Italian forces, were joined in ground operations against Iraq by some Arab forces from Egypt, Syria, and Saudia Arabia. Thus the Arab peoples, long wracked by bitter rivalries between nation-building states, came to fight a kind of bloody civil war as the 1990s opened.

IMPERIALISM AND NATIONALISM IN BLACK AFRICA

Most of sub-Saharan Africa won political independence fairly rapidly after the Second World War. Only Portugal's old but relatively underdeveloped African territories and white-dominated southern Africa remained beyond the reach of African nationalists by 1964. The rise of independent states in black Africa—a decisive development in world history—resulted directly from both a reaction against Western imperialism and the growth of African nationalism.

The Imperial System (1900–1930)

European traders had been in constant contact with Africa's coastal regions ever since the Age of Discovery. In the nineteenth century, as trade in so-called legitimate products like peanuts and palm oil increasingly supplanted traffic in human beings, European influence continued to grow. Then came the political onslaught. After 1880 the Great Powers scrambled for territory and pushed into the interior, using overwhelming military force to mow down or intimidate African opposition and establish firm rule (see pages 972–979). By 1900, most of black Africa had been conquered—or, as Europeans preferred to say, "pacified"—and a system of imperial administration was taking shape.

Gradually but relentlessly, this imperial system transformed Africa. Generally, its effect was to weaken or shatter the traditional social order and challenge accepted values. Yet this generalization must be qualified. For one thing, sub-Saharan Africa consisted of an astonishing diversity of peoples and cultures prior to the European invasion. There were, for example, over eight hundred distinct languages and literally thousands of independent political units, ranging all the way from tiny kinship groups to large and powerful kingdoms like Ashanti of central Ghana and Ethiopia. The effects of imperialism varied accordingly.

Furthermore, the European powers themselves took rather different approaches to colonial rule. The British tended to exercise indirect rule through existing chiefs. The French believed in direct rule by appointed officials, both black and white. Moreover, the number of white settlers varied greatly from region to region, and their presence had important consequences. In light of these qualifications, how did imperial systems generally operate in black Africa?

The self-proclaimed political goal of the French and the British—the principal foreign powers in black Africa—was to provide good government for their African subjects, especially after 1919. "Good government" meant, above all, law and order. It meant maintaining a small army and building up an African police force to put down rebellion, suppress tribal warfare, and protect life and property. Good government required a modern bureaucracy capable of taxing and governing the population. Many African leaders and their peoples had chosen not to resist the invader's superior force, and most others had stopped fighting after experiencing crushing military defeat. Thus the goal of law and order was widely achieved. This success was a source of great satisfaction to colonial officials. It strengthened their self-confidence and convinced them that they were serving the common people, who were assumed to want only peace and security.

Colonial governments demonstrated much less interest in providing basic social services than in establishing law and order. Expenditures on education, public health, hospitals, and other social services increased after the First World War but still remained small. Europeans feared the political implications of mass education and typically relied instead on the modest efforts of state-subsidized mission schools. Moreover, they tried to

District Officer on Tour For many Africans, imperialism meant the local colonial official, who might be a vicious, petty tyrant or a relatively enlightened administrator. This humorous wood carving by Thomas Ona grows out of the rich satirical tradition upheld by the Yoruba of western Nigeria. *(Source: Berta Bascom/Lowie Museum of Anthropology, University of California, Berkeley)*

make even their poorest colonies pay for themselves. Thus salaries for government workers normally absorbed nearly all tax revenues.

Economically, the imperialist goal was to draw the vast untapped interior of the continent into the rapidly expanding world economy on terms favorable to the dominant Europeans. The key was railroads, linking coastal trading centers to outposts hundreds of miles into the interior. Cheap, dependable transportation facilitated easy shipment of raw materials out and manufactured goods in. Most African railroads were built after 1900; 5,200 miles were in operation by 1926, when attention turned to road building for trucks. Railroads and roads had two other important outcomes. They allowed the quick movement of troops to put down any local unrest, and they allowed many African peasants to earn wages for the first time.

Efforts to force Africa into the world economy on European terms went hand in hand with the advent of plantations and mines. The Europeans often imposed head taxes, payable in money or labor, to compel Africans to work for their white overlords. No aspect of imperialism was more disruptive and more despised by Africans than forced labor, widespread until about 1920. In some regions, however, particularly in West Africa, African peasants responded freely to the new economic opportunities by voluntarily shifting to export crops on their own farms. Overall, the result was increased production geared to the world market and a gradual decline in both traditional self-sufficient farming and nomadic herding.

In sum, the imposition of bureaucratic Western rule and the gradual growth of a world-oriented cash economy between 1900 and 1930 had a revolutionary impact on large parts of Africa. The experiences of Ghana and Kenya, two very different African countries, dramatically illustrate variations on the general pattern.

Present-day Ghana (see Map 37.4), which takes its name from one of West Africa's most famous early kingdoms, had a fairly complex economy well before British armies smashed the powerful Ashanti kingdom in 1873 and established the Crown colony that they called the "Gold Coast." Precolonial local trade was vigorous and varied,

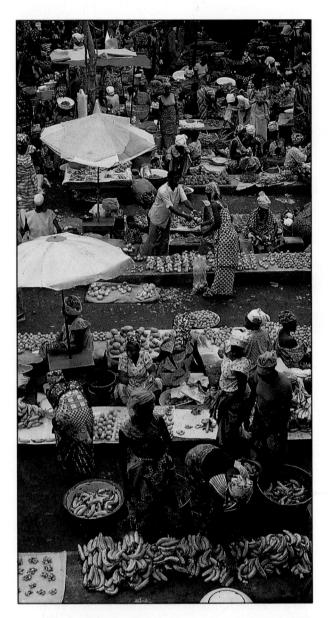

African Traders display their produce in this colorful, contemporary scene, which suggests the competition and the dynamism of a West African market. African traders and peasants have played a key role in the economic development of West Africa since the 1920s. *(Source: Cynthia Johnson/Gamma-Liaison)*

though occasionally disrupted by war and hindered by poor transportation, especially in the rainy season.

Into this sophisticated economy the British introduced production of cocoa beans for the world's chocolate bars. Output rose spectacularly,

from a few hundred tons in the 1890s to 305,000 tons in 1936. British imperialists loved to brag about the railroads to the interior, but recent studies clearly show that independent peasants and energetic African business people—many of the traders were women—were mainly responsible for the spectacular success of cocoa-bean production. Creative African entrepreneurs even went so far as to build their own roads, and they sometimes reaped big profits. During the boom of 1920, "motor cars were purchased right and left, champagne flowed freely, and expensive cigars scented the air."[7] As neighboring West African territories followed the Gold Coast's entrepreneurial example, West Africa took its place in the world economy.

The Gold Coast also showed the way politically and culturally. The Westernized elite—relatively prosperous and well-educated lawyers, professionals, and journalists—and business people took full advantage of opportunities provided by the fairly enlightened colonial regime. The black elite was the main presence in the limited local elections permitted by the British, for few permanent white settlers had ventured to hot and densely populated West Africa.

Across the continent in the British East African colony of Kenya, events unfolded differently. The East African peoples were more self-sufficient, less numerous, and less advanced commercially and politically than Africans in the Gold Coast. Once the British had built a strategic railroad from the Indian Ocean coast across Kenya to Uganda, foreigners from Great Britain and India moved in to exploit the situation. Indian settlers became shopkeepers, clerks, and laborers in the towns. The British settlers dreamed of turning the cool, beautiful, and fertile Kenya highlands into a "white man's country" like Southern Rhodesia or the Union of South Africa. They dismissed the local population of peasant farmers as "barbarians," fit only to toil as cheap labor on their large estates and plantations. By 1929, two thousand white settlers were producing a variety of crops for export.

The white settlers in Kenya manipulated the colonial government for their own interests and imposed rigorous segregation on the black (and Indian) population. Kenya's Africans thus experienced much harsher colonial rule than their fellow Africans in the Gold Coast.

The Growth of African Nationalism

Western intrusion was the critical factor in the development of African nationalism, as it had been in Asia and the Middle East. Yet two things were different about Africa. Because the imperial system and Western education did not solidify in Africa until after 1900, national movements did not come of age there until after 1945. And, too, Africa's multiplicity of ethnic groups, coupled with imperial boundaries that often bore no resemblance to existing ethnic boundaries, greatly complicated the development of political—as distinct from cultural—nationalism. Was a modern national state to be based on ethnic tribal loyalties (as it had been in France and Germany, in China and Japan)? Was it to be founded on an all-African union of all black peoples? Or would such a state have to be built on the multitribal territories arbitrarily carved out by competing European empires? Only after 1945 did a tentative answer emerge.

A few educated West Africans in British colonies had articulated a kind of black nationalism before 1914. But the first real impetus came from the United States and the British West Indies. American blacks struggling energetically for racial justice and black self-confidence early in the twentieth century took a keen interest in their African origins and in the common problems of all black people. Their influence on educated Africans was great.

Of the many persons who participated in this "black nationalism" and in the "Renaissance" of American black literature in the 1920s, the most renowned was W. E. B. Du Bois (1868–1963). The first black to receive a Ph.D. from Harvard, this brilliant writer and historian was stirred by President Woodrow Wilson's promises of self-determination. Thus Du Bois organized pan-African congresses in Paris during the Versailles Peace Conference and in Brussels in 1921. The goals of pan-Africanists were solidarity among blacks everywhere and, eventually, a vast self-governing union of all African peoples.

The European powers were hostile, of course, but so was the tiny minority of educated blacks in French Africa. As the influential Blaise Daigne, a black politician elected to the French parliament by the privileged African "citizens" of Senegal, told Du Bois:

We Frenchmen of Africa wish to remain French, for France has given us every liberty and accepted us without reservation along with her European children. None of us aspire to see French Africa delivered exclusively to the Africans as is demanded, though without any authority, by the American Negroes.[8]

More authoritarian than the British but less racist, French imperialists aimed to create a tiny elite of loyal "black Frenchmen" who would link the uneducated African masses to their white rulers. They were sometimes quite successful.

Many educated French and British Africans, however, experienced a strong surge of pride and cultural nationalism in the 1920s and 1930s, inspired in part by American and West Indian blacks. The Senegalese poet and political leader Léopold Senghor (b. 1906) is an outstanding example.

A gifted interpreter of Catholicism and of the French language in his native Senegal, Senghor discovered his African heritage in the cafés and lecture halls of Paris. He and other black and white students and intellectuals marveled at the accomplishments of American blacks in art, literature, African history, and anthropology. They listened to black musicians—jazz swept Europe by storm—and concluded that "in music American Negroes have acquired since the War a place which one can call pre-eminent; for they have impressed the entire world with their vibrating or melancholy rhythms."[9]

Senghor and his circle formulated and articulated the rich idea of *négritude*, or blackness: racial pride, self-confidence, and joy in black creativity and the black spirit. The powerful cultural nationalism that grew out of the cross-fertilization of African intellectuals and blacks from the United States and the West Indies was an unexpected by-product of European imperialism.

Black consciousness also emerged in the British colonies between the world wars—especially in West Africa. The Westernized elite pressed for more equal access to government jobs, modest steps toward self-government, and an end to humiliating discrimination. This elite began to claim the right to speak for ordinary Africans and to denounce the government-supported chiefs as "Uncle Toms." Yet the great majority of well-educated British and French Africans remained moderate in their demands. They wanted to join the white man's club, not to tear it down.

The Great Depression was the decisive turning point in the development of African nationalism. For the first time, unemployment was widespread among educated Africans, who continued to increase in number as job openings in government and the large foreign trading companies remained stable or even declined. Hostility toward well-paid white officials rose sharply. The Western-educated elite became more vocal, and some real radicals appeared.

Educated Africans ventured into new activities, often out of necessity. Especially in the towns, they supplied the leadership for many new organizations, including not only political parties and trade unions, but also social clubs, native churches, and agricultural cooperatives. Radical journalists published uncompromising attacks on colonial governments in easy-to-read mass-circulation newspapers. The most spectacular of these journalists was the Nigerian Nnamdi Azikiwe, who had attended black colleges in the United States and learned his trade on an African-American weekly in Baltimore. The popular, flamboyant "Zik" was demanding independence for Nigeria as early as the late 1930s.

The Great Depression also produced extreme hardship and profound discontent among the African masses. African peasants and small-business people who had been drawn into world trade, and sometimes profited from booms, felt the agony of decade-long bust. Urban workers, many of whom were disaffiliated from their rural tribal origins, experienced a similar fate. In some areas the result was unprecedented mass protest.

The Gold Coast "cocoa holdups" of 1930–1931 and 1937–1938 are the most famous example. Cocoa completely dominated the Gold Coast's economy. As prices plummeted after 1929, cocoa farmers refused to sell their beans to the large British firms that fixed prices and monopolized the export trade. Instead, the farmers organized cooperatives to cut back production and sell their crops directly to European and American chocolate manufacturers. Small African traders and traditional tribal leaders largely supported the movement, which succeeded in mobilizing much of the population against the foreign companies. Many Africans saw the economic conflict in racial terms. The holdups were only partially successful, but they did force the government to establish an independent cocoa marketing board. They also demonstrated that mass organization and mass protest had come to advanced West Africa. Powerful mass movements for national independence would not be far behind.

Achieving Independence with New Leaders

The repercussions of the Second World War in black Africa greatly accelerated the changes begun in the 1930s. Mines and plantations strained to meet wartime demands. Towns mushroomed into cities whose tin-can housing, inflation, and shortages of consumer goods created discontent and hardship. Africans had such eye-opening experiences as the curious spectacle of the British denouncing the racism of the Germans. Many African soldiers who served in India were powerfully impressed by Indian nationalism.

The attitudes of Western imperialists changed also. Both the British and the French acknowledged the need for rapid social and economic improvement in their colonies; both began sending money and aid on a large scale for the first time. The French funneled more money into their West African colonies between 1947 and 1957 than during the entire previous half-century. The principle of self-government was written into the United Nations charter and was fully supported by Great Britain's postwar Labour government. As one top British official stated in 1948:

The central purpose of British colonial policy is simple. It is to guide the colonial territories to responsible government within the commonwealth in conditions that ensure to the people concerned both a fair standard of living and freedom from oppression from any quarter.[10]

Thus the key question for Great Britain's various African colonies was their rate of progress toward self-government. The British and the French were in no rush. But a new breed of African leader was emerging. Impatient and insistent, these spokesmen for modern African nationalism were remarkably successful: by 1964 almost all of western, eastern, and central Africa had achieved statehood, usually without much bloodshed.

The new postwar African leaders shared common characteristics. They formed an elite by virtue

NATIONALISM IN BLACK AFRICA

1919	Du Bois organizes first pan-African congress
1920s	Cultural nationalism grows among Africa's educated elites
1929	Great Depression brings economic hardship and discontent
1930–1931	Farmers in the Gold Coast organize first "cocoa hold-ups"
1939–1945	World War Two accelerates political and economic change
1951	Nkrumah and Convention People's Party win national elections
1957	Nkrumah leads Ghana—former Gold Coast—to independence
1958	De Gaulle offers commonwealth status to France's African territories; Guinea alone chooses independence
1960	Mali and Nigeria become independent states
1966	Ghana's Nkrumah deposed in military coup
1967	Eastern Region secedes from Nigeria to form state of Biafra
1975	Nigeria's military rulers permit elected civilian government
1980	Blacks rule Zimbabwe—formerly southern Rhodesia—after long civil war with white settlers
1983	South Africa's whites maintain racial segregation and discrimination
1989–1990	South African government begins process of reform; black leader Nelson Mandella freed from prison

of advanced European (or American) education, and they were profoundly influenced by Western thought. But compared with the interwar generation of educated Africans, they were more radical and humbler in social origin. Among them were former schoolteachers, union leaders, government clerks, and unemployed students, as well as lawyers and prize-winning poets.

Furthermore, the postwar African leaders expressed their nationalism in terms of the existing territorial governments. They accepted prevailing boundaries to avoid border disputes and to facilitate building unified modern states. Sometimes traditional tribal chiefs became their worst political enemies. Skillfully, the new leaders channeled postwar hope and discontent into support for mass political parties. These new parties in turn organized gigantic protests and eventually came to power by winning elections held by the colonial government to choose its successor.

Ghana Shows the Way

Perhaps the most charismatic of this fascinating generation of African leaders was Kwame Nkrumah (1909–1972). Under his leadership the Gold Coast—which he rechristened "Ghana"—became the first independent African state to emerge from colonialism. Having begun his career as a schoolteacher in the Gold Coast, Nkrumah spent ten years studying in the United States, where he was deeply influenced by European socialists and by the Jamaican-born black leader Marcus Garvey (1887–1940). Convinced that blacks could never win justice in countries with white majorities, Garvey had organized a massive "Back to Africa" movement in the 1920s. He also preached "Africa for the Africans," calling for independence. Nkrumah returned to the Gold Coast immediately after the war and entered politics.

And the time was ripe. Economic discontent erupted in rioting in February 1948; angry crowds looted European and Lebanese stores. The British, embarking on their new course, invited African proposals for constitutional reform. These proposals became the basis of the new constitution, which gave more power to Africans within the framework of (eventual) parliamentary democracy.

Meanwhile Nkrumah was building a radical mass party appealing particularly to modern elements—former servicemen, market women, union members, urban toughs, and cocoa farmers. Nkrumah and his party injected the joy and enthusiasm

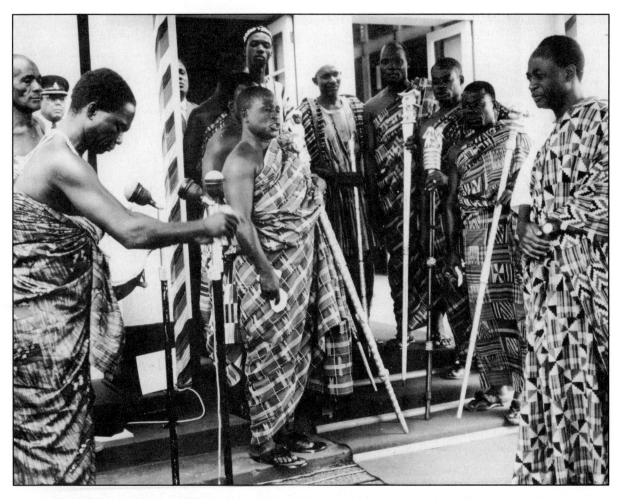

The Opening of Parliament in Ghana As part of an ancient ritual, two medicine men pour out sacred oil and call upon the gods to bless the work of the Second Parliament and President Kwame Nkrumah, standing on the right. The combination of time-honored customs and modern political institutions has been characteristic of African states since independence. *(Source: Wide World Photos)*

of religious revivals into their rallies and propaganda: "Self-Government Now" was their credo, secular salvation the promise.

Rejecting halfway measures—"We prefer self-government with danger to servitude in tranquillity"—Nkrumah and his Convention People's party staged strikes and riots. Arrested, the "Deliverer of Ghana" campaigned from jail and saw his party win a smashing victory in the national elections of 1951. Called from prison to head the transitional government, Nkrumah and his nationalist party continued to win victories in free elections, defeating both Westernized moderates and more traditional "tribal" rivals. By 1957 Nkrumah

had achieved worldwide fame and influence as Ghana became the first African state to emerge from colonial control.

After Ghana's breakthrough, independence for other African colonies followed with breathtaking speed. As in Algeria, the main problem was the permanent white settlers, as distinguished from the colonial officials. Wherever white settlers were at all numerous, as in Kenya, they sought to preserve their privileged position. This white hope was fed by a substantial influx of white settlers after 1945, especially in central Africa. Yet only in Southern Rhodesia were whites numerous enough to prevail long. Southern Rhodesian whites declared independence illegally in 1965 and held out for more than a decade until black nationalists won a long guerrilla war and renamed the country Zimbabwe. In Zambia (formerly Northern Rhodesia) and East Africa, white settlers simply lacked the numbers to challenge black nationalists or the British colonial office for long.

French-speaking Regions

Decolonization took a somewhat different course in French-speaking Africa. France tried hard to hold on to Indochina and Algeria after 1945. Thus, although France upped its financial and technical aid to its African colonies, *independence* remained a dirty word until de Gaulle came to power in 1958. Seeking to head off radical nationalists, and receiving the crucial support of moderate black leaders, de Gaulle divided the federations of French West Africa and French Equatorial Africa into thirteen separate governments, thus creating a "French commonwealth." Plebiscites were called in each territory to ratify the new arrangement. An affirmative vote meant continued ties with France; a negative vote signified immediate independence and a complete break with France.

De Gaulle's gamble was shrewd. The educated black elite—as personified by the poet Senghor, who now led the government of Senegal (see Map 37.4)—loved France and dreaded a sudden divorce. They also wanted French aid to continue. France, in keeping with its ideology of assimilation, had given the vote to the educated elite in its colonies after the Second World War, and about forty Africans held seats in the French parliament after 1946. Some of these impressive African politicians exercised real power and influence in metropolitan France. The Ivory Coast's Félix Houphouét-Boigny, for instance, served for a time as France's minister of health. For both cultural and practical reasons, therefore, French Africa's leaders tended to be moderate and in no rush for independence.

Yet political nationalism was not totally submerged. In Guinea (see Map 37.4), an inspiring young radical named Sekou Touré (1922–1984) led his people in overwhelming rejection of the new constitution in 1958. Touré had risen to prominence as a labor leader in his country's rap-idly expanding mining industry; he had close ties with France's Communist-dominated trade unions and was inspired by Ghana's Nkrumah. Touré laid it out to de Gaulle, face to face:

We have to tell you bluntly, Mr. President, what the demands of the people are. . . . We have one prime and essential need: our dignity. But there is no dignity without freedom. . . . We prefer freedom in poverty to opulence in slavery.[11]

De Gaulle punished Guinea as best he could. French officials and equipment were withdrawn, literally overnight, down to the last man and pencil. Guinea's total collapse was widely predicted— and devoutly hoped for in France. Yet Guinea's new government survived. Following Guinea's lead, Mali asked for independence in 1960. The other French territories quickly followed suit, though the new states retained close ties with France.

Belgium tried belatedly to imitate de Gaulle in its enormous Congo colony, but without success. Long-time practitioners of extreme paternalism, coupled with harsh, selfish rule, the Belgians had discouraged the development of an educated elite. In 1959, therefore, when after wild riots they suddenly decided to grant independence, the fabric of government simply broke down. Independence was soon followed by violent tribal conflict, civil war, and foreign intervention. The Belgian Congo was the great exception to black Africa's generally peaceful and successful transition to independence between 1957 and 1964.

BLACK AFRICA SINCE 1960

The ease with which most of black Africa achieved independence stimulated buoyant optimism in the early 1960s. As Europeans congratulated themselves on having fulfilled their "civilizing mission," Africans and sympathetic Americans anticipated even more rapid progress.

A generation later the outlook was different. In most former colonies, democratic government and civil liberties had given way to one-party rule or military dictatorship. Even where dictatorship did not prevail or was overturned, political conduct in Africa often seemed to slip into reverse gear. In many countries it was routine for the winners in a political power struggle to imprison, exile, or murder the losers. Corruption was widespread; politicians, army officers, and even lowly government clerks used their positions to line their pockets and reward their relatives. Meanwhile, the challenge of constructive economic and social development sometimes appeared overwhelming in a time of global crisis (see Chapter 39).

Some European and American observers, surveying these conditions, went so far as to write off Africa as a lost cause. Such a dismissal betrayed a limited vision and a serious lack of historical perspective. Given the scope of their challenges, the new African countries did rather well after achieving political independence. Nationalism, first harnessed to throw off imperialism, served to promote some degree of unity and ongoing modernization. Fragile states held together and began to emerge as viable modern nation-states with their own distinct personalities.

Building National Unity

The course of African history after independence was complex and often confusing. Yet the common legacy of imperialism resulted in certain basic patterns and problems.

The legacy of imperialism in Africa was by no means all bad. One positive outcome was the creation of about forty well-defined states (see Map 36.3, page 1180). These new states inherited functioning bureaucracies, some elected political leaders, and some modern infrastructure—that is, transportation, schools, hospitals, and the like.

The new African states also inherited relatively modern, diversified social structures. Traditional tribal and religious rulers had generally lost out to a dynamic Westernized elite whose moderate and radical wings faithfully reproduced the twentieth-century political spectrum. Each new state also had the beginnings of an industrial working class (as well as a volatile urban poor population). Each country also inherited the cornerstone of imperial power—a tough, well-equipped army to maintain order.

Other features of the imperialist legacy served to torment independent Africa, however. The disruption of traditional life caused real suffering and resulted in postindependence expectations that could not be met. The prevailing export economies were weak, lopsided, and concentrated in foreign hands. Technical, managerial, and medical skills were in acutely short supply. Above all, the legacy of political boundaries imposed by foreigners without regard to ethnic and cultural groupings weighed heavily on postindependence Africa. Almost all of the new states encompassed a variety of peoples, with different languages, religions, and cultures. In such circumstances, building up the central government and forging a truly unified country could conflict with ethnic loyalties. As in the Austrian Empire in the nineteenth century or in British India before independence, different peoples might easily develop conflicting national aspirations.

The multi-ethnic character of the new states had a powerful impact on African political development after 1960. Great Britain and France had granted Africa democratic government in the belief that, if Africans insisted on independence, they might as well get the best. Yet Western-style democracy served poorly. Political parties often coalesced along regional and ethnic lines, so that political competition encouraged regional and ethnic conflict and promoted political crisis. Many African leaders concluded that democracy threatened to destroy the existing states, which they deemed essential for social and economic progress in spite of their less-than-perfect boundaries. These leaders imposed tough measures to hold their countries together, and free elections often gave way to dictators and one-party rule.

After Ghana won its independence, for instance, Nkrumah jailed without trial his main opponents—chiefs, lawyers, and intellectuals—and outlawed opposition parties. Embracing the totalitarian model, Nkrumah worked to build a dynamic "revolutionary" one-party state. His personality, his calls for African unity, and his bitter attacks on "Western imperialists" aroused both strong support and growing opposition. By the mid-1960s Nkrumah's grandiose economic projects had almost bankrupted Ghana, and in 1966 the army suddenly seized power while Nkrumah was visiting China. Across the continent in East Africa, Kenya and Tanzania likewise became one-party states with strong leaders.

The French-speaking countries also shifted toward one-party government to promote state unity and develop distinctive characteristics that could serve as the basis for statewide nationalism. Mali followed Guinea into fiery radicalism. Senegal and the Ivory Coast stressed moderation and close economic and cultural ties with France.

Like Nkrumah, many of the politicians at the helm of one-party states were eventually overthrown by military leaders. "The man on horseback" became a familiar figure in postindependence Africa. Between 1952, when Egypt's King Farouk was overthrown by Colonel Nasser, and 1968, Africa experienced at least seventy attempted military takeovers, twenty of which succeeded. The trend continued after 1968 with important coups in Ethiopia, Liberia, Uganda, and elsewhere. The rise of would-be Napoleons was lamented by many Western liberals and African intellectuals, who often failed to note that military rule was also widespread in Latin America, Asia, and the Near East.

As elsewhere, military rule in Africa was authoritarian and undemocratic. Sometimes it placed a terrible burden on Africans. In Uganda, for instance, Idi Amin (b. 1925?), a brutal former sergeant, seized power, packed the army with his tribal supporters, and terrorized the population for a decade. Yet military government often had redeeming qualities. African military leaders generally managed to hold their countries together, and they worked to build existing states into viable nations.

Equally important, and like their counterparts in Latin America (see pages 1205–1209), military regimes were usually committed to social and economic modernization. Drawing on a well-educated, well-organized, and highly motivated elite, they sometimes accomplished a good deal. Finally, African military leaders often believed in the ultimate goal of free, representative civilian government, which they sometimes restored after surmounting a grave national crisis. It was a question of priorities: unity came first, democracy second.

Nigeria, Africa's Giant

The history of Nigeria illustrates just how difficult nation building could be when state and ethnic boundaries were at odds with each other. "Nigeria" was a name coined by the British to designate their conquests in the Niger River basin (Map 37.4). The peoples of Nigeria encompassed many ancient kingdoms and hundreds of smaller groupings. The northern region was part of a great open plain, devoted to grazing and intensive farming. The much smaller southern region was a combination of coastal swamp and inland forest belt. Most of the peoples of the north were Muslims; most southerners were Christians or animists. The south was dominated by two very different peoples: in the west the proud Yorubas, with a military tradition and strong, well-defined kingdom; in the east the Ibos, with a tradition of business enterprise and independent villages.

Modern Nigeria came into being in 1914, when the British arbitrarily consolidated the northern and southern territories for administrative convenience. One British governor described Nigeria in 1920 as a

collection of self-contained and mutually independent Native States, separated from one another, as many of them are, by differences of history and traditions, and by ethnological, racial, tribal, political, and religious barriers.[12]

Such a land, the governor believed, could never be welded into a single homogeneous nation.

In spite of its internal divisions, by 1945 Nigeria had spawned a powerful independence movement. The British responded receptively, and Nigeria entered into a period of intense but peaceful negotiation. In 1954, the third constitution in seven years set up the framework within which independence was achieved in 1960.

The key constitutional question was the relationship between the central government and the various regions. Some Nigerians, like the fiery Ibo journalist Azikiwe, wanted a strong centralized state, but the Yorubas in the west and the Muslim Hausa-Fulani leaders in the north wanted real power concentrated at the regional level. Ultimately Nigeria adopted a federal system, whereby the national government at Lagos shared power with three regional or state governments in the north, west, and east. Each region had a dominant tribe and a corresponding political party. The parties were expected to cooperate in the national parliament, and the rights of minorities were protected by law.

With a population of 55 million in 1963, "Africa's Giant" towered over the other new African nations. But after independence, Nigerians' bright

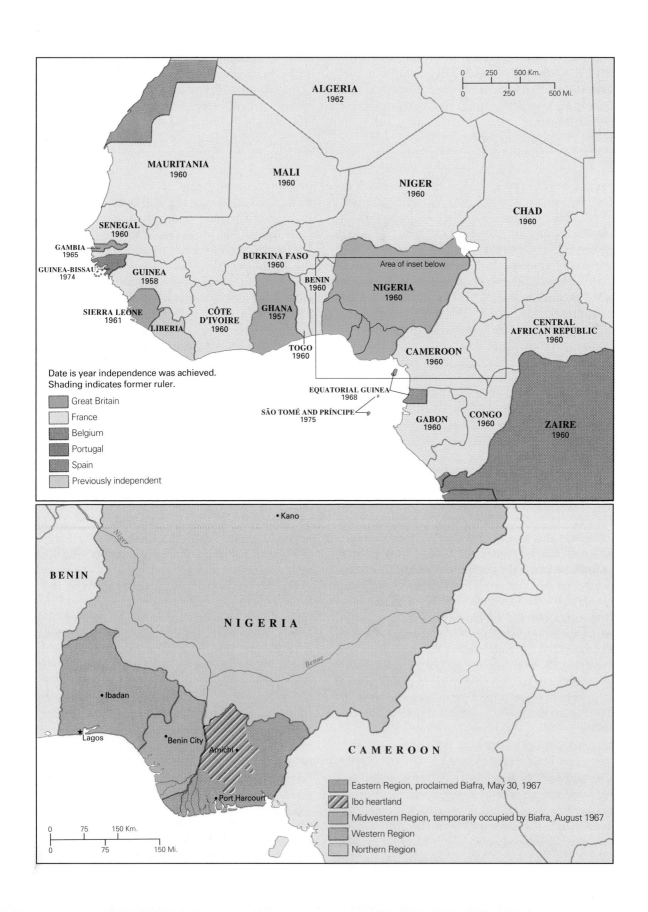

ALGERIA
1962

0   250   500 Km.
0   250   500 Mi.

MAURITANIA
1960

MALI
1960

NIGER
1960

CHAD
1960

SENEGAL
1960

GAMBIA
1965

GUINEA-BISSAU
1974

GUINEA
1958

BURKINA FASO
1960

Area of inset below

NIGERIA
1960

SIERRA LEONE
1961

CÔTE
D'IVOIRE
1960

BENIN
1960

GHANA
1957

CENTRAL
AFRICAN REPUBLIC
1960

LIBERIA

TOGO
1960

CAMEROON
1960

Date is year independence was achieved.
Shading indicates former ruler.

EQUATORIAL GUINEA
1968

SÃO TOMÉ AND PRÍNCIPE
1975

GABON
1960

CONGO
1960

ZAIRE
1960

Great Britain
France
Belgium
Portugal
Spain
Previously independent

• Kano

BENIN

Niger

N I G E R I A

Benue

• Ibadan

★
Lagos

• Benin City

Amichi •

CAMEROON

• Port Harcourt

0   75   150 Km.
0   75   150 Mi.

Eastern Region, proclaimed Biafra, May 30, 1967
Ibo heartland
Midwestern Region, temporarily occupied by Biafra, August 1967
Western Region
Northern Region

Mobilizing in Biafra A Biafran officer, himself only nine years old, drills a column of fresh recruits in 1969 during the Nigerian civil war. The boy soldiers were used for spying and sabotage, as Biafra struggled desperately against encirclement and starvation to win its independence. *(Source: Pictorial Parade)*

hopes gradually dimmed. Ethnic rivalries made for political tensions. In 1964, minorities in the Western Region began forming their own Midwestern Region in an attempt to escape Yoruba domination (see Map 37.4). Tribal battles ensued, and in 1965 law and order broke down completely in the Western Region. At this point a group of young army officers seized power in the capital city of Lagos, executing leading politicians and all officers above the rank of major. In an attempt to end the national crisis, the new military council imposed martial law and abolished the regional governments.

At first the young officers were popular, for the murdered politicians had been widely considered weak, corrupt, and too pro-Western. However,

MAP 37.4 Nationalism and Independence in West Africa Most of West Africa achieved independence by 1960. Borders inherited from the colonial era were generally accepted, although the Ibo people tried unsuccessfully to break away from Nigeria in the bitter Nigerian civil war.

most of the new military leaders were Ibos. The Muslim northerners had long distrusted the hard-working, clannish, non-Muslim Ibos, who under the British had come to dominate business and the professions throughout Nigeria. Thus every town in the Muslim north had its Ibo "strangers' district." When the Ibo-led military council proclaimed a highly centralized dictatorship, angry mobs in northern cities went wild. Thousands of Ibos were brutally massacred, and the panic-stricken survivors fled to their Ibo homeland. When a group of northern officers then seized the national government in a counter-coup, the traumatized Ibos revolted. Like the American South in the Civil War, the Eastern Region seceded from Nigeria in 1967 and proclaimed itself the independent state of Biafra (see Map 37.4).

The war in Biafra lasted three long years. The Ibos fought with heroic determination, believing that political independence was their only refuge from genocide. Heavily outnumbered, the Ibos were gradually surrounded. Perhaps millions starved to death as Biafra became another name for monumental human tragedy.

But Nigeria, like Abraham Lincoln's Union, endured. The civil war entered the history books of the victors as the "War for Nigerian Unity," not the "War for Biafran Independence." Whatever its name, the conflict in Nigeria showed the world that Africa's "artificial" boundaries and states were remarkably durable.

Having preserved the state in the 1960s, Nigeria's military focused on building a nation in the 1970s. Although the federal government held the real power, the country was divided into nineteen small, manageable units to handle local and cultural matters. The defeated Ibos were generously pardoned, not slaughtered, and Iboland was rebuilt with federal money. Modernizing investments of this kind were made possible by soaring oil revenues; Nigeria became the world's seventh largest oil producer.

In 1979, after thirteen years of military rule, Nigeria's army leaders were confident enough to relinquish power to an elected civilian government. Yet four years later the army again seized control, arresting the civilian politicians at the head of Nigeria's Second Republic. Once again, the coup was popular, for the politicians had mismanaged the economy and lined their pockets with bribes and kickbacks. But the military rulers soon imposed a harsh dictatorship that violated human rights as badly as the greedy politicians had abused the public trust. The military dictatorship was dominated by Hausa-Fulani Muslims, and these northerners practiced a tribal favoritism that threatened to reignite regional and ethnic tensions that were never far beneath the surface. Thus a group of reforming officers engineered another coup in 1985, promising more liberty and less favoritism. The new generals showed greater respect for basic rights, but they repeatedly postponed national elections and maintained military rule to hold Nigeria together.

The Struggle in Southern Africa

After the great rush toward political independence, decolonization stalled. Meanwhile, southern Africa remained under white rule, largely because of the numerical strength and determination of its white settlers. In Portuguese Angola and Mozambique, the white population actually increased from 70,000 to 380,000 between 1940 and the mid-1960s as white settlers using forced native labor established large coffee farms.

As economic exploitation grew, so did resentment. Nationalist liberation movements arose to wage unrelenting guerrilla warfare. After a coup overturned the long-established dictatorship in Portugal, African guerrillas managed to take control in Angola and Mozambique in 1975. Shortly thereafter, a coalition of nationalist groups also won in Zimbabwe after a long struggle.

This second round of decolonization in black Africa was bloodier than the first, and a third round in South Africa threatened to be still worse. The racial conflict in the white-ruled Republic of South Africa (Map 37.5) could be traced back in history—to the seventeenth-century Dutch settlers, to complex rivalries between black tribes, to settler wars of extermination and enslavement in the eighteenth and nineteenth centuries, and to the surging British imperialism that resulted in the Boer War (see page 973). Although the British finally conquered the inland Afrikaner republics, they had to compromise to avoid a long guerrilla war. Specifically, the British agreed to grant all of South Africa self-government as soon as possible and to let its government decide which non-whites, if any, should vote. It was to be a tragic compromise.

Defeated on the battlefield, the embittered Afrikaners elaborated a potently racist nationalism. Between 1910—when South Africa became basically a self-governing dominion, like Canada and Australia—and 1948, the Afrikaners gradually won political power from their English-speaking settler rivals. After their decisive electoral victory in 1948, Afrikaner nationalists spoke increasingly for a large majority of South African whites, who supported the political leadership with varying degrees of enthusiasm.

The goals of Afrikaner nationalism in the twentieth century were remarkably consistent: white supremacy and racial segregation. In 1913, the new South African legislature passed the Native Land Act, which limited black ownership of land to native reserves encompassing a mere one-seventh of the country. Poor, overpopulated, and too small to feed themselves, the native reserves in the countryside served as a pool of cheap, temporary black labor for white farms, gold mines, and urban factories. A black worker—typically a young single person—could leave the reserve only with

MAP 37.5 The Republic of South Africa and Apartheid, ca 1960 Despite repressive apartheid laws, many blacks managed to leave the reserves for South Africa's growing cities, where most Indians and coloureds already lived.

special permission. In the eyes of the law, he or she was only a temporary migrant who could be returned at will by the employer or the government. Thus so-called pass laws required every black outside the reserves to carry at all times an up-to-date pass approved by the white police. The native reserves system, combining racial segregation and indirect forced labor, formed the foundation of white supremacy in South Africa.

After 1948, successive Afrikaner governments wove the somewhat haphazard early racist measures into an authoritarian fabric of racial discrimination and inequality. This system was officially known as *apartheid,* meaning "separation" or "segregation." The population was dogmatically divided into four legally unequal racial groups: whites, blacks, Asians, and racially mixed "col-

oureds." Afrikaner propagandists claimed to serve the interests of all racial groups by preserving separate cultures and racial purity; marriage and sexual relations between races became criminal offenses. Most observers saw apartheid as a way of maintaining the lavish privileges of the white minority, which accounted for only one-sixth of the total population.

After 1940, South Africa's cities grew rapidly in conjunction with its emergence as the most highly industrialized country in Africa. Urbanization changed the face of the country, but good jobs in the cities were reserved for whites. Moreover, the whites lived in luxurious modern central cities; the blacks, legally classified as temporary migrants, were restricted to outlying black townships plagued by poverty, crime, and white policemen.

In spite of pass laws and segregation, the growing cities produced a vibrant urban black culture, largely distinct from that of the tribal reserves. As a black journalist in Johannesburg explained in 1966:

I am supposed to be a Pondo, but I don't even know the language of that tribe. . . . I am just not a tribesman, whether I like it or not. I am, inescapably, a part of the city slums, the factory machines and our beloved shebeens [illegal bars].[13]

South Africa's harsh white supremacy elicited many black nationalist protests from the 1920s onward. Black nationalists began as moderates, seeking gradual reforms. By the 1950s, blacks—and their coloured, white, and Asian allies—were staging large-scale peaceful protests. A high point came in 1960, when police at Sharpeville fired into a crowd of demonstrators and killed sixty-nine blacks. The main black nationalist organization—the African National Congress (ANC)—was outlawed but sent some of its leaders abroad to establish new headquarters. Other members, led by a young black lawyer named Nelson Mandela (b. 1918), stayed in South Africa to set up an underground army to oppose the government. Captured after seventeen months, Mandela was tried for treason and sentenced to life imprisonment. With harsh laws, a powerful police force, and an army of spies, the government defended and strengthened the apartheid system.

By the late 1970s, the white government had apparently destroyed the moderate black opposition within South Africa. Operating out of the sympathetic black states of Zimbabwe and Mozambique to the north (see Map 37.5), the militant ANC turned increasingly to armed struggle. South Africa struck back hard. It used its awesome economic and military strength to support separatist movements that destabilized its neighbors, and it forced Marxist Mozambique in particular to curtail the ANC's guerrilla activities. Fortified by these successes, South Africa's white leaders launched in 1984 a program of "reforms"—changes designed to ensure continued white domination by means of a few strategic concessions.

The main reform was constitutional. The government set up a new parliament consisting of one house for the 5 million whites and, for the first time, two much less powerful houses for the 3 million coloureds and the 1 million South Africans of Asian descent. But no provision was made for any representation of the country's 22 million blacks, on the grounds that they were citizens of "black homelands"—the new name for the tribal reserves. The government also made cosmetic adjustments to apartheid, permitting marriage between races, for example. But the hated pass laws were replaced only by a new identity card, which still controlled black movement and settlement.

The government's self-serving reforms provoked black indignation and triggered a massive reaction. In the segregated townships surrounding white cities, young black militants took to the streets, attacking in particular black civil servants and policemen as traitorous agents of white oppression. White security forces, armed with tear gas, whips, and guns, clashed repeatedly with black protesters, who turned funerals for fallen comrades into mass demonstrations. Foreign governments and opinion leaders urged fundamental changes that would move South Africa toward universal suffrage and black majority rule.

Instead, the white government dug in. In 1985, it imposed a state of emergency, which gave the police and army virtually unlimited powers to put down protest. In late 1986, the government imposed unlimited press censorship and took a gigantic step toward dictatorship for all, regardless of race. The state security force and the secret police hammered away at protesters in the black townships. Between 1985 and 1989, 5,000 died and 50,000 were jailed without charges because of the political unrest.

By 1989, the white government and the black opposition had reached an impasse. Black protesters had been bloodied but not beaten, and their movement for democracy had gathered worldwide support. The U.S. Congress had applied strong sanctions against South Africa in October 1986 and the Common Market had followed. The white government still held power, but the white population was increasingly divided. White South Africans had long prided themselves on their basic freedoms and parliamentary democracy even though they excluded blacks. Being rejected as outcasts by the world community wounded the pride of some whites and, more importantly, harsh repression of the black resistance had obviously failed.

A major step toward breaking the political stalemate came in September 1989 with the election of a new state president, Frederik W. de Klerk, an Afrikaner lawyer and politician. A late-blooming reformer, de Klerk moved cautiously toward reducing tensions and opening a dialogue with the ANC leaders. He began by freeing some prominent black prisoners, lifting the ban on black political demonstrations, and integrating public beaches. Negotiating with Nelson Mandela, whose reputation had soared among urban blacks during his long years in prison, de Klerk then lifted the state of emergency in most of the country, legalized the ANC, and freed Mandela in February 1990. Emerging from prison as a proud and impressive leader, Mandela received a hero's welcome in South Africa and then in the United States and Europe.

In August 1990, Mandela showed again his courage and statesmanship. Overriding the doubts of some militant supporters, he suspended the ANC's armed struggle, thereby meeting de Klerk's condition for more talks and eventual negotiations on South Africa's political future. The two leaders were still far apart, especially on the question of universal adult suffrage and majority rule. But striking progress had been made, more than had been thought possible, and the prospects for a multiracial democratic state in South Africa had never seemed brighter.

Soweto, 1990 Angry black protesters are forced to retreat in the face of tear gas fired by police. With a population today of more than 2 million, the sprawling black township near Johannesburg has for many years been the center of the struggle against the white minority government. *(Source: Wide World Photos)*

SUMMARY

This chapter focuses on the remarkable resurgence of Asian and African peoples after the Second World War, a resurgence that will almost certainly stand as a decisive turning point in world history. The chapter examines how the long-developing nationalist movement in China culminated in a social revolution led by communists who went on to pursue innovative and fiercely independent policies that redeemed China as a great power in world affairs. Meanwhile, Japan, defeated, demilitarized, and democratized, took a completely different path to the rank of economic superpower in a no less spectacular renaissance. Elsewhere—in India, Indonesia, and the Philippines—Asian peoples won their freedom and self-confidently charted independent courses. The Muslim world was also rejuvenated, most notably under Nasser in Egypt. In black Africa, a generation of nationalist leaders guided colonial territories to self-rule so successfully that by the middle of the 1960s only the Soviet Union still retained a large colonial empire.

The resurgence and political self-assertion of Asian and African peoples in revitalized or developing nation-states did not proceed without conflict. Serious regional and ethnic confrontations erupted, notably between Hindus and Muslims in India and between Arabs and Israelis in the Middle East. Moreover, the vestiges of Western colonialism and cold war struggles resulted in atypical but highly destructive conflicts in Algeria, Vietnam, and Zimbabwe. The revitalized peoples of Asia and Africa continued to face tremendous economic and social challenges, which had to be met if the emerging nations were to realize fully the promise of self-assertion and independence.

NOTES

1. S. Schram, *Mao Tse-tung* (New York: Simon and Schuster, 1966), p. 151.
2. Quoted in P. B. Ebrey, ed., *Chinese Civilization and Society: A Source Book* (New York: Free Press, 1981), p. 393.
3. Quoted in W. Bingham, H. Conroy, and F. Iklé, *A History of Asia*, vol. 2, 2d ed. (Boston: Allyn and Bacon, 1974), p. 459.
4. Quoted in S. Wolpert, *A New History of India*, 2d ed. (New York: Oxford University Press, 1982), p. 330.
5. Quoted in K. Bhata, *The Ordeal of Nationhood: A Social Study of India Since Independence, 1947–1970* (New York: Atheneum, 1971), p. 9.
6. Quoted in B. D. Nossiter, *Soft State: A Newspaperman's Chronicle of India* (New York: Harper & Row, 1970), p. 52.
7. G. B. Kay, ed., *The Political Economy of Colonialism in Ghana: A Collection of Documents and Statistics* (Cambridge, England: Cambridge University Press, 1972), p. 48.
8. Quoted in R. W. July, *A History of the African People*, 3d ed. (New York: Scribner's, 1980), pp. 519–520.
9. Quoted in J. L. Hymans, *Léopold Sédar Senghor: An Intellectual Biography* (Edinburgh: University of Edinburgh Press, 1971), p. 58.
10. Quoted in L. H. Gann and P. Duignan, *Colonialism in Africa*, vol. 2 (Cambridge, England: Cambridge University Press, 1970), p. 512.
11. Quoted in R. Hallett, *Africa Since 1875: A Modern History* (Ann Arbor: University of Michigan Press, 1974), pp. 378–379.
12. Ibid., p. 345.
13. Ibid., p. 657.

SUGGESTED READING

Many of the works mentioned in the Suggested Reading for Chapter 33 are also valuable for considering postwar developments in Asia and the Middle East. Three other important studies on developments in China are C. Johnson, *Peasant Nationalism and Communist Power: The Emergence of Revolutionary China, 1937–1945* (1962); L. Dittmer, *China's Continuous Revolution: The Post-Liberation Epoch, 1949–1981* (1987); and W. L. Parish and M. K. Whyte, *Village and Family in Contemporary China* (1978). M. Meisner, *Mao's China: A History of the People's Republic* (1977), is an excellent comprehensive study, and C. P. FitzGerald, *Communism Takes China: How the Revolution Went Red* (1971), is a lively, illustrated account by a scholar who spent many years in China. Recent developments are ably analyzed by J. Spence, *The Search for Modern China* (1990), and F. Butterfield, *China, Alive in a Bitter Sea* (1982), a journalist's perceptive eyewitness account. Yueh, T. and C. Wakeman, *To the Storm: The Odyssey of a Revolutionary Chinese Woman* (1985) is the poignant drama of a participant. R. Lardy, *Agriculture in China's Economic Development* (1983), carefully examines the poor performance that led to Deng's reforms, and A. Smith, ed., *The*

Re-emergence of the Chinese Peasantry (1987), considers the rural transformation.

K. Kawai, *Japan's American Interlude* (1960), and R. P. Dore, *Land Reform in Japan* (1959), consider key problems of occupation policy. Three excellent and thought-provoking studies of contemporary Japanese society are E. Reischauer, *The Japanese* (1977); F. Gibney, *Japan, the Fragile Superpower* (1977); and E. Vogel, *Japan as Number One: Lessons for America* (1979). G. Bernstein, *Haruko's World: A Japanese Farm Woman and Her Community* (1983), probes changing patterns of rural life. Akira Iriye, *The Cold War in Asia: A Historical Introduction* (1974), and M. Schaller, *The United States and China in the Twentieth Century* (1979), analyze international conflicts in the postwar Pacific Basin.

F. G. Hutchins, *India's Revolution: Gandhi and the Quit India Movement* (1973), is an excellent account of wartime developments in India, which may be compared with J. Nehru, *An Autobiography* (1962), the appealing testimony of a principal architect of Indian freedom. F. Frankel, *India's Political Economy, 1947–1977* (1978), intelligently discusses the economic policies of independent India. There is a good biography of Indira Gandhi by D. Moraes (1980). H. Tinker, *South Asia: A Short History,* 2d ed. (1990), is a good guide to the states of the Indian subcontinent. For Southeast Asia there are solid general accounts by C. Dubois, *Social Forces in Southeast Asia* (1967), and R. N. Kearney, *Politics and Modernization in South and Southeast Asia* (1974). C. Cooper, *The Lost Crusade: America in Vietnam* (1972), and F. FitzGerald, *Fire in the Lake* (1973), probe the tragic war in Vietnam. Two valuable works on other Asian countries are B. Dahm, *Sukarno and the Struggle for Indonesian Independence* (1969), and T. Friend, *Between Two Empires: The Ordeal of the Philippines, 1929–1946* (1965).

Recommended studies of the Middle East and Israel include a cultural investigation by R. Patai, *The Arab Mind* (1973); a balanced account by C. Smith, *Palestine and the Arab-Israeli Conflict* (1988); and an excellent biography of Israel's inspiring leader during its war for independence by A. Avi-Hai, *Ben Gurion, State Builder* (1974). A. Goldschmidt, Jr., *Modern Egypt: The Formation of a Nation-State* (1988), treats the post-Nasser years extensively and H. Munson, Jr., *Islam and Revolution in the Middle East* (1988), compares Iran and Arab countries.

The studies by July and Hallett cited in the Notes are outstanding interpretations of modern Africa's rich and complex history. Both have extensive bibliographies. Important works on the colonial era include J. A. Langley, *Pan-Africanism and Nationalism in West Africa, 1900–1945: A Study in Ideology and Social Classes* (1973); R. O. Collins, *Problems in the History of Colonial Africa, 1860–1960* (1970); T. Hodgkin, *Nationalism in Colonial Africa* (1957); and the monumental investigation edited by L. H. Gann and P. Duignan, *Colonialism in Africa, 1870–1960,* 5 vols. (1969–1975). W. E. B. Du Bois, *The World and Africa* (1947), and J. Kenyatta, *Facing Mount Kenya* (1953), are powerful comments on African nationalism by the distinguished American black thinker and Kenya's foremost revolutionary and political leader. R. July, *The African Voice: The Role of the Humanities in African Independence* (1987), focuses on intellectuals and artists struggling against cultural imperialism. A Hopkins, *An Economic History of West Africa* (1973), is a pioneering synthesis. C. Dewey and A. Hopkins, eds., *The Imperial Impact: Studies in the Economic History of Africa and India* (1978), is an innovative comparative study. R. Olaniyan, ed., *African History and Culture* (1982), is a valuable recent collection. M. Crowder, ed., *The Cambridge History of Africa,* vol. 8, examines the struggle for independence and nationhood between 1940 and 1975 in broad perspective. Major works on specific countries include M. Crowder, *The Story of Nigeria,* 4th ed. (1978); P. Hill, *Migrant Cocoa Farmers in Ghana* (1963); and R. W. Johnson, *How Long Will South Africa Survive?* (1977). P. C. Lloyd, *Africa in Social Change* (1972), is a useful study on the contemporary era, and F. Willett, *African Art* (1971), is a good introduction.

38

Life in the Third World

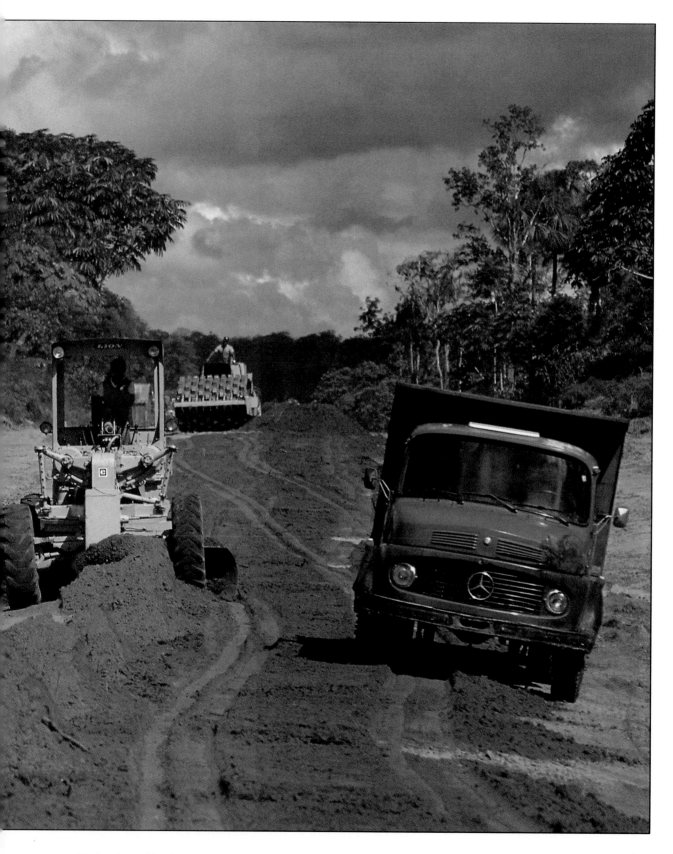

Destruction of the Amazon rain forest, near the Peru border

$\mathcal{E}$veryday life in the emerging nations of Asia and Africa changed dramatically after the Second World War as many peoples struggled to build effective nation-states. Some of the changes paralleled the experiences of Europe and North America: science and modern technology altered individuals' lives in countless ways, and efforts to raise the standard of living by means of industrialization profoundly affected relations among social classes. Yet most observers stressed the differences in development between the emerging nations and the industrialized nations. In the new nations, which—along with the older states of Latin America—suffered widespread poverty and had a heritage of foreign domination, life remained very hard. Moreover, many discerned a widening economic gap between the industrialized nations of Europe and North America on the one hand and most of the emerging nations on the other, especially in the economically difficult 1970s and 1980s. Some writers even argued that the gap between North and South— that is, between rich nations and poor nations — had replaced the cold war between East and West and its immediate aftermath as humankind's most explosive division.

This chapter concentrates on shared problems of development and everyday life in Asia, Africa, and Latin America—a vast geographical expanse commonly known as the "Third World." Three key questions guide the investigation:

- How have the emerging nations of the Third World sought to escape from poverty, and what have been the results of their efforts?

- What has caused the prodigious growth of Third World cities, and what does their growth mean for their inhabitants?

- How have Third World thinkers and artists interpreted the modern world and the experiences of their peoples before, during, and after foreign domination?

DEFINING THE THIRD WORLD

Can Africa, Asia, and Latin America be validly and usefully lumped together as a single entity—the Third World? Some experts prefer to speak of "emerging nations" or of "less developed countries"—deliberately vague terms suggesting a spectrum of conditions ranging from near-hopeless poverty to moderate well-being. Others now add a "Fourth" and even a "Fifth World" in order to distinguish more closely among the less developed nations. Nevertheless, the countries often termed "Third World" share characteristics that make it generally valid to speak of them jointly.

First, virtually all the countries of the Third World experienced political or economic domination, nationalist reaction, and a struggle for independence or autonomy. This shared past gave rise to a common consciousness and a widespread feeling of having been oppressed and victimized in dealings with Europe and North America. This outlook was nurtured by a variety of nationalists, Marxists, and anti-imperialist intellectuals, who argued forcibly that the Third World's problems were the result of past and present exploitation by the wealthy capitalist nations. Precisely because of their shared sense of past injustice, many influential Latin Americans have identified with the Third World, despite their countries' greater affluence. Indeed, "Third World" was first widely used by Latin American intellectuals in the late 1950s. They picked up the term from a French scholar who likened the peoples of Africa, Asia, and Latin America to the equally diverse but no less oppressed and humiliated French third estate before the revolution of 1789. The term also came into global use in the cold war era as a handy way of distinguishing Africa, Asia, and Latin America from the "First" and "Second" worlds—the capitalist and communist industrialized nations, respectively. (With the end of the cold war in 1989 eastern Europe has thrown off its former communist unity and is in flux. Some east European countries like Hungary may succeed in joining the capitalist First World; others like the Soviet Union may fall to Third World status as their planned economies collapse.)

Second, a large majority of men and women in most Third World countries live in the countryside and depend on agriculture for a living. Agricultural goods and raw materials are still the primary exports of Third World countries. In Europe, North America, and Japan, by contrast, most people live in cities and depend mainly on industry and urban services for employment.

Finally, the agricultural countries of Asia, Africa, and most of Latin America are united by awareness

An Indian Family walking barefoot across the countryside captures the human dimension of Third World poverty. Quite possibly they are landless laborers, searching for work, and carrying all their meager belongings. *(Source: Harmit Singh/Black Star)*

of their common poverty. By no means is everyone in the Third World poor; some people are quite wealthy. The average standard of living, however, is low, especially compared with that of people in the wealthy industrial nations, and massive poverty remains ever present.

ECONOMIC AND SOCIAL CHALLENGES IN THE THIRD WORLD

Alongside the tough postindependence task of preserving political unity and building cohesive nation-states, the emerging countries of the Third World faced the enormous challenges of poverty, malnutrition, and disease. These scourges weighed especially heavily on rural people, who depended on agriculture for survival and accounted for most of the Third World's population. Stirred by nationalism and the struggle for political freedom, peasants and landless laborers wanted the brighter future that their leaders had promised them.

Most Third World leaders and their advisers in the 1950s and 1960s saw rapid industrialization and "modernization" as the answer to rural poverty and disease. Industrialization and modernization also kindled popular enthusiasm and thus served nation building, which in turn promised economic self-sufficiency and genuine independence. For these reasons, the leaders and peoples of the Third World in the 1950s and 1960s set themselves the massive task of building modern factories, roads, and public health services like those of Europe and North America. Their considerable success fueled rapid economic progress.

Yet social problems, complicated by surging population growth, almost dwarfed the accomplishment. Disappointments multiplied. By and large, the poorest rural people in the poorest countries gained the least from industrialization, and industrial expansion provided jobs for only a small segment even of the urban population. By the late 1960s, widespread dissatisfaction with policies of all-out industrialization prompted a greater emphasis on rural development. The economic downturn of the 1970s and the crisis of the early 1980s reinforced this trend. More generally, different approaches proliferated from the late 1960s onward, as the Third World became less unified and more complex.

Poverty

It is easy to lose sight of the true dimensions of poverty in the Third World in a fog of economic statistics. In the 1950s and 1960s the United Nations and the emerging nations began collecting national income statistics. Dividing those estimates by total population yields a nation's average per capita income. These figures received enormous attention because they were stunningly low compared with those of wealthy nations. In 1960, for example, average annual income per person in all of Africa and Southeast Asia was about $100. In North America it was $2,500—twenty-five times more. Using such figures, journalists, politicians, and scholars often concluded that Third World people were unspeakably poor and verging on mass starvation.

Such comparisons, however, exaggerated the economic gap between the North and the South. They made a hard, sometimes desperate situation seem utterly hopeless. For example, average income per person in the United States in 1973 was about $5,000; in India it was about $100. Yet the average American was not necessarily fifty times better off than the average Indian. As an English and an Indian economist jointly pointed out, "Merely to survive, to be able to buy enough basic food, clothing and shelter in the United States would cost over $1,000 while $100 would suffice for these in India, so that someone with $1,000 in

America may be worse off than someone in India with $100."[1] Basic necessities cost considerably less in poor countries than in rich countries.

Reliance on national income statistics also promotes distorted comparisons because the statistics on poor countries are less complete and tend to leave out many wage-earning activities. Furthermore, fewer economic activities involve money transactions in poor countries than in rich ones, and only wage-earning work shows up consistently in national income statistics. In industrialized countries, only housewives do not receive money wages and thus do not show up in income statistics; there are many such "housewife" groups in the Third World.

A deeper understanding arises from considering Third World poverty not in statistical terms but in human terms, as did the postwar generation of nationalist leaders. To them, poverty meant, above all, not having enough to eat. For millions, hunger and malnutrition were harsh facts of life. In India, Ethiopia, Bolivia, and other extremely poor countries, the average adult ate fewer than 2,000 calories a day—only 85 percent of the minimal requirement. Although many poor countries fared better, in the 1960s none but Argentina could match the 3,000 or more calories consumed in the more fortunate North. Even Third World people who consumed enough calories often suffered from the effects of unbalanced high-starch diets and inadequate protein. Severe protein deficiency stunts the brain as well as the body, and many of the poorest children grew up mentally retarded.

Poor housing—crowded, often damp, and exposed to the elements—also contributed significantly to the less developed world's high incidence of chronic ill health. So too did scanty education and lack of the fundamentals of modern public health: adequate and safe water, sewage disposal, immunizations, prenatal care, and control of communicable diseases. Infant mortality was savage, and chronic illness weakened and demoralized many adults, making them unfit for the hard labor that their lives required.

Generally speaking, health status in Asia and Latin America was better than in the new states of sub-Saharan Africa. As one authority described the situation in the early 1960s:

In the African social drama, sickness has a strong claim to being archvillain. . . . In tropical Africa, most men, women, and children are habitually unwell.

Many are unwell from the day of their birth to the day of their death. . . . Most of the sick are sick of more than one disease.[2]

The people of poor countries were overwhelmingly concentrated in the countryside, as small farmers and landless laborers. These rural people were often unable to read or write, and they lacked steady employment. Even with hard work, simple tools limited productivity. Basic services like safe running water were uncommon: village women around the world spent much of each day carrying water and searching for firewood or dung to use as fuel, as they must still do in many countries.

Mass poverty represented an awesome challenge to the postwar leaders of the newly emerging nations. Having raised peoples' hopes in the struggle for independence, they had to start delivering on their promises if they were to maintain trust and stay in power. A strong commitment to modern economic and social development, already present in parts of Latin America in the 1930s, took hold in Asia and Africa in the postwar era.

The Medical Revolution and the Population Explosion

The most thoroughgoing success achieved by the Third World after the Second World War was a spectacular, ongoing medical revolution. Immediately after winning independence, the governments of emerging nations began adapting modern methods of immunology and public health.

The One-Child Family   China's continued moderate rate of population increase resulted in the early 1980s in drastic laws that generally prohibit Chinese families from having more than one child. The happy grandmother and the government posters behind preach the joys of the one-child family, which is at odds with Chinese tradition. *(Source: Jin Xuqi/Picture Group)*

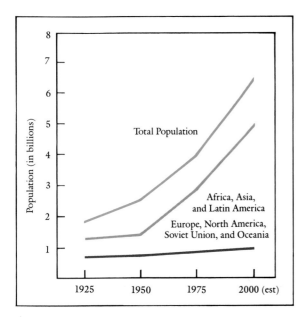

FIGURE 38.1 The Increase of World Population, 1925–2000 Since the first quarter of the twentieth century Africa, Asia, and Latin America—the Third World—have been growing much more rapidly than industrialized Europe, North America, and the Soviet Union. Compare with Figure 30.2 for a long-term perspective. *(Source: Data from United Nations,* Concise Report on the World Population Situation in 1970–1975 and Its Long-Range Implications, *New York, 1974, p. 59.)*

These methods were often simple and inexpensive but extremely effective. One famous measure was spraying DDT in Southeast Asia in order to control mosquitoes bearing malaria, one of the deadliest and most debilitating of tropical diseases. In Sri Lanka (formerly Ceylon), DDT spraying halved the yearly toll of deaths in the very first postwar decade—at a modest cost of $2 per person. According to the U.N. World Health Organization, which helped provide medical expertise to the new states, deaths from smallpox, cholera, and plague declined by more than 95 percent worldwide between 1951 and 1966.

Asian and African countries increased the small numbers of hospitals, doctors, and nurses that they had inherited from the colonial past. Large African cities' biggest, most modern, and most beautiful buildings were often their hospitals. Sophisticated medical facilities became symbols of the commitment to a better life.

Some critics, however, maintained that expensive medical technology was an indulgence that Third World countries could not afford, for it was ill suited to the pressing health problems of most of the population. In recent years, such criticism has prompted greater emphasis on delivering medical services to the countryside. Local people have been successfully trained as paramedics to staff rural outpatient clinics that offer medical treatment, health education, and prenatal and postnatal care. Most of the paramedics are women: many health problems involve childbirth and infancy, and villagers the world over consider it improper for a male to examine a woman's body.

The medical revolution significantly lowered death rates and lengthened life expectancy. In particular, children became increasingly likely to survive their early years, though infant and juvenile mortality remained far higher in the Third World than in rich countries. By 1980 the average inhabitant of the Third World could expect at birth to live about 54 years; life expectancy varied from 40 to 64 years depending on the country. In developed countries, by contrast, life expectancy at birth averaged 71 years.

A much less favorable consequence of the medical revolution was the acceleration of population growth. As in Europe during the nineteenth century, a rapid decline in the death rate was not immediately accompanied by a similar decline in the birthrate. Third World women generally continued to bear from five to seven children, as their mothers and grandmothers had done. The combined populations of Asia, Africa, and Latin America, which had grown relatively modestly from 1925 to 1950, increased between 1950 and 1975 from 1,750 million to 3,000 million (Figure 38.1 and Map 38.1). Barring catastrophe, the population of the three continents is expected to surge to about 5,200 million in the year 2000—an unprecedented explosion.

The population explosion aroused fears of approaching famine and starvation. Thomas Malthus's gloomy late-eighteenth-century conclusion that population always tends to grow faster than the food supply (see page 872) was revived and updated by "neo-Malthusian" social scientists. Such

MAP 38.1 World Population Density

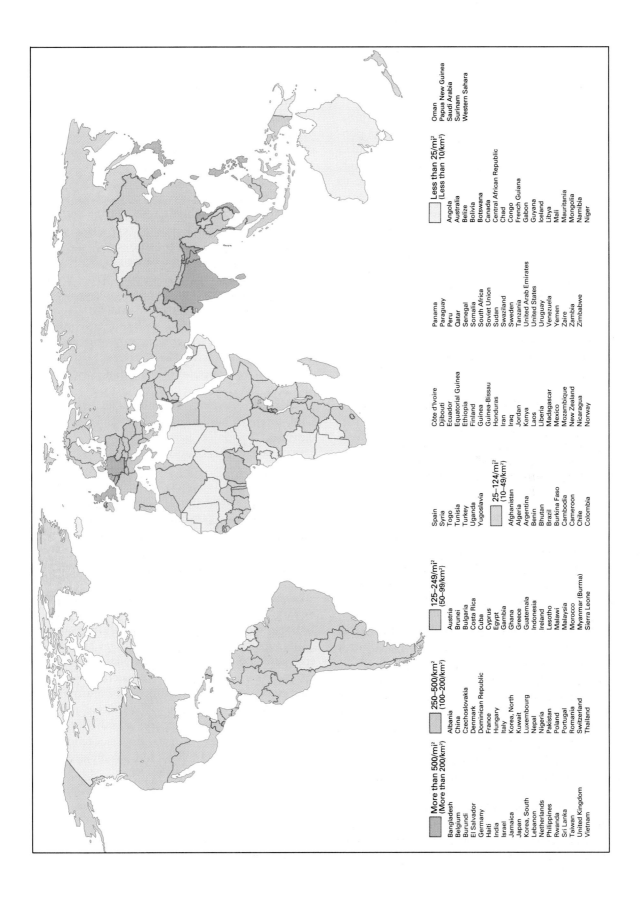

More than 500/mi²
(More than 200/km²)

Bangladesh
Belgium
Burundi
El Salvador
Germany
Haiti
India
Israel
Jamaica
Japan
Korea, South
Lebanon
Netherlands
Nigeria
Philippines
Rwanda
Sri Lanka
Taiwan
United Kingdom
Vietnam

250–500/km²
(100–200/km²)

Albania
China
Czechoslovakia
Denmark
Dominican Republic
France
Hungary
Italy
Korea, North
Kuwait
Luxembourg
Nepal
Pakistan
Poland
Portugal
Romania
Switzerland
Thailand

125–249/mi²
(50–99/km²)

Austria
Brunei
Bulgaria
Costa Rica
Cuba
Cyprus
Egypt
Gambia
Ghana
Greece
Guatemala
Indonesia
Ireland
Lesotho
Malawi
Malaysia
Morocco
Myanmar (Burma)
Sierra Leone

Spain
Syria
Togo
Tunisia
Turkey
Uganda
Yugoslavia

25–124/mi²
(10–49/km²)

Afghanistan
Algeria
Argentina
Benin
Bhutan
Brazil
Burkina Faso
Cambodia
Cameroon
Chile
Colombia

Côte d'Ivoire
Djibouti
Ecuador
Equatorial Guinea
Ethiopia
Finland
Guinea
Guinea-Bissau
Honduras
Iran
Iraq
Jordan
Kenya
Laos
Liberia
Madagascar
Mexico
Mozambique
New Zealand
Nicaragua
Norway

Panama
Paraguay
Peru
Qatar
Senegal
Somalia
South Africa
Soviet Union
Sudan
Swaziland
Sweden
Tanzania
United Arab Emirates
United States
Uruguay
Venezuela
Yemen
Zaire
Zambia
Zimbabwe

Less than 25/mi²
(Less than 10/km²)

Angola
Australia
Belize
Bolivia
Botswana
Canada
Central African Republic
Chad
Congo
French Guiana
Gabon
Guyana
Iceland
Libya
Mali
Mauritania
Mongolia
Namibia
Niger

Oman
Papua New Guinea
Saudi Arabia
Surinam
Western Sahara

fears were exaggerated, but they did produce uneasiness in the Third World, where leaders saw that their countries had to run fast just to maintain already low standards of living.

Some governments began pushing family planning and birth control to slow the growth of population. These measures were not very successful in the 1950s and 1960s. In many countries, Islamic and Catholic religious teachings were hostile to birth control. Moreover, widespread cultural attitudes dictated that a real man keep his wife pregnant. There were also solid economic reasons for preferring large families. Farmers needed the help of plenty of children at planting and harvest times. And sons and daughters were a sort of social security system for their elders; thus a prudent couple wanted several children because some would surely die young.

The Race to Industrialize (1950–1970)

Throughout the 1950s and most of the 1960s, many key Third World leaders, pressed on by their European, American, and Soviet advisers, were convinced that all-out industrialization was the only answer to poverty and population growth. The masses, they concluded, were poor because they were imprisoned in a primitive, inefficient agricultural economy. Farm families' tiny holdings were too small for modern machinery. Large landowners showed more, but still limited, promise. Only modern factory industry appeared capable of creating wealth quickly enough to outrace the growth of numbers.

The two-century experience of the West, Japan, and the Soviet Union seemed to validate this faith in industrialization. Economic history became a popular subject among Third World elites. It taught the encouraging lesson that the wealthy countries had also been agricultural and "underdeveloped" until the Industrial Revolution had lifted them out of poverty, one by one. According to this view, the uneven progress of industrialization was primarily responsible for the great income gap that existed between the rich countries of North America and Europe (including the Soviet Union) and the poor countries of the postindependent Third World.

Theories of modernization, particularly popular in the 1960s, also assumed that all countries were following the path already taken by the industrialized nations and that the task of the elite was to speed the trip. Marxism, with its industrial and urban bias, preached a similar gospel. These ideas reinforced the Third World's desire to industrialize.

Nationalist leaders believed that successful industrialization required state action and enterprise. Many were impressed by socialism in general and by Stalin's forced industrialization in particular, which they saw as having won the Soviet Union international power and prominence, whatever its social costs. In Asia and Africa, furthermore, capitalists and private enterprise were equated with the old rulers and colonial servitude. The reasoning was practical as well as ideological: in addition to high-paying administrative jobs for political allies, modern industry meant ports, roads, schools, and hospitals, as well as factories. Only the state could afford such expensive investments—as, indeed, the colonial governments had begun to realize in the twilight years of colonial rule. With the exception of the People's Republic of China, however, the new governments recognized private property and also tolerated native (and foreign) businessmen. The "mixed economy"—part socialist, part capitalist—became the general rule in the Third World.

Political leaders concentrated state investment in big, highly visible projects that proclaimed the country's independence and stimulated national pride. Enormous dams for irrigation and hydroelectric power were favored undertakings. Nasser's stupendous Aswan Dam harnessed the Nile, demonstrating that modern Egyptians could surpass even the pyramids of their ancient ancestors. The gigantic state-owned steel mill was another favorite project.

These big projects testified to the prevailing faith in expensive advanced technology and modernization along European lines. Nationalist leaders and their economic experts generally believed that money for investment in rapid industrialization would be squeezed out of agriculture and the farm population. They measured overall success by how fast national income grew, and they tended to assume that social problems and income distribution would take care of themselves.

India, the world's most populous noncommunist country, exemplified the general trends. After India achieved independence in 1947, Gandhi's special brand of nationalism was redirected toward economic and social rebirth through state enterprise and planning. Nehru and many Congress

Building the Aswan Dam Financed and engineered by the Soviet Union, the massive high dam at Aswan was Nasser's dream for Egypt's economic future. Here an army of workers lay the stones that will harness the Nile for irrigation and hydroelectric power. *(Source: Popperfoto)*

party leaders believed that unregulated capitalism and free trade under British rule had deepened Indian poverty. Considering themselves democratic socialists, they introduced five-year plans, built state-owned factories and steel mills, and raised tariffs to protect Indian manufacturers. Quite typically, they neglected agriculture, land reform, and village life.

The Third World's first great industrialization drive was in many ways a success. Industry grew faster than ever before, though from an admittedly low base in Africa and most of Asia. According to the United Nations, industry in the noncommunist developing nations grew at more than 7 percent per year between 1950 and 1970. Because

this growth exceeded the average annual population increase of 2.5 percent, Third World industrial production per capita grew about 4.5 percent per year for a generation. This was very solid industrial growth by historical standards: it matched the fastest rates of industrialization in the United States before 1914 and was double the rate of Britain and France in the same years.

Industrial expansion stimulated the other sectors of Third World economies. National income per capita grew about 2.5 percent per year in the 1950s and 1960s. This pace was far superior to the very modest increases that had occurred under colonial domination between 1900 and 1950. Future historians may well see the era after political emancipation as the era of industrial revolution in Asia and Africa.

This was certainly the case for a few small Asian countries that downgraded government control and emphasized private enterprise and the export of manufactured goods. South Korea, Taiwan, the city-state of Singapore, and the British colony of Hong Kong were genuine "economic miracles," industrializing rapidly and remarkably improving the living standards of ordinary people.

South Korea and Taiwan were typical underdeveloped countries after the Second World War—poor, small, agricultural, densely populated, and lacking in natural resources. They had also suffered from Japanese imperialism. How did they manage to make good?

Radical land reform drew the mass of small farmers into a competitive market economy, which proved an excellent school of self-reliance and initiative. As in Japan, probusiness governments in South Korea and Taiwan cooperated with capitalists and helped keep wages low. American aid also helped, as did almost free access to the large American market. And like Japan, both countries succeeded in preserving the fundamentals of their traditional cultures even as they accepted and mastered Western technology. Tough nationalist leaders maintained political stability at the expense of genuine political democracy.

Nevertheless, by the late 1960s, disillusionment with the Third World's relatively rapid industrialization was spreading, for several reasons. In the first place, the experience of a few small states like South Korea and Taiwan was the exception. The countries of Asia, Africa, and Latin America did not as a whole match the "miraculous" concurrent advances of western Europe and Japan, and the great economic gap between the rich and the poor nations continued to widen.

Also, most Third World leaders had genuinely believed that rapid industrial development would help the rural masses. Yet careful studies showed that the main beneficiaries of industrialization were businessmen, bureaucrats, skilled workers, and urban professionals. Peasants and agricultural laborers gained little or nothing. In fast-growing, dynamic Mexico, for instance, it was estimated that about 40 percent of the population was completely excluded from the benefits of industrialization. Moreover, the very poorest countries—such as India and Indonesia in Asia, and Ethiopia and

the Sudan in Africa—were growing most slowly in per capita terms. The industrialization prescription appeared least effective where poverty was most intense. Economic dislocations after 1973, and especially the worldwide economic crisis of the early 1980s, accentuated this trend, visiting particularly devastating effects on the poorest countries.

Perhaps most seriously, industrialization failed to provide the sheer number of jobs needed for the sons and daughters of the population explosion. Statisticians estimated that the growth of Third World manufacturing between 1950 and 1970 provided jobs for only about one-fifth of the 200 million young men and women who entered the exploding labor force in the same period. Most new enterprises employed advanced technology that required few workers. One person on a bulldozer could do the job of hundreds with shovels. For the foreseeable future, most Third World people would have to remain on the farm or work in traditional handicrafts and service occupations. All-out modern industrialization had failed as a panacea.

Agriculture and Village Life

From the late 1960s onward, the limitations of industrial development forced Third World governments to take a renewed interest in rural people and village life. At best, this attention meant giving agriculture its due and coordinating rural development with industrialization and urbanization. At worst, it fostered a resigned second-best approach to the unrelenting economic and social challenge, especially in the very poorest countries. The optimistic vision of living standards approaching those of the wealthy North gave way to the pessimistic conclusion that it was possible to ease only modestly the great hardships.

Nationalist elites had neglected agriculture in the 1950s and the 1960s for various reasons. They regarded an agricultural economy as a mark of colonial servitude, which they were symbolically repudiating by embracing industrialization. They wanted to squeeze agriculture and peasant producers in order to provide capital for industry. Thus governments often established artificially low food prices, which also subsidized their volatile urban supporters at the expense of the farmers.

In addition, the obstacles to more productive farming seemed overwhelming to unsympathetic urban elites and condescending foreign experts: farms were too small and fragmented for mechanization, peasants were too stubborn and ignorant to change their ways, and so on. Little wonder that only big farmers and some plantations received much government support. Wherever large estates and absentee landlords predominated—in large parts of Asia and most of Latin America, excluding Mexico, though not in black Africa—landless laborers and poor peasants who had no other choice than to rent land simply lacked the incentive to work harder. Any increased profits from larger crops went mainly to the absentee landowners.

Most honest observers were convinced that improved farm performance required land reform. Yet ever since the French Revolution, genuine land reform has been a profoundly radical measure, frequently bringing violence and civil war. Powerful landowners and their allies have generally succeeded in blocking or subverting redistribution of land to benefit the poor. Land reform, unlike industrialization, has generally been too hot for most politicians to handle.

Third World governments also neglected agriculture because feeding the masses was deceptively easy in the 1950s and early 1960s. Very poor countries received food from the United States at giveaway prices as part of a U.S. effort to dispose of enormous grain surpluses and help American farmers. Before 1939, the countries of Asia, Africa, and Latin America had collectively produced more grain than they consumed. But after 1945, as their populations soared, they began importing ever increasing quantities. Crops might fail, but starvation seemed a thing of the past. In 1965, when India was urged to build up its food reserves, one top Indian official expressed a widespread attitude: "Why should we bother? Our reserves are the wheat fields of Kansas."[3]

In the short run, the Indian official was right. In 1966 and again in 1967, when the monsoon failed to deliver its life-giving rains to the Indo-Pakistan subcontinent and famine gripped the land, the United States gave India one-fifth of the U.S. wheat crop. More than 60 million Indians lived exclusively on American grain. The effort required a food armada of six hundred ships, the largest fleet assembled since the Normandy invasion of 1944. The famine was ultimately contained, and instead of millions of deaths there were only a few thousand.

That close brush with mass starvation sent a shiver down the world's spine. Complacency dissolved in the Third World, and prophecies of disaster multiplied in wealthy nations. Paul Ehrlich, an American scientist, envisioned a grisly future in his polemical 1968 best-seller *The Population Bomb*:

The battle to feed all of humanity is over. In the 1970s the world will undergo famines—hundreds of millions of people are going to starve to death in spite of any crash programs embarked upon now. At this stage nothing can prevent a substantial increase in the world death rate.[4]

Other Western commentators outdid each other with nightmare visions. One portrayed the earth as a crowded lifeboat in a sea of hungry poor who would have to drown in order not to swamp the lifeboat. Another vision compared truly poor countries like Bangladesh, Ethiopia, and Haiti to hopelessly wounded soldiers on a gory battlefield. Such victims were best left to die so that scarce resources could be concentrated on the "walking wounded" who might yet be saved. Such crude and brutal Social Darwinism made it easy for Third World intellectuals to believe the worst about the rich industrialized nations and their economies.

Yet there was another face, a technological face, to the European and American interest in the Third World's food supply. Plant scientists and agricultural research stations had already set out to develop new hybrid seeds genetically engineered to suit the growing conditions of tropical agriculture. Their model was extraordinarily productive hybrid corn developed for the American Midwest in the 1940s. The first breakthrough came in Mexico in the 1950s, when an American-led team developed new high-yielding dwarf wheats. These varieties enabled farmers to double their yields from one year to the next, though they demanded greater amounts of fertilizer and water for irrigation. Mexican wheat production soared. Thus began the transformation of Third World agriculture—the so-called Green Revolution.

In the 1960s an American-backed team of scientists in the Philippines turned their attention to rice, the Asian staff of life; they quickly developed

Peasant Farming in Ecuador   Cultivating the land with simple hand tools, these peasant women in Latin America appear doomed to poverty despite backbreaking labor. In many cases, a high rent to an absentee landlord reduces the peasants' income still further. *(Source: Bernard Pierre Wolff/Photo Researchers, Inc.)*

a "miracle rice." The new hybrid also required more fertilizer and water but yielded more and grew much faster. It permitted the revolutionary advent of year-round farming on irrigated land, making possible two, three, or even four crops a year. The brutal tropical sun of the hot dry season became an agricultural blessing for the first time. Asian scientists, financed by their governments, developed similar hybrids to meet local conditions.

Increases in grain production were rapid and dramatic in some Asian countries. In gigantic India, for example, farmers upped production more than 60 percent in fifteen years. By 1980, thousands of new grain bins dotted the countryside, symbols of the agricultural revolution in India and the country's new-found ability to feed all its people. China followed with its own highly successful version of the Green Revolution under Deng Xiao-ping.

The Green Revolution offered new hope to the Third World, but it was no cure-all. At first it seemed that most of its benefits flowed to large landowners and substantial peasant farmers who could afford the necessary investments in irrigation and fertilizer. Subsequent experience in China and other Asian countries showed, however, that even peasant families with tiny farms could gain substantially. The new techniques of year-round cropping required more work, but they enabled a peasant family to squeeze more food out of its precious land. For any family lucky enough to have even three acres, the ongoing Green Revolution proved a godsend.

After early breakthroughs in Mexico, the Green Revolution's greatest successes have occurred not in Latin America but in Asia, most notably in countries with broad-based peasant ownership of land. The technical revolution has shared relatively few of its benefits with the poorest classes—landless laborers, tenant farmers, and tiny landholders. Lacking even the two or three acres necessary to feed themselves with intensive effort, the very poorest groups have gained only slightly more regular employment from the Green Revolution's demand for more labor. Pakistan, the Philippines, and other countries with large numbers of landless peasants and insecure tenant farmers have experienced less improvement than countries like South Korea and Taiwan, where land is generally owned by peasants. This helps to explain why the Green Revolution failed to spread from Mexico through-

out Latin America: as long as 3 or 4 percent of the rural population owned 60 to 80 percent of the land, which is still the case in many Latin American countries, the Green Revolution will probably remain stillborn.

The same fatal equation of property ownership has prevailed in Bangladesh. There an elite tenth of the population owns half of the land, and the poorest half owns nothing at all. People eat less today than in 1970, yet land reform remains a political and social minefield. One member of a big (fifty-acre) landowning family in Bangladesh told an American reporter in 1981: "They talk of removing property markers. It cannot happen. I will kill you if you move my property markers one inch."[5]

Old and New With a fetish statue designed to frighten off evil spirits standing by, the proud owner of a two-acre plot in southern India shows a visiting expert his crop of miracle rice. As this picture suggests, the acceptance of modern technology does not necessarily require the repudiation of cultural traditions. *(Source: Marc and Evelyne Bernheim/Woodfin Camp)*

Black Africa has benefited little from the new agricultural techniques, even though land reform has been a serious problem only in white-ruled South Africa. Poor transportation, inadequate storage facilities, and low government-imposed agricultural prices have to bear much of the blame. Also, the climatic conditions of black Africa have encouraged continued adherence to dry farming and root crops, whereas the Green Revolution has been almost synonymous with intensive irrigation and grain production.

The Green Revolution, like the medical revolution and industrialization, represented a large but uneven step forward for the Third World. Most unfortunately, relatively few of its benefits flowed to the poorest groups—black Africans and the landless peasants of Asia and Latin America. These poor, who lacked political influence and had no clear idea about what needed to be done, increasingly longed to escape from ill-paid, irregular work in somebody else's fields. For many of the bravest and most enterprising, life in a nearby town or city seemed a way out.

THE GROWTH OF CITIES

Life in the less developed countries has been marked by violent contrasts, and it is in urban areas that such contrasts are most striking. Shiny airports, international hotels, and massive government buildings were built next to tar-paper slums. Like their counterparts in the North, these rapidly growing cities were monuments to political independence and industrial development. Unfortunately, they were also testimonials to increasing population, limited opportunities in the countryside, and neocolonial influence. Runaway urban growth has become a distinctive feature of the Third World.

Urbanization in the Third World

The cities of the Third World expanded at an astonishing pace after the Second World War. Many doubled and some even tripled in size in a single decade. The Algerian city of Algiers jumped from 300,000 to 900,000 between 1950 and 1960;

Accra in Ghana, Lima in Peru, and Nairobi in Kenya grew just as fast. Moreover, rapid urban growth has continued. Thus the less developed countries have become far more thoroughly urbanized in recent times than most people realize. In Latin America, three out of four people lived in towns and cities by 1975; in Asia and Africa, as Table 38.1 shows, one in four lived in an urban area by the same year.

The urban explosion continued in the 1980s, so that by 1990 fully 60 percent of the planet's city dwellers lived in the cities of the Third World, according to U.N. estimates. Rapid Third World urbanization represents a tremendous historical change. As recently as 1920, three out of every four of the world's urban inhabitants were concentrated in Europe and North America.

In most Third World countries the largest cities grew fastest. Gigantic "super cities" of 2 to 10 million persons arose. The capital typically emerged as the all-powerful urban center, encompassing all the important elite groups and dwarfing smaller cities as well as villages. Mexico City, for example, grew from 3 million to 12 million people between 1950 and 1975, and it will probably have a staggering 31 million in the year 2000. The pattern of a dominant megalopolis has continued to spread from Latin America to Africa and Asia (though not to Asia's giants, China and India).

In the truly poor countries of Africa and Asia, moreover, the process of urbanization is still in the early stages. However populous the cities, the countryside still holds most of the people. But if present trends continue, a city like Jakarta, the capital of Indonesia, will have about 17 million people by the end of this century. Calcutta and Bombay could be equally large. In the year 2000, the world will have 25 megalopolises with more than 10 million people—20 of them in the Third World, by World Bank estimates. Such growth poses enormous challenges for the future.

This urban explosion has been due, first of all, to the general growth of population in the Third World. Urban residents gained substanially from the medical revolution but only gradually began to reduce the size of their families. At the same time, the pressure of numbers in the countryside encouraged millions to set out for the nearest city. More than half of all urban growth has been due to rural migration.

TABLE 38.1 URBAN POPULATION AS A PERCENTAGE OF TOTAL POPULATION IN THE WORLD AND IN EIGHT MAJOR AREAS, 1925–2025

Area	1925	1950	1975	2000 (est.)	2025 (est.)
World total	21	28	39	50	63
North America	54	64	77	86	93
Europe	48	55	67	79	88
Soviet Union	18	39	61	76	87
East Asia	10	15	30	46	63
Latin America	25	41	60	74	85
Africa	8	13	24	37	54
South Asia	9	15	23	35	51
Oceania	54	65	71	77	87

Little more than one-fifth of the world's population was urban in 1925. In 1990 the urban proportion in the world total was about 45 percent and, according to United Nations experts, it should reach one-half by the century's end and two-thirds by about 2025. The most rapid urban growth will come in Africa and Asia, where the move to cities is still in its early stages. (Source: United Nations, Concise Report on the World Population Situation in 1970–1975 and Its Long-Range Implications, New York, 1974, p. 63.)

Even more than in Europe and North America in the nineteenth century, great cities became the undisputed centers of industry in the less developed countries. Half of all the industrial jobs in Mexico were concentrated in Mexico City in 1980. The same kind of extreme concentration of industry occurred in many Third World countries. Yet careful study leads scholars to play down industrialization as a cause of urban explosion. In the words of a leading authority:

After about 1930 a new phenomenon which might be termed "urbanization without industrialization" began to appear in the Third World. This phenomenon very rapidly acquired an inflationary character and in the early 1960s began to present most serious problems of urban employment and underemployment.[6]

In short, urban population grew much faster than industrial employment. It was a lucky migrant who found a real factory job.

Nevertheless, newcomers continued to stream to the cities. Many were pushed: they simply lacked enough land to survive. Large landowners found it more profitable to produce export crops, like sugar or coffee, for wealthy industrialized countries, and their increasingly mechanized operations provided few jobs for agricultural laborers. The push factor was particularly strong in Latin America, where the neocolonial pattern of large landowners and foreign companies exporting food and raw materials to the industrialized nations worked against peasant agriculture. More generally, much migration was seasonal or temporary. Many a young person left home for the city to work in construction or serve as a maid, planning to return shortly with a modest nest egg. Higher wages and steadier work in the city also strongly influenced most decisions to migrate.

Yet the magnetic attraction of Third World cities was more than economic. Their attraction rested on the services and opportunities they offered, as well as on changing attitudes and the urge to escape from the traditional restraints of village life. Most of the modern hospitals, secondary schools, and transportation systems in less developed countries were in the cities. So were most banks, libraries, movie houses, and basic conveniences. Safe piped water and processed food were rare in rural areas, for instance, and village women by necessity spent much of their time carrying water and grinding grain.

The city held a special appeal for rural people who had been exposed to the seductive influence of modern education. In Africa, a European economist concluded that "the number of people who are prepared to go back to the land after more than three or four years in the classroom is infinitesimal."[7] One survey from the 1960s in the Ivory Coast found two out of three rural high school graduates planning to move to the city; only one in ten of the illiterates expressed the same intention. Africa was not unique in this. For the young and the ambitious, the allure of the city was the excitement and opportunity of modern life. The village took on the curse of boredom and failure.

Overcrowding and Shantytowns

Rapid population growth placed great pressure on already inadequate urban social services, and in many Third World cities the quality of life deteriorated. Many people lacked running water, paved streets, electricity, and police and fire protection. As in the early days of England's industrial revolution, sanitation was minimal in poor sections of town. Outdoor toilets were shared by many. Raw sewage often ran in streets and streams.

Faced with a rising human tide, government officials and their well-to-do urban allies sometimes tried to restrict internal migration to preserve the cities. Particularly in Africa, politicians talked of sending newcomers "back to the land" in order to reduce urban unemployment, crime rates, congestion, and environmental decline. In Africa as elsewhere, these antimigration efforts proved unsuccessful, and frustrated officials often threw up their hands in despair.

Surging population growth had particularly severe consequences for housing. As in western Europe in the early nineteenth century, overcrowding reached staggering proportions in a great many Third World cities. Old buildings were often divided and redivided until population density reached the absolute saturation point. Take, for example, this vivid description of an old inner-city area, Singapore's Chinatown, in the late 1950s:

Chinatown . . . consists almost entirely of two or three story shop-houses. These shop-houses, originally intended to house one or two families, have been divided by a maze of interior partitions into cubicles, the ma-jority of which are without windows and in permanent semi-darkness. Most of these cubicles are about the size of two double beds, placed side by side. In one such cubicle—dark, confined, unsanitary, and without comfort—may live a family of seven or more persons. Many of them sleep on the floor, often under the bed. Their possessions are in boxes, placed on shelves to leave the floor free for sleeping. Their food . . . is kept in tiny cupboards, which hang from the rafters. Their clothes hang on the walls, or from racks.[8]

Makeshift squatter settlements were another manifestation of the urban housing problem. These shantytowns sprang up continuously, almost overnight, on the worst possible urban land. Mudflats, garbage dumps, railroad sidings, steep hills on the outskirts, even polluted waterfronts—these were the dismal sites that squatters claimed. Typically, a group of urban poor "invaded" unoccupied land and quickly threw up tents or huts. Often beaten off by the police, they invaded again and again until the authorities gave up and a new squatter beachhead had been secured.

Squatter shantytowns grew much faster than more conventional urban areas in most Third World cities. In the giant Brazilian city of Rio de Janeiro, for example, the population of the shantytowns grew four times faster than the population of the rest of the city in the 1950s and 1960s. As a result, the Third World's squatter settlements came to house up to two-fifths of the urban population. The proportion was particularly high in Asia. Such settlements had occasionally grown up in American mining towns and in Europe, but never to the extent of Latin America, Asia, and Africa. The Third World created a new urban form.

The meaning of squatter housing has been hotly debated. For a long time "pessimists" stressed the miseries of squatter settlements—the lack of the most basic services, the pitiful one-room shacks, the hopelessness of disoriented migrants in a strange environment, the revolutionary discontent. More recently, detailed case studies have presented a more "optimistic" interpretation, stressing the vitality of the settlements and the resourcefulness of their inhabitants. In this view, shantytowns appeared to be real neighborhoods, whose residents often share common ethnic origins and kinship ties.

Moreover, the shantytowns themselves evolved, most notably in Latin America, where they have

Shacks and Skyscrapers   This striking view of Bombay, India, has many counterparts in the Third World. Makeshift dwellings coexist with luxurious high-rise apartments, and the urban landscape expands rapidly as newcomers pour into the swollen city from rural areas. *(Source: Camera Press London/Globe Photos. Photograph: Alan Whicker)*

existed longest. There poor but enterprising inhabitants relied on self-help to improve their living conditions. With much sweat labor and a little hard-earned cash, a family replaced its mud walls with concrete blocks and gradually built a real home. Or the community pressured the city to install a central water pump or build a school. Low-paid office workers in search of cheap housing sometimes moved in and continued the upgrading process.

Few members of squatter communities have been particularly attracted to revolutionary doctrines, despite widespread fears (and hopes) to the contrary. Making a living and holding the family together have been challenges enough. Indeed, one observer described squatters' beliefs as resembling those of the classic small businessman:

These beliefs can be summed up in the familiar and accepted maxims: Work hard, save your money, trust only family members (and them not too much), outwit the state, vote conservatively if possible, but always in your own economic self-interest; educate your children for their future and as old-age insurance for yourself.[9]

Thus the optimists have counseled politicians to abandon their hostility to squatter settlements and help them to help themselves. The rush to the city cannot be stopped, they say. However bad life in the city is, it appears desirable to the millions of rural people who "voted with their feet." Since hard-pressed Third World governments can provide only a fraction of the urban masses with subsidized housing, they should support the creativ-

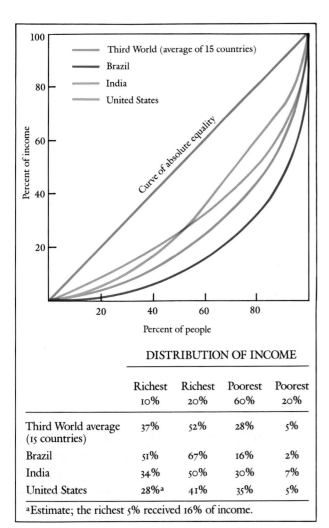

DISTRIBUTION OF INCOME

	Richest 10%	Richest 20%	Poorest 60%	Poorest 20%
Third World average (15 countries)	37%	52%	28%	5%
Brazil	51%	67%	16%	2%
India	34%	50%	30%	7%
United States	28%[a]	41%	35%	5%

[a]Estimate; the richest 5% received 16% of income.

FIGURE 38.2 The Distribution of Income in the Third World, Brazil, India, and the United States, ca 1975 The Lorenz curve is useful for showing the degree of economic inequality in a given country. The closer the actual distribution lies to the (theoretical) curve of absolute equality, the more nearly equal are incomes. In general, Third World countries have a high degree of income inequality, as great as that in Europe before 1914 (see Figure 28.2). However, there are important differences among Third World countries in the degree of income inequality, as may be seen here in the comparison of Brazil and India. *(Source: Data from M. Todaro,* Economic Development in the Third World, *4th ed., (New York: Longman, 1989), p. 155 and references cited therein; U.S. Department of Commerce,* Historical Statistics of the United States: Colonial Times to 1970, *(Washington, D.C.: GPO, 1975), Part I, p. 291.)*

ity of the "spontaneous settlement." However squalid such settlements appear, they are preferable to sleeping on sidewalks.

Rich and Poor

After the less developed countries achieved political independence, massive inequality continued, with few exceptions, to be the reality of life. Rich and poor were separated by a monumental gap, a gap that could be measured, to some extent, as Third World governments began gathering better statistical information. As Figure 38.2 shows, in about 1975 in most developing countries, the top 10 percent of all households received more than one-third of all national income, and the top 20 percent took more than 50 percent. At the other end of the scale, the poorest 60 percent received on average less than 30 percent of all income, and the poorest fifth got about 6 percent. Thus the average household in the top fifth of the population received almost ten times as much monetary income as the average household in the bottom fifth in the 1970s. This situation did not change significantly in the 1980s.

Such differences have been the rule in human history. A comparison of Figure 38.2 with Figure 28.2 on page 907 shows that the situation in the Third World in our time has strongly resembled that of Europe prior to the First World War, before the movement toward greater equality accelerated sharply. It is noteworthy that the usual distinctions between rightist and leftist governments in the Third World, or between capitalist and socialist economies, have had limited significance where shares of income are concerned. For example, in the 1970s income inequality was almost as pronounced in Mexico with its progressive, even revolutionary, tradition, as in Brazil with its rightist military rule.

Differences in wealth and well-being have been most pronounced in the towns and cities of the Third World. Few rich or even middle-class people lived in the countryside. Urban squatters may have been better off than landless rural laborers, but they were light-years away from the luxury of the urban elite.

Consider housing. In the sober words of one careful observer, "The contrast between the opulent housing enjoyed by the tiny minority of the rich and the conditions under which the vast majority of the urban poor must live is extreme."[10] In Asia and Africa, the rich often moved into the luxurious sections previously reserved for colonial administrators and white businessmen. Particularly in Latin America, upper-class and upper-middle-class people built fine mansions in exclusive suburbs, where they lived behind high walls, with many servants, protected from intruders by armed guards and fierce dogs.

A lifestyle in the "modern" mold was almost the byword of the Third World's urban elite. From French perfume and Scotch whiskey to electronic gadgets and the latest rock music, imported luxuries became the unmistakable signs of wealth and privilege. In Swahili-speaking East Africa, the common folk called them *wa Benzi,* "those who ride in a Mercedes-Benz." Even in Mao Tse-tung's relatively egalitarian China, the urban masses saved to buy bicycles while government officials rode in chauffeur-driven state-owned limousines. The automobile became the ultimate symbol of the urban elite.

Education also distinguished the wealthy from the masses. Young people from the elite often studied abroad at leading European and North American universities, or they monopolized openings in local universities. While absorbing the latest knowledge in a prestigious field like civil engineering or economics, they also absorbed foreign customs and values. They mastered the fluent English or French that is indispensable for many top-paying jobs, especially with international agencies and giant multinational corporations. Thus Third World elites often had more in common with the power brokers of the industrialized

A Sleek Automobile fascinates four boys in an African village. The most ambitious youngster may already dream of acquiring power and wealth in the city. *(Source: Marc and Evelyne Bernheim/Woodfin Camp)*

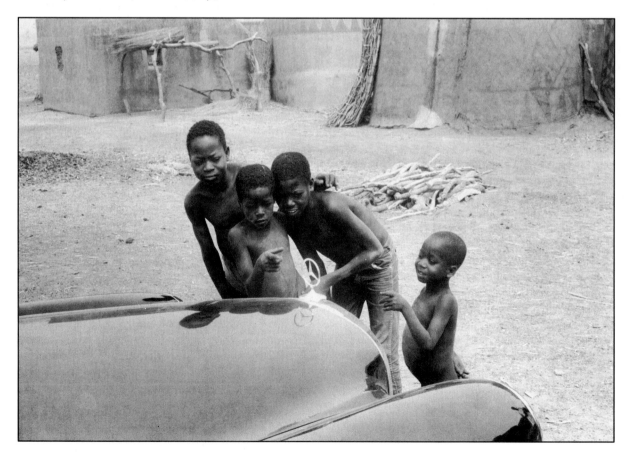

nations than with their own people. Willing tools of neocolonial penetration, they became "white men with black faces," in the words of Frantz Fanon, one angry critic (see page 1275).

The middle classes of the Third World remained quite small relative to the total population. White-collar workers and government bureaucrats joined the traditional ranks of merchants and professionals in the urban middle class. Their salaries, though modest, were wonderfully secure and usually carried valuable fringe benefits. Unlike recent migrants and the rural poor, white-collar workers often received ration cards entitling them to cheap subsidized food.

An unexpected component of the urban middle classes was the modern factory proletariat, a privileged segment of the population in many poor countries. Few in number because sophisticated machines require few workers relative to agriculture or traditional crafts, they received high wages for their skilled work. On the Caribbean island of Jamaica in the late 1960s, for example, aluminum workers in big, modern American-owned plants earned from $60 to $65 a week. Meanwhile, cane cutters on sugar plantations earned $3 a week and many laborers on small farms only $1 a week. Little wonder that modern factory workers tended to be self-satisfied in the Third World.

The great majority, the urban poor, earned precarious livings in a modern yet traditional "bazaar economy"—an economy of petty trades and unskilled labor. Here regular salaried jobs were rare and highly prized, and a complex world of tiny, unregulated businesses and service occupations predominated.

As in industrializing Europe a century ago, irregular armies of peddlers and pushcart operators hawked their wares and squeezed a living from commerce. West African market women, with their colorful dresses and overflowing baskets, provided a classic example of this pattern. Sweatshops and home-based workers manufactured cheap goods for popular consumption. Maids, prostitutes, small-time crooks, and unemployed former students sold all kinds of services. This old-yet-new bazaar economy showed no signs of dying out in the late twentieth century. Indeed, it continued to grow prodigiously as migrants streamed to the cities, as modern industry provided few jobs, and as the wide gap between rich and poor persisted.

Migration and the Family

Large-scale urban migration had a massive impact on traditional family patterns in the Third World. Particularly in Africa and Asia, the great majority of migrants to the city were young men, married and unmarried; women tended to stay in the villages. The result was a sexual imbalance in both places. There were several reasons for this pattern. Much of the movement to cities (and mines) remained temporary or seasonal. At least at first, young men left home to earn hard cash to bring back to their villages. Moreover, the cities were expensive and prospects there were uncertain. Only after a man secured a genuine foothold did he become married or call for his wife and children.

Kinship and village ties helped ease the rigors of temporary migration. Often a young man could go to the city rather easily because his family had close ties with friends and relatives there. Many city neighborhoods were urban versions of their residents' original villages. Networks of friendship and mutual aid helped young men (and some women, especially brides) move back and forth without being overwhelmed.

For rural women, the consequences of male out-migration were mixed. Asian and African women had long been treated as subordinates, if not inferiors, by their fathers and husbands. Rather suddenly, such women found themselves heads of households, faced with managing the farm, feeding the children, and running their own lives. In the east African country of Kenya, for instance, one-third of all rural households were headed by women in the late 1970s.

African and Asian village women had to become unprecedentedly self-reliant and independent. The real beginnings of more equal rights and opportunities, of women's liberation, became readily visible in Africa and Asia. But the price was high and progress uneven. Rural women often had only their children to help in the endless, backbreaking labor. And their husbands, when they returned, often expected their wives to revert to the old subordination.

In economically more advanced Latin America, the pattern of migration was different. Whole families migrated, very often to squatter settlements, much more commonly than in Asia and Africa. These families frequently belonged to the class of landless laborers, which was generally larger in

The Power of Television   An enterprising merchant in West Africa uses television to attract a crowd to a tiny shop in Dakar, Senegal. Only the man passing on the right, suggestively clad in the traditional dress of the Muslim believer, appears oblivious to the siren call of the modern age. *(Source: Philip Jon Bailey/Stock, Boston)*

Latin America than in Africa or even Asia. Migration was also more likely to be once-and-for-all. Another difference was that single women were as likely as single men to move to the city. The situation in Mexico in the late 1970s was typical:

They [women] leave the village seeking employment, often as domestic servants. When they do not find work in the cities, they have few alternatives. If they are young, they frequently turn to prostitution; if not, they often resort to begging in the streets. Homeless peasant women, often carrying small children, roam every quarter of Mexico City.[11]

Some women also left to escape the narrow, male-dominated villages. Even so, in Latin America urban migration seemed to have less impact on traditional family patterns and on women's attitudes than in Asia and Africa. This helps explain why the women's movement lagged behind in Latin America.

MASS CULTURE AND CONTEMPORARY THOUGHT

Ideas and beliefs continued to change dramatically in the Third World after independence. Education fostered new attitudes, and mass communications relentlessly spread the sounds and viewpoints of modern life. Third World intellectuals, in their search for the meanings of their countries' experiences, articulated a wide spectrum of independent opinion in keeping with growing national diversity.

Education and Mass Communications

In their efforts to modernize and better their societies, Third World leaders became increasingly convinced of the critical importance of education. They realized that "human capital"—skilled and educated workers, managers, and citizens—played a critical role in the development process.

Faith in education and "book learning" spread surprisingly rapidly to the Third World's masses, for whom education principally meant jobs. Asked how their lives differed from their mothers' and grandmothers' lives, poor and often illiterate peasant women in several countries in the late 1970s testified to the need for an education, along with the need to earn money and have fewer children. A young African woman in Kenya was quite typical of Third World women when she explained it this way.

My mother has eleven children. She is my father's only wife. She works in the fields and grows the food we eat. She plants cabbage, spinach, and corn. She works very hard, but with so many children it is difficult to get enough food or money. All of my brothers and sisters go to school. One is already a teacher. . . .

My life is very different from my mother's. . . . Women have to get an education. Then if you get a large family and don't know how to feed it, you can find work and get some cash. That's what I will teach my children: "Get an education first."[12]

As this voice suggests, young people in the Third World headed for schools and universities in unprecedented numbers. Latin America, in keeping with its higher incomes and greater urbanization, had the highest percentage of students in all age groups, followed by Asia and then by Africa. There still remained, however, a wide education gap with the rich countries, where more than 90 percent of both sexes attended school through age seventeen.

Moreover, the quality of education in the Third World was often mediocre. African and Asian universities tended to retain the old colonial values, stressing law and liberal arts at the expense of technical and vocational training. As a result, many poor countries found themselves with large

numbers of unemployed or underemployed liberal-arts graduates. These "generalists" competed for scarce jobs in the already bloated government bureaucracies while less prestigious technical jobs went begging.

A related problem was the Third World's "brain drain": many gifted students in vital fields like engineering and medicine ended up pursuing their careers in the rich countries of the developed world, which needed their talents far less than their native lands needed them. For example, in the early 1980s, as many Indian-trained doctors practiced abroad, mainly in advanced countries, as served India's entire rural population of 480 million. The threat represented by the brain drain helped explain why the Third World's professional elite received high salaries even in very poor countries.

In recent years many observers have concluded that the education drive, like its forerunner, the industrialization drive, served the rural masses poorly. It sometimes seemed that its greatest beneficiaries were schoolteachers, who profited from the elite status provided by a permanent government job. Instruction was often impractical and mind-numbing. The children of farmers generally learned little about agriculture, animal raising, or practical mechanics. Instead, students often memorized passages from ancient literary works and religious texts and spewed back cut-and-dried answers. No wonder children stayed away from school in droves. Village schools succeeded best at identifying the exceptional pupils, who were then siphoned off to the city for further study and lost forever to the village.

Whatever its shortcomings, formal education spread hand in hand with another influential agent of popular instruction: mass communications. The transistor radio penetrated the most isolated hamlets of the Third World. Governments universally embraced radio broadcasting as a means of power, propaganda, and education. Relentlessly, the transistor radio propagated the outlook and attitudes of urban elites and in the process challenged old values.

Moreover, the second communications revolution—the visual one—is now in the process of reaching rural people everywhere. Television is bringing the whole planet into the bars and meetinghouses of the world's villages. Experience elsewhere—in remote French villages, in Eskimo communities above the Arctic Circle—seems to show that television is likely to have a profound, even revolutionary impact. At the very least the lure of the city seems certain to grow.

Interpreting the Experiences of the Emerging World

Popular education and mass communications compounded the influence of the Third World's writers and thinkers, its purveyors of explanations. Some intellectuals meekly obeyed their employers, whether the ministry of information or a large newspaper. Others simply embellished or reiterated some received ideology like Marxism or free-market capitalism. But some Third World intellectuals led in the search for meanings and direction that has accompanied rapid social change and economic struggle.

Having come of age during and after the struggle for political emancipation, Third World intellectuals have been centrally preoccupied with achieving genuine independence and freedom from outside control. Thus some Third World writers argued that real independence required a total break with the former colonial powers and a total rejection of Western values. This was the message of Frantz Fanon (1925–1961) in his powerful study of colonial peoples, *The Wretched of the Earth.*

Fanon, a French-trained black psychiatrist from the Caribbean island of Martinique, was assigned to a hospital in Algeria during the bloody war for Algerian independence. He quickly came to sympathize with the guerrillas and probed deeply into the psychology of colonial revolt. According to Fanon, decolonization is always a violent and totally consuming process whereby one "species" of men, the colonizers, is completely replaced by an absolutely different species—the colonized, the wretched of the earth. During decolonization the colonized masses mock colonial values, "insult them, and vomit them up," in a psychic purge.

Fanon believed that the battle for formal independence was only the first step. The former imperialists and their local collaborators—the "white men with black faces"—remained the enemy:

The mobilization of the masses, when it arises out of the war of liberation, introduces into each man's consciousness the ideas of a common cause, of a national destiny, and of a collective history. In the same way

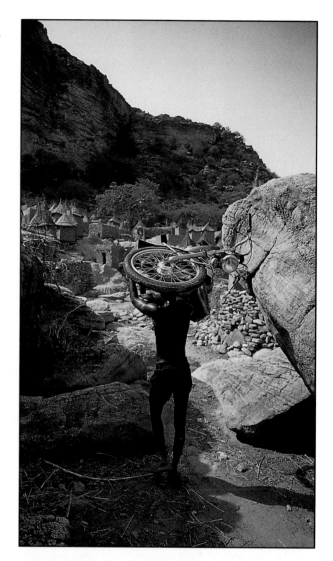

The Revolution in Communications Although this young man must carry his motorbike up a rocky path to reach his home, he has gained access to speed and excitement, to roads and cities. The messages of the modern world easily reach remote villages by transistor radio. *(Source: Pern/Hutchison Library)*

the second phase, that of the building-up of the nation, is helped on by the existence of this cement which has been mixed with blood and anger. . . . During the colonial period the people are called upon to fight against oppression; after national liberation, they are called upon to fight against poverty, illiteracy, and underdevelopment. The struggle, they say, goes on. The people realize that life is an unending contest.

. . . The apotheosis of independence is transformed into the curse of independence, and the colonial

power through its immense resources of coercion condemns the young nation to regression. In plain words, the colonial power says: "Since you want independence, take it and starve."

. . . We are not blinded by the moral reparation of national independence; nor are we fed by it. The wealth of the imperial countries is our wealth too. . . . Europe is literally the creation of the Third World. The wealth which smothers her is that which was stolen from the underdeveloped peoples.[13]

For Fanon, independence and national solidarity went hand in hand with outrage at the misdeeds and moral posturings of the former colonial powers. Fanon's passionate, angry work became a sacred text for radicals attacking imperialism and struggling for liberation.

As independence was gained and nationalist governments were established, some later writers looked beyond wholesale rejection of the industrialized powers. They too were "anti-imperialist," but they saw colonial domination as only one chapter in the life of their people. Many of these writers were cultural nationalists who applied their talents to celebrating the rich histories and cultures of their people. At the same time, they did not hesitate to criticize their own leaders and fellow citizens, with whom they often disagreed.

The Nigerian writer Chinua Achebe (b. 1930) rendered these themes with acute insight and vivid specificity in his short, moving novels. Achebe wrote in English rather than his native Ibo tongue, but he wrote primarily for Africans, seeking to restore his people's self-confidence by reinterpreting the past. For Achebe, the "writer in a new nation" had first to embrace the "fundamental theme":

This theme—quite simply—is that the African people did not hear of culture for the first time from Europeans; that their societies were not mindless but frequently had a philosophy of great depth and volume and beauty, that they had poetry and above all, they had dignity. It is this dignity that many African peoples all but lost in the colonial period, and it is this that they must now regain. The worst thing that can happen to any people is the loss of their dignity and self-respect. The writer's duty is to help them regain it by showing what happened to them, what they lost.[14]

In *Things Fall Apart* (1959) Achebe achieves his goal by bringing vividly to life the men and women of an Ibo village at the beginning of the twentieth century, with all their virtues and frailties. The hero, Okonkwo, is a mighty wrestler and a hard-working, prosperous farmer, but he is stern and easily angered. Enraged at the failure of his people to reject newcomers, and especially at the white missionaries who convert his son to Christianity and provoke the slaying of the sacred python, Okonkwo kills a colonial messenger. When his act fails to spark a tribal revolt, he commits suicide. Okonkwo is destroyed by the general breakdown of tribal authority and his own intransigent recklessness. Woven into the story are the proverbs and wisdom of a sophisticated people and the beauty of a vanishing world.

In later novels, especially *A Man of the People* (1966), Achebe portrays the postindependence disillusionment of many Third World intellectuals. The villain is Chief The Honorable Nanga, a politician with the popular touch. This "man of the people" lives in luxury, takes bribes to build expensive apartment buildings for foreigners, and flim-flams the voters with celebrations and empty words. The hero, an idealistic young schoolteacher, tries to unseat Chief Nanga, with disastrous results. Beaten up and hospitalized, the hero broods that the people "had become even more cynical than their leaders and were apathetic into the bargain."[15] Achebe's harsh but considered judgment reflected trends in many Third World nations in the 1960s and 1970s: the rulers seemed increasingly corrupted by Western luxury and estranged from the rural masses, and idealistic intellectuals could only gnash their teeth in frustration.

The celebrated novelist V. S. Naipaul, born in Trinidad in 1932 of Indian parents, has also castigated Third World governments for corruption, ineptitude, and self-deception. Another of Naipaul's recurring themes is the poignant loneliness and homelessness of uprooted people. In *The Mimic Men* (1967), the blacks and whites and the Hindus and Chinese who populate the tiny Caribbean islands are all aliens, thrown together by "shipwreck." As one of the characters says:

It was my hope in writing to give expression to the restlessness, the deep disorder, which the great exploration, the overthrow in three continents of established social organizations, the unnatural bringing to-

On Location Third World countries responded to the overthrow of foreign domination with a renewed interest in their own cultures. Here director Marcela Fernandez Volante is shown shooting a film set in Mexico. *(Source: Courtesy of John Mosier)*

gether of peoples who could achieve fulfillment only within the security of their own societies and the landscapes hymned by their ancestors . . . has brought about. The empires of our time were short-lived, but they altered the world for ever; their passing away is their least significant feature. It was my hope to sketch a subject which, fifty years hence, a great historian might pursue. . . . But this work will not now be written by me; I am too much a victim of that restlessness which was to have been my subject.[16]

Naipaul and Achebe, like many other talented Third World writers and intellectuals, probed Third World experiences in pursuit of understanding and identity. A similar soul-searching went on in other creative fields, from art and dance to architecture and social science, and seemed to reflect the intellectual maturity of genuine independence.

SUMMARY

As Third World leaders and peoples threw off foreign domination after 1945 and reasserted themselves in new or revitalized states, they turned increasingly inward to attack poverty and limited economic development. The collective response was an unparalleled medical revolution and the Third World's first great industrialization drive. Long-neglected agriculture also made progress, and some countries experienced a veritable Green Revolution. Moreover, rapid urbanization, expanding educational opportunities, and greater rights for women were striking evidence of modernization and fundamental human progress. The achievement was great.

Yet so was the challenge, and results fell far short of aspirations. Deep and enduring rural poverty, overcrowded cities, enormous class differences, and the sharp criticisms of leading Third World writers mocked early hopes of quick solutions. Since the late 1960s there has been growing dissatisfaction and frustration in Third World nations. And, as the final chapter will examine, the belief grew that the Third World could meet the challenge only by reordering the entire global system and dissolving the unequal ties that bound it to the rich nations.

NOTES

1. A. MacBean and V. N. Balasubramanyam, *Meeting the Third World Challenge* (New York: St. Martin's Press, 1976), p. 27.

2. P. J. McEwan and R. B. Sutcliffe, eds., *Modern Africa* (New York: Thomas Y. Crowell, 1965), p. 349.

3. Quoted in L. R. Brown, *Seeds of Change: The Green Revolution and Development in the 1970s* (New York: Praeger, 1970), p. 16.

4. P. Ehrlich, *The Population Bomb* (New York: Ballantine, 1968), p. 11.

5. *Wall Street Journal*, April 16, 1981, p. 17.

6. P. Bairoch, *The Economic Development of the Third World Since 1900* (London: Methuen, 1975), p. 144.

7. R. Dumont, *False Start in Africa* (London: André Deutsch, 1966), p. 88.

8. B. Kaye, *Upper Nankin Street, Singapore: A Sociological Study of Households Living in a Densely Populated Area* (Singapore: University of Malaya Press, 1960), p. 2.

9. W. Mangin, "Latin American Squatter Settlements," *Latin American Research Review* 2 (1967): 84–85.

10. D. J. Dwyer, *People and Housing in Third World Cities: Perspectives on the Problem of Spontaneous Settlements* (London: Longman, 1975), p. 24.

11. P. Hudson, *Third World Women Speak Out: Interviews in Six Countries on Change, Development, and Basic Needs* (New York: Praeger, 1979), p. 11.

12. Ibid., p. 22.

13. F. Fanon, *The Wretched of the Earth* (New York: Grove Press, 1968), pp. 43, 93–94, 97, 102.

14. C. Achebe, *Morning Yet on Creation Day* (London: Heinemann, 1975), p. 81.

15. C. Achebe, *A Man of the People* (London: Heinemann, 1966), p. 161.

16. V. S. Naipaul, *The Mimic Men* (New York: Macmillan, 1967), p. 38.

SUGGESTED READING

Many of the suggested readings for Chapter 37 discuss themes considered in this chapter. P. Bairoch, *The Economic Development of the Third World Since 1900* (1975), is a valuable historical study. A. B. Mountjoy, ed., *The Third World: Problems and Perspectives* (1978), and A. MacBean and V. N. Balasubramanyam, *Meeting the Third World Challenge* (1976), are reliable, even-handed introductions to contemporary trends and policies. R. Gamer, *The Developing Nations: A Comparative Perspective*, 2d ed. (1986), is a stimulating synthesis. Two excellent works from a truly Third World perspective are especially recommended: E. Hermassi, *The Third World Reassessed* (1980), and M. ul-Haq, *The Poverty Curtain: Choices for the Third World* (1976). The many clear and compelling works of B. Ward, notably *The Rich Nations and the Poor Nations* (1962) and *The Lopsided World* (1968), movingly convey the hopes and frustrations of sympathetic Western economists in the 1960s. Equally renowned are studies by the Swedish socialist G. Myrdal: *Asian Drama: An Inquiry Into the Poverty of Nations*, 3 vols. (1968), and *The Challenge of World Poverty: A World Anti-Poverty Program in Outline* (1970). Valuable introductions to world agriculture and population are found in various works by L. R. Brown, notably *Seeds of Change: The Green Revolution and Development in the 1970s* (1970) and *In the Human Interest: A Strategy to Stabilize World Population* (1974). R. King, *Land Reform: A World Survey* (1977), is a useful introduction to key problems.

Three valuable studies on African questions are R. Austen, *African Economic History: Internal Development and External Dependency* (1987); K. Patterson, *History and Disease in Africa: An Introductory Survey and Case Studies* (1978); and P. Lloyd, ed., *The New Elites of Tropical Africa* (1966). C. Turnbull, *The Lonely African* (1962), provides intimate portraits of Africans caught up in decolonization and rapid social change; J. Iliffe, *The African Poor: A History* (1987), is an original and important work that is highly recommended. Critical aspects of contemporary Indian economic development are carefully considered by M. Franda, *India's Rural Development: An Assessment of Alternatives* (1980), and A. G. Noble and A. K. Dutt, eds., *Indian Urbanization and Planning: Vehicles of Modernization* (1977). China's economic and social problems are skillfully placed in a broad and somewhat somber perspective by two Chinese-speaking journalists, F. Butterfield, *China: Alive in the Bitter Sea* (1982), and R. Bernstein, *From the Center of the Earth: The Search for the Truth About China* (1982).

For the prodigious growth of Third World cities, J. Abu-Lughod and R. Hay, Jr., eds., *Third World Urban-*

ization (1977), and the lively studies of D. J. Dwyer, *People and Housing in Third World Cities: Perspectives on the Problem of Spontaneous Settlements* (1975) and *The City in the Third World* (1974), are highly recommended. Similarly recommended is a fascinating investigation of enduring urban-rural differences by M. Lipton, *Why Poor People Stay Poor: Urban Bias in World Development* (1977), which may be complemented by C. Elliott, *Patterns of Poverty in the Third World: A Study of Social and Economic Stratification* (1975).

A good introduction to changes within families is P. Hudson, *Third World Women Speak Out: Interviews in Six Countries on Change, Development, and Basic Needs* (1979), a truly remarkable study. Other useful works on Third World women and the changes they are experiencing include L. Iglitzen and R. Ross, *Women in the World: A Comparative Study* (1976); A. de Souza, *Women in Contemporary India and South Asia* (1980); N. J. Hafkin and E. Bay, eds., *Women in Africa* (1977); J. Ginat, *Women in Muslim Rural Society: Status and Role in Family and Community* (1982); and M. Wolf, *Revolution Postponed: Women in Contemporary China* (1985). K. Kakar, *The Inner World: A Psychoanalytic Study of Childhood and Society in India* (1978), is a fascinating interpretation of Indian dependence on family and personal relations, which is provocatively compared with the compulsive individualism of Western society.

The reader is especially encouraged to enter into the contemporary Third World with the aid of the gifted writers discussed in this chapter. F. Fanon, *The Wretched of the Earth* (1968), is a particularly strong indictment of colonialism from the 1960s. The wide-ranging work of C. Achebe illuminates the proud search for a viable past in his classic novel of precolonial Africa, *Things Fall Apart* (1959), and the disillusionment with unprincipled postindependence leaders in *A Man of the People* (1966). G. Moore and U. Beier, eds., *Modern Poetry from Africa* (1963), is a recommended anthology. In addition to his rich and introspective novels like *The Mimic Men* (1967), V. S. Naipaul has reported extensively on life in Third World countries. His *India: A Wounded Civilization* (1978), impressions gleaned from a trip to his family's land of origin, and *A Bend in the River* (1980), an investigation of the high price that postcolonial Africa is paying for modernization, are especially original and thought provoking. Finally, L. Heng and J. Shapiro, *Son of the Revolution* (1983), brilliantly captures the drama of Mao's China through the turbulent real-life story of a young Red Guard.

PERIOD (CA 1920–1990)	AFRICA AND THE MIDDLE EAST	THE AMERICAS
1920	Cultural nationalism in Africa, 1920s Treaty of Lausanne recognizes Turkish Republic, 1923 Reza Shah leads Iran, 1925–1941	U.S. "consumer revolution," 1920s Stock market crash in U.S.; Great Depression begins, 1929
1930	African farmers organize first "cocoa hold-ups," 1930–1931 Iraq gains independence, 1932 Syrian-French friendship treaty, 1936	Revolutions in six South American countries, 1930 New Deal under U.S. President Franklin D. Roosevelt, 1933
1940	Civil war between Arabs and Jews in Palestine; state of Israel is created, 1948 Apartheid system in South Africa, 1948 to 1991 Libya gains independence, 1949	Surprise attack by Japan on Pearl Harbor; U.S. enters World War Two, 1941 U.N. established, 1945 Marshall Plan, 1947 Perón regime in Argentina, 1946–1953
1950	Egypt declared a republic; Nasser named premier, 1954 Morocco, Tunisia, Sudan, and Ghana gain independence, 1956–1957 French-British Suez invasion, 1956	Fidel Castro takes power in Cuba, 1959
1960	French maintain powerful presence in Africa, ca 1960–1980 Mali, Nigeria, and the Congo gain independence, 1960 Biafra declares independence from Nigeria, 1967 Arab-Israeli Six-Day War, 1967	Cuban Missile Crisis, 1962 Military dictatorship in Brazil, 1964–1985 U.S. escalates war in Vietnam, 1964 Separatist movement in Quebec, 1967 to present
1970	"Yom Kippur War," 1973 Mozambique and Angola gain independence, 1975 Islamic revolution in Iran, 1979 Camp David Accords, 1979	Military coup in Chile, 1973 U.S. Watergate scandal, 1974 Revolutions in Nicaragua and El Salvador, 1979
1980	Iran-Iraq War, 1980–1988 Reforms in South Africa, 1989 to present	U.S. military buildup, 1980 to present Argentina restores civilian rule, 1983

EAST ASIA	INDIA AND SOUTHEAST ASIA	EUROPE
Kita Ikki advocates ultranationalism in Japan, 1923 Chiang Kai-shek unites China, 1928	Mohandas "Mahatma" Gandhi launches nonviolent resistance campaign, 1920	Mussolini seizes power in Italy, 1922 Treaties of Locarno, 1925 Stalin takes power in U.S.S.R., 1927 Depths of Great Depression, 1929–1933
Japan invades Manchuria, 1931 Mao Tse-tung's Long March, 1934 Sino-Japanese War, 1937–1945	Mahatma Gandhi's Salt March, 1930 Japanese conquer empire in southeast Asia, 1939–1942	Hitler gains dictatorial power, 1933 Civil war in Spain, 1936–1939 Germany invades Poland; Britain and France declare war on Germany, 1939 World War Two, 1939–1945
U.S. drops atomic bombs on Hiroshima and Nagasaki, 1945 Chinese civil war, 1945–1949 Mao Tse-tung proclaims People's Republic of China, 1949	Philippines gain independence, 1946 Vietnam War, French phase, 1947–1954 India (Hindu) and Pakistan (Muslim) gain independence, 1947; violent clashes continue	Yalta Conference, 1945 NATO alliance, 1949 Soviet Union and Red China sign 30-year alliance treaty, 1949
Korean War, 1950–1953 Japan begins long period of rapid economic growth, 1950 Mao Tse-tung announces Great Leap Forward, 1958	Vietnamese nationalists defeat French at Dien Bien Phu; Vietnam divided, 1954 Islamic Republic of Pakistan declared, 1956	Death of Stalin, 1953 Warsaw Pact, 1955 Revolution in Hungary crushed by Soviets, 1956 Creation of the Common Market, 1957
Sino-Soviet split becomes apparent, 1960 Great Proletarian Cultural Revolution in China, 1965–1969	Vietnam War, American phase, 1963–1975 Indira Gandhi Prime Minister of India, 1966–1977, 1980–1984	Construction of Berlin Wall, 1961 Student revolution in France, 1968 Soviet invasion of Czechoslovakia, 1968 German Chancellor Willy Brandt's Ostpolitik, 1969–1973
Communist victory in Vietnam War, 1975 China pursues modernization after Mao Tse-tung's death, 1976	India-Pakistan war, 1971 Republic of Bangladesh, 1972 Chinese invade Vietnam, 1979	Fall of Polish government of Gomulka, 1970 Détente reaches apogee in Helsinki Agreement, 1975 Soviet invasion of Afghanistan, 1979
Japanese foreign investment surge, 1980 to present China crushes democracy movement, 1989	Sikh nationalism in India, 1984 to present Corazón Aquino takes power in the Philippines, 1986	Soviet reform under Mikhail Gorbachev, 1985 to present Anticommunist revolutions sweep eastern Europe, 1989

39

One Small Planet

Kano Airport, Kano, Nigeria

The idea of visitors from elsewhere in the universe has kindled the modern imagination. Motorists swear that they have seen unidentified flying objects; the alchemy of imagination even lands the crew of the starship *Enterprise* on our earth in our era. A best-selling author spins preposterous theories about "ancient astronauts" who landed on earth and built everything from the pyramids at Giza to the temples of the Aztecs. It is as if we earthlings, believers in the power of technology but weighed down by apparently insoluble human conflicts, have been yearning for some superior intelligence to decipher our little world and set it straight while there is still time.

Yet perhaps our yearning for enlightened interstellar visitors can be put to good use. We can imagine how superior intelligences, easily able to grasp our world and its complex history, would view the planet and its talented but quarrelsome human race. Surely interstellar observers would take a genuinely global perspective, free from our customary biases of creed and nation. If we try to do the same, perhaps we too can gain insight into our world's ongoing development.

From a global perspective, three questions might seem particularly important.

- How has the planet organized itself politically, and will competing nation-states continue to dominate world politics?
- How has the human race been using its resources to meet its material needs?
- What key ideas are guiding human behavior as our planet moves toward an uncertain future?

WORLD POLITICS

Although many earthlings are deeply impressed by our recent scientific and technological achievements, highly advanced space travelers might be less so. They might instead be astonished that accelerated technological achievement has not been matched by any corresponding change in the way the human race governs—or fails to govern— itself. Sovereign nation-states reign supreme, as assertive and as competitive as ever, and are con-tinuously reinforced by ever more destructive weapons. The embryonic growth of an effective global political organization, of a government that could protect the world's nations from themselves, appears permanently arrested. The tension generated by powerful, warlike states in a fragile and interdependent world remains one of the most striking—and dangerous—characteristics of this small planet.

Nation-States and the United Nations

The rise of the nation-state and the global triumph of nationalism have been a grand theme of modern world history. The independent territorial nation-state—sometimes containing separatist ethnic groups striving for nationhood in their own right—is clearly the fundamental principle of political organization in our times. Yet from a global perspective we must surely question what we take for granted. Has the nation-state system, with its apparently inevitable conflicts, become a threat to life on the planet?

Some have thought so. It is one of history's ironies that nationalism has been widely condemned in the twentieth century, especially in Europe, just as it has triumphed decisively in world politics. In *Mankind and Mother Earth* (1976), his last work, the renowned British historian Arnold Toynbee (1889–1975) poignantly expressed the post-1914 disillusionment of many European and American intellectuals. At the time of his birth, Toynbee wrote, his middle-class countrymen "supposed Earthly Paradise was just around the corner." They also assumed that the national state was "the natural, normal, rightful political unit."

Toynbee's generation of Europeans, however, lived through an era of "self-inflicted tribulation," war and genocide, largely due to their "explosive, subversive" faith in national self-determination. Toynbee borrowed a term from the ancient Greeks to explain that the spread of the western European political idea of the national state, first to eastern Europe and then to Asia and Africa, had created a fatal discrepancy—

the discrepancy between the political partition of the Oikoumené [the habitat of the human race] into local sovereign states and the global unification of the Oikoumené on technological and economic planes. This misfit is the crux of mankind's present plight. Some form of global government is now needed for keeping the peace . . . and for reestablishing the balance between Man and the rest of the biosphere.[1]

Similar views prevail among a small but articulate group of intellectuals and political scientists. Thus we should probably take the "unrealistic" question of world government seriously. Let us look more closely than usual at the United Nations for signs of the emergence of a global authority transcending sovereign states.

When the United Nations was founded in San Francisco in 1945, the United States was the driving force behind its creation. President Roosevelt and Democrats in the Wilsonian tradition believed that the failure of the United States to join the League of Nations had contributed to the tragic breakdown of "collective security" in the 1930s. A resurrected League, they believed, would facilitate Allied cooperation in the postwar era.

It was to be the prime purpose of the new organization "to maintain international peace and security." Primary responsibility for this awesome task was assigned to the twelve-nation Security Council. According to the U.N. charter, the Security Council had the authority to examine any international conflict, impose economic and political penalties on an aggressor, and even "take such action by air, sea, or land forces as may be necessary to restore international peace and security." In short, the Security Council had the power to police the world.

Yet this theoretical power was severely restricted in practice. China, Great Britain, France, the Soviet Union, and the United States were all made permanent members of the Security Council, and all five had to agree on any peacekeeping action. The veto power of the Big Five has been criticized for preventing the United Nations from ever regulating its most powerful members. But that was precisely the point: none of the Big Five, and certainly not the United States, was willing to surrender sovereign power to a potential world government.

Indeed, the United Nations affirmed and reinforced the primacy of the national state in world politics. The charter directed the United Nations to pursue "friendly relations between nations based on the principle of equal rights and self-determination of peoples." Every "peace-loving" state was eligible to join and to participate in the General Assembly, the United Nations's second main body. Founded with 50 members, the General Assembly reached 122 members in 1965 and 159 in 1990. Each member state, whatever its size, always had one voice and one vote on all resolutions. However, the resolutions of the General Assembly became legally binding on states only if all five of the Security Council's permanent members agreed. The General Assembly was a world debating society for nation-states, not a lawmaking body for the peoples of the planet.

The third express purpose of the United Nations testified to the expanded scope of government tasks since the late nineteenth century, as well as to global interdependence. According to its charter, the United Nations was "to achieve international cooperation in solving international problems of an economic, social, cultural, or humanitarian character, and in promoting and encouraging respect for human rights and for fundamental freedom for all without distinction as to race, sex, language, or religion." This open-ended assignment was the province of a Social and Economic Council, whose eighteen members were to be elected periodically by the General Assembly. The council was also to work with such specialized affiliated agencies as the World Health Organization in Geneva and the Food and Agriculture Organization in Rome.

The scope of its original purposes helps explain the evolution of the United Nations. Hopes of effective Allied cooperation in the Security Council faded as cold war rhetoric and vetoes by the outnumbered Soviet Union began to paralyze that body. The Security Council proved somewhat more successful at quieting bloody conflicts between smaller states where the interests of the superpowers were not directly involved, such as the dispute between India and Pakistan over Kashmir and that between Greece and Turkey over Cyprus. In 1960, it even sent military forces to re-establish order in the former Belgian Congo. This ambitious undertaking, criticized from all sides, marked an early high point of Security Council peacekeeping.

With the Security Council often deadlocked, the rapidly changing General Assembly claimed ever greater authority. As decolonization picked up speed and the number of member states more than doubled by the early 1960s, a nonaligned, anticolonial Afro-Asian bloc emerged. Reinforced by sympathetic Latin American countries, the bloc succeeded in organizing a coherent Third World majority in the General Assembly by the mid-1960s. This majority concentrated on economic and social issues, passing many fiery and fine-sounding resolutions often directed against the former colonial powers, the United States, Israel, imperialist Portugal, and racist South Africa.

The long-term significance of these developments at the United Nations was by no means clear. The Third World majority, predominantly composed of small and poor countries, clearly mistook the illusion of power at the United Nations for the substance of power in world affairs. By the

late 1970s, many of the General Assembly's resolutions were simply ignored. Meanwhile, many critical international issues, such as the Arab-Israel conflict, were increasingly resolved by resort to traditional diplomacy or war. In the mid-1980s, the United Nations experienced a serious financial crisis as the United States and other Western countries cut their contributions in order to retaliate against U.N. policies that they opposed.

Nor did the United Nations generate much popular support around the world. Most people continued to identify with their national states, which may even provide adults with a psychological substitute for the family bonds that nurtured them in childhood. Thus nation-states have continued to weave the powerful social bonds necessary for group action. As two American political scientists put it, "The nation-state may all too seldom speak the voice of reason. But it remains the only serious alternative to chaos."[2]

And yet the United Nations has also proved to be a remarkably hardy institution. Particularly significant in long-term perspective was the Third World majority's successful expansion of the scope of the organization's economic, social, and cultural mission. By the early 1980s, an alphabet soup of U.N. committees, specialized agencies, and affiliated international organizations was studying and promoting health, labor, agriculture, industrial development, and world trade, not to mention disarmament, control of narcotics, and preservation of the great whales. These U.N. agencies and affiliated organizations derived their initial authority from treaties and agreements between sovereign states, but once in operation they took on a life of their own.

Staffed by a talented international bureaucracy, U.N. agencies worked tenaciously to consolidate their power and to serve their main constituency—the overwhelming Third World majority in both the General Assembly and the world's total population. Without directly challenging national sovereignty, they exerted a steady pressure for more "international cooperation" in dealing with specific global issues, and the world's big powers sometimes went along. The United Nations also emerged as the central forum for the debate on the world economic order and the relations between rich and poor countries, issues of fundamental importance in the late twentieth century. Thus sharp-eyed observers detected a grad-

Learning About Nutrition The United Nations expert in the center is showing women with hospitalized children in Mali how to prepare meals providing maximum nourishment. *(Source: United Nations/Ray Witlin)*

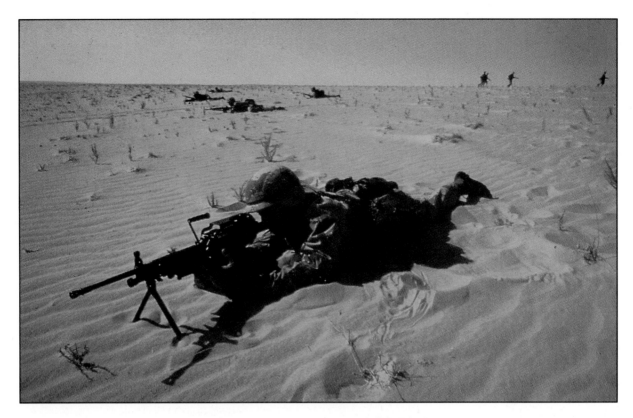

Desert Warfare   American soldiers practice the art of desert warfare in Saudi Arabia as the U.N.-authorized coalition builds up its forces and Iraq's army defiantly remains in Kuwait. After Saddam Hussein's forces were smashed and expelled in a lightning attack, the Security Council continued to punish and discipline Iraq. *(Source: U.S. Air Force)*

ual, many-sided enlargement of U.N. involvement in planetary affairs.

This development marked time in the 1980s, but as the 1990s opened the United Nations suddenly took fresh and almost unprecedented action. In response to Iraq's invasion and annexation of the small state of Kuwait, the five permanent members of the Security Council agreed in August 1990 to impose a strict naval blockade on Iraq. Naval forces, led by the United States but augmented by ships from several nations, then enforced the blockade and halted all trade between Saddam Hussein's country and the rest of the world. Receiving the support of ground units from some Arab states as well as from Great Britain and France, the United States also landed first 200,000—and then a total of 500,000—American soldiers in Saudia Arabia near the border of Kuwait. At the same time the United States and its allies pushed a series of resolutions through the

U.N. Security Council, which ordered Iraq to withdraw from Kuwait and pay reparations. When a defiant Saddam Hussein continued to claim that Kuwait had become an Iraqi province, the Security Council authorized the U.S.-led military coalition to attack Iraq.

The subsequent war (Map 39.1) and the Soviet Union's unsuccessful attempt to mediate an Iraqi retreat from Kuwait received saturation coverage in the world's media. But the most notable feature of the war from a truly global perspective was that it could not have occurred—at least under U.N. auspices—without the permission of China and the Soviet Union. Once before, in the Korean War, the United States and its Western allies had fought with U.N. authorization. But that was only because an angry Soviet Union had walked out of the United Nations and was not present to cast its veto—a tactical error that none of the five permanent members ever repeated when their far-flung

MAP 39.1 The Persian Gulf War   The United States' most valuable ally in the Gulf war was the kingdom of Saudia Arabia, which feared it might be next on the list after Iraq suddenly seized Kuwait. Providing U.S. commanders with both bases and troops, Saudi Arabia emerged from the war with increased regional influence and unique superpower status in the world oil industry.

interests appeared threatened or even challenged. Did five-power agreement to punish Saddam Hussein severely mean the triumph of the original American idea of using the United Nations as a means for the great states to police the world? Or was the Security Council's unified response to Iraq's Kuwaiti invasion something of a fluke, the result of special circumstances? Only time will tell. In any event it seems possible that dramatic military action in the Persian Gulf has only reinforced the gradual expansion of U.N. action in world affairs, and that the early steps toward some kind of world government have already been taken.

Complexity and Violence

In between territorial nation-states and international organizations that concentrate on specific problems there has stretched a vast middle ground of alliances, blocs, partnerships, and ongoing conflicts and rivalries. Although it is often difficult to make sense of this tangle of associations, certain fundamental developments have structured a complexity sometimes bordering on chaos.

First, East-West competition and the mutual hostility of the bloc leaders, the Soviet Union and the United States, was one of the planet's most enduring realities until very recently. The cold war raged in the 1980s, when Soviet armies decimated Afghanistan and the United States modernized its military might. Yet even then it was clear that neither bloc was as solid as it had been a generation earlier. China had long since broken with the Soviet Union, and Poland's effort to chart its own course testified eloquently to tensions within the East bloc. As for the West, serious differences on military matters surfaced within NATO (which France had long since quit), and economic quarrels flared between the Common Market and the United States. Thus the hostile superpowers were restrained by their allies as well as by the possibility of nuclear self-destruction. When, therefore, Mikhail Gorbachev launched his reforms in the Soviet Union—reforms that unexpectedly snowballed into successful anticommunist revolutions in eastern Europe in 1989—the scene was set for the unification of the two Germanys and the end of the cold war. Joyously welcomed, and rightly so, the sudden end of the cold war removed nonethe-

less a basic principle of global organization and signaled a new era in world politics.

The long cold war contributed to the ideology of Third World solidarity, a second significant factor in planetary affairs. A critical step was taken in 1955, when Asian and African nations came together in Bandung, Indonesia, to form a "third force" of nonaligned nations. The neutralist leaders of Asia and Africa believed that genuine independence and social justice were the real challenges before them, and they considered the cold war a wasteful and irrelevant diversion. African, Asian, and Latin American countries learned to work together at the United Nations, and they called for a restructuring of the world economic system. These efforts have brought mixed results (see below), but a loose majority of Third World countries has coalesced around some global issues.

A striking third development has been the increasingly "multipolar" nature of world politics. Regional conflict and a fluid, complicated jockeying for regional influence have been the keynotes. While the two superpowers were struggling to control their allies and competing for global power and influence, a number of increasingly assertive "middle powers" were arising around the world. Often showing by their actions limited commitment to Third World solidarity, these middle powers strove to be capable of leading or dominating their neighbors and of standing up to the world's superpowers on regional questions. The rise of middle powers reflected the fact that most of the world's countries are small and weak, with fewer than 20 million people. Only a few countries have the large populations, natural resources, and industrial bases necessary for real power on a regional or global scale.

Latin America presented two striking examples of middle powers. Brazil, with more than 140 million people, vast territory and resources, and one of the world's most rapidly industrializing economies, emerged rather suddenly as South America's dominant nation-state. Even more striking was the rapid rise of Mexico, with its population of over 80 million, its substantial industrial base and oil wealth, and its proud nationalism. Although the world recession of the early 1980s hit hard, Mexico clearly saw itself as the natural leader of the Spanish-speaking Americas. As a major regional power, it challenged the long-dominant influence of the United States in Central America.

Strong regional powers like France and West Germany had re-emerged in western Europe by the early 1960s. The unification of Germany in 1990 created a dominant economic power in Europe, with far-reaching implications for the Common Market and Europe's role in world affairs. Resurgent Nigeria was unquestionably the leading power in sub-Saharan Africa. Heavily populated Egypt and much smaller Israel were also regional powerhouses. Iran sought under the shah to dominate the Persian Gulf but came out of the long, bitter war with Iraq in the 1980s a bloodied loser. This defeat encouraged Saddam Hussein to launch his surprise attack on tiny Kuwait as part of Iraq's unsuccessful bid to become the dominant power in the region. China, India, and Japan were all leading regional powers, and several other Asian countries—notably Indonesia, Vietnam, Pakistan, and the Philippines—were determined to join them.

A high degree of conflict and violence characterized the emerging multipolar political system. Conflict in Europe remained mainly verbal, but in Africa, Asia, and Central America blood flowed freely. Of the 145 wars that occurred worldwide between 1945 and 1979, 117 were in the Third World. As Germany was in the Thirty Years' War, some countries were literally torn apart. Lebanon, which had long been considered the most advanced state in the Arab world, was practically destroyed by endless war, civil conflict, and foreign occupation. Cambodia (Kampuchea), invaded by American armies in 1970, then ravaged by the savage Pol Pot regime and finally occupied by Vietnamese armies, became another terrible tragedy.

Beirut: The Fruits of Civil War Savage conflict between rival militias divided and decimated the Lebanese capital in the 1980s. This Muslim family is walking along the previously fortified "green line," which separated the city's warring Muslim and Christian quarters for fifteen years before it was dismantled by a resurgent national government in 1990. *(Source: Wide World Photos)*

The ongoing plague of local wars and civil conflicts caused great suffering. Millions of refugees, like Vietnam's "boat people," fled for their lives. The war for independence in Bangladesh temporarily created over 10 million refugees, who fled into India toward Calcutta. Hungry, homeless people overwhelmed the Indian relief centers, sleeping in trees, huddling in the rain, starving to death. After the Soviet invasion of Afghanistan, fully one-tenth of that country's population of 1.7 million people fled. In 1981, the United Nations's commission for emergency relief counted 10 million refugees in Asia and Africa. It was an appalling commentary on organized violence in our time, which continued unabated in the 1980s.

The Arms Race and Nuclear Proliferation

Regional competition and local hot wars brought military questions once again to the forefront of world attention. Indeed, nearly every country in the world joined the superpowers in the ever-intensifying arms race. In garrison states like Israel, South Africa, and Vietnam, defense expenditures assumed truly fantastic proportions. Unified Vietnam, having defeated the Americans and battled the Chinese to a standstill, emerged as a modern-day Prussia or Sparta. In the early 1980s, Vietnam was spending half of its national income on the military; its standing army of a million men was the world's third largest, after the Soviet Union and China, and one of the best. Vietnam, with its population of 54 million, had achieved the status of a major Asian power for the foreseeable future. In both India and Brazil, there developed a widespread belief that heavy defense spending spurred economic growth because such outlays created more sophisticated weapons for which there was a strong international demand.

A particularly ominous aspect of the global arms race was the threat of nuclear proliferation. For a generation after 1945, nuclear weapons were concentrated mainly in the hands of the two superpowers, who learned a grudging respect for each other. But other states also developed nuclear weapons, and by the 1970s many more were capable of doing so. Some experts then feared that as many as twenty countries might have their own atomic bombs in a few brief years. As the 1990s opened, these fears had not come true. But the specter of nuclear proliferation and ever-increasing chances of nuclear war clearly haunted the planet. How, a superior intelligence would surely ask, had this frightening situation arisen? And what was being done to find a solution?

Having let the atomic genie out of the bottle at Hiroshima and Nagasaki in 1945, a troubled United States immediately proposed that it be recaptured through effective international control of all atomic weapons. As American representative Bernard Baruch told the first meeting of the United Nations Atomic Energy Commission in 1946:

We are here to make a choice between the quick and the dead. . . . We must elect World Peace or World Destruction. . . . Therefore the United States proposes the creation of an International Atomic Development Authority, to which should be entrusted all phases of the development and use of atomic energy.

The Soviets, suspicious that the United States was really trying to preserve its atomic monopoly through its proposal for international control and inspection, rejected the American idea and continued their crash program to catch up with the United States. The Soviet Union exploded its first atomic bomb in 1949. As the cold war raged on in the 1950s, the two superpowers pressed forward with nuclear development. The United States exploded its first hydrogen bomb in 1952; within ten months the Soviet Union did the same. Further American, Soviet, and then British tests aroused intense worldwide concern about nuclear fallout. There was well-founded fear that radioactive fallout entering the food chain would cause leukemia, bone cancer, and genetic damage. Concerned scientists called for an international agreement to stop all testing of atomic bombs.

Partly in response to worldwide public pressure, the United States, the Soviet Union, and Great Britain agreed in 1958 to stop testing for three years. In 1963 these three powers signed an agreement, later signed by more than one hundred countries, banning nuclear tests in the atmosphere. A second step toward control was the 1968 Treaty on the Non-Proliferation of Nuclear Weapons, designed to halt their spread to other states and to reduce stockpiles of existing bombs. It seemed that the nuclear arms race might yet be reversed.

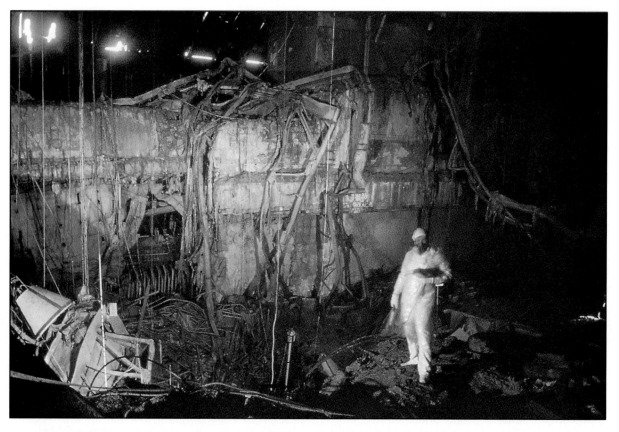

Chernobyl, Five Years Later A specialist measures the level of deadly radiation in the reactor hall, sixty yards from the center of the nuclear accident. Contaminating a large part of the Soviet Ukraine, the Chernobyl meltdown provided an ominous warning of the dangers of nuclear proliferation. *(Source: V. Ivleva/Magnum)*

Unfortunately, this outcome did not come to pass. De Gaulle's France and Mao's China, seeing themselves as great world powers, simply disregarded the test ban and refused to sign the nonproliferation treaty. By 1968, they too had hydrogen bombs. In 1974, India exploded an atomic device, reversing its previous commitment to nuclear arms limitations.

India's reversal was partly due to the failure of the Soviet Union and the United States to abide by the terms of the 1968 treaty on nuclear nonproliferation. According to the terms of the treaty, the nuclear powers agreed "to pursue negotiations in good faith on effective measures relating to cessation of the nuclear arms race at an early date and to nuclear disarmament, and on a treaty on general and complete disarmament under strict and effective international control." The non-nuclear states, which had seen serious efforts at disarmament by the superpowers as their payoff for promising not to go nuclear, had offered a whole series of proposals ranging from a complete test ban to a freeze or reduction on nuclear weapons before agreeing to sign the treaty.

In fact, the nuclear arms race between the Soviet Union and the United States surged ahead after 1968. According to American officials, the United States was capable in 1974 of dropping 36 bombs on each of the 218 Soviet cities with populations of 100,000 or more. The Soviet Union had 11 nuclear weapons for each American city of comparable size. The much-discussed SALT talks confined themselves to limiting the rate at which the Soviet Union and the United States produced more nuclear warheads. After 1980, when the second Strategic Arms Limitation Treaty failed to be ratified by the United States Senate, the superpowers appeared once again to be locked into a nuclear arms race.

Partly out of fear for their own security, many near-nuclear powers appeared poised to go nuclear in the 1980s. The worldwide energy crisis of the 1970s had played a part: peaceful use of the atom to generate electric power had created as a by-product large quantities of plutonium, the raw material for bombs. Ominously, some countries began to regard nuclear bombs as just another weapon in the struggle for power and survival.

India, for instance, developed its atomic capability out of fear of China, which had manhandled India in a savage border war in 1962. India's nuclear blast in 1974 in turn frightened Pakistan, which regarded India as a bitter enemy after 1947 and which lost Bangladesh because of Indian armies. Pakistan's President Zulfikar Ali Bhutto (1928–1979) was reported to have said that Pakistan must have the bomb even if its people had to eat grass. In the 1980s, Pakistan was clearly on the verge of producing nuclear weapons. It was also widely believed that both Israel and South Africa had arsenals of nuclear bombs. Israel's apparent nuclear superiority was profoundly distasteful to the Arabs. Hence Iraq pushed hard, with help from France, to develop nuclear capability. In June 1981, Israel reponded suddenly, attacking and destroying the Iraqi nuclear reactor. When Iraq subsequently used deadly chemical weapons against Iran and against its own dissatisfied minorities, the terrible dangers of nuclear proliferation were driven home to all.

If countries like Iraq developed nuclear arms, and if regional conflicts remained so intense, would not some nation use the dreadful weapons sooner or later? And if so, was there not a danger that such a nuclear war would spread to the superpowers? And what about nuclear terrorism and blackmail? In a world full of nuclear weapons and nuclear potential, might not fanatical political groups and desperate states resort to nuclear blackmail to gain their demands? None of these ominous possibilities came to pass in the 1980s, but in a world of bitter political rivalries they made the hardheaded observer grimly apprehensive. Was the human race, as one expert on nuclear arms warned, "an endangered species"?[3]

The end of the cold war offered new hopes and dangers. Some observers worried that a disinte-grating Soviet Union might lose control of its vast nuclear stockpile, but the likelihood of nuclear war between the United States and the Soviet Union seemed greatly reduced. In addition, effective Soviet-American cooperation presented the possibility of a reduction in existing nuclear arsenals along with a corresponding renunciation of such weapons by non-nuclear countries, as already spelled out in the 1968 Treaty on the Non-Proliferation of Nuclear Weapons. A major step in this direction was quite possibly taken in July 1990, when the Soviet Union, no doubt with U.S. support, required West Germany to renounce forever the manufacture of nuclear arms in return for Soviet agreement to German reunification. That Germany—mighty, unified, and with a tragic history of aggression in the twentieth century—was forever refusing to produce nuclear weapons raised the hope that nuclear proliferation might yet be mastered.

GLOBAL INTERDEPENDENCE

Alongside political competition and the global arms race, a contradictory phenomenon unfolded: as Toynbee suggested, the nations of our small world became increasingly interdependent both economically and technologically. Even the great continental states with the largest land masses and populations and the richest natural resources found that they could not depend only on themselves. The United States required foreign oil, and the Soviet Union needed foreign grain. All countries and peoples had need of each other.

Mutual dependence in economic affairs was often interpreted as a hopeful sign for the human race. Dependence promoted peaceful cooperation and limited the scope of violence. Yet the existing framework of global interdependence also came under intense attack. The poor countries of the South—the Third World—charged that the North continued to receive far more than its rightful share from existing economic relationships, relationships forged to the South's disadvantage in the era of European expansion and political domination. The South demanded a new international economic order. Critics also saw strong evidence of neocolonialism in the growing importance of the North's huge global business corporations—

the so-called multinationals—in world economic development. Thus global interdependence has been widely accepted in principle and hotly debated in practice.

Pressure on Vital Resources

During the postwar economic boom of the 1950s and the 1960s, the nations of the world became ever more dependent on each other for vital resources. Yet resources also seemed abundant, and rapid industrialization was a worldwide article of faith. Only those alarmed by the population explosion predicted grave shortages, and they spoke almost exclusively about food shortages in the Third World.

The situation changed suddenly in the early 1970s. Fear that the world was running out of resources was widely voiced. In a famous study aptly titled *The Limits to Growth* (1972), a group of American and European scholars argued that unlimited growth is impossible on a finite planet. By the early twenty-first century, they predicted, the ever-increasing demands of too many people and factories would exhaust the world's mineral resources and destroy the fragile biosphere with pollution.

Meanwhile, Japan was importing 99 percent of its petroleum, western Europe 96 percent. When the Organization of Petroleum Exporting Countries (OPEC) increased the price of crude oil fourfold in 1973 (see page 1185), there was panic in many industrial countries. Skyrocketing prices for oil and other raw materials seemed to confirm grim predictions that the world was exhausting its vital resources.

In much of the Third World, the pressure to grow more food for more people led to piecemeal destruction of forests and increased soil erosion. Much of the Third World suffered from what has been called "the other energy crisis"—a severe lack of firewood for cooking and heat.

A striking case is the southern edge of the Sahara. Population growth caused the hard-pressed peoples of this region to overgraze the land and denude the forests. As a result, the sterile sand of the Sahara advanced southward as much as thirty miles a year along a 3,000-mile front. Thus land available for cultivation decreased, leaving Africa all the more exposed to terrible droughts in the 1980s. Crops shriveled up and famine stalked the

land. Yet an interdependent world mobilized, and international relief prevented mass starvation.

A recognition of interdependence was also reinforced by a common dependence on the air and the sea. Just as radioactive fallout has no respect for national boundaries, so pollution may sully the whole globe. Deadly chemicals, including mercury, lead, and arsenic, accumulated in the biosphere. Some feared that pollution of the oceans would lead to the contamination of fish, one of the world's main sources of protein. Others, worried that the oceans had been overfished, feared that the significant decline in the worldwide fish catch in the 1970s indicated abuse of the sea, the common heritage of humankind.

Of all the long-term pressures on global resources, the growth of population was probably the most serious. Here recent experience offered some room for cautious optimism. Population growth in the industrialized countries slowed markedly or even stopped. Of much greater importance from a global perspective, the world's poor women began to bear fewer children. Small countries like Barbados, Chile, Costa Rica, South Korea, Taiwan, Tunisia, and the British colony of Hong Kong led the way. Between 1970 and 1975, China had history's fastest five-year decline in the birthrate. The rate fell from 32 births per thousand people to only 19 births per thousand and stayed level thereafter.

There were several reasons for the decline of the birthrate in many Third World countries. Fewer babies were dying of disease or malnutrition; thus couples needed fewer births to guarantee the survival of the number of children they wanted. As had happened earlier in the industrialized nations, better living conditions, urbanization, and more education encouraged women to have fewer children. No wonder that the most rapidly industrializing countries, like Taiwan or South Korea, led the way in birthrate declines. On the other hand, state-run birth control programs proved most successful in authoritarian China. The birth control pill, borrowed from the West but manufactured locally, was widely used in conjunction with heavy financial penalties for couples who exceeded the birth quota, increasingly fixed at one child per couple. As in most communist countries, abortion was free and on demand.

Elsewhere—in Africa, the Muslim world, and North and South America—contraception and abortion remained controversial. This helps ex-

Famine in Ethiopia   These desperate Ethiopians, fleeing from drought and starvation in 1985, hoped to find enough food to escape death in makeshift refugee camps sponsored by international relief organizations. Huddling together after a night exposed to the bitter desert cold, the recent arrivals in the foreground are completely exhausted from hunger and fatigue. *(Source: Sebastio Salgado/Magnum)*

plain why birthrates and population growth remained much higher in Africa and South America than in Asia. In 1985, Africa led the world with a population growth of 3.2 percent per year—enough to double the continent's numbers in only twenty-two years.

Indira Gandhi's fiasco with compulsory sterilization (see page 1226) suggests that, barring catastrophe, worldwide population growth will decline only gradually, as a result of billions of private decisions supplemented by government policies. This means that world population will continue to grow for a long time, as the Third World's current huge population of young adults form their own families. Thus the world's population—5 billion in 1987, as opposed to 1.6 billion in 1900—will probably not stabilize until the

mid-twenty-first century at the earliest, when it will have reached 10 to 12 billion people. Such continued growth will put tremendous pressure on global resources.

Yet gloom is not the only possible perspective. Even with 11 billion people, the earth would be less densely populated than Europe is today, and only one-fourth as densely populated as small, prosperous countries like Belgium and the Netherlands, which largely feed themselves (see Map 38.1). Such countries, often overlooked in world politics, are promising models for life on a crowded planet. Moreover, the human race has exhibited considerable skill throughout its history at finding new resources and inventing new technologies. A striking example was the way that conservation, alternative energy sources, and world recession in the early 1980s at least temporarily belied gloomy prophecies about dwindling energy resources. An optimist could conclude that, at least from a quantitative and technical point of view, the adequacy of resources is a serious but by no means insoluble problem.

North-South Relations

The real key to adequate resources is probably global cooperation. Will the world's peoples work together, or will they eventually fight over resources like wild dogs over meat?

Since the late 1960s there has been dissatisfaction in Asia, Africa, and Latin America not only with the fruits of the industrialization drive but also with the world's economic system. Scholars imbued with a Third World perspective and spokesmen for the United Nations majority declared that the international system was unjust and in need of radical change. A brilliant Pakistani, World Bank official, and member of the international bureaucratic elite sympathetically articulated this position in 1976:

The vastly unequal relationship between the rich and the poor nations is fast becoming the central issue of our time. The poor nations are beginning to question the basic premises of an international order which leads to ever-widening disparities between the rich and the poor countries and to a persistent denial of equality of opportunity to many poor nations. They are, in fact, arguing that in international order—just as much as within national orders—all distribution of benefits, credit, services, and decision-making becomes warped in favor of a privileged minority and that this situation cannot be changed except through fundamental institutional reforms.[4]

The subsequent Third World demand for a "new international economic order" had many causes, both distant and immediate. Critics of imperialism like J. A. Hobson (see page 980) and Third World writers on decolonization like Franz Fanon (see page 1275) had long charged that the colonial powers grew rich exploiting Asia, Africa, and Latin America. Beginning in the 1950s, a number of writers, many of them Latin American Marxists, breathed new life into these ideas with their "theory of dependency."

The poverty and so-called underdevelopment of the South, they argued, were not the starting points but the deliberate and permanent results of exploitation by the capitalist industrialized nations in the modern era. Third World countries produced cheap raw materials for wealthy, industrialized countries and were conditioned to buy their expensive manufactured goods. As in the case of Latin America since the nineteenth century, the industrialized nations perpetuated this neocolonial pattern after Third World countries gained political independence. Thus the prevailing economic interdependence was the unequal, unjust interdependence of dominant and subordinate, of master and peon. Declining economic aid, smug pronouncements about the overpopulation of the Third World, and the natural resentment of the poor toward the rich also fostered calls for radical restructuring of the international order.

It was the highly successful OPEC oil coup of 1973–1974 that ignited Third World hopes of actually achieving a new system of economic interdependence. From the industrialized North's point of view, OPEC's action in quadrupling the price of oil was a dangerous attack. It brought an end to the postwar economic boom and created serious social problems. From a global perspective, however, the sudden price rise brought a massive global transfer of wealth unprecedented since the looting of Mexico and Peru by the Spanish conquistadors. Perhaps 2 percent of all the income of the rich nations was suddenly forwarded to the OPEC countries (Map 39.2). Third World critics of dependence and neocolonialism were euphoric. For years the developed countries had gradually been reducing their economic aid. They had never seriously tried to meet the goal suggested by the U.N. General Assembly of earmarking 1 percent of their income each year for foreign aid. OPEC's success suggested that radical change was possible.

In 1974, a special session of the General Assembly rammed through two landmark resolutions calling for a "new international economic order" and a "program of action" to attain it. Among the specific demands were firm control by each country of its own natural resources, higher and more stable prices for raw materials, and equal tariff treatment for manufactured goods from the Third World. These demands were subject to "collective bargaining," but the Third World vigorously insisted on new terms. As one sympathetic scholar observed in 1980:

There has taken place a unionization of the Third World that has marked a profound shift in international relations. It looks as if the confrontation between unions and employers that stirred capitalist societies in the nineteenth century is being reenacted, but this time on a world scale between developed and developing nations. The question this time is whether the new nations command as many assets and opportunities as did the laboring classes of capitalist nations.[5]

That profound question remained unanswered in the late twentieth century. The developing countries did negotiate some victories, notably a Common Fund under U.N. auspices to support the prices of raw materials and a scaling down of their enormous debts to the industrial nations. But the North, deeply troubled by inflation and by its own economic problems, proved a very tough bargainer when it came to basic changes.

For example, in the late 1970s the South laid great hopes on a long, complicated conference to formulate a new Law of the Sea. The proposed new law was based on the principle that the world's oceans are "a common heritage of mankind" and should be exploited only for the benefit of all nations. In practice, this was to mean that a U.N.-sponsored authority would regulate and tax use of the sea and that a global organization would even mine the ocean floor. Some wealthy countries and their business firms were reluctant to accept such an infringement of their economic sovereignty and scope of action. The United States withdrew from the negotiations in 1981, and in 1982 the Reagan administration and the governments of several other developed nations refused to sign the final draft of the new Law of the Sea.

Increasingly frustrated in their desire to fashion a new international economic order quickly, some

MAP 39.2 OPEC and the World Oil Trade   Though much of the world depends on imported oil, Western Europe and Japan are OPEC's biggest customers. What major oil exporters remain outside of OPEC?

Major Trafficking Routes

— Cocaine
— Marijuana
— Opiates
— Hashish

Principal Cultivation Areas

● Coca
● Marijuana
● Illegal opium
● Hashish

▨ Major drug source region
• Selected cities involved in drug trafficking
▫ Money laundering center

Third World leaders predicted more confrontation and perhaps military conflict between North and South. Some alarmists in the North voiced similar concerns. For example, these alarmists charged that many Third World governments secretly condoned the production of illegal drugs for sale in the industrialized nations, and they predicted that this behavior would dangerously increase the tensions existing between the rich and the poor countries (Map 39.3).

In considering these ominous predictions, an impartial observer is initially struck by the great gap between the richest and poorest nations. That gap was built on the coercive power of Western imperialism as well as on the wealth-creating achievements of continuous technological improvement since the Industrial Revolution. In the face of bitter poverty, unbalanced economies, and local elites that often cater to Western interests, Third World peoples have reason for anger.

Yet close examination of our small planet hardly suggests two sharply defined economic camps, a "North" and a "South." Rather, there are several distinct classes of nations in terms of wealth and income, as may be seen in Map 39.4. The former communist countries of eastern Europe form something of a middle-income group, as do the major oil-exporting states, which still lag behind the wealthier countries of western Europe and North America. Latin America is much better off than sub-Saharan Africa, having a number of middle-range countries to match their counterparts in highly diverse Asia.

When one adds global differences in culture, religion, politics, and historical development, the supposed clear-cut split between the rich North and the poor South breaks down further. Moreover, the solidarity of the Third World is fragile, resting largely on the ideas of some Third World intellectuals and their supporters. As one writer put it,

in the advocacy of growth and equalization at the international level . . . Third World states have aston-

MAP 39.3 World Drug Trade As the drug trade has grown, the area of production has greatly expanded from the traditional Asian centers—the Golden Crescent and the Golden Triangle—to include many Third World countries. Poverty provides the drug lords with an army of drug runners.

ished everybody, their enemies and their friends alike, for no one has ever believed that such a diverse congress of countries, separated by geography, geopolitics, cultural traditions, size, ideology, and a host of other factors, could ever manage to build a cohesive alliance.[6]

The oil cartel's achievement rested in large part on regional (and perhaps temporary) Arab solidarity, for example, and duplicating its success with less vital raw materials and more complicated issues proved impossible.

Thus continuing global collective bargaining seems more likely than international class (and race) war. The poorer nations will press to reduce international economic differences through taxation, redistribution measures, and special aid to the most unfortunate countries. And because global interdependence is a reality, they will gradually win concessions, as has occurred domestically for the working classes in the wealthy nations since the late nineteenth century.

The international debt crisis suggests how this global bargaining is already occurring. The economic dislocations of the 1970s and early 1980s worsened the problems of many Third World countries, especially those that had to import the oil they needed. Growing unemployment, unbalanced budgets, and large trade deficits forced many Third World countries to borrow rapidly from the wealthy industrialized nations. By the middle of 1982, Third World nations—led by Mexico, Brazil, and Argentina—owed foreign banks and governments about $600 billion. Moreover, much of this staggering debt was short-term and could not possibly be repaid as it fell due.

When Mexico closed its foreign exchange markets in August 1982, unable to keep up with the payments on $80 billion of foreign debts, default and financial chaos in Mexico seemed at hand. Yet the Reagan administration, consistently opposed to Third World calls for a new international system, quickly organized a gigantic rescue operation to pump new money into Mexico and prevent default. The reason was simple: Mexico's failure to service its foreign debt would cripple or even bankrupt some of the large American banks that had lent Mexico money. Such a failure promised to touch off such massive debt repudiations in the Third World and corporate losses in the industrialized countries that the whole world would be

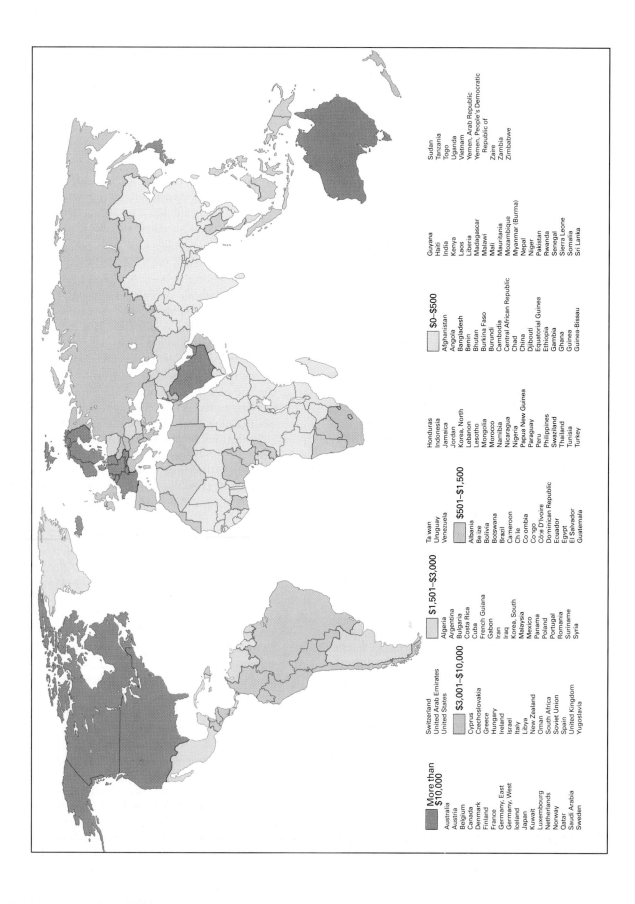

More than
$10,000

Australia
Austria
Belgium
Canada
Denmark
Finland
France
Germany, East
Germany, West
Iceland
Japan
Kuwait
Luxembourg
Netherlands
Norway
Qatar
Saudi Arabia
Sweden

Switzerland
United Arab Emirates
United States

$3,001–$10,000

Cyprus
Czechoslovakia
Greece
Hungary
Ireland
Israel
Italy
Korea, South
Malaysia
Mexico
New Zealand
Oman
Panama
Poland
Portugal
Romania
Suriname
Syria

Taiwan
Uruguay
Venezuela

$1,501–$3,000

Algeria
Argentina
Bulgaria
Costa Rica
Cuba
French Guiana
Gabon
Iran
Iraq
Korea, South
Malaysia
Mexico
Panama
Poland
Portugal
Romania
Suriname
Syria

Honduras
Indonesia
Jamaica
Jordan
Korea, North
Lebanon
Lesotho
Mongolia
Morocco
Namibia
Nicaragua
Nigeria
Papua New Guinea
Paraguay
Peru
Philippines
Swaziland
Thailand
Tunisia
Turkey

$501–$1,500

Albania
Belize
Bolivia
Botswana
Brazil
Cameroon
Chile
Colombia
Congo
Côte D'Ivoire
Dominican Republic
Ecuador
Egypt
El Salvador
Guatemala

$0–$500

Afghanistan
Angola
Bangladesh
Benin
Bhutan
Burkina Faso
Burundi
Cambodia
Central African Republic
Chad
China
Djibouti
Equatorial Guinea
Ethiopia
Gambia
Ghana
Guinea
Guinea-Bissau

Guyana
Haiti
India
Kenya
Laos
Liberia
Madagascar
Malawi
Mali
Mauritania
Mozambique
Myanmar (Burma)
Nepal
Niger
Pakistan
Rwanda
Senegal
Sierra Leone
Somalia
Sri Lanka

Sudan
Tanzania
Togo
Uganda
Vietnam
Yemen, Arab Republic
Yemen, People's Democratic
    Republic of
Zaire
Zambia
Zimbabwe

plunged into depression and even social turmoil. Thus a series of ongoing negotiations began all over the globe to reduce Third World debts, stretch out repayments far into the future, and grant desperately needed new loans. Lenders and borrowers, rich and poor, North and South, have realized that they are bound together in mutual dependence by the international debt crisis.

The Multinational Corporations

One of the most striking features of global economic interdependence has been the rapid emergence of multinational corporations since the early 1950s. Multinationals are business firms that operate in a number of different countries and tend to adopt a global rather than a national perspective. Multinational corporations themselves were not new, but their great importance was. By 1971, each of the ten largest multinational corporations—the IBMs, the Royal Dutch Shell Petroleums, the General Motors—was selling more than $3 billion worth of goods annually, more than the total national incomes of four-fifths of the world's countries. Multinational corporations accounted for fully a fifth of the noncommunist world's annual income, and they have grown even more important in the last two decades.

The rise of multinationals has aroused a great deal of heated discussion around the world. Defenders see the multinational corporations as building an efficient world economic system and transcending narrow national ties. In the words of a top manager of Royal Dutch Shell, the multinational corporation is

a new form of social architecture, matching the world-girding potential inherent in modern technology. . . .

In an age when modern technology has shrunk the world, and brought us all closer together, the multinational corporation and the nation state must get used to living with each other[7]

Critics worry precisely that the nation-state is getting the worst of the new arrangement. Pro-

MAP 39.4 Estimated GNP per Capita Income in the Early 1980s

vocative book titles portray *Frightening Angels* holding *Sovereignty at Bay,* while building *Invisible Empires* and extending their nefarious *Global Reach.* As usual whenever a major development attracts widespread attention, exaggerations and unreasonable predictions abound on both sides.

The rise of the multinationals was partly due to the general revival of capitalism after the Second World War, relatively free international economic relations, and the worldwide drive for rapid industrialization. The multinationals also had three specific assets, which they used to their advantage. First, "pure" scientific knowledge unrelated to the military was freely available, but its highly profitable industrial applications remained in the hands of the world's largest business firms. These firms held advanced, fast-changing technology as a kind of property and hurried to make profitable use of it wherever they could. Second, the multinationals knew how to sell, as well as how to innovate and produce. They used their advertising and marketing skills to push their products relentlessly, especially the ever-expanding range of consumer products, around the world. Finally, the multinationals developed new techniques to escape from political controls and national policies. Managers found ways to treat the world as one big market, coordinating complex activities across many political boundaries so as to reap the greatest profits.

Multinational industrial corporations began in the last quarter of the nineteenth century. U.S. businessmen took the lead, for reasons rooted in the nature of the American economy and society. Above all, the United States had a vast, unified market and the world's highest standard of living by 1890, so that U.S. businessmen were positioned to pioneer in the mass production of standardized consumer goods. Many of the most famous examples—such as kerosene (John D. Rockefeller and Standard Oil), sewing machines (Singer), and farm machinery (Cyrus McCormick and International Harvester)—date from the 1880s. Others—like the cheap automobile (Henry Ford), the mass retailer (Sears), and standardized food (Coca-Cola, Wrigley's chewing gum)—were thriving by 1914.

Having developed mass-marketing techniques as well as new products, the biggest, most monopolistic American corporations quickly expanded abroad. They created wholly owned subsidiaries to

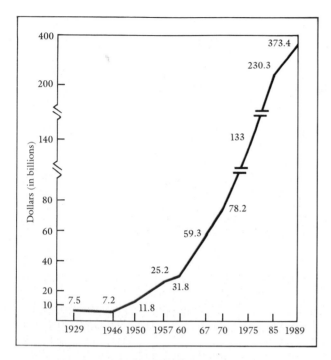

FIGURE 39.1 Total Investment by American Corporations in Foreign Subsidiaries *(Source: Data from U.S. Department of Commerce. Survey of Current Business.)*

produce and sell American-style consumer goods in foreign lands before 1914, and they continued to do so between the world wars. With ever more products and the attractions of the European Common Market, there followed a mighty surge of American investment in Europe after 1945. Nor were other parts of the world neglected by the giant American manufacturing firms: there was continued multinational investment in raw-material production in Latin America (particularly copper, sugar, and bananas) as well as in the Middle East and Africa (primarily oil and gold). By 1967, American corporations—mainly the largest, most familiar household names—had sunk $60 billion into their foreign operations (Figure 39.1).

A few European companies, notably German chemical and electrical firms, also became multinationals before 1900. Others emerged in the twentieth century. By the 1970s these European multinationals were in hot pursuit. Some, like Volkswagen, pushed directly into the American heartland and also into the Third World. Big Japanese firms like Sony also rushed to catch up and go multinational in the 1960s and 1970s. Whereas

American investment had been heavily concentrated in Europe, Canada, and the Middle East, Japanese firms turned at first to Asia for raw materials and cheap, high-quality factory labor. By the 1970s Japanese subsidiaries in Taiwan, Thailand, Hong Kong, and Malaysia were pouring out a torrent of transistor radios, televisions, cameras, and pocket calculators.

Fearful of a growing protectionist reaction in their largest foreign market, the United States, where unemployed autoworkers symbolically demolished a Japanese automobile with sledgehammers in 1979, a host of Japanese firms followed Sony's example and began manufacturing in the United States in the 1980s. The Japanese inflow was so great that by 1989 Japanese multinationals had invested $70 billion in their subsidiaries in the United States, which far surpassed the $19 billion that American multinationals had invested in Japan. In 1989 investment by European multinationals in the United States was also about 50 percent greater than American multinational investment in Europe. The emergence of European and Japanese multinational corporations alongside their American forerunners marked the coming of age of global business in an interdependent world.

The impact of multinational corporations, especially on Third World countries, has been heatedly debated. From an economic point of view, the effects have been mixed. The giant firms have provided advanced technology, but the technology has been expensive and often inappropriate for poor countries with widespread unemployment.

The social consequences have been quite striking. The multinationals helped spread the products and values of consumer society to the elites of the Third World. Moreover, they fostered the creation of islands of Western wealth, management, and consumer culture around the world. After buying up local companies with offers that local business people did not dare to refuse, multinational corporations often hired Third World business leaders to manage their operations abroad. Critics considered this practice an integral part of the process of neocolonialism, whereby local elites abandoned the national interest and made themselves willing tools of continued foreign domination.

Some global corporations have used aggressive techniques of modern marketing to sell products

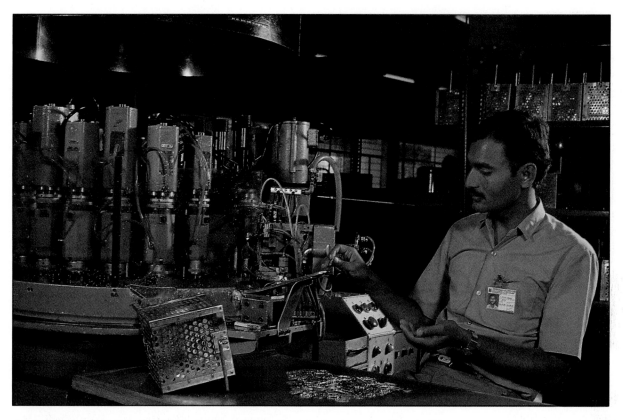

Japanese Investment in India An Indian worker carefully feeds a machine in this Japanese-owned plant. The high cost of labor in Japan encourages Japanese companies to manufacture a growing number of products in low-wage countries like India. *(Source: P. R. Gansham/Dinodia Picture Agency)*

that are not well suited to Third World conditions. For example, Third World mothers have been urged to abandon "old-fashioned, primitive" breast-feeding (which was, ironically, making a strong comeback in rich countries) and to buy powdered milk formulas for their babies. But the use of unsanitary bottles and contaminated water and the dilution of the expensive formula to make it last longer tragically resulted in additional infant deaths. On this and many other issues, the multinationals have come into sharp conflict with host countries.

Far from acting helpless in such conflicts, some poor countries have exercised their sovereign rights over the foreign multinationals. Many foreign mining companies, like the fabulously profitable U.S. oil companies in the Middle East, were simply nationalized by the host countries. More importantly, Third World governments began to learn how to make foreign manufacturing companies conform to some of their plans and desires. Increasingly, multinationals have to share ownership with local investors, hire more local managers, provide technology on better terms, and accept a variety of controls. Governments have learned to play Americans, Europeans, and Japanese off against each other. Frustrated by such treatment, one American managing director in Malaysia pounded his desk in 1979 and sputtered, "This little country and her little people need help, but they must be reasonable, otherwise we will get out of here." A Japanese manager in the same country expressed a more cooperative view: "We came here as guests, and our nation is small and needs natural resources, as well as foreign trade and investment to survive."[8] A growing proliferation of multinationals has opened up new opportunities for Third World countries that want to use these powerful foreign corporations without being dominated by them.

PATTERNS OF THOUGHT

The renowned economist John Maynard Keynes often said that we live by our ideas and by very little else. True or not, a global perspective surely requires keen attention to patterns of collective thinking. As Keynes saw, we need to be aware of the ideas that are shaping the uncertain destiny of this small, politically fragmented, economically interdependent planet.

To be sure, human thought can be baffling in its rich profusion. Nevertheless, in the late twentieth century, three distinct patterns on a global scale can be identified: the enduring strength of the modern world's secular ideologies, a vigorous revival of the world's great religions, and a search for mystical experience. The human race lives by these ideas.

Secular Ideologies

A good deal has been said in this book about the modern world's great secular ideologies. Almost all of these bodies of ideas, including liberalism, nationalism, and Marxian socialism, as well as faith in scientific and technical progress, industrialism, and democratic republicanism, took form in Europe between the eighteenth-century Enlightenment and the revolutions of 1848. These ideologies continued to evolve with the coming of mass society in the late nineteenth century and were carried by imperialism to the highly diverse societies of Asia and Africa. There they won converts among the local elites, who eventually conquered their imperialist masters in the twentieth century. European ideologies became worldwide ideologies, gradually outgrowing their early, specifically European character.

All this can be seen as an aspect of global interdependence. The world has come to live, in part, by shared ideas. These ideas have continued to develop in a complex global dialogue, and champions of competing views now arise from all regions. This has certainly been true of nationalist ideology and also of Marxism. Europe, the birth-place of Marxism, has made few original intellectual contributions to Marxism since Stalin transformed it into a totalitarian ideology of forced industrialization. Since 1945, it has been Marxists from the Third World who have injected new meanings into the old ideology, notably with Mao's brand of peasant-based revolution and the Marxist theory of Third World dependency. Leftist intellectuals in Europe have cheered and said "me too."

It is primarily as critics that Europeans contributed to world Marxism. Yugoslavs were particularly influential. After breaking with Stalin in 1948, they revived and expanded the ideas of Stalin's vanquished rival, Leon Trotsky. Trotsky had claimed that Stalin perverted socialism by introducing "state capitalism" and reactionary bureaucratic dictatorship. According to the influential Yugoslav Milovan Djilas (b. 1911) Lenin's dedicated elite of full-time revolutionaries became Stalin's ruthless bureaucrats, "a new class" that was unprecedented in history. Djilas's powerful impact stemmed from his mastery of the Marxian dialectic:

The social origin of the new class lies in the proletariat just as the aristocracy arose in peasant society, and the bourgeoisie in a commercial and artisans' society. . . .

Former sons of the working class are the most steadfast members of the new class. It has always been the fate of slaves to provide for their masters the most clever and gifted representatives. In this case a new exploiting and governing class is born from the exploited class. . . .

The communists are . . . a new class.

As in other owning classes, the proof that it is a special class lies in its ownership and in its special relations to other classes. In the same way, the class to which a member belongs is indicated by the material and other privileges which ownership brings him.

As defined by Roman law, property constitutes the use, enjoyment, and disposition of material goods. The communist political bureaucracy uses, enjoys, and disposes of nationalized property.[9]

Non-Marxian criticism of communism also continued to develop, as in Jean François Revel's provocative *The Totalitarian Temptation* (1977). According to Revel, the application of the Marxist-Leninist-Maoist model, which came to be adopted by many countries not strictly belonging to the Communist camp, brought about phony revolution. Under the guise of supposedly progressive socialism, it built reactionary totalitarian states of the Stalinist variety. Critics of Marxism-Leninism like Revel and Dijlas undermined the intellectual appeal of communism and thereby contributed to its being overthrown in eastern Europe in 1989.

As the varieties of Marxism lost considerable luster in the 1980s, old-fashioned, long-battered liberalism and democracy survived and even thrived as a global ideology. In every communist country small, persecuted human rights movements bravely demanded the basic liberties first set into law in the American and French revolutions, preparing the way against all odds for the renewed triumph of liberal revolution in eastern Europe in 1989. And there have always been some African and Asian intellectuals, often in exile, calling for similar rights even in the most authoritarian states.

The call for human rights and representative government coincided with a renewed faith in market forces and economic liberalism as effective tools of economic and social development. That countries as highly diverse as Brazil, China, Ghana, and the Soviet Union all moved in this direction in the 1980s was little short of astonishing.

Efforts to combine the best elements of socialism and liberalism in a superior hybrid have also been important. The physicist Andrei Sakharov (1921–1990), the father of the Russian atomic bomb, who in the 1960s became a fearless leader of the human rights movement in the Soviet Union, was an eloquent spokesman for what might be called the "convergence school." According to Sakharov, humanity's best hope lay in the accelerated convergence of liberal capitalism and dictatorial communism on some middle ground of welfare capitalism and democratic socialism, like that which has flourished in the small, close-knit societies of Scandinavia, Iceland, and New Zealand.

Solzhenitsyn in Vermont After he was forcibly expelled from the Soviet Union in 1974, Solzhenitsyn settled in Vermont, which recalled to him the beauty of Russia. Although an uncompromising opponent of communism, Solzhenitsyn criticized the West for its materialism and restless greed. *(Source: S. Bassouls/Sygma)*

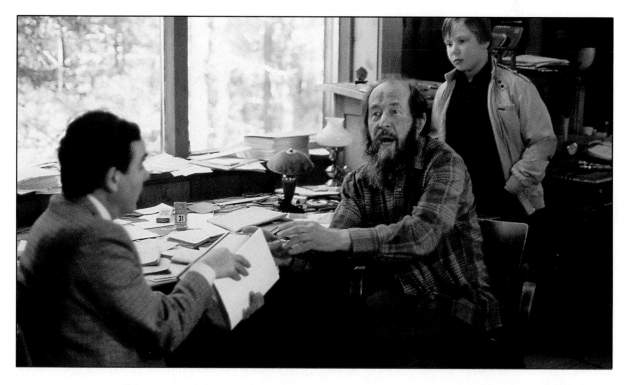

This outlook waxes and wanes in influence, but it has deep historical roots in society and remains a potent force in world thought.

Finally, there has been a many-sided global reaction to the dominant faith in industrialization, consumerism, and unrestrained "modernization." The disillusionment of the Third World has been matched by disillusionment in the developed countries and a search for alternative secular visions of the future. The student revolt of the 1960s (see page 1185), with its vague ideology of broad participation in community decisions, coincided with widespread nostalgia for simple, close-knit rural societies. The great Russian novelist Alexander Solzhenitsyn, caught up in the vanishing-resources doctrine of the 1970s, called on Soviet leaders to renounce Western technology and return to the earth:

Herein lies Russia's hope for winning time and winning salvation: In our vast northeastern spaces, which over four centuries our sluggishness has prevented us from mutilating by our mistakes, we can build anew: not the senseless, voracious civilization of "progress"—no; we can set up a stable economy without pain or delay and settle people there for the first time according to the needs and principles of that economy. These spaces allow us to hope that we shall not destroy Russia in the general crisis of Western civilization.[10]

Communes sprang up in the United States and Europe in the late 1960s. There were many advocates of alternative technologies and lifestyles. E. F. Schumacher, an English disciple of Gandhi, in *Small Is Beautiful* (1973) urged the building of solar-heated houses to conserve nonrenewable oil. Africa and Asia increasingly stressed "appropriate technologies" tailored to village life rather than borrowed from large-scale urban industrialized society—such as small, rugged, three-wheeled motorized carts suited to existing country lanes, rather than large trucks requiring expensive modern highways, elaborate maintenance facilities, and large amounts of imported fuel.

Perhaps the most striking aspect of the worldwide reappraisal of industrialization was the heretical revival of Jean-Jacques Rousseau's belief in the superiority of the simple, frugal "noble savage." As Robert Heilbroner poignantly put it in 1974 in his otherwise gloomy *An Inquiry into the Human Prospect:*

One element [of hope] . . . is our knowledge that some human societies have existed for millennia, and that others can probably exist for future millennia, in a continuous rhythm of birth and coming of age and death, without pressing toward those dangerous ecological limits, or engendering those dangerous social tensions, that threaten present-day "advanced" societies. In our discovery of "primitive" cultures, living out their timeless histories, we may have found the single most important object lesson for future man.[11]

Other writers from the industrialized countries reassessed traditional cultures and found nobility and value similar to that championed by the Nigerian novelist Achebe (see page 1276). It was another striking example of the globalization of intellectual life.

Religious Belief: Christianity and Islam

The reaction to industrialism and consumerism was part of a broader religious response to the dominance of secular ideologies in general. The revival of Christianity among intellectuals after the First World War (see pages 1109–1110) was matched in the 1970s and 1980s by a surge of popular, often fundamentalist, Christianity in many countries. Judaism and Islam also experienced resurgence, and Buddhism and Hinduism stopped losing ground. The continuing importance of religion in contemporary human thought—an importance that has often escaped those fascinated by secular ideology and secular history—must impress the unbiased observer.

Pope John Paul II (r. 1978–) exemplified several aspects of the worldwide Christian revival. A jet-age global evangelist, John Paul journeyed to Africa, Asia, and North and South America, inspiring enthusiatic multitudes with his warm sincerity and unfailing popular touch. John Paul's melding of a liberal social gospel with conservatism in doctrinal matters also seemed to reflect the spirit of the age. Thus the pope boldly urged a more equitable distribution of wealth in plutocratic Brazil and more civil liberties in Marcos's authoritarian Philippines while reaffirming the church's long-standing opposition to mechanical contraception and women in the priesthood. Many of Christianity's most rapidly growing Protestant churches also espoused theological fundamentalism, based on a literal reading of the Bible.

Pope John Paul II The man of peace and good will arrives in Warsaw in 1983 for a second pilgrimage to his homeland. John Paul drew vast and enthusiastic crowds, demonstrating their opposition to an oppressive system as well as their deep-rooted Christian faith. *(Jean-Claude Francolon/Alain Mingam/Chip Hires/François Lochon/Gamma-Liaison)*

It was also emblematic that the "Polish Pope" came from an officially atheist communist country. Yet after thirty-five years of communist rule, Poland was more intensely Catholic than ever before. Lech Walesa, the courageous leader of Poland's trade union Solidarity, said that he never could be a communist because he was a devout Roman Catholic. Poland illustrated the enduring strength of spiritual life in the face of materialistic culture and secular ideologies, of which communism was only the most openly hostile.

The attempted assassination of the pope in 1981 by a mysterious Turkish terrorist, possibly connected with the Soviet KGB in an effort to undermine the Catholic church in Poland, also dramatized the appeal of religious thinking. In a frightening, violent world, faith and prayer offer comfort and courage.

Islam, the religion of one-seventh of the earth's people, also experienced a powerful resurgence in the 1970s and 1980s. Like orthodox Christianity, Islam had been challenged by the self-confident secular ideologies of the West since the early nineteenth century. And although the acids of modern thought did not eat as deeply as in Europe and North America, they etched a seductive alternative to Islam. Moderate Muslim intellectuals advocated religious reforms; radicals wanted drastic surgery. The most famous and successful of the radicals was the twentieth-century Turkish nationalist Kemal Atatürk (see pages 1079–1081), who reflected and accelerated the impact of secularism on the Muslim world.

The generation of Muslim intellectual and political leaders born in the interwar years, who reached maturity after the Second World War, agreed that Islam required at least some modernizing. They accepted the attractively simple Muslim creed, "There is no god but Allah and Muhammad is his Prophet," but they did not think that the

Ayatollah Khomeini The apostle of Islamic regeneration and the unwavering critic of the shah returns in triumph to Teheran from exile in February 1979. The shah had visions of making Iran a major military power, but all his military might crumbled before the emotional appeal of Islamic revolution. *(Source: Black Star/Sipa Press–Setboun)*

laws of the Qur'an should be taken literally. The prohibition on lending money at interest, the social inferiority of women, even cutting off the hands of thieves and public beheading of murderers, had made sense for the Arabian peninsula in the Middle Ages. But such practices did not suit the modern age. It became necessary for Islam to adapt.

These views were still common among educated elites in the 1970s, and they remained dominant in Turkey and probably in Egypt. Yet throughout much of the Middle East they have had to bow before a revival of Islamic fundamentalism, the critical development of recent years. Like some of their Christian and Jewish counterparts, orthodox Muslim believers wanted to return to unalterable fundamentals. In taking the Qur'an literally, they demanded that the modern world adapt to the

Prophet's teachings, not vice versa. And because the masses remained deeply religious and distrustful of change, Islamic fundamentalism aroused a heartfelt popular response.

Iran provided a spectacular manifestation of resurgent Islamic fundamentalism. In the 1970s, Iran's religious leaders, notably the charismatic Ayatollah Khomeini, catalyzed intense popular dissatisfaction with the shah's all-out industrialization and heavy-handed religious reform into a successful revolution. An "Islamic Republic" was established to govern according to the sacred laws of the Qur'an. State and church were tightly bound together. The holy men and their followers were absolutely serious: they sanctioned the stoning to death of prostitutes and adulterers and proposed revising the legal code along strictly Qur'anic lines.

Iran's fundamentalism was exceptionally rigid and antimodern, partly because the country adhered to the minority Shi'ite version of Islam. But similar movements developed in every Muslim country. Even where the fundamentalists are unlikely to take power, as in Indonesia or Pakistan, and where they have been co-opted and neutralized, as in Saudi Arabia, they have found enthusiastic support among the masses and have revitalized the Muslim faith. Islamic religious thought remains extremely vigorous and continues to win converts, especially in black Africa.

Searching for Mystical Experience

Alongside secular ideologies and a revival of the world's great religions, the third powerful current of intellectual attraction has consisted of an enormous variety of religious sects, cults, and spiritual yearnings. Some of these new outpourings welled up within one or another of the great religions; many more did not. Though widely divergent, these movements seemed to share a common urge toward nonrational experiences, such as meditation, spiritual mysteries, and direct communication with supernatural forces.

Not that this is new. So-called primitive peoples have always embraced myths, visions, and continuous revelation. So too have the world's main religions, especially those of the ancient East—Taoism, Hinduism, and the Zen form of Buddhism. What is new is the receptiveness of many people in the rationalistic, scientific industrialized countries (and their disciples, the Third World elite) to ancient modes of mystical experience. Some of this interest stems from the doubt about the power of the rational human mind that blossomed after the First World War. By the 1960s, it had struck deep roots in the mass culture of Europe and North America.

In this sense, the late twentieth century is reminiscent of the initial encounter of West and East in the Hellenistic Age. Then, the rationalistic, humanistic Greeks encountered the Eastern mystery religions and were profoundly influenced by them. Now, various strains of mystical thought are again appearing from the East and from "primitive" peoples. It can be said that the non-Western world is providing intellectual repayment for the powerful secular ideologies that it borrowed in the nineteenth century.

Reflecting on this ongoing encounter, the American social scientist Robert Heilbroner was not alone in suggesting startling implications for the future:

It is therefore possible that a post-industrial society would also turn in the direction of many preindustrial societies—toward the exploration of inner states of experience rather than the outer world of fact and material accomplishment. Tradition and ritual, the pillars of life in virtually all societies other than those of an industrial character, would probably once again assert their ancient claims as the guide to and solace for life.[12]

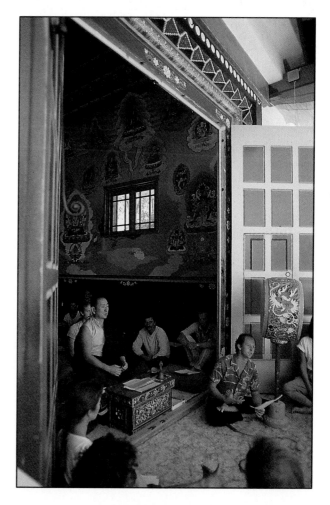

Buddhism in the West   Americans from different backgrounds come together for worship in this Buddhist temple in Santa Fe, New Mexico. This temple adheres to the Tibetan form of Buddhism, which combines mysticism and colorful ceremony. *(Source: Mimi Forsyth/Monkmeyer Press)*

Some observers see the onrush of science and technology as actually reinforcing the search for spiritual experience. Electronic communications demolish time and distance; information itself is becoming the new global environment. According to the philosopher William Thompson:

Culture is full of many surprises, because culture is full of the play of opposites. And so there will be scientists and mystics in the New Age. . . . To look at the American counterculture today, one would guess . . . that the East was about to engulf the West. But in fact . . . America is swallowing up and absorbing the traditional Eastern techniques of transformation, because only these are strong enough to humanize its technology. In the days before planetization, when civilization was split between East and West, there were basically two cultural directions. The Westerner went outward to level forests, conquer nations, and walk on the moon; the Easterner went inward and away from the physical into the astral and causal planes. Now . . . we can glimpse the beginnings of a new level of religious experience, neither Eastern nor Western, but planetary.[13]

Many people have doubts about the significance of such views. But it is just possible that the upsurge of mysticism and religious searching will exert a growing influence in the coming era, especially if political conflict and economic difficulties continue to undermine the old secular faith in endless progress.

SUMMARY

Whatever does or does not happen, the study of world history puts the future in perspective. Future developments on this small planet will surely build on the many-layered foundations hammered out in the past. Moreover, the study of world history, of mighty struggles and fearsome challenges, of shining achievements and tragic failures, imparts a strong sense of life's essence: the process of change over time. Again and again we have seen how peoples and societies evolve, influenced by ideas, human passions, and material conditions. Armed with the ability to think historically, students of history are prepared to comprehend this inexorable process of change in their own life-

times, as the world races forward toward an uncertain destiny.

NOTES

1. A. Toynbee, *Mankind and Mother Earth* (New York: Oxford University Press, 1976), pp. 576–577.
2. D. Calleo and B. Rowland, *America and the World Political Economy* (Bloomington: Indiana University Press, 1973), p. 191.
3. W. Epstein, *The Last Chance: Nuclear Proliferation and Arms Control* (New York: Free Press, 1976), p. 274.
4. M. ul-Haq, *The Poverty Curtain: Choices for the Third World* (New York: Columbia University Press, 1976), p. 152.
5. E. Hermassi, *The Third World Reassessed* (Berkeley: University of California Press, 1980), p. 76.
6. Ibid., p. 185.
7. Quoted in H. Stephenson, *The Coming Clash: The Impact of Multinational Corporations on National States* (New York: Saturday Review Press, 1973), p. 60.
8. Quoted in A. R. Negandhi, *The Functioning of the Multinational Corporation: A Global Comparative Study* (New York: Pergamon Press, 1980), p. 142.
9. M. Djilas, *The New Class* (New York: Praeger, 1957), pp. 41–42, 44.
10. A. I. Solzhenitsyn, *Letter to the Soviet Leaders* (New York: Harper & Row, 1974), p. 33.
11. R. L. Heilbroner, *An Inquiry into the Human Prospect* (New York: Norton, 1974), p. 141.
12. Ibid., p. 140.
13. W. I. Thompson, *Evil and World Order* (New York: Harper & Row, 1980), p. 53.

SUGGESTED READING

Many of the books cited in the Suggested Reading for Chapter 38 pertain to the themes of this chapter. Three helpful and stimulating studies on global politics from different viewpoints are R. Barnet, *The Lean Years: The Politics of the Age of Scarcity* (1980); F. M. Lappé and J. Collins, *Food First: Beyond the Myth of Scarcity* (1977); and S. Hoffman, *Primacy or World Order: American Foreign Policy Since the Cold War* (1978). An excellent if ominous introduction to international negotiations for the control of nuclear arms is W. Epstein, *The Last Chance: Nuclear Proliferation and Arms Control* (1976). Two clear and judicious studies on the evolving nuclear policies of the two great superpowers, by relatively impartial British scholars, are D. Holloway, *The Soviet Union and the Arms Race* (1983), and L. Freedman, *The Evolution of Nuclear Strategy* (1982), a history of American thinking about nuclear weapons and nuclear war. J. Hackett, *The Third World War, August 1985* (1978), is a gripping but all-too-optimistic best-selling account of limited nuclear war by a retired British general, writing "in consultation with NATO experts."

M. ul Haq, *The Poverty Curtain: Choices for the Third World* (1976), is an excellent presentation of Third World demands for a new economic order. This position is expanded in J. Tinbergen and A. J. Dolman, eds., *RIO, Reshaping the International Order: A Report to the Club of Rome* (1977), and *North-South: A Program for Survival* (1980), a report calling for increased help for the South by the blue-ribbon Independent Commission on International Development Issues, under the chairmanship of Willy Brandt. Such views do not go unchallenged, and P. T. Bauer, *Equality, the Third World, and Economic Delusion* (1981), is a vigorous defense of the industrialized nations and their wealth. J. K. Galbraith, the witty economist and former U.S. ambassador to India, argues simply and effectively that poor countries have important lessons to teach rich countries in *The Voice of the Poor* (1983). Common problems and aspirations are also the focus of E. Laszlo et al., *Goals for Mankind* (1977). The important study by R. Ayres, *Banking on the Poor: The World Bank and World Poverty* (1983), shows how this international financial organization has emerged as a standard-bearer for the poorest countries. *World Development Report,* which the World Bank publishes annually, is an outstanding source of information about current trends. Valuable studies on multinational corporations and global indebtedness include L. Solomon, *Multinational Corporations and the Emerging World Order* (1978); A. R. Negandhi, *The Functioning of the Multinational Corporation: A Global Comparative Study* (1980); R. Barnet and R. Muller, *Global Reach: The Power of the Multinational Corporations* (1975); and A. Sampson, *The Money Lenders: The People and Politics of the World Banking Crisis* (1983).

Contemporary thought is so rich and diverse that any selection must be highly arbitrary. Among works not mentioned elsewhere, G. Blainey, *The Great Seesaw: A New View of the Western World, 1750–2000* (1988), uncovers a cyclical pattern of optimism and pessimism and is recommended as an introduction to the history of ideas. E. Banfield, *The Unheavenly City Revisited* (1974), is a provocative and influential reassessment of urban problems and solutions in the United States. D. H. Meadows and D. L. Meadows, *The Limits of Growth* (1974), argue that the world will soon exhaust its natural resources. E. F. Schumacher, *Small Is Beautiful: Economics as If People Mattered* (1973), advocates conservation and a scaling down of technology to avoid disaster. R. M. Pirsig, *Zen and the Art of Motorcycle Maintenance: An Inquiry into Values* (1976), is a stimulating exploration of the tie between modern technology and personal development.

E. Rice, *Wars of the Third Kind: Conflict in Underdeveloped Countries* (1988), is a thoughtful inquiry into the dynamics of guerrilla movements. T. R. Gurr, *Why Men Rebel* (1970), skillfully reworks the idea that revolutions occur when rising expectations are frustrated. M. Djilas, *The New Class* (1957), criticizes the ruling Communist bureaucracies from a Marxist point of view. J. Revel, *The Totalitarian Temptation* (1977), claims that many Western intellectuals have been seduced into seeing Communist dictatorships as progressive socialist societies. A. Sakharov, *Progress, Coexistence, and Intellectual Freedom,* rev. ed. (1970), soberly assesses the prospects for improved relations between the Soviet Union and the United States.

The Islamic revival may be approached through the sympathetic work of E. Gellner, *Muslim Society* (1981); and the reservations of V. S. Naipaul, *Among the Believers: An Islamic Journey* (1981); H. Algar, ed., *Islam and Revolution: Writings and Declarations of Imam Khomeini* (1982); and J. Stempel, *Inside the Iranian Revolution* (1981). Muslim writers address issues in the Islamic world in J. Donohue and J. Esposito, eds., *Islam in Transition: Muslim Perspectives* (1982).

Studies of the future are so numerous that M. Marien, *Societal Directions and Alternatives: A Critical Guide to the Literature* (1977), is a useful aid with its annotated bibliography. The many future-oriented works of the members of the Hudson Institute usually combine optimism and conservatism, as in H. Kahn et al., *The Next Two Hundred Years* (1976), and H. Kahn, *The Coming Boom* (1982). J. Lorraine, *Global Signposts to the 21st Century* (1979), and R. L. Heilbroner, *An Inquiry into the Human Prospect* (1974), are especially recommended as stimulating and intelligent studies. L. Stavrianos, *The Promise of the Coming Dark Age* (1976), is especially suited to those with cataclysmic dispositions.

Chapter Opener Credits

Chapter 25: *Musée Carnavalet/Bulloz.* Locked out of their meeting hall, members of the Third Estate meet at an indoor tennis court, June 20, 1789.

Chapter 26: *The Bridgeman Art Library. Reproduced by courtesy of the Royal Holloway & Bedford New College, Surrey.* Paddington Station, London, 1862, bustling with middle-class travellers.

Chapter 27: *Historisches Museen der Stadt Wien.* Citizens of Vienna astride the barricades during the revolution of 1848.

Chapter 28: *Museum of London.* Urban growth, 19th-century London.

Chapter 29: *Fabio Lensini/Madeline Grimoldi.* The meeting of Garibaldi and Victor Emmanuel.

Chapter 30: *Peabody Museum of Salem. Photo: Mark Sexton.* Flags of various countries flying in front of factories at Canton Harbor.

Chapter 31: *E. Williamson/The Picture Cube.* Governor's Palace, Plaza de Armas, Lima, Peru.

Chapter 32: *Trustees of the Imperial War Museum.* World War One trench warfare.

Chapter 33: *Bettmann/Hulton.* Turks surrounding victory flag made to celebrate the victory at Smyrna, October 1922.

Chapter 34: *Collection of Whitney Museum of American Art.* The unemployed seeking jobs during the 1930s Depression in the United States.

Chapter 35: *Archiv/Photo Researchers. Cindy Pardy, Artist.* Adolf Hitler at Bueckeberg (Westphalia).

Chapter 36: *Leonard Freed/Magnum.* A young *Grepo,* an East German border guard, at the Berlin Wall in the 1960s.

Chapter 37: *Gary Sawhney, Hertfordshire, England.* Construction of Asia's longest river bridge, spanning the River Ganges in India.

Chapter 38: *John Maier, Jr./Picture Group.* Destruction of the Amazon rain forest, near the Peru border.

Chapter 39: *Frank T. Wood/Superstock.* Kano Airport, Kano, Nigeria.

Notes on the Illustrations

Pages 794–795: After David, and probably the work of a collaborator of David, *The Tennis Court Oath.* This is a slightly smaller painting than the famous pen drawing with sepia was by David, 1791. It gives some idea of the intended color scheme of David's great project, which remains only as the famous drawing.

Page 800: John Trumbull (American, 1756–1843), *Signing of the Declaration of Independence,* 1786. Oil on canvas, 21⅛ × 31½ in. John Trumbull was considered to be one of the most significant American artists of his time.

Page 807: A primitive but contemporary representation of the taking of the Bastille, by "Cholet" who was a participant in the attack.

Page 811: This was the first portrait of Mary Wollstonecraft, by an unknown artist, commissioned by William Roscoe.

Page 814: "Un Comité révolutionnaire sous la Terreur," after Alexandre Évariste Fragonard, French historical painter (1780–1850).

Page 819: Jacques-Louis David (French, 1748–1825), *Napoleon Crossing the Alps.* Oil on canvas.

Page 822: Francisco de Goya y Lucientes, *The Third of May, 1808* (1814–1815). Oil on canvas; 8 ft. 9 in. × 11 ft. 3½ in. Goya was known in the Spain of his day as a portraitist, history painter, and church painter.

Pages 826–827: William-Powell Frith (British, 1819–1909), *The Railway Station* (detail), completed 1862. Oil on canvas; 45¼ × 98¼ in.

Page 833: Samuel Scott (English, 1702–1772), *Old East India Quay, London,* Victoria and Albert Museum. Samuel Scott was the most distinguished native English topographical view painter in the eighteenth century. Such painting was popularized in England by Canaletto during his residence there from 1746–1755.

Page 844: Honoré Daumier (French, 1808–1879), *The Third-Class Carriage.* Oil on canvas. Daumier was both a caricaturist and a serious painter.

Page 857: From *Parliamentary Papers,* 1842, vol. XV.

Pages 862–863: Anton Ziegler, *Barricade in the Michaeler Square on the Night of 26 to 27 May 1848.* Oil on canvas; 68 × 55 cm.

Page 865: Isabey, *Congress of Vienna.* Royal Library, Windsor Castle, RL.21539.

Page 869: *Count Clemens von Metternich (1773–1859)* by Sir Thomas Lawrence, English painter (1769–1830).

Page 875: Left to right: K. Marx, F. Engels (rear), with Marx's daughters: Jenny, Eleanor, and Laura, photographed in the 1860s.

Page 877: John Constable (English, 1776–1837), *The Hay Wain.* Constable was one of the two great romantic painters of the period (Joseph Turner being the other), and was the first artist of importance to paint outdoors.

Page 879: Joseph Danhauser (German, 1805–1845), *Liszt am Klavier,* 1840.

Page 882: Eugene Delacroix (French, 1789–1863), *Les Massacres de Scio.* Delacroix was leader of the Romantic school. This dramatic interpretation of a contemporary event scandalized Paris Salon visitors in 1824.

Page 887: Eugene Delacroix (French, 1789–1863), *Liberty Leading the People,* 1830. Oil on canvas; 10½ × 128 in. Exhibited at the Paris Salon of 1831, the painting was acquired by the French Government.

Page 889: Honoré Daumier (French, 1808–1879), *Legislative Belly,* lithograph, 1834, 42 × 52.5 cm. Charles Deering Collection (1941.1258).

Pages 896–897: John O'Connor, *St. Pancras Hotel and Station from Pentonville Road.*

Page 900: "The Court for King Cholera," cartoon from *Punch,* XXIII (1852), 139.

Page 904: Cross-section of a Parisian house, about 1850, from Edmund Texier, *Tableauade Paris,* Paris, 1852, vol. I, p. 65.

Page 909: Paul-Emile Chabas (French, 1869–1937), *Un Coin de Table,* 1904. Oil on canvas. Bibliothèque des Arts Decoratifs.

Page 913: Pierre-Auguste Renoir (French, 1841–1919), *Le Moulin de la Galette à Montmartre,* 1876. 4 ft. 3½ in. × 5 ft. 9 in. Bequest of Gustave Caillabotte, 1894.

Page 917: After a drawing by C. Koch, 1890.

Page 925: Hilaire Germaine Edgar Degas (French, 1834–1917), *Les Repasseuses.*

Pages 928–929: Wall painting from the Town Hall and Civic Museum, Siena.

Page 932: Demolition of part of the Latin Quarter in 1860. Engraving from a drawing by Félix Thorigny.

Page 935: R. Legat, *Battle of Calatafim,* 1860.

Page 944: Merchants of Nijni-Novgorod drinking tea. From *L'Illustration,* 29 August 1905.

Pages 958–959: Oil painting on glass, post 1780, by unknown Chinese artist.

Page 965: Townsend Harris, the American Consul, meeting with representatives of the Tokugawa Shogunate. Color on paper, 1857. Artist unknown. Tsuneo Tamba Collection, Yokohama.

Page 975: A. Sutherland, *Battle of Omdurman,* September 2, 1898. Colored lithograph.

Page 979: From "The Graphic," November 9, 1895.

Page 984: Ichiyosai Kuniteru, *Tomioka raw-silk reeling factory,* ca 1875. Painted wood black. Tsuneo Tamba Collection, Yokohama.

Page 1009: Richard Caton Woodville (1815–1855), *War News from Mexico,* 1848. Oil on canvas, 27 × 25″.

Page 1010: Alfred Boisseau French (1823–1901), *Louisiana Indians Walking Along a Bayou.* Oil on canvas. (NOMA # 56.34).

Page 1013: Winslow Homer (1836–1910), *The Cotton Pickers,* 1876. Oil on canvas, 26 1/16 × 38 1/8″. Los Angeles County Museum of Art, Acquisition made possible through Museum Trustees: Robert O. Anderson, R. Stanton Avery, B. Gerald Cantor, Edward W. Carter, Justin Dart, Charles E. Ducommun, Mrs. F. Daniel Frost, Julian Ganz, Jr., Dr. Armand Hammer, Harry Lenart, Dr. Franklin D. Murphy, Mrs. Joan Palevsky, Richard E. Sherwood, Maynard J. Toll, and Hal B. Wallis.

Page 1017: Thure de Thulstrup, *The Battle of Gettysburg,* from the *CIVIL WAR, Gettysburg* (Time-Life Books, Inc.). Courtesy, The Seventh Regiment Fund, Inc.

Page 1029: Thomas Rowlandson (1756–1827), *Convicts Embarking for Botany Bay.* Pen and wash drawing, 17.3 × 15.7 cm. Rex Nan Kivell Collection, National Library of Australia.

Pages 1036–1037: John Nash (English), *Over the Top.*

Page 1039: Anton von Werner (German, 1843–1915), *The Congress of Berlin,* 1878.

Pages 1070–1071: Cheering Turks mass around a Turkish victory flag made to celebrate the victory at Smyrna, October 1922.

Page 1091: "Anti-Reds" wrest Canton from the Communists, with over 3,000 casualties. This January 1928 photo shows the dead strewn in the principal streets of Canton.

Page 1101: Philippine "West Pointers" on parade: cadets of the Baguio Military Academy march in a parade to celebrate the second anniversary of the Philippine Commonwealth.

Pages 1104–1105: Isaac Soyer (American, 1907–), *Employment Agency,* 1937. Oil on canvas; 34 ¼ × 45 in. Whitney Museum of American Art (Purchase 37.44). Photo: Geoffrey Clements, New York.

Page 1111: Edvard Munch (Norwegian, 1863–1944), *The Dance of Life,* 1899.

Page 1114: Frank Lloyd Wright (American architect, 1869–1959), Falling Water, Bear Run, Pennsylvania—perhaps the greatest modern house in America, 1936. The largely self-taught Wright was an exponent of what he called "organic architecture": the idea that a building should blend in with its setting and be harmonious with nature.

Page 1115: Pablo Picasso (Spanish, 1881–1973), *Guernica,* 1937. The original oil on canvas, 11 ft. 5 ½ in. × 25 ft. 5 ¾ in., is in the Museo del Prado, Madrid.

Page 1135: 100,000 Nazi Storm Troopers gathered in the Luitpodarena in Nuremberg, Germany, to hear Adolf Hitler on Brown Shirt Day at the Nazi Party convention, September 20, 1936.

Page 1137: French caricature by C. Leavdre, 1898.

Page 1141: Arkady Aleksandrovich Plastov (Russian 1893–1972) *Collective Farm Threshing,* 1949. Oil on canvas, 200 × 382 cm. Plastov's career was entirely in the Soviet era; his great paintings were calls to action—icons of socialism.

Page 1157: The cartoon "Stepping Stones to Glory" by Sir David Low (1891–1963) appeared in the London *Evening Standard* on 8 July 1936.

Page 1163: I. Toidze (Russian), *For the Motherland's Sake, Go Forward, Heroes,* 1942 poster.

Page 1204: Detail from Diego Rivera's monumental fresco painting (8.59 × 12.87 m), *History of Mexico: From the Conquest to the Future,* 1929–1930. From the West Wall, Stairway of the Palacio Nacional, Mexico City. In this detail, the priest Hidalgo presides over the cause of independence. In the center the Mexican eagle, symbol of nationality, holds the Aztec emblem of ceremonial war. Rivera was a painter, printmaker, sculptor, book illustrator, as well as a political activist.

Index